AMERICAN ADMIRALSHIP

AMERICAN ADMIRALSHIP

The Art of Naval Command

Edgar F. Puryear Jr.

ZENITH PRESS

This edition first published in 2008 by Zenith Press, an imprint of MBI Publishing Company, 400 First Avenue North, Suite 300, Minneapolis, MN 55401 USA.

This book was previously published by Naval Institute Press in hardcover under the title *American Admiralship: The Moral Imperatives of Naval Leadership* (2005).

Zenith Press titles are also available at discounts in bulk quantity for industrial or sales-promotional use. For details write to Special Sales Manager at MBI Publishing Company, 400 First Avenue North, Suite 300, Minneapolis, MN 55401 USA.

To find out more about our books, join us online at www.zenithpress.com.

Credits:
front cover image © Vincent Giordano courtesy of Shutterstock.com

Library of Congress Cataloging-in-Publication Data

Puryear, Edgar F., 1930–
   American admiralship : the art of naval command   / Edgar F. Puryear Jr.
      p. cm.
   Includes bibliographical references and index.
   ISBN 978-0-7603-3220-7 (pbk. : alk. paper)
   1. Leadership. 2. Admirals—United States. 3. United States.
Navy—Officers. I. Title.
   VB203.P87 2008
   359.3'310973—dc22

                                                           2008000876

Printed in the United States of America

To all of those leaders at every level of the U.S. Navy throughout its glorious history who have been responsible for the magnificent fleet that today controls the oceans of the world to ensure the security of our great nation.

CONTENTS

Preface ix

Foreword xi

Acknowledgments xvii

1 Decision 1

2 Sixth Sense 51

3 Yes Men 86

4 Books: The Importance of Reading 154

5 Mentorship 193

6 Consideration 232

7 Delegation 272

8 Fix the Problem, Not the Blame 298

9 Rickover and Zumwalt: Contrast and Contradiction . . 381

10 Selflessness 481

11 Elements of Command: Self and Family 541

12 The Pattern 572

Notes 607

Index 633

Thousands of books and articles have been written on leadership, and hundreds of autobiographies, memoirs, and biographies exist on our military leaders. What does *American Admiralship: The Art of Naval Command* have to say about leadership that they have not already said? The most important aspect of this book is its pervading theme: the role of character in successful leadership within the American military. Character is a leadership quality that cannot be defined, it must be described; the descriptions of leaders and their words quoted herein give life and discernible meaning to the term. The personalities of these prominent and successful leaders in war and peace capture the eternally elusive definition of "true character."

This volume represents forty years of research on successful leadership in the U.S. military. Over this period I had personal interviews with more than 125 officers of four-star rank and discussions or personal correspondence with more than 1,000 officers of one-star rank and higher. I corresponded with military leaders of all ranks and services, and consulted many diaries as well as hundreds of autobiographies, biographies, memoirs, and military histories. It is the objective of this volume to focus the insights and thoughts of these senior naval leaders on why they personally believe they were successful leaders and how they analyze the success of other senior naval officers. How, in other words, does one lead successfully in the American military, and what role does character play in that success? This book concentrates on the leadership of the top naval commanders in World War II: Fleet Admirals William D. Leahy, Ernest J. King, Chester W. Nimitz, and William F. Halsey, and Adm. Raymond A. Spruance; and postwar Chiefs of Naval Operations Arleigh A. Burke, Thomas H. Moorer, Elmo R. Zumwalt Jr., James L. Holloway III, Thomas B. Hayward, James D. Watkins, Carlisle A. H. Trost, Frank B. Kelso II, and Jay L. Johnson. Also included in this study are admirals who held significant positions of leadership responsibility in the postwar period such as Hyman G. Rickover, Kinnaird R. McKee, Bruce DeMars, Stansfield Turner, Henry G. Chiles, Paul David Miller, Stephen Angelo White, and Chairman of the Joint Chiefs of Staff William J. Crowe Jr.

There is a pattern to successful naval leadership. My interviews, combined with the leadership insights of American admirals taken from interviews and oral histories conducted by the U.S. Naval Institute, yield demonstrable evidence of that pattern. Comparative analyses dictate that there are indeed requisite qualities for successful American military leadership. Among them are (1) willingness to put service before self; (2) the desire and strength of character to achieve positions that require making tough decisions; (3) a "sixth sense" that enhances the judgment required for most sound decisions; (4) an aversion to "yes men"; (5) maturity in perception and judgment attained through lifelong professional reading; (6) mentorship, which reflects an understanding of the need to develop successors from among the most promising men and women under one's command; (7) delegation of authority in leadership responsibility among one's most responsible subordinates; and (8) true character, the cardinal requisite of leadership, as illustrated by a leader who fixes problems and does not blame others or look for a scapegoat when things go wrong. Acceptance of personal accountability is the prerequisite for character. I do not contend that mere study of these eight qualities will ensure attainment of the greatness achieved by these admirals. It will, however, make any officer a better leader.

When I was chief of naval operations on one of my routine trips to the fleet, I visited a squadron of eight frigates in Pearl Harbor. It was not an inspection, just a walk-through to get a feel for the morale and material condition of our fleet units. The eight ships were as alike as if they had been produced by a giant cookie cutter. They had been constructed in the same year from the same set of plans, were manned by crews produced by the same recruit depots and training schools, and operated in the same theater under the same chain of command. Yet one of these six-thousand-ton frigates stood out from all the rest. The exterior showed no stains of rust or grime, the interior was spotless and shipshape. The crew looked happy. The quality of this ship went well beyond her appearance. The capital initial *E*s on her bridge, gun mounts, and stack were evidence that her battle efficiency was top among her class in the fleet. A few questions confirmed her overall quality: reenlistment rate double the fleet average; score in the most recent Operational Readiness Inspection better than any other ship in the squadron.

What made this particular ship, one of eight identical frigates with a crew drawn from the same sources and operating under similar conditions as its squadron mates, so much better than all the others? Leadership. The one factor that made this ship superior to the rest of the litter was her commanding officer: he was an outstanding leader. It was his personal ability that constituted the margin of excellence between his command and the others in the squadron.

What is leadership?

Leadership is a complex attribute that is not confined to naval commanders. Every profession has its leaders—the church, the government, business, law, medicine, and, unfortunately, even crime. There are good leaders and evil ones—Charlemagne and Attila, Eisenhower and Hitler. There are leaders at every level—Gen. John Pershing and Sgt. Alvin York, Gen. George C. Marshall and Lt. Audie Murphy. And there are charismatic leaders and introspective types—Gen. Douglas MacArthur and Adm. Hyman Rickover. This book, however, is about naval leadership, a particular niche in this universal subject and a category to which almost all of the general rules of leadership apply, but conversely, a brand of leadership with many sharply unique tenets of its own.

How do we define leadership?

In its sense most relevant to the Navy, leadership is "the ability to influence people to do things they would not otherwise want to do." That is the essence of military leadership at all levels. In its most benign application it is getting the crew ready for inspection by having them take pride in the appearance of themselves and their equipment. In the ultimate it is inspiring men to risk their lives in attacking an enemy or holding an outpost at all costs.

In the United States, the military establishment exists to defend the nation. The mission of our military forces is to be able to fight to win. Winning will require defeating the enemy in battle. Battles mean that people will die on both sides. Our troops cannot shrink from battle or avoid casualties. The ultimate aim of military leadership is to inspire our people in uniform to be willing to give their lives in the service of their country. So, military leadership is at the core of our national defense. Without military leaders, the national defense establishment would be toothless.

Where do we get such leaders—the lifeblood of our Army, Navy, Marine Corps, and Air Force?

There is an old saw that "leaders are born, not made." The truth is that leaders *are* made. But the proper material is required for their making. There are certain physical attributes within the human race—some genetic, some environmental, and some seemingly spontaneous—

that when identified can be built on and developed into powerful traits of military leadership.

Principal among these innate attributes is intelligence. I have never known a leader who was not intelligent. A second essential attribute is energy. Armchair strategists are not very helpful when active leadership is required. And a third essential trait is character, a moral outlook and sense of integrity. A person without a sense of moral responsibility cannot become a military leader—a crime king, perhaps, but not a successful military leader. There are other attributes that contribute to the makeup of a competent leader, but these are the substance of military leadership.

I have known people in leadership positions who were neither intelligent nor energetic nor moral. They created as much havoc among our own forces as an enemy. In most cases they were quickly found out and summarily removed, but their mere existence represented a failure of leadership on the part of their seniors, the ones responsible for or who tolerated their appointment.

Once potential leaders in the military have been identified by their personal attributes, the service begins the process of leadership training. Enlisted people so recognized are promoted to noncommissioned officers, learning on the job. The next step can be a formal course, a petty officer or NCO leadership training school. With officers, the identification of potential military leaders takes place during the admissions process for a service academy or while the person serves in the ROTC at a civilian institution. Candidates are selected for precommissioned training on the basis of their high school academic grades (a measure of intelligence), their school activities and public service (an indication of energy), and an essay (to express their moral convictions). At the service academy or university, leadership is taught as an accredited course, and the newly minted officer joins the operating forces with a substantive appreciation of his or her leadership responsibilities.

Ultimately, through combat or the arduous demands of peacetime deployments, the true leadership qualities of each officer will emerge. Some will be better leaders than others. Those who prove unsatisfactory will leave the service when their obligated time is done—or before; the superstars will go on to CNO and theater commands; those in between will fall somewhere on a bell curve.

As an officer's career in the service progresses, his or her effectiveness as a leader improves as well, up to a certain point. It is a maturing process based on innate capabilities, experience, education, and training. Some naval officers will hit their limit as a division officer or, for aviators, a flight section leader, and will progress no further. They will not screen for a ship or squadron command. Those who are selected for command and who are successful in that tour of duty will later be considered for a major command, and upon a commendable tour of duty will be eligible for consideration for selection to flag rank.

Line officers constantly face the challenges of leading people. Those who are successful will move on to the next plateau of more important command assignments under more demanding conditions. Those who lead well are considered for larger responsibilities. It is the familiar hierarchal pyramid structure, with CNO at the top. One person—at a time—can be CNO. It was my experience as vice chief, later as the chief of naval operations, and then as a confidant of subsequent CNOs that there were never more than three individuals seriously considered as candidates for the appointment to CNO, and usually only two. Yet as an officer proceeds up the naval hierarchy he has equal opportunity with all of his year group contemporaries to compete for selection to the next rank, which will take him one step closer to the top.

This selection process is to my mind scrupulously fair for the individual and remarkably healthy for the naval officer corps. It is based on an individual's accomplishments as a matter of signed record, not on word-of-mouth advocacy. Furthermore, the selection board is primarily influenced by the person's accomplishments *for the Navy,* not for him- or herself. A fitness report showing that a young officer's division won the majority of the CO's kudos at captain's inspections will mean infinitely more than graduation from a war college correspondence course in world affairs. *Leadership* is the governing factor throughout the U.S. Navy's officer promotion system. This selection process ensures that the best of the Navy's leaders are promoted to the next rank so that each officer grade comprises individuals demonstrably qualified to lead the naval units, staffs, and officers at that level of seniority.

There is another way of looking at leaders in the Navy. It is equally informative to examine the leadership factor from a "vertical" view. When going over the fitness report records of an individual four-star admiral, my prerogative when I was CNO, I invariably found the record to show outstanding accomplishments by the senior flag officer from the earliest days of his commissioned service. No tour of duty, no matter how mundane, had been unsuccessful, and the man himself had always been an important component of that success. The most impressive single factor in defining success was *getting things done*—winning the *E,* getting high marks on the ORI, demonstrating impressive reenlistment rates and few disciplinary cases, even leading the ship or squadron in per capita contributions to Navy Relief. The real measure of an officer's leadership qualities was represented in his fitness report record by concrete achievements as opposed to a thesaurus of complimentary adjectives.

This landmark volume by Edgar F. Puryear Jr., *American Admiralship: The Art of Naval Command,* for the first time to my knowledge presents a practical discussion of leadership for naval officers. First, it is based on the premises that "leaders are made, not born," and that the making of a leader is not a perfunctory process. Puryear further accepts the fact that every leader has his own personality and style. But certain elements of good leadership are common to the persona of every acknowledged naval leader, and Puryear's treatment of these qualities is both scholarly and realistic.

This is not a leadership handbook or a "how-to" tract. It is a serious work on a subject of central concern to our military establishment, and one that has long suffered from superficial treatment. One of the book's most important aspects is that it relates to leadership at every level of a commissioned officer's responsibility. We must remember that the success of every great naval leader in the final analysis depended on the subordinates beneath him in the chain of command who effectively carried out their leader's brilliant strategies—such heroes as carrier captain Jocko Clark, submarine skipper Dick O'Kane, squadron CO Jimmy Flatley, destroyer commander Arleigh Burke, and the thousands of Navy petty officers who refused to leave their battle stations on sinking ships. Every officer and petty officer in the U.S. Navy is a leader. Some are better leaders than others, but even those least accomplished in the skills of leadership have critical responsibilities for the people under their control, whether it be in the magazine of a destroyer or as flight leader of an alpha strike from a carrier. To win a war, which is the Navy's reason for existence, the Navy must depend on these leaders at every level. If they lack leadership ability, the Navy must make them better. They are all part of the bell curve. The primary responsibility of a naval officer in every grade is to help move that curve to the right, to improve leadership at every echelon. Understanding the principles and lessons in this book will be of inestimable help in enabling naval officers to do just that.

Adm. James L. Holloway III, USN (Ret.)
Chief of Naval Operations, 1974–78

ACKNOWLEDGMENTS

This book is a collaborative effort, and I have been assisted by too many people to mention them all, particularly each of the more than 130 generals and admirals whom I have interviewed over the last forty years. These great leaders are the epitome of character, and their selfless service has made the American people admire them, believe in them, and follow them. These exceptional men have shown a never-ending commitment to the development of the future generations of young men and women who have chosen the military as their career. We owe an enduring debt of gratitude to each of them.

I appreciate the association and support of the National Defense University (NDU) and its presidents: Lt. Gen. Ervin J. Rokke, USAF (Ret.), president 1994–97; Lt. Gen. Richard A. Chilcoat, USA (Ret.), 1997–2000; and Vice Adm. Paul Gaffney, USN (Ret.), 2000–03. Vice Adm. Paul Gaffney and Chief of Naval Operations Vern Clark were particularly important in endorsing and encouraging the manuscript. I owe a sincere debt of gratitude to James Keagle, Vice President for Academic Affairs, for his insights, counsel, and judgment in the development of the concept for *American Admiralship: The Art of Naval Command,* and for his assistance in handling so many administrative details, which allowed me to research, write, and lecture on naval leadership. I also had invaluable administrative help from Col. Clyde Newman, USA (Ret.), chief of staff to the president of NDU, who assisted me with numerous details as the book progressed and provided me with the research assistance of Yvonne Eaton, who coordinated my requests to the NDU Library for books and articles, found valuable source material, and took care of research details as well. I am sincerely grateful to the staff of the NDU Library for their assistance.

My family collaborated in the making of this book as well, and I offer my thanks to each of them. My wife, Agnes G. Puryear, has been patient during the years of research, traveling, and writing. My son Beverly Spotswood "Chug" Puryear has offered a superb example of the character an individual needs to succeed in the business world. Special thanks to my son Edgar F. "Chip" Puryear III, who provided me with invaluable scholarly research help in tracking down reliable leads. My soldier son S. Braxton "Colt" Puryear continues his selfless service to his country in the Virginia National Guard. And my soldier son Alfred A. "Cotton" Puryear, teacher, reporter, photographer, and computer genius, offered editorial and computer skills and journalistic abilities that proved indispensable.

I continued to receive editorial support from the founder of Presidio Press, Col. Robert V. Kane, USA (Ret.), who made a lasting contribution to the education of America's military forces by establishing the press. I owe a debt of gratitude to Comdr. Thomas J. Cutler, USN (Ret.), of the U.S. Naval Institute for his frequent counsel and good judgment. The oral histories conducted by Paul Stillwell and John T. Mason Jr. offered enormous insight into the leadership and character of our senior naval admirals.

Helen M. Slaven gave meaningful assistance in typing letters and relieving me of duties and challenges that arose, allowing me time to focus my attention on the book.

I pay special tribute to Deborah L. Foster, whose commitment to this endeavor has been exceptional. She typed, revised, and polished my work, all with a turnaround speed that was invaluable in completing the manuscript. The copy editing by Melinda N. Conner has been most valuable and has made this a better book.

A constant model for me has been my friend Brig. Gen. Philip J. Erdle, USAF (Ret.), whose character and leadership have made a lasting contribution to our country and who is the embodiment of the concept of his West Point alma mater's motto: "Duty, Honor, Country."

AMERICAN ADMIRALSHIP

Decision

Making decisions is of the essence in leadership.

General of the Army Dwight D. Eisenhower

While this is a study of naval leadership, the thoughts and insights of General of the Army Dwight D. Eisenhower, who served as D-day commander, U.S. Army chief of staff (1946–47), the first NATO commander (1949–52), and president of the United States (1953–60), are relevant. His words provide a foundation for the study of naval leadership at the highest level. In my interview with General Eisenhower on May 2, 1963, he commented:

> I have pondered the question of leadership quite a bit, and I think I can come back to take as my starting point the statement that Napoleon is reputed to have made: "Genius in leadership is the ability to do an average thing when everyone around you is going crazy. . . ." When you come right down to it, leadership is, of course, being exerted all the time in the capacity of boosting morale, confidence, and all that, but leadership is most noticeable when tough decisions finally have to be made. This is the time when you get conflicting advice and urgent advice of every kind. Now this is the kind of leadership that's often concealed

from the public. . . . *But making decisions is of the essence in leadership*—that is, handling large problems whether or not you are at war or at peace. When you make these decisions it is not done with any reaching for the dramatic. It is almost everyday and commonplace. You reach a conclusion based upon the facts as you see them, the evaluations of the several factors as you see them, the relationship of one fact to another, and, above all, your convictions as to the capacity of different individuals to fit into these different places. You come to a decision after you've taken all these things into consideration. Then you decide and say, "That's what we'll do."[1]

The position of command is a lonely one. At no time does a leader feel loneliness more deeply than when having to make a critical, high-level decision dealing with life and death, success or failure, victory or defeat. It is an overwhelming responsibility that few people desire and for which considerably fewer are qualified. But making decisions is part of leadership. In time of war, the admiral who does not have the strength to make decisions and the judgment to be right a large percentage of the time does not remain long in a position of high command. Admirals are human and are subject to the same strains and stresses that lesser beings face. Their mistakes, however, can be counted in deaths and destruction; it is a responsibility that no sane person takes lightly.

The wartime admirals I discuss here had to make difficult and grave decisions. We must take into consideration two facts, however, in evaluating these decisions. First, the decisions were based on the information *immediately available* to them, not the volumes of information that a historian has available for evaluation. A commander must act on the facts available at that time. Second, to one who has never been involved with making high-level decisions, the process looks easy. Those in lower echelons are mostly ignorant of the complexity of the commander's problems and become impatient when they receive a late or unclear decision. It is easy to criticize but hard to do better if placed at a similar level of responsibility.

Wartime commanders do have a significant advantage: normally, they can select key staff members, and the advisers they choose are generally the most competent people available, dedicated and strong professionals. One cannot take the advice of such people lightly. When these advisers are all opposed to a top admiral's conclusion, the decision-making process becomes far more difficult.

President Franklin D. Roosevelt's decision-making methodology in World War II illustrates the value of good advisers. His most important move was establishing the Joint Chiefs of Staff in February 1942. Its initial members were Army Chief of Staff Gen. George C. Marshall; Chief of Naval Operations Adm. Ernest J. King; and Gen. Henry H. Arnold, chief of the Army Air Corps (the Air Force was not then a separate service).

Marshall advised Roosevelt to appoint an adviser to the commander in chief for the purpose of coordinating all U.S. military forces, and suggested Adm. William D. Leahy for the position. He was a superb choice. Leahy had served as chief of naval operations from 1937 to 1939; governor of Puerto Rico; ambassador to France from January 1941 to May 1942 (a difficult period because of the German occupation); on the Joint Chiefs of Staff; and as a member of the Combined Chiefs of Staff, which included military officers from the Allied countries, primarily the British. As chief of staff to the commander in chief, an office without precedent in American military annals, Leahy contributed his knowledge and judgment to the awesome decisions that had to be made. "Mr. Roosevelt," he later said, ". . . made decisions after careful consideration of requested or volunteered advice"; much of that advice came from his military counselors. Leahy noted that his duties as the president's chief of staff

> required careful selection of all military dispatches of sufficient importance to be read by the President. Also involved was the screening of numerous and on occasion, insistent demands from many persons—military, diplomatic, and civilian—for conferences with the President on matters having a real or supposed military angle. It was natural that this close, daily association with both war Presidents brought all manner of men and causes to my office, seeking intercession in their behalf. Among these were representatives of defeated and exiled governments, as well as our active allies, who often pleaded for more American dollars, more American arms, and sometimes for American troops.[2]

How did this position, so important to U.S. military decision making, evolve? Leahy later reflected on his appointment:

On Monday, July 6, 1942, the President telephoned to my little office in the State Department Building and asked that I come over at noon for a conference. We talked for a half-hour. He had made up his mind. He wanted me to serve on his staff as a military and naval adviser to the Commander-in-Chief. He did most of the talking—he always did. He asked me pertinent questions and I replied as best I could. We reviewed the French situation and at the end of the half-hour it was obvious that the discussion was not completed, so the President asked me to come to lunch with him the next day.

On July 7 we had lunch together in his office. I do not recall that he recommended the actual title "Chief of Staff," but the duties he outlined, such as daily contact with the three branches of the armed services, the reading of reports and giving him summaries and digests, added up to the kind of post that we referred to in the Navy as a "chief of staff." It does not carry command authority. A chief of staff in the Navy acts in an advisory capacity. The Army definition of "chief of staff" is somewhat different. General Marshall had that designation and he was the active commander of the Army. It was planned that as soon as the East Wing of the White House, then under construction, should be completed, I was to move in so that I could be near the President. The President talked at length about the military and naval situation and what he hoped I would be able to accomplish for him in the direction of coordinating the effort of the military and naval arms in our national defense.

Later, in a talk with General Marshall, the question of designation of the office arose and I think I suggested the title "Chief of Staff." Marshall thought that a very accurate designation and we all agreed on it.[3]

Leahy reported for duty July 20, 1942:

Almost immediately it developed that there were matters to take up with the President every day, so I made arrangements to meet him every morning at about a quarter of ten. I usually arrived at the office between 8:30 and 8:45. My aide already would have gone over the accumulation of overnight dispatches and reports. There would be cables from people in many parts of the world addressed directly to Roosevelt, copies of cables from the theater commanders to Marshall, King, or Arnold, and dispatches going out to them. . . .

From this mass of colored papers I would select those which should be brought to the attention of the President, place them in a tan portfolio, and usually meet Mr. Roosevelt as he emerged from the elevator on his way to his study. After a cheery "Good Morning" (he called me "Bill" and I addressed him as

"Mr. President") we would start our discussions as he was wheeled over to his office. Many mornings he would prefer to go directly to the Map Room, which was one of the best-guarded portions of the White House.

The President kept himself informed minutely on the progress of the war. The maps in the Map Room were so hung that he would not have to get out of his wheel chair to look at them. There were flags and pins of various colors showing the disposition of our land, naval, and air forces over the entire globe. While looking at them he and I would talk about some overnight development that seemed at the time to have significance.

There were a number of young officers assigned to the White House Map Room who received military dispatches twenty-four hours a day. The President could have instant information any time he needed it. From this Map Room also messages would be sent by him all over the world, as there was a relay from this point in the White House to the Communications Center in the Pentagon Building.

War is no respecter of schedules, and there were many mornings when I went up to the President's bedroom to discuss urgent matters. More than once when I would arrive, the President would be in the bathroom shaving. I would pull out my papers and we would start talking while he continued shaving. (The President used an old-fashioned straight razor.)

Whenever the President left Washington I usually went with him, except for some weekends at Hyde Park. One of the bedrooms on his private car was assigned to me. His train always was equipped with communication facilities, and we would receive on the train all of the important dispatches that were coming into my office. If those communications had an important bearing on the conduct of the war or on international implications affecting the war, I would so inform the President.

It soon became known that the President's Chief of Staff conferred with him every day. This brought a stream of callers to my office. Many problems were presented to me with the thought that I would pass them on to the President and perhaps get a favorable decision on behalf of those presenting the problem. I did take up with the President many complaints that I thought were serious. Many high officials who themselves had frequent access to the Presidential ear would come to me with their troubles. I would listen sympathetically but in most cases reminded them that the President was already thoroughly informed on the particular situation they were discussing.[4]

Leahy's contributions were essential to the decisions made by the commander in chief in the conduct of the war:

The most important function of the Chief of Staff was the maintaining of daily liaison between the President and the Joint Chiefs of Staff. It was my job to pass on to the Joint Chiefs of Staff the basic thinking of the President on all war plans and strategy. In turn I brought back from the Joint Chiefs a consensus of their thinking. . . .

The Joint Chiefs became the principal agency for Army-Navy–Air Force coordination. Its duties during the war never were defined precisely. I have heard that in some file there is a chit or memorandum from Roosevelt, setting up the Joint Chiefs, but I never saw it. The absence of any fixed charter of responsibility allowed great flexibility in the JCS organization and enabled us to extend its activities to meet the changing requirements of the war. The Joint Chiefs of Staff was an instrument of the Commander-in-Chief and was responsible to him. I was his representative on that body. As the senior officer present, I presided at its meetings, prepared the agendas, and signed all of the major papers and decisions. . . . The Joint Chiefs would assign problems to . . . subsidiary groups. The latter would work up studies covering the subject. They generally did an excellent job, but their papers were too long. There were times when meetings of the JCS seemed rather like a Chautauqua gathering as the chairman of one of these committees "lectured" on his findings. They gave us so much stuff to read that I had to take the reports home. There simply wasn't time during the day to digest them, and part of my duty was to give the President a summary of the findings of these various committees and the action of the Joint Chiefs of Staff thereon.[5]

President Roosevelt died on April 12, 1945, and was succeeded in office by Harry S. Truman. The Joint Chiefs and the chief of staff to the commander in chief provided continuity to the war effort. Leahy commented:

That was the team which, under the constant direction of the President of the United States, ran the war. One tribute I shall never forget came from President Truman. Shortly after he became Commander-in-Chief, following the death of President Roosevelt, I explained to him in detail the functioning of his Joint Chiefs of Staff. He listened intently. When I was through, Truman said, "Why, Admiral, if the South had had a staff organization like that, the Confederates would have won the Civil War. Lee would not have had Johnson, Beauregard, Longstreet, and the other generals running around on the loose." The same statement could be made in regard to Lincoln's difficulties. Lincoln tried to create a chief of staff and a chain of command. Congress thwarted his effort.[6]

Tough decisions were not confined to the White House, of course. Fortunately for the United States, there were men qualified and able to make them at all levels of the chain of command. As commander in chief, Pacific (CinCPac), Adm. Chester W. Nimitz had equally difficult decisions to make. On July 20, 1943, for example, the Joint Chiefs of Staff ordered Nimitz to prepare plans for the invasion and occupation of the Marshall Islands in the Pacific Ocean. The timeline of the plan was to be presented by August 20, 1943, and the invasion had as a target date January 1, 1944. Three islands—Kwajalein, Wotje, and Maloelap—were to be taken simultaneously.

Nimitz had been appalled by the tremendous losses suffered by U.S. forces in the taking of Tarawa and opposed the idea of taking all three islands at once. He preferred invading Kwajalein first. His advisers—Marine Maj. Gen. Holland M. Smith, Adm. Raymond A. Spruance, and Vice Adm. Richard K. Turner—disagreed and strongly recommended first taking Wotje and Maloelap and using these islands as support bases for the effort to take Kwajalein. Spruance reasoned:

> The schedule of operations set up by the JCS called for the Pacific Fleet, after the capture of Kwajalein, to leave the Marshalls and proceed to the South Pacific, in order to support an operation under Admiral Halsey. Under these conditions, I argued as strongly as I could with Admiral Nimitz against Kwajalein, proposing instead Wotje and Maloelap. My argument was based, not on any anticipated difficulty in taking Kwajalein rather than Wotje and Maloelap, but on the insecurity of our line of communications into Kwajalein after the withdrawal of the Pacific Fleet. Kwajalein would have stood encircled by Japanese airfields on Mili, Maloelap, Wotje and Ponape, further away but still in range. A field on Kusaie was under construction but was never completed. With the air pipeline through Eniwetok open back to Japan and with the activity which had been shown by Japanese air in their attacks on our fleet during the Gilberts operation, I felt that our support shipping moving into Kwajalein would have a tough time of it. In my arguments I was supported by Admiral Turner and General Holland Smith, but I was overruled by Admiral Nimitz.[7]

Nimitz's biography provides further insight regarding his decision:

Spruance tried to convince Nimitz that if any objective was to be omitted, it better be Kwajalein, not the outer islands, and Turner and Smith supported him. Nimitz refused to be persuaded. His decision was confirmed by new radio intelligence showing that the Japanese were strengthening their outer islands at the expense of Kwajalein. Evidently it was against one or more of the outer islands that the enemy expected the attack to come.

At last, at a meeting on December 14, Admiral Nimitz polled the Fifth Fleet flag and general officers concerning where they should hit.

"Raymond," he asked, "what do you think now?"

"Outer islands," replied Spruance.

"Kelly?"

"Outer islands," replied Turner. (Turner would lead the amphibious beach landing.)

"Holland?"

"Outer islands," replied Smith.

And so it went around the room, every one of the commanders recommending an initial assault on the outer islands of Wotje and Maloelap. When the poll was completed, there was a brief silence. Then Nimitz said quietly, "Well, gentlemen, our next objective will be Kwajalein."

But Nimitz's staff wouldn't give up.

When the meeting was adjourned, Turner and Spruance stayed behind to argue some more. Turner insisted to Nimitz that the decision to go straight into Kwajalein was dangerous and reckless. He argued and argued. He raised his voice. Spruance asserted that Kelly was right.

When Ray and Kelly had exhausted their arguments, Nimitz said calmly, "This is it. If you don't want to do it, the Department will find someone else to do it. Do you want to do it or not?"

Kelly Turner frowned for a moment, then relaxed his knitted brows and smiled, "Sure I want to do it."[8]

The invasion was a stunning success. The Marines lost 196 killed and 550 wounded; the Army, 177 killed and 1,000 wounded. In contrast, the Japanese lost 8,000 men; only 100 Japanese surrendered.

Admiral Nimitz followed a distinctive methodology in his decision making. Outside the door of his office was a sign that stated: "Nations, like men, should grasp time by the forelock instead of the fetlock." Inside on the wall was a sign with three questions he expected his staff to answer when a decision was being discussed: (1) Is the proposed operation likely to succeed? (2) What might be the consequences of failure? (3) Is it in the realm of practicability of material and supplies? Under the glass top of his desk were several cards with military quotes. In the center was a card with a list that stated: "Objective, Offensive, Surprise, Superiority of Force at Point of Contact, Simplicity, Security, Movement, Economy of Force, Cooperation." His biographer, E. B. Potter, noted that "Nimitz thought of these merely as reminders, a check-off list of things to be considered before launching an operation, beginning with a clearly defined objective and ending with full cooperation among forces involved—this last being particularly important in a theater of operations in which there were two separate commands, his and MacArthur's."[9]

One of the gutsiest decisions Admirals Nimitz and Halsey ever made was to approve the bombing raid on Tokyo in 1942. The main objective of the raid was psychological. The people of Japan had been told by their government that they were invulnerable, that they could never be invaded or bombed. Hitting the capital of the Japanese homeland would cause Japanese citizens to doubt the reliability of their leaders. In addition, it would provide Americans with sorely needed good news. After the surprise attack on Pearl Harbor, the losses of Wake Island and Guam, and the situation in the Philippines, where Bataan had surrendered and U.S. forces were making a last stand on Corregidor, the bombing of Tokyo would be a great morale booster. The planners also hoped that a raid on Tokyo would make the Japanese divert aircraft, shipping, and military forces from offensive operational activities to homeland defense.

Leading the sixteen B-25 bombers was Lt. Col. James H. Doolittle of the U.S. Army Air Force. The crew members, all volunteers, were trained to take off from the deck of a carrier, something never before attempted by a plane of that size. Nimitz selected Vice Adm. William F. Halsey to lead the naval force assigned to bring the bombers into range.[10]

The plan was to get within four hundred miles of Tokyo to ensure that the aircraft had sufficient fuel to land safely in China after dropping the bombs. When the fleet was spotted by a Japanese picket ship before reaching the desired take-off point, Halsey was faced with a difficult decision. His autobiography provides the following account:

We fueled the heavy ships on the seventeenth, 1,000 miles east of Tokyo, and at 1400 they commenced their run-in at 23 knots, with the destroyers and tankers left behind, as at Marcus. Everything went smoothly until 0300 on the eighteenth when our radars began getting blips from what we assumed were picket vessels. These outliers we managed to dodge, but at 0745 another was sighted, 12,000 yards on our port bow. I directed the *Nashville* to sink it. Before she succeeded, we intercepted a radio transmission which showed, by its strength, that it was originating close aboard, and our inference was that the picket had given the alarm. Although we were then 650 miles from Tokyo, instead of the 400 we had hoped for, the fact that our force had been reported left me no choice. At 0800 I sent "Pete" Mitscher a signal: LAUNCH PLANES X TO COL DOOLITTLE AND HIS GALLANT COMMAND GOOD LUCK AND GOD BLESS YOU.[11]

The bombers had been scheduled to launch in the afternoon, with Doolittle taking off first so that his plane could drop incendiary bombs at night to light up Tokyo for the other fifteen B-25s. The air crews were surprised when they were ordered to take off in the morning. As Doolittle later described it: there was an "ear-shattering Klaxon horn" and a booming voice ordered: "Now hear this! Now hear this! Army pilots, man your planes." Not only were the planes launching earlier than planned, but the weather was miserable. The sea was rough, and the *Hornet,* the carrier loaded with the sixteen B-25s, "plunged into mountainous waves that sent water cascading down the deck. Rain pelted us as we ran toward our aircraft. It was not an ideal day for a mission like this one." Doolittle's aircraft took off first, successfully, at 0825; the last plane left at 0924.[12]

Halsey's decision to launch the mission was one of the most courageous combat decisions in military history, and it significantly lessened Doolittle's chance of success. Not only were the planes 650 miles rather than 400 miles away from the target when they took off, but after dropping their bombs they had to fly 1,400 miles to terribly poor airfields in a strange country. Nor were the Chinese expecting them. China's leader, Generalissimo Chiang Kai-shek, was not informed of the raid for several reasons. First, the information might have been leaked to the Japanese. In addition, Chiang would have opposed it because he feared reprisals against China's people, a concern that time showed was justified; it was estimated that the Japanese assassinated

250,000 men, women, and children in reprisal. Halsey, who felt bad about his decision to launch 668 miles (his figure) from Tokyo rather than the planned 400 miles, apologized to Doolittle in a letter written several days after the launching: "I hated to dump you off at that distance, but because of discovery there was nothing else to do. . . . I stated to my staff that on landing, you should have two-stars pinned on each shoulder, and the Medal of Honor pinned around your neck. . . . I am highly honored in having had you and the very gallant and brave lads with you, serve under my command for a short period of time. It is something I shall always remember. I do not know of any more gallant deed in history than that performed by your squadron."[13] Halsey's comment was prophetic. Doolittle was secretly called to Washington, where President Roosevelt presented him with the Medal of Honor and promoted him from lieutenant colonel to brigadier general.

There is no more difficult decision for a commander than to relieve a senior flag officer, particularly when he is a close friend. Admiral Nimitz did not hesitate to act when the situation arose on Nouméa, a small Pacific island whose harbor was a crucial port for U.S. Navy ships. When Nimitz flew into Nouméa on September 28, 1942, for meetings, he found the harbor in a state of chaos. There were eighty cargo vessels tied up, all desperately needed for Operation Torch, the invasion of North Africa. The ships had been improperly loaded—for example, with guns in one ship and ammunition in another— but could not be unloaded because the port lacked the necessary piers, cranes, barges, trucks, and workers. The ships were sent to Wellington, New Zealand, for unloading and reloading, but the longshoremen at that port were on strike. Vice Adm. Robert Ghormley, as the fleet commander, was blamed for the mess, although the real blame lay in Washington. Nimitz arrived to find Ghormley "haggard with fatigue and anxiety," and thought it poor judgment that Ghormley's office was a small "hot box." During the meeting with Nimitz, Ghormley received several high-priority messages. Rather than reacting to them with the appropriate commands, he said out loud, "My God, what are we going to do about this?" Nimitz was disturbed enough to consider relieving Ghormley.[14]

On October 15, 1942, Nimitz met with his senior flag officers to obtain their views on whether Ghormley was capable of handling the challenges he would face as commander South Pacific, particularly the need to hold Guadalcanal. Was it within Ghormley's ability to handle the leadership responsibility ahead? The consensus among those at the meeting was that Ghormley did not have the necessary qualities. Then Nimitz hit the issue head-on, asking each of them, "Is it time for me to relieve Admiral Ghormley?" Each replied, "Yes." Nimitz did not announce his decision at that time.[15]

That evening, Nimitz had already dressed for bed when a small group of staff officers who had not been at the meeting arrived and asked to be heard. Specifically, they asked Nimitz to "put aside any thoughts of sympathy or understanding for Ghormley, a brother officer, and order Halsey to take over the SoPac command." Nimitz told the group that he appreciated their coming to see him, knew that their motives were the best, and would give every consideration to their suggestions. The fact that these officers were not afraid to approach Nimitz speaks well of his rapport with them. In any event, Nimitz had already made up his mind. The next day, October 16, he wired Admiral King for permission to relieve Ghormley and replace him with Halsey. King immediately fired back: "Affirmative."[16]

Admiral Nimitz next sent a dispatch to Ghormley:

> After carefully weighing all factors, have decided that talents and previous experience of Halsey can best be applied to the situation by having him take over duties of ComSoPac as soon as practicable after his arrival Nouméa 18th your date. I greatly appreciate your loyal and devoted efforts toward the accomplishment of a most difficult task. I shall order you to report to Halsey for the time being, as I believe he will need your thorough knowledge of the situation and your loyal help. CINC has approved this change. Orders will follow shortly.[17]

It could not have been an easy decision. Nimitz and Ghormley had begun serving together as midshipmen at the Naval Academy. Nimitz laid out his private feelings in a letter to his wife: "Today I have replaced Ghormley with Halsey. It was a sore mental struggle and the decision was not reached until after hours of anguished consideration. Reason (private): Ghormley was too immersed in detail and not sufficiently bold and aggressive at the right times. I feel better now that it has been done. I am very fond of G. and I hope I have not made a life enemy. I believe not. The interests of the nation transcend private interests." Several days later, Nimitz was informed that Ghormley would be stopping in Nouméa. Nimitz wrote to Mrs. Nimitz, "It will be a tough time for G. and probably for me also, but we both must face it."[18]

When they met, Nimitz told him: "Bob, I had to pick from the whole Navy the man best fitted to handle that situation. Were you that man?" Ghormley replied, "No. If you put it that way, I guess I wasn't." That evening, Nimitz again revealed his feelings in a letter to his wife: "G. is taking it in fine style and his fine manner has saved me much embarrassment. . . . Ghormley left at 2 P.M. and while he was not too cheerful, I am sure no one could have borne the disappointment."[19]

Rear Adm. Arleigh Burke was jumped over ninety-two admirals senior to him when he was selected by President Eisenhower to be chief of naval operations in 1955. Seniority is an important element of the military hierarchy, and such a jump is almost certain to generate antipathy in those passed over, in turn presenting real challenges in decision making. Burke was asked, "Wasn't there resentment among the admirals who were senior to you before you became CNO?" He replied:

> Sure, they were all resentful. Why not? No man reaches a position like that without feeling he is qualified. They're all good people. They all spent a lifetime—thirty, thirty-five years of working. Of course they resented that they had been passed over. Now there was my biggest job—to get rid of that resentment. You can't order it out. It's natural. . . . Your destiny is dependent on those admirals. The most important thing I had to do was get the confidence that what was being done were the correct things to be done for the Navy—for the country. They had to believe that. *No organization can go very far unless it has a cause that's bigger than itself.*[20]

The first step he took toward mitigating the resentment toward him was to retain all of the staff of Adm. Robert B. Carney, his predecessor as CNO, except for the flag lieutenant.

> This one young fellow was due to go so I looked down the list. I had a list of all my destroyer captains. A flag lieutenant is very close to the admiral. He has to know how the admiral thinks, what he's going to do. He has to act for him lots of times, so it ought to be somebody with the same sort of background. I chose my flag lieutenant from the list of captains of COMDESLANT, that I'd just been

with, and I chose a man I had never met, I chose him because he had such a hell of a good reputation. . . . So I looked down there and picked Weschler. He turned out to be a hell of a man. They were loyal to Carney. They were used to doing it his way. They thought he had gotten a raw deal, a dirty deal and I was a usurper—knowing damn well it wasn't my fault, I didn't do it, but still I was a usurper. They resented the hell out of me but they were experienced and they were loyal to the Navy. I called them in and said, "Now look, I don't give a damn whether you like me or not. That's not the point. What I'd like you to do is the very best job you can—advise me." That group of people never did like me like they liked Admiral Carney—I couldn't expect it. But they did a good job. I had a group that was experienced, but a group I had to always be careful with. They didn't give a damn if they were pleasing me or not. They were operating strictly from a duty proposition and that's good. Uncomfortable, but good. Later on, they left.[21]

When Admiral Burke was asked to describe his first priority as CNO, he replied:

I realized that my most difficult job was to obtain the maximum effort out of the senior officers toward a common direction. Sometimes you lose a friend, but you usually get him back. You have to make choices. One of my friends is an excellent admiral—four-star admiral. He felt he should have had a job that I gave to someone else. To this day I don't know. The other man did a very good job but you have to make a choice. I did what I thought was right, but I could be wrong. Lots of times there are things that other people know and you don't know and you make the wrong choice. But you've got to make it based on what you know and not what somebody else knows. You've got to make sure you know as much as you can but neither can you wait forever until you find out. You lose sometimes.[22]

Admiral Burke understood that the human factor, toughness in particular, is a vital part of decision making: "You have to make tough, hard decisions and make them after you've analyzed as much as you can within the time that you've got, make them as right as you can, but then you have to stand by them, and sometimes force the decisions on people that hurt people. You can't do anything productive without adversely affecting some people."[23]

Realizing the importance of his staff for making good and informed decisions, Burke had no tolerance for mediocrity. Asked, "How did you handle the cases of people who weren't pulling their weight?" he responded:

I got rid of them, summarily. The first thing that a commander must learn is not to tolerate incompetence. As soon as you tolerate incompetence—it doesn't matter why—you have an incompetent organization. It's quite natural that the level of performance of an organization always goes down if you have mediocre people. It's quite natural. It doesn't take very many mediocre people—if you permit it. I'd rather have that incompetent person near me if I'm going to tolerate incompetence at all. I'll put the competent person way out where he makes decisions and I don't have to watch over him. It's not good to surround yourself with competent people—that doesn't do it. You must put competent people in your organization in the right spots. You'll make mistakes. Some people can't do it. Some people are not equally capable of all things. You can't assume that a man is suitable for all types of work, so you make mistakes.[24]

Asked: "Where does a flag officer who's just been canned go?" Burke replied: "Out. He's had it. War is that way. It may be beyond his capability, but that's too bad. When you permit improper performance of duty you accept an excuse and excuses get poorer and poorer and people don't try very hard. This is why it's absolutely necessary that you have very high standards and you make sure those standards are met or you cut throats."[25]

Admiral Burke was a firm believer in the importance of input from his junior officers when he was making decisions. He commented in his oral history:

One of the things we had trouble with in our own commands, when they were uncertain about an action they were taking, they would sometimes conceal it by an attitude "I know best, I know what I'm doing." This was particularly true when a commander issues an order to a subordinate, and the subordinate questions it. Some commanders may say: "Look, I know what I'm doing. I gave you that order. Carry it out." The subordinate does—but may lose some confidence in the judgment of his senior. The junior has got to be able to, not to protest the order, but to make sure he understands it, and if he thinks it to be in error, he should inform his senior with his reasons for doing so. Confidence of juniors in their seniors builds military effectiveness. The commander has got to generate that confidence.

I think it is very difficult for a very junior officer to write to a senior officer giving his early thoughts on a subject when he was not quite sure he was on the right path. He could not be certain his ideas were sound—and he had not yet examined the whole problem. Yet his early impressions—or off the cuff judgments—could be very useful. And of course sometimes the senior officer was bound to be in error.

Decision making for the Joint Chiefs of Staff is often most challenging when a consensus is necessary. When the Joint Chiefs cannot reach a decision because there are differences of opinion among the service chiefs, the president as commander in chief has to make the decision. Admiral Burke remembered:

> Now, this President Eisenhower did not want to do. He didn't want these problems coming up to him, he wanted them settled down below, and it was one of the things that we had difficulty—he had difficulty with me the whole time, and with the other chiefs, too. Naturally a man who's brought up in the Air Force, if he's a good Air Force officer (and he was or he wouldn't be chief of their service), he believes in what the Air Force can do. He believes the Air Force is the best damned service in the whole world, and when he sees a job, when he sees something needs to be done, he thinks of how can the Air Force do it? And the same is true with the Army and Navy.

Admiral Burke commented further that President Eisenhower wanted the service chiefs to be unanimous in their decisions, but added, "I believe now that it's not so important to have unity; what is important is to make sure that all the facts and all the factors pertaining to the problem are each brought out very clearly and then if there are differences of opinion, the president has to make a decision."[26]

Adm. William J. Crowe Jr. served as chairman of the Joint Chiefs under President Ronald Reagan. His remarks regarding a presidential decision quoted below offer insight into decision making at the highest level.

> Preparations for Reykjavik were nothing like those for full-dress encounters between heads of state. The several meetings I attended seemed more or less pro forma; the reviews of issues and positions being prepared for the president were sparse and less thorough than usual. When President Reagan and his party left for Reykjavik, no one expected the dramatic weekend that was in store.
>
>   At the first session between Reagan and Gorbachev it quickly became apparent that the Soviet leader had come to talk business, particularly in regard to strategic arms limitations. Reagan was responsive, and in a series of face-to-face

meetings the two leaders moved much farther than anyone had ever anticipated. On the next to last day, Reagan surfaced a proposal to eliminate all ballistic missiles in ten years, and Gorbachev accepted it. The following day Gorbachev came back with a proposal to eliminate not just ballistic missiles but all nuclear weapons. Reagan apparently answered in a positive vein, though no one present seemed quite clear if he meant to do anything more than express his basic sympathy for the idea. Though the press subsequently devoted considerable space to this exchange (their information all came through leaks), for the arms control people the crux of the discussions remained the president's offer to go to zero ballistic missiles in ten years.

During these extraordinary meetings, George Schultz was encouraging the President to exploit the breakthrough that seemed to be developing, as was National Security Adviser John Poindexter. Overnight, Richard Perle and Colonel Robert Linhard, an NSC staff expert, drew up talking papers for the president. My own representative, Lieutenant General John Moellering, did not know about the ballistic missile proposal until well into the evening. He had had no advance notice and took no part in drafting the talking paper. Nor had anyone seriously discussed such an idea prior to Reykjavik. Neither the Joint Chiefs nor the Secretary of Defense's office had given it any consideration whatsoever. But despite this sudden and groundbreaking development, in the end the Reykjavik summit adjourned with no agreement. At the last moment Gorbachev made all the breathtaking advances dependent on severely restricting SDI (Strategic Defense Initiative, or Star Wars) research, and President Reagan angrily refused.

When the American delegation returned to Washington, the events at Reykjavik were handled in an oddly secretive fashion. Although accounts of what had happened made their way through the rumor mill and into the newspapers, the administration never did inform the Joint Chiefs of what had transpired. No one called to discuss the proposals that had been made, or to ask for an opinion. By inference, I concluded that various people in the President's inner circle had become agitated that he had gone too far, and that the political tacticians had decided the best way to manage the situation was to act as if it had never happened. The President's zero-ballistic-missiles-in-ten-years (ZBM) formula was being treated as a nonevent—the idea apparently being that if it were ignored long and hard enough it would eventually go away (which is essentially what did happen).

However, it did not go away instantly. ZBM was news, and it became the subject of considerable media speculation and commentary. A number of commentators opined that the President was badly off base in not consulting with the

Joint Chiefs before making such a radical departure. The fact is, of course, that the President does not have to consult with anybody. Despite the traditional approach of preparing arms control positions with the utmost care, the President is not compelled to consult, and if he finds himself at a meeting where an attractive opportunity suddenly appears to further American interests, he has the right to grasp it. I suspect President Reagan looked at what happened at Reykjavik in exactly that fashion.

At the same time, it always puzzled me that I was not consulted even after the president returned. Casper Weinberger was also cut out of the official loop. Donald Regan, the president's chief of staff, had warned the entire delegation that while the summit was in process nobody was to communicate with his boss back in Washington about anything. As a result, John Moellering did not inform me until he returned, though apparently Richard Perle ignored Regan and did keep Weinberger updated throughout the talks.

Nevertheless, with the continued speculation in the media, I took the subject up with the chiefs. "We weren't consulted about this," I said. "We aren't even sure exactly what happened in Reykjavik, but there are quite a few references to us in the papers, and I think it's incumbent upon us to decide what our position is. If in fact a zero-ballistic-missile offer was made, what is our position on it? Does the proposal we've been reading about appeal to you or appall you?" "Why?" said Weinberger. "Why tell the President that? We all think it's a mistake. But it's going to go away, don't worry about it."

"You may think it's going to go away," I answered, "but it is not going to go away for me. I'm going to be asked by Congress what the chiefs think and whether I told the President what they think. And I'm going to have to say that the chiefs deliberated on the subject and we're against it. There's a hearing scheduled, and I believe that is what Aspin [i.e., Rep. Les Aspin, chair of the House Committee on Armed Services] is going to ask."

Weinberger just sort of looked at me for a moment, then said, "Are you sure you have to do this?"

"Yes, I think so." I was a little put off that he was not being as supportive as I wanted him to be.

"O.K.," he said, "if that's what you think you have to do, it's your privilege."

Ordinarily when I spoke at these meetings, I did so extemporaneously, but I felt so strongly about the importance of this issue that I carefully wrote out the chiefs' objections. I did that for the sake of clarity, and also because if this became a true confrontation I wanted to be able to deduce exactly what I had said. If I was about to gain immortality by being fired, I at least wanted to document my demise. I was really quite apprehensive about what reaction this might precipitate.

The NG meeting of October 27 focused on other topics. When it was almost over the President asked, as he usually did, whether anybody had anything else. I said that I did have something I'd like to say, that I wanted to talk about Reykjavik. Discussions at NSPG meetings were most often dominated by the principals—the secretaries of State and Defense and the National Security Adviser, so my taking the floor like this was a bit unusual, and when I announced that I wanted to address Reykjavik, the room quieted.

I began reading the statement, to the effect that the chiefs had deliberated on the ten-year zero ballistic missile concept, and that we felt such a proposal, while theoretically attractive, would be ill-advised. I then launched into a four-page description of the problems we believed such a commitment would entail, including the need to vastly restructure our forces and develop new weaponry. Our current posture and strategy had evolved over a long period of time, and a sudden, dramatic change had the potential to jeopardize our deterrent capability and destabilize the equilibrium between Great Power forces. "As your chief military adviser," I concluded, "I do not recommend that you submit this proposal, Mr. President. It is not my intention to make your burdens any greater than they normally are, but this subject is of sufficient significance and the feelings of the Joint Chiefs are strong enough that I feel I would not be carrying out my responsibilities without informing you."

When I finished, Ken Adelman, the young and brash head of the Arms Control and Disarmament Agency, said, "I agree with that." Everybody stared at him, wondering why someone else would gratuitously stick his neck out. Then all eyes turned to the President. I thought to myself, "Well, I've done my duty, now here it comes."

"Admiral," the President said, "I really love the US military. I have always loved it. Those young men and women do a wonderful job for our country, and everywhere I go I tell people how proud I am of our armed forces. You oversee a superb organization, one that is not adequately appreciated. But I am constantly trying to get the country to recognize and understand the true value of our military."

I looked at him and said, "Thank you, Mr. President," and that was the end of the meeting. I think the most relieved man in the room was Weinberger. All my fears evaporated. If the President was angry, it was not obvious to me. If he had heard my remarks, it was not obvious to me. If he simply did not wish to respond, that was not clear to me either. Nor did I know where the controversial proposal stood now.

In fact the ZBM concept slipped quietly into oblivion and was not heard from again. On the other hand, I was called before the Aspin committee, where I was asked about the chiefs' opinion and whether I had communicated them to the President. And I did have the satisfaction of saying that I most certainly had informed the President, face to face. In a number of respects, I felt this was the most crucial event of my chairmanship, at least in personal terms. I had weathered a crisis and had decided to take the risk. Afterwards I found it was much easier to speak out at NSPG meetings. It seemed to me that an indefinable but real change had taken place around the table. For the first time as Chairman I felt I had been accepted by the Secretary of State and the others as a full member of the group.

Although the Reykjavik proposal seemed to fade away, the INF Zero Option (zero SS-20s for zero Pershings) gathered momentum. In July 1987 the Soviets formally agreed to eliminate all intermediate missiles in Asia as well as Europe. The talks moved toward closure. But the debate in our own councils had not yet run its course.

At the very end of the process, Bernie Rogers issued a final blast, loudly reaffirming his view that we should not be giving up a weapon that had become so important in maintaining the balance in Europe. Although I disagreed with Rogers, I admired his integrity and courage. He believed strongly in his position and was not afraid to say so, even at personal cost. For several reasons I thought it was imperative that we not ignore him.

In my talks with Frank Carlucci, who was still the National Security Adviser, I suggested that since Rogers was going to make his voice heard during the ratification process, we could put ourselves in the best position by inviting him in to see the President now. Carlucci agreed and Rogers came to Washington, where the chiefs and the Secretary of Defense heard him out. The President was angry about his public blast and did not see him, but Rogers did get to talk to Carlucci. In fact, Rogers' arguments had been fully taken into account during the earlier discussions on INF, but I did want to give him the opportunity to make his points in person. I also wanted the administration to be able to say in the ratification hearings that we had given his position our fullest consideration, even to the extent of having him back for a direct exchange of views.

In the end, the administration accepted the INF principles. Then we fought our way through a variety of verification details and procedures for destruction—

very involved and complicated—and reached closure. Although the INF Treaty did not do much to reduce the total nuclear inventory, it was a milestone in terms of breaking the deadlock on nuclear weapons. Happily, many of the issues that seemed so weighty, regarding both INF and strategic arms reduction, have now disappeared with the collapse of the Warsaw Pact and disintegration of the U.S.S.R.[27]

Adm. Kent L. Lee left an exceptional legacy to the U.S. Navy. He became commander, Naval Air Systems Command, with the rank of vice admiral on August 31, 1973, and was primarily responsible for the development of the F-18, an aircraft that is still the finest carrier aircraft in the Navy's inventory. My interview with Admiral Lee illuminates some aspects of the decision making involved in weapon systems procurement.

Perhaps the F-18's development really began with Lee's enlistment as a sailor in 1940 and his work in aircraft mechanics. Few who reach the rank of admiral know aircraft from the ground up as he did. Admiral Lee grew up on what he called a "small family subsistence farm" in Florence County, South Carolina. He enlisted in the Navy immediately on graduation from high school, signing up on August 15, 1940. "There wasn't much for me to do," he reflected, "except farm or join the Navy." He liked aviation and went to aviation machinist maintenance school right out of boot camp in 1940.[28]

Lee rose to the rank of E-5, second-class petty officer, and became an aviation cadet on November 12, 1942. He had to wait until then because application for aviation cadet training required two years of college. Acceptance also required passing an aviation selection board, a series of written tests, and the recommendation of his commanding officer. In preflight, students were graded in three areas: physical conditioning, academics, and military aptitude. Many of the preflight cadets were college graduates, but his high school education proved sufficient for Lee. "I was worried that I wouldn't make it, didn't know what the competition would be like. There were 250 to 350 cadets in preflight. I decided this was my big chance. I wanted to be a flier, and I had been an aircraft mechanic knowing a lot about airplanes. I didn't have much trouble, however, and came in number one. I still remember my grade, 3.43 on a 4.0 scale."[29]

Lee added expertise that few could match as his career progressed: mechanic, carrier pilot, group commander, and captain of a carrier.

Commanding the *Enterprise,* which carried seven different types of aircraft, all with different maintenance demands, was a tremendous challenge. The A-5, for example, described by Lee as a "colossal dog," was more than a maintenance problem; it was a dangerous aircraft to fly off a carrier. "One of the most spectacular things I've ever seen in my life," he recalled, took place "one night in the Mediterranean on the second cruise. . . . We had an A-5 hit the ramp. Balls of fire and airplane came up the ramp and went over on the two pilots, including the executive officer in the squadron. . . . It came in at much too high a speed, and you had to be very precise to get it aboard a carrier."[30]

Aircraft maintenance was a continuing problem during Lee's two years on the *Enterprise.*

> I made many hangar deck tours to see how maintenance was coming along. It was just backbreaking. We could not maintain the RA-5C, which was a dog of an airplane in the first place. But with the F-4s, A-6s, and A-7s, we always had a hangar deck full, the A-7s being a little better than the others. But almost without exception, an A-6 would make one flight and have to go to the hangar deck for repairs, the F-4 almost as bad. Maintenance man-hours per flight hour were running around forty to forty-five, which is just unbelievable. . . . For instance, take the engines in the F-14, A-7, and A-4. Takes a three-man crew three days, roughly, to tune them up, and trim them, as it's called, afterward. The reason being that it has so many connections to it and in some airplanes, like the A-4, you've got to take the airplane apart to get the engines out, take the tail apart and the fuselage. In the Harrier you have to take the wing off to get an engine out. . . . I didn't realize at the time that an airplane is hard to maintain if, in the initial design, the builders don't take maintainability into account, to include proper testing and ease of replacing parts.
>
> When we designed the F-18, our plan initially was to build an engine which, number one, could be tuned up in a test stand, because to tune up an engine in an aircraft you have to maneuver the aircraft into position on the hangar deck or flight deck and direct the exhaust overboard. That requires a lot of extra work. In the F-18 we said, number one, the engine should be tuned in a test cell after it comes out of overhaul or rework. When it's put in the airplane, it's ready to go. It doesn't have to be retuned. Just the engine itself should be pulled off, so it should take no more than two hours to replace it.

The F-18 was designed and built with those ground rules. . . . But, of course, once an airplane has been built, such as the F-14, it's not possible to change that. I decided that something had to be done in this area. We were failing. We had to carry altogether too many maintenance people to keep these planes going, so I decided that I would seek a job in naval aviation which had to do with procurement, maintenance, reliability, to see if I could do something about this. I applied for work in that particular area on leaving *Enterprise.*

The wisdom was in undertaking the development of an appropriate aircraft. The F/A-18 was the first airplane we designed in the Navy with its number-one priority being maintainability and reliability. We put a lot of money into it. It really paid off. Maintenance man-hours per flight hour and overall reliability of the F-18 now are just unbelievable compared to other airplanes, the reason being that we did it all up front. We made the spark plugs easy to change; we made changing the oil and the filter as well as troubleshooting easy. In the F-18, we decided that the fuel control, the generator, the starter, the hydraulic pump, all these accessories that are normally bolted to an engine, would be put on a pad [to the] rear [of] the engine. The engine is only fastened in about four places like an automobile engine, using four mounting brackets. You then only need to disconnect maybe a dozen pipes and tubes. All the accessories remain right in the airplane on a pad, a technique never done before. You can change that engine, have a new one in and off again, in less than two hours. It might have cost us a few pounds in weight by putting that accessory pad there, but I doubt it.[31]

Aircraft selection involves more than a prototype's reliability, maintenance, and combat effectiveness. Politics plays a big part, with competitive aircraft manufacturers spending many dollars lobbying the congressmen and senators who allocate the money for aircraft construction. These politicians rely on the votes of constituents who work in factories where aircraft and aircraft parts are manufactured. "Grumman," Lee explained,

fought the F-18 the entire time I was at NavAir, because they could see it taking business away from them. They paid millions, I bet, in lobbyists to fight the F-18. The A-7 people were fighting against the F-18. I've never seen anything like it. Industry was arrayed against it. They had their congressmen alerted. And then there were a whole bunch of people—the F-14 pilots—in OP-05 who didn't like the F-18. The F-18 was a very controversial airplane for a while. And, yes, we flinched. But I felt we had a world beater—if you'll pardon the expression, a world-class airplane except for fuel. And it's proved itself.[32]

Lee's role in furthering the adoption of the F-18 did not end with his retirement. "I retired on 1 November 1976," he reflected,

> and was relieved by a good friend, Forrest Petersen, who . . . had also relieved me as commanding officer of *Enterprise*. I thought the F-18 program was in good shape and in good hands when I left, because we had signed the contract, and McDonnell Douglas was in the process of putting it together. I received a telephone call from . . . McDonnell Douglas [asking] if I had been keeping up with the F-18 program. I said no, that I'd been away and had decided that the F-18 was not my responsibility anymore. He told me that they thought the program was in jeopardy; that the Navy was trying to kill it. So I then called Forrest Petersen, who was commander, Naval Air Systems Command. He told me that, yes indeed the F-18 program was in trouble. Petersen was a great backer of the F-18, but they had put together the budget for the following year excluding the F-18.[33]

Adm. James L. Holloway III was chief of naval operations during this period. I asked him for his input on the F-18 and Vice Adm. Kent Lee's role. "As commander of the Naval Air Systems Command," he told me, Lee

> personally took charge of the design effort to fulfill the Navy's carrier fighter requirements. The military requirements for the aircraft and its characteristics were set forth by the CNO's staff, OpNav, and specifically the deputy CNO for air warfare. This is the normal procedure. Then the technical bureau, in this case the Air Systems Command [NavAir], converts those military characteristics into an aircraft design to fulfill the military requirements. Then NavAir develops a procurement program, determines the cost, and OpNav integrates the F-18 program into the budget. Then it is up to the CNO to justify the aircraft, the program, and the budget to the OSD [Office of the Secretary of Defense] and the Congress. NavAir is an essential contributor to that process, backing up the CNO and his staff with the technical justification for the plane's projected military performance and cost data. It is a complex and tightly orchestrated operation and Kent Lee was instrumental in its success. He carried a lot of technical credulity as a congressional witness. . . . Kent Lee's personal commitment as commander of the Air Systems Command . . . really created the F-18 as we know it. However, selling the aircraft to the OSD was another matter.

In September 1974, SecDef Schlesinger had accepted the General Dynamics F-16 as the winner of the lightweight fighter [LWF] competition and authorized production of the F-16 for the services. The Navy preferred the Northrop F-17 design and proceeded to upgrade the F-17 concept to satisfy its VFAX requirements. As CNO, I had approved a scaled-up version of the F-17 which was then designated the F-18. The F-18 included substantial additions and improvements over the F-17 to make it carrier suitable and all-weather-capable with Sparrow III. Although I made this decision independent of the SecNav, the secretary accepted the decision as with my responsibility for military requirements.

Initially the majority of the Congress wanted a single LWF to lower program costs. I had testified that "the Navy wasn't interested in a fighter that could only get on and off a carrier by means of a crane, no matter how little it cost." Congressional opposition to a single LWF for both services (with probably the F-111 debacle in mind) was neutralized. But the SecDef's office . . . [was] adamant that the Navy [would] be forced to take the F-16. By spring this appeared to be a fait accompli to the extent that Secretary of the Air Force McLucas, encountering me by chance in the "E" Ring, proclaimed in a loud voice to ensure that both I and the two USAF four-stars in his company could clearly hear, "Admiral, the Air Force is the program manager for the F-16, and I can promise you we are not going to screw up the design and performance by adding a lot of stuff that the Navy wants. It's an Air Force lightweight fighter, and we are going to keep it that."

By April the situation had become critical; [the] Navy had not yet received the OK for the F-18. OSD was making plans for the Navy to procure a slightly modified version of the F-16. The main spokesman for this position was a civilian in OSD, "Chuck" Myers, a member of the "Fighter Mafia" and a longtime critic of naval aviation.

I appealed to Schlesinger and he agreed to hear out the issue "like a country judge," letting both sides argue their cases. The CNO was to represent the Navy, and Leonard Sullivan, another longtime carrier critic . . . would be the F-16 protagonist.

The meeting was held in April 1975 in Schlesinger's office. It was to begin at 1330 and go on until neither side "had anything more to say." Then Schlesinger would make the decision. CNO was allowed to bring only two people "because of the size of the room." I selected Vice Admirals Tom Hayward (OP-090) and Kent Lee (ComAirSysCom). When the three of us arrived at the SecDef's office, we were stunned to find more than a dozen OSD people assembled—Leonard Sullivan, Chuck Myers, plus analysts, engineers, and finance types. It looked like an attempt to overpower Navy with sheer volume of testimony. The first part of the meeting involved lengthy discussions on the carrier suitability of the F-16. Naval test analysis indicated the F-16 would bang the tailpipe on the deck every thirteenth landing. OSD claimed this could be solved by faster landing speeds and better pilot technique. Then came the discussion of the program costs and the synergy of a single type of LWF for all services.

The CNO was to be the only witness to speak for the Navy side. When I complained [that] the short legs of the F-16 would reduce the carrier air wing's striking radius by several hundred miles from even its current capabilities, Leonard Sullivan told SecDef that . . . [was] a plus; it would get the carriers back where they belonged, conducting ASW [antisubmarine warfare] and covering amphibious landings.

I had saved my blockbuster until PA&E had run through all of their arguments. I then announced the F-16 was not acceptable as a carrier fighter because it lacked all-weather capability. There was dead silence in the room. Schlesinger said, "Say that again and explain." I pointed out that the F-16 carried only the AIM-12 Sidewinders and they were clear-air-mass missiles. In the clouds, a radar missile like the AIM-3 Sparrow was required. This capability, with the necessary guidance system and heavier pylons, had been incorporated in the F-18 design, but the F-16 would not accommodate an all-weather missile system without extensive redesign and added weight. Schlesinger was incredulous and asked Sullivan to explain. There was silence and then confusion; then Myers said, "Most of the time, maybe two-thirds, and the weather on the average would be suitable for Sidewinder. Why should we assume the enemy would attack in bad weather?"

I replied that if the enemy knew our air defense was no good in cloudy weather, that is when they would choose to attack. The debate was over. There was another hour of perfunctory discussion, but the suggestion that Sparrow III be installed on the F-16 was never mentioned. I believe it would have altered the design and degraded the aerodynamics of the F-16 to the extent it could no longer by considered a lightweight fighter.

By 1630 both sides had run out of discussion points and SecDef adjourned the session. He called me into his inner office alone. He said, "Admiral, you've got your F-18." After a pause he added, "PA&E never pointed out to me the all-weather limitations of the F-16." On May 2, 1975, OSD announced that the Navy had DoD approval to develop the F-18 for production.

The F-18 is still the Navy's premier aircraft. Admiral Holloway was enthusiastic in his praise for it.

It has filled the carrier decks as a fighter attack aircraft, replacing the A-7 attack plane and the F-14 fighter with a single plane that can perform both of its predecessors' functions. This gives the carrier enormous flexibility in its air wing, capable of launching forty-eight fighters or forty-eight attack planes depending upon the tactical situation or the battle group mission. With four squadrons of F-18s the maintenance and supply support has been dramatically simplified, and the F-18 was designed for ease of maintenance—only a third of the man-hours required by the F-14. Earlier F-18 models performed admirably in Afghanistan and in Iraqi Freedom, and as the F-18E and F versions continue to enter the fleet this will be another step increase in air wing capability.

Admiral Holloway was succeeded as CNO in 1978 by Adm. Thomas B. Hayward. I asked him about his decision-making methodology—how he handled tough decisions. One of the toughest decisions he ever had to make saved not only the Navy, but all the military services. It solved the drug problem, which was having a devastating impact on morale and readiness. "When you face tough decisions," he told me,

the right approach is to go fix it, not to put it off, not to let it drift, but to take on the system and to fix it. That is the right thing to do. There was probably one of four or five priorities of mine that I look back on with particular satisfaction— one that has stood the test of time, where we confronted and corrected a problem for all the services—the drug problem. When I was CinCPacFleet we were getting lots of reports of marijuana and pill use aboard ship, and elsewhere. I'm not talking about cocaine and heroin, the hard stuff, but drugs that could clearly lead to using them. Try as we might, we never could get a handle on the magnitude of the problem. Other than rumors and occasional findings, there was never any evidence of their impact on readiness. Ships weren't having unusual casualties. Airplanes weren't having unexplained accidents and incidents. There was no measurable readiness effect of drug use.

At that time there was an African American reporter for the *San Diego Union,* whose name regrettably escapes me right now, who used to bug me at every opportunity about how I could be so blind as not to see what was going on on the waterfront. When I became CNO he didn't let up. Finally, I was persuaded that I had to do something to get to ground truth. So, I hired one of the big eight accounting firms to do a survey of the fleet to see whether I should believe the rumors or not. I told them, "I don't want one of those sample surveys of 1,700 people, with plus or minus 5 percent accuracy, or whatever it is. I want you to do at least 50,000 sailors on both coasts, all types of units." After their survey, they came back and said, "Admiral, 47 to 48 percent of all your people are using drugs from time to time—some onboard ship and while on watch."

We had been working the problem with drug experts for some time—psychiatrists, medical doctors, and other experts. Their recommendations were uniform and centered on education: Tell the sailors just how bad drugs are for their health and careers. Have your people go on the offensive with extensive lectures and training. And so we did. But that really turned me off. I said, young sailors don't listen to that crap from their seniors. You're talking about seventeen-, eighteen-, nineteen-year-old kids. They'll sit in class all right, pretend to listen to you, and then go out saying to themselves and their shipmates, "What do these old guys know about it?" That's not going to solve the problem. And it didn't.

Luckily, about this time the solution arrived at our doorstep. Urinalysis. After months and years of development work and testing, the urinalysis procedure had been perfected sufficiently to give us some confidence that the number of false findings could be managed. We finally had the club that would get everyone's attention. In fact, initially, as we were developing our plans, the other services and OSD expressed their strong disagreement in the direction we were heading, believing that we would encounter enough false charges to create a loophole that would bring lawsuits ad nauseum. The commandant of the Marine Corps, General Bob Barrow, and I were not to be intimidated. We were prepared to take the risk. So, we developed a policy based largely on conducting random urinalysis tests that would serve as a hammer to detect almost all of the drug users. Concurrently, we established the policy of no tolerance.

We had a singular belief, the belief that these kids were no different from other kids; they were responding to peer pressure, which got them to do drugs. These kids want an excuse to stop. We were determined to give them one. They can blame us all they want, but by God, they were going to stop using drugs.

The no-tolerance policy was to hit the officers hardest. It became a policy of zero tolerance. If you are caught once, your career is over, so think about it. You're out. We don't need you anymore. For the chief petty officers, we planned to give them one chance. For other petty officers, we gave them two chances. For new recruits coming into the Navy, if they tested for drugs, they were ushered out the gate. It was a great day when prior to issuing the policy directives the Master Chief of the Navy, Tom Crow, came to me and said, "Admiral, the command master chiefs of the Navy want me to deliver a message to you. We don't want a first or second chance. We want the same policy as for the officers: zero tolerance." When I heard that, I knew we were on the right track.

To be fair in the implementation of a policy that held such demanding consequences, the directive was issued three months from "go" to give those who so chose [time] to turn themselves in to a drug treatment center to beat the habit by February 1, the start date. If you figure you have a drug problem, turn yourself in for help. We will give you the treatment necessary, the schooling necessary, and it will not affect your career—this guaranteed by the CNO.

The next challenge was how to disseminate the message in such a way that everyone down the line would know this is for real. This isn't just another message from Washington that will be lost in the files as fast as it is issued. Two lines of approach were employed. I am a great believer in the necessity of and effectiveness of the chain of command. In fact, reinvigorating the chain of command was one of Jim Holloway's and my most critical challenges, it having been seriously eroded during the days of Z-grams and the like, however well intended they might have been. So, first I did a TV piece with a simple message, "Not in my ship, not in my squadron, not in my division, not in my Navy." Then, the directives and TV went out to admirals and captains in command to pass down personally to the senior officers, then chief petty officers, then senior petty officers, who were to make the policy clear. No tolerance. Not in our Navy.

The results were immediate and extremely rewarding. We went from 48 percent to 7 percent within six months. And the Navy is still at that low level, or even better. Why? Because you had every commanding officer, and the chief petty officers, and the first-class petty officers sending out the message, "We're not going to put up with this anymore." As I said earlier, the secretary of defense's staff was terrified we'd have all kinds of class action suits thrown our way, and prior discharges reversed, and the like. To my knowledge, we never had a one.[34]

Adm. Stansfield Turner was selected by President Jimmy Carter to head the CIA, a position in which he kept his four-star rank and was considered to be on active duty. He continued to have the same values he had always had as a naval officer as well. When I asked him about his most difficult decisions, he responded:

Some of my toughest decisions were ethical decisions. I'd only been in the CIA a couple of months when I found out we had three cases of CIA officers who had seriously broken the rules months before I got there and everybody knew about it. They had investigated them, and they had found that they were guilty. My predecessor, George Bush, had not taken any action on these cases. Nobody had raised the issue with me. They were just lying fallow until Bob Woodward of the *Washington Post* wrote an article, which tipped me off that there was something askew here. I told my staff, "Look into this." I thought it would take them a week. They came back in a couple of hours because they had already looked into it, but they had not decided what to do. So, the question was, did I fire these people? The director of the CIA is the only authority in the government to fire people with no recourse. Should I reprimand them, punish them, or let them off? I called in the highest people in the CIA, professionals that were involved with these three individuals, and said, "What do I do?" They all said, "Slap them on the wrist." I fired them.

It was a matter of ethics. Number one, the CIA was in bad repute. I was a new director. I had reasonably good publicity coming in. Could I do this ethically? Number two, it would help improve the image of the agency if I fired them because it would show we were cleaning house. I wanted to improve the image of the agency. Can you tamper with people's careers and lives and wives and children and the whole works in order to improve the image of the agency? It would help me to get control of the agency if I did. I will put down a marker: this is a new standard. If I let these people, as they all had, lie in the system covering up their malfeasance, how could I be sure that the people between them and me weren't lying to me? If I tolerated lying, I've lost control of the organization. In order to get control of this organization, can I throw this guy out who's got a family? Who has put in the fifteen years or something like this toward retirement? A tough decision, but I did it—although I wrestled with it.[35]

I asked Adm. Carlisle A. H. Trost (CNO 1986–90) about his decision-making methodology: "If you are going to make a decision," he said,

first of all, you should know all that you can find out about the subject that you have to decide on, and seek advice as you feel necessary. You take advice as given, whether or not requested, and it depends on what the topic is, and how familiar you are with it. And then you make that decision based on what you know and what your experience dictates to be the proper course of action. I am a bug on honor and integrity being the underlying basis for any leader's viability. If there is any question of whether or not this was something that should be done because it was the right thing to do, I had no question about it. If I had some doubts as to what was right, then I just got myself a little further educated.

What was Admiral Trost's toughest decision?

The one that sticks in my mind is the face-off between me and Secretary of the Navy John Lehman. This had to do with promotion boards, and the integrity of the promotion system in the Navy. It has been protected by senior officers throughout my career. It is inappropriate for anybody in a senior position to interfere with the proceedings of a promotion board, to attempt to influence the selection. In this particular instance, we were dealing with a captain selection board, for promotion from commander to captain.

The secretary has the opportunity to modify and approve the guidance to the board. It is his board. They are statutory boards. In this particular instance, the secretary had put out pretty normal guidance, the kind of guidance a board should have—select the best fitted, best suited. He, unbeknownst initially to me, had then approached or called in two members of that board and told them that he wanted them to report personally to him on the proceedings of the board as it evolved, which again is immoral, illegal, and just plain damn wrong. This was done, as it turns out, and as a result, he knew that his preordained—mentally preordained—split of people among the warfare communities was not taking place the way he wanted it.

After the board had completed its deliberations and prior to reporting out, the board results were sent to the chief of naval personnel, whose legal people, including the JAG lawyers, reviewed the package for legality of the proceedings, then checked it to make sure that everyone was properly eligible for promotion. There were no irregularities, and the president of the board reported personally to the vice chief of naval operations. Together they then reported to the CNO, telling him, here are the selection board results. Once the CNO approves, they go to the secretary for his approval.

That is as high as it has to go for a new 0-6 [i.e., captain] promotion. In this particular instance, when he left me, the president of the board, . . . Vice Admiral Bruce DeMars, a career submariner, went next door to report out to the secretary. He came back to see me shortly thereafter and said that the secretary had told me to reconvene the board and change the split. The secretary was unhappy because he considered there were too many nuclear submariners selected, and instructed that five of these guys should be replaced with five aviators. Lehman was an aviator in the Naval Reserve.

So Bruce asked me, "What do I do?" and I said, "Come with me," and we went through the back door into Lehman's office, and I said, "John, what the hell are you trying to do?"

He started explaining, "Well, here we have this submarine three-star (meaning DeMars) who was president of the promotion board." I said, "Wait a minute. You had five aviators on that board, and there were more aviators than there were people in any other specialty. There were one or two other submariners under the three-star. So are you saying this minority drove the selection of submariners?" He told me, "I don't know how they did it, but they did it, and I want the board to reconvene."

I said, "That is inappropriate and it is illegal."

"Well," he said, "I have got the JAG right here." And sure enough, he had the JAG, the senior lawyer in the Navy, right outside the door. He came in and handed the secretary a memo, which I never saw because it was not given to me, and he sat there and said it is perfectly legal for me to send DeMars back and reconvene. He said, "If you won't reconvene the board, I will reconvene it and I will name and convene a new board." I said, "You can't do that." He, nonetheless, had already picked the new board. I said that this was illegal. It was about six o'clock at night. He said, "Well, that's what I am doing!"

I instructed Vice Admiral DeMars and his board . . . not to leave Washington until I released them. I also instructed the members of the new board convened by Secretary Lehman not to report to Washington.[36]

Admiral Trost approached the Navy JAG about his report to Secretary Lehman.

The JAG did what the secretary told him to do. When I later confronted him, he said, "You know, basically I work for the secretary." I said, "You are absolutely right. The secretary selected you for the job, but you also work for the Navy. . . ." Anyway, he went along with it, and I got back to the office and called Don Jones, who was a Navy vice admiral then working for the secretary of defense, Casper Weinberger, as the senior military assistant. I said, "I have a major problem, and I want to talk to the secretary." And he said, "He is off to the White House right now, and he has got a dinner later on." But I said, "Can I get a memo to him this evening? It has to be before tomorrow morning." He said, "I can get it to him."

So I sat down and wrote down the circumstances of what happened in a memo to Secretary Weinberger, and pointed out that it was illegal and unprecedented in procedure to interfere with a valid selection board, and that even though the secretary of the navy had final approval authority, I was putting this under his purview, and that I was bringing it to his attention and asked that he overrule Lehman. I got a call from Weinberger about eleven o'clock that night. He had gotten home, had read the memo, and said that this is bad, and said that John Lehman is coming to see me in the morning. Weinberger supported me. Of course, that didn't make me any kind of a favorite with Lehman. He was absolutely livid because I had gone over his head, and said it was illegal for me to do that. I had violated the chain of command. My administrative chain went via the secretary of the navy, and then to the secretary of defense.

He was absolutely correct that I had violated the chain of command, but it was on a matter of principle. He tried many, many times during my brief time with him as CNO to horn in on Joint Chiefs of Staff matters. He wanted to be briefed and have input before we met on different topics. He was not in that chain. I told him that I wouldn't do it. What we did to partially console him was to give him debriefs of selected items, but after the chiefs discussed them. There were many items that we talked about that had nothing to do with him because he had no operational authority whatsoever, and I did not debrief him on these.[37]

True leaders are willing to make morally correct decisions at their personal peril. Peacetime heroism merely engenders more subtle risks.

I asked Admiral Trost to describe the staff that assisted him in decision making. He told me:

I had a little cadre of six officers to advise me. Frequently I would get a paper on a major policy issue, but it had gone through so many offices for critique and approval, then by the time it got to me as CNO, it was at best a compromise on any topic. It could be so watered down that it was impossible to use. So what I started doing was using this little group when I had to prepare a posture statement for testimony before Congress, or when I had to prepare testimony for a particular thing. We farmed it out to all the normal offices for their input, but then I would separately task this little group to give me their input on what they thought of it. I could tell them what my real concerns were, and what things that I wanted to emphasize, and they would come through.[38]

I asked Adm. Jay L. Johnson (CNO 1996–2000): "When you got input from your staff when you were making a decision, did you limit the report to one page or two pages?" He responded:

I tried to encourage that. Here's the way it really works. You give me one page, and then you can tab it. The one page could, therefore, get quite thick with attachments. I'm a consensus builder, and I like buy-in inputs for the decisions, particularly the tough ones that are being made. I relied very heavily on my fleet CinCs, the CNO staff, along with the vice chief and a couple of the senior three-stars. We really spent a lot of time wrestling with decisions.

I usually held Monday morning meetings, and tried to keep them at an hour or less. Then I'd have a couple more, several more, during the week, with smaller audiences. In those meetings we would roll up our sleeves. If you wait until you are absolutely certain about a problem you'd never make a decision. Sometimes the 80 percent solution has to be good enough.[39]

I asked Admiral Johnson why he thought he had been picked to be vice CNO. His answer provided further insight into his own decision making.

I think a lot of it had to do with my relationship with Admiral Boorda. I'd worked for him before. Generally, the CNO will have as his vice someone who is not of his same warfare area—an aviator CNO would select either a submariner or surface warfare officer, for example. I did that [when] picking my own vice chiefs [Johnson succeeded Boorda as CNO]. I don't believe there's any ironclad rule, but it makes sense. My strength, because of my upbringing, was aviation, carrier aviation. My vice chiefs—Hal Gehman and Don Pilling—were surface warfare officers, and that worked real well. My reliance on their skill and judgment cannot be overstated. This diversified background assisted me in my decision making.[40]

Did Admiral Johnson use a particular methodology in making decisions as CNO?

I tried to make decisions that were in the best interests of the Navy. I was—and still am—fiercely loyal to the Navy. I didn't like anything that got in the way of that. I didn't like outside agendas. . . .

I came to that job in a way that nobody else has ever come. [Admiral Boorda had committed suicide.] As a result of that, I didn't have, at that time, my vision for the future of the Navy. It was this time of tremendous turmoil and tragedy for our Navy. I became the acting CNO the day that Admiral Boorda died, and had my hands full. I was nominated by President Clinton on my fiftieth birthday. We talked that day in the White House. I told him that I'd given this considerable thought in the time between Boorda's death and when it became apparent I would be nominated.

I said I needed something to shape my thinking, something to help shape the Navy's focus on the mission as we overcame the tragedy of losing a very popular CNO. I do some of my best thinking at five o'clock in the morning, when I'm running. That was my "private" time to think, unencumbered by anything else. I put together a very simple vision for the Navy, which I shared with the president. I told him that the Navy was going to steer by the stars that were out ahead of us and not the wake that was behind us. . . . In the constellation of stars that were out ahead of us, I wanted the Navy to focus on four main guide stars that were of equal magnitude in that constellation. And those stars were called operational primacy, leadership, teamwork, and pride. I tried to shape the Navy's focus looking forward, not back from the day I became CNO.

One of the things that I was particularly focused on was building trust and confidence within and throughout the Navy chain of command from four-stars to seamen. As a result of that, I worked hard to ensure that everybody was part of the solution and everybody was invested with each other and what . . . we were doing. I was very much not of a mind to cut out parts of the chain of command as we went forward.[41]

Adm. Henry G. "Hank" Chiles Jr., formerly commander in chief of the Strategic Command, also had a well-thought-out philosophy on leadership in decision making.

For example, when I went to Strategic Command, I took an all–Air Force office staff and picked folks who worked for me when I was deputy CinC and were working for my predecessor, but they were all Air Force officers. I figured I knew the Navy's strategic program sufficiently well to be comfortable making decisions on Navy strategic issues. . . . My thought was: "Hey, get people to complement your weaknesses and reliable people that you can depend on. Use them wisely; get their input frequently."

We brought in the best Air Force three-star general available, Lieutenant General Dirk Jameson, to be my deputy. He was a missileer. The Air Force had picked him to be the CinC, but General Lee Butler (my predecessor) had considerable input. Dirk was the finest person with an Air Force strategic background in every conceivable way. He was a very good guy, a complement to me in experience. I don't mind leaning on my good people who are experts in their fields to help me make decisions, to provide insight and a different perspective. . . .

I believe you make the decision when you believe you need to make the decision, and that is a key responsibility of being a senior officer in a top leadership position. If you can afford to get more information before you make the decision, then that's your prerogative as the commander.

Based on long years in submarines, I'm convinced that for matériel problems, first reports are always wrong. I know we have a problem and an idea of the consequences. You probably don't know what was at fault and you probably don't know exactly who was at fault. So take the initial corrective action you need to take, stabilize the situation, and then think your way through the problem. Some situations necessitate immediate actions, quick decisions: fire and flooding aboard ship, smoke-filled aircraft as examples. You've got to react instantaneously on what you know. You could make the wrong initial decision, but you've got your job and must be darn careful you don't. You may not have all the knowledge to make the decision, but you want to make sure that you're not going to make the problem worse. I believe in making the decision when I needed to. It's a judgment call; I trusted that more after long sea tours in submarines.[42]

Adm. Charles R. Larson, who served an unprecedented two terms as superintendent of the Naval Academy, was selected for that post because of his successful naval career. In his first-class year he was elected president of the senior class and selected as brigade commander, the highest midshipman rank. One Academy classmate said of him, "The day that Chuck Larson walked on the Naval Academy grounds everyone knew he would be a great leader." He began his career as a carrier pilot, but switched to nuclear submarines and became commander in chief of all U.S. forces in the Pacific. I asked Admiral Larson if decision making is a talent or something you can develop. He reflected: "I think it's something you develop. It comes with self-confidence and competence. I think you have to develop confidence in yourself, and in your instincts, as well as your ability to weigh all sides of an issue. This makes you able to make decisions."

When asked about key decisions he had made and the methodology he used, he responded:

What I really tried to do was to get the pros and cons given to me from my people. One of the things I was doing, and was, I think, particularly relevant when I was commanding a submarine, when I faced a difficult technical or tactical problem, I would bring together a group of the most talented people available, normally leaders from our chain of command. There might be other particular technicians or people present who have the required talent. I would hold what I call a "Council of War" where we discussed all the options. I got recommendations of pros and cons from everybody. But they didn't know how I felt until I made the decision, at which point, I marched off.[43]

In the grade of commander, Larson was an aide to President Nixon. I asked him what he learned in that assignment.

What I learned from Nixon is, if you go into a meeting and you let people know right up front how you think about something and about how you're going to make a decision; or if you say to some people, "I think this, what do you all think?" then you're going to get a "yes man" answer. So I learned from him to be quiet until all others have had a chance to express their opinions.

The second thing I learned from him and a number of people under whom I served is to convey to people at every new command that they shouldn't think just because I'm the commander that I'm perfect and never make a mistake. I really need to hear from people who disagree with me. I want people who have the courage to say, "Wait a minute. Does that really look like that's the right thing to do? Let's think about this." I found in going back on the rosters of my commands, that they were likely the people who worked for me in senior advisory positions more than once. Those were the people that felt quite free to come and argue with me, and particularly, if they felt strongly, to be able to close the door, and I would listen to them.[44]

Admiral Larson commented on his most difficult decisions:

Probably the toughest one I made as a four-star, and one made pretty much independently, . . . was related to the POW-MIA business in Southeast Asia. It was probably the ugliest, dirtiest business I've ever been involved in. A lot of people preyed on families and made millions of dollars with this stuff telling families that they knew of prisoners in secret camps, that your loved one is really alive over there somewhere and we can get them out; that kind of stuff.

Unsavory people were taking advantage of and preying upon the families. I had one particular person in my organization, a civilian, who had been around for a long time. He was blackmailing me for a position that I knew he did not deserve. He let me know that if I didn't give him the job, he would go public and expose a lot of ugly things that had gone on about the POWs.

It was the election year of 1992. We were told that the administration didn't want us to be in the headlines about this business. I couldn't fire the guy because he was a civil servant. But I did not give him the job he wanted. I ordered him to another position in the organization which I knew he wouldn't accept. He retired, but he did carry out his threat. It did not, however, get much play. Until this day, he will surface with some comments, but his words have become less relevant over the years.[45]

Leaders with character never yield to blackmail threats.

One of the most significant decisions Admiral Holloway made during his tenure as CNO involved a 1976 incident that might have started another war with North Korea if handled incorrectly: the ax murder by North Korean soldiers of American soldiers in the Demilitarized Zone (DMZ). I was able to discuss this crisis at length with Admiral Holloway. The events unfolded as follows.

On August 18, 1976, Washington, D.C., was preoccupied with political matters. President Gerald Ford, together with Secretary of State and National Security Adviser Henry Kissinger, was departing for Kansas City to attend the National Republican Convention. Ford was expected to be nominated as the Republican Party's candidate in the upcoming presidential elections. Secretary of Defense Donald Rumsfeld was in Michigan recovering from a thyroid operation; the chairman of the Joint Chiefs of Staff, Gen. George Brown, was in Europe attending one of the frequent and mandatory meetings of NATO. Admiral Holloway, the CNO, was acting chairman of the Joint Chiefs of Staff in the absence of General Brown. This was an established policy of President Ford, who disliked having the acting chairman's responsibilities rotated among the other members.

Late that afternoon, the routine of the Pentagon—and all of official Washington—was shattered by a flash message from Gen. Richard G. Stillwell, the commander of United Nations forces in Korea, who reported that two U.S. Army officers had been murdered by North Korean soldiers in the DMZ in plain view of hundreds of troops on both sides. The intentions of the North Koreans in attacking a U.S.–South Korean patrol without provocation were unknown. Stillwell put all of his forces in South Korea on full alert, then reported the incident to Washington, warning of a potential crisis that could widen to the dimensions of a full-scale attack on all UN forces in South Korea.

The full story soon followed. The UN forces responsible for the surveillance of the DMZ had been concerned because foliage was obscuring their full view of the zone from the observation points on its southern boundary. The truce agreement governing the DMZ specified that both sides had the right of unobstructed observation of all areas within the zone, and also the right to remove any obstructions to surveillance. In this case, a large tree had grown to the extent that its branches were blocking the view of a sizable segment of the DMZ. The North Korean representatives at Panmunjom were advised that an unarmed patrol would be sent to clear the foliage. The soldiers would carry only axes and chain saws. When the party of nine South Koreans, two U.S. engineering officers, and four American MPs walked forward, the DMZ was calm. A North Korean lieutenant and seven men entered the DMZ from their side, walked up to the two U.S. lieutenants, and demanded that the work be halted. When the Americans refused, a North Korean trotted across the northern boundary and returned with a truckload of troops. A North Korean officer then shouted, "Kill them," and his soldiers jumped the two U.S. Army officers, ripped the axes from their hands, and hacked them to death. The remaining U.S. and Korean members of the working party, outnumbered by the North Koreans, made a brief attempt to defend themselves, then ran to the southern boundary and escaped through a gate in the fence. The U.S. Army routinely covered operations in the DMZ with photography and was able to get a complete depiction of the American officers' skulls being crushed by the North Koreans.

Ford and Kissinger had already left Washington when the details of the incident reached town; the only communications available to the president were unsecured phone lines. Full discussion of the available intelligence and the U.S. options was impossible until a secure telephone could be installed. This was not an easy task, as the president was fulfilling a complex schedule of meetings and open sessions in Kansas City. Ford directed Deputy Secretary of Defense William Clements to call a meeting of the Washington Special Action Group (WSAG) and keep him informed.

The WSAG was convened by Director of Central Intelligence George Bush; its principals consisted of Secretary Bill Clements for the DoD, Admiral Holloway for the JCS, Gen. Brent Skowcroft (Kissinger's deputy) for the National Security Council, and Ambassador Philip Habib for the State Department.

Before heading for the WSAG, Admiral Holloway called a meeting of the Joint Chiefs and briefed them on the situation. He had already directed that DefCon [defense condition] 3 be set in the Pacific command, and DefCon 4 worldwide. He asked that the JCS, through the Joint Staff, earmark all available forces that could be moved to Korea for a show of strength and could be committed to the conflict if shooting started. However, no action was to be taken other than identifying and alerting units until the National Command Authority issued the executive orders.

The WSAG deliberated until late in the afternoon but reached no conclusion regarding the probable intentions of the North Koreans. Still lacking a secure means of communication, the WSAG dispatched a White House aide to brief the president on the current situation and made plans to meet again on the morning of the nineteenth.

At this point I will let Admiral Holloway take over the story. On the way back to the Pentagon in the car, Holloway told Secretary Clements that

> the JCS wanted to send additional forces to Korea and needed his authority to do so. It would be justified on the basis that we were simply prepositioning forces to be in a better posture to respond to any eventuality. Bill was reluctant but realized that he would have to rely on their judgment. So he authorized the JCS to redeploy forces as necessary to improve readiness, but to avoid any actions that could be interpreted as being provocative. He was to be kept informed.
>
> The evening of the eighteenth, the JCS met again. We decided of the forces available, that the most effective moves that could be undertaken immediately would be to send a squadron of twenty-four Air Force F-4 Phantoms from the Kadena Air Force base on Okinawa, twenty F-111s to fly trans-Pac to Korea from the U.S., refueling en route. B-52s based on Guam would be scheduled to conduct training runs on the strategic bombing target range located just south of Korea. These would be highly visible on the North Korean radar. The USS *Midway* and its accompanying task force of destroyers and cruisers would be diverted from a port call in Yokosuka, Japan, and proceed at high speed to the east coast

of Korea off the DMZ, bringing about fifty more fighter and attack planes into the theater. The level of readiness would be maintained at DefCon 3 in the entire Pacific theater.

On the next day, the nineteenth of August, General Dick Stillwell, a combat-experienced Army general whom I personally knew and professionally admired, called me on a secure line from Korea to discuss the options available. He urged that he be given the authority to immediately go back into the DMZ with a heavily armed infantry patrol and, again with engineers, cut down the offending trees as we had originally intended. We both agreed that there could be no other solution to this incident. The U.S. had to go in and do what we had originally intended to do. To do anything less would be to demonstrate a lack of resolution and virtually invite North Korea to take further advantage of our weakness with some further bizarre incident. I explained to Stillwell, however, that I had assured the other members of the WSAG that the JCS would not plan any moves that could be considered threatening or provocative without getting clearance from the president.

At noon on the nineteenth the WSAG met in Secretary Clements's office. Clements and Scowcroft reiterated their position that the U.S. must avoid any provocative actions that might upset the North Koreans. They considered Stillwell's proposal, supported by the JCS, to remove the offending trees was too risky. We still did not know the real reason for the original North Korea reaction. So the discussion that afternoon examined other alternatives. Bill Clements was being largely influenced by his Army aide, a lieutenant colonel who had served with the MPs in Panmunjom and therefore carried a great deal of weight with him. He suggested that we fill a body bag with napalm and have a helicopter drop it on the tree and then, using tracer ammunition, set it on fire and thus burn it down. The rationale was that we could eliminate the tree without having any U.S. ground forces enter the Demilitarized Zone. The unorthodoxy of the scheme— the intrusion by a helicopter and the use of napalm in the DMZ—eventually caused his approach to be set aside by Clements, although it appealed to him as being "imaginative." As an alternative, Clements turned to me and said, "Why don't we shoot one of your guided missiles from a ship at sea to take out the tree?" I explained to him that we didn't have a guided missile with the accuracy to take out a particular tree, and there was just as good a chance it would take out a North Korean observation point as the offending poplar.

The meeting broke up late in the afternoon at an impasse, with Holloway supported by the chiefs, and Stillwell adamant that the only acceptable course of action at this time was to reenter the DMZ with engineers and cut down the tree.

> To do anything less than our original plan would be a clear sign of lack of resolution bordering on irresponsibility. It would certainly be a capitulation to a blatant violation to the signed agreement and a crime against the UN forces by the North Koreans. Clements would not agree with this plan, feeling it was too risky. In his view it invited an armed reaction by the North Koreans. In any case, he felt we should probably take no action until we could fathom the motivations and intentions of the North Koreans. Brent Scowcroft supported Clements, but not enthusiastically. Ambassador Habib, another distinguished public servant with whom I had worked successfully on many other occasions, took the predictable State Department line, which was we should do nothing until tempers had cooled off on both sides. He implied that the uniformed military was by nature hotheaded, and had to be restrained from rash decisions and precipitous action. I could only reply that unless the U.S. took action, and took it promptly, we would lose the initiative. To wait would give the North Koreans their desired opportunity to barrage us with rhetoric and threats that would somehow make it all our fault. We could not afford to lose this confrontation. Our reputation and our credibility depended upon our being resolute and unafraid to assert our rights.

> On the morning of the twentieth of August I again had a long conversation with Dick Stillwell, who made an emotional appeal for immediate authority to send our troops into the DMZ to cut the tree down. He said the morale of his forces depended on it. They felt that having been run out of the DMZ, where they had every right to be, it was a point of honor to return, prepared to fight if necessary, to carry out their mission. I reported to Stillwell the substance of the discussions at the WSAG and reassured him that the chiefs would do all they could to convince the National Command Authority that the only solution was to move quickly with our original plan. Stillwell was also convinced that there was little chance the North Koreans would react with armed force. It was only the unanticipated opportunity for a surprise attack with superior numbers that had led them to undertake the initial assault on the unarmed patrol. We both considered that the most dangerous course to follow was either to do nothing or to remove the tree by some other means.

> Later on the morning of the twentieth, I again met again with Clements and Scowcroft. Ambassador Habib had essentially given his proxy to Clements and was attending the WSAG sessions only sporadically. As forcefully as possible

I urged that he agree to send an armed patrol in that afternoon (Korean time) and chop down the tree. He again demurred. I then asked him to allow us to present this alternative to the president as soon as we could arrange secure communications. We would also explain to the president the division of the WSAG into two distinctly different views. Bill was perfectly agreeable to go forward with the two alternatives and to get presidential guidance as soon as possible.

Late that afternoon of the twentieth the breakthrough occurred. Henry Kissinger called the JCS War Room, where I was meeting with the Joint Staff. He was sitting next to the president in the convention hall in Kansas City and wanted to hear the WSAG recommendations. He would then brief the president and we could expect an early decision. I explained the two different approaches that had divided the WSAG between the JCS and the theater commander on one side and the position of the acting secretaries of defense and state on the other. He responded immediately by saying, "I will recommend to the president that a heavily armed patrol be sent into the DMZ to cut down those trees with axes and chain saws. Hold the line while I get the president's answer."

Less than a minute later Kissinger came on. "The president directs the Joint Chiefs of Staff to order the theater commander to proceed with his plan of going into the DMZ with the necessary protective force and remove those trees. In doing so, he wants to be assured that all U.S. and UN forces in Korea will be alerted to respond to any reaction that the North Koreans might take in response to our operation."

I immediately informed the other chiefs and called Stillwell. It was agreed that the operation would take place at 10:00 A.M. (9:00 P.M. Washington time), which was then about four hours away. Stillwell said his people would be ready in every respect for any eventuality. I advised him that the JCS would be meeting in the War Room with the secretary of defense present to monitor the operation, which had been nicknamed "Paul Bunyan."

By nine o'clock on the evening of the twentieth of August the Joint Chiefs of Staff plus the members of the Joint Staff who were associated with operations had gathered in the War Room. Clements joined us along with certain selected civilian aides. We had General Stillwell on the loudspeaker, and large electronic charts in the room were displaying the situation throughout the Pacific Command, Korea, and the DMZ. Stillwell was airborne in his helicopter. He had put all of the military units in the UN command in DefCon 2, the highest condition of readiness short of general war. Ammunition was . . . distributed to the troops, all of whom were in full battle gear. A U.S. Army infantry division backed up by an ROK division was moved into fighting positions. Spotting planes and command helicopters were flying overhead, and communications was tested and contact established among all units. The combat units in the reserve marshaling areas were equally ready.

Dick Stillwell reported that his troops were ready to go and morale had never been higher. He assured the chiefs that the UN command would not cause an incident, but he was fully prepared to respond appropriately to any actions taken by the North Koreans. As H-hour approached, the tension in the JCS War Room was palpable. The North Koreans had given no hint of what their reaction might be. We were presuming they wouldn't start shooting, but we were also aware of the unpredictability of these people and the possibility that a nervous trigger finger might start a firefight. On the dot of H-hour, 1000 local Korean time, the engineers along with three hundred American soldiers went directly to the tree, and as the infantrymen set up in a defensive perimeter, the engineers turned to with their chain saws and cut down the tree in about twenty minutes. Then the group marched out of the DMZ.

A large number of North Korean troops gathered along the fence on their side of the DMZ and in their observation posts. However, they were not in military formation, nor did any of them display a weapon. They were all obviously unarmed. It was clear that the North Koreans did not want to start an incident and were being careful not to be misunderstood as being aggressive.

Secretary Clements was delighted with the outcome. He was impressed with how smoothly the Joint Staff had worked and with the close coordination between the JCS command center in Washington and the forces in the field. It was a good lesson, too, for the number of civilians from the OSD staff who were present to see how a military operation works. The force commanders in the field conduct the operations and the JCS is kept informed. If help is needed or if things go awry, the full support of the Department of Defense is available to the theater commander. In a matter of two hours the business was all wrapped up: the F-111s were prepared to fly back across the Pacific to their U.S. bases, the squadron F-4 Phantoms would leave the next morning for Okinawa, the B-52s would have completed their training flights on the South Korean bombing range, and the USS *Midway* and its cruisers and destroyers would return to Japan for a port visit in Yokosuka and liberty in Tokyo.

By the next day there were no tag ends in Washington. The president and Secretary Kissinger had been informed of the resolution of the incident. There was little left to do except to write a report and be prepared to brief the president in detail upon his return to the White House.[46]

I pointed out at the beginning of this chapter that the position of command is very lonely. Some of the toughest decisions ever faced by an American commander in chief were those faced by President Harry S. Truman, whose position as an outsider put an additional burden of loneliness on his shoulders. At the time of Roosevelt's death, Truman had been vice president for eighty-three days. He had not been to Europe since his service there as an Army captain in World War I; he had never been invited into the War Room in the West Wing of the White House, which daily kept the president informed of the war's progress; he had not been invited to or briefed on the Yalta Conference; he was not aware of the confrontation between the United States and the USSR over Poland; he knew nothing of the development of the atomic bomb; and he had never had a day of college.

During the first month after being sworn in as president, Truman was presented with an awesome number of critical decisions that required immediate attention: Should the United States drop the atomic bomb? How to handle the occupation of a defeated Germany? Should the Soviet Union be encouraged to declare war against Japan? What should be done about the Soviet Union's establishing a puppet communist regime in Warsaw? And there were subsequent crises as well, with the Berlin Airlift and Korean conflict. It is no wonder that Truman appropriately entitled the first volume of his memoirs *Year of Decisions.* In the preface to that book he wrote: "The presidency of the United States carries with it a responsibility so personal as to be without parallel. Very few are ever authorized to speak for the President. No one can make decisions for him. No one can know all the processes and stages of his thinking in making important decisions. Even those closest to him, even members of his immediate family, never know all the reasons why he does certain things and why he comes to certain conclusions. To be President of the United States is to be lonely, very lonely at times of great decisions."[47]

Dean Acheson, an assistant secretary of state for Truman and later his secretary of state, responded to a friend's question about Truman's leadership by describing him as "straightforward, decisive, simple, entirely honest"— all qualities essential for effective decision making.[48] Averell Harriman, the U.S. ambassador to the Soviet Union during World War II and an adviser to eight U.S. presidents, had worked closely with Roosevelt and his administration for almost fourteen years. Contrasting the two men, he said of Truman, "You could go into his office with a question and come out with a decision from him more swiftly than any man I have ever known."[49]

Among the most difficult decisions made by an Allied commander in World War II was General Eisenhower's on when and where to launch the Allied forces' invasion of France. The invasion had been tentatively scheduled for June 5, 1944. The meeting at which the final decision was to be made was held at 4:00 A.M. on June 4, although some of the forward elements had already embarked. The weather was bad; low clouds, high winds, and high waves all presaged a hazardous landing. Air support would be impossible and naval gunfire inaccurate. General Eisenhower consulted his key advisers: Admiral Ramsay, representing the naval forces, was neutral; General Montgomery said "go"; and Air Marshal Tedder said "no go." But they could only advise; the final decision was Eisenhower's. He decided to postpone the attack.

The staff met again the next morning. The weather outlook for June 6 was good, but the fair weather was predicted to last only about thirty-six hours. Gen. Walter B. Smith, Eisenhower's chief of staff, described the scene on the morning of June 5:

> All the commanders were there when General Eisenhower arrived, trim in his tailored battle jacket, his face tense with the gravity of the decision which lay before him. Field Marshal Montgomery wore his inevitable baggy corduroy trousers and sweatshirt. Admiral Ramsay and his Chief of Staff were immaculate in navy blue and gold.
>
> The meteorologists were brought in at once. There was the ghost of a smile on the tired face of Group Captain Stagg, the tall Scot. "I think we have found a gleam of hope for you, sir," he said to General Eisenhower, and we all listened expectantly. "The mass of weather fronts coming in from the Atlantic is moving faster than we anticipated," the chief meteorologist said and he went on to promise reasonable weather for twenty-four hours. Ike's advisers then started firing rapid questions at the weatherman. When they had finished asking questions there was silence which lasted for a full five minutes while General Eisenhower sat on a sofa before the bookcase which filled the end of the room. . . . *I never realized before the loneliness and isolation of a Commander at a time when such a momentous*

decision has to be taken, with full knowledge that failure or success rests on his judgment alone. He sat there quietly, not getting up to pace with quick strides as he often does. He was tense, weighing every consideration of weather as he had been briefed to do during the dry runs since April, and weighing with them those other imponderables.

Finally he looked up, and the tension was gone from his face. He said briskly, "Well, we'll go!"[50]

What goes on in a commander's mind after such a monumental decision? Ike said of the occasion in his memoirs, "Again I had to endure the interminable wait that always intervenes between the final decision of the high command and the earliest possible determination of success or failure in such ventures."[51] He then occupied himself with visiting his troops, wishing them well and in return receiving joshing comments from the men telling him that he had no cause to worry. Although people were all around him during, before, and after decisions, it is easy to see why Ike wrote to a friend during the war, "The worst part of high military command is the loneliness."

Loneliness was certainly something Admiral Nimitz faced as commander of U.S. naval forces in the Pacific in World War II. His daughter, Catherine Nimitz Lay, recalled a wartime experience. Some teachers had asked her if Admiral Nimitz would speak at a local elementary school attended by her son, Jimmy, Nimitz's grandson:

Dad came up in his Fleet Admiral's uniform and talked and this is one of the few times that I actually heard him talk. I went and sat in the front row. And after he had finished talking, the kids were allowed to send up questions on 3 x 5s and he would read the question, and answer. And one of the questions, I remember, was, "How did you feel when you found that you were the commander-in-chief?" And he said, "*Lonely*," and then went on to say, you know, "It's all on you," and that a person in that position is bound to be lonely even though you have wonderful people to help you.[52]

In one of his oral history interviews with John T. Mason Jr., Adm. Arleigh Burke succinctly and perceptively pulled together the importance of decision making in naval leadership at all levels:

Decision-makers are all up and down the line, from a seaman all the way up. A seaman makes decisions and some of them are important decisions. Everybody is a decision-maker. Not everybody makes all decisions, but they have to make some decisions, and the more experience you get in making decisions, the more capable you become at making decisions. So it's possible and frequently true in a bureaucracy that no decisions are made at lower levels because they aren't competent and they never become competent because they aren't permitted to make decisions, and so when . . . they are promoted to upper levels they aren't used to making decisions. So, after a while, in the upper levels they don't make decisions either because they're no longer competent to do so. And soon nobody can make decisions really, except the top man. This is what happens with centralized control. It's fatal in the navy. It's fatal in any military service because there always comes a time when the man on the spot, whoever he happens to be, whether he's a petty officer, second class, or flag officer, when the man on the spot is confronted with a situation in which he's got to make a decision. And he's got to know he's got to make a decision. He's got to realize that this is a decision-making point and it goes through his mind in about half a second. So he's got to make a decision as best he can, qualified or not, he's got to make it, so he does. If he can't do it, then it's got to be made topside, some place up the line.

More likely the situation will get out of hand right quickly. This is why you should have decisions made at the lowest possible level, nearly always. There are some decisions that should be reserved for the higher levels, but those should be known in advance. When a man's at sea as officer of the deck, he's got a lot of decisions to make. Some of them are minor, but every once [in] a while one becomes very important and he might feel unqualified, he doesn't know quite what to do, but he's got to do something very fast. He can't wait for the captain to get to the bridge, he must take action quickly. If he makes a decision not to make a decision but call the captain, it's frequently the wrong thing to do, where in the little time that he did have he could have saved the situation but he didn't, because he made the decision not to take the responsibility for it.

I tried to push authority down. It's hard to do because lots of times I felt I could make a better decision than some of my subordinates. I knew the subject, I'd had more experience, but I didn't have the time to follow through, didn't know the detailed situation as well, and so the net result [was] I tried to keep as many decisions at the lowest levels possible. Sometimes I thought that if I had been in a subordinate's job, I could do a better job than the man who was there could do it. But, I wasn't in that job and couldn't take over his job, and if I started to make decisions for him he would never improve. He would never be able to make good decisions if he kept bucking them to me. This is why I got rid of people who could not make decisions in their jobs, because I didn't have time to make their decisions for them.[53]

The admirals I interviewed who were responsible for making life-and-death decisions invariably sought out and assigned good people—and good leaders—to do the particularly tough jobs. One of the qualities of a good leader is that he is always training someone to follow him, so leadership begins to snowball. There are many ways of promoting leadership. Some leaders conduct monthly reviews of the operations of their commanders and key staff. Others examine problems, express their leadership philosophy, and keep everybody abreast of the facts and problems that have been dealt with at that particular time. Generally, people are a lot better than they think they are, so the responsibility of the top leader is to create an atmosphere in which his or her subordinates can use their full horsepower. That involves giving them some knowledge of the problems the leader is dealing with, the factors that surround these problems, and the leader's personal philosophy. They avoid "yes men." One of the hazards of command is that too many people will tell the commander what they think he or she wants to hear. So one has to work very hard to create an atmosphere in which subordinates are willing to disagree. This is not easy. If the leader takes decisive action, they are apt to think he or she will hold it against them if they disagree. The successful commander wants everybody to say what he or she thinks, because no one is smart enough to think about everything. Somebody will have an idea or a thought that might change the course if the commander knows it. But once the commander makes the decision, subordinates are expected to carry it out as their own. If a leader has created an atmosphere conducive to drawing out ideas from those below, his or her subordinates are more likely to be happy; and happy people work far better than unhappy ones.

Leadership decisions in both peacetime and wartime may cost human lives. It takes courage to be a decision maker. It also is inevitable that wrong decisions will sometimes be made. General of the Air Force Henry H.

"Hap" Arnold had this philosophy: "What I can't change, I don't worry about. The . . . Chinese have a proverb . . . which runs something like this, 'What will not matter a thousand years from now does not matter now.' Certainly one has to have a philosophy such as this in making decisions where human lives are involved."[54]

CHAPTER 2

Sixth Sense

The ship talks to you.

Adm. James L. Holloway III, USN (Ret.)

Chief of Naval Operations, 1974–78

After more than one hundred personal interviews with Army and Air Force generals and Navy admirals, it became clear to me that these proven leaders had a "feel" or "sixth sense" for their commands that helped them in decision making. This chapter addresses that sixth sense. Is it an inborn talent or can it be developed through leadership training? How important is it for decision making?

The leadership approaches of Adm. Chester Nimitz, commander in chief of U.S. naval forces in the Pacific, and General of the Army Dwight D. Eisenhower, commander of the Allied invasion on June 6, 1944, provide superb insight on the question of a feel for command. Leading a military force of more than 1.5 million soldiers, sailors, airmen, and marines to free Europe from Hitler's grasp and Asia from Japan's presented a colossal leadership and decision-making challenge.

In a personal interview with General Eisenhower I learned that personal contact with the troops played a significant role in his decision making. Just before he was to transfer from the Mediterranean area to London to assume his duties as supreme commander of the Allied invasion of Europe, he became uneasy over the Anzio project. He was disturbed to hear that his plan for concentrating Air Force headquarters in Caserta was to be dropped. "To me," General Eisenhower commented,

> this decision seemed to imply a lack of understanding of the situation and of the duties of the highest commander in the field: regardless of preoccupation with multitudinous problems of great import, he must never lose touch with the *feel* of his troops. He can and should delegate tactical responsibility and avoid interference in the authority of his selected subordinates, but he must maintain the closest kind of factual and spiritual contact with them or . . . he will fail. This contact requires frequent visits to the troops themselves.[1]

Eisenhower did visit the soldiers in his command frequently. In the fall of 1944, for example, he went to the front to talk with several hundred men of the 29th Infantry Division. He spoke to them on a muddy, slippery hillside. After he had finished talking, he turned to go back to his jeep, slipped, and fell on his back in the mud. The soldiers he had been talking with could not refrain from laughing, but this did not upset him. "From the shout of laughter that went up," he reflected, "I am quite sure that no other meeting I had with soldiers during the war was a greater success than that one."

Once SHAEF (Supreme Headquarters, Allied Expeditionary Forces) had been set up, it was Eisenhower's policy to devote about a third of his time to visiting the troops. When he did so, he insisted on no parades or formal inspections. He wanted routine training to continue as usual, and thus his visits were normally made without press coverage. He spent little time with the brass, instead concentrating his attention on the living conditions of the soldiers. His personal interaction with the troops was an enormous asset to morale.

When a unit inspection was scheduled, the standard procedure was to have the men in open-rank formation. Eisenhower would walk along at a moderate pace, up one line and down the next. After every dozen men he would stop and talk with one of the soldiers. The conversation with the soldier would usually go like this:

General Eisenhower: "What did you do in civilian life?"
Soldier: "I'm a farmer, sir."
General Eisenhower: "Fine, so am I. What did you raise?"
Soldier: "Wheat."
General Eisenhower: "Good. How many bushels did you get to the acre?"
Soldier: "Oh, about thirty-five bushels, when we had a good year."
General Eisenhower: "You did? Well, when the war is over I'm coming to you for a job."

Then he would normally close by saying to the soldier, "Do me a favor, will you? Go and finish this war fast, so I can go fishing."

His jeep had a loudspeaker that could broadcast his words to groups of soldiers. He generally emphasized their importance in the war, saying, "You are the men who will win this war." He told them it was a privilege to be their commander. "A commander," he would say, "meets to talk to his men to inspire them. With me it's the other way around. I get inspired by you."

Adm. Chester W. Nimitz possessed leadership qualities equal to Eisenhower's. He was given command of the Pacific Fleet on December 30, 1941, succeeding Adm. Husband Kimmel after the December 7, 1941, surprise attack on Pearl Harbor. The vast command covered hundreds of thousands of square miles of Pacific Ocean, hundreds of islands, more than a thousand ships, and several hundred thousand sailors, soldiers, and marines.

Admiral Nimitz also spent a considerable amount of his time connecting with his people. On May 2, 1942, for example, he visited Midway atoll because he had a "hunch" the Japanese would attempt to invade it. As busy as he was, with a huge sea battle in the Coral Sea looming, he flew from his headquarters 1,135 miles to lonely Midway for a personal inspection of defenses and to get the feel that only personal experience could provide.[2] Nimitz's biographer, E. B. Potter, wrote of the visit:

Nimitz and members of his staff spent May 2 . . . inspecting thoroughly the fortifications of the atoll's two islets, Eastern and Sand. The admiral crawled into gun pits, let himself down into underground command posts, examined the hangars, questioned the Marine defenders, and observed the operations of the communications facilities, especially the priceless cable connection with Honolulu. By means of this cable, a segment of the old transpacific cable system, Midway and Pearl Harbor could communicate in plain English without having to worry about static or enemy interception and traffic analysis.

Nimitz liked what he saw, and was particularly pleased with the obviously close liaison between Commander Cyril T. Simard, the atoll commander, and Lieutenant Colonel Harold Shannon, USMC, commander of the ground forces. At the end of the day he asked them what they would need if they had to defend Midway against a powerful attack from the sea. Shannon, who had already given the problem much thought, reeled off a list.

"If I get you all these things you say you need, then can you hold Midway against a major amphibious assault?"

"Yes, sir," replied Shannon.

Nimitz smiled and appeared to relax. He asked Shannon to put his list in writing and to add to it any other supplies and reinforcements that he or Simard thought would ensure the defense of the atoll. The next morning he and his staff boarded his PBY-5A and flew back to Pearl Harbor. In his usual quiet way, he had thoroughly alerted the defenders of the atoll and at the same time instilled confidence in them.

After the victory at Midway, he waited for the returning B-26 and B-17 bomber crews to award medals: "He was not able to meet them all," Potter noted, but "he saw to it he was at least represented, and that each squadron leader received his personal thanks to pass down to the individual aviators." He then "went aboard flagships and shook hands with the commanders and as many of the officers and enlisted men as possible, thanking them all in the name of the nation for their splendid performance."

Even adverse conditions did not prevent a thorough inspection. When one of the ships in his command, the *Yorktown*, was badly damaged and taking on water, Nimitz "pulled on long boots, and led an inspection party in a sloshing examination of the *Yorktown*'s hull." When the U.S. Marines were engaged in a desperate struggle to hold Guadalcanal, Nimitz flew there in a Coronado flying boat along with the Marine Corps commander, Maj. Gen. A. Archer Vandegrift. They visited the flight headquarters, Bloody Ridge, and the defense perimeter, all in a steady downpour, then went to the makeshift hospital to talk with the wounded and those suffering from malaria and the usual fungal infections that plagued the men who served in the Pacific. He also personally awarded medals. As he approached a sergeant, the marine keeled over in a dead faint. "It turned out that the sergeant was scared to death at finding himself so close to a four-star admiral."[3]

Potter's biography offers excellent insight into how Admiral Nimitz got the feel he needed to lead.

"I would like to see, as *Navy Regulations* specify," he [told his staff], "the commanding officer of any ship that joins the command." His aides thereupon telephoned all the commanders at the base and made the necessary arrangements. Commanding officers of all vessels, from lieutenants (jg) commanding LSTs to senior captains from new battleships, as they arrived at Pearl Harbor reported at eleven o'clock and stayed fifteen minutes. "Some of the best help and advice I've had," said Nimitz, "comes from junior officers and enlisted men."

At precisely eleven, Lamar would escort the visitors into Nimitz's office and try to introduce them, but as often as not the officers would introduce themselves: "I'm John Smith, or whatever, of the USS So-an-So." "Glad to have you with us," Nimitz would reply, shaking hands, and motioning them to chairs.

Admiral Nimitz would open each meeting with a few remarks about what he was thinking of doing. . . . His visitors would listen, fascinated at hearing high strategy from its source. "Now tell me what you're doing," he would say and look at the man he wanted to hear from. Then he would go around the circle, listening to informal reports. He would ask if any of them were unhappy, if there was anything he could do for any of them. When the allotted time was up, he would rise, go to the door, and shake hands again with the officers as they filed out.

The story of the commander in chief's morning receptions spread through the fleet and the stations, giving assurance that the big boss was interested in everyone and was their active partner. The calls gave Nimitz a feel for the operational front which he found invaluable. Moreover, they introduced him to future leaders. "There's an officer we must watch," he would say to Lamar when the visitors had left. "He's going to be one of the good ones."

"He wanted a chance to size them up," another staff officer recalled, "and for them to know they had an identity with the fleet commander. It was an important element in morale."[4]

Nimitz looked for that same feel when he conceived his war plans. At planning sessions with his staff, he

acted like a chairman of the board, guiding and being guided by others. This does not mean that the war was being run like a town meeting. Nimitz made the final decisions, sometimes despite contrary advice, but first he heard the advice and weighed it carefully. He knew that World War II was far too complex for any one man in any theater of operations to do all the high-level thinking, keeping his own counsel and at last handing down Napoleonic decisions.

On quiet afternoons, Nimitz might stroll about headquarters, dropping in on staff members to inquire into their operations and make suggestions. Or he might visit naval and Marine operations around Oahu. If the visit was formal, he would probably go with his driver in his big black official Buick with his flag flying. Otherwise, he was likely to travel in a smaller, unmarked car with Lamar doing the driving. . . .

Admiral Nimitz decided that he ought to go to Tarawa to study the defense that had taken such a heavy toll of American lives. In preparation, he had Lamar type on filing cards the names, ranks, and titles of the principal officers he would be meeting for the first time. He would memorize these details during the flight down and thus would be able quickly to establish a rapport with the men.[5]

Admiral Nimitz did not encourage visiting, however, if he thought it might interfere with the commander on the site of combat operations. Potter noted an incident involving General Vandegrift.

On April 16, Archer Vandegrift, who had become Commandant of the Marine Corps and a four-star general, arrived at Guam with two members of his staff. They had been in Hawaii visiting the 4th Marine Division, sadly depleted by its fighting on Iwo. General Vandegrift informed Admiral Nimitz that he proposed visiting his Marines fighting on Okinawa, and was shocked and angered when Nimitz told him flatly that he would not permit him to go.

"Things are very active up there now," the admiral wrote Mrs. Nimitz that evening, "and I am not willing to have my agents there interfered with—even by me—although God knows I would like nothing better than to go up for a visit."

"I thought I knew what was bothering him," wrote Vandegrift afterward. "It was the Saipan controversy and was probably the main reason Holland Smith was sitting back at Pearl Harbor. In Nimitz's mind, I concluded, a senior Marine general by barging into Okinawa might upset the applecart of command relations.

I subtly tried to quiet his fears, but at the same time I let him know I intended to visit my Marines."[6]

Like Nimitz, Adm. William F. Halsey had a sixth sense when it came to his command. Among other things, he had an indicator that gave him a feel for the morale and readiness of a ship: "You can tell how smart a ship is by the way she maneuvers," he once said, "but if you want to know whether she is clean, the galley and the heads [toilets] are the key places. When I inspect a ship, those are the first compartments I look at."[7]

Halsey, like Nimitz, believed in the importance of visiting the troops, and was similarly unpretentious about it. During the Guadalcanal battle, he made a number of trips to the front lines to become familiar with the situation firsthand. As James A. Merrill, Halsey's biographer, described it, "he had a secondary purpose—to let the men see him in person. Sometimes, however, the staff's purpose was perhaps not served. Since Halsey's informal dress was almost indistinguishable from any private's, his flag lieutenant begged him to stand up in the jeep to wave, to make some self-identifying gesture. Halsey refused. To him it smelled of exhibitionism." Merrill described a visit to Guadalcanal:

> During the lull in operations Halsey decided to tour Guadalcanal as he wanted to get a first-hand impression, unobtainable from scanning reports. General Vandegrift remembered that Halsey *"flew in like a wonderful breath of fresh air."* During the tour of the area, Halsey showed extreme interest and enthusiasm in all phases of the Marines' operations, concurring with Vandegrift's existing positions and future plans. More importantly, Halsey talked to large numbers of leathernecks, and saw their gaunt, malaria-ridden bodies . . . "the most fatigued looking men I have ever encountered."
>
> Halsey could not say enough in praise of these Marines who invaded the island and held without reinforcements for more than a month. He was especially proud of the Army, Navy, and Marine fliers who controlled the air over the island against heavy odds. "I think they are the most superb gang of people I have ever known. I knew they were good, but they are so damn good they have surprised the hell out of me." . . .
>
> The next morning, Halsey, standing in front of Vandegrift's headquarters, decorated thirteen officers and men of the Marines who had distinguished themselves

in the recent fight. He said, "I wish to God that every man, woman, and child in our great country could know and see what you are doing. God bless you." As he pinned on the medals, Halsey had a word of praise for each man. To Pvt. Joseph D. Champayne, who had won the Navy Cross, Halsey expressed the conviction that "you will undoubtedly be more than a private the next time I come here."

At Fleet Headquarters in Pearl Harbor, Nimitz sensed that Halsey had turned the situation around in less than a month. "The situation is critical," Nimitz wrote, "but the determination, efficiency, and morale of our people there is so fine that even the most pessimistic critics must concede that we will win out in the end."[8]

Adm. Arleigh Burke (CNO 1955–61) commented on lessons he had learned from Halsey as a captain:

What I learned from Halsey in the war—the lessons of command, the characteristics of leadership—has served me well in all the years that followed, years in which I held a variety of posts throughout the Navy. For example:

Confidence. Bull Halsey possessed to a magnificent degree the intuition that let him know how to get the best out of his people under any conditions. . . . One night early in 1943, he warned me that a number of Japanese destroyers were coming our way. "Proceed. You know what to do," was all his message said.

We did proceed, at 31 knots, a creditable speed considering the condition of our destroyers' boilers. We found the Japanese force and smashed it. Back at headquarters, Halsey grinned proudly and gave me a nickname: "Thirty-one-Knot Burke." My destroyer squadron had proved what he knew: give men the incentive, the opportunity and the information, and they will exceed themselves as we had done that night, fighting for a commander whom we respected and loved.[9]

Burke also believed in the value of firsthand experience—feel—for a commander. When he learned that he was going to serve with aviators, he decided that he needed to understand what they went through in combat and asked the group commander if he could accompany a group of aircraft on a mission. The group commander did not think he had the authority to allow it, so Burke approached Vice Adm. Marc Mitscher. When Mitscher asked him why he wanted to go on a flight mission, Burke responded: "To get the feel. I don't know anything about air combat, but I want to get the feel of it and I can't do that sitting here on the ship or from listening to somebody else." Merrill described a rather close call that Burke had during the course of one of his visits. On the way to a command conference being held in a destroyer off Hollandia,

> Burke . . . decided I ought to see the front lines and I flew over the battle area in a dive bomber from the *Lexington*—Air Group Six. This was the time that I went up with the squadron commander. We went over and surveyed all the airfields, nothing on them. Went over to find the front lines and couldn't find any front lines. There weren't any front lines. We'd see enemy troops sometimes, but only in small detachments and not very close to Hollandia. So it was obvious there wasn't going to be very heavy opposition there.
>
> I wasn't familiar enough with seeing things from high altitude and I really wanted to know what the hell was happening in the ground, so I asked the pilot if he'd drop a little lower, which he did, but we got no opposition even then. He came down over an airfield quite close to Hollandia and the pilot said: "You know, it would be nice if we were the first airplane to land in Hollandia," so we decided to put our wheels down and land on this field. We did, we just touched down and took off, but when we got above the end of the damned runway and we were climbing a 40-mm, or some small caliber gun, opened up and got our starboard wing.
>
> Well, we climbed and the pilot said: "That was a stupid damned thing that we did. We should have never done that."[10]

In 1960, while the Eisenhower administration was still in office, there was an unexpected fire on the *Constellation* in the New York shipyard. Admiral Burke, as CNO, was contacted immediately. His first concern was for the people—civilians as well as naval personnel—who had been injured: "I went up there," he noted in his oral history, "as soon as I heard there was a fire and a lot of people were hurt. This was a fire in the shipyard. The ship had a lot of civilian workmen aboard and very few crew, . . . and nearly all the people who were hurt were civilians. But what I couldn't understand was how the hell a fire like that could get started and why it should go so long, and why the firemen could not get to it, and I couldn't get a very good answer. So I went up."

He also visited some of the families of those killed. "That's always hard to do," he said. "It's something that's appreciated, but it's very hard on the families, too, to have such people visit them, yet in the long run they appreciate it. I think you always ought to go where the trouble is if you can help."[11]

Adm. Thomas H. Moorer (CNO 1967–70), as commander of the Seventh Fleet in 1966, emphasized personal contact as well. He told me in one of my personal interviews with him, "I visited quite a bit, normally going on board at six in the morning. I went down to the flag deck, had coffee with the boys even though I was in command of the whole fleet. They liked that. I asked them to tell me what they were going to do this morning when their ship launched. I never placed any restraints on them. I wanted them to say what they thought. I didn't want any rank-conscious intervention." As CNO, Moorer took steps to improve the readiness, retention, and quality of life of those in his command. In doing so, he developed a feel for his people.

> I think my ideas were reflected in personnel policies. I would have frequent conferences with Admiral Charles K. Duncan, who at that time was chief of the Bureau of Personnel. We conferred many times with the secretary of the navy with respect to selection criteria. I tried to talk to as many of the young men as I could aboard ship at the various training activities, amphibious activities, submarine activities, and so on, and of course, the war colleges. I emphasized to them that in my view at least, . . . it was not the people that you work for that make you successful but rather the people who work for you, and consequently . . . young officers must bear in mind that by and large the senior officers have only one significant difference so far as they are concerned and that is they are just older. Their times are going to come—I tried to hold out to them the thought that they were inevitably going to be the leaders in the years ahead and that they should focus their thinking to this eventuality that is going to come a lot sooner than any of them thought or anticipated.
>
> I think also there was some effort made to give junior officers greater responsibility. But at the same time, I think that I emphasized through every means of communication I had, the importance of the chain of command and the necessity to back up and support the people that work for you as far as you can, including chief petty officers. I always made a point to talk to the chief petty officers. I had done this frequently, for instance when I was commander in chief of the Pacific and the Atlantic. If I found that a ship was inbound from a period at sea, I would get the roster and I would send a message to the ship that when it arrived I would

like to have Ensign so-and-so or Lieutenant junior grade so-and-so or Seaman or Fireman so-and-so report to me at headquarters. Of course, this caused great furor because they never knew what it was all about. I simply just wanted to talk with them and get the ideas of what they were doing and so on.[12]

His visits with sailors gave Admiral Moorer insight into their needs and ideas for ways to improve the quality of their lives. He reflected:

Of course, we were busy during that time trying to improve housing. Admiral David L. McDonald, CNO from 1963 to 1969, had done a lot in this regard. For instance, I went down with Secretary Chafee and we broke ground for the Navy motel we have in the Norfolk area, which I think has been very successful. . . . Today the sailors have a place to go with their families when they arrive in town to report aboard a ship or to some other billet without having to undergo the expense that one encounters in a regular motel these days. It was conveniently located.

In addition to that, we tried to expand the education of young officers in various management techniques. Quite a bit was done out at Monterey. We had many people going off to postgraduate schools and Harvard Business School and places of that kind. So as I say, . . . there is no end to it.[13]

While Admiral Moorer was CNO, he visited Vietnam at least twice a year, often with the secretary of defense. "Generally speaking," he said, "when I made one of these trips, I would specifically select two or three young sergeants or captains or second lieutenants and talk to them for a while. Then when I got back I would call their families and tell them I had just seen them and so on and what they were doing. Of course, I couldn't do that on a large scale, but I did that as a rule for two or three. But I visited every key point and then talked to the people who had been engaged in an action recently or that were preparing for a specific action. Of course, I always went out to visit the fleet."

Asked if it was dangerous, he responded:

Oh yes. I think that the commands that I was visiting took full care there. Generally speaking, they would parade out the whole works, all armed to the teeth. So there was plenty of security. I had multiple bodyguards all the time. I think they were sensitive to this possibility, too, and didn't want it to happen at their place. So obviously the fact that I'm here today proves that the precautions were adequate. But it was still dangerous. On two occasions I had bullet holes through the helo blades, but we weren't aware of it when it happened. But of course, I think you always are subject to someone blowing up your bunk or something like that in that area. Or having a waiter roll a hand grenade under your table or what-have-you.[14]

While on a visit to Vietnam, Moorer observed something that bothered him:

When I visited Abrams's headquarters in Vietnam and Saigon and visited the various units in Vietnam toward the end of the war, the Air Force made the others look bad in terms of their appearance. I think perhaps the Marines were next and the Army next and the Navy last. I saw sailors walking around there with their shoestrings broken or just through two eyelets of their shoes or something like that. It was very disconcerting to me. I mean sailors that were assigned to Abrams's *headquarters* in Saigon. We had gotten to the point where they were going to have beards and so on and every damned one of them looked like hell.[15]

He saw to it that the situation was corrected, but he would not have learned about it at all if he had remained behind his desk in Washington.

Admiral Moorer took care to ensure that visitors to his command saw more than a briefing room.

We had a constant flood of visitors from the Defense Department itself. But we tried to brief them on the purposes of the fleet, what it was doing, what the general situation was, and kind of tailor the briefing to the audience. We involved the pilots and the officers of the ship. Then we always would take them on a tour of the ships because this had, I think, a very positive morale effect. Any young individual—or individual of any age for that matter, likes to be recognized and observed. If he's worth anything, he will enthusiastically describe his job if you give him the opportunity. If he overstates it sometimes, so much the better.[16]

When Admiral Moorer was asked how a U.S. commander acquires a feel for the nuances that tell him what to do in a given situation, he replied: "I think it's like so many things, it's only through experience. It's the same thing that applied to dealing with the press and testifying before Congress. You can't learn these things in a textbook. It just is not in there, yet you have people come into the government and into the Pentagon that try to learn things like this from a textbook."[17]

I had a lengthy discussion about the leader's feel for command with Adm. James L. Holloway III (CNO 1974–78), who commented on his policy on visiting subordinates as a ship commander:

After twenty years in the Navy, spending most of your time on carriers and finally getting command of one, you have developed certain interests you're especially concerned with. As captain of the ship, I could not afford to spend much time off the bridge, but when I did visit, I would go to the areas where I thought the men needed to see me. [Adm. Hyman G.] Rickover wanted me to spend most of my available time in the nuclear reactor space, but that's one place I felt I really didn't need to go. Those people did not need my attention. The men running that part of the ship were bright, smart, and magnificently trained. They knew they were good and how important their jobs were. Instead I went down to the gasoline pumping station and asked, "How are you guys doing?" They were filthy, overworked, and seldom saw much of the actual flight deck operations. Their work was dirty and smelly. Yet without their total effort, we could never have made a launch operation on schedule. I would tell them results of our missions. . . . The fuel gang seldom saw a strike being launched, and it was important to inform them of the results of their efforts. Once I asked: "How do you like that new piece of equipment there?" They told me, "Well, actually Captain, this gaddamn thing don't work. We pump it by hand." That was useful information that otherwise would not have gotten back to Washington.

I went down to the aircraft maintenance spaces and told them, "I am a nut on neatness and I want to see the inside of your workbench drawer." I emphasize neatness because when you need a $^3/_8$ wrench in a hurry, for example, you want to know just where it is. Too often when sailors saw an inspection party coming, they would throw everything . . . on the workbenches into the drawers and cabinets and shut the doors so the shops looked neat. When I returned to check up three weeks later, the drawers were perfectly arranged. The men were proud of what they had done, and I realized how important it was for an inspecting officer's comments because they knew what the inspecting officer would look for next time.

We had zone inspection every week on Friday. The ship was divided into some thirty or so zones, and each zone was inspected by a team headed by senior officers. As captain, I didn't conduct a zone inspection very often, but occasionally I would. All the ship's officers above the rank of lieutenant were assigned a zone during the weekly inspection and were required to give their assigned spaces a comprehensive going over with a written report. It was a material inspection, checking on cleanliness, preservation, and the good operation of the equipment. The junior officers and chiefs stood by in their spaces. I told the inspectors that they had to be thorough. "You've got to pay attention to the details because these guys have been working hard getting their places cleaned up for you, and if you don't look in the corners, you're letting them down. They have spent considerable time getting things ready and they want you to know it." These zone inspections, properly done, established a good relationship with our sailors throughout the ship and gave me an excellent feel of how things were going.

When I had command of the *Enterprise,* we had about 6,250 souls aboard. I tried to get around so many people in the crew would at least recognize me. The bridge was my normal command post, but I felt confident that I could depend upon the officers of the deck under way to handle the ship in my absence until I could get back to the bridge in an emergency. I roamed the ship from flight deck to the reactor, from the chow lines to the CIC [Command Information Center]. I made these visits on a random basis, unannounced. The sailors like that. They felt free to gripe after initially overcoming their surprise. After all, on a carrier, the skipper is pretty much confined to bridge at sea.[18]

One of Holloway's interactions with a subordinate during this time returned to him years later.

In his book about his POW experience, Lt. Comdr. Red McDaniel relates, "I was operations officer of the A-6 squadron and was manning my plane on the flight deck. Captain Holloway, skipper of the *Enterprise,* climbed on to the cockpit and asked, 'Where are you going, Red,' and I told him, 'Hanoi,' and Holloway said, 'It's a milk run.'

"The first thing I did," the former POW said, "when I got out of the Hanoi POW camp (six years later), was put in a long distance call for then Admiral Holloway and said, 'That was no milk run.'"[19]

Book knowledge may help to develop the feel for knowing what to do and when to do it, but books alone are not enough. I asked Holloway: "As a ship commander, did you have that feel or sixth sense?" He replied:

Yes, absolutely. I agree that intellect alone is not enough to be an effective leader. One of the worst leaders I've ever known was a classmate who graduated high in my class at the Naval Academy. He was very bright and was a good pilot. He got the DFC as an AD [Douglas Skyraider] pilot in Korea, but couldn't stand being a lieutenant. He thought he was smarter than his commanding officer. Then he couldn't stand being a commander; he wanted to be a captain. He thought he was smarter than the CO of the ship. Instead of doing his current job better, he was writing letters to the CNO telling him how he ought to run the Navy. He was determined to be the world's greatest leader, but he was trying to get ahead by driving his people and demanding more than they could physically or mentally produce. He was a great planner, but totally impractical. I succeeded him in his job, a two-star task group commander. He was unpopular and got little accomplished. Yet there wasn't anyone who wanted more to succeed and more to be loved. He was book smart, but that wasn't enough by itself to succeed as a leader.[20]

Adm. Robert L. J. Long, the vice CNO under Admiral Holloway, responded to my inquiry on whether he had the "feel" as follows:

Inspection is a major part of any command. I'd say particularly in the submarine force there's almost a hands-on attitude by division commanders, squadron commanders, and even the force commander. I routinely would ride one or two ships a quarter. I'd go out for a few days and make my own observations, and those were very useful to me. One of the things that I found was that there was almost too much Rickover influence. Rickover was a great pusher for formal discipline in communications. I remember riding one submarine. We were coming into Norfolk, Thimble Shoal Channel. I was on the bridge with the commanding officer, who I think was trying to impress me with his formality of communication. So he turned to the officer of the deck and said, "What's the range and bearing to buoy two?"

The officer of the deck said, "Range and bearing to buoy two, aye, sir."

So he gets on the MC [the ship's speaker system] and he said, "Navigator, Officer of the Deck, what's the range and bearing to buoy two?"

The navigator said, "Range and bearing to buoy two, Navigator, aye."

A little while later the navigator came back and says, "Officer of the Deck, Navigator, the range and bearing to buoy two is range 3,000 yards, bearing such and such."

The officer of the deck repeated that, even though the captain was standing right there. The officer of the deck then turned to the captain and repeated the same thing, whereupon three minutes later we hit the buoy.[21]

The ship's captain was following procedures, but as Admiral Long noted, "There comes a time for common sense. So that skipper didn't do very well. Overall, the quality of the crews was truly outstanding. This was an exception. I won't give you his name, but we got rid of him."

Admiral Long believed it made the crew feel good when he visited their spaces. "But obviously," he said, "like a lot of things, you can carry that too far. If they're involved in some sort of a complex operation, . . . you can sit there and unnerve them to the point where you're looking over their shoulders continuously: 'How are you doing? How are you doing? How are you doing?' I think you have to show some restraint. But fundamentally, if commanding officers are to be responsible, they have to have some appreciation of how the system works throughout the ship."[22]

I told Adm. James D. Watkins (CNO 1982–86) that one of the things I had found among really successful leaders is a sixth sense for knowing what to do and when to do it, and asked if he believed in such a thing.

> Absolutely. I have never, as CNO or any other time, ever doubted (I mean as a senior officer now, I am not talking about as a junior officer) my ability to address or solve problems no matter how thorny they were. I always felt comfortable with whatever challenge. Yes, it was born out of my postgraduate and nuclear power training. It basically calls for the building of a strategic plan within which all my actions can find their proper place. My actions then make sense instead of the "fits and starts" when piecemealing—little bits at a time which cannot add up to a whole. I always believe that there is a strategic concept waiting to be adopted, whether it is military strategy, energy strategy, or health strategy, whatever it is. I have to know what . . . we are doing over the long haul in order to know if my short-term decisions make any cohesive sense to achieve my strategic objective— like winning. I would always demand that my staff help me put those concepts together so as to be part of the team in their implementation.

As an example he offered his responsibility in putting together the Naval Maritime Strategy, which was published in 1986.

> It was the first time we had gone with an unclassified published version. The first two hundred copies were bought by the Soviets! The published strategy, in itself, was a deterrent. I had taken the draft strategy through a vetting process—through the secretaries of navy, defense, and state; through key [Capitol] Hill members—

so that when it came out, it would be found acceptable as the nation's maritime strategy in dealing with the six-hundred-ship Navy initiative. I spent two years putting that strategy together. You don't put such an important strategy together fast.[23]

I asked Adm. Carlisle A. H. Trost (CNO 1986–90) about his policy on visiting the sailors and ships to get a feel for what was going on. As commander, Seventh Fleet, he said:

I was tasked with visiting the countries in Asia, South Asia, and East Asia . . . no less frequently than [every] six months. I visited Korea and the Philippines monthly and Okinawa about once a quarter. So basically I visited a lot of ships, and talked to a lot of people. . . . I tried to get out to the ships deployed in the North Arabian Sea at least once a quarter, and fly aboard the carrier usually from Oman, and then transfer to the other ships in company. I tried to get around and talk to them as much as I could. I visited all our bases, primarily in the Philippines, Okinawa, and Korea.

I generally talked to all the sailors, but in groups because I would not have had the time to go around individually. I usually got pretty well through the ships I visited. My routine varied. What I generally did when I came aboard ship was to give them an update on what was happening in their world and why they were doing what they were doing. I always tried to do it so there was a question-and-answer session. This was done in different ways. On a carrier, for example, it was done sometimes by talking to the crew in a hangar deck, and getting as many as possible there. Then my message was piped throughout the ship so that the people on watch could also hear it. Next, arranging for questions and answers right there from the audience. Another thing I did several times was to go live on the closed-circuit TV discussing issues, and then people could call in with questions and I would respond to them and to the crew. When you don't have the time to be able to go throughout the ship and talk to a lot of people, that is a good way to reach everyone. On shore, I would talk to groups usually in the base theater or wherever.

Admiral Trost had a set procedure as a ship commander:

My routine when I commanded *Sam Rayburn* was basically to make a point of seeing every sailor at least once a day. I saw most of them at least twice a day. In a nuclear sub, we had about 150 sailors. There were six-hour watch schedules and there were basically four watch cycles per day, each man standing two of those. I could readily, in a six-hour time, walk through the boat, and unless otherwise interrupted, I would go all the way through and see everybody on watch.

I also used to make a point of holding sessions with sections of the crew in the crew's mess, sitting down and talking to them about what we were doing, and discussing what was happening in the world, and finding out what their problems and concerns were. In so doing, I had an opportunity to get to know everybody in the crew, to know something about them. When they were on watch, I would stop and talk to them about their job, and talk to them about what was happening back home. On a missile submarine on patrol, it can get pretty lonely out there. In my time (before email), we got two ten-word messages per patrol, "family grams." It was hard for a wife, no matter how fluent she is, to express in her message everything that was happening in twenty words for a period of seventy to eighty days.

One gets a pretty good feeling for how people react and respond. I will tell you one sea story, if I may. It's about one of my sailors, on what turned out be our last patrol since the ship was going into overhaul.

We had one of our sailors, a second-class petty officer whom I used to see on watch. He was the oxygen generator expert, and he maintained the atmosphere control equipment in a compartment on the ship. He was the only one standing watch in that space, and so we used to have some pretty quiet, one-on-one conversations and I felt like I got to know him pretty well.

My executive officer came to me the day that we were sailing out on patrol. We were deploying out of Charleston, South Carolina, going out for a seventy-day trip. We were within, I guess, two hours of sailing, and the executive officer came in and said petty officer so-and-so has been in to see me, and he would like to talk to you. As it turned out, he had a problem with his fiancée. She had told him that if he goes on this trip, she won't be here when he gets back. She was tired of this routine. The sailor tells me that he can't sail. I said to my exec, "Okay, send him in."

He came in and he explained that he loves this lady very much, and wants to marry her eventually, and he can't stand the thought of losing her. He asked me what I was going to do if he didn't go on this patrol. I said, "First of all, let me tell you my side of it. You are a critical watch stander and I don't have an onboard replacement for you. Somebody would have to be pulled off one of the other ships getting ready to deploy to get someone over here fast enough, and it is kind of unfair to that person, and especially if he is a married man who expects to have another couple of weeks at home. The other thing . . . is that you need to be here.

You are part of this crew. You can't decide just an hour or two before sailing that you're not going to go. The Navy doesn't work that way, and we are responsible and we have duties to fulfill."

"Well," he said, "what are you going to do if I am not here when you sail?"

I said, "The first thing I will do is send a message to the squadron commander telling him that you missed sailing, and to put out an alert for you and for your apprehension. Then, if they haven't apprehended you in thirty days, I will ask them to declare you a deserter."

He said, "Oh. Thank you very much, Captain." I didn't say anything more to him, and he left my stateroom.

We got under way and the executive officer reported as we are getting under way that all hands were present and accounted for. I said, "Including petty officer so-and-so?" "Yes, sir."

We set sail, and the first time I saw him was while walking through the ship that evening. He was on watch. He said, "Thanks for the conversation." That was all that was ever said about it. They have to know that, one, they are needed, and two, that they can talk to you. It helped that I knew him so well, having talked with him so many times.

Regarding the sixth sense that all good leaders possess, Admiral Trost said: "I always felt I had a gut feeling for things; what is right and what is wrong, and which way to go." When I asked him why, he said, "When I think back on that, it is directly a matter of how you have been raised, and what you have experienced, and what you have read, and how you reacted to different situations."[24]

Adm. Frank B. Kelso II (CNO 1990–94) discussed his thoughts on visiting to get a feel for one's command:

The higher you get, the harder it is to reach, personally, all the people you would like to see. There is no question of the importance of visiting with your subordinates. They need to see you and know that you respect them and the job they are doing. Their morale and yours is dependent on face-to-face contact. The troops want to know you will listen to them. A couple of examples make the point. When I was CO of Naval Nuclear Power School in Bainbridge, Maryland [a shore command of around 2,500 students and staff], I established a policy that any one who had a grievance he could not get answered could come to my door and it would be open to him. Some of the staff thought I was crazy as they felt the load of visits would dilute my efforts to run the school. What actually occurred was few came to see me and those that did invariably had valid gripes. Turning these issues into actions made an important difference in their minds about their commander. They felt good to know they would be heard, and they also seldom came to me with petty issues. I learned a lot about the good sense of the American sailor.

When reporting as CO on the submarine *Finback*, I asked the ship's yeoman to make me a picture book with a page for each crew member. I wanted to learn their names and be able to walk to their spaces and call them all by name in the first week I was in command. [There were] around 150 [sailors onboard], and I was able to go to where they stood their watch and know their names within the week. I learned everything I could about them. Maybe I did not know every home town, but it was enough for a few to say, "The old man even knew where I was from."

I did not appreciate what an incredible impression this had made upon the crew until I experienced a debilitating back problem requiring me to be relieved after about six weeks in command. I was sent to Portsmouth Naval Hospital for a back operation, and many members of the crew, including the very young members, would come over nightly to see how I was getting along. A commander should never forget the impact made by the simplest of gestures that expresses his respect and care for his subordinates. He should always remember that sailors make him look good; he cannot do it alone.

As a submarine squadron commander I rode all my ships regularly and got to know many of the officers and sailors on those ships. It was always a pleasure to spend some time in the chief petty officer quarters and talk to the crews both individually on their watch stations and in sections in the crew's mess. I wanted them to talk and tell me what they wanted to and to answer their questions. You do not [have to] do much of this to learn that the American sailor is brutally frank and will tell you candidly how he or she feels. One can learn a lot about a ship talking to the ship's crew. Visiting ships and shore stations became an important part of my job as I moved to flag commands. As Sixth Fleet commander my goal was to visit every ship deployed to the Mediterranean at least once. This practice continued when I was Atlantic Fleet commander in Norfolk. Visiting in these capacities involved talks with the crews, usually in groups, maybe lunch with the chiefs or in the crews' mess hall, and sometimes on large ships like carriers in the squadron officers' wardroom. These talks always ended with a question-and-answer period.

I often took the captain's advice as to where he wanted me to visit and generally insisted on seeing some of the engineering spaces. On a carrier the visit often consisted of a talk to the crew on the hangar deck or flight deck depending on the conditions. This often would be an audience of 2,000–2,500. Sometimes a TV interview with the master chief of the command on the ship's entertainment system was set up and the crew could call in with their questions.

It is also important to learn from your trips. When ordered to Sixth Fleet, I understood that my experience with aviation units was quite thin. So I took off for a week's visit on *Nimitz* shortly after arriving to learn as much as possible about carrier operations. My academy classmate Jim Flatley was the battle group commander, and he put me through my paces by scheduling rides in the carrier's aircraft and instructional visits to the aviation spaces and ready rooms. I wanted to try to understand what I was asking the aviators to do when they had to go in harm's way. Of course, a week is not enough, but I had a much better feel after this week. Jim Flatley saw that I got a trip in each of the aircraft and taught me many of the operational requirements of a carrier that helped me tremendously in the months ahead. I wanted the aviators to know that I wished to learn how they did their jobs.

There are many audiences that the CNO must address, but in my opinion his most important audience is the Navy family, including officers, sailors, dependents, and retirees. The more he can visit and have a discourse with those who make the Navy go, the better he can perform his job. These groups want to support the Navy, and they want to know what the leadership thinks and is doing to ensure the Navy's future capability and ensure the people's interest and welfare are respected. Visiting ships and shore stations is essential to maintain a rapport with the audience. He must also reach out to those who face tragedy by his presence. My experience in this endeavor was without doubt difficult, but the survivors often amazed me with their patriotism and pride in their loved ones who had served.

I think Eisenhower's view . . . on visiting is absolutely right. As a commander, you must be seen by the troops. If you have the ability to touch their lives, that makes a big difference in how they will support you and your policies.

When I asked Admiral Kelso if he believed he had the sixth sense instinct, he answered: "Yes, I think so. I don't know how to describe it to you exactly. Some people have it and some people have a hard time acquiring it, some never do." Then I inquired, "Is it a God-given talent or can it be developed?" Admiral Kelso replied, "I don't think it's God-given, I think it's learned. Do you have any children?" he asked me.

I said, "Yes, I have four sons and nine grandchildren."
"When your wife was young," he continued, "did she like to sleep?"
"Yes."
"After that first baby came, she didn't sleep much, did she?"
"No."
"She could hear that baby all the way across the house."
"Yes."

Well, it's the same thing on your ship. A good commander of a ship has got that same sense. I could sleep through anything, but if one blower stopped running that ought to be running, I would wake up. I don't know why that is, but when I get on that ship, I can hear and feel, but you don't get that by not paying attention. The stateroom on the kind of submarine I commanded wasn't very far away because it was close to the control room. If I heard the watch standers sounded scared, then I had to find out what the hell was going on. So you have to pay attention to those signals. You can't be oblivious to them. Some people pick up those signs quickly and others don't see them quite as quickly.

After a ship's been in port a long time, then gets under way, you generally have a younger officer on watch. I cannot tell you how many times when I was the engineer, the young officer would call me and tell me something was wrong. So I'd go back and listen to it, and more often than not, there wasn't anything wrong, it's just been a while since they had been there and heard the sound.

They didn't understand that these sounds didn't mean that much to them to start with because the newer and younger officers hadn't had the experience of listening to them. They're noisier when you hear them for the first time than they are when you've heard them a hundred times. I think it's a sense you learn from having been there. It's an experience level. It's a key factor in driving ships. That's just part of the job. It's a sixth sense to go look, and when I went and looked, there was something different than what I thought it would be, and it was good that I did, because if I hadn't, we might've run aground or we might've done something else incorrectly.

On a ship there are a certain set of reports that a captain ought to get. They are determined, some of them by law, some of them by tradition, and some of them by the captain who has decided to be informed. I'm expecting to hear things or know that something is going to happen or doesn't happen. If I'm paying attention, I know when it didn't happen in the time frame I thought it should've happened. I can give you a very good example. When I was a skipper of the *Blue Fish,* we went into the Mediterranean through the Straits of Gibraltar submerged. It was about 1973.

Our method of getting the ship's position was through satellite navigation. After we headed from Gibraltar to the Straits of Sicily, some 750 to 800 miles or so, we got the ship's position fixed with a satellite observation—you feed that into an inertial navigator, which will then tell you where you are. It is normally quite accurate, but an inertial navigator is like all machines; sometimes they'll break. All ships are going to have this problem, but I had it set in my night orders to tell me what the depth of water was, and to let me know if we got to such and such— a shallow depth. They started giving me soundings that didn't make sense, because we should not have been that shallow. Well, it turns out the inertial navigator was not working right. By just having the sense to set up a system to tell me we were getting into trouble by soundings on how deep the water is . . . I was able to tell them let's go up and get a fix, find out where we really are. . . . So that was a sixth sense that something had gone wrong.

The danger was we were going to run aground if we had continued the way we were. The fix information in the inertial navigator was wrong. . . . It had broken, so it was providing the navigator position information that was incorrect. Remember, the inertial navigator had brought us across the Atlantic and through Gibraltar flawlessly. To realize that we had a problem with those sorts of things, you create a sixth sense. . . . In many cases [it's] forethought—thinking through the situation you're going to be in—which makes some of those indicators that come to you. . . . So you create a situation where you have the ability to have that sixth sense.

Of course, in the situation I just described, the kids that were around me were absolutely amazed, looked at me and said, "How the hell did he know that?" It was a sixth sense that I was able to know something wasn't right, and to do something about it ahead of time. I do believe there are certain people who have that ability where others might, for whatever reason, miss seeing something.

You learn most of those things from experience; but you can have experiences and learn nothing from them, or you can have experiences where you learn a lot from them. In my judgment, what I think happens here, where you're talking about a sixth sense, it's really a set of experiences you put together. It's called a memory bank—that this happened one time, and this happened one time; maybe it could happen to me.

My son is now a captain of a submarine, and I always tell him: "Son, one thing you have to always do is watch your navigator. I don't care how good he is, you look over their shoulder because you need two eyes and not one in this game." I hope he does that.[25]

Adm. Jay L. Johnson (CNO 1996–2000) agreed with the other leaders I have quoted regarding visiting one's command.

> I believe, and I told others, particularly admirals stationed in Washington—indeed, anybody at a headquarters, anywhere—"You have to get out. You have to go to the troops. You have to go to the deck plates to really find out what the heck is going on. Go to their spaces, where they work, where they live. You've got to go to them." Only then can you really find out the truth about all the stuff you're doing on their behalf and how it really translates from the desk in Washington, or wherever it is, right down to them. It's amazing. I would say, probably like any leader would say, I never got to do that enough, because I had to stay in Washington with so much testifying, working the budget, and so forth. That's important, don't get me wrong, but I never could spend enough time out there in the field. That's really where you find out what's going on. It's very helpful to then come back and try to direct or redirect your focus here; I often found the need to recalibrate somewhat on past realities with your previous perception of those realities before the trip.

Regarding a command feel or sixth sense, Admiral Johnson noted: "When in doubt, there is no doubt. If your instinct tells you that it shouldn't be done, put that program aside. If you feel there's doubt, then it's not the thing to do. That's not to say you should never take risks. You can't see too well with your head in the sand!"

I asked Admiral Johnson what he did when he visited troops and ships. "What was your day like? Did you have a particular routine? Did you have certain questions you asked—Where are you from? How do you like your job?" He answered:

> I tried to do all of that, but I didn't have a formal pattern like I'm going to go down to the ejection seat shop, or talk to the parachute riggers, ask them a set of questions. I just tried to stay connected to them as best I could, by being there, thanking them for their service, and trying to be a good listener.
>
> I had a sort of a strategic plan about where I would go. Not always announced. I tried a couple of times to whistle up an airplane and say, "Let's go to Kingsville, Texas, this afternoon." I tried that once or twice, but it was too hard on the system. We had to be a little more predictable—on schedule, some would

say—than that. Whatever ceremony they would like me to be a part of, I'd do that. Then I'd stand up and talk, normally for a half hour or so, on the state of the Navy and things that would be of interest to them. And then, without fail, I'd stop talking—I used to tell them, okay, I'm going to turn my transmitter off and my receiver on, and I want to hear what's on your mind.

And I used to take the master chief petty officer of the Navy with me. The two of us would then get up there, and we'd tag-team on questions and really get the essence of what was on their minds. We'd do that all over the world. It was invaluable to me—and to [the master chief].

I relied very heavily on input, fresh input from the fleet. And that's why I'd go out and talk to them at all-hands calls, and get it unvarnished from them. Over time, they were very open, very straightforward, no sugar-coating—good, bad, or other. I felt, again, that over time we were creating an atmosphere where they felt free to talk with their leadership—be it the CNO, their skipper, or their command master chief.

My wife and I decided that one of the things we would try to do was to spend either Thanksgiving or Christmas overseas. We went to the Arabian Gulf for Christmas holiday. When we'd go, we'd set up a schedule and try to visit every ship that was out there, six, eight, ten a day. . . . It was really the best way to tell them directly how much we appreciated their service and sacrifice. We often got to participate in awards ceremonies, advancements, enlistments; whatever the command wanted. One year in the Gulf we took Santa with us. Everyone loved it. To talk with them, give the sailors advancement certificates, pin medals on folks, whatever good work was needed, they loved it.[26]

I inquired of Adm. James A. "Ace" Lyons, who had 255 ships under his command as commander of the Pacific Fleet, if he followed an organized pattern for his visiting. "I didn't make up a master list and then tick each one going down the list," he told me.

I did it by areas. I would ask myself what area was I in. What was there? I purposely didn't give advance notice because I didn't want them wasting time spending two and three days preparing for my visit. I told my aide to call up the ship I was going to visit, tell them I would be there in five minutes and what I wanted to see. I will ask their names, whether they were married, what their background was, is there anything they needed, were they getting enough liberty.

I had programs like the Fleet Tip Program. I'd ask them if they had any ideas on how to cut costs, and they would tell me. I would go down to the bottom of the ship, particularly the engineering rooms. I'd get the whole crew on the deck and give them a pep talk. What is your next port? I particularly liked for them to go to Perth in Australia, which had a unique thing. It was a program called "dial a sailor," where the locals could call the quarter deck to take the sailors to their homes. Australians were great.[27]

I said to Adm. Stansfield Turner, "Ike had said it was important to get the feel of the troops. One of the things I've learned in my research on generalship is that the top people have a certain sensitivity, or feel, of knowing what to do and when to do it. Do you agree? Did you have that feel or sixth sense?"

"Yes," he replied.

To have it you've got to stay in touch with your people. I'll give you two examples. On the USS *Rowan* I just had a policy where once a day, when we were at sea, I would go to one engine room. There are four rooms. Two engine rooms and two boiler rooms. I would go to each one of those four spaces. They're the undesirable places to work. It's hot, it's dirty and sweaty. Most captains can go months without going into one, some never did unless there was a real problem. I said to myself, "I've got to make those sailors understand that they've got a dirty, gritty job down there, but they're important. I can't run this ship if the engines and boilers don't work." So every day, I went to one space of the engineering department to keep them abreast of the fact that I was concerned. Were they keeping it clean? Were they doing it right? That I loved them, that I cared.[28]

When Admiral Turner moved on to head the CIA, he used focus groups to get a feel for his new job.

I took a page out of my third mentor's book, Admiral Bud Zumwalt. . . . I brought a naval officer captain with me. I had him get groups of CIA people together at the middle and lower grades, a group of secretaries, a group of communicators, a group of spy officers, a group of analysts, ten or twelve at a time. He would get the group of secretaries together and for maybe two days, run a discussion with them about what they thought about this CIA, what they thought about how they were being managed, what they thought about their jobs. At the end of two days of discussions, I would come in for an hour with them. He would have had them focus themselves so they would know what they wanted to say to me. I wanted them able to articulate their views. I would say, "Mary, what have you got to say about how you think this organization is being run?" I said, "I don't want to know anything about your boss, Joe Jones. I mean we're not here to hang people. We're here to talk about the organization."

For instance, I went into one group of spy officers and asked one of them, "What do you have to do to get promoted?" He answered, "I don't know." I said, "What responsibilities did you have to fulfill?" "I don't know." In the military, I pointed out, we have to fulfill certain check-off jobs. The point was this officer had not been informed. He was not given any idea what we expected of him so that he could try to meet those standards to improve himself.

The older people in the agency were not very happy with this because they thought I was bypassing the chain of command. This is what leaders have to do, however, to get a feel of the organization. You have to find a way to bypass the chain of command in order to find out what's really going on, but to do that delicately because the chain of command is important. You can't violate the chain of command lightly. I always said, and made it clear to people, "I don't take action on what this lieutenant tells me, or this communicator, or this secretary. I take it and I then put it into the system and that means that you, the GS-15, have a chance to tell me your view." Because surely the lieutenants and the secretaries don't have a broad enough view of the whole operation. The fact is that they have a view that must be taken into account. That's what I wanted to know; then we'll work on what to do about it together. Those were ways I tried to keep my finger on the pulse, the feel of the organization.[29]

I made the comment to Adm. Henry G. Chiles Jr. that people who get to the top have a feel for knowing what to do and when to do it and asked if he had experienced that sixth sense during his career. He replied: "I'll tell you what Kin McKee will tell you. 'The ship talks to you.' I didn't originate that; I think McKee originated it. [McKee attributed the aphorism to Admiral Holloway.] Admiral McKee would say this to the graduating PCOs at Naval Reactors. 'When the ship talks to you, you'd better listen.'"

I asked him to give me an example, and he described a situation that occurred in late 1972 or 1973.

When I was an executive officer, I remember that our ship was proceeding to periscope depth about 0400 to 0530. The captain, I believe, was still in bed. We were making landfall off San Diego, returning from being out at sea. It was a clear, dark night but something bothered me. I went up into the control room.

We had not surfaced. We were preparing . . . to surface the ship. The officer of the deck [OOD] was on the periscope looking around. I asked to take a look. I swung around and could see all the lights along the California coast because it was so clear. We were maybe about ten to fifteen miles offshore at this time. Something just didn't look right. I took a careful look around at high power and right off the bow was a sailboat on that piece of the horizon where there were no lights. This sailboat was very close to us, and I was worried we were going to hit it. So I did an emergency dive on the ship and got out of the way, and it didn't become a problem. My senses told me to check on things. I just picked the right timing to go take a look.

There was another opportunity when I was in command. We were tracking another ship and it was in an odd part of the world. I can't talk about it particularly, but the OOD was on the scope and he said, "We have a motor boat up here." I said, "A motor boat?" It just didn't fit with the part of the world we were in and the targets in the vicinity. It was the contact we were tracking, but was much larger than a motor boat and close. We were about to get into trouble, but were able to successfully avoid the contact.[30]

I asked Admiral Chiles whether this feel or sense was inborn or something gained through experience. "It's based on doing the job and watching other ships operate so that you understand their tactics, what they're doing and when something's not right, something instinctively tells you, the picture needs better clarification, so I've got to get involved. If it doesn't feel right, a seaman of any rank or rate better find out why not."[31]

A nuclear submarine is small compared with most surface ships, and a sub commander has an unusually good opportunity to get to know his crew. I asked Admiral Chiles how he visited his men onboard the confined space of a submarine without "crowding" them.

As a commanding officer you've got an executive officer [XO]. So you say, "XO, watch the tactical situation. I'm going to walk the ship," and you go back and you talk to the watch. Now, I learned from watching a guy who didn't talk to his people, he could walk 300 feet through the submarine and not talk to many of his enlisted people on any kind of a personal level. You'll lose a lot by that approach. I talked to every one I could, asking them: "Hey, how are the kids at home doing? Are they handling this deployment okay?" [You ask that] if you've just come out of port in the mid-term of your patrol. You don't say that to the guy if you've been submerged for sixty days. Then you take a different approach. [You ask,] "How's it going, got everything you need down here? How's the chow been in the crew's mess?" In a submarine, everybody eats the same food. Officers and enlisted, it's all made in the same place. The food is great, but sometimes the crew gets down, and so I would talk to the folks about what's happening. As the CO of the submarine, I would talk to one off-going watch section every week. You typically have three underwater watch sections, and so I would do this at the crew's mess. It's the only place large enough on a submarine to hold the off-going watch section. It was just the enlisted personnel. The officers came if they wanted to. It was not mandatory for them to come because we'd get together in the wardroom and talk among ourselves.

I would start off by telling them where we are in the deployment, what our successes have been, what I'm worried about in our performance, where I think we can do better. I'd try not to make it laborious. I can do that in five to seven minutes. No notes, speak off the cuff, and then ask: "What's going on, folks that I need to know about? What can I help you with?"

I asked Admiral Chiles if any of the officers thought he was violating the chain of command by talking directly with the enlisted personnel, who could go over their direct superiors' heads.

Well, hey, the wardroom understood that I wanted to talk to the off-going watch section once a week. They were welcome to come. They didn't have to come. Occasionally one or two would. If I was talking about a drill that had occurred in their area and it hadn't gone real well, sometimes the engineer would come if it was an engineering drill, and sometimes the operations officer if it was an operation that I was talking about. Every now and then I would invite the operations officer to come along to fill in details on an aspect of his responsibility.

Usually, I just did it on my own and the chief of the boat would be there at all of those. He's the senior enlisted person on the ship. The leading chief from the nuclear part of the ship and the front end of the ship would always come after my presentation. I'd just throw it open to questions. I encouraged them to be open. The things that were correctly the executive officer's prerogative in administration, getting orders for people, looking at where are we going to go, and who's going to get off the ship to go to school and had to get back into port, I would just turn these matters over to him. We would try to put the answers to the questions in the plan of the day, as appropriate.

You would know when there was something bothering the crew that was substantive, because you'd walk into the crew's mess when they said they had the watch section ready and there would be people hanging off the overhead. It would be more than just the watch crew. Everybody would get up. "Hey, we're going to have a chance to hammer the old man." And that would be great. I loved it. The XO hated it because he always got the action to investigate the suggestions, then he had to implement those ideas that merited attention.[32]

I asked Adm. Charles R. Larson if he had that feel or sixth sense. "I think I had the kind of instinct that if I felt something just wasn't right, I had that feeling in the pit of my stomach. A lot of times it had an ethical and moral dimension to it. I just got that feeling, well, if we do that, it's just not right, I'm just not proud of this."

Asked if the sixth sense is a talent or developed, he answered, "I think it's probably both, but I think a lot of us develop it and experience it." He offered an example:

> I boarded a nuclear aircraft carrier, whose captain was a nuclear-trained aviator. He was a couple of years behind me at the Naval Academy. While onboard ship, a couple of things happened on that same day. A couple of aircraft had a mid-air collision. One of them, the pilot had to eject, and he landed in the water and made it to his life raft. And the other pilot diverted into, I think, Greece, and landed safely.
>
> We were steaming at thirty knots to pick up the first guy in his life raft out there. . . . While we were doing that, we were making a recovery, one of the young ensign pilots was landing onboard . . . as we were steaming off at 30 knots. He overbanked and was killed. So we'd had a mid-air, a guy in the water, a guy killed, and a guy diverted into Greece all in the same day. So the aviators all got their heads together and came to me with the recommendation that we continue flying. I thought about that for a minute. I told them, "My instincts tell me no. We need to just calm down and do a little retraining, and just kind of settle things down, and then we'll go back to flying a day later." So we took a twenty-four-hour stand-down. When it was all over, they came back to me and admitted we had been pushing too hard and the stand-down was a good thing.[33]

I asked Admiral Larson if he saw any value in visiting those under his command:

Oh, absolutely, when I was on the CinCPacFleet staff for a year before I became CinCPac, I visited virtually every naval base in the Pacific. I walked around and visited individual units, talked to the troops as I was doing it. Returning to my headquarters I would say to myself, this is what I've heard, and these are the perceptions. It may not be accurate, but perceptions are important as well as reality. I told them we needed to find out what's behind these perceptions and work on it in a positive way.

I would ask the sailors, Where are you from? How long have you been on the ship? What's your job on the ship? What's the most enjoyable thing about being on this trip? Are you glad you're here? Would you sign up again? I have found that you can also tell a lot about the morale of the ship by taking a walk around it, particularly the enthusiasm with which they describe their job and their contribution to the ship; I noticed this in particular. When I [was] one of the first nuclear submariners . . . after supper I particularly enjoyed just wandering around the sub.[34]

In my interview with him I asked Adm. Kinnaird McKee to elaborate on Admiral Holloway's comment that "the ship talks to you."

If you understand the ship, if you know the boat, as we say on submarines, and you demand the same thing of your crew, when the time comes, she'll talk to you. She'll truly become an extension of your fingertips. . . . When you truly know the boat and her crew, she'll talk to you. Not often; but when it means the difference between success and failure, life and death, you will know. Every truly successful CO can remember at least one instance where something caused him to act. I'll give you an example. Far from home, running at great depths, the commanding officer—and I'm talking in the third person about myself in this instance— the commanding officer suddenly finds himself taking a totally unplanned action. Instinctively and correctly, he reacts. Later, he'll ask himself why, and he'll find no logical explanation.

In this instance, we were returning from our second special operation. It had been very successful, so we were ordered to come back as rapidly as we could—best speed. . . . We didn't even stop to take navigational fixes; we were just riding on the inertial navigational system. We were also keeping several other plots. As we came close to home, we began to approach the hundred-fathom curve, the beginning of the continental shelf. At the time, we were still running fast, and at depth deeper than the continental shelf. I had left instructions with the officer of the deck to watch all of his indicators, then slow and come to a hundred feet and get a fix when the leading navigational indicator got within twenty miles of the continental shelf. We were still running without the fathometers, as a matter of security. I went down and went to bed. This was about one in the morning.

I was sound asleep when all of a sudden, something woke me up. It was just a sense of something different. And as I sat up, I found myself with the telephone in my hand calling the officer of the deck. I told him, "Slow"—and this is a quote—"Slow to one-third speed now, and come shallow now." As it turned out, we were already over the continental shelf. We were just about to run headlong into the ground. Now, the question is, what woke me up? You can say whatever you want to, but I believe it was some sort of sixth sense. . . .

Here's another one. *Dace* was returning to New London from a routine operation. I don't remember exactly when it was. New London is a pretty difficult place to get in and out of because you're often in the fog. As you approach New London, you have to go past Race Rock, a navigational aid, and often that involved running in a very strong tide. We were coming in, in late afternoon, when the fog closed in. . . . You don't want to enter [New London] in a thick fog; the river is just too narrow. So, we put the anchor down outside and left the reactor critical, but ready to go on propulsion on short notice. We had anchored just outside the entrance to the port because of the fog. We were planning to wait until the next morning. We took a round of radar fixes and marked up the radar scope with a grease pencil so it would be easy to see the outline of the land. That way, if the ship started to drift, the outline of the land would move; that way, it's easily visible if you're in some difficulty.

I had left instructions with a young quartermaster on watch and the duty officer to watch the scope carefully. About three or four in the morning, something woke me up. I went to the attack center, and the picture had indeed changed dramatically. The young quartermaster hadn't been paying attention. What had happened was that the anchor chain had broken . . . and we were being carried into shoal water. I told the engineering watch officer to answer bells on the main engines and sent the officer of the deck up to the bridge. We were on the surface at the time with steam in the engine room, but the engines had not run for a while and were not warmed up. I told the engineering officer of the watch to give me the engines, and he said, "I'll warm them up." I said, "Don't warm them up; put them on the line now." Well, if you don't warm them up . . . they may vibrate. But that didn't really matter in this case. He did what I told him to do. The officer of the deck put a standard bell on right away and turned toward deep water.

I asked him: "Had that not been the case, would you have run aground?" "Yes," he said. "We would have run aground." I then inquired: "Would that be the end of your career?" He replied, "Maybe so. It would certainly have hurt the boat, and it would have been bad for everybody."[35]

General Eisenhower put the importance of feel or sixth sense for sound decision making and successful military leadership into perspective perhaps as well as anyone when he said that "regardless of preoccupation with multitudinous problems of great importance, [a commander] must never lose the touch with the *feel* of his troops. He can and should delegate tactical responsibility and avoid interference in the authority of his selected subordinates, but he must maintain the closest kind of factual and spiritual contact with them, or in a vast critical campaign he will fail. This requires frequent visits to the troops themselves."[36]

Our senior naval officers certainly understood the importance of visiting, of being seen, to be effective leaders and to obtain that feel. Admiral Nimitz as commander of the U.S. naval forces in the Pacific in World War II had considerably more territory to cover than Ike, but he visited as much of it as he could: Midway, 1,135 miles from his headquarters, and the fortifications on Eastern and Sand; and everywhere throughout his command. He asked about the needs of his troops everywhere he went; he was present to award medals for successful missions; he asked for input from the troops and listened to their answers, recognizing the value of their comments. He asked, "What do you need?" "Some of the best help and advice I've had comes from junior officers and enlisted men," he said. But he never interfered with them after giving them their mission.

Admiral Halsey visited his outposts to let the men see him in person, flying in "like a wonderful breath of fresh air," as Marine General Vandegrift said of his visit to Guadalcanal.

Admiral Moorer, who as commander of the Pacific and Atlantic fleets often traveled with other senior personnel, military and civilian, reflected, "We always would take them [the VIPs] on a tour of the ships because this had, I think, a very positive morale effect. Any young individual . . . likes to be recognized and observed."

Admiral Holloway 's approach as captain of the *Enterprise* was to "go to the areas where I thought the men needed to see me." "I tried to get around so many in the crew would at least recognize me. . . . I roamed the ship from flight deck to the reactor. . . . The sailors like that."

Admiral Long as vice CNO considered inspection to be "a major part of command."

Admiral Watkins, as a fleet commander and as CNO, "visited a lot of ships, and talked to a lot of people. . . . I generally talked to all the sailors, but in groups. . . . I usually got pretty well through the ships I visited. . . . I always tried to do it so there was a question-and-answer session."

Admiral Trost as a submarine commander made "a point of seeing every sailor at least once a day . . . most of them at least twice a day. . . . One gets a pretty good feeling for people [doing that]."

Admiral Kelso as a ship captain made up a book with a picture of each of the sailors and was able to call them by name. "I didn't realize what an incredible impression this had made upon them until . . . I was sick with a bad back problem and was incapacitated, and I had to be relieved . . . and these kids, these young seamen were coming over to see me in the hospital. I couldn't believe it. They'd come over in bunches to see me and how I was doing."

As CNO, with onerous duties in Washington, Admiral Johnson nevertheless tried to "go to the troops . . . go to their spaces, where they work, where they live. Only then can you really find out the truth about all the stuff you're doing on their behalf and how I really translate from the desk in Washington, right down to them."

Admiral Chiles would walk the ship. "I talked to everyone I could."

Admiral Turner said, "You've got to stay in touch with your people."

Admiral McKee reflected on feel: "If you understand the ship, if you know the boat, . . . and you demand the same thing of your crew, when the time comes, she'll talk to you. She'll truly become an extension of your fingertips."

Is feel or sixth sense an inborn talent, or can it be learned?

Admiral Moorer said: "I think it's like so many things, it's only through experience."

Admiral Trost said he always had a gut feeling for things. "When I think back on that, it was directly a matter of how you have been raised, and what you have experienced, and what you have read, and how you reacted to different situations."

Admiral Larson thought the sixth sense is "probably both, but I think a lot of us develop it and experience it."

Admiral McKee's response was: "It's based on doing it, and watching other ships . . . what they're doing . . . something instinctively tells you, the picture needs better clarification, so I got involved."

Admiral Kelso said, "I don't think it's all God-given, I think it's learned. . . . You learn most of those things from experience, but you can have experiences and learn nothing from them, or you can have experiences where you learn a lot from them . . . it's really a set of experiences you put together. It's called a memory bank."

Feel, sixth sense, intuition, whatever you want to call it, comes from years of experience. Those who have it can make decisions quickly, seemingly without thinking. General of the Army Omar N. Bradley summed up the importance of feel in decision making in an interview I had with him in 1963:

> My theory is that you collect information, little bits of it, and it goes into your brain like feeding information into a 1401 IBM calculator. It's stored there, but you are not conscious of it. You hear some of it over the phone, you see some of it on the map, in what you read, in briefings. It is all stored in your mind; then suddenly you are faced with a decision. You don't go back and pick up each one of those pieces of information, but you run over main ideas that are involved and the answer comes out like when you push the button on the IBM machine. You have stored up this knowledge as it comes in and when you are suddenly faced in battle with a situation needing a decision, you can give it. When people would call me on the phone and give me a situation, I would push a button, and I would have to answer right then. You can't go back and pore over the maps for two or three days.[37]

CHAPTER 3

Yes Men

Admirals are selected not for their politics, but on the basis of their
character and professional competence. I have yet to encounter
a navy secretary or secretary of defense or president who thought it
was in his job description to disregard the advice of his flag
officers. Yet there will be times when otherwise like-minded leaders
will differ, and a CNO must be prepared to disagree.

Adm. James L. Holloway III, USN (Ret.)
Chief of Naval Operations, 1974–78

In his capacity as chief of staff to President Franklin D. Roosevelt, Fleet
Adm. William D. Leahy met with the president every morning in the White
House to brief him. He coordinated with the U.S. Joint Chiefs of Staff and
the Allied Combined Chiefs of Staff, a group of professionals who provided
input in the president's decision making as commander in chief. Leahy
observed that the British military leaders were intimidated by Winston
Churchill, but the American chiefs felt free to speak up to the president
and offer advice and counsel. He reflected in his memoir, *I Was There*:

> This was the first truly worldwide war, and there was no land or ocean that did
> not feel its impact. It was fortunate for our country and particularly for our Army,

Navy, and Air Force, that we had in these critical years a President with a superb knowledge of international affairs and an almost professional understanding of naval and military operations. I believe history will record that he exercised greater skill in the direction of our global war effort than did his gallant and brilliant contemporary Winston Churchill. As we worked in closest liaison with the chiefs of the British armed forces, there was more than one occasion when we felt that our British colleagues were loyally supporting the views of their defense minister only because it was their duty and because they were carrying out orders. On our side, we never labored under any such handicap. There were differences of opinion, of course, but due to the mutual confidence and daily contact between the President and his military chiefs, these differences never became serious. This daily contact was achieved through the creation of a new military office—that of Chief of Staff to the Commander-in-Chief of the Army and Navy. It was my high privilege to be the first to serve in that capacity.[1]

On December 30, 1941, Adm. Ernest J. King became commander in chief of the U.S. Fleet. A brief description of King in E. B. Potter's biography of Adm. Chester W. Nimitz offers insight into King's character and leadership.

King had earned a reputation for brilliance and toughness, not to say harshness. He was generally reputed to be cold, aloof, and humorless. Ladislas Farago, who served under King, in his book *The Tenth Fleet* describes the new commander in chief: "Tall, gaunt and taut, with a high dome, piercing eyes, aquiline nose, and a firm jaw, he looked somewhat like Hogarth's etching of Don Quixote but he had none of the old knight's fancy dreams. He was a supreme realist with the arrogance of genius. . . . He was a grim taskmaster, as hard on himself as others. He rarely cracked a smile and had neither time nor disposition for ephemeral pleasantries. He inspired respect but not love, and King wanted it that way."

The description is, of course, a stereotype, as Farago readily admitted. King could turn a reasonably benevolent eye upon a subordinate who produced to suit him, and in return elicit a degree of wry affection. On the other hand, he was utterly intolerant of stupidity, inefficiency, and laziness. He hated dishonesty and pretension, *despised yes-men,* and had no patience with indecisive Hamlet types. He could be completely ruthless. On one occasion he sent a commander to relieve a rear admiral who, in King's opinion, had failed to measure up—with orders that the admiral be out of the Navy Department building by five o'clock that afternoon.[2]

An aversion to "yes men" is an essential part of successful leadership and is almost universally present in those who earn a reputation as great leaders.

When Admiral Nimitz became commander in chief of the Pacific Fleet in mid-December 1941, it was immediately apparent to everyone in Washington that he was not a yes man. Potter's account of his appointment makes the case.

> Apparently the President and Secretary decided to sleep on the question of who should relieve Kimmel, for the next morning, Tuesday, December 16, Knox [the Secretary of the Navy] was back at the White House. They then quickly agreed on Nimitz for CinCPac. "Tell Nimitz," said Roosevelt, "to get the hell out to Pearl and stay there till the war is won."
>
> Knox hastened to the Navy Department and at once sent for Nimitz. The latter, completely unaware of the decisions reached at the White House, trudged wearily down to the Secretary's office. Knox, seated at his desk and obviously excited, did not ask the admiral to sit down. He blurted out, "How soon can you be ready to travel?"
>
> Nimitz, his nerves on edge from fatigue, answered a little crossly, "It depends on where I'm going and how long I'll be away."
>
> "You're going to take command of the Pacific Fleet, and I think you will be gone for a long time."
>
> Nimitz was startled. The year before he had begged off from the command for lack of seniority. That reason still applied, and now he would have the additional embarrassment of relieving an old friend. But in time of war one does not question an order. He thought of his immediate responsibilities.
>
> "I'll have to get someone to relieve me."
>
> "Whom do you want?"
>
> "Randall Jacobs." Captain Jacobs, until recently Assistant Chief of the Bureau of Navigation, knew the bureau's problems almost as thoroughly as Nimitz did.
>
> "You can't have him," replied Knox. "FDR doesn't like him."
>
> "God damn it," Nimitz exploded, "he's the only man who can do the job!"
>
> "Where is he?"
>
> Nimitz replied that Jacobs was somewhere in the Atlantic and that he would find him. Leaving the Secretary's office, he set out down the corridor, his thoughts awhirl. Suddenly he was brought to a startled standstill at the sight of a

pudgy figure coming toward him. It was Captain Jacobs. Jacobs explained that he was steaming into Norfolk, when he heard the news of the attack on Pearl Harbor. As soon as he could get away, he had come to Washington to find out what was going on.

Said Nimitz, "Come up with me."

The admiral led Jacobs to his own office and sat him down at the desk. "From now on," he said, "you are chief of the bureau. Get your orders drawn up."

Leaving behind a slightly bewildered new chief of bureau, Nimitz spent several hours preparing instructions, getting off correspondence, conferring with Shafroth and others—all necessary to get the new chief off to a clear start. Late in the afternoon he was summoned to the White House with Knox and King for a brief interview with the President. Then he walked home to Q Street, as usual.[3]

One of the most important decisions made during the Pacific campaign was whether to invade Formosa or the Philippines. The decision hinged on Adm. Raymond Spruance's refusal to be a yes man, also described in Potter's biography of Nimitz.

As the *Indianapolis* entered East Loch at Pearl Harbor, the signal station flashed a message of congratulation from CinCPac. When the flagship had moored, Spruance proceeded to Makalapa, and reported to his commander in chief. Nimitz greeted him warmly, then said, "The next operation is going to be Formosa and Amoy. You just hop in a plane, go back to California to see your family, and be back here in a couple of weeks."

Spruance reacted unexpectedly. "I don't like Formosa," he said. "I would prefer taking Iwo Jima and Okinawa."

Spruance saw Iwo Jima as not merely a way station from which fighters could escort the Marianas-based B-29s over Tokyo, but as the focus of an arc extending from Okinawa through the Japanese home islands of Kyushu, Shikoku, and Honshu to Tokyo. Bombers would be able to fuel at Iwo Jima and from there, with fighter escort, reach any of these areas. Fighters based on Iwo would be able to support a fleet operating in Japanese waters, as fighters from the Solomons in late 1943 had supported the carrier groups attacking Rabaul. From Okinawa, the Americans would be able to intercept ships in direct contact between Japan and China. As a bomber base, Okinawa was superbly situated for attacks on southern Japan.

"Well," said Nimitz, having in mind Admiral King's order, "it's going to be Formosa."

Normally Spruance would have set his staff to work at once drawing up plans. Instead, he was so convinced that King would eventually see the light and drop Formosa that he told his staff to take leave and not waste their time on an operation that would never take place. He then headed for home.[4]

Later the decision controversy came to a head:

The CinCPOA planners liked Spruance's suggestion of taking Iwo Jima and Okinawa, but those islands were too close to Japan to be assaulted until Japanese air power had been further reduced. Meanwhile MacArthur had offered, using the force he had and relying on support from the Third Fleet, to invade Luzon on December 20, the date originally assigned for the invasion of Leyte. The planners accepted that date and tentatively scheduled a target date of January 20, 1945, for Iwo Jima and a target date of the following March 1 for Okinawa.

Admiral Nimitz, summoned to San Francisco for another CinCPac-CominCh conference, took with him Admiral Forrest Sherman; General Harmon, who had come up from SoPac headquarters to command the Army Air Forces in the Central Pacific; and General Buckner, who had been appointed to command the new Tenth Army. To Spruance, Nimitz, preparing for the ticklish chore of talking King out of his Formosa project, had the arguments carefully marshaled and then summarized on a single sheet of paper.

When Spruance arrived in the Federal Building on September 29, he found CinCPOA and CominCh staff members chatting in the conference room while awaiting the arrival of Nimitz and King. Sherman handed him the summary sheet. "Read it carefully," he said, "and tell me what you think of it."

Spruance studied the sheet with obvious satisfaction. "I wouldn't change a word of it," he said, giving it back to Sherman.

Admiral Nimitz came in presently followed by Admiral King, and the meeting came to order. Nimitz took the paper from Sherman and handed it to King, who frowned as he read it. In the discussion that followed, Nimitz and Sherman did most of the talking, very tactfully pointing out why King's proposed strategy should not be adopted. King turned to Spruance, who had been sitting quietly. It was Spruance, King recalled, who had first suggested Okinawa. What did he have to say now? Spruance replied that Nimitz and Sherman were presenting the case very well; he had nothing to add.

Nimitz called on Harmon for the Air Force view and on Buckner for the Army view. Both opposed Formosa. Buckner pointed out that the crack Japanese Kwantung army had gone into garrison on Formosa. Judging from recent

American experience in attacking elite troops, Buckner concluded that at least nine divisions would be needed to conquer Formosa and that, even with that large a force, the invaders might well suffer 50,000 casualties. King at last gave in. He agreed that Iwo Jima and Okinawa should be attacked instead of Formosa, and said that he would recommend it to the Joint Chiefs.[5]

A wartime commander cannot permit distractions, even if he has to say "no"—quite emphatically "no"—to his service secretary. After the Navy and Marine Corps had conducted a very successful raid against several Japanese-held islands, Secretary of the Navy Frank Knox, a newspaper publisher before becoming secretary, wanted the success publicized, but Spruance was opposed to it.

> Nimitz, under pressure from Secretary Knox, who was eager to publicize the raid, asked repeatedly for details and even ordered Spruance to break radio silence [to provide the details]. The latter suspected that the source of the pressure was newspaperman Knox. "I'm not going to tell them anything," Spruance told Captain Moore, his chief of staff. "My job is to report to my superiors precisely what I have accomplished. When I have an accurate assessment, then I will report. If they want somebody to come out here and fight a publicity war, then they can relieve me."[6]

Admiral Nimitz was also opposed to publicity, and not afraid to say so.

> In the midst of the busy spring of 1945, the publicity-minded Secretary of the Navy Knox decided that CinCPac should publish a daily newspaper, or at least a Pacific Fleet magazine. Nimitz admitted that he had a good public relations staff and that they could do the job, but, he said, ". . . we are trying to run a war and, besides, we get daily press and radio and plenty of magazines." The most forward areas received miniaturized, overseas editions of *Time* and *Newsweek,* and Nimitz had no desire to compete with these.
>
> "The publicity side of the war is getting so large," said Nimitz, "it almost overshadows the fighting side." The more Mr. Forrestal insisted that Nimitz go into the publishing business, the more the admiral dug in his heels and refused to do anything of the sort. At last the Secretary gave up, having concluded that, with the possible exception of Ernie King, Nimitz was the most stubborn officer he had to deal with.[7]

Adm. William Halsey could be adamant when confronted with opposition to his personnel decisions. On one occasion, Nimitz, his superior, had to intervene in a running feud Halsey was having with the Bureau of Naval Personnel over obtaining the services of his old friend Commander Oliver Owen "Scrappy" Kessing, with the temporary rank of captain, to command the naval base at Tulagi. After an exchange of snappish radio messages, Scrappy finally arrived, but without the requested temporary rank. Halsey told Nimitz that he was fed up and that if the promotion had not been confirmed by the time he returned to Nouméa, he would send Scrappy a message, with an information copy to the Bureau of Naval Personnel: "You will assume rank, uniform, and title of captain, U.S. Navy."

Nimitz threw up his hands. "No! For God's sake, don't do it!" he exclaimed, "You'll foul up everything."

"You wait and see," replied Halsey.

Fortunately confirmation of the promotion came through in time to prevent a showdown between ComSoPac and the bureau.[8]

The media and certain historians have made much of the fact that MacArthur and his Navy counterparts did not always get along during World War II. "Bull" Halsey, however, so named by the media because of his tenacious, outspoken personality and take-charge leadership, was charmed by MacArthur's eloquence and logic. After the war Halsey reflected:

> The overall strategy of the whole area was in MacArthur's hands; the Joint Chiefs of Staff had put tactical command of the Solomons sub-area in mine. Although this arrangement was sensible and satisfactory, it had the curious effect of giving me two "hats" in the same echelon. My original hat was under Nimitz, who controlled my troops, ships, and supplies; now I had another hat under MacArthur, who controlled my strategy.
>
> To discuss plans for New Georgia with General MacArthur, I requested an appointment at his headquarters, which were then in Brisbane, Australia, and I flew across from Nouméa early in April. I had never met the General before, but we had one tenuous connection: my father had been a friend of his father in the Philippines more than forty years back. Five minutes after I reported, I felt as if we were lifelong friends. I have seldom seen a man who makes a quicker, stronger, more favorable impression. He was then sixty-three years old, but he could have passed as fifty. His hair was jet black; his eyes were clear; his carriage was erect. If he had been wearing civilian clothes, I still would have known at once that he was a soldier.

The respect that I had for him that afternoon grew steadily during the war and continues to grow as I watch his masterly administration of surrendered Japan. I can recall no flaw in our relationship.

We had arguments, but they always ended pleasantly. Not once did he, my superior officer, ever force his decisions upon me. On the few occasions when I disagreed with him, I told him so, and we discussed the issue until one of us changed his mind. My mental picture poses him against the background of these discussions; heels pacing his office, almost wearing a groove between his large, bare desk and the portrait of George Washington that faced it; his corncob pipe in his hand (I rarely saw him smoke it); and he is making his points in a diction I have never heard surpassed.

One had to be very persuasive to convince MacArthur. On one occasion he had a meeting with Halsey concerning a jurisdictional issue between MacArthur's "turf" and that of the Navy. Halsey wrote of this session:

When he had finished, he pointed his pipe stem at me and demanded. "Am I not right, Bill?" Tom Kinkaid, Mick, Felix, and I answered with one voice, "No, Sir!"

MacArthur smiled and said pleasantly, "Well if so many fine gentlemen disagree with me, we'd better examine the proposition once more. Bill, what's your opinion?"

"General," I said, "I disagree with you entirely. Not only that, but I'm going one step further and tell you that if you stick to this order of yours, you'll be hampering the war effort!"

His staff gasped. I imagine they never expected to hear those terms this side of the Judgment Throne, if then. I told him that the command of Manus didn't matter a whit to me. What did matter was the quick construction of the base. Kenney or an Australian or an enlisted cavalryman could boss it for all I cared, as long as it was ready to handle the fleet when we moved up New Guinea and on toward the Philippines.

The argument had begun at 1700. By 1800 when we broke up, I thought I had won him around, but next morning at 1000 he asked us to come back to his office. (He kept unusual hours from 1000 until 1400, and from 1600 until 2100 or later.) It seemed that during the night he had become mad all over again, and again was dead set on restricting the work. We went through the same arguments as the afternoon before, almost word for word, and at the end of an hour we reached the same conclusion: the work would proceed. I was about to tell him goodbye and fly back to Nouméa when he suddenly asked if we would return at 1700. I'll be damned if we didn't run the course a third time! This time, though, it was really final. He gave me a charming smile and said, "You win, Bill!" and to General Sutherland, "Dick, go ahead with the job."[9]

Among all the senior admirals I have interviewed, I do not believe there is one who would challenge an assertion that Adm. Arleigh Burke was America's most exceptional post–World War II naval leader, or that he made significant contributions to the Navy's mission to protect America. Admiral Burke learned very early the importance of having no "yes men" on his staff.

In his oral history Burke recounted a fateful World War II encounter with an officer who was no yes man: "I was down in Purvis Bay in the Solomons and a big man came over, said he was from the PT boats and he wanted to go with me because the PT boat war was pretty much over, he thought, in his area." The man turned out to be Byron R. "Whizzer" White, who went on to become a U.S. Supreme Court justice.

Byron White was a remarkable man. Like Burke, he was born and raised in Colorado, growing up in Willington, near the Wyoming border. In high school he worked summers in the sugar beet fields and as a railroad section hand. White graduated with a straight-A average and was valedictorian of his class, and won a scholarship to the University of Colorado. He played varsity football at Colorado and in 1937 was selected All-America, Colorado's first player so honored. As a senior he was the first varsity football player at a major college to have the highest number of yards per rush, the best pass completion percentage, and the best average of yards per punt for the season. To this day that achievement has never been equaled in Division I college football. In addition, White was a superb basketball player who led the Colorado team to the championship game in the National Invitational Tournament in New York's Madison Square Garden in 1938—the most prestigious tournament in college basketball at the time.

He was a true scholar-athlete at Colorado, again had a straight-A average, and won a Rhodes scholarship for study at Oxford University in England. He deferred the scholarship for a semester to play professional football with the Pittsburgh Steelers of the newly formed National Football League. His salary was an unprecedented $15,800 a year, twice what most of the other players received. He proved his worth, leading the league in rushing with 567 yards in eleven games, and was selected Rookie of the Year. After the season was over, he sailed to Oxford to begin study as a Rhodes scholar. He left his studies to play pro football again, this time with the Detroit Lions in the 1940 and 1941 seasons. In the 1940s he led the league in rushing and was named to the NFL All-Pro Team. In 1954 he was admitted to the College Football Hall of Fame.

When Lieutenant White asked if he could become Burke's intelligence officer, Burke agreed right away:

"Fine, you can come aboard and be my intelligence officer." He asked, "You rate an intelligence officer?" I said, "No, I don't, but . . ." He said, "When do I come?" I said, "Now." He said, "I don't have any clothes." I said, "If that bothers you don't bother to come."

Well, we went up the slot that afternoon, and of course, he was wonderful. When I went to carriers, I took him with me. His main job besides riding the intelligence circuits, which gave us a lot of valuable information, was to criticize what I was going to do. I explained every action if I had the time. I knew he was going to take the negative point of view. I did what I wanted to do, but he could point out where I might make a mistake. It gave me another dimension. And also sometimes I changed [my mind]. Sometimes . . . he'd say, "Don't drive in so close." For example, I'd tell him, "I'm going to get 45 degrees on the bow of the enemy, I'm going in to 4,000 yards, I'm going to fire torpedoes and turn right, retire to 9,000 yards, then open fire with guns."

He'd say, "Don't do it, 4,000 yards, you're on the wrong course for that, your moon'll be behind you, make it 5,000." Well, those things helped. Or he'd say, "You can drive in closer." Those were tactical things. He could also tell me that, "If you hit as big a group of ships that you think are there, there may be more. I think, although you've been told there are three ships, from reading intelligence reports there may be six, be prepared for six. I don't think you ought to go in with all you've got at the beginning."

This is one of the reasons why I developed the tactics I used of having one division to stand by, to come in hard right now, while the other division was fighting, so you could always have one division as a surprise for the enemy. You might not surprise him, but one outfit to engage him and the other outfit could attack, could stand by to take you off the hook in case you got into trouble. White is a wonderful man. I was lucky on that. I used to think I could pick men pretty well, but I made a couple of mistakes. I was certainly lucky on those people. They were marvelous. And there's an awful lot of things we did that I got credit for in CNO that shouldn't be credited to any individual, but to a group of people who made sure that I had the word.[10]

After World War II, Burke was assigned to the Korean truce negotiations as a delegate to the Military Armistice Commission. During the course of the negotiations, the commission was instructed by Washington to order the UN forces to take up a position that was contrary to the truce line of demarcation. It proved to be a test of Burke's character.

General Ridgway [Matthew Ridgway, UN forces commander] was there and we had to reply back from the Joint Chiefs saying that the United States' position was to be—the United Nations' position was to be, to accept this present battle line as the final line of demarcation.

Well, we said, we just can't do that. We just can't do it. General Ridgway agreed, and we wrote what we thought was a very strong dispatch, but General Ridgway thought it wasn't strong enough, and along about ten o'clock that night he had finished his dispatch, he had changed it, and it was a very strong dispatch. He sent that back, from Ridgway, but stating that everybody connected with the negotiations in the Far East agreed with this dispatch. . . .

The next day we got orders, again with the comment that we hadn't presented anything new in our dispatch. They said they understood our position, but for us to accept the present battle line as the final line of demarcation.

Well, General Hodes [Maj. Gen. Henry Hodes, deputy chief of staff of the Eighth Army] and I dug into concrete. We said we weren't going to do it, we just weren't going to do it, and if they wanted someone to do that, they'd have to [relieve us]. . . . Admiral Joy said he wasn't going to accept it either, so Ridgway talked to all of the negotiating team and said, "You are military people. I dislike these orders just as much as you do, but we are military people. We have stated as clearly as we know how our position. We have now been instructed to do something we believe to be wrong, but you are military people and you will carry out your orders."

Well, he was right.[11]

Burke, Joy, and the others illustrated their character, responding:

"All right, General, we'll do that, but that makes us liars and so we will not stay on this delegation. We cannot, for the good of the United States, for our own good, for many other reasons. We cannot stay on this delegation anymore because we've lied. We've been discredited—so you'll have to get somebody to relieve us. We'll carry out these orders, but that's the last thing we do." He said all right, he'd do that. So Hodes and I went up the next day and accepted the communist position.

Well, of course, Hodes and I and everybody else talked about this thing. We got very little sleep because of what happened. Obviously the communists knew our orders before we did. They knew what we were going to be ordered to do. They came in to the tent cocky. Well, we carried out our orders.

I don't know exactly when I got back, but it must have been the first week in December, I think, and I had six or seven days' leave, they said, which meant that I didn't have a job, but, of course, as soon as I came back I reported in to Admiral William Morrow Fechteler, who was then chief of naval operations [1951–53]. He asked me some questions, but wasn't particularly concerned about my concern that the communists knew our orders before we did. There were several things that I was angry about, really angry. One of them was the communists knowing about our orders and another one was why we would accept their position when it was so obviously not in our country's interest, and another thing, who the hell was running the show in Washington? Who was doing all this? Who, in our government, was responsible for this sort of terrible action? Admiral Fechteler wasn't concerned very much about it and tried to cool me off, but I was still angry and I asked him if I could tell the chiefs what I knew. . . . He arranged for me to meet them, but when I went down there to tell my story to the chiefs, they weren't particularly interested either.

Bradley was chairman, Fechteler was CNO, Collins was the Army chief, [Hoyt S.] Vandenburg was Air Force chief, and Shepherd was the Marine commandant. Anyway, I went down there and they were completely uninterested. I felt that they had let me come down there . . . as a courtesy to Admiral Fechteler, but they weren't interested in what I had to say. Vandenburg darned near went to sleep on me. Of course, he was sick then, too. But they weren't concerned. By that time I was furious. I think I said something about them permitting such disastrous orders to be issued, but . . . I don't know exactly what I did.

Anyway, on the 17th of December, the president [Harry S. Truman] sent for me. Dennison, who was aide to the president, told me that I had about fifteen minutes—the president would like to see me for about fifteen minutes. I think I went in about two o'clock, something like that and he asked me if I'd like to see the President. I said, "You bet I would," so I went in to talk to the president. He asked me some questions and he listened very attentively, particularly when I said:

"Mr. President, who the hell is—are you giving these orders?"

He said: "No, I accept what the chiefs agree to."

So I said, "Who originates it?" And he said the State Department did. So I asked him who in the State Department.

I was grilling the president and that's not what you're supposed to do, but he said, "I don't know exactly." And I said: "Mr. President, somebody in this government is leaking information because I know that the communists got our orders before we did. I just know it. I can't prove it, but I know it."

He talked about what I thought about Korea and what I thought we should do, and I stayed two or three hours. He kept me. At the end of the fifteen minutes—you're supposed, when you're given an allotted time with the president, at the end of that time you're supposed to say, "Mr. President, my time is up," and leave unless he keeps you. Well, he kept me.

The president liked what I had to say. He agreed with it. . . . He agreed to everything. I asked him about Ridgway. I said: "Mr. President, General Ridgway is a wonderful man and he submits recommendations he feels are for the best interests of our country, but nobody pays attention to those recommendations." He said: "Well, I see him and I agree with him, but we've got to do the things that are best for the government as a whole and he doesn't know all of it."

I said: "That's right, Sir."

And he said: "Well, I agree with Ridgway's stand." The president also said that he was all for more firmness on our part, less giving away, and I felt very happy about it.

The point of this incident is that the president was the only man who would pay any damned attention to what I had to say at all. He not only paid attention to it, he started checking. Well, you know, years later I found out what had happened.[12]

One of the most meaningful challenges in Admiral Burke's career was his selection for the General Board, on which he served from April 1947 through July 1948. The board's function was to advise the secretary of the navy and the CNO. Burke was specifically appointed to the board because of his dynamic energy, combat experience, initiative, ideas, willingness to challenge his superiors, and ability to express himself. He said about this assignment:

> Admiral Towers had written to Admiral Mitscher before and asked him if he would release me to go to the General Board, which Towers expected to be ordered to head. He wanted to reinvigorate the board and make it more purposeful than it had been immediately after the war. The General Board had been a very powerful and important influence before the war. During the war, of course, it wasn't, and he wanted to revitalize it. That's what the CNO had asked him to do, either King or Nimitz.
>
> This letter to Mitscher referred to previous correspondence and said that he knew that Mitscher wanted me to stay with him, but that he thought he should consider (since I'd been with him a long time) Towers's needs, and he hoped that he would release me sometime in the coming spring. He'd like to have me report by March, I think it was, anyway in the spring of 1947.
>
> Well, the letter was very embarrassing for me to answer, but I did write to Admiral Towers and told him that I was embarrassed and flattered by the kind remarks about me he made, and that Mitscher was in the hospital. I was opening his mail and that although I didn't think that Mitscher would return to full active duty, as long as he needed me I was going to stay with him. When he did not need me anymore, I'd be happy to go to the General Board if he wanted me to. But I wouldn't leave as long as I could help Admiral Mitscher in any way.
>
> Well, of course, Mitscher died very shortly thereafter. That letter of Admiral Towers's was dated 17 January. . . . At that time, Mitscher was so ill that I couldn't take decisions to him, so I reported it to the CNO orally, and to Admiral Gatch, who was the next senior in the Atlantic Fleet and was Acting CinCLant.[13]

After Mitscher's death Burke took up his assignment on the General Board, which collectively could and would stand up to the hierarchy; it was not a place for yes men. His bosses were the CNO and other senior Navy people; Burke was a very junior rear admiral. Admiral Burke continued:

> All that the General Board could do was to start an action and recommend. This is because it was an advisory committee. It was not responsible for the action taken. But to do that there had to be a small group of very knowledgeable men and that's what Admiral Towers had decided to create. He tried to make the membership knowledgeable, he and Admiral McMorris. The previous members of the General Board had been older people, admirals just about to retire, some

of them active and very good, but all of them looking forward to retirement. The problems that were presented to the General Board were short-range, not major long-term problems. So Towers asked for the people he wanted. . . . We had very little staff and that was good because as soon as you get a big organization to study important problems, it is done by an inexperienced staff of beautiful writers who produce volumes and volumes of paper, but don't arrive at the guts of a problem. Any similarity with the present White House staff and this description is purely coincidental. A very small staff who have to do most of their own work only take on the important things. They soon have to separate the important from the unimportant and they have to arrive at fundamentals. This is the advantage of a small staff in any organization.

This was a big advantage of the General Board. Of course, an advisory group in any organization is very apt to be bypassed. Its recommendations do not have to be accepted, then the man who makes that decision should be and sometimes is, criticized for not doing what it was suggested that he do. An advisory board . . . can't be bypassed just to get the kind of advice that the head man wants. The influence of any advisory board is, correctly, dependent upon the quality of the work that the advisory board does, but primarily it's dependent upon whether the action people, the management, really wants to accept advice. Do they really want advice, or is it just a procedural matter for them?

When I first went on there, the General Board had not been very influential for a long time because of the war. Naturally, it shouldn't have been. And so most people felt it couldn't contribute anything, most of the people in the management of the Navy. There are a lot of people in management in most civilian organizations and military organizations who don't want any advice outside of their own shop. They feel that an advisory group doesn't really have all the knowledge and certainly not the responsibility for carrying out the project and so such a group can be pretty free with its advice.[14]

From December 1951 through March 1954, Rear Admiral Burke was assigned as director, Strategic Plans Division, in the Office of the Chief of Naval Operations, second in importance only to the CNO. It was a critical position for the Navy's future, and it was clear that he was being groomed for higher positions. Burke commented on this experience:

I said that the responsibility of this division is tremendous, for it is our responsibility to determine how the Navy will fight its next war. It is our responsibility and ours alone to ensure that U.S. Navy plans are sound. There is nobody else in the Navy who has this responsibility, including our seniors. Therefore, it was essential that we did some sound thinking and that we did our best to make certain that the papers that were accepted [were] correct. That means that it was not enough just for us to have had good ideas. We had to furnish our bosses with the data in such a manner that they could sell those ideas, after they're convinced.[15]

More specifically, Burke said: "The mission of the Strategic Plans Division was to prepare preliminary positions for the Navy on all matters that pertained to the future security of the United States in which naval forces might become involved. That was a very broad charter."

Burke made it clear he and the board were not reluctant to challenge higher authority:

The ideas of our seniors or the words of our seniors were not sacrosanct. What we wanted was the best possible solution, and sometimes the words given to us by our seniors were not that best solution, because they had not been well considered. Those seniors realized this. Sometimes their words were based on vast experience and were absolutely correct, but we did not make that assumption. If this was true in any individual case, and we modified their words, we would be told about it. But it was our duty to present the very best paper with the very best ideas that we could. It was our further duty to make certain that our seniors understood what we are trying to do and why we thought it sound. *In short, there was no room for a yes man in any outfit like this.*

This was important because a lot of people can have an uneasy feeling that a proposition or a paper may not be quite right, but they don't feel they have enough data to go in opposition to somebody, either senior or junior to them. They can't prove their case, but they should still bring up their doubts. This is what makes an organization work, because one man has a glimmering of an idea he's not sure about and it may be that somebody else can pick it up and eventually a good solid idea is developed. Something else may come out of it and that is also good.[16]

The Strategic Plans Division helped to design the Navy's future.

Our major duty in Op-30 was, of course, war plans, handling Joint Chiefs of Staff papers. We proposed papers to them and had to comment on papers that the other services proposed and on what the Joint Chiefs were doing and make sure that all those papers were distributed in the Navy properly. We originated quite a few of those. There were literally hundreds of these papers in a year, so I don't want to go into any individual paper, but the same process that we used for our own command and other commands; that is, exchanging ideas and getting ideas before positions froze, we tried to use them with the Joint Chiefs of Staff organization, too, and that worked pretty well. . . . Whether your bosses use what you provide for them or not is not something you can control. You can't make them do it, just like you can't make the government of the United States, as a government, do anything, anything at all. You can only persuade them. If you don't succeed you've failed, but if you don't try, you've failed miserably. You've got to do the best you can do and that's all you can do.[17]

The duties of the Strategic Plans Division were far too important to allow yes men to serve there.

There's always a tendency in any organization to follow the directions that come down from on high, from a senior, and doing so without really questioning them or examining the direction very closely. That attitude can be fatal in a planning organization. If this attitude becomes habitual, it becomes deep-seated, and the directions that are issued by the top had not only better be right, but the originator should also have thought out all the possible contingencies and side issues that might arise from those orders. If they're in detail, they are very apt to be carried out blindly and without much deviation from them. This happens in any organization, not necessarily military. Surprisingly enough, I think military leaders are more aware of that pitfall and try to avoid it, but it is a danger, of course. . . .

An organization that doesn't examine its directives from the top will eventually turn out to be a yes man organization. They will do what they're told, they will do it very well, but they don't go beyond that. Dictators run into that trouble soon because they got their office by being forceful and by giving detailed directions. They suffer from the same faults as anybody else because no one man and no one group can know all the ramifications of any complex problem, any major problem.

Quite frequently, the senior commanders themselves do not intend to have their detailed orders carried out absolutely. Yet the assumptions of the commander and his staff when they drew up those orders turn out to be erroneous. What commanders frequently do not understand is that their juniors just as frequently don't know what those assumptions were. They don't have the background that the commander and the staff have.[18]

Service in the Strategic Plans Division was demanding. A man could be effective only for so long. The usual tenure, according to Burke, was

about two years. It takes a person six to eight months to get acquainted with the organization and the way it works, so he ought to be able to produce for at least a year. Our staff officers were all highly motivated in the first place. The only reward for such dedication that such a job has is more work and gaining a sense of achievement, the satisfaction he has that an officer did a good job. There's no way that you can reward a man for planning. It's an intangible reward and it runs counter to human nature. There's a thrill, an excitement in making plans, even little plans, seeing if you can arrange for the contingencies, seeing if your estimates of the situation turn out to be correct. You practice on plans. There is a great deal of satisfaction out of being able to foresee a problem and developing plans on what can be done about it.

One of the board's big problems . . . was how to get good officers. I inherited some wonderful officers, but we had to expand somewhat. I had to get more. Above all, we had to get good people in, our own naval staffs, joint staffs, and NATO staffs, too, and our allies' staffs. We had to encourage them to do their very best. We didn't know who had the motivation and skill to become good planners, so the first thing we did was to consult our own people in Op-30 about possible candidates, "We ought to get Joe in here. Joe's pretty good at this stuff, I know him." So we try to get Joe. Well, first, it's hard to get specific people. Joe's already got a job and his boss is not about to let him go if he doesn't have to. So you have to get people who are just about ready to change, anyway. We did get a few individuals.

One of the first things I did was to write to all the war colleges, not always to the head man but to other people, and say, "Can you give me the names of the five men who wrote the best papers in the last term?" They would then select from among those recommended names for assignment to the board upon graduation.[19]

On August 17, 1955, Burke was jumped ninety-two files and promoted from a two-star admiral to chief of naval operations. He considered himself very lucky to find a good staff already in place, particularly his vice CNO.

I was most fortunate. When I became chief of naval operations, I didn't change the organization nor did I change the people in it very fast. I inherited from Admiral Carney [Robert B. Carney, CNO 1953–55) a fine man who was much older than I, a very experienced, quiet individual, Admiral William Duncan. He was slow. He did not like change very much. He had some characteristics that bothered a lot of people. He would not do anything until he was quite sure that it was the proper thing to do. He kept advising me not to make changes, not to destroy anything until I found a replacement for it—in other words, not to eliminate something until I was sure either that it wasn't needed at all or that the substitute would work. Otherwise we would keep the Navy in a state of flux. He was right on that.

He was wonderful. He stayed for a little while and *then I looked around to find a man who would disagree with me* because the head of any organization is a lonesome individual. You have to make a lot of decisions. You have to make decisions just like the president, but on a lesser scale, . . . and I needed somebody who would disagree with me but who was straightforward and had great integrity as well as great experience. I didn't want just a stubborn man, but I wanted somebody who was very intelligent, from a different background, different personal characteristics, so that I could discuss matters with him.

I knew that was an unpleasant thing to be. It's not an easy way to operate. But I'd seen people in CNO and other high places where they had a group of yes men around them and they'd never work out well unless the head man himself is brilliant. I needed somebody to make sure that we didn't make any serious mistakes. If we made any, I would not take corrective action without knowing that somebody had thought the failed course of action was a serious mistake.

I looked all over the whole flag list in the Navy and came upon a happy choice in [Admiral] Don Felt. Don was an aviator, a small, irascible individual, hardheaded and tough, and he and I used to have a lot of big arguments, but he was extremely loyal to the Navy, which is what I wanted. He was knowledgeable. He had his nose to the grindstone and he would carry out things or tell me when he hadn't [done] things exactly the way I thought they should be carried out. He kept me fully informed. He really ran the detail of the Navy, but he kept me informed so that I could make the decisions that I should make. We had a successful operation going. Now, it wasn't pleasant. It isn't pleasant to fight continuously with a good friend, and after a while you wonder whether he's all that good a friend, and I know it was unpleasant for Don, too. But it operated extremely well.[20]

What does a CNO do if he disagrees with a decision made by the president as commander in chief? He must carry out the orders, and if he cannot, he must resign or retire. But American military officers are free to point out any disagreements they might have with their civilian bosses. Burke commented on that dilemma, remembering what President Eisenhower told him as CNO just before Burke was due to appear before Congress:

> "Once I approve a budget, I don't want you people going up there and undercutting my budget." Each time we'd say, "But Mr. President, what do we answer when they say do you think this is enough? We'll say no. We've got to say no. We don't think it's enough."
>
> President Eisenhower said, "You'd better be asked that question, you'd better not plant it either." Well, of course, it doesn't have to be planted. It's always asked. He would permit it very reluctantly. I had a statement that I wrote out very carefully, which I always read: "I do support the President's budget. But I think it would not be my way of building the budget. The priorities are different. He has made a decision, I will support that decision—I don't think it's the right decision, but I'll support it." The president didn't like that. No president does.[21]

Critics often allege that chairmen of the Joint Chiefs of Staff favor their own service. Admiral Burke, who served as CNO when Admiral Radford was chairman of the Joint Chiefs, was asked if Admiral Radford was able to rise above his loyalty to the Navy in his capacity as chairman. Burke responded:

> Admiral Radford did not want to be a naval officer and stay with the Navy [a chairman belongs to all the services and is often called a purple-suiter], so he was very careful always; if there was any doubt, the Navy lost. He was my hardest antagonist because he was a naval officer, he knew a lot about the Navy, he thought that he knew more about it than I did—well, he might have, I don't know—but he would give a decision to the Air Force and the Army rather than the Navy when it was an even break, because he did not ever want to be accused, or did not ever want to be in a position of favoring the Navy. So he leaned over backward.[22]

A dictator who surrounds himself with yes men is doomed. Admiral Burke waxed eloquent and philosophical on this point, which goes to the crux of the yes men issue:

> There's always a tendency in a big organization to want to run it, to want to centralize. Up to a certain size and if you get good enough people in an organization,

centralized authority will work and work better than any other organization. If you have the proper people, . . . experienced, knowledgeable, intelligent, and with the same objectives, it will work better than any other organization. A dictatorship is the most efficient of all organizations so long as it's headed in the right direction. But when an organization gets so big, not all of it can be directed from the top. The more you centralize an organization, the more you cut down the initiative of subordinates, and eventually it ends up with top people doing all the thinking and all the ordering, and the lower people, junior people, carrying out orders, without any authority themselves to initiate anything to carry it through. That means you've got a lot fewer people working on the problem than you should have when you centralize things. And centralization always comes a cropper eventually—usually when you run out of [the] people that started it.

Now, a dictatorship is usually efficient when it first starts. For three or four years a dictatorship is very efficient. And then people who get into power like power, and I don't mean just the head man, but the people who surround him. They like the prerogatives of power and they like more of it, and they get corrupted by power as the old saying goes. *They become yes men because the dictator at first likes to have people oppose him,* he wants to do the right thing for his government, but after a while, he gets a little irritated at people always opposing him. So he makes a decree, and pretty soon people get the word and they don't oppose him so very much because he controls the destiny of the individuals, and those individuals want a good future. So they say yes, and they give him what they think he wants. And at that time he doesn't have knowledge of what is going on below; he only gets what people want him to hear. So he loses contact with reality. Then he gets arbitrary and he starts to think, and the whole top of the organization starts to think that they have all the answers, that nobody else really knows anything, and . . . that they are endowed with super-knowledge. . . .

Now centralization of the services is not quite that serious, but it has the same tendency. If you centralize the services into one big service, with so many different facets, people lose their knowledge of the individual facets. They end up with too much emphasis on one aspect of war and not enough emphasis on the other aspects. They're bound to make mistakes. They don't have the checks and balances that you would have if you had independent services. Now there's such a thing as being too independent, too. There's got to be a compromise. You've got to reach a happy medium where people take independent action, but in coordination with other people who are working within the same policy that you're working in. Somebody knows, when the top people lay down policy, but the ways of accomplishing that policy are different in different areas of work.[23]

Admiral Burke was certainly not a yes man as CNO—not with the secretary of the navy, the secretary of defense, or the commander in chief. His oral history offers a remarkable illustration of his character and his willingness to fight hard for what he believed was vital to the Navy's survival.

I had a very unfortunate experience when I first became CNO. At that time we were short of people. The Navy was short of people and we were laying up ships. It was a question of whether we lay up more ships and agree to a much reduced number of personnel, or go to the draft. The secretary of navy, secretary of defense, and the president had agreed, upon advice of Admiral Carney (my predecessor), that the Navy would not go to the draft, but instead would remain a volunteer service and would reduce its number of ships to fit whatever it could get as volunteers. They expected that the volunteers would level off at a rather high position and we would not have any great difficulty in manning most of our ships.

Well I had studied that damn problem backward and forward. It was one of the worst ones that I was confronted with. The decision had been made, but I wasn't so sure that we wouldn't have to go to the draft. Well, in the time between—I don't know exactly when, the president made that decision, probably June of 1955. Our Navy kept going down, the situation got worse. By the time I took over, I thought we were in a very bad way, and I talked with Admiral Holloway who was chief of BuPers then, as to what he thought the answers were. BuPers felt that we should go to the draft, but not very strongly, although Admiral Holloway himself felt rather strongly about it.

Well, I was convinced after listening to their reasons and their analysis of the problem that we would have to go to the draft. So I went up to see the Secretary of the Navy and told him so and he said, "No, we've settled that question. This has been a very serious thing and we've worked on it, and we've studied it."

I said, "Well, I think it's wrong, I think we should go to the draft."

He said, "Your predecessor agreed that we should not go to the draft, that we should have a volunteer Navy."

I said, "The situation's a little bit different now."

He said, "No, it hasn't become much different. Now, you just go back and work on those problems you can do something about. Don't worry about this one, this decision's been made."

So I did. I went back for a couple of days. It didn't get any better. I thought it over and I asked for some more data, all the data I could get, and I came to my previous conclusion. So I went back to Navy Secretary Charles S. Thomas, and he was still insistent that we not go to the draft. I said, "Mr. Secretary, I must see the president."

He said, "You can't do that."

I said, "It says in the law that I, any time I want to, can see the president. And this is something that I think is serious enough so that the president should know, and I think what's being done here is wrong."

So he said, "Well, let's go down to see Charlie Wilson [the secretary of defense]." So I went down to see Mr. Wilson and explained to him, with Mr. Thomas, and Mr. Wilson tried to dissuade me and I said, "No, I want to see the president."

So we called up and made an appointment to see the president that afternoon, and Mr. Wilson took us over to the White House in his car. This was maybe within a week after I'd become CNO.

It was something that needed to be done. I went over there, and, of course, we got over there a little early, and I walked up and down the outer office for fifteen to twenty minutes, and I thought, "Who am I? The president has made the decision and the secretary of defense, the secretary of the navy, they all think the decision is right, and who am I to pit my knowledge, which is incomplete, and I've just found out I don't know very much, . . . against their knowledge and be so damn stubborn? Maybe I'm wrong, and I shouldn't have done this."

I seriously thought maybe I ought to go tell them forget it. Then I realized I'd brought up the subject, I'd taken a stand, and if I back down now, I've had it. I will never again be able to make a decision. And damn it, I was really right. What worried me is not the fact that I thought I was wrong, but the fact that I might have been wrong and that I was scared of bucking the organization.

So I met with the president and they asked me to explain my position courteously to the president first, and I did. Then Mr. Thomas and Mr. Wilson explained their position, why they thought I was wrong.

Eisenhower understood exactly what position I'd put him in. We discussed the thing a little bit more. He understood all about the draft, too. He said, "Well, we can go to the draft. We'll go to the draft."

He made his decision right then. He had to. I put him in a spot where he had to fire me right then, or he had to do what I asked him to do. It wasn't quite that, but nearly that. The lines were clearly drawn. And if he fired me, all hell would break loose. They'd just gone through the turmoil of dipping deep for me, and if they fired me in a week or so, it would have been a hell of a thing. He couldn't do it. He also, I think, realized that I was right. But the Navy was very proud of being a volunteer service and we have probably leaned over too far to keep it that way and been hurt in the process.

Well, anyway, I put him in a terrible spot, because he had to change a decision that had been made and he had to go against the secretary of defense and secretary of the navy, both of whom were civilians, both good men. I remember it so well because the president asked me to stay for a minute after the other two had left. I've forgotten what he told me, but I got the import. "Young man, you put me in a hell of a spot." And he didn't like it at all. He was furious. I had forced him into a position which he didn't like.

When I went out, Mr. Wilson and Mr. Thomas had left. I guess they were saying to hell with me. They left me over there without a car. So I had to call up and get a car to go back to the Pentagon. Mr. Thomas, particularly later, was distant, official, and very cold. He thought he had probably made a big mistake in recommending me in the first place. Not impolite, not rough or anything like that, but he didn't like what I had done.

Well, the nice part about that was, . . . I was supposed to be the secretary's man. I was Thomas's boy and Mr. Wilson's boy. And this indicated to the Navy and to the president that I was not. I was independent and probably a wrong and stubborn bastard, which I had warned them about in the first place.

So later on, after I'd gotten to know the president, he sometimes sent for me on problems that had nothing to do whatsoever with the Navy. Sometimes not even with the military. And usually about five o'clock in the afternoon, just before dinner, sometimes six o'clock—I'd come over. I liked old-fashioneds, he liked old-fashioneds, and we'd have a drink, and he would bring up the problems he wanted to discuss. First they were all connected with the military. When they were not Navy problems I'd say, "Mr. President, I'm not familiar with all the details of this."

He said, "I don't want you to be. I want to get an off-the-top-of-your-head opinion."

And I would give it to him as well as I knew how. Mostly I never knew what decision he finally took. But the nice part about that was that after a little while, I realized that what he was doing, he could trust my statements insofar as they were the best I could give him.

It was integrity, . . . somebody to talk to, to play things against, and he needed that, somebody who had some knowledge of some of the things. Now, a president needs that very much. I wasn't the only one that he did that with by any means. But this is one of the things that's needed, is somebody to give you their opinion, even though it's not an expert opinion, based upon a general observation; what's good for the country is hard to find out, hard to determine, and you have to make sure you're not letting some personal prejudice ride in it.

President Eisenhower recognized that. And because he did, he was a fine president. He was not a brilliant man, and he'd get mad as hell sometimes. He'd get awfully furious. He'd forget it pretty soon, too, when he got mad. But his decisions were based upon what he thought was good for the United States, not on what was good for Eisenhower.[24]

How did Admiral Burke's stand on the volunteer Navy versus the draft affect his relationship with the secretary of the navy?

It took a couple of weeks for better relations. . . . He's a fine man. I had a lot of trouble with Mr. Thomas. We had lots of differences of opinion. But we're good friends now. He's one of the best friends I have now, I think. But we had trouble, particularly when he wanted to see me move fast in replacing some of the older officers, and I had had that as a condition on which I took office. Some of them, I would have removed sooner if he hadn't tried to force me. But when he would get me on a particular man and say, "You've got to get rid of him," I'd say, "No." So I'd hang on too long, longer than I really should have because I wouldn't—didn't want to be pressured into doing something.[25]

Military leaders must stand up to their civilian bosses when they think that the best interests of the nation are threatened. The SALT II Treaty provides an illustration of how U.S. military leaders respond to a treaty on which they disagree with the secretary of state. In a 1979 interview Admiral Burke reflected on the newly signed treaty:

Would we support SALT II? . . . I'm going to be asked about that and they're going to expect that I will say the Joint Chiefs are dead wrong. But that's not what I can say because they aren't wrong. The Joint Chiefs are confronted with a fait accompli, and what they have to look at, the one thing that they have to keep in front of them all the time, the one factor, is what is to the best interest of the United States ten, twenty, years from now. They must ask themselves, "What can I do that's in the best interest of the United States?"

That sounds easy, but it isn't, because you must start from where you are when action is required, whether it's mechanical work, negotiations, or anything else, and the same thing is true of a decision. You start from where the country is, not where you wish it were, and the country had negotiated a treaty. The treaty is not a good treaty, it is not the treaty that we should have gotten, that we could have gotten, perhaps, but it has been negotiated. For seven years they've been negotiating. The president has signed the treaty. He has put the United States' signature on that treaty. He has committed the United States, both in the treaty and more vehemently by his statements.

Now, supposing the chiefs disagree and think that's a bad treaty. But they are not just individuals—they are important officials with heavy responsibilities for the security of our country. But what can they do about that? They can't say: "Mr. President, I'm going to oppose this treaty when I testify before the Senate," because that would be worse for the United States at this stage than accepting it reluctantly and then build up our military power. The important point now for the Joint Chiefs is to consider what can be done within that treaty, within the limits of that treaty, to protect the interests of the United States, and that is, we've got to build up our military capability somehow. I mean we've got to get stronger, relatively, than the communists, which can be done within the treaty. But if the chiefs oppose the treaty, what will the United States administration probably do? They sure as hell won't increase the military capability of the United States. They will decrease it. So if you're a chief sitting there in this position, you've got to think that if I oppose this bad treaty will it do harm or good for the United States, and you've got to come to the conclusion that it will do harm . . . because the net result, if he opposes, will be that the relative military power of the United States will be decreased.[26]

After World War II, efforts were made by members of the Truman administration, the Army, and the Air Force to "unify" the nation's air defense by transferring some of the Navy's duties to the Air Force. There was a tremendous blowup about it in the spring of 1949 that resulted in extensive congressional hearings. At issue was the future role of the Navy in U.S. national defense. The events are worthy of extensive discussion because they highlight the roles played by some senior naval officers who were willing to risk their careers for the good of their service and the nation.

The first signs of discontent appeared in April 1949 when an anonymous letter was circulated to congressmen, senators, industrial leaders, and the press. The letter accused Floyd B. Odlum, president of the Atlas Corporation—a holding company that included as a subsidiary the company that manufactured the B-36—of being "unscrupulous." Odlum, the letter said, had made contributions to the Democratic Party during the most recent campaign amounting to "very large sums, ranging up to the extraordinary figure of $6.5 million," for the alleged purpose of influencing aircraft contracts for the benefit of his corporation. The letter further stated that Air Force Secretary Stuart Symington and Odlum "have been much in each other's company. The log of Mr. Symington's plane . . . shows frequent trips between Washington and Palm Springs, allegedly to visit with Mr. Odlum . . . [and] on one occasion this year Symington and General Vandenberg spent a week at Odlum's ranch in California." The letter suggested that the Air Force and its leaders had lied about the capabilities of the B-36 and that even some members of the Air Force were not convinced that it could perform its stated mission. There were many other allegations implying corruption, incompetence, and payoffs.

In May 1949 Congressman James E. Van Zandt, a Republican from Pennsylvania, cited this anonymous letter in a speech to the House, adding further insinuations about Secretary Symington, the Air Force high command, and its civilian counterparts. These allegations led to a prompt investigation by the House Armed Services Committee, which was chaired by Congressman Carl Vinson, a Democrat from Georgia and a senior and powerful man.

Much more was involved than the utility of the B-36. At the heart of the investigation, which began in early August, lay the balance of power in the U.S. military establishment. At issue was the importance of strategic bombing and the high priority it received in budget allocations. Was too much attention being paid to the long-range heavy bomber, which carried the atomic bomb great distances, at the expense of medium-range attack bombers, fighter bombers, and fighters? Equally controversial was the Navy's tactical air power and its *Midway*- and *Essex*-sized fleet carriers. The force had already been reduced from eleven ships to eight. Were more cuts contemplated?

Secretary Symington vigorously defended the B-36 bomber program. In spirited language he answered the attacks made on him, the Air Force leadership, and the B-36. In his testimony before Congress he insisted that the B-36 had lived up to its predicted bomb load and had successfully accomplished a ten-thousand-mile round-trip bombing mission. He also emphasized that, in view of the limited amount of money available for new aircraft, building the B-36 would require sacrifices by the Air Force and the other services; there would be less money for other bombers and for tactical, cargo, and reconnaissance aircraft.

Symington's thirty-two-page statement categorically denied the fifteen accusations against his personal character made in Van Zandt's speech and challenged the besmirching of the reputations of Vandenberg and other Air Force leaders. He demanded to know the identity of the person responsible for the anonymous charges.

The anonymous letter had been written by Cedric R. Worth, formerly a special assistant to the assistant secretary of the navy. Worth was subsequently suspended from his employment by the Navy Department, and the congressional committee concluded that the anonymous letter contained not "one iota, not one scintilla of evidence . . . that would support charges that collusion, fraud, corruption, influence or favoritism played any part whatsoever in the procurement of the B-36 bomber. There has been very substantial and compelling evidence that the Air Force procured this bomber solely on the ground that this is the best aircraft for its purpose available to the nation."

Although Worth stated that his superiors in the Navy Department had had no part in writing his anonymous letter, the controversy did not end with that denial, because the admirals soon entered the fray. When Secretary of Defense Louis Johnson canceled the production of the USS *United States*, the admirals leaped to the carrier's defense. The chairman of the Joint Chiefs of Staff at that time, General of the Army Omar N. Bradley, supported the secretary's decision. He defended his view in his autobiography:

> An unstinting air-power advocate, Johnson was determined first and foremost to remove the Navy from the strategic air mission. He could best do that by canceling the Navy's new supercarrier, now named the USS *United States*, whose keel was laid only days after Johnson took office. After checking with Ike by telephone

(apparently obtaining Ike's approval), on April 15 Johnson sent the JCS a memo asking for our opinion. On April 22, the JCS responded with a formal "vote": Van and I against the carrier, Denfeld for. In my remarks, I concluded that it is militarily unsound to authorize at this time the construction of additional aircraft carriers or to continue expenditure on the USS *United States*. The very next day, April 23, Johnson ordered construction of the carrier canceled.[27]

Navy Secretary John L. Sullivan and the admirals were stunned by this *coup de foudre*. Johnson had not forewarned a soul—not the president, not Sullivan, not Denfeld. The Navy turned on Johnson as though he were a madman (which later events would indicate that he may well have been). Truman's naval aide, Robert L. Dennison, who had not been forewarned either, later summed up the Navy's opinion of Louis Johnson: "He was just a criminal." Outraged, Navy Secretary Sullivan resigned in protest, an idealistic gesture that dismayed not only Johnson but the whole military establishment. Sullivan asked Chief of Naval Operations Louis Denfeld to resign with him—to increase the impact—but Denfeld thought he could help the Navy more by remaining where he was.[28]

Sullivan was replaced by Francis P. Matthews, a choice the admirals, in the words of Bradley, considered "another slap in the face." They angrily derided Matthews, who had never served in the military and was not considered knowledgeable about the Navy, as Johnson's "errand boy." Matthews was a prominent Catholic who had long been active in Democratic politics, and, also according to General Bradley, "some sources believed Johnson had deliberately chosen Matthews to please and court the Catholic vote should Johnson run for President."[29]

The senior Navy leaders decided that their service's mission and perhaps its very survival were at stake. Taking a stand that showed they were definitely not yes men, they fought a battle that ultimately resulted in the firing of the CNO, Adm. Louis Denfeld; endangered the further advancement of one of the most exceptional naval leaders of World War II, then-Capt. Arleigh Burke; and exposed Adm. Arthur W. Radford, then commander of the Pacific Fleet, to damaging public criticism. There is no better example of the strong character of America's senior naval officers, who put their careers at risk by challenging higher authority to protect the Navy's mission.

Admiral Denfeld's appearance at the congressional hearings was awaited with great anticipation. Secretary Johnson expected him to be a yes man and follow the position of the secretary's office, but he was not entirely sure what Denfield would say, telling a friend before the hearing: "Denfeld hasn't been disloyal—yet." When Denfeld made a strong statement before the House Armed Services Committee on behalf of the Navy, the reaction in the Defense Department was described as "profound shock." The secretary of the navy was said to be "visibly flushed when he left the hearing room that afternoon." Admiral Denfeld emphasized that his perspective, though it differed from those of the other services, should be brought out in public hearings, stating: "I believe . . . it would be immeasurably more regrettable had these issues remained hidden and a false sense of security been permitted to prevail."[30] The other witnesses who appeared before the congressional committee included the Navy's most powerful leaders. World War II heroes Admirals King, Nimitz, Halsey, Spruance, Kinkaid, and many others either appeared or supplied statements in support of Navy aviation.

General Bradley viewed the admirals' actions as "insubordinate, mutinous." *Time* magazine entitled the controversy the "Revolt of the Admirals," and so it is remembered today. *Time* quoted one high-ranking general's comment on Denfeld's testimony, "Personal relationships have gone to hell. I don't see how they can ever be repaired within the Joint Chiefs of Staff." Bradley's most biting comment challenged the Navy's concerns: "This is no time for 'fancy dans' who won't hit the line with all they have on every play, unless they can call the signals."[31]

Admiral Radford was among those present when Admiral Denfeld spoke. "The hearing room was crowded for the testimony of Admiral Denfeld," he noted, "because of interest generated by stories in the press about what he was going to say. His statement was a remarkable document, a clear and objective analysis of the Navy's predicament and its problems, which had been brought about by unification." Denfeld made an eloquent plea for the role of the U.S. Navy in the nation's defense:

> We [the Navy] endorse the spirit of unification as Congress conceived it and the public demands it. We maintain that those principles and objectives are not being

realized and will not be achieved unless the Navy is admitted to full partnership. Gentlemen, the Navy is not seeking to destroy unification, as has been publicly charged. The Navy, whose inherent functions are as old as sea power, knows from experience the valuable results which follow the spirit of real unification, real coordination of effort. Our functions have long required operations on the sea, under the sea, on the land, and in the air, utilizing the basic principles of unity of effort. The success the navy has achieved can be directly attributed to avoiding arbitrary separation of functions on the basis of elements, the land, the sea, the air.

The fact that the Navy is not accepted in full partnership in the national defense structure is the fundamental reason for the apprehension you have heard expressed here. The entire issue is the Navy's deep apprehension for the security of the United States. This apprehension arises from the trend to arrest and diminish the Navy's ability to meet its responsibilities. . . .

On April 15, 1949, the Joint Chiefs of Staff were asked for their individual opinions on the flush deck carrier project which was well under way. . . . It is no secret that General Bradley reversed his earlier approval of this project. I again strongly recommended its construction, pointing out in detail its importance to the evolution of carrier aviation and naval warfare. General Vandenberg again opposed its construction. As senior member of the JCS, it fell to me to sign the forwarding letter to the Secretary of Defense enclosing the three opinions. It was delivered to the Secretary. . . . Forty minutes later, I was handed the already mimeographed press release of the cancellation order. . . . Unification should not mean that two services can control a third. Up to now, there have been many instances in which that has happened . . . . The Army and the Air Force have disapproved proposals advanced by the Navy pertaining to naval aviation and the Marine Corps. There is no intention to impugn the motives of any person in this respect; rather, [the problem] arises from lack of study or lack of experience in naval matters, or both. Nevertheless, these disapprovals constitute a pattern which I cannot ignore. . . .

In the present stage of unification, it must be recognized that the views of a particular service are entitled to predominant weight in the determination of the forces needed by that service to fulfill its missions.

The accomplishment of these points will not in itself solve all our national security problems. It will, however, go far toward providing a framework which will permit a unified approach to the grave problems of national security. We must get on with these problems, for in their solution lies in the whole hope of life, liberty, and the pursuit of happiness—not only for this great country but for the entire world. The time is now!

I express the wish of the entire Navy when I say that we not only hope, but sincerely believe, that the opportunity afforded the Navy to make this presentation can but lead in the final analysis to a clearer understanding of unification and hence to a more expeditious realization of its sound objectives.[32]

Admiral Radford, who was present for the entire hearing, made a point in his memoir to emphasize the respect Congress had for Denfeld. The chairman of the congressional hearing, Carl Vinson, said, "Admiral Denfeld, in my judgment, you have rendered a great service to the nation by making this statement . . . putting chips on the table and letting the country know the facts." Minority leader Dewey Short also complimented the admiral: "Amen . . . to his magnificent statement . . . this committee is sympathetic to your problems, and I personally appreciate the frankness and courage that you have exhibited here. It is something that needed to be said and it was forcefully and beautifully said."[33]

Admiral Radford offered additional support for Admiral Denfeld in his memoir:

Secretary Symington and General Vandenberg had, it seemed to me, made their statements too strong. Consequently, during the question periods, committee members cornered both of them, to their embarrassment, in several instances.

To keep the record straight, the Navy had no objection to the purchase of the first hundred B-36s; that was water over the dam. But it did feel that the hurried procurement of 75 additional ones, before any of the first had undergone a thorough evaluation test, was a great mistake. [As a member of the JCS] Admiral Denfeld had not voted against this procurement because he thought it was Air Force business. Further, the Navy did not think the B-36 would pass a strict evaluation test as an intercontinental bomber and was prepared to prove its point.

Regarding the carrier *United States,* the Navy felt it had been approved by the President, the Secretary of Defense, and Congress as a *new development.* Under the Key West Agreement each service was permitted to carry a new weapon through the development stage. Air Force representatives had heard Secretary Forrestal say on several occasions that he approved the building of one such carrier. Additional carriers would be built only if the first one proved a great success. The Navy thus felt that Generals Bradley and Vandenberg had violated the Key

West Agreement in voting to stop construction of the carrier when asked for their opinions by Secretary Johnson. The Navy felt too that Secretary Johnson had handled the matter in an arbitrary and unfair way.

General Bradley, Chairman of the JCS, was the next witness. He read a long, involved statement which he said was entirely his own and which he had not shown to anyone, from the Secretary of Defense to the JCS. He must have been fuming when he wrote it. There was evidence throughout of an almost uncontrollable temper. His military arguments suffered, either for this reason or because his overall knowledge of some subjects was insufficient.[34]

General of the Army Dwight D. Eisenhower, who also appeared as a witness, did not take sides or suggest solutions. He believed in unification and thought that, ultimately, it would work. He inferred that the services *had* to learn how to work together. His views would prove to have a significant effect on the futures of two of the strongest supporters of the Navy's position, Admiral Radford and Captain Burke. When General Eisenhower was elected president and commander in chief, he would play a significant role in service unification and would show his appreciation for senior officers who were not yes men.

On January 10, 1950, Congressman Carl Vinson signed and sent on to Speaker of the House Sam Rayburn a report of the House Armed Services Committee's investigation of the B-36 bomber program. The committee concluded that Cedric Worth was the author of an anonymous document that leveled unsubstantiated charges at many public officials and recommended that he be fired by the Navy Department.

The committee's Report of Investigation on Unification and Strategy, the second part of the hearings, was extensive. It was dated March 1, 1950, more than five months after the hearings ended, and specifically addressed the "revolt of the admirals."

> The committee wishes . . . to emphasize that it solicited from each witness his own personal viewpoint and urged that his testimony be presented without restraint or hesitation . . . therefore, the fact that the presentation of Navy views revealed fundamental disagreements within the Pentagon Building should not, in the view of the committee, be distorted into a charge against the witnesses that they were performing in any manner unbecoming their positions in the government. . . .

Should the time ever come when personnel of the Army, Navy, Air Force, or Marine Corps, or other officers or employees of the Executive branch, are fearful of, unwilling to, or restrained from voicing their frank opinions and convictions before congressional committees, then will be the time when effective representative government in this country is gravely imperiled. . . .

Civilian control of the Nation's armed forces is integrally a part of the nation's democratic process and tradition; it is strongly supported by the committee. But in supporting civilian control of the armed forces, the committee does not mean preventing free testimony before congressional committees by members of the armed forces. . . . The committee deplores the manner of cancellation of the construction of the aircraft carrier *United States,* but because of the pressure of other shipbuilding programs at the present time and the existing budgetary limitations on the Navy Department, will withhold further action—for the present—as regards the construction of this vessel. The committee considers it sound policy, however, for the Nation to follow the advice of its professional leaders in regard to this subject in the same manner as has been heretofore done in respect to the B36 bomber. In the committee's view, the Nation's leaders in respect to naval weapons are the leaders of the United States Navy.[35]

General Bradley could not forgive the Navy's open rebellion. "The leader of the Navy's mutiny," he noted in his memoirs,

. . . was Arthur W. Radford, a distinguished and brilliant naval aviator. He was assisted by many other admirals and senior captains, notably aviators Ralph A. Ofstie and John G. Crommelin, and a destroyerman, Arleigh A. (31 Knot) Burke, hero of the Pacific war. Burke and Crommelin, both skilled propagandists, attempted, with varying degrees of success, to enlist the media in the Navy's cause. In any event, they kept the pot boiling with leaks or rebellious public statements, attacking Johnson's budget cuts, the Air Force, the B-36 and the nuclear retaliatory strategy.[36]

Shortly after the hearing, Admiral Denfeld was fired as the CNO. That did not sit well with the chairman of the Armed Services Committee, Carl Vinson, who told the press: "Admiral Denfeld has been made to walk the plank for having testified before the Armed Services Committee. . . . Suffice it to say that the reprisal against Admiral Denfeld for having painted the picture as he sees it in the Navy will be dealt with in the committee's report and on the floor of the House in January."[37] The congressional report to which Senator Vinson referred stated:

> The removal of Admiral Denfeld was a reprisal against him for giving testimony to the House Armed Services Committee. This act is a blow against effective representative government in that it tends to intimidate witnesses and hence discourages the rendering of free and honest testimony to the Congress; it violated promises made to the witnesses by the committee, the Secretary of the Navy, and the Secretary of Defense; and it violated the Unification Act, into which a provision was written specifically to prevent actions of this nature against the Nation's highest military and naval officers.[38]

Although a great many influential people were upset by Denfeld's firing, not even Congress could save his position as CNO. When Denfeld testified before Congress without first discussing what he planned to say with Secretary of the Navy Matthews as the secretary had requested, his fate was sealed. Essentially, the CNO worked on his congressional hearing testimony up to the last minute, but even if he had informed the secretary what he planned to say, he had no intention of changing his testimony. The crux of Denfeld's testimony was, as he stated: "As the senior military spokesman for the Navy, I want to state forthwith that I fully support the broad conclusions presented to this committee by the naval and Marine officers who had proceeded me." Admiral Denfeld was relieved as CNO, but his efforts were not without success. The Navy got its carrier; Congress authorized it in March 1951, and a contract was let in July 1951.

And when it was time for General Bradley to step down as chairman of the Joint Chiefs, he showed his respect for Admiral Radford, who had stood against him in support of the Navy: "Who, then, would replace me as chairman of the JCS? . . . In terms of seniority, prestige and Pacific and Far East background made the logical candidate Arthur Radford (Naval Academy 1916). At first it was hard for me to agree that my arch foe in the B-36 hearings, a man I had publicly castigated, should succeed me. But I had to concede that Radford was the best-qualified admiral the Navy had. Moreover, since 1949, he had broadened and matured; he clearly had the potential to grow into the job and shed his service bias."[39]

Although Admiral Radford had put his career at risk by refusing to back down when he knew he was right, no permanent damage was done. President Eisenhower selected him to succeed General Bradley as chairman of the Joint Chiefs of Staff. Radford reflected on this turn of fortune:

> From the time Mr. Wilson [Secretary of Defense Charles Wilson] had spoken to me in Honolulu about the possibility of my becoming the next Chairman, I knew my name would be considered when the selection was made. But, looking at the matter cold-bloodedly, I had decided that my chances were slim. I knew there would be strong opposition from Air Force sources and that it was possible that President Eisenhower himself might be reluctant to nominate me. I talked it over with Mrs. Radford. She agreed that my chances were minimal. We decided that if the nomination came to pass it would be a great compliment, but that in the meantime it was best that I not try to get it. I had put it out of my mind entirely for the next few months and was busy with CINCPAC responsibilities. In spring 1952, nearing the end of my third year at Pearl Harbor, I had written to Bill Fechteler [the CNO] and told him that if he felt it desirable for any reason to make a change in the CINCPAC assignment to just let me know. I had thoroughly enjoyed the assignment, but realized it had to be rotated, and I would gladly ask for retirement whenever he felt it best that I should. I was similarly relaxed about the Chairman's job. If it came my way, I'd do my best. If it did not, I would be glad to step aside.[40]

Admiral Radford spent an afternoon with Frank Nash, assistant secretary of defense for international affairs, who told him:

> "On Tuesday morning your telephone will start ringing a little after seven. It will be the press in Honolulu asking for comments on your nomination as Chairman of the Joint Chiefs of Staff by President Eisenhower, which will have just been announced by the White House at twelve noon, Washington time." When I suggested that he was trying to kid me, he swore he was not and said he had been authorized to tell me in advance.
>
> I could hardly believe the news and said nothing to anyone, not even Mrs. Radford. But on Tuesday morning the telephone rang just as Frank had predicted, and it was the Associated Press office in Honolulu telling me of my nomination and asking for my comment. I said in response to a question: "I sincerely and deeply appreciate the honor of being nominated by the President as Chairman of the Joint Chiefs of Staff. My first reaction is an awareness of the

tremendous responsibilities involved, and I can only promise to do my best." I was completely overwhelmed, even though I had had nearly 48 hours to think it over. . . .

I was notified that the Senate Armed Services Committee would begin hearings on my nomination on 25 May. I accepted an invitation from the Pentagon press corps to attend a stag dinner in my honor at the Carleton Hotel the evening of 27 May. I knew this would be quite an occasion and that I could expect almost anything. I was not disappointed. One gentleman who had been imbibing freely offered to bet me $50 that my nomination would not be confirmed. He said he knew that Senator Symington, former Secretary of the Air Force, would oppose it and that he, Symington, could undoubtedly convince a majority of the committee to agree with him. I tried to stall the man off politely, but finally had to be blunt. I told him that I would not take his bet and that I myself was not at all certain I would be confirmed, as I knew there would be a good deal of opposition in the committee. . . .

The next morning I appeared before the Senate Armed Services Committee for the confirmation hearings. I was expecting and was prepared for a thorough questioning and I was given one. The Senators explored in considerable detail my views on strategic bombing, the strategic air force, unification, and many variations in those subjects. A few brief examples will suffice to show how it all went.

Question: Admiral Radford, anyone who reads the daily papers is aware that in 1949 you expressed certain views with respect to strategic bombing by long-range bombers and the so-called atomic blitz. Prior to these 1949 hearings, testimony you had given regarding the 1947 Unification Act was regarded by some as being in opposition to the bill then under consideration. Do you still hold the same views on those subjects?

Answer: It is almost four years since the hearings you refer to. There have been developments, improvements in material, and other changes that would naturally cause me to modify some positions. We are going ahead too fast for fixed ideas. I did not say anything I did not honestly believe. Under conditions as they exist today I probably would modify some of my statements. There have been references in the newspapers that I was against unification. It has never been clear to me exactly what people meant when they said you were for or against unification. If they mean as the object uniformity in all aspects of the Defense Department, then I am against it. I think you have to have three very strong independent services and can expect differences of opinion. *I do not think that you want men in the Defense Department who are going to agree for agreement's sake.* Military men who have years of experience and training behind them have very strong feelings about certain aspects of their work, and I think that is proper. . . . My ideas in 1947 were certainly that the status quo was not satisfactory. We had to have an improved defense organization. I felt that the bill before Congress was not the best bill that could be drawn. I stated my objections to it frankly. Congress passed the bill, and I have tried to make it work ever since.

Question: In the event the Chiefs of Staff were of the opinion that a certain minimum military strength was necessary to defend the country and they were overridden by the Secretary of Defense, do you think there is any obligation on the chiefs to talk to the President?

Answer: I do. . . .

In due course Senator Symington questioned me. He said, "Admiral, when you were with the Navy, you worked hard for the Navy. What I would like to know is this: in this new job, will you consider it your duty to work as hard for the Army and Air Force as for the Navy?

I said: "Senator Symington, in this new job I will work primarily for the United States and I will do my best not to favor any particular service. I will try to call my shots as impartially as I can." Senator Symington then told the committee chairman that he had no further questions. I was over that particular hurdle, in spite of what my friend of the night before had predicted. . . . On 2 June 1953, the Senate unanimously approved my nomination as Chairman of the JCS. By that time I had returned to Pearl and was waiting for my relief and trying to say goodbye to my friends in the Far East.[41]

President Eisenhower made it quite clear to Radford he did not want a yes man as chairman:

On Saturday 15 August 1953, I was sworn in as Chairman of the Joint Chiefs of Staff. The oath was administered by my predecessor, General Bradley. Although I had been preparing for this ceremony ever since the Senate's confirmation, I was overwhelmed by the actual event. The full realization of my enormous responsibilities suddenly dawned on me and never left me for four years, until I turned them over to my successor, General Twining.

President Eisenhower made it plain to me that he expected me, as Chairman, to call him directly whenever I felt it necessary, day or night and wherever he was. What a splendid and thoughtful man he was to work for. Secretary Wilson gave me the same orders, saying, "Whenever you feel you have to see me, come into my office. If I have someone else there and you tell me you must see me I will see you alone at once." During my four years' tenure I had quite the same relationship with Secretary of State Dulles, who also expected me to consult him whenever I felt it necessary. . . .

The fact that the President had ordered me to consult with him whenever I thought it necessary or advisable was known by members of his cabinet, consequently, I had no difficulty communicating with key men in the whole administration. From my point of view this was a great safety factor for the country, and it made my responsibilities much easier to carry out.

At one of my first meetings with the President in July he asked if I would like to have a weekly meeting with him. Surprised, I answered that I had not realized I would have to see him that often. He said, "Well, Raddy, if you don't mind, I'd like to continue the arrangement I've had with Brad, a meeting with you at 9:30 every Monday morning when we're both in the city." For one thing, it would seldom then be necessary for him to call me for a special meeting, which would always cause speculation by the press. Finally, he said, if I did not have anything in particular to take up with him he could just talk with me; it would be relaxing for him in the midst of a heavy schedule of appointments with individuals who generally wanted something! My regular appointment on Mondays continued until his first heart attack, after which I saw him at more irregular intervals. But he was always available, and on short notice.[42]

Arleigh Burke, at that time still a captain, also put his career at risk by publicly protesting against the cancellation of the new carrier—certainly not the act of a yes man. For a time, it appeared that his testimony before the Armed Services Committee might be his swan song. On November 14,

1949, a nine-member selection board met to choose a group of captains for promotion to rear admiral, and Arleigh Burke was one of the officers up for consideration. Vice Adm. Henry W. Hill was the board's president, and eight rear admirals made up the rest of the group. Selection required a yes vote by six of the nine members; Burke received nine favorable votes.

Secretary of the Navy Francis P. Matthews sent for Admiral Hill when he learned the board's decision. "You gentlemen are responsible for my having had no sleep last night," the secretary said. "Why you would select an officer who . . . has done the things that Captain Burke has done, I don't know." And he struck Burke's name from the list. Once the board had made its decision, only President Truman, the commander in chief, had the authority to remove a name from it. But Matthews did not stop there. He also ordered the board to reconvene to specifically promote Capt. Richard Glass, Matthew's public relations officer, who had previously been passed over for promotion to rear admiral. On November 28, 1949, the board, under duress, promoted Glass.[43]

The promotion list was given to Truman's naval aide at the time, Rear Adm. Robert L. Dennison, to pass on to the president. Dennison and Burke had been classmates, and Dennison held Burke in high regard. Normally President Truman asked Dennison, when such a list was presented to him, if any injustice had been done. On this occasion Dennison spoke up, as Jeffrey G. Barlow noted in his book *Revolt of the Admirals*: "This time, Mr. President, . . . I'd have to say yes. But I want to do some special pleading. And may I step out of my role as your Naval Aide for a moment?" Then Truman said, "Well, take the stuffing out of your shirt and sit down and tell me what the problem is." When he had heard what Dennison had to say, Truman responded: "You told me that Burke was Chief of Staff for Admiral Mitscher. And if Burke was good enough to be his Chief of Staff he must be a real good officer."[44]

After his conversation with Dennison, Truman put the promotion list in his drawer, and there it remained for weeks. The president usually returned promotion lists to the secretary of the navy within a few days, and when it did not reappear, Secretary Matthews became concerned. He had good reason to be: the press had gotten wind of Burke's removal. Burke was well known as an exceptional officer, and the media attacked Truman, Johnson, and Matthews for the injustice. The president, who had been at his Key West White House, returned on December 20, 1949, and instructed Johnson and Matthews to meet with him. After that meeting he called Dennison in and told him, "Guess what happened? Burke's name has been reinstated on the list and this other officer [Captain Glass] . . . also remains selected. . . . And the best part of it is that Johnson and Matthews think that they thought the whole thing up themselves."[45]

Burke's reaction, expressed in a letter to his close friend Adm. J. W. Reeves dated January 5, 1950, was, "It was a big surprise to find my name on the list under the circumstances. I still haven't recovered." Not only was Burke's career not over, but as described above, President Eisenhower selected him as CNO in 1955 and called on him to serve an unprecedented three two-year terms in that office.

To put the "revolt of the admirals" into perspective it is necessary to understand, first, why President Truman appointed Louis Johnson secretary of defense, and, second, the nature of the military's relationship with the civilian secretaries. The president's first choice to serve as chairman of his finance committee to raise funds for his 1948 election campaign was the philanthropist Bernard Baruch, who refused. This infuriated Truman, who wrote to Baruch: "A great many honors have passed your way . . . and it seems when the going is rough it is a one way street." Three other men had turned down the president's request to serve as chairman, perhaps because the polls were indicating victory for the Republican candidate, Governor Thomas Dewey. Louis Johnson accepted.

Johnson's credentials were quite impressive. He had served in the U.S. Army as a captain in World War I, as had Truman; he was undersecretary of war from 1937 to 1940; served as commander of the American Legion; was successful in the legal and business worlds; was independently wealthy; and was chairman of the finance committee for President Franklin D. Roosevelt from 1936 to 1940. Truman's biographer, David McCullough, described Johnson as a "booming, bald-headed, headstrong corporation lawyer and millionaire who stood over six feet tall and weighed 250 pounds. A subject of controversy in the past, he would be again . . . to

Truman's regret. But he took the job now when nobody else would, and he achieved amazing results, given the fact that no one other than Truman thought the ticket had the slightest chance."[46] After the election, Johnson's financial assistance and background earned him the position of secretary of defense; it was in essence a political payoff.

The Navy was right to oppose Johnson with such vigor. His lack of judgment surfaced over an appointment to Truman's cabinet. The president's assistant secretary of the army in 1948 was Gordon Gray, who made a significant contribution to his role by studying the combat readiness of the U.S. Army and making recommendations for its improvement. This impressed Truman favorably. When Secretary of the Army Kenneth Royall left that post to return to North Carolina to enter politics, Truman wanted Gray to succeed him. Gray declined the position because he had been offered the deanship at the University of North Carolina. What General Bradley referred to as "the most bizarre episode I had ever seen in Washington" followed. Johnson went to see Truman and in the words of General Bradley "dishonestly" informed the president that Gray wanted to be secretary of the army so bad "he could taste it," and that Gray was "delighted" with the appointment.[47] Based on this information, and relying on the assurance provided by Johnson, Truman sent Gray's nomination to the Senate for confirmation without further checking with Gray. When Gray returned to Washington, he was "stunned" to learn what had happened and immediately informed Truman that he did not want the position. Bradley said the president was "dumbfounded," but typical of Truman's character, said he would "take the rap," inform the Senate he had made a mistake, and withdraw Gray's nomination.[48]

Gray, in the meantime, decided "that you don't do that kind of thing to the President of the United States" and changed his mind. To avoid embarrassing the president, Gray gave up the deanship he wanted and agreed to serve as secretary of the army for a "respectable time." Truman was grateful to Gray and, as General Bradley commented, "must have certainly had some second thoughts about Louis Johnson's integrity and methods." In fact, "what it boiled down to was that Johnson, for whatever reason, had lied to Truman and thereby placed the President in an extremely awkward position." "As time passed," Bradley noted, "there were many in Washington who sincerely believed Louis Johnson was mentally ill. Truman was one."[49] In his private diary, Truman wrote of the incident, "Something happened. I am of the opinion that Potomac fever and a pathological condition are to blame. . . . Louis began to show an inordinate egotistical desire to run the whole government. He offended every member of the cabinet. . . . He never missed an opportunity to say mean things about my personal staff."[50]

Johnson was hoping to use his position of secretary of defense as a stepping stone to the presidency. When he decided that Secretary of State Dean Acheson, who was clearly Truman's most trusted cabinet officer, was standing in the way of his ambition, Johnson tried to solicit the aid of Averell Harriman, Truman's secretary of commerce, to get Acheson fired. Harriman related in his memoirs that Johnson, in return for Harriman's "help in forcing Acheson out of office," promised to make him secretary of state. Harriman, who had a clear understanding of loyalty, immediately reported this to Truman. In addition, while Harriman was sitting in Johnson's office, Johnson attacked Acheson during a telephone conversation with Senator Robert A. Taft of Ohio, the main Republican critic of Truman's foreign policy. This, too, Harriman reported to Truman.[51]

Truman's biographer, David McCullough, described how the events that led to the revolt of the admirals came to a head.

In late April, with no advance warning to the President or the Secretary of the Navy, Johnson suddenly canceled construction of a new $186 million supercarrier, *United States,* a major component in the Navy's whole program—with the result that the Secretary of Navy, John Sullivan, resigned in a rage. Truman, who liked Sullivan and did not blame him for resigning, nonetheless approved the cancellation. Still, Johnson's manner troubled him greatly.

In May, to the disbelief of the Joint Chiefs, Johnson ordered another $1.4 billion slashed from the military budget. To those who charged he was weakening the country's defense, Johnson boasted that the United States could "lick Russia with one hand tied behind our back."

Where Forrestal had been small, introverted, and apolitical almost to a fault, Johnson was a great boisterous bear of a man who shouted to make his point to an admiral or general, and exuded such overt political ambition, stirred such speculation as to his true motives, that he felt obliged after only a few months on the job to state publicly several times that he was *not* running for President. The press quoted an unnamed high official who said Johnson was making two enemies for every dollar he saved.

It was rapidly becoming apparent that Louis Johnson was perhaps the worst appointment Truman ever made. In a little more than a year, many who worked with him, including Truman and Dean Acheson, would conclude that Johnson was mentally unbalanced. "Unwittingly," wrote General Bradley later, "Truman had replaced one mental case with another."[52]

Secretary of State Dean Acheson provided another example of Johnson's mental instability. President Truman had ordered an evaluation of the U.S. defense posture and wanted it to be coordinated in particular between the State and Defense Departments, as well as with other cabinet members. Secretary Acheson arranged for the other cabinet officers to review the plan before it was presented to the president. Acheson's description of the meeting is quite revealing of Johnson's mental condition:

After apparently friendly greetings all around, I asked Nitze to outline the paper and its conclusions. Nitze, who was a joy to work with because of his clear, incisive mind, began to do so. Johnson listened, chair tilted back, gazing at the ceiling, seemingly calm and attentive. Suddenly he lunged forward with a crash of chair legs on the floor and fist on the table, scaring me out of my shoes. No one, he shouted, was going to make arrangements for him to meet with another Cabinet officer, and a roomful of people, and be told what he was going to report to the President. Who authorized these meetings contrary to his orders? What was this paper, which he had never seen? Trying to calm him down, I told him that we were working under the President's orders to him and me and through his designated channel, General Burns. As for the paper, he had had it for a week. But he would have none of it and, gathering General Bradley and other Defense people, stalked out of the room. The rest of us were left in shocked disbelief. General Burns, who had stayed behind, put his head in his hands and wept in shame. I was then summoned into my own office, where Louis Johnson began again to storm at me that he had been insulted. This was too much. I told him since he had started to leave, to get on with it and the State Department would complete the report alone and, explain why.

Rejoining the still shell-shocked group, I reported the latest episode to Admiral Souers and James Lay, who left, in turn, to inform the President. Within the hour the President telephoned me, expressing his outrage and telling me to carry on exactly as we had been doing. At the slightest sign of obstruction or foot-dragging in the Pentagon I was to report to him. From this time on until the President felt it necessary in September to ask for Johnson's resignation, evidence accumulated to convince me that Louis Johnson was mentally ill. His conduct became too outrageous to be explained by mere cussedness. It did not surprise me when some years later he underwent a brain operation.[53]

Truman faced a difficult decision. Johnson had raised a large sum of money for his campaign when several others had refused to help, and had been conspicuous in carrying out Truman's desire to cut the Pentagon budget. But Truman finally had to fire him. Things were not going well in Korea, and he needed a rational and effective secretary of defense. McCullough described the scene.

On Monday the 11th, Truman summoned Louis Johnson and told him he must quit. Further, in announcing his resignation, Johnson was to recommend General Marshall as his successor.

Johnson looked as if he might faint. Truman felt dreadful. Johnson pleaded for time to think it over. He could have a day, Truman said, but there would be no change. Returning the next afternoon with an unsigned letter of resignation in hand, Johnson begged Truman not to fire him. When Truman insisted he sign the letter, Johnson broke down and wept. He had seldom ever been so miserably uncomfortable, Truman later said. He had known Johnson for thirty years.[54]

The resignation of Johnson and the nomination of Marshall were announced at once.

Admiral Denfeld was fired as CNO because he challenged the authority of the secretary of defense, Louis Johnson, and insisted on the Navy's proper role in the defense of the nation. A decade later, another CNO was to suffer the same fate: Adm. George W. Anderson (CNO 1961–63).

On August 2, 1961, the *New York Times* announced in a small headline, "Anderson Takes Top Post in Navy." Adm. George W. Anderson was a fifty-four-year-old Navy flyer when President John F. Kennedy elevated him from his command of the Sixth Fleet in the Mediterranean, jumping him over ten more senior admirals. Anderson accepted the Navy's highest leadership position with "a mixture of pride, of inspiration, of humility and confidence," telling the *Times*, "I recognize the tremendous challenge which I accept."[55]

Admiral Anderson, a 1927 graduate of the Naval Academy, began his naval career as a surface officer on the cruiser *Cincinnati*; after two years he entered pilot training and won his wings in October 1930. He served throughout the 1930s in various aviation assignments. In 1942 he met and favorably impressed then–Brigadier General Eisenhower, who was serving as war plans officer for Army Chief of Staff Gen. George C. Marshall. Army war plans had to be closely coordinated with the Navy, which was responsible for transporting men and supplies, and Anderson performed well in that job. Eisenhower wrote a special letter of commendation on Anderson's performance.

When Ike became NATO commander in 1949, he specifically asked that Anderson be the senior American officer for plans and operations on the staff of the supreme allied commander in Europe. When President Eisenhower selected Adm. Arthur W. Radford to be chairman of the Joint Chiefs of Staff, Radford brought Anderson to Washington as his special assistant. He was selected as CNO by President John F. Kennedy when Admiral Burke declined a fourth two-year term. Anderson had served in diverse assignments: in the surface Navy and as a combat carrier fighter pilot in World War II; he had an extensive operational background and had commanded a carrier fleet and a fleet air wing; he had been involved in antisubmarine warfare; and he had served on joint and international staffs. His operational and staff ability made him well qualified to be CNO.

It was prophetic that in his acceptance speech Anderson pledged to "keep the Navy on course and steaming strong, regardless of what the future may portend," because he put his career at constant risk to protect the best interests of the Navy.[56] He was certainly not a yes man. His tour as CNO involved numerous confrontations with Secretary of Defense Robert S. McNamara. It was expected that he would serve two two-year terms, as most CNOs did. Some even speculated that the administration planned to appoint Anderson chairman of the Joint Chiefs of Staff to succeed Gen. Lyman L. Lemnitzer.

On May 7, 1963, however, several months shy of the end of Anderson's first term, the front page of the *Washington Post* carried the headline: "Anderson Is Dropped from the Chief Navy Post." The article began: "President Kennedy jolted the Pentagon yesterday by dropping Admiral George W. Anderson as Chief of Naval Operations." The following day, the *Post*'s headline read: "Dropping of Anderson Is Viewed as Warning." The article went on to state: "The dropping of Admiral George W. Anderson as Chief of Naval Operations is being interpreted as a warning to military leaders to conform—or else."[57]

Several reasons were given for the decision, all related to Anderson's refusal to be a yes man. First, he had protested when the secretary of defense and his key civilian subordinates had bypassed traditional Navy channels. They had no military experience, did not know what they were doing, and were arrogant to boot. During the October 1962 Cuban missile crisis, when the Navy blockaded Cuban ports, McNamara communicated directly with local Navy commanders. Anderson insisted that McNamara should have gone through the Atlantic commander, Adm. Robert Dennison.

Lawrence Korb's profile of Admiral Anderson in *The Chiefs of Naval Operations* offers a vivid description of the conflict between Anderson and McNamara over the handling of the blockade:

> Anderson's frustrations with the conduct of the blockade came to a head on Wednesday night, 24 October, when McNamara and Gilpatric came unannounced into the flag plot to explore the Navy's procedures and routine for intercepting. Anderson reminded McNamara that he had outlined the procedures at the meeting of the Security Council on Sunday, and he saw no need to discuss the subject further. McNamara then asked a number of detailed questions about what the Navy would do under certain circumstances. Anderson refused to be drawn into specifics and explained that the Navy had long-standing regulations that covered blockades. This sequence angered both men and led to some harsh exchanges. The sharp encounter ended when Anderson told McNamara that he and his deputy ought to go back to their offices and let the Navy run the blockade.

After that, Gilpatric reported to the president that Anderson and McNamara could no longer work in an atmosphere "of mutual confidence and loyalty."[58]

Second, Anderson and McNamara had major differences over the TFX (Tactical Fighter Experimental). In a move to save money, McNamara had decided that the Navy and the Air Force should have *the same tactical aircraft*— that is, that the same fighter would simultaneously fulfill the needs of both services. The decision might have saved money, but it illustrated McNamara's ignorance of the different operational requirements of each service.

The TFX, designed by the Air Force's Tactical Air Command, "could operate from sod fields, fly non-stop without refueling across the Atlantic, carry large quantities of ordinance, and operate equally well at high and low altitudes at speeds in excess of 1,700 miles per hour. On the other hand, the Navy wanted a tactical fighter with long endurance and a very complex missile system."[59] Air Force and Navy planners informed McNamara that one aircraft design could not be used by both services. Anderson, believing himself more competent than McNamara to judge the Navy's needs, refused to back down. Lawrence Korb wrote of this controversy:

> After thirty-six years of commissioned service, Anderson considered himself better qualified than a businessman or a scholar to decide questions concerning the specific characteristics of weapon systems and tactics for operational units. Finally, as a service chief and member of the Joint Chiefs, Anderson was responsible not only to the Secretary of Defense but also to the president and to Congress, and the chief executive and members of the legislature had a right to hear the opinions of their senior naval adviser, even when these opinions differed markedly from those of the Secretary of Defense. As Anderson noted on one occasion, the full force of recommendations made by the service chiefs to the president and Congress should not be "dulled in any way in transmission."[60]

Admiral Anderson favored the fighter designed by Boeing, but McNamara favored the model presented by a consortium of General Dynamics and Grumman. There was outrage when McNamara overruled the unanimous recommendations of a study group of twenty-one Air Force generals and Navy admirals on the appropriate design each needed. The controversy was ultimately resolved by Congress after nine months of hearings. The General Dynamics design of the TFX did not meet the Navy's requirements for a tactical fighter, and it was Anderson's forceful and well-articulated arguments that convinced Congress of that. He even took his fight beyond Congress to the administration and to the public in speeches. In his presentation to Congress, the *New York Times* reported, "Anderson spoke out strongly against McNamara's decision in such a way as to anger Pentagon chiefs. They think he 'got out of line' by reading a statement giving his views instead of simply answering questions."[61]

A third reason for Admiral Anderson's firing was his opposition to the Department of Defense's attempt to reorganize the Navy into a logistics agency, bolstering the secretary of the navy's office and the material side of the service at the expense of the role of the CNO and the seagoing line admirals. A fourth factor was Anderson's testimony before Congress that the Kennedy administration's pay bill was inadequate to maintain skilled men in the Navy.

The *Washington Post* article of May 8, 1963, noted that Admiral Anderson and Air Force Chief of Staff Curtis E. LeMay "disagreed frequently and strongly with their civilian superiors—but always according to the rules! That is they voiced their dissent only within command channels or when asked by Congress for their views."[62] But Anderson, fighting to preserve the Navy's role in the defense of the nation, took the cause beyond that. Of all the reasons for Admiral Anderson's failure to be appointed to a second term as CNO, his testimony against the TFX was probably the most important. The implications of his firing were alarming. The *Post* article of May 8, 1963, concluded that "many at the Pentagon felt President Kennedy's command appointments, taken on McNamara's recommendations, *may discourage military men from dissenting* and further downgrade the Joint Chiefs of Staff."[63]

Apparently, McNamara wanted to replace all of the incumbents: in October 1962, Gen. Lyman Lemnitzer, after only one year as chairman of the Joint Chiefs, was moved to command NATO forces; Army Chief of Staff George H. Deckers was summarily retired; Air Force Gen. Curtis E. LeMay's appointment was extended for only one year rather than the usual two, but McNamara had to tread cautiously there because General LeMay was a national hero, the last truly great battle-tested leader still on active duty. Joseph Alsop, the nationally syndicated columnist, commented in the *Washington Post* on May 8, 1963, that "recent harsh lessons have taught

McNamara to be more deferential to congressional and public opinion."[64] LeMay was virtually untouchable because of his popularity, but Anderson was largely unknown to the man on the street.

Although the May 7 *Washington Post* article announced that Anderson was being "dropped" as CNO, White House spokesman Andrew T. Hatcher reported that Anderson had been offered a new position by President Kennedy. In response to reporters' questions about a possible new assignment, Anderson stated, "I am highly honored by the position the President has offered me, and am, of course, considering it. I will make my reply to him personally."[65]

The position was ambassador to Portugal, and Anderson accepted. Some of the Navy brass were disappointed because this overseas posting would prevent Anderson from continuing to present his cause to Congress and the American people, something he had done with great success, but unfortunately at the expense of his Navy career. The naval community vigorously and openly questioned the firing. When the controversy showed no signs of ending, Anderson himself finally put a stop to it, imploring "all hands" in the Navy "to avoid any remarks, comments, or assumptions relating thereto. Let me assure each and every man in the Naval service that our Commander in Chief has made clear to me not only his confidence in our Naval leadership, but his pride in our service, and it is unbecoming of the Naval profession to engage in any actions or reactions which could do damage to our service reputations—collective and individual—as well as to the prestige of the armed forces of these United States and our civilian leadership."[66]

Adm. James L. Holloway III (CNO 1974–78) told me in one of our many interviews that "admirals are selected not for their politics, but on the basis of their character and professional competence. I have yet to encounter a navy secretary or secretary of defense or president who thought it was in his job description to disregard the advice of his flag officers. Yet there will be times when otherwise like-minded leaders will differ, and a CNO must be prepared to disagree." He described several incidents that occurred during his tenure as CNO when he clearly put his career at risk by challenging his seniors. In doing so he could have suffered the same fate as Admirals Denfield and Anderson. For example:

> In early 1976, President Gerald Ford was running hard for nomination facing a very strong challenge from Ronald Reagan and he was anxious to consummate some sort of a SALT II agreement to show progress in his administration for arms limitations and reduction. At that time, Secretary of State and National Security Adviser Henry Kissinger was in Europe negotiating with the Soviets. Kissinger cabled back from Vienna the outlines of a new treaty to which [he] had tentatively agreed. This agreement would ban the deployment of the Tomahawk missile on U.S. submarines and limit its deployment on surface ships to only ten cruisers with ten Tomahawks each.
>
> Kissinger had previously sent the outline of this agreement to the Pentagon for comment, and Secretary of Defense Donald Rumsfeld and Gen. George S. Brown, chairman of the Joint Chiefs, indicated their agreement by initialing the draft. General Brown preliminarily shared this information with me, aware that the Navy was the principal service affected. I told him that the Navy would definitely oppose such an agreement, as the Tomahawk was very important in the future plans of the Navy. It was essential to provide our submarines, cruisers, and destroyers with standoff weapons, which were absolutely necessary to give them an offensive capability into the twenty-first century and thus to extend their usefulness in the fleet.
>
> I told Brown, and this was in my authority as a member of the JCS, that I wanted a meeting of the chiefs to review this proposal and to develop a formal position for the JCS, based upon all of the members participating. He agreed. However, very shortly after that, both he and Secretary Rumsfeld left Washington to attend a NATO ministerial meeting in Oslo, Norway. It was at that juncture that the president called a meeting of the National Security Council to formally review Kissinger's proposed agreement. In the absence of the secretary of defense and the CJCS, Deputy Secretary Bill Clements and I attended. President Ford had previously directed that I was to be the acting chairman of the JCS whenever George Brown was out of town.
>
> The announcement of the NSC meeting came on short notice, and I had less than an hour to prepare myself before going to the White House. I immediately tried to call all the chiefs, but I could locate only Lou Wilson, the commandant of the Marine Corps, and the vice chief of staff of the Army. They both felt we should not agree to this treaty without a formal review by the Joint Staff

and a meeting of the JCS. Armed only with this backing, I was to represent the Joint Chiefs of Staff in an NSC meeting chaired by the president.

President Ford first made a pitch in favor of the proposal, remarking on the fortunate political timing of the agreement prior to the election. Then, he went around the table, asking each representative for his position. I was under tremendous pressure. All of the other members and advisers, as they were queried, were voting in favor of the Kissinger agreement. I was one of the last members the president called on, and he probably expected me to echo General Brown's position. But the chairman had not brought the matter before the Joint Chiefs, so it was only his position, not that of the JCS. I replied that I was aware of the president's desire for a SALT II agreement, and how important it was to the nation that we have one. But in representing the chiefs, I had to say that our responsibility was to secure a SALT agreement that was best for the security of the nation, both now and in the future, and that I was persuaded that this was an unbalanced agreement in that we were giving up a tremendous military capability in the cruise missile for a transient reduction . . . on the part of the Soviets. I was concerned that the potential for the cruise missile in the U.S. Navy was virtually unlimited. We saw it as the principal weapon of the future for cruisers, destroyers, and submarines and were considering an airborne version to be flown off the carriers. I added that after an opportunity to review that treaty, the chiefs would all agree with me.

The president was obviously upset. But he . . . said, "Admiral, I asked for your view and you gave it to me, but I want you to think about it very carefully, because this is a vitally important decision we are making today." I replied that there was no question in my mind that the chiefs were not in favor of it, but I pointed out in words to the effect that, "Mr. President, you are the person who has to weigh the views from all sides, domestic, political, our allies, and the eventual relationship with the Soviet Union. You can certainly make the decision to go with this agreement with the chiefs registering their disagreement. It is a presidential decision. If you say it will be done, the treaty will be approved by the NSC. But in the ratification of the treaty in the Congress, the chiefs will be called upon for their views. It is the responsibility of each member of the Joint Chiefs of Staff to give his personal professional opinion, and the chiefs will have to say we disagree, and we advised the president of our disagreement."

The president then said, "We have everybody in the room for it except for the chairman of the Joint Chiefs of Staff, but I have to say, I will not go against the judgment of the JCS in matters such as this. Jim, will you go back and meet with your colleagues and discuss this with them again, and make sure you are

accurately representing their position? We will reconvene the NSC meeting at
4:00 P.M. this afternoon."

When I arrived at the Pentagon, the other chiefs were standing on the front
steps of the River Entrance to meet me, and we immediately went into executive session in the tank. The chiefs to a man were positive in their position that
we should not give up the cruise missile for the tradeoff that was offered in the
proposal. At the 4:00 P.M. White House NSC meeting, I reiterated the fact that
the chiefs were positive in recommending in the strongest terms that the president not agree to this proposal. So, the NSC meeting was adjourned with the NSC
staff being directed to send a message to Secretary Kissinger that the chiefs were
opposed to the agreement and that the president had determined that he would
not go against their advice.

As you can imagine, I was not very popular at that time. The only people
who told me that I did the right thing were Fred Ikle, who was the head of the
Arms Control and Disarmament Agency, and his deputy, John Lehman, who was
eventually to become the secretary of the navy.

As a sequel to this story, many years later in 1988, I was a member of the
Commission for Long Term Integrated Strategy along with Henry Kissinger
among others. During one of our meetings, Dr. Kissinger whispered to me,
"Admiral, at one time I was very mad at you." And I knew he was referring to the
cruise missile incident. I said, "Mr. Secretary, I know you were, but we all have
to do what we have to do." He chuckled and said, "Well I'm not sure your decision wasn't the right one. Things seem to have worked out for the best."

The Tomahawk cruise missile has become the most important weapon in
the arsenal of the U.S. Navy's surface combatants—the frigates, destroyers, and
cruisers—as well as all attack submarines. It is effective against ship and land targets. Modern warships carry up to 80 of these missiles in vertical launchers.
During the U.S. campaign in Afghanistan, the submarines, destroyers, and cruisers of the Fifth Fleet, operating off the coast of Pakistan in the Arabian Sea, fired
176 Tomahawks in the first hour of the war against targets in Afghanistan with 90
percent effectiveness, to pave the way for the carrier strikes and the airborne
assault.[67]

A second incident Admiral Holloway related to me concerned
President Jimmy Carter's military budget:

In January 1978, I was chief of naval operations when President Carter called a
meeting of the Joint Chiefs of Staff to have lunch with him at the White House.

It was typical of President Carter to meet personally with the chiefs. He seemed to like to engage us in professional discussions over breakfast, lunch, or coffee in the White House or at the Pentagon. On this occasion he had included Secretary Harold Brown; National Security Adviser Zbigniew Brzezinski; Gen. Dave C. Jones, chief of staff of the Air Force; the vice chief of the Army; Gen. Lou Wilson, the commandant of the Marine Corps; and myself as CNO; Gen. George S. Brown, the CJCS, [was] not . . . available.

After greeting us, the president announced that the purpose of this get-together was to explain to the chiefs that the fiscal year 1979 defense budget was going to have to be cut by nine billion dollars. The current version of the budget was considered by his fiscal advisers to be too large and required reduction. Nine billion dollars would be the military's share of the cut. Carter went on to say he was going to defend the reductions by saying that our military would be even stronger with this belt tightening. It would eliminate waste and make the services leaner and more efficient. He wanted the chiefs to get this message out to the service troops, and to back him up with the press and the Congress.

The initial reaction among the chiefs was silence. The president then made some comment designed to elicit our reaction, and when no one else spoke up, I stated, "Mr. President, I am sure you realize that when you make a decision to cut the budget, that is your presidential judgment and that every one of us here is going to accept it. That is what we are going to support, and that is what we are going to work with. But you must realize that it is our responsibility in testifying before the Congress that we must provide, when asked, our own personal professional views. My concern is that if I am questioned whether I believe that the nation will be even stronger in a military sense with a nine-billion-dollar cut, I do not believe I can say that I agree with that. Frankly, I would rather have those additional dollars than not. We are already underfunded for the Navy's minimum operational commitments. But that is a decision you have to make, and you have made it. We will support your budget. But you should realize that we will be under great pressure from the Congress when we are asked to support the statement that a nine-billion-dollar cut will make our military stronger."

The president was clearly upset. I don't think he understood the chiefs' responsibility to the Congress, and that we were hauled over the coals each year on every aspect of the budget that affects our service. I was taken aback by the president's rebuke. I had hoped there would be an opportunity for discussion. However, one of the other service chiefs jumped in and said, "Now, Mr. President, you must not worry about this. We chiefs will be able to handle it OK. . . . We will find a way to support your statement that the nine-billion-dollar cut will make us stronger."

I considered trying to make the point that a cut in defense of nine billion dollars could make the nation stronger by reducing the national debt and improving the economy. That probably was a true statement, and the chiefs could have supported a presidential statement like that because it was above our pay grade. But I didn't, and the president dropped the subject. I'm sure he did not want any more dissents such as mine from the other chiefs.

The upshot of this was that we did take a nine-billion-dollar cut and among other things, the readiness of the Navy distinctly suffered. Our share of the cut was about three and a half billion, and that meant a reduction in training, in flying hours, in ship steaming days, in practice ammunition fired, in technical training school quotas, and in the essential spare parts to keep our aircraft and ships operating, just to cite a few examples. . . .

There is a very important point to be learned from this incident, which caused considerably more damage than was immediately evident—to the president's credibility, to the reputation of the JCS, and [to] the readiness of the military. The members of the Joint Chiefs of Staff as a body had failed to carry out their important single function—to act as the principal military advisers to the commander in chief. We were simply being yes men.

The chiefs did not question the president's statement that "a nine billion dollar cut will make our military stronger." The chiefs did not pursue the president's rationale for this statement or question his justification. The patent illogic of the statement should have elicited a request for further explanation. Did the president really believe this assertion, or was it a political ploy to shift the burden of a budget cut to the military, which would evoke less public sympathy? If President Carter really believed that there was . . . nine billion dollars of waste and excess in his . . . defense budget, the chiefs had an obligation to point out that this was the lowest level of defense spending since the post–World War II drawdown before the Vietnam War. Yet the military's responsibilities had not correspondingly decreased. We still faced a threatening USSR and unrest throughout the Third World.

I have characterized the Joint Chiefs as being yes men in what I consider to be a misguided effort to please their commander in chief. Yet, I must point out that we were all aware that disagreeing with the president could bring its own difficulties. From that day on, I never enjoyed a cordial relationship with President Carter and my access to him became limited. A service chief must accept the fact that such may be the price to pay for not being a yes man, but there is no honorable alternative.

The reduced defense budgets during the Carter years did substantially reduce the capability of the U.S. Armed Forces. The chief of staff of the Army [Gen. Charles C. Meyer] in his annual posture statement referred to his "hollow divisions." As CNO, I testified before Congress in response to questioning that we were no longer a two-ocean navy. In the event of a general war with the Soviet Union, the U.S. could not control the Pacific. At best we would be able to keep open some military lines of communication with Japan. The secretary of defense subsequently ordered the transfer of some naval units from the Atlantic to the Pacific to assuage the concerns of our Japanese allies. This simply weakened our posture in NATO, but President Carter had left office before this could become an issue.[68]

Admiral Holloway described a third confrontation, this time with Secretary of Defense Harold Brown:

In February 1977 I was in my third year as chief of naval operations, working for my third president and third secretary of defense. The president was Jimmy Carter, and the secretary of defense was Harold Brown, who previously had been director of defense and research engineering and later secretary of the air force. President Carter, who considered himself an expert in naval matters, in spite of his very limited duty in the Navy in training submarines, was not favorably disposed toward aircraft carriers. In getting ready for the FY 1979 budget, I was scheduled to testify before the Military Subcommittee of the Appropriations Committee of the Senate, a small but very powerful committee on the Hill. The session was scheduled for 10:00 A.M., and Secretary of the Navy Graham Claytor and Secretary of Defense Brown decided to accompany me to this hearing. I'm not sure if the three of us had been invited as a group or it was their decision to appear with me to make sure I said the right thing.

I was told by the secretary of defense's office that the subject of an aircraft carrier probably would come up and that Dr. Brown wanted to reaffirm to me that the president's position was that there were no plans for the immediate construction of a new aircraft carrier, certainly not in the 1979 budget, and that the program in the future would be for a small, nonnuclear carrier, years later at some unspecified time. . . . If I were asked a question on aircraft carriers, that was to be the guidance for my response.

On the day of the hearing, Secretary Claytor, with whom I had a pleasant and straightforward relationship, asked me to ride over to the Senate with him.

I knew it would be an opportunity for us to talk, and I was not keen on letting myself in for any additional instructions. True gentleman that he was, Graham Claytor on the trip over never brought up the subject of the testimony to be given at the hearings. We did talk about the state of the Navy in general, but there was no pressure on me from him to provide any set answers for the committee.

In the course of the hearings, for which there had been only an innocuous statement prepared for submission for the record, one of the senior senators said, "Admiral, I do not see an aircraft carrier in this budget, aren't you concerned about this?" My response was that the budget I submitted to the secretary of the navy included a nuclear-powered aircraft carrier, but it had been taken out during the budget review. The senator then said, "Well, if you had your way, would you like to see a carrier in the president's budget?" My answer was, "Yes, Sir." Then the senator turned to the secretary of defense and said, "What are your feelings about including a carrier in this FY '79 budget?" Secretary Brown responded: "We don't share Admiral Holloway's view; you must understand he is only the chief of naval operations and we have to look at the bigger picture. It is our position, we don't need another carrier now, but that we are not ruling out a carrier in the future. The senator then said, "What kind of a carrier would that be?" Harold Brown responded: "We think it should be a much smaller carrier without nuclear power and probably designed for VSTOL aircraft only." Then the senator said, "Admiral Holloway, how do you feel about Secretary Brown's position? Now I want the truth." And I said, "Senator I can only repeat what I have consistently stated in . . . appearances before this committee for the past three years: I would prefer without question a new nuclear-powered carrier in this budget rather than a smaller, nonnuclear carrier sometime in the indeterminate future." I immediately realized that Harold Brown was upset because he felt that I had not followed his guidance.

When the hearing adjourned, Secretary Brown asked me to ride back to the Pentagon with him. Although Harold Brown was a very positive and somewhat didactic person, he was also a gentleman and did not become unpleasant in the car. He merely said, "Jim, you did not support the president's budget as we had intended you to do." I said, "Mr. Secretary, there is a requirement for a chief of service when testifying before the Congress, that he is not just privileged but that he is obligated to provide his own personal professional view when so requested by the Congress." Harold Brown said, "I have never heard of that before, I will have to check with the general counsel."

Secretary Brown never got back to me on the issue of the obligation of the uniformed head of service to express his own personal professional views before the Congress. I did, however, have the Navy's judge advocate general call the general counsel's office to reaffirm that this was the rule. The response was that I had been correct.

President Carter's position on carriers held firm. He canceled the carrier in the FY 1978 budget he inherited from President Ford, and would not include any kind of carrier in FY 1979. But the Congress on its own initiative added a nuclear carrier in the 1979 budget, and Carter vetoed the entire defense budget to get rid of the carrier. The next year, the Congress put a large nuclear-powered carrier in the 1980 budget, and Carter again vetoed it. But this time, Congress passed the appropriations and authorization bills overriding Carter's veto in order to include that nuclear-powered carrier. That ship became the *Theodore Roosevelt,* which in 2002 established an all-time record off Afghanistan for 241 consecutive operating days without a day in port. We got that nuclear carrier because of the uniformed Navy stepping up and legally and properly not saying yes to the president's naval program.

In saying no to the president and risking his personal disfavor, the CNO made a convincing argument to Congress of the depth of the Navy's conviction that the carrier was needed and the degree of its determination to make that point. "Also a matter of personal integrity was at stake," Holloway continued. "If after ten years of stating in my professional opinion that a large-deck nuclear carrier was the only acceptable carrier, what would the senators have thought of me as a professional officer if I suddenly said that a small, nonnuclear carrier was really better?[69]

I also had the opportunity to discuss the concept of yes men with Adm. William J. Crowe Jr. (chairman of the Joint Chiefs of Staff 1979–83), who pointed out that being a "no man" sometimes requires caution. When I inquired about the value of candid input, he responded:

I'm human. Sometimes a "no man" really upsets me. You have something you want to do and here comes some wise son of a bitch and tells you that's a dumb idea. That gets under your skin. But those are the kind of guys who really matter. But it is so hard to fill out a good fitness report on an abrasive guy.

But I did run into several people who were not yes men who just cut their own throats. They got so enamored with being disagreers that they didn't give a great deal of thought to how they disagreed. There are ways to let people know you are not aboard and that you think you have a better idea without just totally pushing them off a cliff. That's an art.

The secretary of defense will depend on your advice, and if he's smart will depend a lot on your advice; he'll always seek it. But if you go in there and tell him he's wrong every time he asks a question, you lose your credibility. He doesn't have to seek your advice; then pretty soon he's going to say I don't know why I want to talk to Crowe about this, he's a disagreeable son of a bitch. The secretary of defense can cut the chairman right out of the problem. When dealing with the secretary, you . . . agree with him on most things that don't matter one way or another and when you have something that matters, you've got to step up. That doesn't come naturally. You have to work at that. You have to work at getting your guts up to speak up. . . .

Admiral Haywood had a vice commander by the name of Bob Long. I'm great admirer of Bob Long. I did not know him before my assignment to the Office of the Chief of Naval Operations. . . . He had been there about a week and had called me up and started telling me something about my business and I really stood up to him. His executive assistant came down, a friend of mine, and said Bob Long doesn't like that—nobody talks to him that way. I said to myself, "Well, that's the end of that." I thought I was finished. It didn't turn out to be the end at all.[70]

Adm. Robert L. J. Long had no reservations about standing up to the strong and forceful personality of Adm. Hyman G. Rickover. He told me about an incident that took place when he was commander of a nuclear submarine and Rickover came aboard for an inspection. There was a disagreement over the lighting.

Rickover wanted white lights rather than red lights on because people could see better. There's no question, you can see better. He wanted to get the submarine under way before sunrise, and he wanted the ship rigged for white. I said, "No. If you want that ship to get under way before sunrise, it will be rigged for red. If you want it rigged for white, I'll get it under way after sunrise," to which Rickover said, "Are you telling me how to conduct sea trials?"

I said, "No, but I'm telling you how I'm going to operate this submarine."

"Well, goddamn it, I'll take it to the CNO."

I said, "You damn well take it to the CNO. Go right ahead." So, I mean, that was the kind of dialogue that we would have. It was the typical Rickover. Of course, he never did anything about it. It was a bluff. . . . I didn't have that sort of baloney with his people. They were very fine. . . . But you had to deal with Rickover, though, and a lot of people never learned how, which was too bad.[71]

Adm. Stansfield Turner established that he was no yes man while he was still a lieutenant.

One of my earliest ethical decisions in the Navy was when I was on a destroyer as a very junior officer. I had just completed my studies at Oxford University [he was a Rhodes scholar]. So, at this stage in my career, I had very few what we call fitness reports, efficiency reports. I had one year at sea, two and half years at Oxford. I mean, nobody could touch me as a naval officer. I was coming up for my first fitness report on this ship. It seemed important to me to get a good fitness report, because the Navy was skeptical of the whole Oxford program. If I came back and fell flat on my face as the first Rhodes scholar that came out after World War II, the Academy might close the opportunity again.

My skipper committed some bad errors and was hauled up before a court of inquiry like the *Greenville* skipper was for hitting the Japanese fishing boat. I was called to testify, and in the course of my testimony the members of the court didn't ask me anything about his most egregious action. I just sat there and I had to make up my mind as to whether or not I volunteer this, because this was going to determine what would happen to the captain. It had already been decided he was not going to stay on our ship. The issue was would he be given another command.

The captain had already showed me my fitness report, and it was outstanding. I got along well with the captain. I liked the captain, but just before the board of inquiry, the executive officer told me, "You ought to know that the captain kept your fitness report. He didn't give it to me to mail in." All the officers realized this was obviously a threat. The question in my mind was, do I raise this egregious action of the captain before this court because it's very relevant to his fitness to command? I don't know that I thought this through, but I blurted it out. Because of this, the captain tore up my fitness report and . . . changed it from the outstanding rating and put one in that was just high enough that I wasn't required to comment on it. If it was really unsatisfactory, I could challenge it. I was really scared because I'd only had . . . probably two other fitness reports up to that point in my career. . . . I said to myself, I've had it because this one bad report out of half a dozen, there is going to be enough to say he won't be in the top 5 percent. Fortunately, that didn't happen. I weathered it.

The egregious error by the captain was he had come back to the ship drunk at 2:00 A.M. in the morning after having spent the evening on the French Riviera. A sailor who didn't like him had put a fire hose in his cabin and turned it on before he came back. The cabin flooded. It was a malicious act. Upon his return, the captain went down to the quarter deck and pulled a pistol out of the petty officer's hand and said you go find the son of a bitch who did this, pointing the pistol at this petty officer. He then sounded the general alarm and got all of us up at two in the morning. We thought we were in some kind of an emergency. This was seven days after the Korean War had started. We were in the Mediterranean, not in a war zone, but nonetheless, it was unsettling. I was up at my gun station getting ready to load bullets. Then he called us all together on the fantail and berated us in a terrible way. None of us knew what he was talking about. What the captain did was unconscionable, and fortunately it ended his career.[72]

I asked Admiral Turner what advice he would give to an ensign just beginning his or her career. Like Admiral Crowe, he cautioned that a young officer has to be careful when challenging a senior officer.

It is really important to develop your leadership skills by looking out for and being interested in your people. One piece of advice for leadership that I've always given people that I would give to a young officer is, always look at your present job as much as you can through the eyes of your immediate superior. The people who only can look at it from their own perspective will top out pretty early. But, if you can, understand why your superior is differing with you on why and how you're doing your job. You've got a responsibility to your people, so if your boss may be asking you to do something that's bad for your people, you may fight that, but fight it after understanding why he's doing that. Even if you decide still to fight it, you may not understand that there really may be bigger reasons for doing it his way. Then what you have to do is try it in a way that will accomplish his objective, not to undermine it, but at the same time protect your people, if that's an issue.[73]

Adm. Frank B. Kelso II (CNO 1990–94) offered the following remarks regarding yes men:

I've always felt the most disloyal subordinates are the ones who won't tell you what's the truth, but what they think you want to hear. That can create an atmosphere where nobody tells them anything, and that results in the worst of all leaders. I tried to make it clear to people who worked for me that I could take bad news. I needed to know the bad news if we're going to be able to carry on well. Keeping bad news from me was not a very good tactic. Then they could not use my experience, nor could I help them if they needed help. I tried to make myself available to them so they could talk to me because, most unfortunately, when you're starting out, most young officers and young enlisted people can be a little bit intimidated. I don't want to say seriously afraid, but they're a little bit afraid because of their inexperience, and have a little period of anxiety. The only way that you can set their anxiety aside is for a senior to be available to them when they need him. . . . They learn from their experiences, but because most of us have made the same mistakes in our careers we are able to point out to them they are not the first ones that had this problem and there's a methodology of approaching it. You may want this to happen, but unless you have a personality that will allow people to see you as one who wants to listen, it will not work.

You had asked earlier if leaders are born or made. Actually I think it takes a certain set of traits to be willing to accept that and to be willing to accept [subordinates'] mistakes without faulting them for it all the time. The worst thing you can do, I think, is to put young officers in an embarrassing position in front of their enlisted people. To help the officer so he can be right more often than wrong is one of the major functions of a ship captain or executive officer or department head; to help the young ones coming along to understand that this is the way it's done and you want them to do it right. You want a young officer to understand that if he or she doesn't know how to do it, stop and ask. . . . To me, that's the only atmosphere to encourage.

. . . Creating fear sometimes makes people do things right as well, but that was never my approach. I couldn't do that. I had one captain who . . . had an incredible knack for making people feel good. He just had a knack of being able to joke but be effective. It's very rare for an officer to have the ability to do that and not be misunderstood, but he could do that. . . . He served as a wonderful example for everybody around there. I don't know anybody that ever served with him that didn't fundamentally just love him. He was one of those people, but I would say the majority of the people that I had to work for were extremely competent and made an effort to try to make people understand that they wanted to work with them and help them.[74]

I asked Adm. Carlisle A. H. Trost (CNO 1986–90) how he felt about having yes men on his staff. He told me:

The CNO or any other senior officer doesn't need people who do what they think you want them to do. They want people who do what they know to be right, and will have the guts to stand up to you if you are wrong, and in private, hopefully. I brought people into my office who were known entities who knew my thought process, and who would disagree with me when appropriate, people who were professionally competent, competitively minded, and straightforward, who could come in and talk to me. I am not that hard to talk with, and I don't have an ego that needs stroking, and so they could come and talk with me if they disagreed with something.[75]

Adm. James D. Watkins (CNO 1982–86) commented on Admiral Moorer in his role as CNO and chairman of the Joint Chiefs of Staff: "They loved him on Capitol Hill because he was a straight-shooter, straight-talker. You talk about someone who can say no; he is one of them. He was terrific. And you know, all of us have different leadership characteristics. I had the reputation at the Department of Energy, they called me "Radio-Free Watkins." But I don't mind taking on issues. I understand politics, but I don't like it. I don't like what some people have to do. I would never prostitute myself."

Admiral Watkins was even willing to take on the Catholic Church in defense of the Navy.

One of the first things I got into when I was CNO involved the impact on the Navy of the first edition of the draft paper by the Conference of Catholic Bishops on the subject of nuclear war. I am a Roman Catholic. In the first draft, it was stated that you could not be a practicing Roman Catholic if you were involved in a military that had nuclear weapons. Well, we had people who started to leave, officers and enlisted men, on the basis of what their bishops had said in this first draft. I got into it with . . . Bishop O'Connor, who had been the former chief of chaplains for the Navy. I had taken it on publicly right away because I wanted the Navy and others to know that there was no final edition of that paper until "the fat lady sang," and that wasn't going to come for some time. The second and subsequent drafts that finally came out were balanced and reflected many more of our views that made their paper an acceptable one. As a matter of fact, there were more clarifying footnotes than narrative in the bishop's final paper on nuclear warfare.[76]

Like Admiral Long, Adm. Charles R. Larson had experience as a junior officer with strong-willed Admiral Rickover. Even though Rickover ruled with an iron hand, Larson was not a yes man. "There are two incidents that come to mind immediately," Admiral Larson told me.

> When I was commanding officer of a submarine, we had an incident back in the electrical plant where my engineer violated one of the safety procedures, and they didn't do a proper job of tagging off some of the electrical systems. One of my electricians was almost electrocuted, and so badly burned he had to go to the hospital. He ultimately fully recovered. Admiral Rickover called me up right after that incident and said, "I want you to fire your engineer." I said, "No, sir, I'm not going to do that. He's a very fine engineer. He's a young officer, and still learning. It's early in his tour. I think this was a one-time lapse. I don't think it's indicative of his overall performance or his conscientious nature. And he's going to be fine, and we're going to move forward." So Rickover said, "All right, goddammit. It's your responsibility," and hung up.
>
> On another occasion, I was commissioning a submarine. It was having some engineering problems. It was about the time I was giving them operation readiness instructions and getting them ready for their first commission. Rickover called me up and said, "That ship's not doing well in engineering and not coming along as nice as I expected. Fire that skipper." I said, "No, sir, I'm not going to do that. I've got confidence in that skipper. He is coming along just fine." And again he said, "OK, goddammit, you're going to be responsible." I said, "Yes, sir," and hung up on him. And of course, the ship went on to do wonderful things, and the skipper got two distinguished service medals.[77]

I asked Adm. Jay L. Johnson (CNO 1996–2000) what he had done as CNO to encourage input from his staff. "I tried not to shoot messengers," he answered.

> I probably wasn't 100 percent successful there, but I think I was pretty successful. I always felt that shooting messengers was a waste of ammo! I like what Gen. Colin Powell . . . says. . . . "Unlike wine, bad news does not get better with age." I try to remember that when somebody's telling me something I may not like to hear. I think it's very useful, particularly when you're making big decisions, to get both the inputs you want and the inputs you need. They probably aren't the same. I encourage that. I was not very kind to people who discourage that in their own circles by shooting messengers. Only when you receive the full spectrum of input can you really get to the basis of what I call an informed decision.[78]

Adm. Henry G. Chiles (commander in chief, U.S. Strategic Command, 1994–96) began his Navy career in a nuclear submarine. In his early career he had extensive experience with Admiral Rickover, who, as noted, had a reputation for irascibility. I asked Admiral Chiles, "Did Admiral Rickover tolerate people who would stand up to him?" He replied:

> I think he did. I mean, there were times when you had to raise your voice to be heard. He was a man who showed his emotions. When he was angry, he showed it, but he got over it fairly quickly, in fifteen minutes he'd get over it. I never felt any hesitation about telling him what I thought. There was no intimidation or fear on my part. I believe very strongly that he appreciated it when you challenged him. He appreciated the fact that you would stand up for what you believed to be right and not only say, "I believe this is right," but follow that up with crisp arguments, concrete, well-reasoned scenarios, and situations that would help him to understand where you were coming from. So you needed to be able to not only tell him what you thought, you needed to be able to reason it through in crisp terms.[79]

Admiral Rickover was succeeded as head of the nuclear program by Adm. Kinnaird R. McKee, who also stressed the importance of being a "no man," even at a price to one's career. Specifically, he related an incident that took place when he was a young lieutenant assigned to the submarine *Sea Cat*:

> Shortly after I reported aboard, we had an ORI [Operations Readiness Inspection] re-exam and passed. Soon after that a new skipper came aboard. I don't know whether the CO who had the boat when I got the unsatisfactory left because of the ORI failure or because he was at the end of his tour. The new CO was an unusual man. He had been sent to *Sea Cat* to square her away. He did not do that. I found myself at odds with him several times. (By that time I was the engineer.) We crushed a fuel tank because somebody made a mistake on rig-for-dive. He didn't want to report it. His comment was, "Well, I think we just went through a layer."
>
> Another time, we took the ship to sea to ride out a hurricane that was approaching Key West. I had the deck. I got word that the captain wanted us to steer a course that would take us into the dangerous semicircle. I didn't change course. He came to the bridge and ordered me to change course. We discussed the situation in increasingly heated terms. I told him that his ordered course

would take us into the dangerous semicircle. We had a real problem up there. He insisted, so I finally said, "Either relieve me or get off the bridge." The captain got off the bridge.

After that I decided that I needed to leave the *Sea Cat* just as soon as I could. I knew the XO of *Marlin* (SST 2) was about to leave, so I asked for his job. Orders came for me to go to *Marlin,* but the CO of *Sea Cat* told the detailers he would not let me leave unless they could provide two officers to relieve me. They didn't do that. They left my orders in force, and I . . . went on to *Marlin.* I lost track of *Sea Cat* after that. I really didn't think much more about that tour until the end of my *Marlin* tour, when I received orders to the X-1 as OinC [i.e., CO]. I stopped in Washington en route to X-1 to read my fitness reports for the first time, and found that the CO of *Sea Cat* had given me a virtually unsatisfactory fitness report. My marks were down the right-hand side of the report, but one notch over, because in those days if they weren't all the way to the right the reporting senior didn't have to inform the officer concerned. I did not have an opportunity to rebut the report. After reading all that, I went back to the detailer and asked, "What do I do with this?" The detailer told me to forget about it. "Everybody knows that guy." Not long after that, that CO committed suicide. I came out okay, but it could have been a really bad situation.[80]

One of the best illustrations of an effective "no man" was provided to me by Admiral Holloway.

The foundations of this metamorphosis in the U.S. Navy can be attributed to a small number of naval aviators who had the vision, wisdom, aggressiveness, and leadership to make it happen. Jimmy Flatley was one of the architects of the sweeping changes. Along with a handful of others—Jimmy Thach and Butch O'Hare among the most prominent—Flatley fought the war on several fronts. Leading his fighter squadron in successful combat against the acknowledged superiority of the Japanese Zero, he established his credentials for his passionate but articulate battles with the bureaucrats in the shore establishment and the entrenched staff officers. In most cases their professional stubbornness in resisting change was due to a lack of combat experience, which Jimmy Flatley had in vast amounts. Yet Flatley differed from many others of his combat-experienced contemporaries. He spoke out, but when he did, he was temperate, practical, and reasonable. Flatley was smart enough to realize when something was wrong, astute enough to know whether it could be corrected, and wise enough to propose the solution. Then he would muster the boldness to pursue his convictions

with a gritty persistence. Perhaps most important of all, Jimmy Flatley had credibility. He had earned the respect of his policy-making seniors by his brilliant
combat record and the demonstrated validity of the changes he espoused.[81]

Admiral Leahy, President Franklin D. Roosevelt's wartime chief of staff,
observed of a U.S. military tradition: "British colleagues were loyally supporting the views of their defense minister only because it was their duty
and because they were carrying out orders. On our side, we never labored
under any such handicap."

Adm. Ernest King, CNO—and thus the senior U.S. naval officer—
throughout World War II, "despised yes men." The naval leaders who
served beneath him illustrated the value of his view. Adm. Raymond A.
Spruance, for example, challenged King's decision to invade Formosa and
prevailed, and history proved him correct.

When Arleigh Burke was assigned to the Strategic Plans Division he
commented that there was "no room for a yes man" in the group. When
he became CNO, he said, "I looked around to find a man who would disagree with me." When the secretary of defense and secretary of the navy
denied Burke's request for a draft to fill the Navy's ranks, he took it to the
president, and President Eisenhower sided with him.

The decision of the Navy leadership to fight the secretary of defense's
decision to cancel construction of the USS *United States* is a superb example of the character of senior U.S. naval officers. Time has clearly established
the importance of our carriers. But CNO Denfeld was made to "walk the
plank" for refusing to be a yes man. Admiral Anderson suffered the same
fate for standing up to Secretary McNamara. Admiral Radford, who fought
so hard to save the *United States* at the congressional hearing, spoke up candidly: "I do not think you want men in the Defense Department who are
going to agree for agreement's sake." He won confirmation as CNO, and
President Eisenhower told him "to call him directly whenever . . . necessary,
day or night." Ike did not want a yes man as chairman.

Admiral Holloway illustrated his character many times during his
tenure as CNO, standing up to Secretary of State Henry Kissinger on the
SALT II Treaty, to President Carter on the budget cut of nine billion dol-

lars, and to Secretary Brown on the future of the carrier—all terribly important matters for the Navy's readiness.

Admiral Turner showed incredible courage as a young officer in challenging the competency of a captain under whom he served. It was a risk, but that demonstration of character eventually took him to the top.

Rank can give validity to decisions, but too often it stifles contrary opinions from subordinates. Successful leaders and decision makers need the inputs and thoughts of those who work for them, and must create an atmosphere and relationship that allows for free exchange of ideas until such time as a decision is made. Very few leaders are successful when deprived of the opinions of their subordinates. There must be a willingness to challenge cherished beliefs without disparagement and without equivocation. The greatest deterrent to the development of dedicated young leaders is a system that encourages our young officers to be yes men and not to "rock the boat."

CHAPTER 4

Books

The Importance of Reading

Education has for its object the formation of character.

Herbert Spencer

There is no history: there is only biography

Ralph Waldo Emerson

In a personal interview I asked General of the Army Dwight D. Eisenhower, "How does one develop as a decision-maker? Is it a God-given talent or can it be developed, and if so, how does one grow and improve as a decision-maker?" He assured me that decision making can be developed and offered two cornerstones for its development. First, he stressed the importance of being around people making decisions. He certainly had that experience in his career. He worked for General of the Army Douglas MacArthur when he was chief of staff from 1932 to 1935; then served three years under MacArthur as field marshal of the Philippine Army from 1935 to 1938; and worked as Gen. George C. Marshall's plans officer from 1940 to 1942 when Marshall was chief of staff. Second, Eisenhower stressed the importance of reading books, particularly history and biography.[1]

Eisenhower's book *At Ease: Stories I Tell My Friends* includes a chapter entitled "The Key to the Closet" that describes his love for books: "My first reading love was ancient history. At an early age, I developed an interest in the human record and I became particularly fond of Greek and Roman accounts. These subjects were so engrossing that I frequently was guilty of neglecting all others." Because his voracious reading led him to neglect subjects like spelling and geography, as well as his chores, his mother locked the books in a closet. When she was working in the garden or shopping in town, he would find the key and get his books.

Out of that closet and out of those books has come an odd result. Even to this day, there are many unrelated bits of information about Greece and Rome that stick in my memory. Some are dates. I have a sort of fixation that causes me to interrupt a conversation when the speaker is one year off, or a hundred, in dating an event like Arbela; and often I put aside a book, until then interesting enough, when the author is less than scrupulous about chronology.

In any case, the battles of Marathon, Zama, Salamis, and Cannae became as familiar to me as the games (and battles) I enjoyed with my brothers and friends in the school yard. In later years the movies taught children that the bad guy was the one in the black hat. Such people as Hannibal, Caesar, Pericles, Socrates, Themistocles, Miltiades, and Leonidas were my white hats, my heroes. Xerxes, Darius, Alcibiades, Brutus, and Nero wore black ones. White or black, their names and those battles were fresh news, as I could never seem to get it into my head that all these things had happened two thousand years earlier—or that possibly I would be better advised to pay attention to current, rather than ancient, affairs. Among all the figures of antiquity, Hannibal was my favorite.

Since those early years, history of all kinds, and certainly political and military, has always intrigued me mightily. When a historical novel is well written and documented, I am apt to spend the whole evening in its reading. The campaigns of the more modern leaders—Frederick, Napoleon, Gustavus Adolphus, and all of our prominent American soldiers and statesmen—I found absorbing.

When I got around to the Americans, Washington was my hero. I never tired of reading about his exploits at Princeton, at Trenton, and particularly in Valley Forge. I conceived almost a violent hatred of Conway and his cabal and could not imagine anyone so stupid and so unpatriotic as to have wanted to remove Washington from command of the American Army. The qualities that excited my admiration were Washington's stamina and patience in adversity, first, and then his indomitable courage, daring, and capacity for self-sacrifice.[2]

Eisenhower's reference to Washington is interesting, because George Washington was a great reader as well. At the time of his death he had a library of more than nine hundred books, a significant number for that day. Washington very early developed a habit of reading, ordering new books from London by the trunkload. The books he selected made him knowledgeable in military affairs, English history, and agriculture. He even read the popular English novels of the period, such as *Tom Jones*.[3]

It is noteworthy that a recent biography of George Washington by Richard Brookheiser, *Founding Father: Rediscovering George Washington* (1996), has a chapter entitled "Ideas" that discusses at length his education. Brookheiser quoted Thomas Jefferson, who said of Washington, "His time was employed in the action chiefly, reading in agriculture and English history."[4]

Washington was essentially self-educated. His formal education was limited, and we know very little about it. He apparently attended a country day school for the equivalent of grade school, and then had a tutor until he was about fifteen. His family could not afford much more schooling after that. Certainly Washington was not a college graduate, although most of his contemporaries had attended college: Thomas Jefferson at William and Mary; John Adams at Harvard; James Madison and Aaron Burr at the College of New Jersey, now Princeton University (as were nine of the twenty-four delegates to the Constitutional Convention who were college educated); Alexander Hamilton at King's, now Columbia University. But it was Washington who was selected to preside over the convention.

His reading also included the controversial literature of the time, particularly the many pamphlets discussing the issues of the day. Brookheiser commented: "Though Washington's experience as Commander in Chief disposed him in favor of a stronger national government, *reading showed him the way*." During the debate over the Constitution, he read, besides *The Federalist*, the essays of half a dozen other polemicists, pro and con, and cited them in the first draft of his inaugural address. Washington encouraged the idea that newspapers should be free to readers. Visitors to Mount Vernon after his retirement found that he subscribed to ten newspapers.[5]

After George Washington, perhaps the most famous American of the eighteenth century was Benjamin Franklin, who, among other things, served as America's ambassador to France and was one of the framers of the Constitution. While his public service contributions were significant, and included service as a colonel in the Pennsylvania militia, he was also an inventor. Franklin developed the Franklin stove, still in use today, which gave more warmth than an open fireplace; conceived of the lightning rod and was well known in Europe for his research in electrical experiments and theories; and invented bifocal glasses. In Philadelphia, his residence for most of his life, he established the first volunteer fire department and started the first public library, the first hospital, and Philadelphia's first academic academy (now the University of Pennsylvania). His *Poor Richard's Almanac,* which offered suggestions on how to get ahead in life, was a "best seller" and contributed to his substantial fortune.

In her biography on Franklin, entitled *The Most Dangerous Man in America* (1974), Catherine Drinker Bowen noted: "In an era when the fomenting and support of the revolution are claimed by youth as their special attributes, it is significant to recall that two hundred years ago the person feared by the crowned heads of England and many parts of Europe as the most dangerous man in America was Benjamin Franklin—age sixty-eight to eighty."[6]

In view of his extraordinary achievements, most people find it astonishing that Franklin's formal education ended at the age of ten and was limited to one year of formal education and one year with a tutor. Where did his ideas and intellectual depth originate? How did he prepare himself for such significant positions of responsibility? He loved to read. Franklin's autobiography, published after his death, provides considerable insight into the importance he assigned to reading. "I do not remember when I could not read," he wrote. "From my infancy, I was passionately fond of reading, and all the money that came into my hands was ever laid out for books." His father's library was limited to books in polemic divinity, "most of which I read. I have often regretted that, at a time when I had such a thirst for knowledge more proper books had not fallen my way."[7]

As a youth, he entered the printing vocation as an apprentice. "I now had access to better books," he recalled; " . . . often I sat in my chamber reading the greatest part of the night when the book was borrowed in the evening and to be returned in the morning, lest it should be missed or wanted." Young Franklin developed his writing skill by copying the style of other writers, which, he said, "encouraged me to think I might possibly in time come to be a tolerable English writer, of which I was extremely ambitious. My time for these exercises and for reading was at night, after work or before it began in the morning, or on Sundays, when I contrived to be in the printing house alone."[8]

In the spring of 1724 Franklin sailed for England, where he continued his interest in books. "While I lodged in Little Britain," he wrote in his autobiography, "I made acquaintance with one Wilcox, a bookseller, whose shop was at the next door. He had an immense collection of second-hand books. Circulating libraries were not then in use; but we agreed that on certain reasonable terms, which I have now forgotten, I might take, read, and return all of his books. This I esteemed a great advantage, and I made as much use as I could."[9]

On returning to Philadelphia from England, he formed a group of twelve who met once a week for dinner and discussed books assigned for the evening. He persuaded them to "club" their books to a common library convenient to the entire group, so "each had the use and advantage of using the books of all the other members, which was nearly as beneficial as if each owned the whole." When that idea did not work out, he "set foot my first project of a public nature, that for a subscription library," which, he commented, "was the mother of all North American subscription libraries . . . these libraries have improved the general conversation of the Americans, made the common tradesman and farmers as intelligent as most gentlemen from other countries, and perhaps have contributed to some degree to the stand so generally made throughout the colonies in defense of their privileges." Franklin further reflected, "This library afforded me the means of improvement by constant study, for which I set apart an hour or two each day, and thus repaired in some degree the loss of the learned education my father once intended for me. Reading was the

only amusement I allowed myself. I spent no time in tavern games, or frol-
ics of any kind."[10]

Although this book is a study of naval leadership, the reading habits of
some of America's best-known generals offer a great deal of insight into
the development of character, leadership, and success. Among America's
most remarkable soldiers was Lt. Gen. Arthur MacArthur, father of
General of the Army Douglas MacArthur. The senior MacArthur won the
Medal of Honor in the Civil War at age eighteen and by nineteen was the
youngest full colonel in both the Southern and Northern forces. He
achieved the rank of major general in the Spanish-American War
(1898–1900), then, as a lieutenant general, was appointed military governor of the Philippine Islands. When William Howard Taft was sent as the
islands' civilian governor, there was considerable friction between the two.
The very idea of the United States having an overseas territory caused a
controversy that resulted in a Senate investigation, with extensive confrontations between Republicans and Democrats over the matter. Because
of his role as military governor, Arthur MacArthur was a frequent and natural choice to appear as a witness at the hearings. As a witness in 1902, for
example, he showed the breadth of his knowledge by lecturing to the senators on political theory and the principles of democracy. When the senators asked him if the United States should have annexed the Philippines,
he showed great vision by lecturing to them eruditely on the political, economic, and military importance of the islands. He thought they held great
potential as a market for American goods, as a strategic base in the Far East
to increase trade with China, as a base to protect Hawaii, and as a political base to spread democracy. In summary, he informed the senators, the
Philippines were "the stepping stone to a commanding influence—political, commercial, and military supremacy in the East."[11] Arthur
MacArthur's formal education stopped after high school. He was a self-
made man, and his education derived from a lifetime of serious study
through independent reading.

On February 8, 1904, the Japanese Navy attacked the Russian Pacific
fleet at Ports Arthur and Darren in Manchuria, igniting a war between the
two countries. President Theodore Roosevelt, prior to offering his "good

offices" to bring about peace in 1905, sent Lieutenant General MacArthur to Japan and Russia to study the war. MacArthur's observations were invaluable, as his biographer, Kenneth Ray Young, noted: "For thirty years, he had read nearly every book published on East Asia, and his deep interest in China and Japan had been reinforced by experience in the Philippines." Indeed, as early as 1882 he tried to obtain an assignment as the military attaché to Peking.[12]

Arthur MacArthur was accompanied on his trip to Asia by his son, Lt. Douglas MacArthur, who served as his father's aide. Douglas was ordered by his father "to purchase every book he could find on the countries they visited, and in the evenings, they read, talked and analyzed the experiences. The general insisted that Douglas keep meticulous records, and each day his reading list grew. By the end of the trip, the MacArthurs had read dozens of books." Father and son had voracious appetites for books on Greek and Roman history, the history and culture of China, and anything else they could find of value on each country they visited. The trip lasted eight months, and they traveled twenty thousand miles.[13]

Douglas MacArthur wrote in his memoirs that the Asian tour was "without a doubt the most important factor in preparation for my entire life . . . the strength and weakness of the colonial system, how it brought law and order, but failed to develop the masses along the lines of education and political economy."[14] His reading established an important foundation for a man who would eventually have the responsibility for the occupation of Japan and the establishment of democracy there after World War II.

Throughout his military career, Douglas MacArthur sought to emulate his father's brilliant contributions as a soldier, and his father's example was a significant factor in his own development. Immediately after the Civil War, Arthur MacArthur was stationed out West fighting Indians. While he was there, one biographer said, he was "a great reader of other men's books, and sends for them by the trunkful. It is not light fare."[15] What did he read? An efficiency report filed in the adjutant general's office the year after the closing of the frontier noted that MacArthur had pursued investigations in political economy; the colonial and Revolutionary periods in American history; a comparison of the American and English constitutions; an extensive investigation into the civilizations and institutions of China; and the works of Gibbon, Macaulay, Samuel Johnson, Thomas Mathers, David Ricardo, John Stuart Mill, Henry Carey, English economist Walter Bagenot, Thomas Leslie, and William Jevons.

At his father's death, Douglas MacArthur inherited more than four thousand books! A library of that size was a remarkable achievement for a man who spent so much of his career on the western frontier. Douglas MacArthur was equally dedicated to reading. Throughout his life he followed a rigid schedule, devoting his evenings to reading history, literature, and military science; and just as his father had done, he selected difficult books covering a wide range of subjects.

While Douglas MacArthur was stationed in the Philippines in the 1930s, his biographer William Manchester noted, Jean, his wife, "was forever giving him biographies of Confederate generals, among them Douglas S. Freeman's four volume life of Lee, G.F.R. Henderson's two volumes on Stonewall Jackson, and J. A. Wythe's *Nathan Bedford Forrest*. A speed reader," commented Manchester, "MacArthur could get through three books a day."[16]

After the Allied forces were driven from the Philippines by the Japanese in 1942, MacArthur moved to Australia to organize the effort to retake the islands. He moved into a bungalow that included an extensive library and spent his evenings reading: "the shelves were packed with books in several languages. . . . Phrases from this cultural smorgasbord would find their way into the articulate communiqué he dictated . . . each morning." He could "quote Shakespeare, the Bible, Napoleon, Mark Twain, and Lincoln in expounding a single idea," sometimes drawing on "a statement by Plato, or sometimes on a passage from Scripture."[17]

One staff officer who served under him described MacArthur's tour as chief of staff in Washington, D.C.: "He worked long hours at his office and seemed content to spend most of his evenings at his quarters at Fort Myer across the Potomac. Always a prodigious reader and student of history, he would relax with a book in his library, or spend the evening chatting with old friends on his staff who would drop in and stay for hours discussing the problems of the War Department and the national and international situations in general."[18]

As I noted above, Gen. Dwight D. Eisenhower had a lifelong love for books and reading. In a personal interview he discussed the importance of reading in his development as a professional soldier.

> I was not a particularly good student at West Point. They had a course at West Point called Military History that was different from what it is now. One of the things we studied was the Battle of Gettysburg. The first thing we were required to do was memorize the name of every general officer or acting general officer. You had to know what he was commanding. Then they gave you the situation or the position of each of the commands at such and such an hour on such and such a day. I always hated memorizing, although I have a pretty good memory, but this wasn't the kind of thing that interested me; so I didn't pay any attention to my history and I almost got found [flunked]. I despised it the way it was taught.[19]

In 1913, when Eisenhower was a sophomore, he was injured playing football and decided several times to resign, but his classmates always convinced him to stay. Because of his injury, however, there was some question as to whether he would be commissioned, because some of those in authority felt he might be a burden on the government. After considerable discussion, he was commissioned. "Then," General Eisenhower told me,

> I made up my mind that if I was going to have a military career, I was going to have a good one. I don't mean to say I stopped having fun. I guess I was just as frolicking as anyone, in my way. But when I put myself down to study I wasn't doing anything else. I was searching new plans, new ideas. I was very impatient about the idea of trench warfare and why we didn't break away from it. I read everything I could on trench warfare. I didn't get into that war at all; so I just accepted the training end of it because they said I had such special ability as a trainer. This was cold comfort to a young officer. . . .
>
> There was no question that Army Major General Fox Conner got me started in better methods of preparing myself. . . . He was the one that gave me a systematic plan of study. He had just been in the war as the operations officer of the American Expeditionary Force [AEF]. He was a smart, patient man, and he decided that I ought to amount to something, so he was going to see if I would.[20]

Fox Conner, with whom Eisenhower served in Panama, was an avid reader of military history. He gave then-Major Eisenhower books on the subject and then asked him questions about them. He gave him a Civil War book, for example, and asked, "How were the soldiers armed? When did the revolving pistol come in? When did the breech-loading rifle come in? What was the general character of the armaments in the South and North? How did the South get them?" He set aside for Eisenhower a room in his quarters in Panama that served as a study and placed maps on the wall for the study of world strategy, and he had Eisenhower teach classes to the post officers. Ike and Conner were constant companions on exploration expeditions in the jungles of Panama. At night, sitting by the campfire, Fox Conner would quiz Ike on the books he had assigned.[21]

It was a unique experience for a young man to receive the tutelage of one of the most brilliant, well-educated, and sage officers in the Army at that time. Of all the training Eisenhower received, perhaps the most valuable was the result of Conner's understanding that the key to the next world war, which he considered the Treaty of Versailles had made inevitable, would be allied command. Twenty years before the event, Eisenhower began the study of allied unity; and it served him well as the supreme commander in World War II.

Eisenhower's love of books and reading continued throughout his career. When Ike returned to Washington for assignment as plans officer for General Marshall, he and Mamie, his wife, established residence in the Wardman Park Hotel. One of his biographers, his grandson David Eisenhower, provided a description reflecting Ike's continuing love of books:

> Mamie had set up house in an annex of the Wardman and furnished it with her husband's favorite keepsakes: the silver tea service Eisenhower had painstakingly saved for, buying a piece a year since their fourth anniversary, in 1920; two blue Chinese rugs purchased while they were in the Philippines; the family piano; and his favorite overstuffed chair in the living room. She displayed their bound set of Harvard classics, purchased in the early 1930s, in a bookcase next to several framed French prints acquired when they had lived in Paris on the Rue d'Auteil twelve years earlier.[22]

Probably no single person had more crucial decisions to make in World War II than General of the Army George C. Marshall in his capacity as army chief of staff from 1939 through 1945. Marshall, like the MacArthurs and Eisenhower, also considered reading important to his professional life and a factor in his sound decision making. "In [my] home life, I realize today," Marshall reminisced, "I got a great deal of benefit from reading. My father read aloud, very well, and liked to do it, strange to say. . . . He read a great many things. I can recall some of them. I remember the Saracinesca series—*Sant Ilano* and *Don Orsino* by . . . F. Marion Crawford. . . . I remember the Fenimore Cooper stories that he read to us, and particularly the famous story by Sir Arthur Conan Doyle [*The Refugees* (1893)]."[23]

In an interview Marshall described some of the books he read as a boy; it was not always serious reading: "In those days there were large, thin paper novels—the Nick Carter series, the Frank Merriwell series, the Old South series. We were forbidden from reading all but the Frank Merriwell series and those were highly recommended. . . . In order to read the Nick Carter series, which was very much like Jesse James at his best, we would retire to the spring house." His love for Nick Carter novels got Marshall into trouble during that period. Marshall was employed in Saint Peter's Episcopal Church as an organ pumper.

> The place for the pumper was in a very narrow region in the rear of the organ and the pump was just a handle like the tiller of a boat. The pumping was not difficult, except you had to be there. But there was a long period of waiting during the sermon. One of those mornings, I was occupying this period of waiting with a five-cent novel of that day about Nick Carter. Just in the most exciting portion . . . my attention was called to the organ by the thump, thump which the organist, Miss Fanny Howe, could make from the keyboard. And I realized that she had started to play at the end of the sermon and no music was coming out . . . she was not only displeased but rather outraged . . . she relieved me from my duty with the organ.[24]

In high school, Marshall was an average student in math, spelling, and grammar, but "if it was history, that was all right. I could star in history. Benjamin Franklin and Robert E. Lee were my personal heroes." As a cadet at the Virginia Military Institute (VMI), Marshall read

> pretty much anything I could get my hands on, particularly the last year and a half. I didn't discover until about then that my roommate Nicholson—he and his brothers were orphans and they owned the *Times-Picayune* . . . of New Orleans—

he made a casual remark one day that they got all these books to review and they sold them for five cents apiece. So we immediately got him to contact a friend of his on the paper and he, the friend, would send us a barrel of books at a time. You will find on the register there [at VMI] the record of books contributed to the library by Nicholson. That's the way it came about. I was a very rapid reader and Peyton was a rapid reader and Nicholson was a very slow reader. Peyton and I just read through the barrel.

Finally, a very thin, stern, sort of Creole-like character, a lawyer, a Mr. Rapier, arrived at VMI and was Nicholson's guardian. It was a few days . . . before we discovered, Peyton and I, that we were being investigated, because Nicholson was not standing well and they thought maybe we were a poor influence. But it developed that Peyton was third in the class and I was about twelve or fifteen and Nicholson was next to last. So Mr. Rapier gave up the idea that we were a bad influence. . . . I read a little in the library. I remember coming across Rudyard Kipling for the first time, and I read every book they had by Kipling. I don't remember the others that I read there, though I think I did read some historical accounts of life in Virginia in the early days.[25]

General of the Army Omar N. Bradley was also an avid reader. In his autobiography he described his father, John Smith Bradley, a teacher in a one-room schoolhouse in Missouri, as "a curious blend of frontiersman, sportsman, farmer and intellectual." He was a superb hunter and shot, and a pioneer in baseball. He carved his own bats, organized teams, and was a star. In the summer, when school was out, he worked for farmers as a hired hand or sharecropper. While doing all these things, John Bradley "was an omnivorous reader and lover of books. Everywhere he taught, he encouraged his students to read and created small libraries for them."[26]

His father passed his love of reading to General Bradley, who recalled:

I idolized him. He succeeded very quickly in inculcating in me a love of books. After I could read fairly well, I devoured books such as Sir Walter Scott's *Ivanhoe*, Kipling's *Jungle Books,* and the like. I was particularly fascinated by history—tales of the French and Indian Wars, the Revolutionary and Civil Wars. I would act out many of the battles on the living room rug, using dominoes to build forts and empty .22 cartridges to represent lines of soldiers. I made "heavy artillery" from hollow elderberry reeds or brass tubing and would bombard the domino forts with navy beans. In any mock wars, the Americans always won.[27]

Bradley's interest in reading continued in his first assignment after graduating from West Point. On September 12, 1915, he reported to Fort George Wright in Spokane, Washington, where he shared duplex quarters with Edwin Forrest Harding, Class of 1909. Harding was still a second lieutenant after six years of service, although that was not unusual in those days. "Forrest Harding was a serious student of history, a fine writer and a compulsive teacher," Bradley recalled.

> Soon after we arrived, Forrest organized an unofficial weekly gathering in his home to which he invited about six lieutenants on the post. For several hours under his guidance we would discuss small unit tactics, squads and platoon in attack on a variety of terrain and so on. These meetings were immensely stimulating and educational, often turning into broader discussions of military history. No single person in my early Army career had a more salutary influence on me than Forrest Harding. He instilled in me a genuine desire to thoroughly learn my profession.[28]

Bradley did not see combat in World War I, and he thought it likely that he was "professionally ruined" because of it. Stationed at Fort Grant in 1918 at the end of World War I, he saw his battalion shrink as many of its members were discharged. He had time on his hands in the months following the armistice on November 11, 1918, and he spent a "bitterly cold, inactive winter, reading a great deal." He commented on his tour of duty between 1920 and 1924: "In those years, I began to seriously read and study military history and biography, learning a great deal from the mistakes of my predecessors. I took a particularly keen interest in one Civil War general, William T. Sherman, who despite his infamous reputation in the South, was probably the ablest general the Union produced."[29]

In a personal interview General Bradley emphasized the importance of reading and studying in developing the sixth sense necessary for high-level decision making. "You first study the theoretical handling of troops," he said; "you study the principles of war, principles of tactics, and how certain leaders applied them. You are never going to meet with that exact situation, but when you know all these principles and how they were applied in the past, then when a situation faces you, you apply those principles to your present situation and hope you come up with a good solution. I think the study of military history, and what the great leaders did, is very, very important for any young officer in developing this quality."[30]

Gen. Matthew B. Ridgway succeeded Gen. Walter H. Walker as commander of the Eighth Army in Korea in late 1950 after Walker was killed in an accident. Ridgway performed brilliantly in the role, turning a series of defeats into victory and driving the North Koreans back to the Yalu River. Like the other generals we have been discussing, he was a serious reader. As a cadet at West Point, he later recalled:

> I did a prodigious amount of reading . . . which probably detracted from my class standing, but paid off much greater dividends in the long run. I read a tremendous amount from my yearling year on—almost all on biography and military history. Books such as Hamilton's *A Scrapbook of an Officer.* He was the military attaché of Great Britain with the Japanese in Manchuria, and incidentally, of course, I couldn't possibly foresee this, but forty years later as commander of Korea some of these things he had written about then came back vividly. Probably indirectly, and without my being aware of it, they were helpful. For instance, his description of the stoicism and the endurance, physical endurance and acceptance of deprivation of the Japanese soldier on the march there in the bitter winter weather. I could look back on that winter in trying to tell our people that these hardships in Korea that you are enduring are no more than other troops of other nations have endured [in] years past, and you can do it, too.[31]

The role of consideration in successful leadership is discussed in chapter 6, but one of Ridgway's comments on the value of reading is relevant to the development of that quality.

> I also mentioned the great amount of reading I did outside of my curriculum at West Point when I was a cadet. There are a series of books written by German professional military officers . . . toward the end of the eighteenth century, one on *Letters on Artillery, Letters on Infantry, Letters on Cavalry.* . . . *Letters on Infantry* is still fixed strongly in my mind with the principle. Hohenlohe, I think, was the last name of the author. But anyway, . . . this man came of a noble German family and yet his regard for his men [would be a] credit to any company commander of that day. He advised that the unit commander should learn the background of the recruit's family (well-to-do, shoemaker, butcher, whatever he

might be) . . . should learn the man's problems at home if he had any. Just wonderful insights. Now this is just absolutely contrary to what you would have thought to be the norm of the higher-ranking Prussian-type officer. . . . Books like that made a tremendous impression on me and had a very strong influence in my own career from the time that I reported for duty in the 3rd Infantry. It was a great book.[32]

General Ridgway went on to serve as supreme allied commander in the Far East, 1951–52; as supreme allied commander in Europe, 1952–53; and as chief of staff of the U.S. Army, 1953–55.

Let us now turn to our real focus in this chapter—U.S. naval leaders and their views on the importance of reading for the development of leadership qualities. Chester W. Nimitz, one of America's great World War II admirals, loved to read and passed that love on to his children. In 1922, then-Commander Nimitz traveled with his family to his next assignment. Their journey from Honolulu to Newport, Rhode Island, via the Panama Canal, took place aboard the *Argonne*, with the family occupying two rooms and a bath—very pleasant accommodations for that lengthy trip. His biographer, E. B. Potter, wrote that "the long voyage provided leisure for much reading." Nimitz's posting at Pearl Harbor had been an enjoyable one, Potter noted.

> Nimitz always retained pleasant memories of his first tour at Pearl Harbor. He worked hard there, as hard as he ever worked in his life, but he successfully met a severe challenge and left behind a completed base as testimony. Equally important to him was the fact that for a fairly extended period he had a real home where he could entertain his friends and enjoy his family.
>
> Nancy was still a toddler, but Chet and little Catherine were approaching school age. Either Commander Nimitz or Mrs. Nimitz read to them every evening at bedtime. Once, when the two older children had chicken pox together, Nimitz found time to read to them both at considerable length. He thus helped them to forget their itching, but they never forgot his reading to them.
>
> "I can remember my father sitting in a straight-back chair in the hall outside our two rooms on the ground floor of the house in the hills of Honolulu and reading *Robinson Crusoe* to us," Catherine said long afterward. "He read the whole thing from start to finish. The other book that he tried to read to us on this occa-

sion was an adaptation of Maeterlinck's *The Blue Bird,* which my great-aunt from Cambridge had sent us. And he got halfway—oh, not even halfway—into it and just couldn't stand it, and now that I'm grown up I think he had impeccable taste. I hate it myself."

Nimitz continued to read aloud to the children, one of his choices in the early days at Berkeley being a translation of the *Odyssey.* He also took time to help them with their school lessons. On one occasion Kate felt that her father had been a little *too* helpful in this area. As they were clearing the dining room table after dinner one evening, she happened to mention that she had to prepare a report on the Battle of Jutland—forgetting, if she ever knew, that her father had spent months at the War College researching and writing a thesis on that battle. "It was just like putting gasoline on a fire," she said.

When she returned with the *J* volume of the *Encyclopedia Britannica,* she found the dining room table cleared except for quantities of salt and pepper-shakers. This was unusual because after dinner her father normally left the table set for breakfast. "What's the matter?" she asked.

"Don't you have to do a report on the battle of Jutland?"

"Oh, yes. Half a page."

"I'll tell you about the Battle of Jutland."

"All I could think of in later years, " Kate recalled, "was the old story about 'Thank you for the book; it told me more about penguins than I cared to know.' We had saltshakers and peppershakers, and the German High Sea Fleet was here and the British Fleet here. We went through the whole thing, and I was weakly saying, 'half a page.' But I never forgot it, and I never brought up the Battle of Jutland again."[33]

While plans were being made for the defense of Guadalcanal during World War II, Adm. Raymond Spruance was serving as Nimitz's chief of staff. "One evening," noted Potter,

they were entertaining a group of the officers on his staff. When three of the young lieutenants were leaving, one of them asked Nimitz: "I understand you read a lot at night. Do you?"

"Yes, I do," replied the admiral. "I read from three until five every morning."

"Three until *five*! When do you sleep, sir?"

"Well, I turn in at ten and I sleep till three, and then I catch another wink from five till 6:45."[34]

Nimitz's schedule as naval commander in the Pacific was incredibly full, but there was always time to read.

> The officers often worked till midnight. Nimitz and Spruance had their normal busy days, but they mainly kept aloof from the planning drudgery. They took their long walks as usual, and in the evening read, listened to music, or entertained guests. This kept their minds clear for their regular duties and for the stresses to come. Nimitz was thinking ahead to the attack on the Marshalls and beyond, but he kept himself available for consultation on the planning in hand.
>
> A group of dignitaries visiting Nimitz at Guam in 1945 included congressmen, labor leaders, publishers, and executives of some of our defense industries. One of the publishers was Douglas Southhall Freeman, then editor of the Richmond, Virginia, . . . *News Leader* and author of the four-volume biography of Robert E. Lee. Having just read this biography, [Nimitz] very much enjoyed his visit with him."[35]

After he retired from the Navy, Nimitz was a regent at the University of California at Berkeley. His daughter Nancy reflected:

> The amount of work he brought home in his briefcase from the regents' meeting would not keep a man of his ability busy more than two days. Of course at this time he was reading. This was the time when books on the war were coming out in great numbers. All these books were sent to him, so he had a lot of reading to do. He wrote his own letters longhand, and he was an extremely punctilious correspondent. If you wrote a letter to him, you got a letter back within two days. When he liked a book, he would write a letter of appreciation to the author, then, usually, paste the author's answer inside the cover of the book.[36]

Adm. Raymond A. Spruance was an avid reader of history and biographies, but his tastes covered a much wider area than that, as his biographer E. P. Forrestal noted:

> Although inherently a quiet man, he was even then inquisitive and informed and an interesting conversationalist on a wide range and variety of subjects. An avid reader, he kept up to date on and was conversant with world affairs. It was his expressed belief that every well-educated U.S. citizen had a duty to familiarize himself with the broad field of government, extending into the field of international relations. He recognized that in a democratic government like ours, based upon universal suffrage, foreign policies cannot be expected to be much in

advance of the thinking of the majority of the voting public, and that, therefore, knowledge of political and economic happenings and trends outside the United States is essential to a realization of the lines of foreign policy along which the real interests of the country lie. *He believed that those with the mental equipment to do so had a special duty to inform themselves on world affairs and to help educate and guide the rest of the country in that respect. During his first tour of duty in the Philippines he inquired into and took great interest in Filipino politics and legislative affairs, an interest which helped make him an understanding and informed ambassador to the Islands forty years later.*[37]

Thomas B. Buell also described the importance of reading in Spruance's life and career:

Other personality traits emerged. His high-minded integrity, honesty, and morality were uncompromising. He was strong-willed and stubborn, and when he felt he was right, he would insist that things be done his way. Margaret soon was persuaded that he rarely was wrong. He was unselfish and industrious, but he would neither work overtime nor bring work home. He was insatiably curious about the world and loved to explore things and places while he walked, or to pursue abstract ideas in men's minds—and in books.

He was an avid reader but had no personal library, other than books given him after retirement by publishers and admirers. Public libraries provided biographies and histories, which he preferred in early years, but he was not familiar with commonly accepted great works of literature. He chose books indiscriminately, perhaps selecting one whose subject had attracted his momentary interest. Other times he simply read whatever was readily available to occupy his idle hours.

Early on, Margaret found he owned two well-thumbed books that reflected his beliefs on religion, politics, and economics. One was the Bible, which he knew intimately, read often, and kept by his bed. But he read it for its beauty and not its doctrine. He was an agnostic and could not accept Christianity by faith alone. He needed proof, and there was none to his satisfaction. . . .

Spruance was one of seventy students in his Naval War College class. One of the objectives of the curriculum was to provide a great deal of time for reading; to reflect at a more leisurely pace, but most importantly to discuss among themselves their careers, where the Navy was going, how to prepare for what the future had to offer. . . .

Spruance was an intellectual in the purest sense of the word. He was a person with superior mental power. He was deeply interested in fields of knowledge outside the technicalities of the naval profession. He once told some university students, "I think it is most other fields where you may have a natural interest." He explained that those with a liberal education in art, literature, and music had an advantage over people—such as himself—with only a technical education. "A knowledge and appreciation of these subjects enriches their lives," he said, "and makes them more interesting individuals to their friends and acquaintances." . . .

As Commander of Task Force 16, he left Pearl Harbor on February 14, 1942, to Wake Island, a trip of 2,000 miles. Spruance kept himself from boredom since his responsibilities were not pressing by collecting every book and paperback he could find and devoted his waking hours to reading.[38]

His chief of staff during World War II, then-Capt. Charles J. (Carl) Moore, commented on Spruance's reading habits:

> He turns in about eight and doesn't like to be disturbed except for something most important. He won't sleep in his emergency cabin because it is stuffy. He has read dozens of books and doesn't like to be interrupted. I refer almost nothing to him except matters of vital importance, and he lets me strictly alone except on those matters. He is most appreciative of my efforts and says, "I don't know how I could have gotten along without you, Carl." As long as I will stay and do the work and he can walk and read and sleep, he'll be contented.[39]

In a letter to his wife, Margaret, Spruance wrote:

> "I am getting restless to get on with the war." . . . He had been marking time in Pearl Harbor for two months, and two and a half months remained before D-Day on Iwo Jima. "The trouble now is that I do not have enough work thrust on me to keep me busy, and I am too lazy to dig up work for myself. Hence, I wish the time would come to start moving again. On board ship, if there is not much to do, I can sit down and read a book, but here I feel more or less obliged to keep office hours and reading a book during office hours does not look well."[40]

In January 1945 he traveled from Pearl Harbor to the island of Ulithi: "The tranquil passage to Ulithi required eleven days. Spruance resumed his familiar at-sea practice of reading, exercising, and listening to classical music on the ship's loudspeakers in the early afternoon. 'When there is no excitement going on, a daily routine like this keeps you in shape and helps to pass the time,' he wrote . . . Margaret. 'I must say that, except for the heat and humidity, I enjoy a spell at sea. I am also glad to be getting out where we shall be accomplishing something once more.'"[41]

Adm. Arleigh Burke, who served as CNO for an unprecedented three two-year tours (1955–61), began reading at a young age. His biographer, E. B. Potter, wrote of his early indoctrination:

> Clara [his mother] devoted herself to nurturing his intellect. Under her tutelage he had already in his preschool days begun identifying printed words. At Baseline, stimulated by the competition of his fellow students, he made rapid progress and early began reading in his free time, mostly adventure stories. Clara, ambitious to have him read more substantial fare, obtained a library card for him, and each Saturday when family members went to town for shopping, she had him draw books. She encouraged him to read at least two a week, and when he had read three books of his own choosing, she insisted that he alternate with three she chose for him, often with the willing advice of his teachers. Thus she gradually raised his intellectual appetite so that his own selection of reading material steadily matured.[42]

While he was serving as commander of an immensely successful combat destroyer group, Burke was co-opted to be chief of staff for a carrier task force commander, Vice Adm. Marc A. Mitscher. One of the first things he did as Mitscher's chief of staff was read: "I went in and looked at the op orders, and I talked to the staff watch officers, and I looked to see where all the equipment was—the TBS, the scopes, and all the other things I needed to acquaint myself with on the flag bridge. I didn't know anything about aircraft operations, so I sent for all the publications I could get on all the aircraft that they had aboard, or we'd be operating with, and I started to study." His biographer noted that Burke "*devoted every spare moment to his first rapid reading course,* poring over orders, dispatches, instructions, aircraft operating manuals, and everything else a sympathetic staff could think of that might be helpful. Most daunting were the battle plans, thick volumes, filled with detail."[43]

Two postwar assignments provided Burke with opportunities for intense study, research, and discussion in the fields of international relations, history, economics, and government. In April 1947 he became a member of the General Board. "By the end of 1947," he later recalled, "I had been given the job of honchoing a paper. Admiral Towers and Admiral McMorris had accepted the general idea that we could do a paper on national security in the next ten years [which he entitled 'National Security and Naval Contributions for the Next Ten Years'] outlining factors involved, with the understanding that I would guide it. It was my project but they would help, and they did a marvelous job. Everybody helped."[44]

In December 1951 Burke was assigned to the office of the CNO, Strategic Plans Division, referred to as Op-23. His work there involved an extensive study of French military history with a concentration on the Napoleonic period. While in Op-23 he produced two monographs that remain unequaled in scholarship by any professor at any of the finest universities and colleges in the country. These two assignments offered a unique opportunity for professional development and prepared Burke for continued responsibilities as he continued up the hierarchy. They marked him among his seniors and contemporaries as a young officer to watch, someone destined to rise to the top in the Navy. He certainly devoted his energies to preparing for increased responsibilities.

Potter's biography makes a cogent point about Burke's reading and studying at this point in his career that further clarifies its role in his professional development:

> During much of his career he applied himself so vigorously to the problems at hand that he had little energy left for serious general reading. Within the field of his specialties he was without peer, but he had become somewhat of a narrow specialist. Gradually he came to realize that the world of informed citizens was leaving him behind. Too often he saw references in newspapers or heard references in conversations to things he didn't understand. To rectify this defect, Arleigh took advantage of the occasional periods of respite he had been vouchsafed since the war . . . to devour books and articles that might fill in the blanks in his knowledge of history, economics, science, politics, and international relations.
>
> This recent reading helped Burke in some small measure to judge the future functions of the shore establishment, but it also enabled him to judge how much he and his colleagues had yet to learn. He induced Admiral Towers to bring in experts to brief the General Board on such subjects as the operations of the United Nations and the navy's experiments toward use of atomic energy for weapons and propulsion. As for himself, he joined Washington's Brookings Institution for the study of economic, governmental, and international problems

and attended its weekly lectures and discussion periods. All of these studies had a bearing on what to do about the shore establishment.[45]

But not all Burke's reading was scholarly: "I have forgotten to report," Burke reflected on his tour as chief of staff to Mitscher,

one of Admiral Mitscher's vices I had also become addicted to by this time. As you know, battles are going on all the time, and a man can't study plans and think of nothing but his work all of his waking hours either. I soon found after I . . . joined Admiral Mitscher, that he was an ardent detective story reader. There were a few old magazines aboard, of course no newspapers, and if a man started to read a book, something would happen and when whatever had happened was over, the book was gone. Somebody else had started to read it—or it had been in the road and it was chucked someplace else, or something. Books simply didn't stay put when they weren't actually being read.

The Admiral solved the reading problem by bringing a couple of cases of detective stories aboard each time we got back to any place that had detective stories—which wasn't very often. When he finished one he would put it in flag plot. Of course, we on the staff would pick them up and start to read them, too. I doubt if you are a detective story fan—and if you are not you have missed a lot in life—none of it very useful. The big advantage to these time passers is that it doesn't make any difference whether you finish them or not. Also if a few pages are missing the story doesn't lose much thereby. So it was not unusual for us to pick a detective story up and read it for awhile and when it disappeared another one would do just as well—even one you'd read before. Of course they became dog-eared and torn, but nobody threw them away because of that.

Well, in the last cruise we all had read all that Admiral Mitscher had, maybe some of them several times, because you can't be positive you've actually read it before. The press put out a news story on Admiral Mitscher's devotion to that trash literature and deplored the fact that he had run out of them and had been reduced to reading them over. Our mail service during the war was very good— most of the time—and shortly after that story hit the streets, many kind people mailed him lots and lots of detective stories. We never ran out again. Cigarettes yes, bombs sometimes, but detective stories we had plenty of.

Naturally I, and I expect most of the rest of the staff, became detective story addicts. I gave up cigarettes with little trouble, I can go on a diet and lose weight if I have to—and sometimes I've had to—but I still subscribe to detective stories. I really know they don't improve the quality of refinement or culture an iota, and they are a waste of money, but, in spite of the pressure that has sometimes been put on me by well meaning friends, I still waste my time on them. Perhaps they are as valuable as some of the modern historical novels, though. Nor did Admiral Mitscher ever give them up.[46]

Admiral Burke believed strongly that Naval Academy midshipmen should learn about naval history, and his ideas for encouraging its study were often quite innovative. He commented:

There are a lot of things that I tried to start [as CNO], and some of them have been very successful. A lot of these things improved the operations, the support of one country to another, . . . by improving mutual support among navies, and to do that you must know people. You must know how they operate and how they think, so every time I could, I'd have mutual operations with other navies, whether we were allied with them or not. Starting with the Mexicans, we exchanged instructors in the Naval Academy. A young Mexican lieutenant I brought up as my aide I sent to the Naval Academy, not to teach Spanish but to teach American naval history, because our young American boys who see a Mexican teaching our naval history, are a hell of a lot more impressed than if he teaches [something] . . . like Spanish.[47]

Adm. Thomas H. Moorer (CNO 1967–70 and chairman of the Joint Chiefs of Staff 1970–74) agreed on the importance of history in leadership development.

"One of my main concerns in the country today," he said in his oral history, was described in

a big article in the *New York Times* . . . that the enrollment in the universities in history . . . has gone down. And that's bad, very bad, because there's no point in having to learn the same thing twice and that's what the young people today are inclined to want to do. There's one of the old clichés that the generals always want to fight today's war with yesterday's tactics and so on. Today's thinking is always a search for a new way, a new and easy way to fight war. There is no such thing. You can change the technology, but the fundamental principles remain. People ask me what did I learn from the Vietnam War. I say, "Nothing." I mean all that I saw happen proved that the principles of war are sound. They were violated and we didn't succeed. But I didn't learn the principles of war in Vietnam. I already knew them.[48]

He went on to describe what he saw as the value of studying history: "I'm a big believer in learning from other people's mistakes, even if they happened a century ago. I'm not anxious to go out there and experiment myself if I already know the answer. And it's very dangerous."[49]

Effective and successful contributions to one's profession require constant study. Although he conceded the importance of history, Admiral Moorer believed strongly in learning the technical side of the Navy profession as well.

> I think it is particularly important for a naval officer. . . . Although the Naval Academy curriculum emphasizes the technical side of the house—in fact, that's the reason I went to the Naval Academy in the first place—I think that you can't let it stop after you graduate. You have to pursue this further. . . . Any successful operator or commander at sea must have a burning technical curiosity about how things work, including his bilge pump, his steering engine, right on up to his supersonic jet. No one is going to tell him those things. He's got to go out and find out for himself.
>
> I think the Naval Academy has gone way overboard in trying to "me too" the universities. It's not a university. If you're going to give fifty-nine electives or something like that, you might as well close it up and go to some of the universities. I would be heartily in favor of moving back the other way. It's nice to know Shakespeare and so on, and I guess it's good to have that, too, but that's not number one priority. There's only one priority, one reason for midshipmen existing, and that's to learn how to fight. Anything that they teach down there that doesn't teach the midshipman how to fight is a waste of time.[50]

In a personal interview, I asked Adm. James L. Holloway III (CNO 1974–78) to tell me how reading became important in his life, what books he read, and what impact they had on the development of his character and leadership qualities. His answer indicated that love of books and reading was a Holloway family tradition.

> My grandfather was superintendent of schools in Fort Smith, Arkansas. That's where he married my grandmother, who was a schoolteacher. My grandfather went to medical school late in life and became a medical doctor. The family moved to a small town, Oakcliff, which later became a suburb of Dallas, Texas. My grandmother encouraged my father to read, and his father had an extensive

library (for those days). My father loved school. Living in the country, schooling became his main interest. I think he became the teacher's pet because he loved to read. I probably inherited that. When I was young, I enjoyed reading enormously. I was in China as a very young child, [and] I contracted dysentery and rickets. In my early school days I was puny and I stayed home and read rather than go to the playground and get beat up by the neighborhood kids. My family would give me books for Christmas instead of a baseball glove.

I attended boarding school in the country, before the days of good roads. So on weekends I usually stayed at school with the other boarders and threw a lacrosse ball around. I read books. The pleasure of reading never left me. . . . I discovered when I was fifteen years old, the weekly periodicals. At boarding school I had a subscription to *Time* magazine, and I even had a subscription to the *New Yorker*. Yes, the *New Yorker,* and not for the cartoons! I think it included some of our finest authors.

In high school I also discovered the great fiction author, Ernest Hemingway. In the 1930s, Hemingway was popular, although we were forbidden to read some of his novels at school because of what were deemed to be several salacious passages. There was a lot of schoolwork that involved reading, so there wasn't too much opportunity to read a lot on our own time. Also, at Saint James we were required to go out for a sport every semester. That consumed a lot of time and boyish energy. Plus, we had tons of homework every night. I was fortunate in that I had a teacher who greatly encouraged me in reading, not only Hemingway, but other fiction authors like J. D. Salinger and H. H. Munro (Saki), both of whom I still enjoy reading.

At the Naval Academy there just really wasn't much time for anything but what our officers scheduled and our professors assigned. When I went to sea, I did a lot of reading. The book that I best remember was *Vanity Fair* because it took me almost a whole cruise to finish it. I was particularly taken with the similarity between the cavalry officers in the British Army during the Napoleonic era and the naval aviators of my own day. We lived dangerously and led a fast life.

When I was CNO, Herman Wouk and Mrs. Wouk invited Dabney [his wife] and me to dinner at their home in Georgetown, D.C. As we were chatting before dinner, I said, "Let me say how nice it is to meet the author of one of my favorite books." He said, "Oh, did you enjoy the *Caine Mutiny*?" I said, "Well, I did, but that's not the book I'm talking about." He reacted with surprise and asked what book it was. I said, "*Marjorie Morningstar.*" He sat back and looked amused, and he asked, "You liked it?" When I replied, "Yes," he asked, "Why?" I was a little embarrassed, but I told him it reminded me a lot of *Vanity Fair* and I thought that he wrote a great deal like Thackeray. He called over to his wife, who was talking to Dabney. "Betty Sarah, did you hear that?" She laughed and said to Dabney, "Herman has always prided himself in the fact that I thought he was writing like Thackeray in those days, too."

I asked Admiral Holloway to tell me about his mentors. Reading was again a factor in his answer:

The term "mentor" doesn't resonate with me. I can't really say I ever had a mentor. My father was not. He was gone so much of the time. When he was home, he didn't play catch with me because I don't think he could catch a ball. But he did inspire me to read. In my library, you can see one-half a bookshelf on the Roman Army. This was his influence. He was fascinated by the Roman Legions. One day, he took his lunch time off from his office in the Navy Department to walk ten blocks to the Library of Congress, to get a book titled *The Roman Soldier* that was only available in the U.S. in the Library of Congress. Looking back on this, I thought it was really a great thing for him to do. He was a busy man at the office and usually worked late. So I always appreciated the time he took to talk to me. He was very interested in my reading, and strongly encouraged it. He was determined that I should go off to boarding school where I would have good teachers in small classes and would be able to study without the distractions of living at home. A good school education and capacious reading were his objectives for me, and both were important as I grew up. My father made sure I was always reading. Once when he was rereading Gibbon's *Decline and Fall of the Roman Empire* for the umpteenth time, he would read it to me, and he made history sound so wonderful.

I asked Admiral Holloway what books interested him the most. "It's hard to pin down a single book," he replied. "I've enjoyed so many, and my tastes always seem to be changing. Each good book seems better than the last. One that I particularly enjoyed was *Winston Churchill* by Randolph Churchill. I also liked Winston Churchill's *History of the English Speaking People*. It is written with such obvious pride and eloquence. I have read *The Diary of Samuel Pepys* over and over again. I love to pick it up open it at random and read it."

I asked him, "What did you get out of it?"

I was impressed with the immutability of naval careers. *The Diary of Samuel Pepys* is a classic, but most people don't realize that Samuel Pepys was in the late eighteenth century the British equivalent of the secretary of the navy. The problems that he had with shoddy contractors, manning the fleet, and the failure of politicians to provide funds for the navy are so reminiscent of the difficulties we still run into today.

Then I enjoyed particularly the Scottish author James Boswell. Almost everything he's written I've enjoyed. I liked Will Durant's *The History of Civilization*, all seven volumes. I took that set with me on a cruise, and it was a real standby. Again, a biography I really loved, and which has impressed me as much as any I've ever read, is Douglas Southall Freeman's *Life of George Washington*. It is so completely substantiated by the footnotes of Freeman's meticulous research. Many Americans aren't aware of the bitter sacrifices that George Washington had to make to hold his army together and the terrible trials that he went through as commander in chief. It is so sad to read about his soul-wrenching decision to hang the deserters at Valley Forge.

Surprisingly, Holloway said that he did not read naval officers' biographies.

As a naval officer myself, I probably had a much better feel for the thought processes and motivations of these naval officers than the authors, who can only use their imagination in areas where they really lack familiarity. So often I feel that they have misinterpreted the reasoning of their protagonist's decision, and quite often the technicalities that influenced those decisions. My father served with and knew people like King, Nimitz, Spruance, and Burke. I had heard my father talk about them in contemporary terms after a day in the office with them in Washington. Therefore, I lacked the motivation to explore their personalities through an author's conjectures.

I really didn't read as much at sea as one would suppose. On destroyers during World War II, I stood two four-hour officer-of-the-deck watches every day, was at my battle station for an hour each at sunset and sunrise General Quarters, and had to run the gunnery department and do my ship's administrative duties. Otherwise, I slept. There wasn't much time for reading.

My first aircraft squadron immediately after World War II was a carrier dive-bomber squadron flying SB-2Cs—Helldivers. The skipper was only a lieutenant instead of a lieutenant commander, which the Table of Organization called for; so many of the more experienced officers had been demobilized. The squadron included a dozen or so pilots left over from the war waiting to get out, plus a dozen new pilots just out of flight training who were either Naval Academy graduates or reserves who had several years of obligated service. Discipline was nonexistent.

If a scheduled flight was going out, the flight leader might say, "Smith, why aren't you ready?" The reply could be, "I'm not going. I've got a hangover." Then somebody else would speak up, "I can't fly this morning. I have to take my wife to the commissary." The squadron commander would say, "But you're on the flight schedule." And the reply was, "Well, get somebody else." I just couldn't believe it, the lack of respect for authority. Demobilization was having a terrible effect on the Navy.

Things moved very fast after I reported to the squadron, because in the first two months, we had three pilots killed in aircraft accidents. The squadron commander was relieved by a more senior lieutenant commander who was an Academy graduate. Then the executive officer flew into the after gun mount, landing aboard a carrier. His plane blew up. With his loss, I, as a lieutenant, became executive officer of the squadron. The skipper told me, "Jim, we've got to get some professionalism in this outfit." During World War II, one of the unique things about naval aviation in the carrier squadrons was that the pilots had no responsibilities except to fly. I think it was the same in the Army Air Corps. Although in the post–World War II Navy pilots were expected to be officers as well, and every officer in the squadron was assigned administrative duties, . . . the habits of World War II lingered on, and in this squadron the pilots would sit in the ready room and sleep off their hangovers or play a dice board game called "acey-deucey" [a variant of backgammon].

I considered acey-deucey the world's worst waste of time. The pilots would ask me as exec, "Well, if we don't play acey-deucey, what do you want us to do?" I said, "I want you to read and study." And they said, "What?" I said, "This," and I gave them maintenance manuals, tactical doctrines, or FAA procedures. "Also I don't want you in the ready room unless you are getting ready for a flight or debriefing. I want you in your office learning your administrative job or out in the shops getting to know the men. I want you looking after the men." I asked them, "When's the last time you were down in the hangar?" Many of them had never been down to the hangar.

This was in 1946 as a lieutenant. I was very young for an executive officer of the squadron. Normally the XO was a lieutenant commander. Professionalism had been instilled in me in the fleet as a destroyer gunnery officer during the war, and I was just beginning to grasp the distinction between training and education.

Training covers the technical side of the specifics of your plane and your job in the squadron. Education is acquiring the ability to comprehend more obtuse subjects, leadership, engineering, principles, and the art of writing. This education was gained from reading books. Training was the first essential for the squadron pilot. It was a question of survival in the air. Learning was for when you left the squadron area. The evening was the time to settle down with a good book, not hang out at the bar.

. . . The pilots in the squadron . . . needed to be trained to survive. They needed education to get ahead. For some, education came from the professional curriculum at the Naval Academy and postgraduate university courses in advanced professional subjects. But for everyone, reading a broad selection of books across the spectrum of good literature was essential. It is all the education many officers will get after their baccalaureate degrees. I include all kinds of books—histories, biographies, technical treatises, and fiction. Yes, fiction. Thackeray's *Vanity Fair,* Tolstoy's *War and Peace,* and even Shaw's *Androcles and the Lion*—all have persuasive lessons in leadership.

Continuing our discussion of books, Admiral Holloway described some of the events that influenced his love of reading.

I was going through advanced flight training in Corpus Christi, Texas, in 1944. It was after I had come back from two years in destroyers in World War II. Academy graduates had to wait for two years before going into aviation. When we got to Corpus Christi, there was a polio epidemic in the area. The movie theaters were closed because of the quarantine, nor could we enjoy dinner out because of the food rationing. Furthermore, Dabney was expecting and we had to be careful about going places where she could be exposed to polio. There was no vaccine then. The little house we rented had no air conditioning, so just sitting around home in the one-hundred-degree heat and humidity of the Texas Gulf Coast was grim. But we had the La Retama Public Library in Corpus Christi. Dabney and I discovered it early during our stay in Corpus, and every night, as soon as dinner was over, we were at the library. It was magnificently stocked with the widest variety of books. The library itself had been the elegant home of a wealthy Texan, and its atmosphere of quiet culture had been retained.

What I discovered was that there were more books than I had ever been exposed to at home, Saint James, or the Naval Academy. I discovered marvelous books on art. I became fascinated by the reproductions. I had joked about the impressionists and modern art, but after I had a chance to take home these art books, sit down, and study the development of the genres from the beginning, it all made sense to me. It was a marvelous education which I really enjoyed because I was learning something totally new.

One of my greatest discoveries was the world of drama, especially the plays of George Bernard Shaw. I had never read Shaw before, because drama was not taught at the Naval Academy. After I had read Shaw, I didn't consider his works "plays." They are biting social commentaries in dialogue form. My two favorite Shaw works are *Androcles and the Lion* and *Arms and the Man.* I still crack up when I read them again after all these years. One of the great contributions of the La Retama Public Library was that it opened for me the whole scope of dramatic literature and tactile art. . . .

Reading in general, a wide exposure to fiction, drama, and art gave me an opportunity to socialize with a wider group of people. When we went out to a party, I didn't have to go in the kitchen with the men and drink bourbon and talk about the Navy or flying. Dabney and I could make friends with people outside the Navy and talk about things other than flying and babies. . . .

When I was stationed in the Seventh Fleet in Japan, during 1972 and 1973, I became fascinated with Japanese culture. It brought me close to the Japanese people. As commander of the Seventh Fleet and a vice admiral, I had quarters on the former Japanese naval base in Yokosuka. Over the years I have maintained a close relationship with the Japanese, which began with that tour of duty. I attribute our ability to mix with the Japanese to our familiarity with their culture and history, to what we had gained through reading and through their art. The French impressionists were very much influenced by the Japanese woodblock artists such as Hiroshige. You will see a lot of Japanese woodblocks on the walls of our home in Annapolis. Secretary of the Navy Middendorf was an ardent collector of Oriental art—in fact, objects of art of all forms and cultures—he traded me this excellent Japanese samurai print for an autographed picture of the Joint Chiefs of Staff.

Few men have had more impact on the careers of U.S. naval officers than Adm. Hyman G. Rickover, who was for many years the head of the Navy's Naval Reactors program. Admiral Holloway provided insights into Rickover's reading habits:

Admiral Rickover was an avid reader. He told me that as a young officer he preferred to stay aboard ship and read while his fellow junior officers went ashore and caroused. Even after he was married he and his wife preferred to remain at home and read rather than join his fellow officers and their wives at bridge or dinner parties. The Rickovers did not play bridge or enjoy cocktail parties. They preferred to read or visit historical or cultural sites. He admitted that apparent lack of sociability with his contemporaries marked him as a loner and a nonconformist the rest of his life, and he realized this made for some difficulties during his career. Yet Rickover never regretted his introspective ways. As a matter of fact, I personally believe he relished them. He told me several times that it enabled him to pick and choose his company and talk on topics of his choice. He was interested in everything. He often talked to me about flying and the aviator's fatalist philosophy.

. . . Rickover put great store in his wide knowledge of books. He was essentially an engineer, but his broad familiarity with books made him a humanist—in his view—and gave him the ability to work with and influence the Congress and the senior civilians in the Navy. He had the support of every secretary of the navy he served under. An examination of his congressional testimony will disclose that his most trenchant observations to the committee were most often not of an engineering nature, but parables which explained his work in a way the nonengineering layman could understand.

Admiral Rickover interviewed every officer who worked for him in the Navy and each civilian in the Nuclear Reactor Directorate. These interviews have become famous because they were the basis upon which a person was selected for the nuclear program. Going nuclear or not would determine whether a young aspiring submariner would have a successful career in the Navy. One question Admiral Rickover invariably asked during an interview was, "What books have you read lately?" This question was so standard that many officer candidates tried to prep for their interview by cramming—reading a *Readers Digest* condensation of good books. Rickover always found them out, as far as I could tell, and . . . I sat in on hundreds of interviews. Rickover had read virtually every book of consequence that an interview[ee] ever cited, including *Lady Chatterley's Lover.*

When an officer told him he didn't have time to read anything but technical manuals because of the intensity of his current duty assignment, Rickover was not impressed. An aspirant's book report during the interview process was not necessarily a deciding factor in the interview process. An otherwise bright, acceptable young man whose recent reading was deficient would be told he could be reinterviewed in a year if he would promise to read a few of the books on a list provided by Admiral Rickover. I never saw a candidate turn down this offer, and

I'm sure they were shocked when they saw the length of the list and the variety of the books. Yet I don't know of any who failed to accomplish their assigned reading and get selected for the program.

Rickover's list of acceptable books was eclectic. The only requirement was it had to be well written. No comic books or gossipy trash, and he was the arbiter of what was good—history, biography, essays, and novels, mainly. He could generally size up an officer by what he had read, and Rickover seemed to have an affinity for those who had read the classics. I think he approved of their taste.[51]

I discussed books and reading with Adm. Thomas B. Hayward (CNO 1978–82) as well. "I love to read," he told me, "but I was not what you would classify in the same context as these people, avid readers. . . . Most of the stuff I read was nonfiction. Occasionally, I'll read fiction. It's fun to read. I just read a whole series on the history of Egypt, a lot of political military stuff, things of that nature."

When I asked Admiral Hayward to name some biographies that had made an impression on him, he responded:

I think I probably liked the best books on President Harry S. Truman, General of the Army Douglas MacArthur, and Fleet Admiral Chester W. Nimitz. Books about things going on in Washington, that kind of thing; the really prominent leaders of America. I read about Admiral Raymond A. Spruance. I didn't read a lot on Halsey. I probably read a book every three weeks. When I was in Korea, for instance, we were just busy all the time. I didn't have time to read. I didn't grow up reading a lot, nor did my family. I look back on that and say it's too bad because that's clearly where reading starts.[52]

I discussed books and reading with Adm. Carlisle A. H. Trost (CNO 1986–90) and asked what role reading had played in the development of his character and leadership. He reflected:

At the Naval Academy, one of the things that I admired about the way the curriculum developed during my years as a midshipman was that I was there at a time when everybody took the same subjects. I had a year of very intense engineering training at Washington University in St. Louis before entering the Naval Academy. I had a lot of math there, and also in high school I had advanced math courses. So really, I had more math than they even offered at the Naval Academy. I also already had had college physics and college chemistry, mechanical drawing, and descriptive geometry courses, all basic core courses in our first year.

Because of this educational background, Trost had already taken all of the technical courses offered to plebes. "Fortunately," he said,

> there was the option for me to take a literature course, so I got to do more independent reading. I read an awful lot about Admiral Nimitz and books about General of the Army Douglas MacArthur. I even read books about Japanese military leadership and some of the World War II leaders, such as DeGaulle, Montgomery, and Pétain. There was a whole series of books on World War II. After I graduated from the Naval Academy, I started reading history, like European history. In elementary and high school, you learn just what you have to learn. I found when I reflected back on certain books, I was now better able to put things in perspective, especially after I was commissioned and traveled to the places I had read about. For example, I went back and read about European history because of my cruise to Europe as a midshipman. I found it fascinating. I didn't have a specific schedule, but I read whenever I could, and always had a book open. I read numerous professional journals throughout my career such as the *Naval Institute Proceedings, Naval History* magazine, *Time, Newsweek*, and other periodicals that kept me up on naval and current events.

But serious reading was a part of Trost's life before he entered the Naval Academy. In the *St. Louis Post-Dispatch* announcement on July 7, 1986, reporting his selection as chief of naval operations, his aunt, Arlena Trost, was quoted as saying of him, "He was always reading, always studying whatever he could get his hands on." Admiral Trost's sister, Mardelle L. Trost, stated, "He was very much a bookworm." In his high school yearbook, he stated that his ambition was "to be successful." He certainly achieved that goal, rising to the number-one position of responsibility of the U.S. Navy, and his interest in reading was a significant factor in his professional development and career success. "There are so many different thoughts and ideas you are exposed to in reading that are often helpful in one's career," he told me. "I would say that it had a very definite input in my development."[53]

Adm. Jay L. Johnson (CNO 1996–2000) told me that he loves to read.

> I consider myself to be a reader. . . . I failed miserably with my reading program when I was the CNO. It was frustrating . . . not having time to read. When I could, I read things about leadership. I read more recent books, like some of the books

that were written by Senator John McCain and Bob Woodard. One of my favorites is *Soldiers Once and Young* by Hal Moore and my friend Joe Galloway. It gave this Vietnam fighter pilot a real good combat perspective. . . .

I had to take care of myself physically as well as mentally, so I would be in the best position to make sound decisions for the Navy. As a result of that, my reading suffered. Instead of getting up at 3:30 to read a book, I got up at 4:30 or 5:00 to go run five miles. . . . I had to do that. It cleared my head and gave me an opportunity to think. I didn't get to keep the full balance of things I enjoy doing like reading. But I'm catching up now.

I'm currently reading McCullough's book on John Adams, which I really like. And I just bought *Wild Blue* by Steven Ambrose, the story of B-24 pilots (in particular, Senator George McGovern) in World War II. I love Ambrose; he does remarkable things describing what it was like for them. What hooked me on that book, aside from the fact it was written by Mr. Ambrose, was the review that I read in the *Wall Street Journal,* written by my good friend Congressman Duke Cunningham. He was one of only two Navy MiG aces in Vietnam, and Duke is about as far on the opposite side of the political spectrum from George McGovern as a man can get. But after reading *Wild Blue,* Duke said he'd gladly fly Mr. McGovern's wing. That convinced me to add it to my reading list.[54]

"I honestly love to read," was Admiral Stansfield Turner's answer to my question about reading.

I love histories and biographies. I don't want to pretend that I read . . . [at] 3:30 in the morning like Admiral Nimitz did; nor do I have four thousand books in my library. I'm more inclined to read things like Barbara Tuchman's *The Month of August* or Herman Wouk's *The Winds of War.* Herman Wouk, in that book, not only tells you about military strategy, but he tells you about the American character. Another book that influenced me very much is *Men, Machines, and Modern Times* by B. Elton Morrison, a Yale professor. It's a series of anecdotes of military resistance to change. I read this in the mid-1960s when I was working at systems analysis for McNamara, and was watching the military resistance to the changes McNamara was trying to make.

I do like to read. When I became president of the Naval War College, I threw the existing curriculum out. This was totally lock, stock, and barrel. This was from 1972 to 1974. I divided [the curriculum] into three segments: strategy, management, and tactics. You have to decide what you want to accomplish and to decide how you use what you have. But the strategy course was the best, and was based on historical case studies. I'm an avid person for adapting or understanding history in order to understand today.[55]

All of the admirals I interviewed agreed that reading is essential for a successful Navy career. Vice Adm. Kent Lee provided an important example when he commented:

> The education to be a commanding officer of an aircraft carrier is a kind of do-it-yourself thing. I got all the literature available on the technical aspects of running the ship. There are various things like that, that you're supposed to read when you go through AirPac. There are various instructions on how to handle storms, and you get all the books on ship handling. But I think all ships' captains do a great deal of reading in this area, especially carrier captains. So, yes, I had read and reread all the instructions on books in this area. You have to play with it a little bit, but all captains, especially of aircraft carriers, have impressed on them that you don't plow one of those big ships into these walls of water at high speed. You can wreck your ship. We've had carriers wrecked like that, flight decks peeled back. You just want to sit there where the ship rides as comfortably as possible and maintain steerageway and wait it out.[56]

Admiral Lee stressed the importance of reading for all naval personnel, officers and enlisted men and women alike. He received command of the USS *Alamo* in May 1964. "One of the things I did on the USS *Alamo*," he commented, "was build a library. We had no library. My philosophy is that any reading is better than no reading, especially for the youngsters we get in the Navy. If they'll read comic books, we'll stock comic books. But I built a library and got BuPers to send me a whole batch of books. We put together a nice library for *Alamo*, lot of good books in it, but a little bit of everything. That was fun, picking the books to go in this library." Shipboard life provides ample opportunities for reading. "In *Alamo* normally, except for that Vietnam tour, we'd have an exercise about once a month or so, and you'd work very hard for three or four days, or a week on one of those exercises. Then life was fairly simple, and you didn't have a lot to do. So I had a lot of free time. I could do a lot of studying, a lot of reading, and lots of other things."[57]

Command of an aircraft carrier, Lee said, allowed far less time for reading.

> When you're at sea on an aircraft carrier, you're usually working ten or twelve hours a day in a squadron, or the captain of the ship much longer, because you have lots of flight operations. That's the name of the game, flight operations. That's an all-hands evolution and requires a lot of work from everybody from airplane mechanics on up. So the workload on a ship, such as an *Alamo,* versus the work on an aircraft carrier for the average officer, I would say on an aircraft carrier on a scale of one to ten, about nine and a half. On a ship like *Alamo,* maybe four. So it's an easy life in comparison. But *Alamo* was one of the happiest tours in my naval career.[58]

Lee emphasized that reading alone does not make a leader, offering an experience that occurred after he received command of a carrier aircraft squadron as an example.

> One of the embarrassing events in my naval career I'll now talk about. I was still a lieutenant commander, hadn't made my number yet. When I had command of the squadron, I thought I was really king of the hill. I had read lots of books about leadership and command. I thought the thing to do when you go in and take command is to gather all the troops around and tell them how it's going to be— Hollywood style. After I'd been there a few days, maybe a week, I got all the officers together in a ready room. I had written out everything I was going to say. So I told them, "This is how we're going to do it. This is how it's going to be." And even today, when I think about that, I'm embarrassed. I learned a good lesson.
>
> There was a saying in the old Navy that "you don't change the sails for the first half hour of your watch." The watch officer before you might have known what he was doing. And if you've got something that's working, don't fiddle with it. Over the next few weeks and months I found out that it wasn't going to be that way I had planned. After you've had a little experience, you learn to take one problem at a time. And there's no correct answer for most problems. You know, you can solve most problems several different ways. You solve them in the best interests of the individual and the squadron, in the circumstances.[59]

In his oral history Lee reflected on his tour on Rickover's staff:

> Somebody always goes in when Rickover interviews a candidate. There's always a third man, at least during my time there. . . . I did that a number of times. One time a man came into his office, and Rickover asked him what his hobby was, . . .

knowing full well what it was [already]. . . . He said reading the Bible. "What other hobbies do you have?" "That's it. When I'm not working, I read the Bible." Rickover says, "That's all," and wrote a big "NO" across it. His comment to me afterward was, "We don't need people like that in the nuclear program." He didn't believe there was anything wrong with reading your Bible, but he didn't want somebody that single-minded, and another way to look at it is unbalanced.[60]

After interviewing more than one hundred four-star generals over a thirty-five-year period, I concluded that those who were avid readers were superior in depth and perception to those who were not readers. I have reached the same conclusion with my study of naval leaders. Their interest in reading biography and military naval history had a role in the development of their character and leadership abilities, but so did their interest in the works of Socrates, Plato, Aristotle, and Shakespeare. As youths they all read the adventure books of such authors as Sir Walter Scott, Rudyard Kipling, and James Fenimore Cooper, which sparked their interest in the adventures of a military career. While these men were warriors, their love of reading and wide-ranging tastes—including poetry—showed them to be sensitive and caring individuals as well.

In the United States we take for granted the unlimited opportunity we have to own and read books. In the late 1990s a foreign exchange student from formerly communist Bulgaria arrived in the United States to study at Princeton University. In an award-winning essay that was published for alumni and friends of Princeton University in spring 1997, Krassimira J. Zourkova described her passion for books:

> I still wonder whether growing up under communism in Bulgaria was something I should regret or something I should be thankful for. I tell my American friends how in second grade my diploma came with a compulsory enrollment in the children's sub-division of the Communist party, and about my grandfather who was expelled from medical school because he was "politically unreliable." Yet, what I never managed to get across is the positive side: this special, intangible appreciation of life—this awe for the ordinary things—that communism brought into my childhood.
>
> I remember the surprised look on my roommate's face when she saw me sliding my hand up and down the cover of one of my textbooks, as if caressing it. She

laughed and asked me whether I was daydreaming. In fact, I had been thinking about the book itself, because I was opening it for the first time. This initial encounter with a book, from the first touch of its smooth cover to the brief crack of the glue as one opens the front page and presses the leafs down, was a moment which had turned almost into a ritual—long ago, when I would come home from school, and on the rare, "lucky" nights as I called them, would find a book which my father, after hunting for it for days, had left on the table to surprise me. In those days, it was almost impossible even to find the books for purchase. Often I had to wait in line for hours, and then, when the store opened and the crowd rushed in I would have to snatch as many books as possible (hoping the title I was looking for happened to be among them) before the shelves got swept shining-empty within minutes.

For me, learning to feel the special individual significance of any given book took growing up in the years when books were at the same time a rare commodity, an unattainable luxury, and a small, romantic, everyday dream. So, when my friends ask me what it was like back in those years, I tell them to go into our University library, and to find, on one of the thousands of shelves, a book with folded pages, with stains on the paper, and with someone's careless, red-ink notes over the text. I tell them that if upon seeing all that, they feel a strange, inexplicable ball of anger roll up in their throat—they will have known.[61]

The discussion of reading and books in this chapter should make it evident that great military leaders are also great readers. The importance to the young military officer of reading and building a professional library was perhaps best explained by William Lyon Phelps, a professor at Yale University for more than forty years and the owner of a library of more than six thousand books. In a radio broadcast on April 6, 1933, Phelps described the importance of reading and building one's own library:

> The habit of reading is one of the greatest resources of mankind; and we enjoy reading books that belong to us much more than if they are borrowed. A borrowed book is like a guest in the house; it must be treated with punctiliousness, with a certain considerate formality. You must see that it sustains no damage; it must not suffer while under your roof. You cannot leave it carelessly, you cannot mark it, you cannot turn down the pages, and you cannot use it familiarly. And then, someday, although this is seldom done, you really ought to return it.
>
> But your own books belong to you; you treat them with that affectionate intimacy that annihilates formality. Books are for use, not for show; you should

own no book that you are afraid to mark up or afraid to place on the table, wide open and face down. A good reason for marking favorite passages in books is that this practice enables you to remember easily the significant sayings, to refer to them quickly, and then in later years, it is like visiting a forest where you once blazed a trail. You have the pleasure of going over the old ground, and recalling both the intellectual scenery and your own earlier self.

Everyone should begin collecting a private library in youth; the instinct of private property, which is fundamental in human beings, can here be cultivated with every advantage and no evils. One should have one's own bookshelves, which should not have doors, glass windows, or keys; they should be free and accessible to the hand as well as to the eye. The best of mural decorations is books; they are more varied in color and appearance than any wallpaper, they are more attractive in design, and they have the prime advantage of being separate personalities, so that if you sit alone in the room in the firelight, you are surrounded with intimate friends. The knowledge that they are there in plain view is both stimulating and refreshing. You do not have to read them all.

There are, of course, no friends like living, breathing, corporeal men and women; my devotion to reading has never made me a recluse. How could it? Books are of the people, by the people, for the people. Literature is the immortal part of history; it is the best and most enduring part of personality. But book friends have this advantage over living friends: you can enjoy the most truly aristocratic society in the world whenever you want it. The great dead are beyond our physical reach, and the great living are usually almost as inaccessible; as for our personal friends and acquaintances, we cannot always see them. Perchance they are asleep, or away on a journey. But in a private library, you can at any moment converse with Socrates or Shakespeare or Carlyle or Dumas or Dickens or Shaw or Barrie or Galsworthy. And there is no doubt that in these books you see these men at their best. They wrote for you. They "laid themselves out," they did their ultimate best to entertain you, to make a favorable impression. You are as necessary to them as an audience is to an actor, only instead of seeing them masked, you look into their heart of hearts.[62]

CHAPTER 5

Mentorship

How does one develop as a decision maker?
Be around people making decisions.
General of the Army Dwight D. Eisenhower

Several years ago I was a scheduled speaker at the Air Force Squadron Officer's School (SOS) at Maxwell Air Force Base, Alabama. SOS is intended for lieutenants and captains and is the only company-grade course for all branches of the Air Force. The Army, in contrast, has company-grade schools for its officers at Fort Benning for the infantry, Fort Knox for armor, Fort Sill for artillery, Fort Bliss for air defense, and so on.

The man who spoke just before me was an Air Force general who advised the class that to get ahead in the Air Force, you should get yourself a "sponsor and to hitch your wagon to a star." In other words, he was telling them that success depends on whom you know rather than your job performance and what you know. This concerned me, and it also upset the five hundred or so students, who during the subsequent break expressed their disillusionment.

The question of how to succeed in the military is an important one for the younger generation of officers. To answer it, this chapter will explore the careers of some of the twentieth century's most successful admirals. In interviews with seven retired chiefs of naval operations and some other four-star admirals, I asked each whether he thought his success was the result of a mentor. Not one of the admirals who achieved four-star rank—CNOs, chairmen of the Joint Chiefs, or Atlantic or Pacific commanders—believed his achievement in rank and responsibility was because of whom he knew, or the way he parted his hair, his school, his family, or his golf game. All believed their success was based on job performance; outstanding job performance led to knowing the right people and subsequent career advancement.

One of the most perceptive insights into sponsorship came from Gen. Edward C. "Shy" Meyer, Army chief of staff from 1979 to 1983, whom I interviewed in July 1997. Having jumped over fifty-seven senior flag officers for the position, the general preferred the term "mentor" to "sponsor." I agreed that "mentorship" is a better term. Mentorship is associated with "meritocracy," while "sponsorship" is associated with politics.

"First of all," General Meyer said to me,

> you have to define what the components of mentorship are. One component is in the area of guidance, counseling, advice, and teaching. How did you learn from that individual, why did that individual take time to teach you? What guidance, counseling, and advice did you receive? That's one facet of mentorship. The second facet is door opening; it's providing opportunity for an individual. . . . Mentoring in practical terms is all of the things that occur when you get into those two brackets. That's different than your normal relationship can be with your boss or your commander. Your boss or your commander can handle you as a competent, capable individual and tell you what to do and so on without taking the time to teach, advise, counsel, or he can do it without feeling the obligation to open doors for you.[1]

By "opening doors" he meant providing the opportunity for responsibilities and assignments that assist in professional growth. In practical terms, that means seeing that the person being mentored gets the toughest and most demanding jobs and works longer hours than most of his or her contemporaries. And it means taking the time to guide, counsel, advise, and teach that person in preparation for increased responsibility and thus higher rank.

A turning point in the career of Lt. Comdr. Chester W. Nimitz was his assignment to the USS *Maumee* on August 10, 1917, to become engineering aide to then-Capt. Samuel S. Robison, Commander, Submarine Force, Atlantic Fleet. Nimitz's biographer noted: "The new billet proved in some respects the most fortunate of Nimitz's career, for in Robison he acquired a sage advisor, an influential patron, and a lifelong friend. Through the older man's influence, Nimitz shifted the direction of his career away from engineering, which could prove a dead end, and set his feet on the rungs of the ladder to high command. From this point on, he was concerned less with machinery than with people, less with construction and maintenance than with organization, and thus he found his true vocation."[2]

Captain Robison's responsibility was to ready the infant U.S. submarine fleet for operations with our allies in the Atlantic. Initially headquartered in New London, Robison went to Europe in February 1918 and took Nimitz with him as his chief of staff. Their tour in Europe involved meeting with British submarine leaders to study their tactics, including techniques for evading depth charges, and learn their diving methods. The war ended before the U.S. Navy could make a contribution, so the mission "dissolved." At Robison's insistence, Nimitz received a commendation from the secretary of the navy for "meritorious service."[3]

Nimitz's relationship with Robison did not end with World War I, however, as illustrated in a letter dated November 18, 1919, in which Nimitz wrote to his mother: "Admiral Robison, under whom I served as chief of staff in the submarine service, is now commander of the Boston Navy Yard, and he has offered me a job as his industrial aide, whatever that means, and I have told him I would be glad to go, providing he can get the Bureau of Navigation [the name at that time for what became the Bureau of Personnel] to send me there." The assignment did not happen, but it reflected the high esteem in which the two men held one another.[4]

Admiral Robison continued to achieve key responsibilities and was eventually selected to be commander in chief of the Battle Fleet, the second most senior operational command in the U.S. Navy. In that post he was "able to pull a few strings to obtain once more the services of his favorite young officer." Nimitz reported on June 30, 1923, and became

Robison's aide, assistant chief of staff, and tactical officer. It proved to be both a learning experience and an opportunity. Admiral Robison and his wife, who had no children of their own, became "surrogate grandparents" to the Nimitzes' children. The admiral and Nimitz were very close, often taking long walks during which they discussed the Navy's future. In October 1925 Robison received senior operational command as commander in chief, U.S. Fleet (CinCUS), and Nimitz remained his aide, assistant chief of staff, and tactical officer.[5]

The most significant evidence of the Navy's respect for Admiral Robison was his appointment as superintendent of the U.S. Naval Academy in 1928, a post that carried the responsibility for the education of future American naval leaders. He was a superb mentor for Nimitz. His guidance helped develop Nimitz's leadership qualities and prepared him for a stellar career: command of the U.S. Navy in the Pacific in World War II, promotion to five-star rank, and, at the end of the war, appointment as chief of naval operations.

Fleet Adm. Ernest J. King graduated from the Naval Academy in 1901. As his career developed, he aspired in 1925–26 to command a cruiser, but the Bureau of Navigation established a policy that precluded his getting such a command because of his graduation date. He was disappointed at the time, but as events developed, the bad luck became a stroke of fortune.

Rear Adm. William A. Moffett, who had been chief of the Bureau of Aeronautics since its establishment in 1921, became King's mentor. Moffett wanted to interest some senior officers, nonaviators, in naval aviation. It was policy in 1925 that only officers who were pilots could command aircraft carriers, tenders, squadrons, and aviation store establishments, and it became a law by act of Congress in 1926. The Navy had only a few senior officers who had qualified as pilots. Becoming a Navy pilot required two hundred hours of flying time, seventy-five hours of which had to be solo. Moffett persuaded King to enter the program. In January 1927 King entered Pensacola Naval Air Station as a student aviator. Moffett saw to it that the usual ten-month course was compressed into five months, and King received his wings on May 26, 1927. In his memoirs King wrote: "In looking back over fifty years of naval service, the four things that stand out most sharply in [my] memory are the graduation from the Naval Academy, [my] first command at sea, graduation from Pensacola [winning his wings], and the final victory in World War II."[6]

The remarkable career of Adm. Thomas H. Moorer (CNO 1967–70, chairman of the Joint Chiefs 1970–74) is evidence of his character, leadership, and contribution to the Navy's mission to defend the United States. In his oral history Moorer reflected on the men who were his first mentors while he was a midshipman at the Naval Academy:

I have several memories of Admiral Tommy Hart. He was superintendent after Admiral Robison, who was superintendent when I first arrived. Admiral Hart was considered by the midshipmen to be a disciplinarian, which he was. That didn't bother me any. He always was extremely dignified and very firm and insisted on very high standards. Of course, later I had an opportunity to see him in the Dutch East Indies when I was flying in a patrol squadron out there. Then later on when I was chief of naval operations, Admiral Hart became ill, down in the Carolinas, I think. Something down there was giving them some run-around. I heard about it so I sent a plane and some doctors right away to get him. I just thought that Admiral Hart was the kind of man that's hard to find today. He had principles and he stuck with them and he didn't compromise with anybody. As superintendent his objectives were to train young men to be leaders of men and to be gentlemen. He certainly set the pace. So I have nothing but the highest esteem and respect for Admiral Hart, . . . and it's unfortunate that we don't have more people like that today. I always admired him, and I thought he was the kind of a man to emulate.[7]

Admiral Moorer's career in naval aviation actually began at the Naval Academy:

We had what we called "Second Class Summer." The Second Class didn't go on the cruise, so a large part of the summer involved flying in patrol planes at the Academy. Of course, at that time, while we were there, Williams [Maj. Alfred Williams, a famous Navy and Marine Corps aviator] brought down a floatplane with which he was going to try to break the world's speed record and we went out and watched that quite a bit. My class ring, as you may note, shows the propeller and the radial engine. So the motif of the "Lucky Bag" was naval aviation, which I had become vitally interested in. I applied right away, but there again, you were not allowed to go into aviation until you had qualified as a deck watch officer, what we call "top watch," and that is to be able to stand alone in port and at sea.[8]

Admiral Moorer's first cruise exposed him to an officer who was to play a significant role in his career:

I was only aboard for six months. When I went to the *Salt Lake City,* I already had orders to the *New Orleans.* She was being built in the Brooklyn Shipyard in New York. It was a six-month assignment, but my first department head aboard ship was Admiral Jerauld Wright, a wonderful person—I've worked for him several times since, including SACLant, CinCLant, and so on. But he was also president of my selection board to rear admiral. . . . But in any event it gave me an opportunity to qualify for watch and it helped me when I went to the *New Orleans.* I was better qualified to handle many of the assignments.[9]

Another one of Admiral Moorer's early mentors after graduation was a Commander Reeves, a man of initiative and vision who became the Navy's foremost expert on damage prevention.

He went around the ship and disposed of all the flammable material. There was an awful lot of material that would burn like mad. He promoted the development of fireproof paints and things of that kind, scraping off paint where it wasn't necessary. So he just got that done in the nick of time because it was right before World War II. This was his own initiative. The commander in chief of the U.S. Fleet was very high on Commander Reeves and what he was doing in this area. . . .

To give you an example of how he performed, I recall one time he had a fire drill and he decided that the fire extinguishers were totally inadequate. So he called a supply officer and directed him to survey them or dispose of them. The supply officer said, "Commander, I can't do that because the regulations say they must be unfit for use and these aren't unfit for use. They are practically brand new." So Commander Reeves sent for a working party and equipped them with hammers. He just lined the extinguishers up and had these sailors beat them to pieces. He then called the supply officer and said, "Now, do you think they are fit for use?" He said, "No, they're unfit for use." So [Reeves] said, "Well, get rid of them and get me this new kind." That's the way he operated. Of course, he'd be good for five pages in Jack Anderson today. But, by gosh, he got the job done.[10]

Admiral Moorer also learned from Commander Reeves the "hard nose" approach—how to teach humility when it was called for. "For instance," he said,

> . . . we'd have a new group of ensigns come aboard after each graduation at the Naval Academy. After I had been on there a year, a new group came aboard. He called me over and said, "Moorer, I want you to do such-and-such." I've forgotten what it was, but I didn't consider it to be in my realm of responsibility at the moment. I said, "Commander, you've overlooked one thing. I'm the senior ensign on this ship." He said, "There is no such thing."
>
> But he did a hell of a job with that ship. He really was the father of damage control. You see, the basic change that he made was this: in the old days we had fire drills and collision drills and things that were separate and apart from the battle drill. He quite properly reasoned that the time you are most likely to have a fire and collision is during battle. If those drills don't work during battle, they won't work at all. So he rewrote the whole organization. He had in effect a damage control group. Of course, this was done just in time, right before the war. . . . When he had a fire drill, he really had a fire drill. He'd set the ship afire.[11]

Adm. Marc A. Mitscher, commander of a carrier fleet in World War II, was a combat mentor for Moorer.

> At the time Mitscher was at the peak of his career, I was a very junior officer. The main thing I remember about Admiral Mitscher is that he had managed to more or less inject, you might say, a feeling of confidence in the young officers as to their capabilities vis-à-vis the Japanese. Consequently, I believe he was one of the main spark plugs that permitted the carrier forces to succeed as well as they did against the Japanese. He was a quiet man, very methodical, who had a tremendous amount of genuine common sense and with it a tremendous amount of courage and concern for his people. I saw him on two or three occasions in exercises after World War II. He died, however, shortly after the war. . . . In any event, I think he's one of the heroes of naval aviation, and certainly was a man who was in the right place at the right time. We should name a carrier after him.[12]

Adm. Arleigh Burke was another of Moorer's mentors. "Burke was so wonderful to me," he recalled.

> He's always taken an interest in me. Strangely enough, we really didn't cross paths during World War II at all, but subsequent to that time, we've been very closely

associated. . . . I just can't say too much good about Admiral Burke. I don't think anyone has made the same impact on the Navy that he did, certainly not in this century. He represented a combination of the aggressive fighter—31-Knot Burke; the one who was technically competent since he pushed the installation of missiles aboard ship, antiaircraft missiles, SAMs; and he certainly [inspired] not only great respect, but also, I think, great love . . . by all who had anything to do with him because he had a terrific feel for people. He understood people, and he, I think, certainly made a special effort—he was always very curious about why they acted like they did, and he always developed for himself an explanation that satisfied him as to why they acted like they did under certain circumstances and judged people accordingly.

After he became CNO, in particular, I saw him . . . almost daily and worked very hard to try to help him. I remember I was on staff in Norfolk when Admiral Jerry Wright was SACLant, and I was giving a briefing on the nuclear capabilities of the Atlantic Fleet, the nuclear-weapon capabilities, and Admiral Burke was present there. Jerry Wright got called away from the meeting to answer the telephone. It was a call from the CNO saying that the president had approved Arleigh Burke as the next CNO. I was sitting right there and they interrupted my briefing, and Jerry Wright then came up to the microphone and announced that Admiral Burke was going to be the next CNO.

But of course, the fact that he was . . . asked to serve for six years is indicative of what reputation he built up. . . . Arleigh had everything. He had a great sense of humor, great compassion, he was a technical expert in many fields, which most naval officers, to be successful, must be . . . because the Navy's a technical service, not a manpower service. He understood all aspects of naval warfare. By that I mean destroyer operations, amphibious operations, submarine operations, aviation, etc., etc., and was, of course, very, very skillful at bureaucratic infighting here in Washington. Subsequent to his retirement, he has continued this kind of influence and impact. He's one of the great men of our time, to my mind. Of course, having served with Admiral Mitscher like Arleigh did, he had been in the very thick of the most active campaigns conducted by naval aviation.[13]

Admiral Burke was someone an officer was fortunate to have as a role model and mentor. Admiral Moorer spoke about Burke's "deep selection"—that is, his selection as CNO over ninety-two more senior admirals; it caused many problems for the first couple of years:

Well, I think that's always the case when they make a deep selection. Of course, at that time, . . . there was a feeling among many of the civilians in the Defense Department that . . . it might be well to get people who were younger. I think that Tom Gates, who at that time was undersecretary of the navy, later became secretary and then secretary of defense, was a big promoter of that. I don't think that Admiral Burke's statement about it causing him trouble was any different from what it causes in every corporation and every other organization when they reach down and get a junior vice president and make him chairman. That happens all the time in the corporate structure as well as in the military. What all that highlights is that the most difficult task of the senior people in an executive structure is to put the right man in the right place, rather than just . . . take one at a time as they die off. I'm sure it's because people don't like it when they're passed over or skipped over. So they have [a tendency] sometimes, if they happen to be of that character, to not be too cooperative. . . . That doesn't bother me because you just can't be the boss without having to contend with that problem. . . . You can't build the most efficient organization and, at the same time, make everybody totally happy. It can't be done. Everybody thinks he ought to be steering, you know.[14]

Secretary of the Navy Thomas H. Gates was another of Admiral Moorer's mentors. His service as the secretary's aide involved far more than just carrying his boss's briefcase and mixing drinks at cocktail parties.

I had to screen all the papers and keep up with what was going on so I would know when his presence was required, and . . . he would have the necessary backup materials to take with him to these various and sundry conferences, so we got into just about everything you can imagine.

We used to write speeches for him all the time. It was a very, very varied assignment. Of course, we traveled quite a bit. We went to the Orient, Saigon, Bangkok, Philippines, Japan, Korea, and so on; and certainly the same thing in the eastern Atlantic. But it was a very meaningful experience—I would go with him when he had to testify before the Congress, which was useful to me later on. In other words, it wasn't strange to me when I had to go myself as CNO and chairman. . . . I learned a lot from having the opportunity to watch. On occasion, I would go with him up to meetings held by the secretary of defense, Mr. Wilson at the time, and that was helpful, too.

I always went with him to the hearings before Congress. The preparation was very extensive. We would, of course, start out with our budget and then try to develop a series of questions which he might be asked by the Congress. Then we would have a session where we would get people who were knowledgeable and then [have them] ask the questions, and if he didn't give the right answer, we would tell him what it was.[15]

Moorer's duties included writing speeches for Secretary Gates; indeed, he wrote almost all of them. Although he did not enjoy doing it, he "had a pretty good idea of what message [the secretary] was trying to get across. I made his speeches up in modular form, you might say. I tailored the beginning to the audience and the occasion, and in the center you would put in three key points that he was broadcasting at the time or thinking about at the time, and then wind up with a paragraph to terminate the thought. I always tried to make them reasonably short because I think the worst thing you can do is write a long speech."

Admiral Moorer commented that "an aide is not in any kind of a chain of command or executive line, but you can have tremendous influence if you do your homework. You've got to handle it in such a way that you don't develop any antagonism outside toward you. If you do, then what you are doing becomes counterproductive. So I found it very interesting. It was the first time I had been an aide. As a matter of fact, it was the first time I had ever been in Washington." I asked him if his promotion to rear admiral in Washington was a factor in his selection, to which he replied, "Well perhaps. It didn't hurt, I'm sure."[16]

Obviously, promotions are a factor of mentorship, but Admiral Moorer said: "I bent over backward when I was chief of naval operations to make certain I never got involved in the flag officer promotion, and I wouldn't even talk to the president of the board about individuals. I'd never mention an individual to a president of a board prior to the selection."

As CNO, Admiral Moorer had a policy of mentoring promising young officers.

I tried to do that. I found, when I was chief of naval operations, that the most difficult assignment was placing flag officers because you're faced with a situation where you have a limited number to deal with, and . . . you never know what minute one of them is going to have a serious illness and get retired as a result or be plucked out by some other agency of the U.S. government to take a job over in the

White House or State Department. Frequently, you order a man all the way to, say, London, and then three months later wish to hell you hadn't done that; you've got another job that it would be better to assign him to. I spent almost every Saturday from eight o'clock to noon just trying to make certain that we . . . didn't assign a person to this spot without anticipating where he might go next.

It is difficult to do, and the best-laid plans can fall apart. We had a hard time with Bob Baldwin, who was undersecretary of the navy at the time. He wanted to have a board where you would, for all practical purposes, lay out a man's entire career, so you'd know where he was going to be ten years hence. Of course, that's absolutely impossible, because for one thing, they don't all live. They're individuals, but you do have to think about it, and I believe that our system in the Navy is by far the best in terms of promotion. For instance, it's difficult for me to convince people of it sometimes, but I would very meticulously avoid talking to a selection board before they met. I mean, I shook hands with them, some of them had come from CinCLant or whatever, but never did I discuss an individual with them. Many people think the CNO more or less directs promotions. The secretary of the navy does sometimes.

That's what happened to Rickover. You can write up instructions for the board, and you can word it so that you must select one officer who does this and this and this, and there's only one. That happens sometimes from a political point of view. But, speaking only for myself, I never tried to influence them at all. I didn't think it would be fair. We have, I think, the fairest system because you don't have to expose yourself before the same people twice. If you fail this year to get selected, then you've got an entirely new group to look at you the next year.

Asked about his philosophy as CNO on personnel assignments and promotions, Admiral Moorer responded:

I have always had the concept that it's not the people you work for that contribute to your success so much as the people who work for you. I am one that likes to delegate authority to others to do the work. Of course, in that position, in selecting officers for this assignment, if you happen to be an aviator, people suspect you are partial to aviators, if you happen to be a submarine officer, they suspect you are partial to submarine officers, and so on. But people don't believe that I never checked to see whether someone was a Naval Academy graduate. . . . I couldn't tell you whether half the captains were Naval Academy graduates. I didn't know it and I really didn't care so long as he did his job.

Another thing I tried to maintain inviolate was the selection system. I think we have the best selection system of any service or any organization, despite the fact you will see . . . good people, and many will say, "Why didn't he get selected?" But I felt that the integrity of the system was vital insofar as the younger people were concerned and . . . I never talked to the selection board before they met. I never once mentioned to one, "Well, you know old Jack Johnson. He's a good boy and I'd sure like to see him selected." I kept absolutely hands off. I just didn't think it was fair to try to tilt the support like that.[17]

Arleigh Burke's oral history interviewer asked: "Admiral Burke, one of the great challenges of leadership is picking good people and putting them in the right positions. How did you accomplish this?" He responded:

Think among your associates—people you know. You can eliminate 75 percent of them for any position you know a little bit about—probably more than that. Your field comes down pretty fast. You may feel sorry for "poor old Joe" and let him have a crack at it, but if you do, the chances of his failure are much greater. That's one thing you've got to avoid like poison. I had to tell my very best friend he was finished—he couldn't hack it. That didn't mean I didn't like him personally—I did—but he didn't have it. I said, "Sorry, Joe," and he said, "Dammit, you're not giving me a fair shake." Maybe you to lean over a bit too far backward, but you've got to do that so that the good people will realize it all has to do with excellence, not who you know.[18]

Sometimes a single act by a friend can be an act of mentorship that alters a career. After World War II, when Burke was to be reassigned, Capt. William R. Smedley warned him to leave Washington right away.

Later, when I got back from the fleet, six or eight months later, I talked to Smeddy and I said—of course, he never wrote and told me anything—"What was the crisis?"

He said, "Admiral, I overheard Mr. Forrestal asking where you were. He called the General Board to see whether you had been detached and you had been, and he was saying, 'Where in the hell is he?' Then I overheard, I guess Charlie Buchanan, say that he'd found out where you were, and he was told to get you down as soon as possible and you'd be put to work. I don't know what the job was at the time, but now I know. The job you got out of was doing the research on his biography for the Forrestal papers."

That was the luckiest thing. I couldn't have refused the job, and if he'd put me on that it would have been a year or two years doing research on his papers instead of going to sea, and that would have been disastrous.[19]

When Adm. James L. Holloway III (CNO 1974–78) was asked to name his mentors, he replied:

> I just thought the world of Admiral Burke. Whatever he did was right. I also was a great admirer of Admiral Tom Moorer. I was a rear admiral when he was CNO. He called on me quite often for special jobs, and of course, I was flattered. I was director of the Strike Warfare Division in 1967–70, which was probably the best job in the Navy. I had just returned from command of the *Enterprise*. I made two combat tours in command of *Enterprise* and was selected for rear admiral on the first tour. BuPers decided not to send me immediately to a flag job because Rickover said, "I want him to go to sea for the second tour." I had the votes to be selected for admiral the year before, but the aviators on the selection board said, "No, don't select him this year because then he would not get to go to *Enterprise* and that would be a shame, . . . wait until next year." Of course there was always the possibility I wouldn't be picked the next year! . . .
>
> The prize duty assignment for a naval aviator was command of an aircraft carrier. An aviator couldn't make admiral without a successful carrier command. In the 1950s, ever since the end of World War II, when a naval aviator was promoted to captain he was screened for the carrier command list. This was done by an informal selection based upon the performance of the officer and the responsible nature of his assignments. The carrier list, numbered from one to thirty, and these were the top captains in the aviation Navy. The list was in order of merit, and the one who was number one on the list got the finest carrier, usually the newest.
>
> The man who really ran naval aviation personnel was the deputy chief of naval operations. When I made captain, it was Vice Admiral Bob Pirie. He headed a selection board of former carrier skippers who reviewed the records. He was Burke's deputy for aviation. I had been ordered to the Pentagon after my squadron command, and was assigned to be Pirie's executive assistant. This was flattering because I, a commander, relieved a captain in his office. I enjoyed working for Pirie, and I guess I could say he was one of my mentors. He's right up there with Rickover and the lady I worked for in Historic Annapolis after I retired as being the three toughest people I've ever had to work for.[20]

I asked Admiral Holloway to describe the Holloway Plan, a framework within the Navy for mentoring young officers from their initial commissioning through their junior officer years that had been designed by his father, also Admiral Holloway.

During World War II, my father had command of the *Iowa*, the largest and newest battleship in the fleet. Under his command, *Iowa* operated with the fast carrier task forces in the Pacific and eventually participated in the bombardment of the Japanese home islands. He was promoted to rear admiral and when the war ended given responsibility for the demobilization for the Navy.

Demobilization of the armed forces after World War II was a very fast-moving and demanding assignment, and of course it was very important that it be done well. There was enormous pressure to get the troops home without totally destabilizing the services. My father did a good job and caught the eye of the CNO. He was ordered to head up a board in Washington to formulate officer personnel policies and systems for the post–World War II Navy. The program he set up, known as the Holloway Plan, mentored many thousands of young officers over the years.

There were two major components of the plan. One was known as the "Regular NROTC" program. The Naval Academy could produce only a thousand new officers for the fleet each year, only half of the projected requirements for the postwar Navy. So fifty or so top-ranked universities were contracted to produce regular officers for the Navy through their NROTC courses. The candidates were vigorously and competitively selected from physically qualified applicants [who] gain[ed] academic acceptance to one of the Navy's fifty designated universities. When accepted by the Navy and the school, the candidates were enlisted as NROTC midshipmen and paid a monthly stipend as well as having tuition covered by the Navy. The midshipmen could select their own courses as long as they were in the engineering or scientific fields. On graduation from college, these "contract NROTC midshipmen" were commissioned ensigns in the regular Navy and ordered to active duty with the same status and prerogatives of Academy graduates. It was very popular and effective program and within five years copied by both the Army and Air Force. One of my responsibilities as a governor of the Metropolitan Club in Washington from 1988 to 1992 was every Wednesday afternoon to meet with candidates for membership at the club. These candidates were generally young lawyers with the local law firms, investment bankers, corporate executives, and senior government officials. I was truly amazed at the number of these prospective members who asked if I were any relation to the admiral who founded the Holloway Plan. When I answered yes, they would tell me they wouldn't be sitting there today if it weren't for the Holloway Plan. . . . It had put them through college—schools like Princeton, Duke, Cal Tech, and Stanford. After the Korean War and Vietnam the opportunities were so great on the outside, that many of them left the service and became quite successful in their civilian careers.[21]

Another component of the Holloway Plan was designed to overhaul aviation officer input into the Navy. The World War II experience had shown that the best combat pilots were in the nineteen- to twenty-three-year-old age bracket. In a competitive process, fully qualified high school graduates—physically, academically, and with aviation motivation—were selected and sent to designated universities (World War II V-5 schools) with the tuition paid and a stipend furnished by the government. The candidates were commissioned "aviation midshipmen" and ordered to flight training in an active military status. They served as aviation midshipmen for two years and were then promoted to ensign and sent to the fleet. After completing one full tour of sea duty in a squadron, the young officer, now probably a lieutenant, junior grade, would be returned to college at the government's expense to earn a baccalaureate degree.

Admiral Holloway believed that most of these aviation midshipmen remained in the Navy. "The love of flying was an influence. Neil Armstrong, first man on the moon, had been a naval aviation midshipman, and so had astronaut Jim Lovell. Several went on to become four-star admirals. Gus Kinnear was an aviation midshipman who went on to four stars. He was the Navy's chief of legislative liaison and after retirement a vice president of Grumman Aircraft and eventually a college president."[22]

As a junior officer, Adm. William Crowe Jr. (chairman of the Joint Chiefs of Staff 1985–89) was an aide to three senior admirals. One was Vice Adm. Stuart S. Murray, with whom he served for eighteen months. At that time Murray was commander of the submarine force in the Atlantic. Crowe described him as "a marvelous man" and "so considerate and cheerful that he was known throughout the Navy as 'Sunshine.' He was one of the kindest, most gracious men I had ever met; he stood out. In those days, kindness was not a trait too many admirals favored. . . . I remember on one of our trips, we started rushing back to the airplane to take off for our next destination. As he began climbing up, he stopped, telling me, 'I forgot something.' He ran back to the staff car that brought us to our plane, thanked the driver who had taken us to the airport, turned around, and got on the airplane." It is no wonder that Crowe said Murray was "the best model I ever had."

Crow next went to work for Vice Adm. George Clifford Crawford, nick-named "Turkey Neck Crawford" because he was skinny and had a prominent Adam's apple. This tour as aide was not a pleasant one. "I learned a lot from him—what not to do," Admiral Crowe said.

> He was a decision-maker, but he was a "sundowner" because he fired people right and left. He was hard to live with and hard to work with. I thought he was going to fire me a half dozen times. I was aide to him about eight months. I was trying to get out of there. When he came in, Murray said to Crawford, "This aide (meaning me) is leaving, he has to go to a submarine." Turkey Neck called me and said, "I'm not sure I agree with that, I will get you on a submarine, but I've got to keep you until I find an aide." Well, Christ, he didn't find one for six months. Admiral Crawford, during World War II, commanded a submarine division in combat. He knew what he was doing, but he had a short fuse. His motto seemed to be "Never apologize."

Once, Admiral Crowe, said, Crawford inspected a base and "flunked the entire base after giving its hundred-plus buildings a white glove inspection. For three days personnel had nowhere to eat on base because he even closed down the mess hall." But Crowe also commented, "Crawford was imbued with the Navy ethos."

Crowe's third tour as an aide, beginning in September 1958, was with Vice Adm. Bernard Austen, Deputy Chief of Naval Operations for Plans, Policy, and Operations. The aide's responsibility was to coordinate political-military relations with the Departments of Defense and State, the Joint Chiefs of Staff, and the National Security Council. Crowe, who "jumped at the opportunity," noted that the tour with Austin "changed my whole career because I decided I wanted to go to graduate school, and I wanted to get into political-military work." He did go on to graduate school at Princeton University, receiving a PhD in political science.[23]

One of Adm. Robert L. J. Long's mentors, he told an interviewer, was "Hal Bowen, a 'very much older' officer, born in October 1912; he must have been in his forties. He had qualities I wanted to emulate. Of course, he was very mature, but he probably was one of the most perceptive officers that I had known, very much an open mind, easy to talk to. He had the characteristics that I admire: that is, smart, showed great respect for the people working for him, encouraged them to voice their views, rewarded performance."

Later in his career, Long said, he

received a call to come over to be interviewed by the undersecretary of the navy to be assigned as his executive assistant. I never will forget that interview. This was with Robert H. B. Baldwin, and I was to relieve a classmate of mine, David Bagley. The conversation went on for some period of time, and then Bob Baldwin, who subsequently has become a very close friend of mine, said, "Well, Captain, would you like to be the executive assistant to the undersecretary?"

I said, "Well, frankly, no."

That took him aback a little bit, and he said, "Why? I don't understand."

I said, "I'm working for the best program manager in the Department of Defense. I think I have an awful lot to learn from him, and I'd just as soon stay where I am." His response was a classic, and he still reminds me of it today. He said, "Wouldn't you like to learn a little something more than that?"

Well, I came back and I told my boss, Levering Smith, of my interview with Mr. Baldwin. Levering at that time was a heavy cigarette smoker. He took a big drag on his cigarette, blew the smoke out, and said, "Well, I've lost you." Sure enough, within a matter of days I had orders to report to the undersecretary as his executive assistant.

Bob Baldwin was a unique individual and I learned a great deal from him. He's a guy of tremendous drive, energy, almost a compulsive nature to tell people how to do things. He's the kind of guy that gets in a taxicab and invariably will tell the taxicab driver how to get to the airport. He was the undersecretary under Paul Nitze, two rather different personalities. Nitze is almost an academic, loves studies, loves to sit and discuss things conceptually, was very reflective. Bob Baldwin, on the other hand, was a hands-on, let's-get-it-done kind of guy. He loved to get into the details, and is extremely effective when he believes in something and can be very antagonistic if he does not believe in it. He didn't always get along with the OpNav admirals. They looked upon him as somewhat too independent at times. He asked a lot of hard questions. He was not one that took everything on blind faith. Sometimes his personality was such that he rubbed people the wrong way just by his rather aggressive personality. I established a good rapport with him. I wouldn't say that I'm a terribly aggressive personality, but he and I established a rapport early, but I was not a yes man. I felt absolutely no compulsion about telling him where I thought he was wrong, and he appreciated that. Obviously, I told him that not in a large crowd.[24]

Long was exposed to other mentoring influences during this period as well in the form of outstanding civilians in the assistant and deputy secretary positions. He reminisced:

> At that time McNamara was the secretary of defense. . . . When I reflect on the presidential appointees—Paul Nitze, Bob Baldwin, Chuck Baird, Bob Frosch, Jim Bannerman—these were people who had achieved a measure of success outside the government. Paul Nitze was . . . wealthy in his own right. Bob Baldwin was a young, upcoming executive at Morgan Stanley. Chuck Baird was a young executive at Exxon Standard Oil of New Jersey. Chuck Bowsher was with Arthur Anderson, successful there, and Frosch had come from DARPA.
>
>   . . . I learned a great deal being exposed to such talented men. Although people will criticize Robert McNamara for a variety of things, one . . . great strength was that he tried to select the very best people he could, regardless of their political affiliation. Of course, as we all know, we don't always do that today. So these people were recruited . . . not from congressional staffs, but they came from being successful people on the outside, many in the financial community.
>
>   When these people left office, Bob Baldwin went back to being the chairman and CEO of Morgan Stanley in New York, probably the most prestigious international investment house in the world. After Chuck Baird left the under secretary's job, he went on to become the chairman and CEO of International Nickel. Chuck Bowsher went back to Arthur Anderson, and, of course, he currently is the comptroller general of the United States. Bob Frosch has also enjoyed continued success. So it was a very impressive bunch of civilians that we had up there.

Admiral Long had talented people working for him, as well, and he tried to be a good mentor to them. Many went on to do well in their careers. They included "Jim Flatley, who was the famous Admiral Flatley's son. He had some younger assistant executive assistants, Vernon Clark, who is now a chief of naval operations; Jerry Smith was then a commander and became a two-star. I also had a young man by the name of Commander Paul David Miller, who was sort of the administrative assistant, who became a four-star. So those are the kind of people that you surround yourself with, and if you screw it up, you're pretty dumb. Wonderful talent."[25]

Admiral Long's guiding principle was that it was in the best interest of any officer to serve where he could make the greatest contribution to the Navy. He offered as an example Arthur S. Moreau Jr., a lieutenant at that time, who wanted to be in nuclear submarines but was turned down by Rickover.

I think that he always resented the fact that he was not chosen as a nuclear officer. But he clearly, I think, among the weapons officers of all of those early crews, he was considered to be the number-one guy. He was the most knowledgeable. He and I had conversations about his future, and early on I told him: "Your future is not in the submarine community. My recommendation is get out, establish yourself in the surface Navy. You'll be outstanding there." And that's what he did.

At that time Rickover was offered . . . the very best, and blindfolded he could almost just point to that one or that one. Essentially, they were all outstanding, and I think he had to have a certain number that didn't make it. Because I can assure you that as far as Moreau versus some of the nuclear-trained officers I had of the same vintage, Moreau was equal or superior. So it's one of those things. Rickover had to have this mystique that he was somehow a mystic in being able to pick these people. But as I say, if you're sent over only the top 5 percent, it's hard to go wrong.[26]

Admiral Long's intuition was sound. Moreau benefited from his mentorship; he went on to serve as commander in chief of Allied Forces, Southern Europe, achieving the rank of admiral.

I asked CNO Adm. James D. Watkins about mentors. He replied:

Admiral Clarey was one of my first mentors. He went on to be vice CNO and then commander in chief, U.S. Pacific Fleet. He was a Navy Cross winner, a fabulous person, as was his wife. He was not only great professionally, but great personally and socially. He never forgot a name. He would remember Ensign Watkins, both he and his wife. He was someone you would want to emulate. He was my first division commander. We were fortunate indeed. He then went on to take command of our squadron of submarines. I was blessed by being with World War II–experienced officers who had demonstrated their capabilities to lead men. . . . They sank enemy ships and did things right—taking risks, yes, but with the idea, "I take this risk, win, and bring my sailors safely back home again." That was the feeling you got from people like Chic Clarey. He was inspirational to me and one of the reasons why I decided to make a career of it. Initially, I did not think that I was ever going to stay in the Navy after the war ended in 1945. But having just entered the Academy that year, . . . I didn't like to be a quitter.[27]

Another of Admiral Watkins's mentors was Capt. Gene Fluckey:

I was a division engineer on the submarine tender in Gene Fluckey's division. Gene was a Medal of Honor winner, skipper of *Barb* during the war, a submarine that penetrated the antisubmarine nets in Tokyo Bay. He sent a select crew ashore and blew up a railroad bridge, incredible stuff. He was one of the great World War II submariners. He was my division commander when I was aboard the new diesel submarine *Volador*, and he had me ordered up to his staff. He thought that I was a bright light, I guess. He was a mentor by setting an extraordinary example. . . . He was a terrific leader . . . natural and friendly. You could talk to him and he listened to you. For example, we both had an idea on how to defeat the first passive acoustic torpedoes. The U.S. was just then bringing the Mark 18 torpedo on line. Other nations, Russians in particular, were fielding passive torpedoes as well, ones that chased the noise of the submarines, crew noises, and so forth. So, we figured a way to decoy it. We went out and tested our device. We shared ideas and he was quick to pick up on them and move. I wrote an inscription for his book, *Thunder Below*, about how he is the kind of person with whom I would want to go to war. Put him in charge of a submarine and I'll get on it, because he is going to win and come back.

Admiral Watkins believed that he had a responsibility to mentor future leaders:

Your leadership qualities mature significantly once you have experienced the breadth of duties I was privileged to have both at sea and shore. For example, I received a graduate degree in engineering from the Navy's postgraduate school. I first began to understand the technology, the excitement, and to see the larger picture and the worth of the Navy. I was, in turn, able to convey this newfound understanding to my sailors, the kids that came under my command. Rickover's idea was that his number-one job, for example, was to educate and train the people that came under him. I learned from serving under him that . . . a professional's number-one job [is] to train his men properly, whether in war fighting or in how to motivate his subordinates, or how to maintain his ship so as to keep its state of war-fighting readiness high. His leadership techniques to get there, however, were unique to Rickover. While I would never directly apply the Rickover techniques as my own, I agreed with his principles of leadership, which I learned over my three and a half years working for him. . . . He would accept only the best and brightest from those the Navy sent to him for interview. Those on the margin were invariably rejected. I believe that some of these "marginals" could have been successful nuclear power candidates because of the . . . intense education and training regimen that Rickover demanded. This was often a point of disagreement between [us].[28]

Adm. Stansfield Turner, who was selected by President Jimmy Carter to head the CIA, might have left the Navy early in his career, but a good mentor persuaded him to stay.

The first time I wanted to get out of the Navy was after winning the Rhodes scholarship. I went to the Mediterranean on a cruiser, and the cruiser came back from the Mediterranean and happened to go into New York. I was now two months from going to Oxford and I went up to see [Ferd] Eberstadt. I said, "I don't like this Navy. I had a terrible skipper. I want to postpone my Rhodes scholarship a year, which will complete my total obligation to the Navy, . . . then I'll go to Oxford a free man. Then I can do what I want." Eberstadt looked me in the eye. I'll never forget this. He said, "Turner, we've worked hard to get you this Rhodes scholarship. You get your ass to Oxford." Those were his exact words. I went to Oxford. If it hadn't been for my mentor, I'd have been a civilian.[29]

Turner had other important mentors as well.

The next and the most important mentor in my career was Vice Admiral William R. Smedberg. He was aide to Secretary Forrestal and had a hand in my competing for the Rhodes. I mean he knew about me and the Rhodes thing. When I came back from Korea in 1953, I knew I was coming up for my first shore duty. I came to Washington from the West Coast and started walking around the Pentagon. Where can my education be put to use here as opposed to going to a recruit training center, or marching people around, or doing something silly?

By happenstance I ended up in then-Captain William R. Smedberg's office in the Office of Political Military Affairs, which was the liaison with [the] State Department. I walked into his office and stood at his desk and said, "I'm Lieutenant Turner, sir." He said, "Yes, Stansfield, brigade commander, Rhodes scholar." This was eight years after I'd seen him! Within twenty minutes, he had called the Bureau of Personnel and told them, "I want this young officer on my staff." At that point, there were no lieutenants in the Pentagon except in minor administrative jobs. It wasn't done in those days, but he changed that. I came to work for Smedberg, and there's nobody I've ever known who had a greater love or sense of people than he. I mean the guy . . . remembered my name eight years after the fact!

When I was working for Smedberg, one day a friend came in to see me, another lieutenant. We're standing there talking and Smedberg happens by and he looks at this lieutenant and said, "I know you. Where do I know you?" And this lieutenant says, "Well, one night when you were captain of your cruiser, I was standing on the pier in Vilesmash waiting for a liberty boat to take me back to my destroyer. You came along and you had your gig there. You said would you like a ride? You dropped me off at my destroyer." Smedberg didn't remember his name, but remembered his face. There were four officers standing there with us, and they couldn't believe this. Smedberg set such a role model.

. . . The first job Smedberg gave me in the Pentagon was to tell me, "I'm going to give a speech this morning to a group of admirals. You're going to sit in the back row and you're going to take notes and when it's over, you're going to tell me what I did wrong and I don't want you just to tell me it was good." This kind of model was just terribly important to me. After he had had me there for six or nine months, and I was apparently doing well for him, he went to the chief of personnel, telling him: "I want to chair a committee to downgrade billets, by assigning lieutenants to the Pentagon. I've proved it will work with Turner. We've got to have some younger officers in here on the Navy staff." They did and they went through every office, and if it was a commander's job, they said, "We'll make it a lieutenant's job." They brought in thirty or forty lieutenants. Now, of course, they're common. It was a real phenomenon in the Navy Department, and I was the catalyst for this change.[30]

I asked Adm. Frank B. Kelso II (CNO 1990–94) about mentorship during his career. "It's impossible to run any kind of personnel system without having some support from the people you work for," he told me.

I had my first job as an officer out of the submarine world as an executive assistant to Admiral Isaac Kidd, when he was commander in chief, Atlantic [CinCLant]. It was a very good job for me. Did Admiral Kidd open any doors for me as far as promotion is concerned? I don't think so. He just wasn't that type of individual. Would he tell you if you asked him what kind of officer is Kelso? Yes, he told you that—what he thought. He openly said that his job was to teach me, and he spent a lot of time providing me with information that was of use to me in latter parts of my career.

When mentorship became an issue with the leadership chair at the Naval Academy several years ago, Kidd just didn't like the word "mentor" at all because he felt that mentor meant you were trying to push an individual for promotion, and he felt the right word was "instructor," or "teacher," or "trainer," not "mentor."[31]

Mentorship is really a controversial issue in the Navy. What does a mentor do for you? Does a mentor shepherd your career? Does that mean that every guy that gets out of Annapolis or OCS gets a mentor assigned to him? It has a connotation in the Navy that you're going to try to get him promoted; contrast this with an instructor or adviser to provide the young people information and knowledge about how to do the job better. If the latter is a mentor, I like it. If a mentor is trying to get me promoted or trying to get my counterpart promoted because he knows somebody, then I'm not very much in favor of the mentor idea.[32]

As our interview continued I described my earlier conversation with Gen. Edward C. Meyer and his philosophy on mentorship (above). Admiral Kelso's response was:

The "open doors" part of it bothers me because it implies whoever is the highest rank that I work for provides the greater opportunity, like a mentor seeing that I get assigned to the right jobs. That doesn't mean I'm better than anybody else, it just happens to mean that I got that job because of whom I knew. I believe the role General Meyer talks about, instruction and counseling, is absolutely there, but every officer has that responsibility to teach their subordinates. . . .

I tried to use my senior subordinate leaders to assist in identifying those who would be the most successful. You can't know everybody, you don't have the ability to know everybody that well, so you need, in my judgment, other leaders to tell you what kind of leaders their subordinates are, what kind of leaders they think will provide the greatest success in the next assignment.

At least twice a year the four-stars met so that I could hear their personal input on who should be assigned to jobs needing to be filled through the process with each reassignment. If we changed jobs and selected someone for a new job, it was discussed. What I'm trying to say is that I felt, to be fair to the officers, that I needed to hear what the other senior Navy leaders thought of them.[33]

Mentorship also came up in my interview with Adm. Carlisle A. H. Trost (CNO 1986–90), who offered his own ideas on mentoring.

To me, a mentor is first of all a leader who is responsible for developing those subordinate to him. The concept of a mentor as somebody who says, "You are my guy, and I am going to take care of you for the rest of your life," I don't like that. I disavow that as a concept that is valid, although it is a very popular one. Mentors to me were guys like Lando Zech, whom I was first exposed to when he was my company officer at the Naval Academy, then with the rank of lieutenant. Another major influence . . . that I considered a mentor was a man named Shannon Cramer. Shannon, who retired as a vice admiral, was a diesel and nuclear submariner. He was my first submarine commanding officer, on *Sirago,* which was a diesel-powered . . . sub.[34]

Asked how he would describe Cramer's leadership, why he admired him, and which of Cramer's qualities he wanted to emulate, Admiral Trost responded:

First, was his consideration for people. He was an exceptionally competent professional, not dashing, but solid, a very active leader and a forthright man. He was extremely honest and he had the highest possible integrity. When Shannon was relieved at a change of command which took place about a year after I reported in, I don't think there was a dry eye on the deck when he walked along between two rows of sailors and shook everyone's hand and left. One of the sailors told me: "He never made us do anything. We did things for him because we didn't want to do it wrong and let him down."

On my first sub with him, a diesel boat, there was a crew of seventy-eight, eight of whom were officers. He made a point to "walk the ship," which was very important to get the "feel." It is important on any ship, but in a submarine even more so. He made a point of walking through the entire ship, which is not too difficult in a sub, but he did it several times a day. He knew everybody onboard, and knew something about each man there, . . . about his family and his professional development. He had a great interest in the professional development of the people who worked for him. He was extremely helpful to all of us, but he could be a taskmaster. I never had to see that side of him because he was satisfied with my own performance. But he was just extremely concerned about people, a good people man, more than perhaps any other person that I know of.

People are the key to any officer's success. Even a lousy officer can be made to look good by good people. The officer who has concern for his people, and clearly evidences that concern, gets from his people a degree of performance that sometimes they don't even know they have in them.

As CNO, Admiral Trost tried to pass on to his aides what he had learned about mentorship.

> In meetings and briefings, at my discretion, my executive assistant came in and I encouraged anybody else—the officers on my immediate staff—to attend my meetings. But, specifically, the one that I brought in was the aide. The aide does lots of things, and it's a somewhat thankless job. The responsibilities of my aide were more than just social. I felt the best way to develop these young guys, and I had three, was to get them in there so they would see what was going on, and so they would see the thought process. This was mentorship on my part, to help them along and get in and keep them in sync on what is happening. They were present in my meetings with three-stars, two-stars, and my senior executive council. The captain would also sit in on those meetings to keep others as informed as possible.

Did Adm. Charles R. Larson, former superintendent of the Naval Academy, have a mentor in his remarkable career? Not really, he told me.

> My career was extremely unusual in that I . . . never really had a mentor. I never . . . worked for any high-level people or people who went on to senior levels of command until I was an admiral or captain. I only had one aide job, and that was to the president, Richard M. Nixor. So I wasn't aide to an admiral at some point early in my career where I kind of stayed attached to that admiral. My first staff job was as commodore of a submarine squadron. It was comprised of two nuclear submarines, a diesel research sub, two submarine rescue vessels, all the Dietz emergence vehicles. I was stationed in San Diego, and my command was spread out from there. So I really started picking up mentors as I finished my major command, my squadron command, and headed back for Washington, D.C. Then I started to become influenced by people like Bob Long and Vice Admiral Chuck Griffis, Jim Watkins, later on, Carl Schultz, folks like that.[35]

I inquired of Adm. Jay L. Johnson (CNO 1986–90), "Who are your mentors, or people who, in your naval career, you wanted to emulate? What qualities did they have that had an impact upon you?"

> The officers that set the best example for me were those who looked after their people. Probably the most indelible imprint ever made by a leader was a wonderful human being and a great naval officer—Rear Admiral John Barrow, now deceased. He was a mentor of the class of 1949, U.S. Naval Academy, a fighter

pilot, and an extraordinary leader. He was the commanding officer of USS *Oriskany*, CVA-34, back in Vietnam. I was a young lieutenant (jg) fighter pilot flying F8-J Crusaders off *Oriskany*. Captain Barrow was our CO and was impressive to look at, but he was also a man of great substance. . . . I was just a kid, a jg I remember . . . walking down the passageway of *Oriskany* one night, and here comes the captain. In those days, when the captain came along, I hit a bulkhead at attention. He called me by name! My first name! I had on a name tag, but not with my first name on it. I had on a flight suit, as I recall. I found out later that Captain Barrow used a picture book to study his men. He learned who we were.

He was sending us into combat every day, and it was important to him that he made that personal connection, and he did. I thought, what a wonderful trait and what a great example of caring for your people. When we got finished with a line period and went to the Philippines, for example, or wherever we were going to get a little bit of R&R, as we taxied the aircraft up to the catapult to fly off the ship, it wasn't the catapult officer taking our salutes and firing us off the deck; it was Captain Barrow. He taught me a lot about how to be a leader.[36]

Chief Petty Officers are also important mentors. In a commencement address given at the Citadel in 1988, Adm. William J. Crowe Jr. told the student graduates, many of whom were about to enter military service: "I would recommend that early in the game every ensign latch on to the leading petty officers in your unit and absorb their wisdom. You will benefit greatly from what experience has taught them and the depth of their knowledge. If you are genuinely willing to learn, they will be happy to share it with you. In return they will expect enlightened leadership."

Fleet Adm. Ernest J. King (CNO during World War II) learned as a midshipman at the Naval Academy the importance of learning from the enlisted personnel. One morning he was responsible for taking the market boat—a four-oar dinghy—into Provincetown. Steering, using a straight-cross till and tiller ropes, was his responsibility. It was a challenge to manage, and he missed the landing because of a strong tide. He reflected of the experience: "The next time I also missed, and I shall always remember how the acting coxswain, who was an old seaman, coached me on how to get the boat alongside the float. There was a good example of the courtesy of the 'Old Navy,' and I have never forgotten that to this day. Indeed, I was helped very much by many other enlisted men who knew what to do, especially in engineering, but also in seamanship."[37]

Admiral Trost benefited from the mentorship of his first chief petty officer.

I was a new ensign, fresh out of the Naval Academy, aboard a destroyer. . . . When I first came to the ship, I was assigned as the antisubmarine warfare [ASW] officer of a ship that was ASW oriented, and was especially built for that purpose. . . . They were World War II long-hull destroyer designs . . . modified to carry more of an antisubmarine warfare capability, . . . and there was a special experimental fire control system. Two ships of this type were built in 1949, . . . *Robert A. Owens* and . . . the *Carpenter.* There was one on each coast, and I was assigned to the *Owens,* a destroyer, in Norfolk, Virginia. I was initially sent off to eight weeks of antisubmarine warfare officers' school down in Key West, Florida. I came back to the ship, and we deployed to the North Atlantic, and then to the Mediterranean, and I was the antisubmarine warfare officer and assistant gunnery officer. This was in 1953. About . . . three months after I had been aboard, I was called in by the exec one day and told, "You are going to be the navigator."

Well, navigators were normally more senior than a new ensign onboard, and I was one of the newest. He said that the exec was technically the navigator, and he would sign the logs. The "official navigator" had been a motor machinist's mate in World War II and was commissioned during [the war], . . . and, as an engineering expert, all he had ever served prior to this tour was in engineering departments. So he said, "I don't know anything about navigation, but we have Chief Glasgow here who is a chief quartermaster, and he is really the navigator." . . . Chief Glasgow taught me an awful lot. He was an amazing guy, a man of few words, and very competent professionally. He taught me more about navigation than I had ever been exposed to before, certainly more than at the Naval Academy. I became a reasonably good navigator. This chief petty officer was clearly a mentor for me.

There was a second petty officer who was a mentor for me. I also became the gunnery officer slightly later on the same ship. I became a gunnery officer because we were getting ready for a short overhaul period up in Philadelphia, to install some new equipment. The gunnery officer had been reassigned, and his replacement had not yet arrived. So I simply fleeted up to become the gunnery officer, and that was fortunate. Again, I had a chief petty officer, a chief gunner's mate, who had been my division chief in my gunnery division. He was quite a fine gent. I was still

a fresh-faced new ensign, and one day at morning quarters, where I had addressed
my troops, he said he would like to see me in the gun shack. The gun shack was a
little two-by-four—literally two-by-four—office up next to the after stack on the ship
on the 0-1 level. I thought that was a funny tone for a chief to use to an officer, "I
would like to see you." I thought I had better go.

So I went on up and said, "What is on your mind, Chief?" And he said,
"Something has got to change or one of us has got to go." I said, "Oh. That
sounds pretty serious. Be more explicit." He said, "You are the division officer
and I am the division chief. There are some things that you ought to do and some
things that I ought to do. You are trying to do too many of the things that I am
supposed to be doing." He said that he could handle this division without me if
he had to. So it was clear to me that I was the one he figured might have to go.
So I said, "Let's be a little more specific, Chief. Where am I getting into your business?" He was specific and he was right. The specifics were things like record
keeping and specific counseling of people. He felt that I should, if I had a problem with somebody's performance, deal with it through him, and go through
him, and he was right.

We did not have the cream of the crop at that point in time. It was just at the
tail end of the Korean War. We were starting to release people. A lot of people in
the crew, the experienced ones, had signed on just to stay on for that last trip to
the Mediterranean, and then they were leaving the Navy. In many cases they were
petty officers who had served in World War II and had come back in during the
Korean War on recall. So I had a very experienced man who was just frustrated as
the devil with me because I was basically getting into his business. I was playing division chief instead of being the division officer, and so he told me to do my job. "You
are doing your job all right," he said. "Stop doing mine." I thought that was really
great advice. . . . He really was a mentor to me. He was helpful in that sense, because
he was the first guy who ever "caught me up." I give him a lot of credit for squar-
ing away young Ensign Trost and putting him on the right path, so I put a lot of
faith in petty officers. There are some very superb young men and women now
serving this Navy, and when one gives them their lead, and stresses them to the
maximum extent of their competence, they do a really fine job.[38]

Adm. Robert L. J. Long likewise related a meaningful experience he
had with a chief petty officer:

The first day that I was the F Division officer [on the *Colorado*], I talked to the
men at morning quarters and told them I was their new division officer. After

quarters, Chief King came up to me and he said, "Well, Mr. Long, you're the new division officer. I want you to know I'm going to make you a good division officer. The only thing I ask is don't screw it up." That is the attitude of some of the finest chiefs I've known. That is, they consider that they are the ones that train these young officers to be good division officers. Chief King was, in fact, a great adviser to me.

I'm not the most patient guy going. I remember one time we had a problem with one of the main computers. Of course, the computers in those days were wheels and levers. We had one of these main battery computers down, and I wanted to get the damn thing fixed. I kept coming in and buzzing in there and would ask, "What are you doing? How are you doing?" Chief King finally took me aside and said, "Mr. Long, we're working our ass off on this thing. Your coming in here and fussing at us is not doing any good. When this thing is fixed, I'm going to tell you. Do me a favor and how about taking a walk up around on the deck. It's not going to get fixed any faster from your constantly checking on progress." . . .

The chief of the boat is a unique job in submarines. He is the senior enlisted man, and speaks for the crew. His boss is the exec, and the exec normally gives orders and direction for the crew through the chief of the boat. The crew looks to the chief of the boat for direction and guidance. He's sort of a father/mother figure. In every submarine that I have served on—the *Corsair,* the *Cutlass,* the *Sea Leopard, Patrick Henry, Casimir Pulaski*—all of those chiefs of the boat have really been outstanding, and they've been good friends of mine. There is no comparison to other parts of the Navy. I think one of the reasons why there's such a normally good feeling between the crew and officers and the commanding officer is that they all understand that their well-being depends on each other. Any one of those guys can really screw it up for everybody. Therefore, if you don't feel that a certain guy is trustworthy, that's a bad situation, and you'd better get rid of him.[39]

I asked Admiral Holloway if he thought being a Navy junior had given him a good foundation for a Navy career and how he learned the value of petty officers.

No, I don't think so. I have to say that my class was poorly prepared at the Naval Academy to go to the fleet. Perhaps it was the loss of the fourth-year cruise; because of the war we graduated early. When I left the Naval Academy, I really didn't know the organization of a Navy ship. The first ship I went to was a destroyer under construction. I was going to be the assistant gunnery officer. Shortly after I reported aboard, the exec said, "Go up to the shipyard and bring down some blank watch quarter and station bills." Well, as far as I knew, that could have been money, or it could have been posters. It could have been anything. I didn't want to say I didn't know what he meant. So, as soon as I could, I asked the chief yeoman, "What's a watch quarter and station bill?" And he told me. That was my first introduction to the fact that the absolute source of practical lore in the Navy was experienced petty officers.

When I was a new ensign, my position during sea detail was on the fantail. I had charge of a division, which was about fifty sailors. A second-class boatswain's mate was the senior petty officer. I knew absolutely nothing about how to handle a destroyer's lines when getting under way and tying up to a pier. Yet that is what my division was responsible for doing. Initially, there wasn't anything I could do during a sea detail except stand there and watch the bosun, and I realized it was my job to watch him direct the men of the division to handle the lines.

One day this petty officer came up and said, "We got a guy who's a real misfit, Ensign Holloway, and we need to get rid of him. Will you take care of it?" Then I began to realize another role I must fulfill. I was the go-between between the petty officers and the more senior officers. I went to the executive officer with the petty officer and said, "We've got to get rid of this guy. He's a misfit." The exec said, "Okay, Holloway. We'll take care of it."

It began to dawn on me that my main responsibilities were to wait, watch, and learn, and not to interfere with the petty officers until I had learned enough to be sure I knew what I was doing. With all that, I was still responsible for my division doing the proper thing on the fantail. I just got to use my common sense in how I could trust what he was doing.[40]

After discussing the role senior officers had played in his development, Adm. Thomas B. Hayward (CNO 1978–82) told me:

Without any questions in my mind, in my career development, the senior chief petty officers had as much influence on my ability to grow, mature, judge, and deal with whatever was coming along as any group I served with. This was from an ensign on. I worked with a number of fabulous chief petty officers. There is a whole batch of them out there who are great, great professionals. They're a wonderful measuring stick, and they'll be straightforward with you at all times. You can learn an enormous amount by working with them, learning from them, knowing what was going on at the deck plate level, which is where the action really is. So, I start from that premise.

Of course, in your squadron, you're with them every day. I'll give you an example I'll never forget. I was in a fighter squadron at the time as the maintenance officer. I was a lieutenant. This would be the late 1950s, I guess. We were introducing the F8U Crusader into the fleet, and I was in the squadron that was doing that, the precursor to the RAG concept. I had been a test pilot at Patuxent River, and I did some test work on the F8U, so I was one of the first group of guys ordered to this squadron. We always had a maintenance concern, [the F8Us] being brand-new airplanes. . . . I recall we had some real maintenance difficulty with one particular aircraft. I turned to one of our chiefs to see what could be done after we had struggled unsuccessfully for some time with it and I said, "All right, let's go get the experts and bring them over here." "Well, now, Lieutenant," he said, "you're talking to the experts." Man, was he ever right. I'll never forget that. He was one of the best mechanics we had, and I had really put him down unintentionally. From then on we were communicating all the time. I really got a lot out of that experience. From that point on I learned to listen to my chiefs. . . . These are the guys that have the real experience who make the deck plates work. Officers come and go on a job for a year here or two years. Chiefs are there for a career.[41]

Sometimes the chief may be the only one aboard with the knowledge needed for a crucial repair. Adm. Kinnaird McKee remembered such an occasion when his submarine had a mechanical malfunction while on a special operation:

The obvious thing to do would have been to turn around, go back into port, and fix it. The captain (Bill Behrens) said, "If we go back we'll never get out of there. Let's fix it here [at sea]," so we did that. We replaced the seal, under way, without removing the periscope. I don't think anybody has ever done that before or since. When the repair was complete, the periscope was actually easier to train, and tighter. We got through the entire special operation with that seal—even though the scope was up a good 90 percent of the time. After leaving the forward area, we came up to send our operational summary and the scope froze solid. We could get it down, but we couldn't train it. Our jury rig repair had served well—but no longer than it had to.

I've talked about Bill Behrens before. We all learned a great deal from him. His decision at that critical time was characteristic. "We've got a mission to perform; we're not going back into port. McKee, go fix it."

"But, sir, we'd have to pull—"

"Don't tell me about that; just go fix it."

And fix it we did. Most other skippers would have turned around and gone back into port. It took about twelve hours to repack the scope. We got very wet. The lifesaver was the chief. I didn't do the repair by myself by any means. I can't remember the senior petty officer's name. He was the key to the repair success. None of us had ever seen the inside of the new seal. We had a fairly good draft instruction book and a spare boot. We were able to stop the leak.[42]

Admiral Moorer's remarks summed up the important role of the petty officer in maintaining the Navy's stature:

Our sailors were sharp. No one was allowed ashore unless every button was in place, their shoes shined, their hair was cut and [they were] shaven, their hat was on just right, and so on. The point was that this was all taken care of by petty officers. The authority was delegated to the chiefs and the chiefs were told, by gosh, we want those sailors looking good when they go ashore. That's all you had to say.

When I was in my first fighter squadron after I got my wings, the chief's name was Ellington. Ellington now lives in Annapolis. We called him Duke, of course, because every Ellington was Duke. But the time I was in that squadron, for three years, we never had a court-martial. As I recall, we only had captain's mast about three times. Ellington was given authority, and if he wanted to put a young sailor's liberty card in his pocket, he could do it. Or if he wanted to give him about five mid-watches, he could do that, too.

Admiral Moorer had a great appreciation for the innovativeness of the chiefs:

I think that the American sailor is one of the most adaptable and innovative individuals in the world. I'll tell you an experience I had in World War II. There was a field right outside of Darwin, Australia, called Bachelor Field. That's where the Australians had their fighters in 1941 and 1942 in the very beginning of the war when the Japanese came down and captured Java and the Indies. . . . There was a General Wurtsmith in the Army Air Corps—as a matter of fact, there's a big airfield named after him now in the United States. But he was in command of the Army Air Corps contingent. . . . We had a few communications units over there, too. We—the Navy—had planes sometimes coming through there.

Well, I went over there one day, and this old Navy chief in this unit—they had everything. There was the Navy sitting in a screened area to eat in, and the flies and insects over there were unbelievable. But they were sitting there all ensconced behind this screen. They had already put up a shower which was made out of 55-gallon fuel drums with block and tackle, a most ingenious way of starting the water and everything, and getting the water in the tank. They didn't have an icebox, but they had built a beer cooler, which was nothing more than a hole in the ground with leaves on it that they sprinkled water on continuously. Of course, the water evaporated and cooled the beer. But they had all this going, and across the way the Army Air Corps had flies were just buzzing all around their place; they didn't have any place to take a shower; they hadn't really been equal to the occasion. But I'll always remember that as long as I live—I was just a lieutenant at the time—how those sailors in nothing flat had set up shop just as if they were back in the middle of the United States. . . . Generally speaking a ship is nothing more than an iron box full of machines, and sailors are always welding, sawing, cutting, boring holes in the bulkheads and running pipes and electric wires, and shifting the water lines and working on the water fountain and the drains, and so on. This goes on all the time, and they are trained in damage control—how to fix the pipe if it's shot up and so on—and it's natural for them to know how to, let us say, convert wood and iron to their own use, and they are pretty good at it.[43]

During his assignment in Korea as a delegate on the Military Armistice Commission, Adm. Arleigh Burke had an interesting experience with his chief yeoman:

Although the story of Chief Yeoman George Guzowski has not a thing to do with Op-30, I'd better talk about him a bit because all of the correspondence with him was during my tour in Op-30 and if I don't tell it now, I won't be reminded of it any other time.

Guzowski was the chief yeoman on the staff of Com-CruDiv 5 when I took command of that division. When I received orders to the military armistice delegation I was informed we would have to form a supporting staff and it would be much easier if we each could bring several officers, yeomen, and radiomen from our present jobs. That made sense for we would be working with people who knew the routines of our own services. So before I left the *Los Angeles,* I called in Guzowski and asked him who the best yeoman was in the ship. He proudly stated he guessed he was. Then I told him to get ready to go with me to Munsan-ni when I was ordered to go and that I hoped he would improve in taking dictation for there was going to be a lot of that in that new job. Then he tried to get out of it by saying I should know better than to believe him when he was boasting, there was a better yeoman who was a first class and he could take dictation real good. No soap. He added that he got land sick, he didn't like the Army, he was needed in his present job, and other similar very good reasons. It didn't work.

After we had our camp shaken down and got a little bit squared away, Guzowski found himself as the chief yeoman for the negotiating team, but he griped all the time about living in a tent, the lack of heads and too many latrines, nobody in the other services worked hard enough or knew what to do. I always agreed with him and gave him dictation until he was mighty good. Among his other duties he always brought my own mail to my tent after I had returned from Kaesong. I soon found out why. My wife, Bobbie, didn't know anything about the Army either and thought I might starve out there, so she had formed the nice habit of sending me a box of candy or cookies about every three or four days. If Guzowski handed me a package, I always opened it and gave him part of whatever it was. He liked cookies even better than I do—broken cookies included—and probably ended up with his half, all right.

One of the oversights of the Army in establishing the camp at Munsan-ni was no barber, excusable for they didn't think the negotiations would last long enough to require a barber there. As you must know, the Army is a stickler for detail, and when they establish anything they have a TO&E, which means a Table of Organization and Equipment. If it isn't on the list, you don't get it , and there was no barber on the list, and the Army officers in the camp needed haircuts just as much as we did after a couple of weeks. But Eighth Army wouldn't relent for them either. So I called up the Navy headquarters in Tokyo and asked them to buy me a complete set of barber tools and send them over to the camp. They did, and of course Ski brought the package around with his tongue hanging out for cookies as usual. He hadn't looked to see where the package came from. I opened it. He asked what in the devil all of that gear was. I told him. He asked me who was going to use them and when I told him I was, he got the idea right quick and said, "Admiral, you wouldn't do that to me would you?" . . . I told him I had to practice on somebody, and it might as well be him. As a matter of fact, after several false starts, I soon got the hang of it and Ski ended up with a pretty good haircut—a little short, maybe, but good enough so that my next customer was General Hodes, who got a better one. By the time I was through, everybody who had to face the communists at Kaesong had presentable haircuts but Burke. Hank Hodes was the only man who would attempt to cut my hair. It wasn't bad either. Shortly after that there was a barber assigned to Munsan-ni.

When I was detached in December from the delegation, Ski was left behind, and that he did not like at all. He just wasn't cut out for Army-type duty, and before I left he pointed out all the sacrifices he had made on that duty, like the haircut, having to practice every third day with his carbine, the cold weather in a tent, and all the other strange things that a sailor should not be subjected to, and asked if I would help him get recruiting duty in the *Los Angeles.*[44]

Adm. Jay L. Johnson reflected on the role of Navy chiefs during an interview in September 2001.

I spent a lot of time as CNO talking to the petty officers. I have great respect for them, to get their insights of what needs to be done to the Navy. I told them, and I meant it, that I considered them to be the core of the United States Navy, in large measure, how they do what they do really sets the course and speed of the Navy.

I was a young fighter pilot, out at Miramar in San Diego, California, and then to Vietnam. . . . I ended up being the aircraft division officer as a lieutenant (jg) when I started. But the point is I had a division working for me, and I'll never forget, I had a couple of really great chiefs, but one that stuck in my mind was a senior chief named Benny Allen; yeah, Senior Chief Allen. Then I had an ordnance chief named Rob Holdman, as I recall—Holdman. Anyway, I used to tell the chief's mess, when I was the CNO, that for the first year or so, I was really proud of being in charge of that division. It wasn't until years later that I realized that the whole time while I thought Senior Chief Allen was working for me, in one sense, I was kind of working for him because he was teaching me how to be an officer.

I would tell the chief petty officers this, and the senior petty officers, "Don't lose sight of the fact that among your responsibilities is certainly to take care of the men and women who are working for you, and to look out for each other as peers." And I continued, "You've also got a hell of a job to do in grooming the junior officers and teaching them about . . . the role . . . of a petty officer or a chief, and why that's important to them as naval officers." In the past decade, as you probably know, we have put senior enlisted leadership at the Naval Academy. It was a brilliant move, and it's making a huge difference for us.

. . . No matter where I went in the world [as CNO], I'd listen to these petty officers, the young men and women. They would absolutely blow me away. They're smart, they're focused, they're professional. They know what they're doing. They are our national treasures. Period. I remember as a junior officer in 1969, we were having an event one night for the chiefs. I had flown a couple of times that day. I was tired, and I really didn't feel like going. My maintenance officer said, "No, you don't understand; you're going tonight because your chiefs are going to be there and your troops are going to be there, and it's important for you to be there to show them that you care."[45]

The admirals I interviewed agreed that chief petty officers play a key role in the development of naval officers' leadership qualities. A naval officer's success may well depend on the experience and ability of a chief. Adm. Charles Larson reflected:

> I told my wife and my family that I often called all my chief petty officers for input because it took them as long to earn the rank of the rating of chief as it did me to earn captain, and they deserve to have that respect. I was taught at the Naval Academy that your chief is going to be your mentor, so listen to your chief. And I had some tough old chiefs. They would give me advice on things that happened, or say to me, "Here's the way I think we ought to approach this problem." It was very helpful.
>
> One of the primary questions a midshipman used to ask me as superintendent was, "As I head out to the fleet for my first assignment, I need to know more about my relationship with my chief. I will have this person who has fifteen years' experience, but I'm right out of school. Yet, I'm the boss. How do I react to them? How do I meet them? How do I talk to them? What kind of relationship do we establish, and what are the dimensions of our relationship?" As superintendent, one of the most astute things [I] did was to initiate programs they still have at the academy—every company having a chief petty officer.[46]

I asked Admiral Larson how he implemented the program of assigning a chief to each company at the Naval Academy. "It's one of those things that may turn out to be a good result for a bad reason," he told me. "With the perception of the cheating scandal, one of the potential fixes was to bring these people in." He had some leverage in Washington, D.C., and he used it to bring in the chiefs.

> It turned out to be, I think, one of the best programs we've ever had there. It does a couple of things. It's very beneficial for the midshipmen to have that extra level of experience and that enlisted thrust. Now they don't have to ask that question anymore of the superintendent; they ask it of the chief, and they learn that while they're there.

But the other thing is, if we're really doing our job right at the Naval Academy, we have a lot of chiefs going back to the fleet every year. There has been a perception in the fleet that I noticed when I came back in 1994 to the Naval Academy, that some of our graduates are a little arrogant. I had a phrase that I used to use on my first tour as superintendent and I reinstated that phrase on my second tour. I said, "What I expect from our graduates is excellence without arrogance. Let me explain what that means. That means that I want you to be really, really good at what you do, work hard, be confident, have a good work ethic, and have a sense of humility, [realize] that you're not perfect, and you're never going to achieve great results without the help of your subordinates."

I asked him, "How did you do that? How often did you bring the entire group of midshipmen together and talk with them?" He answered: "I probably had the whole brigade together about three or four times a year. But more importantly, I had all the senior class over to my home in groups throughout the year so we could have real interaction, so they could ask questions. This presented a chance for us to really trade thoughts."[47]

I told Adm. William N. Smith about Ensign Trost's experience with his chief, related above. He reflected:

I think that's an interesting account. I think it's a little bit different for pilots, for aviators, because you don't have this relationship of a chief petty officer where you are both trying to do the same thing. When I was a pilot, I had a responsibility for the navigation department and making sure for the squadron that all the charts were up-to-date, that sort of thing. I was never in what I would call a leadership role with respect to troops. . . . My relationship with my petty officer was really one of mutual trust and reliance. I would spend a couple hours briefing for a flight and a couple of hours flying the flight, and a couple of hours debriefing and writing up the reports on the airplane and stuff. Then I would check to see what needed to be done in my division, and usually the chief had taken care of it all, so it was a matter of just sort of keeping an eye out and reviewing what the enlisted people were doing. He did a lot of the paperwork for me and saw to the welfare of the men. I had maybe eight or ten enlisted men. I was a division officer, but he was the guy the men came to when they had a problem. If I had a guy in trouble, he would tell me what he thought I, as the division officer, should try to get accomplished. In fact, I'm sure there are occasions when I tried to do things that I should have left for him to do, just as Carl Trost did.

I don't think the conflicts were ever intense. We didn't have that much personal contact. When you fly a couple of flights a day and do all the ancillary things to get ready for them and get them done, you are pretty well shot.[48]

Adm. Paul David Miller learned about Navy chiefs in an unusual way. When he was almost twelve years old, his mother married a boatswain's mate. The chief adopted him and changed his surname from Lucado to Miller. I asked him about the role the chief played in his development.

He was a strict disciplinarian, which probably helped. He was principled in the Ten Commandments, and I lived by them as a child while being raised at home. There was no lying, cheating, or stealing. The bosun instilled in me that if I served in the military, I should do it as an officer. When I was twelve or thirteen years old, he would take me down to his ships and turn me over to first-class petty officers or second-class petty officers. I would work for them as a seaman. This experience gave me a grassroots understanding of the Navy and drummed into me the importance of an education. Because of this relationship, when I became an officer I was automatically part of the chiefs' quarters, having been in chief quarters when I was a teenager. I knew instinctively how to capture their loyalty almost instantly. Once you did that, then you worked your way up instinctively. . . . With the enlisted ranks, whether they be chief petty officer or lower, you have to give them the time that they have earned and deserved. That is probably the most important part of it, particularly while you're at sea. As I inspected the ship, for example I would ask the sailors as I visited, "Are you proud right now of the number 1 boiler room? Are you proud of the cleanliness of the room, as well as the equipment? Are you proud to bring anybody down there and you can say this is the best looking space not only on the ship but in the fleet? If you're not, then we've got to do something about it."

I didn't say, "The bilges are dirty. Go clean them up." With most of my leadership, I never told somebody to do something unless they finally didn't get what I was telling them. Then I said, "God damn it, do it. Okay?" out of exasperation. But I always went through a question-and-answer session for the individual to come up with what needed to be done so it was his idea to do it. That's a skill. It is a skill to do that, but things get done better. In that one particular instance, I won the hearts of every engineman aboard that ship. There was a boiler in very bad shape, so I went and got my coveralls and I stayed with them until two o'clock in the morning working right alongside them; that had a ripple effect through the ship. I didn't leave that ship until the last seaman did. They wanted something to eat, so I was the one who went down to McDonalds, got them something to eat, and brought it to the ship. There were about a dozen of us pulling together, and we did it in a very short period of time. After we finished I said to them: "Are you proud of the way it looks." They beamed, and the place and those boilers never went down again. . . . The ship can probably run very easily with the captain and the petty officer. You can forget the ensigns. Would the ship run? Would it get from point A to point B without them? Sure it would. Absolutely. It would get there just fine. Some ensigns probably wouldn't think so but it would.[49]

When Admiral McKee was superintendent of the Naval Academy, he heard a perfect definition of the officer–petty officer relationship from his commandant of midshipmen:

My commandant used to pose a question to each graduating class of midshipmen. He framed it this way: When you get to be a division officer, you will probably find a tough, talented chief petty officer who already knows the territory. Why should he take orders from you? What do you bring to the game? Put aside the fact that you are an officer and he is not—what do you have to offer? Are you more experienced? Smarter? Do you know the job better? What do you have that he hasn't got more of? It's not too soon to start thinking about that right now, how would each of you answer those questions? You will probably have a better education. But that doesn't necessarily mean you're better than he is. You've simply had opportunities that he has not. What you have to do is to earn his respect, and do it quickly.[50]

CHAPTER 6

Consideration

In every position, a commander's crew will want to know how much you care for them far more than they will ever care how much you know.

Adm. Thomas H. Moorer, USN (Ret.)
Chief of Naval Operations, 1967–70
Chairman of the Joint Chiefs of Staff, 1970–74

"Consideration" in the context of this chapter is defined simply as a thoughtful and sympathetic regard for others. Adm. James L. Holloway III (CNO 1974–78) set the stage for the discussion of the role of consideration in successful leadership, telling me:

> In general, consideration as a leadership trait means that the leader has a concern for the feelings or comfort of his subordinates that rise above his personal responsibilities. The leader who is "tough but fair" seldom is considerate. He does what the regulations require, and the regulations are mute when it comes to a leader sacrificing his own time or his privileges to go beyond the official requirements of his duties toward his subordinates. For a commander to provide aid, comfort, and benefits to his subordinates simply to conform with regulation is not consideration. There must be some aspect of "giving" or self-sacrifice on his part.[1]

As the senior naval leader in the Pacific in World War II, Adm. Chester W. Nimitz showed enormous consideration and sensitivity when he retained the staff of Adm. Husband Kimmel, the commander in chief, Pacific, at the time of the surprise attack on Pearl Harbor. When Kimmel was relieved, his staff fully expected to be "sacked" as well. E. B. Potter's biography of Nimitz describes what the new CinCPac did on succeeding Kimmel.

> Nimitz promptly dropped a bombshell, but not the sort the assembled officers were expecting. He said that he had complete and unlimited confidence in every one of them and that he did not blame them for what had happened at Pearl Harbor. Moreover, he continued, as former Chief of the Bureau of Navigation (responsible for personnel assignments), he knew that it was because of their competence that they had been sent to the Pacific Fleet. Now he wanted them to stay on with him to provide continuity through their familiarity with their duties. If there were any who wanted to leave he would listen to them individually, discuss their futures, and do what he could to get them the assignments they wanted. "But," he concluded, "certain key members of the staff I insist I want to keep." Somehow, in that simple, short speech, Admiral Nimitz lifted an incubus off the spirits at Pearl Harbor.
>
> Most of the officers who expressed a desire to leave Pearl Harbor did so because they were due for sea duty, which was necessary to the advancement of their careers. Among these was Kimmel's chief of staff, Captain (William W.) Smith, who was up for promotion to rear admiral. As soon as his new commission arrived, Nimitz gave him command of a heavy cruiser division. For his own chief of staff, Nimitz selected Admiral (Milo F.) Draemel. He retained Captain Charles H. McMorris as war plans officer, the post McMorris had held under Kimmel. It is worth noting that Draemel and McMorris had taken diametrically opposed positions regarding the recall of the Wake expedition, the former recommending recall and the latter opposing it.[2]

Rear Adm. William Waldo Drake, who served on Nimitz's staff, provided a firsthand account of these events in an interview on June 5, 1969:

> Well, I think Admiral Nimitz's greatest quality was his sense of leadership coupled with his innate ability to read a man's character, his kindliness towards his shipmates and finally his patience in the face of adversity. The admiral needed

all these tools to pull the fleet out of the low state that he found it when he arrived at Pearl Harbor on Christmas morning 1941. Just after he stepped ashore at the submarine base, he called his staff together in Admiral Kimmel's old office, together with Vice Admiral William S. Pye, temporary commander-in-chief. In a very few minutes, speaking softly and slowly, he convinced all hands of his ability to lead us out of the wilderness. He began by describing the meetings in Washington which led to his selection. He emphasized that he had urged the appointment of Admiral Pye, "but such," he said, "was not to be," with Admiral Pye sitting alongside of him. As to the fleet staff, he said, there were going to be no changes. "I know most of you here, and I have complete confidence in your ability and your judgment. We've taken a whale of a wallop, but I have no doubt of the ultimate outcome." Admiral Nimitz in the first few weeks of his command made every effort to convince his staff and his force commanders that an offensive strategy was the only way to win in the Pacific, despite our huge shortage of weapons and the vast distances to the enemy's strongholds.[3]

Consideration, tolerance, and understanding were qualities Nimitz learned while he was still a midshipman at the Naval Academy. One Sunday, while he was off the Academy grounds violating the rule against the purchase of beer, he noticed that he was observed by a distinguished-looking gentleman in civilian clothes. The following Monday, Nimitz was shocked to find that gentleman, now in uniform, to be Lt. Comdr. Levi Calvin Bertolette, his instructor for that morning's class. Nimitz fully expected to be put on report and his naval career ended. Bertolette either did not recognize him or chose to ignore it, but whatever the case, Nimitz learned a lesson about sensitivity and consideration for others. Nimitz later said of the incident: "This escapade taught me a lesson on how to behave for the remainder of my stay at the Academy. It also taught me to look with lenient and tolerant eyes on first offenders when in the later years they appeared before me as a commanding officer holding Mast."[4]

Admiral Nimitz illustrated his sensitivity and caring for others after the December 7, 1941, attack in more ways than by retaining Kimmel's staff, as Potter's biography notes.

"Whose quarters are these?" asked Nimitz [of Admiral William Pye].
"They are yours. Nobody else is there."
Nimitz asked Pye if he had eaten breakfast. Pye replied that he had.

"Well," said Nimitz, "you'll have another one, for I won't eat alone—after what I've seen."

When Nimitz had completed his first and Pye his second breakfast, Admiral Kimmel joined them. He was wearing two stars instead of the four he had worn as CinCPac. A portly man of imperious presence, he now appeared a little stooped, somehow deflated. On that terrible morning, more than a fortnight earlier, as Kimmel with horrified fascination watched his fleet being smashed, a spent .50-caliber bullet broke through the window and struck his breast. "Too bad it didn't kill me," Kimmel had said quietly.

Nimitz, shocked at his old friend's appearance, warmly pressed his hand. "You have my sympathy," he said. "The same thing could have happened to anybody."[5]

Because so many of the quarters had been destroyed, Admiral Nimitz offered to share his with Admirals Kimmel and Pye and Pye's wife. They refused, telling him the problem would soon be resolved. Nimitz conceded that, but insisted they eat their meals with him, which they did, particularly Christmas dinner.[6]

Command, particularly wartime command, is the goal and the highlight of a naval officer's career. Admiral Nimitz called Adm. Raymond A. Spruance from a successful combat command to be his chief of staff. Although he served patiently in that capacity, Spruance was anxious to return to a sea command. Nimitz assured him that time would come, but not immediately. "Well," replied Spruance philosophically, "the war is the important thing. I personally would like to have another crack at the Japs, but if you need me here, this is where I should be."[7]

It is a great sacrifice for a commander to give up a chief of staff of the caliber of Spruance, who took on a considerable amount of Nimitz's workload. The following morning as they were again coming down from their quarters, Nimitz said, "I have been thinking this over during the night. Spruance, you are lucky. I decided that I am going to let you go after all." On April 8 Nimitz wrote to King: "When Task Force 50m is strengthened, then it is my intention to nominate Spruance as the task force commander with the rank of Vice Admiral."[8] The assignment was approved.

Spruance's new command included the whole central Pacific force. As he assembled his staff, Spruance asked for Adm. Kelly Turner to head the amphibious force, "if I can steal him from Admiral Halsey, and General Holland Smith to command the amphibious troops." For his own chief of staff he wanted his old friend Capt. Charles J. Moore, "an officer who would willingly and capably relieve him of the toil of drafting operation plans."[9]

Nimitz made sure that other regular career officers were assigned to combat positions as well. H. Arthur Lamar, who served as Admiral Nimitz's aide, commented in a 1970 interview: "I was a very unpopular person in the Pacific because many Naval Academy graduates didn't understand why a reserve officer had that job. However, when Admiral Nimitz appointed me his aide in old BuNav, he sent out a dispatch to all flag officers. 'This date I have taken a Reserve officer as my personal aide. Will you please do the same in the shortest possible time, and let your Naval Academy graduates go to sea,' or something to that effect. So that was when we changed over the flag lieutenant position."[10]

Admiral Nimitz's success as a leader was to some degree attributable to his concern and consideration for his subordinates; perhaps nothing expressed that better than his knowing their names. But it did not just happen. "Nimitz had a well earned reputation," commented E. B. Potter,

> . . . for never forgetting a name or face and for never failing to send cards or letters to his friends congratulating them on birthdays, anniversaries, and promotions. Those who marveled most not only at his kindliness but at his memory may not have known that Nimitz maintained a card file containing those important dates that he was credited with carrying in his head. At each station or command, some secretary, yeoman, or aide became the custodian of this file, with the collateral duty of keeping Nimitz posted on the dates and also on published notices of promotions or other honors that came to those listed on the cards.[11]

Rear Admiral Drake remembered:

> When new ships and forces reported in Pearl Harbor he liked to have the commanders in his office for a morning visit—to buoy up their spirits and emphasize the size of the job they had ahead and for insight into their own character. He was a native Texan himself, and he often reminded his callers, if there is a place bigger than Texas, it must be the Pacific Ocean. Another thing, he always remembered the birthdays of his staff and, whether it was at the morning conference or

on his pre-breakfast walks, whenever he would encounter one of us, he'd always remember our birthdays.[12]

As a very junior officer, Vice Adm. Lloyd M. Mustin experienced Nimitz's interest in his men firsthand:

> I had a number of encounters with his senior staff, although I was only a lieutenant, in some general matters of interest to them concerning this new type of ship. I was the assistant gunnery officer. There was a considerable interest in their gunnery capabilities and so on, and, of course, this led to just sort of a courtesy call in his office. And here was this four-star admiral, sitting there running the toughest war that our Navy has ever fought, I guess, and yet one of his, to me, very senior staff officers—might be a commander or even a captain—would say, "Well, the old man wants to see you before you go," and I'd just go in and sit down and have a cup of coffee, and again there would be, "Where is Emily?" and "Where are the children?" and he knew all their names, he never forgot a name. Just a thoroughly remarkable personal impact that came through from that man.[13]

Admiral Nimitz was a firm believer in visiting his troops to get a "feel" for how things were going, as I noted in chapter 3, but he never gave more than an hour's notice of an inspection. This was considerate by design, since it did not allow elaborate preparations that would take time from the men's mission, and he also wanted to know the true situation, which might not be obvious if they spent too much time preparing for the visit.[14]

Commander Lamar, who traveled with Nimitz as his aide, remembered one surprise inspection that arose out of Nimitz's concern for his men:

> One night we were coming back from dinner, after ten o'clock and—of course, in those days Pearl Harbor was still black—Honolulu was still blacked out. There were dim lights and we spotted this drunken sailor walking along the highway. The admiral said, "Stop. Pick him up," which we did. The fellow was obviously intoxicated and didn't know who we were—didn't realize. We found out that he was a Seabee and he was attached to a Seabee battalion, and our driver knew where this battalion was located, so the admiral said, "We will drive you to your camp." And the Seabee was very talkative, and he complained that the commanding officer was no good, the food was lousy, the camp was dirty, and he just made a full exposé of the situation. He thanked us very much when we dumped him out and I don't think he knows to this day who took him home. But the admiral didn't forget those

things, and the next morning he rang for me about ten, and he said, "At eleven, we will inspect Seabee Battalion No. so-and-so," which was the one this fellow belonged to. So, of course, I got the commodore of the Seabees, but he had no time—I mean, we caught him just the way the admiral wanted to catch him. The account was accurate and the commanding officer was relieved.[15]

Nimitz was a frequent visitor to military hospitals to see the sick and wounded. He even visited the sick and wounded Japanese servicemen. On at least one occasion, Potter noted, "the admiral's friendly gesture backfired. The patients, informed that the American head men were coming to see them, were struck dumb with fear."[16]

During one of Nimitz's visits to part of his farflung Pacific command, his airplane had mechanical trouble. His aide, Lamar, recalled:

It later turned out that there was something in the [plane's] ignition harness that was getting wet from the seawater and cracking, and that's why they wouldn't start. But finally, in desperation, Admiral Towers radioed, "The only thing I have left is a Pan American clipper. Do you want me to send that down to bring you home?" And Admiral Nimitz said, "Under no circumstances will I keep the boys from getting their mail." That was the principal source of mail coming in to us— the clippers were loaded with mail. And the admiral wouldn't put up with that, so we spent an extra day at Canton and they made repairs, and we finally got home.[17]

Relaxing the uniform standards in tropical Pearl Harbor was another of Nimitz's kindnesses. Neckties were still required, but at Guam he dropped that requirement and went even further and permitted shorts. Nimitz wrote to his wife: "The concession coming as a surprise, nobody had any stockings except me, and some of the long, hairy legs one sees walking about the place in bobby socks, are amusing or nauseating depending on the state of one's health."[18]

Capt. Edwin T. Layton was the only officer who served with Nimitz throughout all of World War II. Admiral Nimitz was allowed to take only a few of his staff to witness the Japanese surrender, and Layton was one of them, as "some recompense for having so many times refused his request to leave CinCPac staff and go to sea."[19]

One rough morning, Commander Lamar recalled, when things were not going well and he was seeking some diversion for Nimitz, he reported to the admiral that there was a young sailor outside asking to see him. Nimitz told Lamar to send the young man in. Once inside the admiral's office the sailor broke down and admitted that he had bet his shipmates that he could get in to see CinCPac. If he lost the bet, he stood to lose several hundred dollars. "'Well,' said Admiral Nimitz, 'in order to collect your money you've got to have some evidence.' So he buzzed for Lamar and said, 'Get the staff photographer here.' The admiral had his picture taken with the young sailor and gave him several copies to take back to the *Enterprise* as proof that he had won his bet."[20]

Nimitz was quite willing to risk Gen. Douglas MacArthur's wrath when the welfare of American soldiers was at stake. After the announcement of the Japanese surrender, Admiral Halsey went into Tokyo Bay with several ships—the *Missouri, South Dakota,* and *Duke of York*—and immediately learned of the dreadful conditions under which American POWs were being kept. The men were sick and hungry and in desperate need of relief. General MacArthur had directed that the POWs should not be recovered until the Army could be there to participate. Halsey did not want to wait and went to Nimitz, who told him: "Go ahead. General MacArthur will understand." Halsey gave the order, and by midnight nearly eight hundred prisoners had been brought out to the hospital ship *Benevolence*, which was standing by in Tokyo Bay to receive them.[21]

After the war was over, Nimitz flew from Pearl Harbor to Oakland, California, on his way back to Washington, D.C. There was to be a parade to honor him in Oakland on October 2, 1945. He insisted that Commander Lamar, on whom he "had grown increasingly dependent for personal services," accompany him to share the spotlight.[22]

When Fleet Admiral Nimitz succeeded Admiral King as CNO after the war, he continued to be known as a considerate man. His annual salary as CNO was fifteen thousand dollars. Nimitz had no outside income, and a salary raise was impossible because Congress had passed legislation in 1946 that prohibited pay increases for five-star generals and admirals. Entertaining was a vital part of the CNO's responsibilities, but the allowance provided by the government for these obligations was insufficient. Since he could not afford to kick in his own money, he reduced entertaining to a minimum. He limited the number of dinners given and held the meals to three courses. This was greatly appreciated by the foreign representatives, who also had limited funds. "You are making it so much easier for us," they would tell the Nimitzes privately.

> "We can't afford to give the dinners that the people are giving in Washington, and when you do this, you make it so much simpler for us. Now *we* can do it."
>
> Frequently Mrs. Nimitz would call guests and ask them: "Do you want an official dinner, or would you rather bring your children?" Almost invariably they would reply that they would just love to bring their children. Usually the result was a jolly sort of picnic dinner, after which the Nimitzes might conduct their guests to the observatory to look at the moon and stars through the big telescope, an adventure the children particularly appreciated.[23]

After he was relieved as CNO, Fleet Adm. Ernest J. King was made a special aide to the secretary of the navy and given an office in the Navy Department. But as time went on, King was ignored, and "some officers held that this neglect, following years when practically his every waking moment was required in the service of his country was the cause of his declining health." Nimitz was determined not to suffer that fate. "When it comes time for me to give up my job here," he said, "we get out on that day. We're not going to stick around and breathe down the next man's neck." A very considerate gesture.[24]

Nimitz wrote prolifically as CNO, advocating a strong Navy in "Your Navy, as Peace Insurance" in *National Geographic,* "The Navy: Investment in Peace" in *Nation's Business,* and "Seapower Still Indispensable" in the *Washington News Digest.* But he refused to write his memoirs about his World War II experiences, "lest in giving credit to one officer or force he might imply another less deserving. He believed that in the victory of Allied arms there was glory for all, and that the distribution of credit and blame should be left to posterity.[25] His son, Chester W. Nimitz Jr., related his father's position on writing memoirs:

> I think it has perplexed all of his children, . . . this gradually revealed reluctance to participate in any active manner in the recording of his memoirs, because to

us, knowing him as a jovial raconteur, and a man who used to love to tell stories about his childhood in Texas (many of them I've decided are apocryphal), it would have seemed the ideal pastime during his retirement years.

However, the succession of biographies of military and political figures following—some as they were alive, others as they died off—from World War II began to make clear the very thing that Dad wanted to avoid for himself, and that was, to create in the minds of any living close relative, or the individual himself, of anybody with whom he served a feeling of being criticized or revealed in some inadequate capacity, because Dad just felt that no purpose was served by in any way bringing unhappiness to those that had served with him or those that were close to those who had served with him. As, for instance, occurred with respect to most everybody that General Montgomery referred to, in one way or another.[26]

Adm. William F. Halsey was another great leader known for his thoughtfulness. In the introduction to Halsey's autobiography, the book's coauthor, Lt. Comdr. J. Bryan III, wrote of Halsey: "Sailors know their welfare is his vital concern." He offered as an illustration an event that occurred at Pensacola Naval Air Station one evening when Halsey came upon a motorcycle accident in which a sailor had been seriously injured. A Navy ambulance was already on the way, and a Navy doctor drove up as it arrived. The doctor put the sailor in the ambulance and ordered the driver to proceed to the hospital. Admiral Halsey, who had remained on the scene, asked the doctor: "Aren't you going to ride with him?" "No, sir," said the doctor. "I've got my own car." Halsey bluntly told him, "Damn your car! Get into that ambulance!"[27]

Any leader of character realizes that success depends to a large extent on his or her subordinates. Admiral Halsey's thoughts were with his subordinates even as he learned that he had been nominated for his fourth star:

On November 18, President Roosevelt nominated Bill for four stars. The news astonished us as much as it pleased us. Unwritten law forbade the Navy to have more than four full admirals on the active list at the same time, and we already had them—"Betty" Stark, Ernie King, Chester Nimitz, and Royal Ingersoll. However, Congress ignored the law and approved the nomination at once.

The word found Nouméa short of four-star pins, as it was of almost everything else in those days, so I obtained four two-star pins from a major general of Marines and had them welded in pairs, while regulation Navy pins—our stars are smaller than the Marines'—were being cut on a repair ship in the harbor.

When I gave Bill the makeshifts, he handed me his old three-star pins and told me, "Send one of these to Mrs. Scott and the other to Mrs. Callaghan. Tell them it was their husbands' bravery that got me my new ones." (Rear Admirals Norman Scott and William M. Callaghan were killed in action over Guadalcanal.)[28]

Admiral Nimitz surprised and delighted Halsey at a cocktail party in Honolulu "by producing young Bill Halsey, an ensign in the Supply Corps reserves, who unknown to his father, had recently arrived at Pearl Harbor."[29] Bill was assigned to the Pacific theater as an aviation supply officer. Soon after his arrival he was sent out on a torpedo plane to pick up spare parts. Halsey's consideration for all of his troops included not permitting any favoritism for his son, even under the worst possible circumstances. In his autobiography he wrote:

Bill had hardly left when an attack of flu put me to bed. I must have been sicker than I realized, because not until the tenth was my Operations officer, Captain H. Raymond Thurber, allowed to tell me, "Admiral, we have had three torpedo planes missing for two days."

I knew at once. "My boy?"

"Yes sir."

Ray described the searches being made, then asked if I could suggest any additional measures.

I told him, "My son is the same as every other son in the combat zone. Look for him just as you'd look for anybody else."

Another day passed, and another, with no word of the planes. Usually I shared my problems with my staff, but this was personal, and I kept it to myself. I didn't give up hope, but I knew that hope was a double-edged sword. When the families of missing men begged me to hold out hope of their return, I always refused. I considered it too cruel. I would tell them frankly, "Only a miracle can bring him home."

By the afternoon of the twelfth, four days after he had disappeared, this was my feeling about Bill. That evening, though, a search plane reported spotting several rubber rafts ashore on the island of Eromanga, between New Caledonia and Efate, and next day all ten men were recovered, suffering from nothing worse than flea bites, diarrhea, and sore feet. It turned out that they had missed their course and had been forced to make a water landing.

The men were picked up on Friday, August 13, and Halsey noted that "from then on—for a while—I spit in the eye of the jinx."[30]

Admiral Spruance, although not an aviator, was in command of the carriers in his fleet and made a point of being considerate of the pilots. Thomas B. Buell's biography of Spruance describes one of his actions.

> Knowing Nimitz's concern for morale, Spruance made a recommendation that benefited the fleet for the remainder of the war. During the Battle of Midway, the naval aviators had told him that their future was hopeless. If they survived Midway, they simply would continue flying in later operations until their number was up. There was scant possibility of being relieved before they eventually were killed.
>
> When Spruance came ashore as chief of staff, he soon persuaded Nimitz to establish a rotation program that sent fresh aviators to relieve those that had been in the front line for long periods. For the remainder of the war, a substantial reserve of replacement squadrons always was available for the fleet carriers. After the war, Nimitz emphasized to a military audience that his men—especially his aviators and submariners—had been his most important assets. He wanted them to be fresh, alert, and well rested. Rotation and recreation programs had been essential.[31]

Admiral Spruance showed further consideration for the carrier pilots—and doubtless saved some lives—by resolving one of the problems with night landings. Planes returning from their missions were often low on fuel and needed to land immediately, but many of the pilots had little experience in night landings. Policy called for ships to be blacked-out to protect against enemy submarines, but Spruance decided to take the risk: for the welfare of pilots the carrier was to be lighted. Some considered this a rash and dangerous decision; he considered it a humanitarian decision to save the lives of his pilots.[32]

Adm. Arleigh Burke showed sensitivity and consideration when, after being jumped ahead of ninety-two more senior admirals to the post of CNO, he refused to reassign the CNO staff he had inherited. "When I became chief of naval operations," he recalled in his oral history,

> . . . one of the conditions under which I took the job (and I had several conditions) was that because I had such great admiration for a lot of my seniors, I was

not going to clean house. I was not going to fire a lot of people who were my seniors. Well, I had been with Admiral Stump during the war. He was a very good
fighting man. He had some spots that I didn't like, of course, just as I had spots
that he didn't like. He's a tough man. But he was a very fine man, and I have
never had anybody that helped me as much as he tried to do when he was
CinCPac and I was CNO. He did everything he could to make things run the way
I wanted them run. And I had to lean over backwards to make sure that I didn't
suggest something that I didn't intend to suggest because he'd try to do it. It
was remarkable what those senior people did. Admiral Wright was the same way.
But Felix Stump was one of the finest people I've ever known for his support. He
was good.[33]

Vice Adm. Marc A. Mitscher was one of many prominent World War
II leaders who refused to write their memoirs even though they were
offered handsome sums to do so. Before his death, Mitscher instructed
Burke that he wanted his papers to be burned:

> Mitscher told me,"There is stuff in there that would be all right, but there's also
> stuff in there that's detrimental to people. There are statements that I have writ-
> ten without knowing the full story which are critical of people and which I now
> wish I hadn't written and that aren't actually even true. There are other things
> in there that are carelessly worded and people can misinterpret it anyway that
> they want to misinterpret it, and they will. I don't want to leave anything. What
> I've done is all over, it's all finished. Forget it."
>
> He knew he was dying. He was sure he was. Nobody else was, but I'm sure
> that's why he asked me to do this. I didn't burn his papers, he did. The only
> papers he left were a few he left in Mrs. Mitscher's gear in the hotel. . . . But there
> weren't very many there. We had a lot of talks then about people writing. He said
> he would never write anything.[34]

Burke's loyalty and devotion to Mitscher continued after his death. His
consideration for Mitscher's widow benefited her and ultimately many
other Navy widows as well.

> When Admiral Mitscher died, Mrs. Mitscher didn't know . . . anything about
> Admiral Mitscher's affairs, not a damned thing. It was sad. It was very sad. I asked
> a few officers what they did. Well, a lot of them didn't do anything. Their papers
> were in the same sort of mess. So I wrote to several insurance companies . . . who

replied and gave me a lot of data. Then I sent them a rough draft and they gave me a lot of suggestions. So I wrote a pamphlet, a little bit of a pamphlet, maybe half a dozen pages, not what a man should do, but a pamphlet that a man could fill in so that his wife would have all of the dope on his estate and references as to who she should call, what she should do when he died. This was a pretty good little thing. I turned this pamphlet over to the Navy Mutual Aid who distributed it throughout the Navy.[35]

When John F. Kennedy assumed the presidency and the role of commander in chief, he asked Burke to continue as CNO. When Burke respectfully declined, Secretary of Defense Gates asked him for a list of possible replacements.

Well, I spent several weeks on that list, and when I ended up I had about forty people on the list, forty people that I thought were qualified, some better than others. There are a lot of very good people and this depended on what kind of man they wanted, what they wanted him to do, and so forth, but they weren't all equally good.

They said, "This is no good. . . . You give me the name of the . . . best man."

I said, "No, I won't do this, unless you guarantee to appoint him. If he will be appointed, I'll do it, but otherwise I won't, and the reason why is that if I think a man is best and recommend him to you and he is not appointed, there will be a leak. Somehow there will be a leak. And that man will be ruined. He will know he was not selected, that he was offered up and he was not selected, and it would be bad for him. On the other hand, if he were selected, it might be just about as bad because he would be known as Burke's boy. . . ."

Well, they kept working on me so eventually I said, "I'll give you six names," and I worked it down to six, and they were six damn good officers. Any one of them could have been CNO and would have made a good one. I never wrote that list down, never typed it. It was a verbal thing. Even then, there are people who made some very astute guesses as to who the six were. In other words, there were leaks. There are always leaks. One of them was selected. [Adm. George Whalen] Anderson [Jr.] was on my list. He was one of them, yes.[36]

Although Burke valued the services of his vice CNO, Adm. Harry Donald Felt, a man who was willing to challenge Burke's decisions, he recognized when it was time to let Felt leave, and showed consideration in letting him go.

He was extremely good. You can only keep a man in that position so long, because he wears out and after a while you have a doubt as to whether or not this opposition is just a habit or whether he really thinks that way, and so after a couple of years, Don—when CinCPac opened up—Don was the ideal man for that because he was a very hardworking, excellent naval officer, and I couldn't hold him back just selfishly to keep him in the vice chief's job. So he got CinCPac, and I got another man who was just like Don—different personal characteristics, but he was an aviator, hardheaded, experienced, good war record—in Jim Russell. They were both—those were two of the best appointments I ever made, in those two people because they did an awful lot for the Navy.[37]

Admiral Burke was a sensitive and thoughtful CNO in other ways as well. When the son of a friend was killed, for example, Burke bent the rules a bit:

I had a friend whose son was killed in naval aviation right after he had passed his examination as a naval aviator at Pensacola. He wrote to me and asked if it would it be possible for him to get a posthumous commission and designation as a naval aviator for his son. His son had passed all the requirements, it was just that the paperwork hadn't been completed. Well, I could see why he wanted that, so I went to BuPers and, sure enough, they said they could do it somehow. They checked up and found out that the report was correct, so they did give his son a commission and a designation as a naval aviator on the day he died, which shows thoughtfulness in BuPers, which a lot of people don't think it has.[38]

Nor did Burke confine his consideration to his own command. When a conflict arose between Queen Frederica of Greece and her ambassador during a visit to the United States, Burke defused the situation. The U.S. government had decided to assist several NATO allies with a gift of some destroyers that were essentially of no value to the U.S. Navy, and Queen Frederica came to the United States to accept for Greece. Admiral Burke reflected:

Now, I've known Queen Frederica for a long time and I knew all of their navy people, their senior navy people whose names mostly I can't pronounce now. Queen Frederica stayed with us in the quarters. She was furious at her ambassador, because the ambassador had told her that he thought it was not appropriate for a woman to accept men-of-war. We had a dinner for her and then after a dinner we had a reception. . . . We were in a receiving line, and I guess the ambassador, Alexis S. Liatis, apparently had talked to her right after dinner, before the reception started, and by the time she got in the receiving line she was furious. And a furious woman is bad enough, but a furious queen is pretty bad.

I was next to her, of course, and she said, "Admiral, I must talk to you soon by yourself."

I said, "Yes, Your Majesty, but this reception is about to begin."

She said, "Can we excuse ourselves for a few minutes?"

I said, "Certainly." So we went over into the little sun room that we have there, and I said, "What can I do for you?"

She said, "Well, how do you like my ambassador?"

I said, "I think he's a fine man."

She said, "I think he's terrible and I'm about to fire him right now. I'm about to send him home."

I said, "Why?"

She said, "He told me not to give this speech the day after tomorrow in San Diego accepting these ships, that I should give a little short general speech and then let him or some man, some other representative of Greece."

I said, "Well, Your Majesty, I think that's—"

She said, "So, I think I will discharge him and send him home right now."

I said, "Don't do that, Your Majesty; please don't do that. He's a good man. He's made a mistake on this, he's wrong on this" (and I thought he was). "He's wrong on this, but you give the speech and give him hell, but don't humiliate him. It won't do Greece any good or you any good or anybody any good." She didn't send him back.[39]

Admiral Burke understood that successful leaders are considerate of their subordinates.

You can't buy people. They need to feel appreciated. It doesn't take very much to do this. I worked my people very hard, particularly my immediate staff. They worked like hell. That's another thing. You've got to work as hard as your people. Mostly you have to know what you're doing, and be a professional. Professionalism throughout the Navy is what I strived most for. A naval officer—a line officer—should be a professional in combat at sea. He may have a lot of other qualities that might be helpful, but basically he's got to be a good combat officer. That doesn't mean that everybody . . . must be fired if he's not a good combat officer. It means that if he isn't a good combat officer he's got to have some damn superior qualities in other ways to make up for his weakness.[40]

Adm. Thomas H. Moorer, who rose to become CNO and chairman of the Joint Chiefs of Staff, illustrated his consideration for others very early in his career. As a lieutenant in World War II he was called on to perform a dangerous rescue mission. The Japanese had attacked the island of Timor, and a group of sixteen elite Australian troops—men similar in training, courage, and professional ability to U.S. Rangers—had been severely wounded in the battle and had to be taken off the island. In our interview, Admiral Moorer offered a fascinating account of the rescue.

> The Australians asked General MacArthur to send . . . one of our planes over to Timor at night and pick up the wounded. I was selected to do the job. Of course, MacArthur said he wanted to talk to me about it. So I flew all the way from Darwin, Australia, to his headquarters and talked to him. I was amazed. He had four or five doors in his office. He had push buttons there, and he had a push button for every door. He had a colonel in charge of sunrise, another colonel in charge of sunset. It wasn't quite that bad, but anytime there was a question about anything he would press a button and this guy knew the answer. He made me tell him exactly how I was going to do it. I said, "Well, I'm going to send them a signal and I'm going to tell them that I want them to put two fires on the beach close together. Then out one fire up here (pointing to a map of the island) and have the people I'm to rescue on the beach right here." So I took off at sunset from Darwin. I decided that they didn't have any radar, so I was going to fly in real high, then cut the throttle back so I wouldn't make any noise.

He took just one plane with a crew of eight to bring out the sixteen wounded soldiers.

> I had so many [passengers] that I couldn't get in the plane. I had to walk outside, making sure my crew got all of the wounded onboard. Then I couldn't get back in the aircraft because it was so full of Australians. I got in the cockpit from the top. Anyway I told General MacArthur I was going to be back at . . . midnight. I had to take off in a heavy swell and that's not easy since we were way overloaded. Anyway I got airborne, arriving back in Australia at just that time. . . .
>   The wounds were really bad. One guy didn't have any jaw. One of them didn't have any legs. It was a hell of a fix. I had the foresight to cook a turkey and

a ham that I took with me. I gave it to them and boy that thing was gone just like that. When I got back I rejoined my squadron and I continued on to the other operations. . . .

A long time after that, in 1999, I was living in McLean, Virginia, and received a telephone call from the Australian media. They asked me if I knew about this operation. I said yes, I know about it and I'll tell you all about it, that I was the one that did it. After I told him about it, I said, "Okay, I did you a favor. Now I want you to broadcast to the whole Australian community that I would like to have the names of every one of those boys who was on that plane." I received the names and addresses of those that were still alive, which were twelve out of the sixteen [including the man who had lost his jaw and the one who had lost his legs].[41]

Admiral Moorer realized that career officers want to be where the action is, so he had a rotation policy to permit the carrier pilots serving in the Atlantic to have a tour in Vietnam.

Since the Navy was primarily involved in an air war in Vietnam, what we endeavored to do was equalize the exposure for the pilots. In other words, it wouldn't have been right, in my view at least, . . . to not involve the pilots on the Atlantic Fleet carriers in the war and let the ones that happened to get caught in the Pacific find themselves shot at continuously. So I looked on it as a worldwide Navy effort, not as a Pacific Fleet effort. Others tended to look on the Vietnam War as a kind of Pacific Fleet problem. But I think it was a United States Navy problem. Our young pilots should all take their chances, so we had a rotation policy. There was another aspect to that, too. That was the experience gained throughout the Navy and in the Air Force, too. It is invaluable and we will have a stockpile of combat experience and pilots unequaled by any other country in the world for years.

Whereas we talk about personnel quite a bit in the services, I think that personnel are personnel no matter where they are. It just happens that in the services you have more order, you have more complete records, you have more permanence, and consequently you can get a better grip on the problem. But the fundamentals of managing personnel are the same whether you are operating a dog kennel or General Electric. It's the same, people to people.[42]

Admiral Moorer's successor as CNO, Adm. Elmo Zumwalt Jr., wrote a book in which he made the point that he had not been Moorer's first choice for the job. One of Moorer's interviewers asked if he felt that

Zumwalt might have made a better CNO further along in his career. Admiral Moorer replied,

> I did not approve of Admiral Zumwalt. As a matter of fact, I wrote a letter to that effect to the secretary of navy and secretary of defense. When Admiral Zumwalt was called to Washington for an interview, he stayed first with Undersecretary of the Navy John Warner. Then I invited him up to my quarters, the admiral's house. I told him, "Before you come into my house, I want to tell you that I did not recommend you for this assignment. I feel that you have had limited experience in major command. I feel that you are a man of great talents, but that being the case, I think it's unfair to the Navy to put you in a position where you will be retired at an early age and the Navy will not have an opportunity to take advantage of what you can do."[43]

Stating his position openly showed consideration for Zumwalt, who was already aware of Moorer's view.

During his tenure as CNO, Admiral Moorer devoted a considerable amount of his time to improving the quality of life for American sailors. He was responsible for the construction of the Norfolk Navy Lodge, one of the first projects designed to provide affordable housing for sailors and their families. But it was a challenge: "We had to overcome the opposition of the local motel operators, of course. But today the sailors have a place to go with their families when they arrive in town to report aboard ship or to some other billet without having to undergo the expense that one encounters in a regular motel these days."[44]

Admiral Moorer learned from firsthand observations that officers who are inconsiderate of their subordinates cannot be effective leaders. "As I've said many times," he noted, "it's been my experience that it's the people that work for you that make you look good, not the people you work for. If young officers would just remember that point, they would butter up the guys that are working for them. I don't really mean butter them up, but I mean make it quite clear that you are aware of their presence, you know what they are doing, you appreciate their contribution, and you are looking out for their welfare."[45]

Certainly Admiral Moorer tried to be sensitive to the needs of those under his command.

You can't permit any group to feel that they are in a low-priority effort, because if what they are doing is not important then they shouldn't be there. I think that an individual likes to be recognized. He likes to be called by his name, not "hey, you" or lieutenant or something. I always try to call people by their name and try to get them involved in what they are doing. . . . Any leader or boss would do well to spend more time with his juniors than he spends with his seniors. In that way, you don't have to worry about what's going to happen in the pinch. They're going to try to make you look good if they think you know what you are doing, that you're interested in what they're doing, and that you feel that what they are doing is worthwhile.[46]

The U.S. Navy has a firm policy that when pilots go down, no effort is spared to rescue them. That rule gives pilots a sense of security that improves their job performance. Moorer reflected:

There are literally hundreds of young pilots and crewman that are walking the streets of America today who wouldn't be alive if it weren't for the helicopters and . . . the courage and the skill of the young men that were flying these helos. You could write a book about that. I think it is one of the great stories of the Vietnam War, the heroics of these young people. . . . The fact that our people know that there is nothing we won't do to rescue a pilot who goes down or any other individual who is caught in the enemy lines, regardless of the risk, is what I think maintains morale and makes people fight like they do. At whatever cost, we'll get them if this can be done.[47]

Moorer showed a keen understanding of the hardships that deployment and separation from the family can cause.

Generally speaking, I found out over a period of time that as far as the Navy is concerned about five months away from home is the optimum, although by and large most of them averaged six months. But I've always found that the end of five months marks the beginning of a flood of telegrams from wives at home, asking their husband to take leave because their wife is overburdened with the responsibilities. Most of the difficulties, most of the emergency leave and so on, take place right at the end of six-month deployments.

In many cases we had ships that were seven, eight, or even eight and a half months away from home. But after all, most of the people were volunteers. And during the height of the Vietnam disaster there were many in the media and in the government that were so callous as to say, so far as the POWs are concerned, it served them right because they volunteered to go. They didn't have to go. I thought that they conducted themselves in a fabulous way, as anyone can plainly see.[48]

Having experienced superiors who reflected poor leadership and lack of consideration, Admiral Moorer tried as CNO to correct this problem whenever he could.

If I could just make a dent, I didn't have any idea I was going to correct all of the things that bothered me, but at least it would reverse the trend. For example . . . I tried to . . . recognize the importance of engineering officers. Line officers by and large tend to not concern themselves with what goes on in the engineering department of the ship, which is a vital part of the ship. That's where you get your mobility.

I was on a cruiser when I was an ensign. The lieutenant would not permit any of the engineering people to come up above the deck unless they were in whites, treating them as second-class citizens. Those were the days when we didn't have any air conditioning and the kids would be down in the fire rooms, sweating like the devil, and they would come up to get some cool air, and he would chase them below. . . .

I did manage to put some people in engineering spaces who were trained in engineering, engineering-duty-only officers and people like that, trying to build up the competence and enhance the image of the engineering personnel. I think this is important because one person, one component of the ship, is just as important as the other. If you don't have fresh water, if you don't have electric power, and if you don't have mobility, everything else comes to naught. There was a period of time where I think the engineering people were not given the recognition they properly deserved.[49]

Like Admiral Burke, Moorer did not confine his acts of consideration to his own Navy. Immediately after World War II, then-Commander Moorer was assigned to a group charged with surveying the results of the U.S. bombing of Japan. One of the Japanese officers he interviewed during the course of the study was Admiral Tamura. At their first meeting, Tamura surrendered his sword to Moorer:

I think he would probably have been forced to give it up anyway because MacArthur decreed that they had to give up all pistols and swords and so on.

Nevertheless, this sword had been in the family. I think it was about three hundred years old, [made] in the days when it took over a month to make one. It had a gold scabbard and gold hilt. I took his sword and put it in my mother's attic in Alabama. When I found out I was going to be commander of the Seventh Fleet I took it with me. When I got out there, I got the best swordsmith I could find and had it done just right, all polished and tightened and so on. So then I returned it to him.

It was done on national TV with the American ambassador and the Japanese foreign ministry present. They made a big to-do of it. From then on, there was just nothing he wouldn't do for me. It was embarrassing the things he tried to do for my wife and me from then on. It was a very valuable sword. I expect if I had kept it, it would have been worth several thousand dollars. It was worth a lot more to me to see the great joy it gave that fellow to get that sword back, because it was just more than the value of the thing. It meant so much to him. . . . Admiral Tamura . . . became my very good friend. He came over to see me several times, and when I would tour Japan, I would be his guest.[50]

I asked Admiral Holloway how the Navy trained aviators to command aircraft carriers when he was CNO. His response illustrated his concern for young officers and, ultimately, the crews they commanded:

We [first] put them in command of ammunition ships, oilers, and tankers. It was known as their deep draft or qualifying command. It wasn't glamorous, but the crew was much smaller, the tasks an order of magnitude simpler, and the ship handling was the same as a carrier—except the speeds were slower. In this way, the young aviator captains could concentrate on ship handling and maneuvering and also learn about the steam propulsion plant. Aviators are good at mechanical things. They have to be. Their lives depend upon the reliability of their airplane engines, landing gear, flaps, and controls. The difference is that steam plants are new to them. Aircraft engines are either gasoline-powered reciprocating cylinder engines or petroleum-fueled jet engines. A steam plant is much more complicated. Most aviators picked up their ship handling quickly when they went to their deep drafts because it's not too different from flying a plane. They were used to flying compass courses, and the relative motion between an aircraft when making a landing at a field and a ship mooring at a pier was similar. But they didn't understand steam plants.

When I was CNO, working with Admiral Rickover and Jim Watkins, who was chief of naval personnel at the time, we set up three Quonset huts at the nuclear propulsion training site at Arco, Utah, where Rickover's Division of Naval Reactors had a land-based steam plant. We fixed these Quonsets up very nicely, with Admiral Rickover furnishing the money. One hut was a BOQ [bachelor officers' quarters]; another, the officers' mess and wardroom; and the third, their classroom. It was called the Commanding Officers' Engineering Training School. All prospective commanding officers of "deep draft" ships were required to attend a three-week course. We included all line officers going to major surface ship commands because it had come to my attention that many surface officers going to command major combatant ships had never served in a ship's steam engineering department.

The course started out with the absolute fundamentals. A grizzled chief machinist's mate would stand before his class of captains and say, "Gentlemen this is a wrench and this is a monkey wrench." The instruction would go on from there. The captains, properly attired in coveralls, went into the steam plant to observe and learn the operation of the equipment, and then actually started up the plant and controlled it. Finally, the student captains did the troubleshooting, the dirty job of repairing oil leaks and escaping steam. Believe it or not, most of the officers loved it. I talked to virtually everyone who went through [the] school initially, and they felt much more confident in taking command of a large steam-powered vessel.

The real benefactors of the program were perhaps the crews of these deep drafts. Previously, command of an oiler was given to a surface officer, one who didn't screen for a destroyer division or a cruiser command. In addition to being a lower-percentile performer, he was not particularly motivated. Then came the young aviation captains, the top 7 percent of their year group, preselected for a carrier command. They were real leaders. The following anecdote illustrates this.

I'd been CNO for two years, and while touring the waterfront at Pearl Harbor on a routine visit to the Pacific Fleet, I went aboard an old oiler, the *Hasayampa*. As I was leaving, after walking through the ship and talking with the sailors as I went, an old chief machinist's mate with a wrinkled countenance, white hair, and gold bars all the way up his arm for his years of service said to me: "Sir, may I see you a moment?" I turned to the skipper, an aviator captain, who answered, "Would you mind, Admiral Holloway?"

"What's on your mind, Chief?" I asked. He said, "Sir, I want to say that you changed this old man's outlook on Navy life when you started that school to train ship captains. My sailors wouldn't ship over because all our previous skippers did not understand our problems in the engineering spaces. When I would report to the captain, 'Sir, the headers are leaking, we can't get steam up, we can't get under way on schedule at 0800 tomorrow,' the skipper would reply, 'By God, we are going to get this heap of rivets under way on schedule, I don't care if you have to work all night. I want this thing fixed.' I would try to explain that the ship was twenty-five years old and I didn't have the spare parts, no proper tools, no experts, no nothing. So, I'd keep the sailors aboard all night, just spinning our wheels and we still couldn't get under way the next morning. These days, if we've got a leaky header and I come to the skipper and report, 'Sir, we've got a problem,' the skipper says, 'Come on, let's go down and take a look at it.' He walks down onto the gratings and says, 'You know, we've got a hell of a problem, Chief. I'm going up to see the maintenance officer on the fleet staff and tell him I have personally inspected the leaking boiler fronts and that we cannot get under way without outside assistance. They need to send down some people with the proper skills and equipment to give us a hand. We can't go to sea with a twenty-five-year-old power plant in this shape.'" The chief continued: "It's changed the lives for us old chiefs and the engineering gangs on these ships." By this time, tears were rolling down his cheeks. He says, "I just want to thank you, Sir."

When I went to the fleet on an inspection tour, I visited a lot of ships. This appreciation was repeated many times, but that was the most dramatic incident. I'll never forget it.[51]

Admiral Holloway objected strongly to the hazing of midshipmen at the Naval Academy. "When I was CNO," he said, "every six months I'd call up Rear Admiral Kinnaird McKee, who was superintendent of the Naval Academy, and say, 'I just wanted to make damn sure you're not allowing any hazing.' I always had a strong concern, when a new class of plebes was being 'indoctrinated,' because I think it's an open opportunity for bullying. Kin McKee felt the same way I did about hazing and was making sure that the disciplining of plebes stayed within bounds. We had no ugly incidents."

Yet Admiral Holloway also told me that he understood and accepted his treatment as a plebe at the Naval Academy: "I don't consider I was bullied when I went through. Bullying is a case of carrying hazing too far. It is meanness, and can become vindictive and cruel. I have seen bullying by senior petty officers in ships and squadrons, and it can become vicious and break a man's spirit. The bully in these cases was protected by his rank from any reaction by his victims. I didn't like it, and whenever I was in a position of authority throughout my career, I wouldn't tolerate it."[52]

In response to my questions on consideration as a vital element of admiralship, Adm. Thomas B. Hayward (CNO 1978–82) had this to say:

> Of all the lessons on leadership that we got as midshipmen at the Naval Academy, which you can find foremost in any service leadership manual, is to take care of your people first. While no doubt one can find examples of senior officers who make their way to admiral who fail in this test, my recommendation is that we all seek to make this a permanent and spontaneous characteristic. Because it is inbred, one can think of many examples where we did it right, and no doubt examples where we failed the test. For me, the most rewarding examples are those that had a profound effect on large numbers of our people.
>
> For example . . . I was commanding officer of USS *America,* a conventionally powered carrier. Because we frequently would find ourselves conducting flight operations when wind conditions were light to none, the practice had become policy throughout the carrier Navy that all available boiler power had to be on line in order to create as much wind over the deck as possible for the aviators during launch. Sounds logical; safety of our aviators is a foremost concern. What wasn't being given consideration is that such a policy resulted in no general maintenance allowed on boilers except in port. Ergo, the engineers, who already had the dirtiest, toughest job on the ship, had their in-port liberty cut short in order to work on at least one boiler in order to keep up with scheduled maintenance.
>
> I was determined to try to do something about this so as to give the engineers a fair liberty break when we were in port, which by the way was seldom during our Vietnam deployment. Consulting with the air wing commander and air boss, we decided to see if we could still safely conduct launches if we reduced the optimum wind over the deck by two knots, for if we could, the engineers could do scheduled maintenance on one boiler at a time while at sea. We decided it could be done safely, undertook the change carefully and deliberately, and ended up able to conduct combat operations without missing a beat. You can imagine how the engineering force responded to that.
>
> While I was CNO, I had another unique opportunity to let the troops know that their seniors care and are appreciative. This was a time when our deployments were being extended to as much as eleven months away from home port to meet the demands being generated by the crisis in Iran with . . . Americans

being held hostage, and the ensuing effort to affect their recovery. During these long deployments, most of the time was spent in the Indian Ocean and Persian Gulf, not the most hospitable places to work. A battle group would be lucky to spend more than four days in port, in Mombassa or Karachi, once during its deployment. By any stretch of the imagination, that's tough. Breaking with virtually all tradition, I persuaded the secretary of the navy to let us provide beer to the sailors while onboard ship, under way. The concept went like this: for every forty-five days under way continuously without a liberty break, the commanding officers of ships could give everyone onboard two cans of cold beer, almost always scheduled around a fantail barbecue/happy hour–like event. They soon named it "Gonzo Beer" after the Indian Ocean data point, Gonzo, that everyone used for area navigation. This was a tremendous morale booster, as you might imagine, for we were successful in sending the signal to the guys carrying the load that they weren't forgotten. The most rewarding aspect as I look at it in hindsight is that the practice is still being followed today.

I was also able to propose and obtain approval for a new set of rules regarding maximum permitted operational tempo . . . a maximum of six months deployed and a minimum of one year back home before deploying again. This was to be held inviolate. In other words, we were not going to demand of them the kind of rotation imposed during Vietnam—an eight-month deployment, back three months, then back to Vietnam for another eight. In the first place, you'd wreck the readiness of the ships because they could not be maintained properly. We had gotten to the point where sailors would not take that kind of treatment anymore. They were forced to leave the Navy; they had no choice.

We also were given new hope when President Reagan became our commander in chief. I took over as CNO in 1982, and President Reagan had already laid the groundwork for a major boost in defense. We were on the way to a six-hundred-ship Navy, so it was an exciting time for me. We were rapidly emerging from a late-1970s slump. We put a lot of emphasis on the morale, training, and readiness of our human resources. We had to bring ourselves into competitive balance with business and industry that were attracting our people away, particularly the high-tech people. So we needed special recruiting bonuses and skill pays and instituted more benefits comparable to those allowed in the private sector. Retention of key sailors markedly improved.[53]

Adm. James D. Watkins (CNO 1982–86) shared his thoughts on the importance of consideration in leadership:

As far as I know, I was respected in every one of my assignments, ship or shore, by my men because I was sensitive to them. Yes, I was tough on them and demanded a lot. But I also conveyed my respect for them as well. It was just a natural thing for me. I had a reputation for being on the "people" side of things. I spent most of my time in Washington in the personnel business and was the one who was aggressive in getting help for our sailors. That is what I do best. I get needed things done. For example, I was instrumental in working with both the secretaries of defense and navy, with the help of the CNO, to get "sea pay" for sailors. There had not been any sea pay until that time. I also got special pay for nuclear-trained and other high-tech sailors. I was also able to get monies appropriated to enhance reenlistment bonuses, badly needed in the 1970s.

This was when I was chief of naval personnel. I set up computer-assisted distribution mechanisms to be better stewards of our people. When sailors called in and asked for help, they didn't get a bunch of crap out of some detailer. The detailer could now flash up their records on a screen, never before possible. Detailers could no longer, in good conscience or through ignorance, ignore our people's needs or desires. These were now stored in the computer. I don't remember anything I did aboard ship that was as significant as that which I was able to do for sailors while chief of naval personnel or, before, when I was installed as the first director of enlisted personnel in 1971.

Before I was chief of naval personnel, many of these things were not being done for our sailors. Remember, we had suddenly transitioned into the all-volunteer force from the draft but were not ready for this dramatic change. The old adage that "if the Navy wanted you to have a wife, they would have issued you one" was still rampant prior to the early 1970s. We had shifted to the all-volunteer Navy, and the Navy was least ready of all the services. The Army and Air Force were much more ready than we were. We used to draft them in and then get a replacement out of recruiting quickly again if we didn't like our initial draftee. That's the way we handled things. We could not do that anymore after 1973. We were now made up of volunteers only—no draftees. So, we had to get competitive with the private sector. We had to create child day-care centers, family service centers, drug and alcohol rehabilitation centers, and the like. I was able to help set them up with federal funding.

The family service center was created in 1978 as the central place for a spouse to go when the sailor was deployed—to get help, legal help, whatever was needed; to meet with the chaplain; to help with job referrals; to answer such questions as: "I did not get my check. It did not come in from Cleveland.

What do I do?" Well, the family service center would get the check for them. Such a one-stop shop for a family did not exist before. Now they are all over the world. Our people love it, and it shows that we are sensitive to their needs. In most of our families, both spouses work. In particular, it is the enlisted men I am talking about. For example, the enlisted man's wife might be an eighth-grade teacher. So, when she moves to Norfolk from San Diego to get a job, for instance, she needs help, a job referral, . . . to get a job right away . . . so as to keep solvent financially. So those are the kinds of things we started to do for our people, and we received funding support on Capitol Hill. We made the case and got the money.

Admiral Watkins made an exceptional contribution toward the welfare of his seamen:

If . . . you believe that people are the most important product we've got to worry about, . . . you are sensitive to their needs and will do all in your power to help them. To me that is extremely important. Recall that we had sailors on food stamps and welfare programs in the 1970s. No competitive profession can put up with that. We made this a number-one issue with the secretary of defense when I was chief of naval personnel and later as CNO because well-trained and motivated sailors are keys to readiness.

Earlier when I was chief of naval personnel, the CNO and secretary of the navy asked me to give a briefing to the secretary of defense, then Harold Brown, on the urgent need for sea pay to bolster flagging retention. He bought off on it. He let us go forward with the sea pay initiatives He also allowed us to seek other special incentive and retention bonuses.

I was often asked what the Navy was doing going for child care centers. I responded that we were trying to take care of families who were married. Seventy percent of our sailors were married and they did not know how to keep body, soul, and family together, particularly with long deployments from home. Both parents working, what the hell were they supposed to do? They needed help.[54]

Adm. Frank B. Kelso II (CNO 1990–94) offered some thoughts on consideration as well:

I tried throughout my career to help the people who worked for me. Officers who had marital problems or money problems, I always made myself available to talk with them, or give them advice ahead of time if they took the time to ask.

As CNO I made a big effort in a downward-sliding budget to cut money out to improve Navy housing that I thought was inadequate. We had to put a lot of money in homes to do that, and the only [part of] my budget that [was] increasing was military housing. Everything else in the budget was on the way down, but I made an effort to pour more money into morale welfare and recreational facilities. Throughout my career I tried to do things to provide for better health and safety like reducing smoking and auto accidents, but you can't make a horse drink if he doesn't want to. Sometimes they don't want to.[55]

In my interview with Adm. Carlisle A. H. Trost (CNO 1986–90) I offered for his comment Adm. Thomas Moorer's quote: "In every position, a commander's crew will want to know how much you care for them far more than they will ever care how much you know." He responded:

I agree with that wholeheartedly. I have always liked the story about the old cavalry general who told his officers that you first look after your horses, see they are rubbed down, fed, then you look after your people, only then do you eat and bed down. . . . That philosophy is certainly very important. You don't do anything without people. As CNO, I emphasized that people are our top priority. People have to be your top priority because regardless of the equipment you have, or the technology, which serves your mission, without the people who are trained and capable of using that equipment, you have nothing. You have no capability. Readiness is . . . primarily people. You have to have those people who are cared for and know it. The well-being of the troops is critical.

While I worked for Secretary of the Navy John Warner, I was Rickover's point of contact when he wanted to get something to Warner. I was a captain and was promoted while in Warner's office to rear admiral, my first flag command. The ceremony was supposed to start, but we had to wait—I couldn't figure out what was going on because my family was there, my wife and kids, and my father-in-law. Everybody was present. Procedures for a promotion ceremony were fairly consistent—reading the promotion document, then pinning the shoulder boards on the summer uniform.

Admiral Wiesner came in. He was vice chief. It was nice of him to come. Well, we kept waiting. Finally, I turned to my boss and asked him who we were waiting for. "Oh, one more person," he said. About fifteen minutes after the appointed time, Rickover walked into the office. He pinned on one shoulder board, and my wife pinned on the other one. She gave me a kiss, and he looked at me and said, "I am not going to kiss you." And I said, "Thank God."

Admiral Trost told me that as CNO he had many confrontations with Navy Secretary John Lehman in trying to deal with personnel problems:

> I believe he said in one of his books that he was told early on that the way that you control the Navy is to control the flag community, and so he decided to take control, to such a degree that the chiefs of naval operations felt it was a trespass on their prerogatives. At the time that I took over as CNO, there was a backlog of pending flag officer job changes of fifty flag officers. It was a horrendous personnel problem. Lehman was bargaining. He would say to Jim Watkins, when he was CNO, "I will approve this if you will do this." Well the trade-offs he wanted often were unacceptable. So he and I started at loggerheads with this tremendous backlog of admiral assignments. I pointed out to him the difficulty this created in the officer community and in the Navy overall, when officers have short notice of reassignments. It was wrong to suddenly rip out a flag officer on short notice and send him somewhere. That sends a very bad message to his subordinates. It could look like he was reassigned because of poor performance. My stated goal at the time was that a flag officer ought to know six months ahead of time where he is going so he can plan properly. It was simply a considerate thing to me that it should be done as much as possible throughout the Navy. We eventually achieved that goal, but only after John left as the navy secretary.

"If technology is to serve mankind," Trost added, *"people must come first."*[56]

When Adm. Robert L. J. Long was part of the battle group in the North Arabian Sea, he worried about the effects of long deployments.

> We had long deployments coming out of the West Coast. Six months is long enough. . . . You can't operate the fleet and keep the people away from the home port forever. You must permit people to get back to live with their families, take care of their families. I think the worst thing that could happen would be to start driving the fleet without regard to the people, and that's something that the senior naval officers must protect. . . . The truth is that the Navy is normally the force of choice when there is a political or military crisis. As Kissinger used to say, "Where are the carriers?" So there were, and there are today, long deployments, but I submit that that's one area where the chiefs of service, the commanders in

chief, must stand up and say, "Hey, you can't drive this force into the ground. You can do it for a short period of time, but you must give the people an opportunity to be home for a period of time." What we have as a standard is 50 percent, but that has been violated in the past in several instances. You can do it for a short period, but you cannot do it over the long haul.[57]

Not all the admirals I interviewed agreed. In time of war or crisis, Adm. Arleigh Burke's dictum was to send the ships needed to get the job done and make it up to the crews later. Admiral Holloway pointed out that during the Korean War the Navy actually "cross-decked" crew members (mostly flight deck people and engineers) from a carrier returning from a seven-month tour in Korea to a carrier in San Diego that was due to deploy to the western Pacific in a week. "It had to be done," he told me. "The Navy went from seven carriers to twenty-four in eighteen months during the war; pulling them out of mothballs. It was hell, but the need for rotation had to be balanced with the needs of the service—sacrifice! It's hard to be tough, but our job is to win wars."

Admiral Long looked after his subordinates while he was CinCPac, but those who showed poor judgment had to pay the price. When an American submarine was involved in an accident with a Japanese ship, Long noted, "I apologized to the Japanese and also fired the skipper of the submarine. I have rather strong views about commanding officers of ships, submarines particularly. That is, I will try to protect the skipper who is aggressive and has bad luck, but I have no, absolutely no sympathy for a skipper who shows very poor judgment."[58]

For Adm. Charles R. Larson, consideration for subordinates included their families.

You need to really try and make sure that the families are happy and taken care of. I'll tell you a story of something that my wife was probably more responsible for than I was. We were so frustrated with the lack of support sometimes for the Navy's enlisted housing. John Dalton, the secretary of the navy, and his wife came out to visit us out in the Pacific at my headquarters in Honolulu [while] I was CinCPac. . . . Mrs. Dalton [was scheduled for] a tour of Navy housing, and my wife was to accompany her.

Well, they went around and looked at the newest, best Navy housing. After my wife had seen some of the very small number of really nice units we had, she told Mrs. Dalton, "You know, this is ridiculous. Get in the car. I want to show you something else." Then she drove her by the golf course to the awful old, mildewing enlisted housing, very much broken down. They went up and knocked on the door and apologized to the person and asked, "Could we just please come in? We're looking at Navy housing and we want to try to make some improvements." They saw the horrible conditions in the enlisted housing. Then my wife said, "Get back in the car; I'm going to show you something else." And drove her to Hickman Air Force Base and showed her the Hickman House (the style of house for officers) to contrast the disparities.

. . . The next morning when I met with the secretary of the navy, he said, "I don't know what your wife did to my wife. Last night when I came back she was crying." My wife and I went back to Hawaii about a year after I retired and all of that old housing had been bulldozed and there was a brand-new corridor of homes with silver panels on the roof and patios and all this stuff. It had all been re-done. . . . You've got to stick your neck out like that every now and then, and just show people that you're willing to go the extra mile for them."[59]

Admiral Larson, who served an unprecedented second tour as superintendent of the Naval Academy, told his midshipmen:

"Your sailors must know that you truly do care about them. . . . If you honestly don't really care about your people, care about their development, their welfare, then you're in the wrong business. You ought to get out and do something else. That's really what it's all about. You can't pretend that. It's got to be something you really feel." I told them about leadership by walking about. That's how you convey that to the people that you really care for.

. . . I said, "You guys have all these computers. There's going to be a real temptation for you to sit in your station and get on that computer and send e-mails to everybody. . . . Don't forget walking about is important. If you become a slave to that computer and find yourself sending e-mails to a guy that's on the same ship that you are, then something's wrong. Get off that computer, get out of your station, and spend a certain amount of time every day walking around. There's really leadership by walking around. Show the people you really do care. But the other thing, you establish an environment that you really, truly let them know that they're important to your mission; that you're a team. And you're really working hard, but they're working with you, and that they're part of that team, and that they get credit for themselves because you formed that as a team."

I worked very, very hard, and I had a good work ethic. But I tried not to overdrive people. I would encourage them to take breaks, to be with their family. I have a young officer that I'm very close to. He was one of my graduates that I watched for an engineering tour. He was preparing for a big engineering exam. The skipper worked him seven days a week getting ready for his exam. But he was just burning out, and was getting demotivated. And I . . . said, "Even under the most severe circumstances of getting ready for something, never work more than six days a week. You need at least one day off to go home and be with your family. . . . I found that I could get more done in six days than I could in seven because of that. So show that consideration. Show the people that you care." I used to take a briefcase of work home rather than sit on the ship so that other people wouldn't leave because I was still there. I tried to encourage people to go around and ask some of the junior officers, don't you think it's about time for you to go out and be with your family or go do something? I'm going home now, so how about you guys?

An important aspect of mentorship for Admiral Larson was his selection as a White House Fellow, the first naval officer to be selected.

It was a real turning point in my career. It got me with Stuart Udall, then secretary of the interior. He exposed me to things I'd never thought about before and really broadened my horizons. It also taught me what's really important in government and in what's going on in the country, and some things that are not so important. And it allowed me to go back in my Navy commands not getting so worked up about things that weren't that significant. I learned to focus on the important, but also to think a lot more about being a broader person. It also gave me an appreciation for how valuable the military person was.[60]

My interview with Adm. Stansfield Turner included one of the questions I asked all four-star Army and Air Force generals: What makes a man give his life for his commander in wartime, or, in time of peace, work eighteen-hour days, seven days a week for weeks to solve some crisis? Most answered that the reasons include dedication to country and duty, but such devotion is also a response to consideration. Admiral Turner replied:

Looking out for your people is so important. You've got to be careful here, however, because even if you look after your people, if you don't have a genuine interest in them, they will know it. You can do things for them, you can do something like solving a problem they have at home, or you give them time off or, whatever. I think young men and women understand instinctively if you really love them. I use that word pretty generously because I'm old enough to. Do you really care? Do you really have an interest in them? Or are you just going through the formalities? I think they also have to feel whether or not you're honest. There are so many ways to cheat, to try to make your own record look good at the expense of the crew, at the expense of integrity, but if they think you're really pushing Stan Turner . . . then you'll lose them.

Another major element in leading is whenever you take over an organization, whether it's twelve men, a division . . . or a ship, the whole ship, or the whole Navy, I think the most essential step is to set down your objectives and make the crew understand them. First of all, you have to define what you want them to do. You owe it to them. They have to know what you want to do. You don't just do it over the loudspeaker system. It's different in almost every organization. When you're in a ship, you do that individually and collectively, largely with your officers, making sure they know, telling them this is what we want to accomplish, and they in turn inform the men. You do it by example.

I took command in 1962 of a seventeen-year-old destroyer that had been totally neglected, the USS *Rowan*. I was shocked. In our heads, our . . . bathrooms, the toilets were literally a trough of water running down with two boards across it that you sat on. This salt water that ran through here would splash your behind. I mean it was just very awful. . . . This is 1962, long after the war. This ship had been built in the last days of the war. We had . . . throughout the Navy . . . put in regular toilets, but not on this ship. Nobody had bothered. Although my ship was going in to a major overhaul in which this would then certainly be taken care of . . . that was . . . twelve months [away]. It was considered a waste of the Navy's money to repair these toilets for twelve months, because they were scheduled to be torn out by the repairs in the shipyard. . . . There was no question that the Navy thought to put toilet stools in this ship was a noneconomical use of the Navy's money. I had to really talk to get it done, but I persuaded my superiors to let me do it, and I did it.

I'm sitting at my desk a week after I took command of the USS *Rowan* and a blooming cockroach walks right across the desk. I mean he's so bold he doesn't worry about me. I said, this means there's got to be a lot of cockroaches around here. So, I went down one night to the galley. That's where you obviously look for cockroaches. They were all over the place. So, I called in the executive officer and I said, "We got to get rid of the cockroaches." He said, "We can't do that,

Captain. They're in the insulation that's along the side of the hull, and the insulation keeps the hull from sweating." I said, "Pull the insulation off." He said, "Well, we can't. It'll sweat." I said, "Pull the insulation off." In a couple of weeks, we had got rid of the cockroaches. We had other campaigns to clean up the ship for the welfare of the men, and we really worked at it. I mean the crew understood that I cared for them. You might say in fixing the toilets that I took care of their behinds.[61]

Vice Adm. Kent Lee looked out for his sailors when he was the captain of the *Enterprise*:

There were . . . events such as smokers on the hangar deck, and I always went down for those. We published an *Enterprise* newsletter. I wrote a letter once a month for all the families. I still have copies of them. There are two other ways that we communicated on *Enterprise* which I thought were useful. We put out a monthly magazine . . . which described some of the departments on the ship . . . ; sort of a mixture of current events and profile of the department or of an individual, and maybe a short piece by the captain. I found one or more officers who could write fairly well, and I would have them give me a rough draft; we would talk about it. Then I would do the editing and put it in final form. We would send this letter to every dependent once a month. I thought that was very important, because they would hear from me, and that would give them confidence in the ship. They, in turn, would write their men. Those were the tools that I used. We worked at it.

When I asked him how to reward people who consistently overachieve, he responded: "Give them credit for what they did. Nothing more. It's hard to do, because a lot of people have a lot of bosses who say, 'Look what I did.' People like that have people who don't like to perform for them—too much of the personal pronoun. They didn't get credit when they deserved it. Mostly a man wants recognition—by his peers, by his family. There can't be any baloney about this either; it has to be real."[62]

Admiral Holloway, another former *Enterprise* captain, illustrated the importance of consideration by describing an experience he had on that ship during the Vietnam War.

In May 1966, USS *Enterprise* was on its sixth month of an eight-month deployment to Task Force 77 in the Gulf of Tonkin conducting combat operations against the

North Vietnamese. The pattern of operations had been the same since our arrival in December of '65. There were normally four carriers in the western Pacific, the numbers increasing to six or seven during a carrier turnover when the relieving ship and the departing carrier were both available for operations for several days. Of the total number of carriers in the western Pacific assigned to the U.S. Seventh Fleet, a minimum of three carriers were always "on the line." During its line period, the carrier was conducting combat operations against the North Vietnamese for thirty calendar days without a break. Following the thirty days on the line each carrier would proceed to the U.S. Naval Base at Subic Bay for R&R and ship's upkeep. A carrier was given seven days off the line for every thirty days of combat operations, and with two days for transit the carrier netted five days in port.

After the high tempo of operations at Yankee Station flying twelve hours per day followed by under-way replenishment from ammunition ships, oilers, and supply vessels, the crew was ready for R&R when the thirty-first day rolled around. May 1966 was no exception. On May fourteenth the air wing had turned out early for an 0845 deck-load launch against targets in Hanoi and continued flight operations until 2000. After *Enterprise* recovered her last aircraft, we proceeded at high speed to rendezvous with the oiler *Kawishiwi*. Then at four in the morning, with a full load of jet fuel, we broke away and headed for Subic Bay. *Enterprise* was scheduled for five days of R&R beginning May sixteenth in Subic Bay. Then we would depart on the twenty-second of May to be back in the Gulf of Tonkin to commence flight operations at 1000 on Monday the twenty-third.

The crew was really looking forward to this break in the schedule. Sailors live forty to sixty in a single compartment, their bunks stacked four-high with all of their possessions stowed in a locker the size of a high school student's book locker. They line up to shower, brush their teeth, and to eat. There is no beer or liquor for relaxation for them at the end of their sixteen-hour workday. Navy ships are totally dry. And then, there was no femininity to soften the boredom of their all-male society. Liberty ashore was very important.

Shortly after disengaging from the *Kawishiwi* we received a typhoon warning from the fleet weather central in the Philippines that Typhoon Erma was roaring up from the south and would be in the vicinity of Subic Bay on the sixteenth, the day of our scheduled arrival. Consequently we proposed a change of plans to go into Subic on the seventeenth or eighteenth after the typhoon had passed. We needed to get some essential upkeep time for the ship and the air wing in Subic, where we could go alongside Alava Pier. Seventh Fleet quickly okayed our plans, but Mother Nature had a different scheduler. Instead of Erma slicing through the Philippines and heading north, it slowly ground to a halt and interposed itself in a position between *Enterprise* and the Philippines. As a result, we did what all ships do while evading typhoons, maneuvered well clear of the storm, staying at least two hundred miles from the eye, and particularly avoiding the northeast quadrant, meanwhile cursing fate in every term we could conjure up. Every four hours we would get a position report on Erma and a forecast movement of the eye. To our dismay, Erma's projected track did nothing but drive us back toward the Gulf of Tonkin.

Finally, on the twentieth of May, Erma blew through to the north and curved toward the mainland, and the way to Subic was opened. ComSeventhFlt directed *Enterprise* [to] proceed at best possible speed to arrive at Subic on 21 May, offload all dud and battle-damaged aircraft, and then get under way at 1800 that same afternoon to recover a dozen or so replacement aircraft, which would fly out from Naval Air Station Cubi Point to land aboard *Enterprise* that evening. No liberty.

We entered Subic Bay at first light on Saturday, the twenty-first of May. The tugs were waiting and we were able to make up to Alava Pier by 0630. As I stood on the starboard wing of the bridge watching the crew send over the heavy mooring lines to the pier, the exec, Captain Sam Linder, joined me. Sam was an exceptionally fine officer who had stood close to the top of his class at the Naval Academy and gone through flight training before getting his master's and doctorate degrees in nuclear physics at Cal Tech. He had been selected by Admiral Rickover for the nuclear program and been ordered to be executive officer of *Enterprise*. He had been selected early for captain before his arrival onboard. In addition to his being a doctor of nuclear physics, Sam was a fine naval officer, a terrific exec who served me well and dealt harmoniously with the crew.

After lamenting the fickleness of fate that had screwed us out of our five days of hard-earned R&R, Sam, as would be the exec's responsibility, proposed that because of our 1800 departure that night, no one would be permitted off the ship except on business. He suggested that we allow a few especially deserving officers and chief petty officers not in the duty section to go ashore for an hour or so to the PX.

I said to Sam: "I think we should grant liberty to sections 2 and 4 to commence at 0900 this morning and to expire at 1700 onboard this afternoon. We will keep sections 1 and 3 aboard as the duty sections." Sam stepped back a pace, absolutely aghast, and said, "Captain you're joking. Sections 2 and 4 are half the crew—three thousand men. We can't keep them from drinking once they are ashore and we're bound to have some drunks and some may miss the ship's sailing."

I replied "You're absolutely right, Sam, and that's why we're sending them ashore. They deserve to tie one on. They've been working their tails off, and we owe it to this crew to give them every break we can. And frankly, I trust these guys. I think that we can run this liberty in a way so that half the crew can have a real liberty and we'll still get the ship under way without any problems."

Then I added: "Sam, when *Enterprise* went through shakedown training in Guantánamo Bay, Cuba, the Fleet Training Group insisted that we conduct an exercise which required *Enterprise* to get under way with only two sections of the crew aboard." This was to simulate a situation in which there was either a disaster at the naval base or a nuclear accident aboard the ship during normal liberty hours that would require the carrier to be moved for safety purposes. At the time I thought this was ridiculous and questioned whether we should actually try to get this carrier under way with only two duty sections. However, it was a drill that we had to do in order to complete our shakedown check-off list. As it turned out, it was not too difficult during shakedowns in Guantánamo. Now, with almost a year of fleet operations under our belt, the crew was much more competent. I really had confidence in the engineering and reactor departments, where we had enough well-trained and qualified people in the duty sections to handle all at the supervisory tasks in the operation of the nuclear plant. That would be my main concern.

Then, I outlined my ideas on how we would handle the liberty. Sections 2 and 4 would go ashore for a normal liberty which would expire at 1700. This meant that they could go do their shopping, play their sports on the Subic Base, or head for Olongapo to the bars and hot spots that would be open and ready for them. Olongapo bars operated on a twenty-four-hour basis. When the liberty party returned at 1700, we would have sufficient members of the master-at-arms force to meet them as they came aboard and to make sure that all of them went directly to their compartments. They could shower, go to their bunks, and turn in. But no member of sections 2 or 4 would be allowed out of their compartments until midnight, when they would be scheduled for their first under-way watch. By then the sailors in sections 2 and 4 would have had eight hours to sleep it off and a big aluminum tray of mid-rats [midnight rations] under their belt to start off their new day.

If Sam had misgivings, he didn't show them. I called the boatswain's mate of the watch over to me on the wing of the bridge and said, "Boats, I want you to pass the word to all hands that liberty for sections 2 and 4 will commence at 0900 and will expire onboard at 1700 this afternoon." Boats, a twenty-year first-class boatswain's mate, looked unbelieving and just stood there. I repeated my instructions and made it clear that I really intended that liberty be granted as I had indicated. He saluted, went over to the 1MC on the bridge, punched the proper buttons, pushed the lever down, blew his boatswain's call, and piped "All Hands." Then he said in that raspy voice that all boatswain's mates eventually develop: "Now hear this. Now hear this. Liberty will commence for sections 2 and 4 to commence at 0900, and to expire onboard at 1700 this afternoon. I repeat," and Boats growled out his message again. The 1MC lever snapped up, and for about five seconds there was absolute silence about the ship. The normal noises of claxons blowing, hammers banging, and blocks creaking as the ship rigged its in-port gangways were all silent. Then suddenly there was a tremendous cheer as the sailors realized that there would be liberty ashore in spite of our only ten hours in port.

I was interested in the reaction of the men in sections 1 and 3 who would stay aboard with the duty. To their credit, and I think characteristic of this crew, there was no bellyaching. They were just pleased that some of their shipmates were going to get off this iron lady on liberty even if for just eight hours.

At 1630 Sam Linder and I again took station on the starboard wing of the bridge overhanging the Alava Pier. We looked down the road toward the main gate. There wasn't a sailor in sight. Our liberty party had gone ashore in their whites with round hats and black neckerchiefs, looking like a million bucks. They would be easily spotted among the numbers of base sailors and working parties in their blue dungarees. At about 1645 one of the inevitable tropical cloudbursts occurred, a tremendous downpour which covered the entire base. Then we saw them. They came in a crowd, filling up the entire road from curb to curb as they headed toward the ship at a fast walk. By ten minutes to four they had reached the brows and were pouring aboard across the gangways. At two minutes before five the last dozen arrived on the backs and shoulders of their comrades, semi-conscious or unconscious, but on time. They looked awful. Their once spotless white uniforms were drenched with rain and soiled with mud. The only thing that was wonderful was the smiles on their faces.

The officer of the deck called from the quarterdeck to say that most of the men had gotten to the main gate, which was equipped with turnstiles for security, all at the same time. So they were held up for fifteen minutes by the bottleneck, or they would have gotten aboard before the thunderstorms.

At 1700 the special sea detail was called away and I remained on the wing of the bridge to see if we had any latecomers. There was not a single sailor to come aboard the ship after 1700. When I checked with the quarterdeck on any unauthorized absentees the word was that every sailor of that three-thousand-man liberty party was back aboard and accounted for.

By 1730 the eight base tugs had arrived and were making up their lines on our port side. The crew of an ammunition ship tied up astern were down on Alava Pier to handle our lines. By 1755 we were singled up with all systems tested. As the sweep second hand passed by 1800 on the bridge clock, the last line was thrown off and there was a single blast on the ship's whistle, and *Enterprise* was under way for the Gulf of Tonkin and back to the war.

I was sitting in the captain's chair on the bridge at 2345, with the ship fully darkened as we headed west toward the Gulf of Tonkin and Yankee Station, threading our way through the fleets of small native fishing craft. As the mid-watch arrived on the bridge, the young sailors who would man the helm and the engine room telegraphs, operate the radars, and handle the communications chatted with the off-going watch about how much they had enjoyed their strange liberty. They were happy, and their shipmates in sections 1 and 3 were pleased for them. I felt that we had really done the right thing, showing the crew not only how much we thought they deserved a break, but also how much we trusted them. And we did it only after assuring ourselves that it could be done within our approved operating procedures.[63]

Admiral Holloway was not required or even expected to grant liberty to any of the men, and he stuck his neck out a mile by granting it to 50 percent of the crew of a ship operating in a war zone. He was professionally and technically competent to make this judgment and did not put his carrier at risk. It was particularly impressive that the half of the crew that did not get liberty shared in the joy of the other half instead of becoming resentful or jealous.

There is no better way to close this chapter than with the wisdom of Admiral Moorer, who told me: "The most effective leader is the one who gets the most out of his people, often more than they themselves realized. Few people ever live up to their full potential."[64] This statement succinctly puts into perspective the role of consideration in successful leadership.

CHAPTER 7

Delegation

We believe in command, not staff. We ~~believe~~ we have "real" things to do. The Navy believes in putting a man ~~in a position~~ with a job to do, and let him do it—give him hell if he does not perform—but be a man in his own name. We decentralize and capitalize on the capabilities of our individual people rather than centralize and make automatons of them. This builds that essential pride of service and sense of accomplishment . . . this is the direction in which we should move.

Adm. Arleigh A. Burke, USN (Ret.)
Chief of Naval Operations, 1955–61

The commander in chief of the U.S. Armed Forces—the president of the United States—has tremendous responsibility, and never more so than in time of war, particularly a worldwide conflict such as World War II. President Franklin D. Roosevelt, the U.S. commander in chief during that war, oversaw the Allies' strategy, but the war could not have been won had he not delegated command decisions to America's military leaders. Realizing that he could not deal with the mountain of war information that came in every day and still run the country, President Roosevelt selected

Adm. William D. Leahy to serve as his chief of staff. Admiral Leahy reflected that after his appointment:

> I did not see the President again until July 18. That morning he informed me that he had directed the Secretary of the Navy to recall me to active duty as "Chief of Staff to the Commander-in-Chief of the Army and Navy of the United States." That same day I submitted my resignation as Ambassador to France. The President announced my new appointment at a news conference on July 21. I was not present. There was a barrage of questions from the newsmen as to the scope of my authority and activities. The President was cagey, as he always was in dealing with the newsmen, and did not tell them very much. He said that I would be a sort of "leg man" who would help him digest, analyze, and summarize a mass of material with which he had been trying to cope single-handedly. There was considerable pressure at that time for the naming of a supreme commander of all the American forces. Asked if I was to be that commander, the President replied that he still was the Commander-in-Chief. And he was. Asked what kind of staff his military adviser would assemble, he replied he did not have "the foggiest idea." Actually, at no time did my staff number more than two aides and two or three civilian secretaries. Someone suggested I should have a public relations man. To me such an officer could only have been a nuisance! Since I was representing the President at all times, I felt that any talking should be done by Mr. Roosevelt. He was much better at that than I was, anyway.[1]

Admiral Leahy's recollections offer insight into the relationship between Roosevelt, his chief of staff, and the Joint Chiefs of Staff.

> Planning of the major campaigns was always done in close cooperation with the President. Frequently, we had sessions in his study. With the approval of the President, the JCS issued overall directives that sent millions of American men to the various battlefronts and marked the general courses of the thousands of ships that eventually made up the greatest naval armada the world had ever seen. The policy and broad objective were stated by the President; the provisions for transportation, allocation of equipment and munitions were fixed by the JCS; but all details of operations were left to the area commanders. For instance, when it was decided we had to take the Japanese island of Iwo Jima, the Joint Chiefs assigned to Admiral Nimitz the necessary ships and materials and told him to take it. The details of how he was to do it were up to Nimitz. This was in accord with our established principle of single command.[2]

After President Roosevelt's death Vice President Harry S. Truman became the president. Leahy continued in his role as chief of staff to the president.

> Working for three years in daily contact with President Truman in much the same way in which I had worked with President Roosevelt, I found him to be, by every measure of comparison, a great American.
>
> President Truman was thoroughly honest, considerate, and kindly in his approach to problems and in his relations with his assistants. He asked advice in regard to military matters and foreign relations as frequently as did his predecessor. He listened attentively to volunteered advice, and made positive decisions for which he assumed full personal responsibility.
>
> His method of administration differed from that of Mr. Roosevelt in that after reaching a decision he delegated full responsibility for its execution to the department of the government charged by custom or by law with that duty. In my opinion his decisions were usually correct and advantageous to the cause of the United States. Where the results were bad, the fault was in an inefficient handling of details by departmental officials.[3]

Fleet admirals Ernest J. King, Chester W. Nimitz, and William Halsey, and Adm. Raymond A. Spruance were the most important American naval leaders in the Pacific in World War II. Their overwhelming responsibilities could not have been accomplished without delegation. Thomas B. Buell, Spruance's biographer, commented:

> *Their philosophy was to tell the subordinate commander what you wanted done, give him the necessary resources, provide as much information as you could about the enemy, and then let him alone so he could accomplish his mission.* King would upbraid any commander for the sin of oversupervising subordinates with complex, overly detailed directives. The intent was to encourage the on-scene commander to use his initiative and not to inhibit his freedom of action. Spruance's personal belief was that the commander responsible for accomplishing the mission should develop the necessary plans; the proper role of the next highest command echelon was to establish the objective and to suggest how the objective might be achieved.[4]

After assuming responsibility as CinCPac, his biographer noted, Nimitz

> found a few officers who failed to measure up. In due course, he transferred them out, but until he did so he was unable to attain his objective of so delegating authority that he, as commander in chief, would have to do only what nobody

else could do. By spring 1942, however, he had cleared his desk well enough to find time for an occasional game of tennis, and, adjacent to his quarters, he had a space prepared where he could toss horseshoes to work off tension. With the help of such limited exercise he gradually overcame the uncharacteristic insomnia that had vexed him since his arrival at Pearl. . . .

A principle of Nimitz's training plan was to give every man as much responsibility as he could handle, which was often a great deal more than the man thought he was capable of handling. By increasing the competence of his junior officers, he could give them responsibilities their immediate seniors were exercising and thus push the latter into higher responsibilities until, at last, he himself could confine his activities to those broad areas of command, administration, and ceremony that only he, as captain, could carry out. It was Nimitz's abiding rule that he should never do anything his juniors could do, least of all mere shiphandling. "Conning the ship," he said, "is ensigns' work."[5]

As captain of the *Augusta* from 1932 to 1933, Nimitz saw delegation as a key aspect of his leadership. One of his ensigns was Odale D. Waters Jr., who reflected on the ship's condition in an interview on July 14, 1969:

It was a happy ship because everyone was supporting the captain all the time and we just thoroughly enjoyed it. I've always looked back and thought of the tremendous advantage it was to all of us young officers to have had an experience like that. He didn't exactly tell you that he expected you to accomplish certain things, but it was kind of an unwritten thing, you knew instinctively that his standards were high and you'd better measure up.

You did it automatically. You did your very best for him because he was a fine man and a great seaman among other things, a great ship-handler, a great leader. When standing watch on the ship, you were always on your toes trying to do the job right. A junior officer is allowed to make a mistake and sometimes you don't do the job right. But we all tried.

I can give you an illustration. He had a system that was, I think, a very good one, of letting the younger officers handle the ship, and he kept a sort of a record, and you might be getting under way or coming to anchor and you'd hear your name passed over the loudspeaker system to report to the bridge, and he'd say, "Mr. so-and-so, take the ship and get her under way," or "Take the ship and bring her to anchor." I was bringing the ship to anchor one time and I was trying my best to do a good job, but I came in too fast and ended up backing the ship full power astern. I think, I laid out something like 90 fathoms of chain, and finally got her stopped, with no word from the captain at all. He just stood there and watched, and when I got all through and then had to heave back into, say, 60 fathoms to get the ship secure, he said, "Waters, you know what you did wrong, don't you?" And I said, "Yes, Sir, I certainly do. I came in too fast." And he said, "That's fine," and that was the end of it. That was the kind of a man he was.

By his calmness and looking out for his people, I don't mean to imply that he pampered anybody. He could be stern when he had to be. When discipline is required, you have to be that way. He was, but it was in the same calm way he did everything else. It was done on the *Augusta*. There were officers on the ship who were detached and sent other places who didn't measure up. That's the way you have to operate to maintain these things.[6]

H. Arthur Lamar, one of Nimitz's aides in World War II, said that Nimitz showed sensitivity when correcting his subordinates: "He hated to do it, hated to do that sort of thing. In fact he hated to reprimand people, but he did it in such a pleasant way you didn't know you were being reprimanded until it was all over. He had those steely blue eyes and he could look at you with a twinkle and tell you what you were doing wrong and make you realize it without getting mad at you—or without you getting mad. He had a wonderful way with people. He could wrap you around his finger with no effort at all."[7]

As a young ensign James T. Lay served on the battleship *Augusta* beginning in October 1933. He was initially assigned as assistant navigator, a post that provided extensive opportunities to observe the captain, Chester W. Nimitz. Lay's reflections of this experience confirm that Nimitz's leadership included a great deal of delegation:

He used to take pains to let us handle his ship. And I know one thing he used to do. He used to put a box over the side and then we'd maneuver around, each junior officer would have a chance to bring the ship up alongside the box like it was a dock. And this ship-handling experience came in handy later on. He was not critical if the young officer didn't succeed in the handling. He never raised his voice, and he'd say, "Well, if I was doing it, I would have done it this way," and you got the message right away, but he didn't appear to be critical. If you listened, you got the message that this was experience talking. And going in and out of port, he'd let the junior officers handle the ship.

Lay emphasized what every leader responsible for training tomorrow's leaders knows:

It's harder to let somebody else handle your ship than it is to do it yourself. I found this out later on when I had command of a cruiser. It's hard to sit back and watch somebody else, because you have to let him go to the limit, to let him decide when to start backing down or whatever he's supposed to do to keep from hitting a pier. If you jump in too quickly they don't learn, and if you wait too long you're apt to be in trouble. You're always responsible. Later on when I had my destroyer, I found this was good training when he let me handle the ship. I remember the first time I brought [my] destroyer into San Diego. . . . I had an ensign as officer of the deck. He was standing on one foot and then the other; he turned round and said, "Captain, are you going to take the con?" and I said no. And he said, "Well, what do you want me to do?" I said, "I want you to tie the ship up to that buoy." He said, "You mean *me*?" This was almost unheard of, but I had to let him do it. Before we got through we had some good ship-handlers.

Lay was passing on what he had learned from Nimitz: "I learned from Nimitz," he said. "I remember one night that it was dark and we were getting under way in Manila Bay. I had the deck, and he said, 'Take her out,' this through the breakwater and the rest of the obstacles. I thought this was really something to be able to take a cruiser out with the captain standing there. It was the flagship, but he trusted me to do it. Of course, it was comforting to know that I had a nice experienced gentleman standing there watching in case I got in trouble, but it was the way I learned. He was a good teacher."

Lay's interviewer asked him if what Nimitz had done was an unusual thing for a commander to do. "Yes," he answered.

Later on I was surprised at the number of junior officers who had never handled a ship. When I had my destroyer, it was considered a drill if someone other than the captain handled the ship. We were out in Japan, and I used to have them log all these drills, when someone other than I handled the ship. I received a letter from the commander, Destroyer Force, Pacific Fleet, saying that he had noted my last quarterly report; that the ship had gotten under way and come to anchor 121 times during the quarter. Paragraph 2, he had noticed that 91 times during the quarter, someone other than the captain had handled the ship. Paragraph 3, we do not think the commanding officer is getting enough ship-handling experience. The training command staff had this framed, because they asked, what are we trying to do? This is exactly what we were trying to do—train the junior officers to handle a ship.[8]

Nimitz's biographer, E. B. Potter, noted that he

> could match any man on his staff in ability to work hard and put in long hours, *but he refused to let himself get involved in details that others could handle. As during his tour as commanding officer of the* Augusta, *his aim was to do nothing officially that anybody else could do.* He reserved his energies for those activities of decision-making and ceremonial and social obligations that were appropriate only to the captain. As always, he delegated as much authority to his subordinates as he believed they should be able to handle. If they showed they could not, out they went—discreetly if they had seniority, roughly if they were young and needed a shock. "Young man," he would say, "you fail to cut the mustard, and I hereby dispense with your services."[9]

The uncertainty that accompanies delegation may be difficult for the commander to bear. One of the first combat campaigns Nimitz tackled after becoming CinCPac was the defense of Wake Island in March 1942. Nimitz sent Halsey out with Task Force 16 to stop the Japanese. He was annoyed when Halsey did not keep him informed, or even break radio silence. Nimitz knew from Japanese radio traffic that the raid was on, but he wanted an accurate report of what was happening. Potter described the scenario:

> It is not known whether Halsey, while at Pearl, complained to Nimitz about being coached from headquarters during the Marshalls operation. At any rate, his subsequent refusal to make radio contact with CinCPac appears to have been his counterpart to the Civil War general's cutting of the telegraph lines to forestall interference from Washington. On March 5 at last came a brief message from commander, Task Force 16, a request for an oiler with the added laconic report: "This force not, repeat not, damaged."
>
> Nimitz got the point. Thenceforth he made it his firm practice, once a commander had departed on a mission with an approved operation plan, not to send out any directive or advice as to how the mission should be carried out.[10]

During the Marianas campaign in June 1944, Nimitz's chief of staff, Capt. John H. Towers, suggested to Nimitz that he order Admiral Spruance to send Task Force 58 to find the Japanese fleet before it got too close to the Marianas. Nimitz would not do it. "It's poor practice," he said, "to tell a commander on the scene how to fight a battle."[11]

During the battle to free the Philippines, Nimitz was concerned about Halsey's handling of Task Force 34, charged with defending the U.S. invasion force, "but kept his hands off. In the first American carrier counter-attack of the war, he had learned from Halsey himself the wise practice of not interfering with the man at the scene." As the battle continued, Nimitz was frustrated by not knowing the whereabouts of Halsey's force. A Japanese fleet was approaching the San Bernardino strait; was Halsey there to defend? Finally, staff officer Bernard L. Austen said to Nimitz that if he wanted to know whether Halsey had left any force to guard San Bernardino, why not ask him? Nimitz's reply was he did not want to "send any dispatch that would directly or indirectly influence his responsible commander in the tactical use of his forces."[12]

In the spring of 1938, Raymond Spruance was given command of the battleship *Mississippi*. His first voyage turned out to be a scary experience for some of his subordinates. The ship swung at anchor in San Pedro Harbor during the first weeks of his command, and Spruance's officers soon came to regard him as a sort of icon, a dignified gentlemen, remote yet accessible, exacting yet tolerant, all-powerful and all-forgiving, as awesome and as majestic as the battleship he commanded.[13]

Spruance got the *Mississippi* under way for the first time when the ship left harbor for an overhaul at Puget Sound Naval Shipyard at Bremerton, Washington. The crew was anxious to watch his performance at sea. The previous captain had virtually lived on the bridge; Spruance was entirely the opposite. The ship got under way at midnight. Spruance sat wordlessly in his bridge chair while the navigator and senior watch officer weighed anchor and swung the battleship seaward. After the ship cleared the Long Beach breakwater, he went to bed. The exec, navigator, and senior watch officer soon followed suit. When the officer of the day ducked into the charthouse, his ensign assistant suddenly found himself alone, in charge of a thirty-two-thousand-ton ship plowing through the dark, congested waters off Los Angeles.

Later in the voyage, another subordinate had a disconcerting experience as a result of Spruance's policy of delegation:

A lieutenant standing his first OOD watch under Spruance was nonplused by his captain's behavior on the way to Bremerton. *Mississippi* came upon a merchantman which, by the Rules of the Road, was obligated to stand clear while *Mississippi* held course and speed. Merchantmen were notorious for their reluctance to take evasive action. A collision seemed imminent, but the worried OOD could not get Spruance out of bed. Fortunately the merchantman changed course and the OOD entered Spruance's sea cabin to report it would miss the battleship.

"They will do it every time," Spruance responded. "Ease off a little if you think you should. Good night." Spruance rolled over on his side, hitched up the covers around his neck, dug his face into the pillow, and prepared for a comfortable sleep.

"I was stunned," said the officer. "Here was the brand new skipper of a capital ship, underway for the first time with a young watch officer he did not know, and he did not even get out of his bunk."[14]

Obviously, Spruance believed in delegating, but there was an occasion when it almost ended his Navy career. In 1926, while he was commander of the *Osborne,* a dishonest commissary steward stole provisions and submitted false records to cover up his crime of embezzling $3,900. The incident was investigated, and the secretary of the navy blamed Spruance and issued him a letter of reprimand. Spruance fought the charge vigorously. His primary defense was that the commissary officer, not the captain, was responsible for supervising the steward. He did not, however, disclaim his ultimate responsibility since he was the ship's commanding officer.

Delegating, as Spruance's biographer noted, has its downside:

This incident illustrates a potential risk in Spruance's style of leadership. He trusted his subordinates. Having told them what he wanted done, he allowed them to do the job in their own way with a minimum of interference and supervision from him. They were grateful for Spruance's faith and support and responded with intense loyalty, inspired to use their initiative and not to fail Spruance.

This system works when one has able subordinates. It can fail if a subordinate is incompetent and lets down his commander. But Spruance felt that the benefits of trusting his people justified the risk of an occasional betrayal of that trust. His leadership philosophy never changed.

There were many able commanders competing with Spruance for promotion. The letter of reprimand—justified or not—could have tipped the scales against him when the board weighed otherwise equally excellent service records. It could only hurt his chances, and Spruance was pessimistic when the board convened. He needn't have been. The board selected Spruance for promotion to captain in late 1931.[15]

As captain of the *Mississippi,* Spruance had a run-in with an admiral who was unwilling to delegate responsibilities normally given to captains. As described in his biography:

> *Mississippi* was filthy from a dry-docking, and Spruance decided to cancel the usual Saturday morning personnel inspection in order to hold field day. Her life-lines soon were covered with wet, scrubbed canvas, and men in dungarees holy-stoned decks, wiped down bulkheads, and shined brightwork. A message arrived by flashing light from the flagship. "There will be no deviation," it decreed, "from the normal battleship Saturday morning routine."
>
> Spruance was furious. "Pipe captain's personnel inspection," he ordered, then went to his cabin. All hell broke loose: bunk bottoms were jerked from the lifelines, hoses were stowed, dirty water was sloshed down scuppers, men shaved from buckets, and inspection uniforms were grabbed from lockers. In an incredibly short time the decks were dry, gear stowed, and the crew mustered in divisions for inspection.
>
> Spruance popped out of his cabin in his dress whites, carrying rather than wearing his sword. He double-timed up one rank and down the other without breaking stride, his face impassive. The men having been "inspected," he turned to his exec and announced, "Pass the word that the Captain is pleased with the appearance of the ship's company. Have the men leave their quarters and continue field day."
>
> The men loved it.
>
> These kinds of experiences caused Spruance to resent senior officers who interfered in the business of their subordinates. It happened far too often; he would not do it if he ever became an admiral.[16]

But Spruance had a good sense for when responsibility should not be delegated. There were some officers he simply did not trust with responsibility. "A new OOD was looking forward to his one big event of the watch—reversing course in the middle of the ocean in daylight with no other ships in sight. Just before the appointed time Spruance strolled onto the bridge. 'I'll take it, son,' he said. He ordered the new course, then returned to his cabin. The young officer was never allowed to order a course or speed change in his two years aboard."[17] A serious misjudgment earlier in handling the ship had cost him Spruance's confidence.

"Admiral Arleigh Burke," commented Adm. Thomas H. Moorer (CNO 1967–70, chairman of the Joint Chiefs 1970–74),

> had had all kinds of experience in weapons and so on. His strong point was with people because he was a man that knew how to select people and then give them their lead and let them go. He didn't kibitz your move-by-move at all. So it was easy to work for Admiral Burke. I thought it was a very stimulating experience because he didn't try to tell you how to run your business. He wanted certain results and he would say, "I think we ought to go in this direction" in the broadest sense, but he permitted you to make the best use of the people you had. That was his real strong point. It's not totally true that he doesn't want to do things himself, he just wants other people to make him look good—he was a good manager."[18]

When the U.S. Marine Corps commandant, Gen. A. Archer Vandegrift, wanted to visit his men on Guam during the Pacific campaign, Nimitz would not permit it. "Things are very active up there now," he wrote to his wife, "and I am not willing to have my agents there interfered with—even by me—although God knows I would like nothing better than to go up for a visit."[19]

As Nimitz's chief of staff, Adm. Charles H. McMorris shielded

> Nimitz from routine matters, and, indeed from anything else he could handle himself, and he took it on himself to handle a great deal—more, some said, than he had the authority to handle. So many communications sent up the chain of command to Nimitz were stopped by the chief of staff that the latter's office became known as Bottleneck Bay. Nimitz, far from resenting McMorris's presumption, called it initiative and appreciated the fact that it relieved him of many burdens. He did, however, suggest to key staff officers that when they felt strongly that a memorandum should be brought to CinCPac's personal attention, they might pass the original directly to him and send the copy through channels.[20]

On one occasion, at least, Nimitz delegated quite a challenging responsibility to a junior officer—his flag lieutenant, Comdr. H. Arthur Lamar. Plans were being made for the official Japanese surrender to take place on the battleship *Missouri*, and Nimitz's staff was informed that General of the

Army Douglas Macarthur had requested that his flag be flown on the ship. Navy regulations, however, allowed only the flag of the senior naval officer onboard to be "broken at the main." Neither MacArthur's flag nor Nimitz's could be shifted to the forepeak, because neither was senior to the other. The baffled Lamar asked Nimitz, "What do we do now?" The admiral was amused. "You're the flag lieutenant," he answered. "That's your problem." . . . Along with other staff officers, Lamar came up with a solution. He had MacArthur's red flag and Nimitz's blue flag prepared for breaking side by side at the main mast. 'That's the first time in naval history,' said Lamar, 'that there have been two five-star flags on the same mast.'"[21]

Adm. Raymond Spruance continued his habit of delegating as Nimitz's unwilling chief of staff. According to E. B. Potter, Nimitz's biographer,

> Admiral Spruance had two functions at Pearl Harbor—directing the CinCPac staff and advising Admiral Nimitz. In his first capacity he was not the bright, harassed, nail-biting chief of staff of the stereotype. Bright indeed he was; brilliant is probably a better word, but he never let himself become harassed. He was, by his own admission, inclined to be lazy—the kind of smart, indolent character said to make the best commanding officer. When Nimitz passed details down to Spruance, Spruance promptly passed them on down the chain of command. Like Nimitz, he was a master organizer, who organized himself as much as possible out of the staff picture. Also like Nimitz, he was adept at picking men, delegating authority to them, then leaving them alone to perform. . . .
>
> The officers often worked 'til midnight. Nimitz and Spruance had their normal busy days, but they mainly kept aloof from the planning drudgery. They took their long walks as usual, and in the evening read, listened to music, or entertained guests. They thus kept their minds clear for their regular duties and for the stresses to come. Nimitz was thinking ahead to the attack on the Marshalls and beyond, but he kept himself available for consultation on the planning in hand. Even when he was hospitalized in late October with acute prostatitis, officers continually came to consult him in his sick bed.[22]

Spruance learned much about delegation from Nimitz. In drawing up the plans for the invasion of the Gilbert Islands, Spruance's staff members were detached observers rather than harried participants, [and] felt they had a broader, clearer picture than those involved in the actual fighting. They could see situations develop that required action and decisions and they pressed Spruance to send messages to alert Hill and Smith. Spruance refused[,] saying, . . . "I pick men who I believe are competent to do the job, . . . and I'm going to let them do it." The matter was closed. . . .

The most consistent opponent of interference was Admiral Nimitz himself. There were occasions when Spruance would recommend radioing long-range advice to combat commanders whom Spruance thought were missing opportunities or were about to make mistakes. Nimitz consistently said, "Leave them alone. Looking over their shoulder only inhibits them. As long as the local commanders have the responsibility, they must retain the initiative to do what they think best."[23]

When Spruance was about to be relieved as Nimitz's chief of staff to return to a fleet command, he prepared to select his own chief of staff. He wanted a hard worker, a good administrator, and an expert planner for the post. "Spruance functioned best," his biographer noted,

when he talked to others and thought aloud, but the complicated, tedious translation of his decisions and ideas into intricate written plans was a chore he disliked and could not do well. Carl Moore, his chief of staff, was a sound, logical thinker who wrote clearly, just the man to do the work that Spruance wanted to avoid. After seeing Moore in March, he knew that his friend was unhappy in Washington and wanted a change, so Spruance wrote Moore and asked him to be his chief of staff. Moore responded immediately that he accepted the offer. Spruance also asked him to choose the staff officers, except for the flag lieutenant, whom Spruance would personally select.[24]

"Carl likes to commit his thoughts to paper," Spruance said of Captain Moore toward the end of the war, "which is something I never do if I can help it. Details and writing get me bogged down immediately. I hate to write, get my best results by talking to people and thinking out loud, but I get bogged down as soon as I have to assemble my ideas on paper. I can do so if necessary, but I have to go off alone, be completely undisturbed, and labor excessively. My staff has been working up to midnight every night, and I have been working during the day but refuse to go on the night shift. Their labors are almost over now, I hope." Secretary of the Navy James V. Forrestal described Moore's importance to Spruance: "He was a tower of strength. . . . Anything you wanted to know about planning, Carl Moore had at his fingertips. He was the backbone of the staff."[25]

After Admiral King decided that a surface fleet commander's chief of staff should be an aviator, and a carrier fleet commander's chief of staff should be a surface officer, Capt. Arleigh Burke was assigned as chief of staff to Vice Adm. Marc A. Mitscher, and Spruance's chief of staff, Captain Moore, was replaced by Capt. Arthur C. Davis. Davis was in awe of Spruance, whom he viewed as modest, shy, unassuming, and unconceited. He later wrote of the assignment: "Spruance has a genuine super ability . . . to be guarded against all minor distractions. I made up my mind that I would do all in my power to keep his mind free of all deadening inconsequentiality that can waste time and take attention from the things that really matter. Without any discussion of the subject, we had an understanding that I would handle the nits and lice, as it were, and that he would be brought into the ring only on matters of importance."[26]

But Spruance's delegation of responsibility was not always complete. When the plans for the invasion of the Marshall Islands were being made and carried out, he deviated and issued detailed orders, something he usually left to the carrier fleet commander, Vice Admiral Mitscher. Spruance felt that "the Truk raid was extremely dangerous. If Task Force 58 made one bad move, the altered Truk air and sea forces could hit Mitscher before he hit them. He knew that he might be forced to rapidly modify his plans. If quick decisions were needed, he did not want to take the time to discuss alternatives with Mitscher by message. One suspects, also, that Spruance was not entirely confident that the carrier admiral could execute the raid without making a potentially fatal error in judgment."[27]

After World War II, Spruance elaborated on his philosophy of delegation:

Things move so fast in naval actions, and the consequences that hang on the results of these actions are often so momentous, that fast teamwork is essential. Teamwork is something that comes best from association, training, and indoctrination. There are too many variables possible in war for everything to be foreseen and planned for ahead of time. Our plans can be made out in great detail up to the time we hit the enemy. After that, they have to be flexible; ready to counter what the enemy may try to do to us and ready to take advantage of the breaks that may come to us. To do that the man on the spot must know where he fits into the operation, and he must be able to act on his own initiative, either without any orders at all, because radio silence may be in effect, or on very brief orders because there is no time for long instructions.

The most consistent message given by Spruance to his commanders was: "Desire you proceed at your discretion selecting dispositions and movements best calculated to meet the enemy under most advantageous conditions. I shall issue general directives when necessary and leave details to you and Admiral Lee."[28]

Delegation was something Admiral Halsey learned about early in his naval career. In June 1918 Halsey was commander of three ships, the USS *Beale,* a destroyer, and the sloops HMS *Kestral* and HMS *Zephyr.* He wrote in his diary on June 18, 1918, "Had the time of my life bossing them around. . . . My first experience in multiple command in the war zone. I was as proud as a dog with two tails." On July 1, 1918, Halsey's ship received an SOS from USS *Covington* saying it had been torpedoed and giving its position. Without any instructions from his headquarters boss, Adm. Sir Louis Bayly, Halsey went to the ship's rescue. "I'd had every hope of getting her to port," he later stated. "My message to Admiral Bayly, simply informing him that I was proceeding to assist her, may sound presumptuous, but it would have been silly to request instructions. The Admiral himself always pointed out that the man on the spot had so much better information than the man at headquarters, it was impossible for HQ to give proper instructions. This is a lesson that has stood by me all through my naval career."[29]

On November 27, 1941, a "war warning" arrived in Washington. Adm. Husband Kimmel was concerned about the U.S. picket-line islands of Midway, Wake, Johnston, and Palmyra. He did not think they were sufficiently well armed, and in particular wanted to send fighter planes to Wake Island. It fell to Halsey to get them there. Halsey related in his autobiography:

We fully expected that this cruise would take us into the lion's mouth, and that at any moment an overt act would precipitate war. Before we shoved off, I asked

Kimmel, "How far do you want me to go?" His reply was characteristic. "Goddammit, use your common sense!" I consider that as fine an order as a subordinate ever received. It was by no means an attempt to pass the buck. He was simply giving me full authority, as the man on the spot, to handle the situation as I saw it, and I knew that he would back me to the hilt.[30]

In May 1942 the Japanese were making moves toward New Guinea and the Solomon Islands. Admiral Halsey was instructed to watch their maneuvers but was restricted by orders in the operations he could perform. This upset Halsey, and he violated the restrictions. "I was hamstrung and hobbled," he later wrote. "Back in World War I, Admiral Sir Louis Bayly had always given his destroyer skippers full discretion at sea, on the theory that the man on the spot knows the local situation better than the man back at headquarters. I thought of this now, and I deemed it a lot more important to scout a potential breakthrough than to risk the surprise and loss of our bases. I headed north."[31]

Halsey, like Nimitz, was a great believer in delegating. He later described how he organized his command when he was chosen by Nimitz to replace Vice Adm. Robert L. Ghormley as commander, South Pacific:

> I have said that Miles Browning and Julian Brown were the only two officers on my staff who accompanied me to the South Pacific. The rest were aboard the *Enterprise,* which delivered them and certain key enlisted personnel at Nouméa on October 25, the day before the Battle of Santa Cruz. As I dug into my new job, I realized that the tremendous burden of responsibility which Bob Ghormley had been carrying was far beyond my own capacity. I have known too many commanding officers whose epitaph could be
>
> > I am cook and a captain bold
> > And the mate of the *Nancy* brig,
> > And a bo'sun tight and a midshipmite
> > And the crew of the captain's gig.
>
> I believe in delegating all possible authority. I called in my staff and told them, "There's a lot to be done. Look around, see what it is, and do it." Able as they were, the job swamped even them and I had to supply them with more assistants. Before we were running smoothly, Operations alone was getting the full-time attention of twenty-five of my officers.[32]

One might think that Nimitz's relief of Admiral Ghormley was contrary to his policy of allowing commanders in the field to make their own decisions. It was not. If a commander failed to perform successfully, he was fired. Ghormley's "messages had become unduly pessimistic, almost defeatist," and Nimitz believed he was "no longer capable of commanding in time of crises. And if Nimitz ever was slow in replacing a nonperformer (as he sometimes was), King would do it for him. It was a 'perform or perish' policy."[33] One of the reasons for Admiral Ghormley's relief was his inability to delegate:

> Admiral Nimitz next prepared the necessary dispatch orders to be handed Halsey on his arrival in Nouméa. To Mrs. Nimitz he wrote: "Today I have replaced Ghormley with Halsey. It was a sore mental struggle and the decision was not reached until after hours of anguished consideration. Reason (private): Ghormley was too immersed in detail and not sufficiently bold and aggressive at the right times. I feel better now that it has been done. I am very fond of G. and hope I have not made a life enemy. I believe not. The interests of the nation transcend private interests."[34]

Admiral Mitscher, like Raymond Spruance, detested paperwork, and he delegated to his chief of staff, Capt. Arleigh Burke, an incredible amount of authority. "At that time," Burke later recalled,

> he allowed me five minutes a day to present papers to him. He said, "I will sign papers up to five minutes a day, and you will sign the rest of them." He said: "There shouldn't be more than one or two papers that I have to sign. If there are any more than that, then something's going wrong that ought to be corrected. If you can't explain a paper in two minutes, it's not clear." So I did. I got where I was pretty good at putting the concise guts of a paper on the top—if he wanted to read it, it was there—and he'd say, "Do I agree with this?" "Yes, Sir," and he'd sign it and never read it. He never read a whole long paper. I'd give him a concise summary saying what it was if he wanted to read it, and sometimes he did read those. But he had me sign all the rest of them as chief of staff. He said to me: "This will do two things. You'll make sure that I get only the important ones, you'll handle all the trash, and it will make sure that you recognize what's important and what isn't."
>
> That was true enough, and this was another thing that he had done all the way through. In the training of the Eighth Fleet and CinCLant, Burke did the

same thing he had done before. He pushed the responsibility down to give his subordinates just as much responsibility as he could possibly do. He kept the responsibilities that were his, but he gave his subordinates authority and responsibility, and they loved it. This is how he would get so very much done.[35]

Mitscher's failing health led to even greater delegation. "Early in December" 1945, Burke recalled, "Mitscher didn't care much about the fleet. He was obviously tired, and I would tell him what was happening, what I had done, signed. Even the five minutes I didn't take up. He went to the hospital and they thought he had bronchitis in January, but it wasn't bronchitis, he had a heart attack, and he died there on the third of February. He was just sixty years old."[36]

Admiral Mitscher was, along with Admiral Halsey, one of the most successful carrier combat leaders of the Pacific war. Burke's recollections offer insight into Mitscher's leadership style. Along with most of the paperwork, Mitscher delegated to Captain Burke the task of firing those who failed to perform, not an easy task.

> It was my job, as chief of staff, to fly over to tell the unfortunate man who didn't measure up that he was all through—that he was relieved from command at that moment—and that he should take the first available transportation back to Pearl. Not one of them ever argued or objected. They knew why it had to be done. We did not broadcast this action, but, of course, others had seen what had happened—or didn't happen—and could guess what was going on. It was an onerous and unpleasant task for me, but a necessary one. I had to relieve a few senior people in destroyers in the Solomons for lack of combat ability so I knew the necessity for such action. . . . Some men are just not capable of performing properly under heavy stress or great responsibility. That can usually not be determined before a man has operated under the severe conditions of hard-fought battles— and most battles with the Japanese were hard-fought. All men who have been in combat realize this and know that one of the fundamental requirements for winning battles is to have commanders who know how to use their force, have the initiative to press the attack home, have the knowledge to enable them to take proper actions when things go wrong and who are willing to shoulder the heavy responsibility for leading men into battle. Men who fight with skill, vigor and a keen sense of duty must have competent commanders who are themselves inspirational. The responsibility to insure that subordinate commanders do perform

with the requisite skill and judgment is one of the most important, and one of the most distasteful, duties of a combat commander. Admiral Mitscher, during that war, became one of the best battle commanders the United States has ever had, and that was partly due to this demanding very high performance from his commanders and his willingness to peremptorily relieve those who couldn't or didn't measure up. Along with this was a deep appreciation and understanding of those commanders, and all combat personnel as well, who did measure up. With these two characteristics it is no wonder he gained the respect—and then the love—of his command. . . .

After WWII we realized as early as 1946 a Soviet expansion. So we had to build a fleet in the Mediterranean to cope with it. Near the end of that year, the secretary of the navy, Forrestal, made a speech in which he said that Admiral Mitscher was going to go to sea to form a new task force. The first I knew about that speech was in early January . . . when Admiral Mitscher called me up and said he was going to sea. I asked where, and he said the Atlantic. I said, What for? Mitscher delegated the entire task of setting up, from scratch, the Eighth Fleet, ships, personnel supplies, ports, everything.

Mitscher instructed Burke to create a combat-ready task force within three months.

I said: "My goodness, that's a terrific job. Where is the Eighth Fleet now?" Mitscher said: "There isn't any Eighth Fleet now. I want you to be detached as soon as you can, go down to Norfolk, choose a staff, form a staff, find out what needs to be done, get some place to operate from, and get going on this just as soon as you can."

We didn't have any flagship, didn't have any ships, no ships at all. I said: "All right, Admiral, I can leave fairly soon." I went down to Norfolk. About the first of February, I started calling up people I had known before, experienced people, to see if I could get them on the staff, . . . I got hold of as many battle-experienced people as I could get. . . . What I needed were the essential people, about fifteen people, of the various elements, a good gunner, a good aviator, a good operations man, a good communicator. We didn't know how much staff we were going to need. We knew that the smaller the staff, the better. . . .

We knew that the situation in the Atlantic Fleet was pretty sad, but we didn't know how sad. There were really no trained ships. This was just a few months after the war ended, and . . . all the services discharged everybody they could. People were flocking to be discharged and we were putting ships out of commission, and before the ships could get out of commission there was nobody left in the ships to decommission them—let alone mothball them. . . . So we went there . . . with a list of ships that we needed. We needed carriers in our task force, some cruisers, some destroyers, and so forth. Those ships, if they were to be of any value at all, had to be manned well enough with trained men to operate with some degree of efficiency and they had to be trained to be combat-capable. . . .

Of course, when a war is over, everybody lets down. People wanted to go on leave, and should. There was not much urgency. But this requirement of being ready for combat in three months was urgent enough. . . . After years of wartime pressure, you can't put sudden pressure on an organization without a reason. Just telling them that we might have to go into combat in a couple of months is not enough reason. So we wanted to establish a deadline, and we chose the middle of April. We wanted to have an exercise, a real, wartime, combat exercise to determine whether we had any capability at all or not. We asked President Truman if he would be willing to come down and inspect the fleet (which we didn't have yet) in April, and he said he would. He would like very much to do that. So there we had a deadline and we had to prove ourselves.[37]

Admiral Moorer was CNO from August 1, 1967, to July 1, 1970. In that position he had three meetings a week with the Joint Chiefs of Staff, which with preparation and follow-up required considerable time. Delegation was crucial. "The CNO must delegate authority to the deputy," Moorer reflected, "otherwise you just wouldn't have enough time. Many people find it difficult to delegate authority. But in a job of that scope one can't function without delegating authority. You just have to get a feel for what are the critical items of the day that you have to deal with." He considered the ability to delegate authority in a sense a measure of a leader's ability.

After all, you are responsible, but just the same, these other people that you have working with you are well qualified and capable of making decisions. The show must go on and you can't possibly handle it all yourself. . . . I think that there's just too much centralization in our system and not enough delegation of authority. In the military organizations, certainly in the Navy, we have change-of-command ceremonies, and I think it's always significant because you have an instantaneous transfer of authority. But, unfortunately, there are all kinds of people who are clamoring around for authority, but none of them seem to be equally zealous about acquiring responsibility and accountability, which in the Navy we've always considered inseparable. If you've got the authority, then you've got to take the rap if the exercise of authority you performed doesn't produce. But that's not true in the civilian world. It's certainly not true in politics. I think also there was some effort made to give junior officers greater responsibility. But at the same time, I think that I emphasized through every means of communication I had, the importance of the chain of command and the necessity to back up and support the people that work for you as far as you can, including chief petty officers.[38]

In some circumstances delegation is leadership failure. Adm. James L. Holloway III (CNO 1974–78), for instance, learned what not to do from a boss who delegated too many of his responsibilities.

I worked for a vice admiral in the Pentagon who tended to be autocratic and didn't listen to people, which is in a way an unfair criticism because he listened to me. He did some things that I didn't admire that mainly had to do with his work ethics. He was a great golfer and on a nice day he would take off for the afternoon. He would say, "Jim, you run the office." Congressmen would call up the office to talk to the admiral, and they would say, "I have to have an answer right now. How does the admiral feel about it?" As the executive assistant I generally knew the admiral's feelings on the important issues so I would say, "The admiral would be very much opposed to this." I found myself in the business of making major decisions in substantive areas. Of course, I reported to the admiral everything I did in his absence. He'd laugh and say, "Well, you gave the right answer." He believed in delegating, but I am not sure it was for the right reasons.[39]

Adm. James D. Watkins (CNO 1982–86) reflected on the importance of delegating responsibility to subordinates.

I'm a great believer in delegating. I leave my people alone. I can watch what they are doing from a distance and if I don't like what they are doing, I can haul them in and talk about it. I am a great believer in that. You are told to delegate, but a lot of people don't understand delegation. Until you see how effective it can be, you hope that you pick people that have the potential to run things on their own and have the fire in the belly for it and have the commitment for it. Many times, you find that you don't have the right person and have to do the management on your own in that department until you can make the change. For the most part in the Navy, people try to pull on the oars together, trying to carry out the mission, doing the best they can. Some are more mediocre than others in terms of leadership qualities, but they all respond to you. They all try to do the job well. That is quite different from the private sector.[40]

After his retirement, Admiral Watkins was appointed to President Ronald Reagan's cabinet as the secretary of energy. His philosophy on delegation remained the same even in that entrenched bureaucracy.

I set it up so that I learned whom I could listen to and believe and those I couldn't. Those I'd believed, I brought in the close inner sanctum and said, "Give me your ideas." I brought in the laboratory czar, I brought in the best that we had. I allowed them to do things. I also tried to manage . . . the bureau and get them into the modern world. They were declaring sovereign immunity still. But wait a minute, the war is over, guys; there is no sovereign immunity. You guys are lousing up the environment. You guys don't need to do it. You can do both, you can be ready and you can also be clean. I tried to bring in the Rickover model.[41]

While he was CNO (1996–2000), Adm. Jay L. Johnson

tried to let the people around me exercise their skills and judgment. I tried to give them, through example and leadership and guidance, the support they needed to make themselves and our mission successful. I worked hard at that. I believe in trust and confidence in the chain of command. I believe in empowering people. That's not a leadership cop-out. I think it's a very strong element of leadership—developing the future leaders. It was the most important thing that guys like me had to do, and I told the flag officers that every year. We all make weighty decisions and are responsible for running our own ports or running the United States Navy, but don't ever, ever lose sight of the fact that what you're really here for right now is to groom and nurture the next generation of leaders. They're the ones that are going to make it happen.[42]

Adm. Robert L. J. Long commented on delegation:

I think it is a fundamental philosophy in the submarine force, and I'd say . . . was enhanced in the nuclear submarine force. For someone to exercise his responsibility, he needs to know what's going on. You can't know what's going on if you don't understand it. Also, I think it is part and parcel of submarine force philosophy . . . that a commanding officer can delegate every bit of authority that he possesses, but he cannot delegate his responsibility. To exercise that responsibility, he must know what's going on. So, as far as I was concerned, I never tried to tell the chief engineer how to do his job, but I expected he would be meticulous in keeping me informed if there were any problems at all developing.

I think most commanding officers believe this, but I never relied on just the chain of command keeping me informed; in other words, the exec or the engineer or the weapons officer or the communicator. I believe that you have to get information wherever you can. Based on that, I was a great believer in walking my ship and talking to the people, talking to the chiefs. I was absolutely careful never to give orders that bypassed that chain of command. If I wanted something changed, I would go to the chief engineer and direct him. But I always felt that I had free license to get information wherever I could. That's the same philosophy I had when I was the commanding officer of the ship and also as commander in chief of the Pacific theater.[43]

Some comments Admiral Holloway made during an interview sum up the role of delegation in successful naval leadership.

Delegation is a tool of command. Within military organization it is essential for the control of armies and fleets, down to the level of individual administrative offices, ship's divisions, and tactical maneuver units. Delegation as an aspect of leadership can be a two-edged sword. On the positive side, when wisely done it relieves the leader from the burden of minutiae and distributes the command and management workload down to the appropriate level of competency for the various tasks involved in the complex operations of a military organization. Delegation beyond that very fine point of judgment by the commander can actually result in the leader himself being eliminated from the most important decisions of his command. This is not what we are looking for in military leadership. The intent is to have the person in command to be the smartest, the wisest, and the most experienced person in that unit. If too much of his responsibility is delegated, then what gets to the operators is a product of people less wise or less professionally competent as the carefully selected leaders.

Early in my career, just after World War II, I was in a position . . . to exercise an editorial role in the production of written instructions for the military. During the war, paperwork had declined to a minimum. As an example, in the naval squadrons embarked aboard the carriers, none of the pilots with the exception of the CO and the executive officer had any administrative duties. If there were written statements of policy, it is doubtful that the younger officers in the squadrons would have read them. In the intense environment of World War II an individual learned by experience. If a mistake was made it was immediately corrected by a senior and generally with a degree of passion that . . . made a permanent impression.

After World War II there was a great flurry of writing operating procedures, administrative policies, and leadership manuals. This was in fact a good idea, as many of our most experienced and competent personnel were leaving the service. I happened to be between stations for two weeks and was correcting a "leadership manual" when I ran across a chapter entitled "Leaders Must Delegate." I first was tempted to strike out the entire sentence since it certainly did not represent what I had learned in my three years at the Naval Academy and two and a half years in the fleet. There was a better and more immediate solution. I simply added one word so that the new chapter heading was "Leaders Must Delegate Wisely."

In today's Navy, the subordinate officers are detailed to a command just as the commanding officer was, by the Bureau of Naval Personnel. The new commander in reporting to his unit may know some of the people onboard from previous associations and tours of duty, but it is doubtful that he was able to select any of them. In most cases, the bureau simply detailed on the basis of the qualifications of the individual as set forth by his military record and a person's availability for transfer. Even past fitness reports are not available to the detailers in their raw unedited form. So I have always taken with a grain of salt the statement of a commanding officer who says that he was able to walk into a new command and immediately feel comfortable in widely delegating authority because he knew the capabilities of his officers.

The key to delegation is to respect the principle of command. Officers are appointed to command on the basis that they are among the wisest, most experienced, and most competent of their contemporaries. The subordinate officers in the command obviously will have less experience than their commanding officers. They may or may not have above-average intellect and professional potential. That will only be known if they should in the future be screened and selected for command themselves. So I do not consider that diluting the responsibilities of military command by perfunctory delegation is good leadership. Rather, delegation should reflect a careful consideration of a commander's personal commitment to his unit.

I always viewed with suspicion those . . . units I visited when I was commander, Seventh Fleet, during the Vietnam War or later vice chief and then chief of naval operations, when the commander could not give me the details of his command that I felt he should be aware of, with the excuse that one of his technical staff officers handles it. I considered that a commander ought to be aware of every activity in his command, even if by an order-of-magnitude assessment. I felt that these commanders who couldn't give me even a general answer to my questions were deficient in one of two ways. First, they may not have known the answer. Some officers might say, "I'm not really into ship's engineering but the chief engineer will know." The captain ought to know, too. Or secondly, when an officer could not give me a reasonable appraisal of a situation that existed within his command I felt that was perhaps a cover-up for a problem which he did not want to disclose.

Having thus far focused on the negative side of the issue does not mean that I am opposed to delegation; I couldn't be. There is no human being that can know all about everything in his command. But there is a point to which he must have informed himself, so that he can be aware of the capabilities and the limitations of his unit. And this point is a product of the commander's personal judgment. How far must he go in getting into the details that could grow into important facts that he must have at his fingertips? How much time can he afford to spend probing the details, already knowing and understanding the overall status of the situation? It would be my thumb rule that a commander must delegate only those things, which if he tried to handle himself, would bog him down in details not consequential to the immediately successful operation of his command. A fleet commander needs to know generally where his ships are now, and where they will probably be next week. But he does not need to know where his ships and units will be deployed a month from now. First, keeping abreast of future plans is time-consuming. Second, the details of future planning can be conjectural and not essential knowledge for command of a fleet on the daily basis in carrying out its mission. It is the immediate situation that counts, and the future plans may change many times.

While I was at the Naval Academy and again in the early 1950s between World War II and Korea, I often encountered a theory called "completed staff work." I am sure that if one went to an index of past issues of the *Naval Institute Proceedings* he would find a long listing of articles pro and con about completed staff work. It was a fairly prevalent doctrine of leadership and command in the Navy. It most probably began in the 1930s when there was little to do in the fleet except maintain the ships and ensure good order and discipline. There was not enough money for fuel to steam more than a day or two a month, and the idea of shooting up rounds of ammunition for target practice was unthinkable. The powder and bullets had to be reserved for the war with Japan that was sure to come. Even routine fleet maneuvers such as refueling under way alongside a tanker were approached with utmost trepidation. In the case of a collision, money would have to be spent to repair the ships involved, and funds were not budgeted for that purpose. So during that period and the letdown in the Navy after World War II there were a lot of officers trying to gain experience who had very little operating opportunity. So much of an officer's time was consumed with theoretical concepts, and what better way to get one's thoughts organized than to write them out. So the concept of completed staff work was born.

The main point was that the commander never looked at his plans or operation schedules until they were laid on his desk typed in the smooth for him to sign. This was the hallmark of an exquisitely trained and harmonized organization, where all began with the junior men in the plans division or the operations section preparing the concept drafts for future schedules and operations. At each layer of the staff or in the ship's organization, there would be some degree of screening and revision, but basically the papers when they appeared upon the desk of the commander . . . were the product of the most junior people in the organization.

The doctrine of completed staff work seemed prevalent when I was a midshipman at the Naval Academy, and it was suggested to us by some of our military staff instructors as the planning approach we should endorse. However, in the 1940s, when I had joined the Navy as a commissioned officer, I found that those seniors whom I admired and whom I considered to be the real up-and-coming leaders in the Navy were opposed to the concept of completed staff work and made it very clear to me as their junior officer that I was to consult with my seniors as I proceeded with the preparation of any such planning papers. These officers always had in their own minds the concepts . . . they wanted to develop for these operations or training exercises. They wanted to see programs made, not the maintenance of the status quo. And they had the experience and the clout to propose new approaches and imaginative solutions as well as to keep the tried procedures and tactics for which no substitutes had been devised.

In summary, delegation is so essential to the command and administration of military forces that it is an absolute necessity. Yet unlike such leadership factors as integrity, commitment, and even reading, it is not an absolute quality. Delegation can be overdone just as it can be underapplied. . . . The successful leader . . . knows what to delegate, how to delegate, and to whom.[44]

CHAPTER 8

Fix the Problem, Not the Blame

Men will not trust leaders who feel themselves beyond
accountability for what they do.

Adm. Kinnaird R. McKee, USN (Ret.)
Director, Navy Nuclear Propulsion, 1982–89

General of the Army George C. Marshall, throughout his exceptional service to his country—as chief of staff of the U.S. Army from 1939 to 1945, secretary of state from 1947 to 1949, and secretary of defense from 1950 to 1951—followed a policy he frequently emphasized to his subordinates: "Fix the problem, not the blame." It was a significant factor in his leadership success and certainly was to some extent responsible for the loyalty of subordinates.

Is accountability important in the Navy as well? In an interview with me on February 23, 2001, Adm. Kinnaird McKee pointed out: "It is cruel, this accountability of good and well intentioned men. But the choice is that or an end to responsibility. And finally, as the cruel sea has taught us, an end to the trust and confidence in men who lead." Several incidents in U.S. naval history are particularly significant because they focus on accountability: the surprise attack on Pearl Harbor, December 7, 1941; the sinking of the USS *Juneau,* November 12–13, 1942; the sinking of the USS *Indianapolis,* July 29–30, 1945; the Cuban Bay of Pigs invasion in April 1961; the seizure of the USS *Pueblo,* January 23, 1968; and the terrorist attack on the USS *Cole* in Yemen, October 12, 2000.

The objective of this chapter is to assess accountability for these tragedies. It is important to distinguish between accountability and blame. Assessing accountability implies examining events to determine what can be learned from them; fixing blame merely finds a scapegoat to carry the responsibility for mistakes that may have been made by others. If an investigation is channeled so as to find someone to blame or is designed to cover up mistakes, there will be no accountability, and no lessons will be learned. We must learn from our mistakes; we owe that to those whose lives were destroyed by the tragedies discussed here.

The Surprise Attack on Pearl Harbor

On December 7, 1941, the Japanese launched a surprise attack on Pearl Harbor. It was, as President Franklin D. Roosevelt said in his speech before a joint session of Congress on December 8, 1941, "a day that will live in infamy." The U.S. losses were 2,403 dead and 1,177 wounded. Eight battleships, three light cruisers, three destroyers, and four auxiliary craft were sunk, capsized, or damaged. The aircraft losses were 13 Navy fighters, 21 scout bombers, 46 patrol bombers, 4 B-17s, 12 B-18s, 32 P-40s, and 20 P-36s; numerous other aircraft were damaged. The Japanese lost twenty-nine aircraft, one large submarine, and five midget submarines.

Adm. Husband E. Kimmel was commander in chief, Pacific Fleet, on the day of the attack. There was an immediate demand nationwide to know how this debacle had been allowed to occur. The first preliminary investigation was made by Secretary of the Navy Frank Knox, who flew out to

Pearl Harbor on December 8, 1941. He reported his findings to President Roosevelt on December 14. As a result of Knox's findings, Admiral Kimmel was relieved of his command on December 16, as was the Army commander at Pearl Harbor, Lt. Gen. Walter C. Short. Their relief was announced to the public on December 17, and Kimmel was retired on March 1, 1942.

Nine separate investigations of the Pearl Harbor surprise attack were made between December 9, 1941, and May 23, 1946: Secretary of the Navy Frank Knox's investigation, December 9 through 14, 1941; the Roberts Commission's investigation, December 18, 1941, through January 23, 1942; the Hart inquiry, February 22 through June 15, 1944; the U.S. Army Pearl Harbor Board, July 20 through October 20, 1944; the U.S. Navy court of inquiry, July 24 through October 19, 1944; the Clarke investigation, August 4 through September 20, 1944; the Hewitt inquiry, May 14 through July 11, 1945; the Clausen investigation, January 24 through September 12, 1945; culminating in a joint congressional committee's investigation, November 15 through May 23, 1946. The witness testimony, documents, and exhibits from these investigations fill thirty-nine volumes! My discussion of accountability for Pearl Harbor will focus on two of the most important issues.

The Pearl Harbor surprise attack has been, and will doubtless continue to be, the subject of numerous works. Historians have assessed accountability for the success of the Japanese attack surprise in various ways, but most consider Admiral Kimmel and General Short either derelict in their duty to defend Pearl Harbor and Hawaii or scapegoats blamed to shield Washington bureaucrats who suspected the attack was imminent and failed to give the two men the information they needed to prepare for it. My objective is to concentrate on where the accountability lay, and in particular to determine whether Kimmel and Short were derelict, as alleged, in not coordinating to decipher the intent of the warnings both had received and what should have been done to prepare for the attack.

The warning message of November 27, 1941, from the CNO, Adm. Harold R. Stark, to Admiral Kimmel's headquarters in Pearl Harbor stated: "This dispatch is to be considered a war warning . . . and an aggression now by Japan is expected in the next few days." It was clearly the thought in December 1941, however, that any such Japanese aggression would occur in the Philippines or elsewhere in the Far East. The brass in Washington, D.C., did not expect Pearl Harbor to be attacked. Indeed, one of the conclusions of the Navy court of inquiry was that,

> although the attack of 7 December came as a surprise, there were good grounds for the belief on the part of high officials in the State, War, and Navy Departments, and on the part of the Army and Navy in the Hawaiian area, that hostilities would begin in the Far East rather than elsewhere, and that the same considerations which influenced the sentiment of the authorities in Washington in this respect, support the interpretation which Admiral Kimmel placed upon the "war warning message" of 27 November, *to the effect that this message directed attention away from Pearl Harbor rather than toward it.*[1]

Secretary Frank Knox agreed:

> The Japanese air attack on the Island of Oahu on December 7th was a complete surprise to both the Army and the Navy. Its initial success, which included almost all the damage done, was due to a lack of a state of readiness against such an air attack, by both branches of the Service. This statement was made by me to both General Short and Admiral Kimmel, and both agreed that it was entirely true. Neither Army or Navy Commandants in Oahu regarded such an attack as at all likely, because of the danger which such a carrier-borne attack would confront in view of the preponderance of the American naval strength in Hawaiian waters. . . . Neither Short nor Kimmel, at the time of the attack, had any knowledge of the plain intimations of some surprise move, made clear in Washington, through the interception of Japanese instructions to Nomura. . . . There was no attempt by either Admiral Kimmel or General Short to alibi the lack of a state of readiness for the air attack. Both admitted that they did not expect it, and had taken no adequate measures to meet one if it came. Both Kimmel and Short evidently regarded an air attack as extremely unlikely. . . . Both felt that if any surprise attack was attempted it would be made in the Far East.[2]

The five-member Roberts Commission, which met from December 18, 1941, through January 23, 1942, was headed by Owen J. Roberts, a sitting associate justice of the U.S. Supreme Court. The commission interviewed 127 witnesses and examined a large number of documents in its effort to determine whether "any derelictions or errors of judgment on the part of the United States Army or Navy personnel contributed to such successes as were achieved by the enemy . . . and if so, what these derelictions or errors were, and who were responsible therefor." The commission's conclusions were harsh:

> In light of the warnings and directions to take appropriate action, transmitted to both commanders between November 27 and December 7, and the obligation under the system of coordination then in effect for joint cooperative action on their part, it was a *dereliction of duty* on the part of each of them not to consult and confer with the other respecting the meaning and intent of the warnings, and the attitude of each, that he was not required by the imminence of hostilities. The attitude of each, that he was not required to inform himself of . . . the measures undertaken by the other to carry out the responsibility assigned to such other under the provisions of the plans then in effect, demonstrated on the part of each a lack of appreciation of the responsibilities vested in them and inherent in their positions as Commander in Chief, Pacific Fleet, and Commanding General, Hawaiian Department.[3]

The commission's most damaging conclusion was the phrase "dereliction of duty." The report was presented to President Roosevelt on January 24, 1942, and released to the press that same day. Whether it was intended or not, the report appeared to place the blame for the Pearl Harbor disaster squarely on Kimmel and Short. The headline in the *New York Times* on January 25, 1942, read: "Roberts Board Blames Kimmel and Short: Warnings to Defend Hawaii Not Heeded."

No court-martial followed, and no further action was taken against the two men at that time. Both, as mentioned above, had been relieved of their commands on December 16, 1941. Kimmel was retired on March 1, 1942, in his permanent grade of rear admiral. His resignation was accepted by the secretary of the navy "without condonation of any offense or prejudice to any future disciplinary action," and the accusation of "dereliction of duty" went unchallenged. Not one of the nine investigations of the Pearl Harbor disaster fairly presents Kimmel's side, and he was not allowed to defend himself until much later. In short, Kimmel's and Short's reputations were destroyed—sacrificed to the war effort—and there is no evidence that anyone in the government tried to deflect criticism away from them. Both men suffered terribly from the public condemnation that followed the release of the Roberts report. On February 22, 1942, Admiral Kimmel wrote to Admiral Stark:

> I regret the losses at Pearl Harbor just as keenly, or perhaps more keenly than any other American citizen. I wish that I had been smarter than I was and able to foresee what happened on December 7. I devoted all my energies to the job and made the dispositions which appeared to me to be called for. I cannot now reproach myself for any lack of effort.
>
> I will not comment on the Report of the Commission, but you probably know what I think of it. I will say in passing that I was not made an interested party or a defendant.
>
> All this I have been willing to accept for the good of the country out of my loyalty to the Nation, and to await the judgment of history when all the factors can be published.
>
> But I do think that in all justice the department should do nothing further to inflame the public against me. I am entitled to some consideration even though you may consider I erred grievously.
>
> You must appreciate that the beating I have taken leaves very little that can be added to my burden.
>
> I appreciate your efforts on my behalf and will always value your friendship, which is a precious thing to me.
>
> I stand ready at any time to accept the consequences of my acts. I do not wish to embarrass the government in the conduct of the war. I do feel, however, that my crucifixion before the public has about reached the limit. I am in daily receipt of letters from irresponsible people over the country taking me to task and even threatening to kill me. I am not particularly concerned except it shows the effect on the public of articles published about me.
>
> I feel that the publication of paragraph two of the Secretary's letter of February 16 [accepting Admiral Kimmel's retirement "without condonation of any offense"] will further inflame the public and do me a great injustice.[4]

In fact, Admiral Kimmel suffered unspeakable vilification after the Roberts report was published. A "veritable hurricane of charges was hurled indiscriminately at Short and me," he said, along with "many abusive and threatening letters, most of them people quite evidently unbalanced." His memoir offers a few examples: On April 6, 1942, Congressman Andrew J. May of Kentucky, chairman of the Military Affairs Committee, said that Admiral Kimmel and General Short should be shot. Municipal Court Judge Twain Michelsen of San Francisco wrote to Kimmel on February 8, 1942:

> I am confident that the people of America will never forget the cul-
> pability that has been attached to both yourself and Short. Equally
> sure am I that history will forever point an accusatory finger at both
> of you, and to your memory, when each has passed to the realm
> where so many of our men were so suddenly hurled because of your
> joint neglect and utter stupidity.
>
> Surely, there isn't much for you and Short to live for—unless a gen-
> eral court-martial would bring forth a page from the shameful chapter
> of Pearl Harbor that might shed a little more light on the entire picture
> and thus, however possible, clean from the hands of both of you the
> blood of your unsuspecting victims. That would, it seems to me, be the
> honorable thing for you to do, instead of to ask for "retirement."

A former Circuit Court judge, George Edward Mix of St. Louis, Missouri, wrote to Kimmel on February 11, 1942:

> As an American citizen, taxpayer, graduate of Yale University, and as one
> whose ancestors have fought in all the wars in which this country has
> been engaged, I suggest that *instead of your cowardly act in asking to be
> relieved from duty and placed on the taxpayers' payroll at $6000.00 per year, and
> in view of the millions of dollars worth of taxpayers' property destroyed in Pearl
> Harbor by reason of your carelessness, negligence, and thoughtlessness,* that you
> try to show that you are a real man by using a pistol and ending your exis-
> tence, *as you are certainly of no use to yourself nor the American people.*

Kimmel's wife also received letters. Eleanor Overman of New York City wrote:

> My dear Mrs. Kimmel:
> My nephew came back from Hawaii with you on the Clipper and
> reported that because you would leave none of your luggage to fol-
> low by slower route, two Navy wives, who were pregnant were forced

to cancel their passage. This, in addition to the report that you required an unusual amount of service en route, would seem to indicate a type of person not the best influence for a husband!

"My dear Mrs. Overman," Mrs. Kimmel replied on March 23, 1942, "Your letter of January 26th reached me today. Your nephew is mistaken. I have never been to Hawaii and I have never traveled on a clipper." Kimmel added, "Mrs. Overman replied promptly with a profuse apology, but that did not stop this malicious lie."

Even Harry S. Truman, then a U.S. senator, was involved in the calumny. Unfortunately, he spoke without knowledge of all the facts. On August 20, 1944, Kimmel wrote to Senator Truman in defense of his reputation:

My dear Senator Truman,

In an article appearing under your name in *Collier's* Magazine of August 26, 1944, you have made false statements concerning my conduct as Commander in Chief of the Pacific Fleet at Pearl Harbor prior to the Japanese attack.

Your innuendo that General Short and I were not on speaking terms is not true. Your statements alleging failure to cooperate and coordinate our efforts are equally false. General Short and I, as well as our subordinates, coordinated the efforts of our commands in close, friendly, personal and official relationships.

The real story of the Pearl Harbor attack and the events preceding it has never been publicly told. This has not been my decision. For more than two and a half years, I have been anxious to have the American people know all the facts.

The Roberts Report, upon which you rely, does not contain the basic truths of the Pearl Harbor catastrophe. This is evident from the fact that no official action has ever been taken upon the basis of that Report. The Congress of the United States, of which you are a member, has recognized the inadequacy of the Roberts Report by directing that the War and Navy Departments undertake a full investigation of the Pearl Harbor disaster.

Until I am afforded a hearing in open court, it is grossly unjust to repeat false charges against me, when, by official action, I have been persistently denied an opportunity to defend myself publicly.

I suggest that until such time as complete disclosure is made of the facts about Pearl Harbor, you refrain from repeating charges based on evidence that has never met the test of public scrutiny.

I ask for nothing more than an end to untruths, and half-truths about this matter, until the entire story is given to our people, who, I am convinced, will be amazed by the truth.

I am releasing this letter to the press in the belief that the historic American sense of fair play will approve this action.[5]

Admiral Kimmel received no reply to his letter. In his autobiography Kimmel addressed another of the lies spread by the media about him and General Short:

> Again in October of 1945 Bill Cunningham published in his column in the *Boston Herald* a statement to the effect that service hostesses in Hawaii were careful never to include Mrs. Kimmel and Mrs. Short as guests at the same time because their constant state of belligerency was embarrassing to all bystanders. It was only by chance that we heard of this canard and informed Mr. Cunningham that Mrs. Kimmel had never been to Hawaii and that she and Mrs. Short had never met. Mr. Cunningham promptly apologized publicly in his column. But there were hundreds of similar lies which were propagated and never overtaken.[6]

The abuse heaped on Admiral Kimmel was terribly unfair, and his reputation was never really cleared, although efforts eventually were made—and are still being made, as will be discussed later—to exonerate him and General Short.

Adm. James O. Richardson, Kimmel's predecessor as CinCPac, had a high opinion of Kimmel and praised him at the ceremony at which he handed over his command to Kimmel. His words are reprinted in his memoir, published in 1973: "My regret in leaving you is tempered by the fact that I turn over this command to Admiral Kimmel, a friend of long standing, a forthright man, an officer of marked ability and a successor of whom I am proud. Under his leadership, I know that you will continue to so perform your duties as to justify the confidence with which the nation places its security in your hands."

In his memoir Richardson added: "I stand by my words." He also pointed to the failure of Kimmel's bosses in Washington to give sufficient warning:

Kimmel received *the rawest of raw deals* from Franklin D. Roosevelt, in so far as he acquiesced in this treatment from Frank Knox and "Betty" Stark [Harold R., the CNO at the time].

I consider "Betty" Stark, in failing to ensure that Kimmel was furnished with all the information available from the breaking of Japanese dispatches, to have been to a marked degree professionally negligent in carrying out his duties as Chief of Naval Operations. This offense was compounded, since in writing he had assured the Commander-in-Chief of the United States Fleet twice (both myself and Kimmel) that the Commander-in-Chief was "being kept advised on all matters within his own [Stark's] knowledge" and "You may rest assured that just as soon as I get anything of definite interest, I shall fire it along."

The Navy had been expecting and planning for a Japanese surprise attack for many years. However, the subordinates in a military organization cannot stand with their arms raised in protective alertness forever. Some superior has to ring a bell that moves the subordinate members of the organization, trained, ready, and expecting a fight, but in the corners of their fighting ring, out to the center of the ring.

That bell was never rung by Kimmel's superiors in Washington.

I consider that "Betty" Stark, in failing to pick up the telephone and give Kimmel a last-minute alert on the morning of Pearl Harbor, committed a major professional lapse, indicating a basic absence of those personal military characteristics required in a successful war leader. I believe his failures in these respects were far more important derelictions than those of any of his subordinates. I do not assert that Kimmel was without blame for some of the naval aspects of the Pearl Harbor debacle, but his blame was less than that of his superiors.

Richardson did not completely exonerate Kimmel, but he made it clear that the blame should not rest solely on him and Short. He said of the Roberts Commission:

I have been told, and I believe, that Justice Frankfurter suggested to the President the creation, under a carefully drawn precept, of a mixed commission composed of officers of the Armed Forces, with a civilian counsel, and headed by a member of the Supreme Court, to investigate the attack on Pearl Harbor. His objective was to have a commission which would not be limited by the rules of evidence governing either a civilian court or a military court of inquiry. I was also told that the Chief Justice (Harlan F. Stone) was requested to serve, but refused the assignment.

In the impression that the Roberts Commission created on the minds of the American people, and in the way it was drawn up for that specific purpose, I believe that the Report of the Roberts Commission was the most unfair, unjust, and deceptively dishonest document ever printed by the Government Printing Office.

I cannot conceive of any honorable man being able to recall his service as a member of that commission without great regret and the deepest feeling of shame. The military members of the Roberts Commission (Admiral William H. Standley, USN [Ret.], Rear Admiral Joseph M. Reeves, USN [Ret.], Major General Frank R. McCoy, USA [Ret.], and Brigadier General Joseph T. McNarney, USA [Ret.]) were later rewarded for their services by favorable assignment and promotion, or employment after retirement, but I cannot believe that such rewards were adequate compensation for their supine service to the President. Its procedures should have outraged every American.

Its findings had been decided on before it ever met, for the decision to relieve Kimmel and Short was made prior to the initial meeting of the Roberts Commission. Had the Roberts Commission been intended to do a factual job, such a removal would have been untimely, to say the least, since it presented to the Commission a finding of culpability.

A more disgraceful spectacle has never been presented to this country during my lifetime than the failure of the civilian officials of the Government to show any willingness to take their share of responsibility for the Japanese success at Pearl Harbor.

Before the Roberts Commission, the leaders of the Armed Forces of the United States, who were the victims of the initial attack in this aggressive war by the Japanese, were not given a trial, were not permitted to introduce evidence in their behalf, and were not allowed counsel. Yet, these leaders were found guilty of dereliction of duty by the Commission, and were crucified in the public press and at the bar of public opinion in the United States.

Richardson's memoir offers a unique perspective on the aftermath of the Pearl Harbor surprise attack:

Instead of sending out the Roberts Commission to muddy the waters, the reliefs of Kimmel and Short should have been dispatched as soon as possible. The Army and Navy and everyone else would have understood and approved this action, because all would have recognized that, *regardless of where the blame lay, no armed force should remain under the command of a leader under whom it had suffered such loss.*

Had this been done, many hours of labor, thousands of gallons of ink, and tons of paper which were wasted in fruitless inquiries and newspaper reports on them, would have been saved, and the public would have been much better served.

Also, those opposed to the President would have had far less reason to question his integrity and fair-mindedness.

I am convinced that the President would have been quite willing to approve without qualification, the induced requests of Kimmel and Short for retirement, except for the furor aroused by the publication of the Report of the Roberts Commission.

The publication of this report led the uninformed public to believe that Kimmel and Short were largely, if not wholly, responsible for the success of the Japanese attack. They, and the worshippers of Roosevelt, naturally insisted that Kimmel and Short should not be placed on the retired list with retired pay, but should be tried by General Court Martial or otherwise, to determine what if any punishment, less than summary execution should be inflicted upon them.[7]

Kimmel presented his side of the Pearl Harbor disaster in his memoir, published in 1955. His version of events further illustrates how unfairly he was treated by America. Pearl Harbor has been investigated ad infinitum, in millions of words and thousands of pages. In the face of this verbiage, it seems fair to put the issue of blame into perspective by quoting the words of Admiral Kimmel himself regarding the Roberts Commission proceedings. The following statements are lengthy, but considerably less so than the mountain of material covering the years of investigations. Anyone with a sense of justice cannot help but be incensed at the way Kimmel was treated. Kimmel wrote:

The Roberts Commission was not conducted in accordance with the rules governing naval investigations. Indeed it was conducted with complete disregard of all rules of fair play and justice.

I was denied any knowledge of what any witness testified. It was not until 1944 when I was supplied a copy of the proceedings, that I learned what testimony the commission had recorded. I will never know what testimony was not recorded.

I had no opportunity to confront witnesses or to submit evidence on subjects they discussed. Each witness was enjoined by the commission that his testimony was secret.

When I came before the commission I was informed that I was not permitted to have counsel, also that I was not on trial. Rear Admiral [Robert A.] Theobald was permitted to assist me in handling my papers. When Admiral Theobald interposed to correct misunderstandings that are bound to arise when five persons are questioning one, Mr. Roberts reprimanded Theobald reminding him that he was not my counsel as I was not permitted to have counsel. When Theobald refused to be suppressed, Mr. Roberts insisted that Theobald be sworn as a witness. The copy of the record of proceedings supplied to me contains no record of these statements of Mr. Roberts.

Several days after I had completed my testimony I asked when I would be permitted to read and verify the record of my testimony. After considerable argument I was permitted to come alone to see the record of my testimony.

I found the transcript of my testimony incomplete, inaccurate, and misleading. The transcript was so badly garbled and there were such glaring omissions that I requested authority to return the next day with a stenographer (yeoman) and Theobald to assist me to reconstruct the testimony as nearly as possible as it had been presented. An example of what I found was the omission from the transcript of a sixteen-page statement which I had read to the commission and supplied them with a copy.

Late that evening I was informed that Mr. Roberts had ruled that I could return with a stenographer but that I would not be permitted to have Theobald assist me. Next morning I had an interview with Mr. Roberts (Admiral Standley was present) in which I renewed my request. In the course of his reply, Mr. Roberts again assured me that I was not on trial, that the President had expressly told him this was not a trial. My reply was that his statement was just so many words. . . . In the eyes of the American people, I was on trial and no words of his could alter that fact.

Mr. Roberts was not stupid enough to believe what he told me. At least he used the term "trial" in its strictly legalistic sense.

As a result of this interview, Theobald, the stenographer, and I revised the transcript to present the substance of what I actually testified to before the commission. Subsequently, I was informed that the original transcript would remain unchanged and my revision would be attached as an addendum. When I was supplied with a copy of the proceedings in 1944, I found the original transcript considerably revised and the sixteen-page statement added. The remainder of my corrections were placed in an addendum attached to the so-called original.

In 1944 I found in the Navy Department a copy of a letter addressed to the Chief of Naval Operations by the Chief of Naval Intelligence which detailed the testimony he had given to the Roberts Commission. No record of this testimony is included in the copy of the proceedings supplied to me.

The proceedings strangely enough relate that the part of the findings which record that General Marshall and Admiral Stark had performed their duties relating to the attack on Pearl Harbor in an exemplary manner, had first been submitted to them and revised to their satisfaction before being adopted by the commission.

The treatment accorded General Marshall and Admiral Stark is in sharp contrast to that accorded to General Short and to me. While I was testifying before the commission Mr. Roberts' attitude was that of a prosecutor, not a judge. In retrospect it is clear that when he had received what he believed to be damaging admissions he carefully refrained from further questions which would have clarified the statements made.

The conduct of the commission's investigation was without precedent. It was conducted without regard to rules, law, or justice. Scapegoats had to be provided to save the administration. Apparently Short and I were elected before the commission left Washington. How a justice of the U.S. Supreme Court, two generals, and two admirals could lend themselves to such an undertaking is past understanding.

Without affording me the opportunity to defend myself, the Roberts Commission convicted me without trial on secret evidence withheld from me and the public and published the findings to the world.

The conflicting and confusing orders sent to General Short and to me are best illustrated by the indictment in the findings of the commission which states that General Short and I did not consult as to the meaning of the warning messages received. Aside from the fact that we did confer both before and after the receipt of the message, it is strange doctrine that would require the admiral commanding the Pacific Fleet to consult with the commanding general at Hawaii to determine the meaning of a message from the Chief of Naval Operations and equally ridiculous to require the commanding general at Hawaii to consult with the commander of the Pacific Fleet to determine the meaning of a message to sent to him by the Army Chief of Staff. Yet this was the principal indictment used by the Roberts Commission in their attempt to fasten the blame for the Pearl

Harbor disaster upon General Short and me. The mere statement that such consultation was necessary to determine the meaning of an order is an indictment
of the agency which originated it.[8]

In the last chapter of his book Admiral Kimmel described the anguish
he suffered:

> Again and again in my mind I have reviewed the events that preceded the
> Japanese attack, seeking to determine if I was unjustified in drawing from
> the orders, directives and information that were forwarded to me the conclu-
> sions that I did. The fact that I then thought and now think my conclusions were
> sound when based upon the information I received, has sustained me during the
> years that have passed since the first Japanese bomb fell on Pearl Harbor.
>
> When the information available in Washington prior to the attack was dis-
> closed to me I was appalled. Nothing in my experience of nearly forty-two years'
> service in the Navy had prepared me for the actions of the highest officials in our
> government which denied this vital information to the Pearl Harbor commanders.
>
> If those in authority wished to engage in power politics, the least that they
> should have done was to advise their naval and military commanders what they
> were endeavoring to accomplish. To utilize the Pacific Fleet and the Army forces
> at Pearl Harbor as a lure for a Japanese attack without advising the commander-
> in-chief of the fleet and the commander of the Army base at Hawaii is something
> I am wholly unable to comprehend.
>
> While I am still able to do so, I feel that I must tell the story so that those
> who follow may fully realize the imperative necessity of furnishing the naval and
> military commanders at the front with full and clear information. Only in this
> way can the future security of our country be preserved.[9]

Rear Adm. Robert A. Theobald accompanied Admiral Kimmel when
he appeared before the Roberts Commission. Theobald's March 20, 1944,
statement on the proceeding of the Roberts Commission, reprinted in
Admiral Kimmel's autobiography, substantiates Kimmel's description of
the injustice he suffered at the hands of the commission.

> When Admiral Kimmel was informed that the Roberts Commission would arrive
> in Pearl Harbor to investigate the Japanese surprise attack on the United States
> Fleet, December 7, 1941, he asked me to act as his counsel. At the time I
> informed him that I would be very glad to do anything I could, but suggested

that, as I had no legal training, it might be at least desirable to have an assistant counsel with legal knowledge. Admiral Kimmel stated that he did not desire this, that all he wanted was a straightforward presentation of his conduct of Fleet affairs prior to and during the attack of December 7, 1941. I then said that I would be very glad to render any assistance within my capabilities.

If nothing else, this comment illustrates Kimmel's exemplary character. The fact that he did not want someone with legal training showed that he wanted to hit the issues head-on and not rely on the technicalities an experienced lawyer might use to protect his client. Theobald continued:

The preparation of Admiral Kimmel's testimony was rendered most difficult for both of us by our total inability to find out what procedure the Roberts Commission was following: when Admiral Kimmel would be called, the manner in which he would be permitted to present his testimony, etc. We spent two or three days attempting to obtain information concerning these matters.

The Roberts Commission commenced its sittings in the Hawaiian Area by spending several days at Fort Shafter where General Short and other witnesses from the Army were called before the Commission. Neither Admiral Kimmel nor any representative of his was present at any of these hearings. Admiral Kimmel thus had no knowledge of what testimony had been presented to the Roberts Commission, what documentary material, if any, was in evidence before that commission, etc. He had no opportunity whatever to question any other witness before the Commission at any time in the Proceedings before the Commission during the presentation of Admiral Kimmel's own testimony and at no other time. When Admiral Kimmel entered the boardroom, he requested of the Commission that I be permitted to attend him due to the fact that I had facility with and knowledge of the location of papers which he would desire to use in presenting his testimony. My presence in this status was authorized by the Roberts Commission. In the middle of Admiral Kimmel's testimony, Associate Justice Roberts turned to me and asked what my status was before the Commission. I stated that I was there to help Admiral Kimmel locate papers which might be pertinent to his testimony. Associate Justice Roberts replied, "In order that your status may be official, Admiral Theobald, I think it would be well that you be sworn as a witness." This was done at that time. Mr. Roberts then smilingly said to me, "Of course you are not here in the capacity of a defense counsel because you and Admiral Kimmel both understand that as no charges have been preferred against him, he is not in the status of a defendant." I bowed but made no answer to this statement of Associate Justice Roberts. I regarded it at the time and still regard the statement as incomprehensible and totally at variance with the facts. Admiral Kimmel was Commander-in-Chief of the United States Fleet which had suffered severe losses in the surprise attack by the Japanese on December 7, 1941. The Roberts Commission, consisting of Associate Justice Roberts, Admiral Standley, Admiral Reeves, Major General McCoy, and Brigadier General McNarney, with Mr. Howe as Judge Advocate, had been dispatched by Presidential order to the Hawaiian area to investigate the happenings of December 7th. The conduct of the Fleet prior to and during that event, the training of the Fleet, the Fleet's defensive dispositions, were all under scrutiny and inquiry by the Roberts Commission. How any investigation of these matters could be conducted without regarding Admiral Kimmel as a defendant is incomprehensible to me. He was Commander-in-Chief of the Fleet and although charges had not been preferred against him, he stood partially condemned in the public eye as soon as the events of December 7, 1941, were known. Everything that was said before the Roberts Commission, all testimony verbal and documentary, must be a matter of serious interest and import to Admiral Kimmel.

In my opinion, equity, fairness, impartiality, and common justice demanded that Admiral Kimmel be accorded the full rights and status of a defendant before the Roberts Commission. Any finding of that body which concerned the reputation and fair name of Admiral Kimmel after he had definitely been denied the status of a defendant is at variance with basic principles of justice and fair play. . . .

The actions of the Commission were generally fair and impartial in their treatment of Admiral Kimmel during the time he was before the Commission in the capacity of a witness. Late on the afternoon of the first day of Admiral Kimmel's testimony, however, Associate Justice Roberts for a considerable period of time forgot his status as a presiding officer of an impartial commission and questioned Admiral Kimmel in a loud tone of voice; in fact, in a manner more to be expected of a trial lawyer in a lower court. That Associate Justice Roberts was not entirely satisfied with his conduct of the business of the Commission at this particular time was evidenced by certain remarks which he addressed to Admiral Kimmel at the opening of the next meeting of the Commission. These remarks were semi-apologetic in character. I cannot quote Admiral Kimmel's reply exactly, but he stated in effect that he desired to offer no objection to the treatment that he had received from the Commission up to that time.

As another evidence of the fatally defective manner in which the inquiry was conducted, I will cite a further instance:

The general bearing and manner of Brigadier General McNarney gave me the definite impression that the officer had little interest in the inquiry unless matters pertaining to Air Forces were in question. Admiral Kimmel made some remark concerning the Hawaiian Air Warning Service which in accordance with the provisions of "Joint Action, Army and Navy" was an Army responsibility and in wartime was to be operated by the Army. Brigadier General McNarney at this point interrupted Admiral Kimmel with a request to Associate Justice Roberts that he be permitted to read into the record an extract from a yellow-backed publication which was in front of him at the table. Permission for this was granted by Justice Roberts, of course without a reference to Admiral Kimmel. Brigadier General McNarney prefaced his reading with the remark, "I introduce this just to keep the record straight." A member of an impartial commission suggests that the testimony of the witness has to be refuted in order to keep the record straight. He then read certain extracts from this publication which had to do with the presence of the Naval liaison officer at the Air Warning Service Center.

Due to the manner in which the inquiry was conducted, Admiral Kimmel had no knowledge as to whether or not the publication from which Brigadier General McNarney had just read was in evidence before the Commission or not. It was not offered to Admiral Kimmel for examination prior to General McNarney's reading of the extract into the record. During the recess that evening, Admiral Kimmel and I found a copy of the publication. To show the general character of the publication from which Brigadier General McNarney had read, it is only necessary to quote a footnote which appeared at the bottom of page 12 in the publication in question. In effect this footnote read about as follows: "Warning to the reader: It must be recognized that this pamphlet is merely a stab in the dark and the reader must treat it accordingly." Apparently the publication was the first effort of the Interceptor Command to establish some regulations for the conduct of the Air Warning Service. This pamphlet had not been sent to Admiral Kimmel's command officially. It had not been promulgated by an order of any senior officer of the Army, nor by any adjutant or Adjutant General of the Army in the name of a senior officer of the Army.

Later in Admiral Kimmel's testimony, a question of a scouting flight about noon of December 7, 1941, came up in the Commission proceedings. I stated before the Commission that a Naval scouting plane had encountered enemy fighters some 250 to 300 miles north of Oahu. Both Admiral Standley and

Brigadier General McNarney stated that no such flight had been made. Admiral Kimmel had requested that Captain Delaney of his Staff be placed on the witness stand to introduce tracing of flights that had been made on December 7th in an attempt to locate the Japanese attacking surface forces. After this happening in the Commission, I went to Captain Delaney and asked him if he had not placed these tracings in evidence before the Commission. He stated that he had appeared as a witness and had tried to offer the tracings of the scouting operations in evidence to the Commission, but the Commission was uninterested and brushed them aside. I quote this incident to show that except during the time he was a witness, Admiral Kimmel had no control whatever over the testimony that he desired presented to the Roberts Commission. Admiral Kimmel asked that several officers be called and it is believed that this was done. However, he had no opportunity to be present to hear their testimony, to cross question them and to assure himself that they offered in evidence facts which he considered material to his presentation of his case. The Delaney incident is merely an evidence of this condition. Informally, Admiral Kimmel and I knew that several senior officers of the Fleet were called but the character of their testimony was totally unknown to us.

When the transcript of Admiral Kimmel's testimony was presented to him for correction, it was at once seen that a very bad stenographic job had been done. The representatives of the stenographic firm hired by the Roberts Commission never at any time in the court asked Admiral Kimmel to repeat his testimony or intimated in any way that they were not getting all that was said. However, the record could hardly have been worse. Admiral Kimmel and I spent about a day and a half correcting his testimony. Admiral Kimmel had read his main statement which was the main part of his testimony. This was not included in the stenographic report and it was the apparent intention to place the report of this section of Admiral Kimmel's testimony in an addendum to the Commission's report.

I first saw Mr. Howe, the Judge Advocate of the Commission, and told him how bad was the record of Admiral Kimmel's testimony. Mr. Howe saw Mr. Roberts and said that Mr. Roberts was opposed to any extensive correction of Admiral Kimmel's testimony. I tried to explain to Mr. Howe that Admiral Kimmel had no desire to modify his testimony in any respect. All that he desired to do in correcting his testimony was to bring it in accord with what he had originally said before the Commission. Mr. Howe apparently reported this to Mr. Roberts but again stated that Mr. Roberts was opposed to any correction of the testimony other than by numbering the errors and placing the correct statements in an addendum to the Commission's report, a perfectly hopeless proceeding as nobody reading the Commission's report was going to turn to an addendum every three or four words.

Recognizing that what Admiral Kimmel desired in the correction of his testimony was the customary proceeding before military courts, I then took the matter up with Admiral Standley, but had no better success with him than I did with Mr. Howe.[10]

The investigations that followed the Knox and Roberts Commission reports also make it clear that the responsibility for the Pearl Harbor disaster should not fall solely on Kimmel and Short. The naval court of inquiry, for example, was extremely favorable to Kimmel in its conclusions on accountability. The objectives and mandate of this investigation were as follows:

Public Law No. 339, 78th Congress, approved 13 June 1944, directed the Secretary of War and Secretary of the Navy, severally, to proceed forthwith to investigate the facts surrounding the Pearl Harbor catastrophe, and to commence such proceedings against such persons as the facts might justify.

A Court of Inquiry, consisting of Admiral Orin G. Murfin, USN (Retired), Admiral Edwards C. Kalbfus, USN (Retired), and Vice Admiral Adolphus Andrews, USN (Retired), with Commander Harold Biesemeier, USN, as Judge Advocate, was appointed by the Secretary of the Navy on 13 July 1944. The court was directed to convene on 17 July 1944, or as soon thereafter as practicable, for the purpose of inquiring into all circumstances connected with the attack made by Japanese forces on Pearl Harbor, Territory of Hawaii, on 7 December 1941; to inquire thoroughly into the matter, and to include in its findings a full statement of the facts it might deem to be established. The Court was further directed to state its opinion as to whether any offenses were committed or serious blame incurred on the part of any person or persons in the Naval service, and, in case its opinion was that offenses had been committed or serious blame incurred, to recommend specifically what further proceedings should be had. The Court of Inquiry commenced its proceedings on 31 July 1944, and submitted the record of its proceedings on 20 October 1944.

One of the most important conclusions of the court of inquiry's report refuted the Roberts Commission's statement that there was a failure of "joint cooperative action" on the part of Kimmel and Short, and emphatically refuted that there "was a dereliction of duty on the part of each of them not to confer with the other respecting the meaning and intent of the warnings." The court further found that "the relations between Admiral Husband E. Kimmel, USN, and Lieutenant General Walter C. Short, US Army, were friendly, cordial and cooperative, that there was no lack of interest, no lack of appreciation of responsibility, and no failure to cooperate on the part of either, and that each was cognizant of the measures being undertaken by the other for the defense of the Pearl Harbor Naval Base to the degree required by the common interest."

The naval court did not exonerate Admiral Stark of responsibility for the disaster.

> Based on Findings XVIII and XIX, the Court is of the opinion that Admiral Harold R. Stark, USN, Chief of Naval Operations and responsible for the operations of the Fleet, failed to display the sound judgment expected of him in that he did not transmit to Admiral Kimmel, Commander in Chief, Pacific Fleet, important information which he had regarding the Japanese situation and, especially, in that, on the morning of 7 December, 1941, he did not transmit immediately the fact that a message had been received which appeared to indicate that a break in diplomatic relations was imminent, and that an attack in the Hawaiian area might be expected soon. The Court is further of this opinion that, had this important information been conveyed to Admiral Kimmel, it is a matter of conjecture as to what action he would have taken.

Stark was relieved as CNO and sent to command the U.S. fleet in the Atlantic, which the Roosevelt administration must have concluded was sufficient punishment. Adm. Ernest H. King became the new CNO. Of greatest impact was the court's conclusion that, "based upon the facts established, . . . no offenses have been committed nor serious blame incurred on the part of any person or persons in the naval service."[11]

The joint committee of Congress that was established to investigate the conduct of Admiral Kimmel and Lieutenant General Short completed its report on May 31, 1946. The report, which was 1,075 pages long, concluded that "the errors made by the Hawaiian commanders [i.e., Kimmel and Short] were errors in judgment and not dereliction of duty."[12]

Prior to the attack on Pearl Harbor, opinion in the United States regarding the war in Europe and Japanese aggression in Asia was deeply divided. The majority in 1939 wanted no part of that war and strongly opposed U.S. involvement in Europe or in Asia. The allegation has been made that President Roosevelt purposely sought to provoke Japan into attacking U.S. forces in the Pacific so that the United States would be forced to enter the war and could legally come to the aid of Europe. That seems unlikely. Although Roosevelt knew that the United States would eventually become involved in the conflict, he also knew that the nation was far from ready for war and needed time to prepare. Further, he had a great love for the Navy. Would he have risked the existence of the Pacific Fleet to bring the United States into the war?

Certainly Kimmel and Short can—and should—be criticized for being surprised and unprepared. Their failure to institute a better system of reconnaissance is inexcusable. It was well known that the Japanese fleet had moved out of home waters, and the Hawaiian commanders should have been more thorough in their efforts to find it. They should have been alarmed when Japanese submarines were observed in the area. But placing all the blame on Kimmel and Short is grossly unfair when Washington was so culpable in failing to keep them informed.

To say that the responsibility for Pearl Harbor is not Kimmel's and Short's alone does not absolve them of *accountability,* however. A commander is always responsible for the welfare of his or her troops and accountable for what his command does or does not do. If a ship runs aground, the captain is accountable whether he or she was on or off the bridge when the incident occurred. If his unit is attacked and surprised, the commander is accountable, not his intelligence officer or his other subordinate commanders. A commander, particularly in time of war, must have exceptional professional skills, vision, and excellent judgment, and must be ready to accept accountability for mistakes even though he or she could not possibly have had personal knowledge of them.

It is doubtful that the Pearl Harbor controversy will ever be settled. Both Short and Kimmel are dead; Short died on September 23, 1949, and Kimmel on May 14, 1968. Considerable effort has been made by naval officers to exonerate Kimmel—with Short a beneficiary of these efforts—and to have each advanced on the retired list to the rank he held at the time he was relieved of command: four stars for Kimmel and three stars for Short, but without success. The fight to exonerate them from sole blame continues; until that is done, the myth that they were derelict in their duty and were responsible for the success of the surprise attack on Pearl Harbor will be perpetuated.

When the Japanese admiral who led the Pearl Harbor attack, Isoroku Yamamoto, learned that the Americans were blaming Admiral Kimmel for its success, he recorded in his diary: "This tells us much about the shock they received. But it is a gross error for the authorities to want to punish their subordinates when some misfortune occurs. When a government wants to exert its national will, it must be prepared for war, and if it is not fully prepared, then it must be ready for defeat. The responsibility always rests on the chief officer."[13] To Yamamoto, the "chief officer" was President Roosevelt, the commander in chief.

Finally, on December 15, 1995, the results of a Department of Defense study on the events of December 7, 1941, were released. The Dorn report, written by Assistant Secretary of Defense Edwin Dorn, reported on an investigation conducted to determine whether Admiral Kimmel and General Short should indeed be advanced in rank as described above. The report concluded: (1) that Army and Navy officials in Washington were privy to intercepted Japanese diplomatic communications that confirmed that war was imminent; (2) that the way these communications were handled in Washington was inept and revealed lack of coordination at higher levels; and (3) that as a result, the Army and Navy commanders in Hawaii were not informed of the urgency of the situation that the Japanese communications should have engendered.[14]

The Sinking of the USS *Juneau*, November 12–13, 1942

Adm. Chester W. Nimitz's selection as commander in chief, Pacific (CinCPac), in December 1941 placed him in command of all U.S. Navy and Marine Corps forces in the Pacific. Early in 1942 Nimitz was instructed by the CNO, Admiral King, to employ a "defensive-offensive" strategy. As part of that strategy Nimitz gave the highest priority to seizing Guadalcanal in the Solomon Islands from the Japanese. The Joint Chiefs of Staff, at King's urging, directed Nimitz to accomplish this task in the summer of 1942. The seizure became urgent when it became apparent that the Japanese were constructing an airfield on the island.

The 1st Marine Division, under the command of Maj. Gen. A. Archer Vandegrift, landed unopposed on Guadalcanal on August 7, 1942. The Japanese counterattacked with a vengeance, and the marines had to be reinforced by heavily escorted troop convoys. The advantage swung back and forth, with the United States bringing in men and materials every night from submarines, surface ships, and aircraft, and the Japanese fighting viciously during the daytime. The battle reached a climax on the night of November 12 when Rear Adm. David J. Callaghan's cruiser force engaged a Japanese fleet maneuvering to bombard the airfield and then land Japanese soldiers in an attempt to retake the island.

Some naval historians consider the Battle of Midway in June 1942 to be the turning point of the war in the Pacific. Others point to Guadalcanal, the first battle in which the Allies shifted from defense to offense, as the turning point. Certainly the stakes were high there. Between November 12 and November 15 the Japanese sent four battleships, two aircraft carriers, five cruisers, thirty destroyers, and twenty transports carrying twenty thousand soldiers in an attempt to retake the island and destroy Henderson Field. To counter this attack Admiral Halsey sent a fleet of only two heavy cruisers: his flagship, the *San Francisco,* and the *Portland,* along with three light cruisers—*Atlanta* (the flagship of Rear Adm. Norman Scott, Halsey's second in command), *Helena,* and *Juneau*—and eight destroyers.

The battle began at 0130 on the clear night of November 12–13 and was not concluded until November 15. The opposing ships fired at point-blank range, each side methodically shooting salvo after salvo. Although the sea battle lasted only twenty-four minutes, both sides suffered severe damage and casualties. U.S. losses totaled three light cruisers and four destroyers sunk, and seven other ships damaged. Admirals

Callaghan and Scott were killed. It was a furiously fought battle against overwhelming odds, but the Japanese warships and transports were repulsed. The U.S. fleet sank two Japanese battleships, one heavy cruiser, three destroyers, and ten transport and cargo ships, and damaged nine others.

One of the worst tragedies of the entire war in the Pacific occurred in the aftermath of the battle for Guadalcanal. The cruiser *Juneau* was damaged in the initial twenty-four-minute battle but was still afloat with a weakened keel and making eighteen knots, half its normal speed, when it was hit by a torpedo from a Japanese submarine; it sank in just minutes. One of the best accounts of what followed is in Admiral Halsey's autobiography, which perfectly illustrates the concept of accountability:

> I cannot close this account of the Battle of Guadalcanal without adding my confession of a grievous mistake. I have already confessed it officially; now I do publicly.
>
> Early on the morning of November 13, the light cruiser *Juneau*, bringing up the rear of Callaghan's column, was torpedoed and badly damaged. The first I knew of it was that afternoon, when *Helena*'s dispatch included her among the ships limping down to Espiritu. When Espiritu reported their arrival, her name was no longer on the list.
>
> I called Miles Browning [his chief of staff] and asked, "Where's the *Juneau*?" "I don't know, sir," he said. "I'll have to check."
>
> It transpired that she had been torpedoed again and had sunk so suddenly, in such a hail of debris, that the other ships at first thought they were under a high-altitude bombing attack. The senior officer present, Captain Gilbert C. Hoover of the *Helena*, now faced a grim decision. Although in his opinion few men, if any, could have survived the terrific explosion, common humanity urged him to search for them. (Captain Lyman K. Swenson of the *Juneau* was one of Hoover's closest friends.) On the other hand, the *O'Bannon* had been sent off on a special mission, so he had only the *Fletcher* and the crippled *Sterett* as escorts for this crippled force; [a] rescue operation would almost certainly invite a second torpedo attack, and at a critical stage; the loss of another ship—and possibly more—might jeopardize the whole campaign. Hoover chose to continue his withdrawal toward Espiritu. He notified a patrol plane that he was doing so and gave it all pertinent information. This information never went through. As a result, of some 120 men left alive in the water (it developed), only ten made the beach.[15]

The sinking of the *Juneau* and the horrors the survivors endured are documented by Dan Kurzman in his book *Left to Die: The Tragedy of the USS Juneau*, a thorough piece of scholarship that captures and reconstructs this unfortunate incident for posterity. Kurzman interviewed seventy individuals who had knowledge of the event. His bibliography cites eighty books, thirty-one periodicals, seventy-two newspaper articles, and ninety other documents. His description of the suffering of the 120 men who remained alive after the sinking is not pleasant reading; yet it is necessary to understand the extent of the tragedy, the lessons that can be learned from it, and how it can be placed in perspective today. I will not delve into the many blunders made in the failure to rescue the survivors, who remained in the water for eight days, but will instead consider its consequences.

Their anticipation of a rescue that did not come added to the horrible suffering of those still alive. A B-17 flying over the area saw the survivors on the morning after the sinking. The navigator pinpointed the location and wrote in his diary that the heads of the men were like "many, many black coconuts (their faces were covered with oil) floating in the mess like peanuts in brittle . . . men floating, swimming to rafts and pieces of wreckage . . . all of them were waving their arms at us . . . we could see the white-gray of their faces where they had wiped off the oil . . . otherwise they were black and bedraggled." Although he fixed the precise location of the survivors, marked it on his map, and entered it into his log, no rafts or supplies were dropped.

Only those who have experienced such a situation can truly understand the suffering of the men, many badly injured, who were without food and medical supplies, and almost without water. Lt. Charles Wang, for example, the only officer among the ten survivors, was trapped in debris and thought he was finished.

> He popped to the surface just in time. There he met two other men, and together they swam toward a net rolled in canvas. As they clung to it, Wang cut off the canvas with a knife and the three unrolled the net. Shortly, it was swarming with survivors, almost all horribly wounded—legs severed or broken, skulls split open, muscles torn away. . . . His broken leg was bleeding, with the shinbone, the tibia, fractured near the ankle and protruding. The fibula, the smaller bone on the side of the leg, was broken as well.

To stop the blood, he tied his feet together with his shoelaces and placed them on a plank he had grabbed as it floated by. When that didn't work, he held the leg down in the churning water and the bleeding finally stopped. Eventually, his raftmates put a tourniquet on his leg above the knee with a piece of white line that Wang had in his pocket. But the pain maddeningly persisted.

By nightfall, the men were hungry and thirsty. There was a rainstorm and they were able to capture some fresh water in empty cans. The heat of the day turned into severe cold, and some of the sailors left the raft to go into the water (which was warmer) despite the danger of drowning for the badly wounded. "The night hideously rang with screams of men dying an agonizing death." Kurzman described the experience of Seaman C. Wyatt Butterfield on the second night in the water:

> We couldn't see the sharks because it was so dark out there on the water. . . . All we could hear were the sounds of winds and waves, and here we were on what felt like an endless roller coaster, wondering where the hell we were and how long it would be before dawn came. We'd doze off, awaken freezing, duck into the water in the raft to try to warm up, then come up and doze again.
>
> As we drifted, our legs started to swell badly because of continual exposure to water. We all had to try to sleep standing up, which made the first days almost intolerable. Then the thirst hit. Our tongues swelled, we couldn't swallow or salivate. Our eyes were almost totally closed by the combination of oil and the intense reflection of the sun on the water. To obtain some warmth during the night, we would urinate down our legs.

When they ran out what little water they had, some resorted to drinking saltwater, which bloated their stomachs; they became delirious and jumped into the water thinking they were going belowdecks to get fresh water and food; or they tried to swim ashore. They drowned if the saltwater they drank didn't kill them first.

Some of the men had lost their shirts escaping the sinking ship. They became so badly burned that their skin peeled off. "It was just like as if you shaved them with a razor or something, all raw . . . and some of them just decided . . . they'd rather drown themselves than suffer like that." One who decided to swim to an island jumped into the water and swam away. Within twenty-five yards, three sharks attacked him and he screamed: "Help me!

Help me!" as the sharks devoured him. Another survivor described a shark "in a swirling boil of water and blood, vise-like jaws clumped shut on Grycky's right shoulder, removing all of it and leaving his arm suspended only by a couple [of] tendons." One survivor was on a raft with only one shipmate. They had removed the floor slats to use as paddles when suddenly one felt "something scratching at his buttocks. He looked around and, to his horror, saw a shark that had swum into the raft and sunk his teeth into him. "God damn," he said, "he's got me by the ass!"[16]

Less than a week after the tragedy, on November 21, Halsey and his chief of staff, Capt. Miles Browning, boarded the USS *Helena* and entered the cabin of the captain, Gilbert Hoover. The three came out after only five minutes, and Halsey and Browning reboarded the admiral's launch. When it was out of sight, Hoover turned to Comdr. Charles L. Carpenter and said, "I have been relieved of command." Halsey's autobiography records his message to Admiral Nimitz, which summed up his thinking at that time:

> After analysis of the situation presented, I consider that commanding officer *Helena*, senior officer present in the task group, committed a serious and costly error in the action which he took.
>
> He should have made radio report of the torpedoing at once. Radio silence, as a measure of concealment, had ceased to be effective since the enemy was in contact. Only positive action to keep him [the enemy] submerged could be expected to delay his report.
>
> He should have instituted offensive action, together with, or closely followed by, rescue operations, utilizing at least one of his destroyers.
>
> His failure to take prompt action on the above lines was further aggravated by lack of any follow-up to insure that the senior commands were informed of the *Juneau*'s loss. Commander South Pacific [i.e., Halsey] was first apprised of this fact as a result of his own inquiry into *Juneau*'s status when she was not included in the arrival report of the group.
>
> Attempts are still in progress as of this date to locate and effect rescue of any of the approximately sixty survivors who were reported in the water at the scene of the torpedoing by a search plane on the fourteenth.
>
> In view of the above circumstances, I have this date relieved Captain G. C. Hoover of his command of the USS *Helena*, and ordered him by dispatch

to proceed by the first available government air transportation and report to Commander in Chief [Nimitz] for assignment.

Admiral Nimitz was not so hasty to condemn Hoover. He wrote to Admiral King that Hoover "would have shown better judgment if he had broken radio silence immediately to report the loss of the *Juneau*," but that he "was in no way responsible for the failure to report it through a B-17." Nimitz continued by saying that Hoover's failure to look for survivors or to seek out and destroy the submarine, or submarines, "was the result of a decision made by him when confronted by a difficult situation." The need to get his damaged ships safely back to a base was balanced against the natural instinct of every naval officer to go to the rescue of men in distress and danger. Nimitz added: "*Whatever may be the opinion of Captain Hoover's decision, he was the responsible officer on the spot* and, from his war record [he had received three Navy Crosses, the Navy's highest decoration, second only to the Congressional Medal of Honor], his courage may not be questioned. . . . It is recommended that [he] be given a suitable command at sea after he has had a reasonable rest period in the United States."

Halsey later regretted his decision to relieve Hoover. In his autobiography he related:

When the *Helena* eventually reached Nouméa, Hoover reported to my headquarters. After interrogating him thoroughly, my advisers Jake Fitch, Kelly Turner, and Bill Calhoun—agreed that he had done wrong in abandoning the *Juneau,* and recommended his detachment. Reluctantly, I concurred. Hoover's record was outstanding—he had won three Navy Crosses—but I felt that the strain of prolonged combat had impaired his judgment; that guts alone were keeping him going; and that his present condition was dangerous to himself and to his splendid ship. In this conviction, I detached him with orders to CINCPAC.

Much later, when I reviewed the case at the instigation of Rear Admiral Robert B. Carney, who had become my Chief of Staff, I concluded that I had been guilty of an injustice. I realized that Hoover's decision was in the best interests of victory. I so informed the Navy Department, requesting that he be restored to combat command, and adding that I would be delighted to have him serve under me. The stigma of such detachment can never be wholly erased, but I have comfort, slight as it is, of knowing that Hoover's official record is clean. I deeply regret the whole incident. It testifies to Captain Hoover's character that he has never let it affect our personal relations.[17]

Captain Hoover never received another sea command. While the fate of the *Juneau*'s crew was tragic, the sailors in the *Helena* and the other ships remaining afloat realized that had *Helena* remained to search for survivors, their ships might well have been sunk with the loss of hundreds more lives.

Captain Hoover surrendered his command at 5:00 A.M. on November 22. As he prepared to leave, his crew held a surprise farewell party for him. He was a superb leader whose men loved him. There were few dry eyes among those battle-hardened warriors as they said good-bye.

Was Halsey correct in believing that Hoover never allowed his dismissal to "affect our personal relations"? In *Left to Die* Kurzman described a postwar incident:

Captain Hoover was returning by train from an Army-Navy football game. A Navy officer approached him at New York station and said: "You're Captain Hoover, aren't you?"

"Yes," Hoover replied.

"Well, Admiral Halsey is sitting in the next car. He has asked if you will come to see him."

Hoover paled. The man who had ruined his career wanted to see him? "No," he said. "If the admiral wishes to see me, let him come here."[18]

The two did not meet.

It was rumored that, on his retirement, Captain Hoover threatened suicide but was prevented by his wife. He did go to a naval hospital for treatment of battle fatigue. After his recovery he had a successful civilian career, serving as the mayor of Bristol, sitting on the Atomic Energy Commission, and performing other public services; but none of those jobs was in the Navy he loved.

When addressing accountability on Hoover's decision not to stop and determine whether there were any survivors from the *Juneau*, one must, to be fair, consider that Japanese submarines were still in the area and other ships in the fleet might have been sunk if he had done so. Kurzman closed his book *Left to Die* with a cogent thought: "Had he not saved many lives?"[19]

The Sinking of the USS *Indianapolis*, July 29–30, 1945

On the night of July 29–30, 1945, the heavy cruiser USS *Indianapolis* sank after being struck by two torpedoes from a Japanese submarine; its loss is considered one of the worst disasters in the history of the U.S. Navy. Peter Maas, in the introduction to Richard F. Newcomb's *Abandon Ship! The Saga of the USS* Indianapolis, *the Navy's Greatest Sea Disaster*, wrote of the incident: "It would trigger a bitter controversy that rages to this day etched in anger, with allegations of shameful injustice and massive cover-ups, duplicity, personal humiliation, accountability, ruined careers and conveniently selected scapegoats, all within the factual context of unspeakable horror."[20]

The *Indianapolis*, under the command of Capt. Charles B. McVay III, was a very special ship with an exceptional record of service and a brilliant Pacific combat record. Launched in November 1931, the *Indianapolis* was a *Portland*-class heavy cruiser displacing 9,800 tons. One of its first duties after commissioning was to transport newly elected President Franklin D. Roosevelt from his vacation home on Campobello Island to Annapolis, Maryland, in July 1933. The ship became one of the president's favorites.

The *Indianapolis* was selected to carry the nuclear components of America's first two atomic bombs from San Francisco to the advance airfield on Tinian Island in July 1945, then had orders to proceed to ten days of training at Leyte, in the Philippines. En route from Guam to Leyte, in the early morning of July 30, the *Indianapolis* was torpedoed by the Japanese submarine I-58 and sank in twelve minutes.

The *Indianapolis* carried a crew of 1,196 men—82 officers and 1,114 enlisted men. An estimated 300 went down with the ship, leaving approximately 900, many badly burned and wounded, floating in shark-infested waters. These figures are, however, only an estimate. Captain McVay later stated: "How many people actually got off the ship I don't think anybody will ever know, but we tried to make estimates. . . . I think we actually guessed at a figure between five and six hundred, but I don't believe that anybody could definitely say if you pinned them down, that that number did get off, because they weren't seen that night. It was too dark to see anybody until between two or three o'clock in the morning when the moon came out." Whatever the exact number of those who survived the sinking, only 317 out of the crew of 1,196 men survived to be rescued.

The sinking of the *Indianapolis* was tragic enough, but much of the suffering and many of the deaths could have been avoided had the ship been operating under the usual procedures. The *Indianapolis*'s mission and movements had been a carefully guarded secret, however, and its failure to arrive in Leyte went unnoticed. The survivors had to wait four and a half miserable days for rescue. In the meantime they had to swim in the diesel fuel oil that covered the sea. In their struggle to get away from the ship, many of the crew swallowed it, along with seawater, and the subsequent vomiting and wrenching threatened to turn their stomachs inside out. The fuel irritated their eyes, and the inevitable constant rubbing to seek relief only made their suffering worse. During the daytime the glare off the oil caused tremendous pain and blindness. Soon the sharks came, picking off the survivors one by one, taking off arms and legs, in some cases leaving only torsos held up by life belts. Dehydration, lack of food and water, and rubber life belts that failed to inflate caused further misery. The saltwater caused some of the life preservers to deteriorate and become useless; the collars of those that remained inflated rubbed chins and necks raw, causing pain and blisters. Continued exposure to the sun left skin blistered and peeling, and lips puffy and cracked. The survivors developed saltwater ulcers, the pain often lasting for months after their rescue. The lack of water was horrible, and of course with no food there was the hunger.

Some of those overcome with thirst from the lack of fresh water desperately swallowed sea water and suffered a hideous death, thrashing and screaming wildly as they sank into the depths. Nights brought cold; teeth chattered, and some of the men had seizures. They feared sleep. A man who fell asleep might float away from the others and be completely alone, or might drown when he could not keep his head above water. The cold and the lack of sleep brought exhaustion; some men gave up. Those who managed to hold on suffered incredible pain from the sunburn. All of this went on for the four days and five nights.

The survivors sighted no planes until the second day, when they made every effort they could think of to be noticed—flares, signal mirrors, signal flags, and yellow dye on the water. The men splashed vigorously, even burning a fire in a can of pieces of cloth, but the planes continued on, oblivious to the scene below. Ultimately, they were spotted by an aircraft on routine patrol and rescued.

The captain of the *Indianapolis,* Charles B. McVay III, was a second-generation career naval officer, a 1919 graduate of the Naval Academy. His father was a retired admiral. An official court of inquiry held in Guam in August recommended that Captain McVay be held for general court-martial. Captain McVay was tried December 3–19, 1945, by a Navy court-martial composed of seven members. There were two charges, signed by Secretary of the Navy James Forrestal:

Charge 1: Through Negligence Suffering a Vessel of the Navy to Be Hazarded

> Specification: In that Charles B. McVay, 3rd, captain, U.S. Navy, while so serving in command of the USS *Indianapolis,* making passage singly, without escort from Guam, Marianas Islands, to Leyte, Philippine Islands, through an area in which enemy submarines might be encountered, did, during good visibility after moonrise on 29 July 1945, at or about 10:30 P.M., minus nine and one-half zone time, neglect and fail to exercise proper care and attention to the safety of said vessel in that he neglected and failed, then and thereafter, to cause a zigzag course to be steered, and he, the said McVay, through said negligence, did suffer the said USS *Indianapolis* to be hazarded, the United States then being in a state of war.

Charge 2: Culpable Inefficiency in the Performance of Duty

> Specification: In that Charles B. McVay, 3rd, captain, U.S. Navy, while so serving in command of the USS *Indianapolis,* making passage from Guam, Marianas, to Leyte, Philippine Islands, having been informed at or about 12:10 A.M., minus nine and one-half zone time, on 30 July 1945, that said vessel was badly damaged and in sinking condition, did then and there fail to issue and see effected such

timely orders as were necessary to cause said vessel to be abandoned, as it was his duty to do, by reason of which inefficiency many persons on board perished with the sinking of said vessel, the United States then being in a state of war.

At the time and in the years since, many of the survivors have tried to clear McVay's name of the blame that has shadowed it for nearly fifty years. One of the survivors, Paul J. Murphy, chairman of the USS *Indianapolis* Survivors' Organization at the time of his testimony before a congressional hearing in 1999, emphasized that Captain McVay's two most senior bosses had been opposed to the court-martial. Speaking for the organization, he commented:

Captain McVay's court-martial was opposed both by Fleet Admiral Chester Nimitz, commander of U.S. naval forces in the Pacific (CINCPAC), and Admiral Raymond Spruance, who headed the Fifth Fleet and for whom the *Indianapolis* served as flagship. In addition, Admiral Louis Denfeld, Chief of Naval Personnel, recommended against the court-martial.

As background, an initial Court of Inquiry convened in Guam within days after our rescue, and the Judge Advocate, a Captain Hilbert, stated that they were "starting the proceedings without having available all the necessary data." Nonetheless, following closed-door sessions, they recommended a court-martial for Captain McVay.

Upon hearing of this recommendation, Admiral Nimitz, a former sub-mariner who understood the vulnerability of surface ships, immediately disagreed and issued a statement that "in not maintaining a zigzag course Captain McVay at worst was guilty only of an error in judgment and not gross negligence." Nimitz went on to say in a CINCPAC memorandum that the rule requiring zigzag-ging would not have applied in any event since Captain McVay's orders gave him discretion on that matter and thus took precedence over all other orders (a point which was never brought out by Captain McVay's defense counsel).

When Secretary of the Navy James Forrestal and Admiral Ernest J. King, Chief of Naval Operations, ordered the court-martial of Captain McVay, it was unprecedented. There is no record in U.S. naval history of any officer being court-martialed against the recommendation of his immediate superior officers, much less officers holding the high ranks of Admirals Nimitz and Spruance.[21]

The court-martial's verdict was, on charge 1: "The specification of the first charge proved. And that the accused, Charles B. McVay, 3rd, captain,

U.S. Navy, is of the first charge guilty." The decision on the second charge was: "The specification of the second charge not proved. And that the accused, Charles B. McVay, 3rd, captain, U.S. Navy, is of the second charge not guilty, and the court does therefore acquit the said Charles B. McVay, 3rd, captain, U.S. Navy, of the second charge."

Immediately after the court-martial decision was announced, the press attacked the Navy for focusing on McVay and not pursuing the lack of effort to save the shipwrecked men. The *Chicago Sun* wrote: "No evidence was introduced at the trial with respect to possible culpability ashore for the lack of a search for the overdue cruiser at the time it was sunk." The *New York Herald Tribune* stated that the trial "has left a bad impression in Washington. . . . The fact [is] that the greater part of the loss of life in the disaster was due to a failure on the part of others to notice that the *Indianapolis* was overdue at Leyte and to begin a search. The Navy has not brought before a court martial anybody responsible for this costly piece of negligence. Suspicion[s] that Captain McVay was being 'railroaded' or chosen as a 'goat' are the inevitable consequences." The *New York World-Telegram* commented: "Captain McVay either willingly or unwillingly, was fall guy for higher-ups, officers say. Alternatives were to bring an admiral to trial for lapses of his subordinates, or to hang blame on an enlisted man or low-ranking reservist."

A number of books have been written on the incident, including *Ordeal by Sea: The Tragedy of the USS* Indianapolis by Thomas Helm; *Abandon Ship! The Saga of the USS* Indianapolis, *the Navy's Greatest Sea Disaster* by Richard F. Newcomb; *Fatal Voyage: The Sinking of the USS* Indianapolis by Dan Kurzman; and *The Tragic Fate of the USS* Indianapolis: *The U.S. Navy's Worst Disaster at Sea* by Raymond B. Lech. In addition to providing details on the sinking and its tragic aftermath, all are critical of two things: first, that there was a court-martial, and, second, that Captain McVay was found guilty because he was not zigzagging the ship. These books were, and are, enlightening, but McVay remained the Navy's scapegoat until an eleven-year-old schoolboy in Pensacola, Florida, named Hunter Scott created a spark with his ninth-grade research project that ignited a firestorm; it ultimately culminated in a hearing before the Committee on Armed Services of the U.S. Senate. What began as a school project became a cause célèbre. Hunter Scott's project received nationwide newspaper coverage and obtained results far beyond those gained by veterans' groups that had tried for decades to exonerate Captain McVay.

The committee met on September 14, 1999, to hear evidence in support of a Senate resolution addressing the *Indianapolis* disaster. The chairman of the committee at that time was Senator John Warner of Virginia, who had enlisted in the Navy at age seventeen and retained a great love for his former service. He had just turned eighteen and was in recruit training in radio tech school in Chicago when the sinking of the *Indianapolis* occurred. He went on to serve his country and the Navy first as undersecretary and then as secretary of the navy, serving a total of five and one-half years. Another key senator at the hearing was Bob Smith of New Hampshire, who served as a naval officer in the Vietnam War. His father had been a naval aviator in World War II, distinguishing himself in the Pacific before being killed right after the war while in training as a test pilot.

Senator Warner made his views on the hearing and its purpose very clear:

> Frankly, I am opposed to revisionist history. My colleague, here [Senator Smith], likewise. But nevertheless, there are some aspects of this case which, by virtue of the testimony today, require me, as an individual and as one of those trustees, to go back and probe and examine other areas of this historic case. I commit to do that. It may well be in consultation with Senator Smith and my colleagues on the committee that we might have a second hearing, because this hearing is going to receive a considerable amount of attention across the country. There may be others who can come forward and provide their firsthand knowledge to a number of questions that have been answered in good faith today by all present here as witnesses.[22]

Senator Max Cleland of Georgia, a Vietnam veteran who lost one arm and both legs in combat in that war, was another member of the committee. He succinctly stated what the committee was to decide: "The ultimate issue is the responsibility and accountability of a commanding officer for his ship at sea." Was the court-martial, however, meant to determine accountability or to make Captain McVay a scapegoat?

One of the first witnesses called was Richard A. Von Doenhoff of the National Archives and Records Administration. On September 14, 1999, in a prepared statement, Von Doenhoff told the committee,

> The tragic circumstances surrounding the sinking of USS *Indianapolis* by the Japanese submarine I-58 on 30 July 1945 have evoked articles and books too numerous to mention. Yet, for many reasons, this is a story which refuses to die. There is, of course, the lurid specter of sharks in a 5-day feeding frenzy; allegations of Navy blundering in "losing" the cruiser en route from Guam to Leyte Gulf; and finally, sympathetic murmuring that Capt. Charles B. McVay III was allegedly being made a scapegoat for a sloppy and slipshod Navy bureaucracy which allowed this tragedy to happen. With the passage of 48 years and as a result of the declassification of documentation which was never supposed to see the light of day, we are able to place one more piece into the overall *Indianapolis* puzzle.

Of particular interest is the comment about "documentation which was never supposed to see the light of day." The committee went on to address a number of key issues:

1. The *Indianapolis* was denied the escort it requested and was not informed that there were four Japanese submarines operating along the route it would take to Leyte. Nor was the captain informed that the USS *Underhill*, a destroyer escort ship, had been sunk along the same path just a few days earlier. The fact that this intelligence information had been withheld was not brought out in the court-martial.
2. The court-martial convened before a full investigation was completed.
3. Fleet Adm. Chester Nimitz, CinCPac, and Adm. Raymond Spruance, who headed the Fifth Fleet, the command to which the *Indianapolis* was assigned, opposed the court-martial but were overruled by CNO Adm. Ernest King.
4. Announcement of the *Indianapolis* tragedy was withheld until the day the war with Japan ended, allegedly to minimize the impact of the tragedy.
5. Captain McVay was selectively prosecuted; no others were held accountable.

6. Senior naval officers had testified that Captain McVay's court-martial and subsequent sentence were "trivial."
7. An allegation had been made that the prosecution for the court-martial on one occasion attempted to coach a witness.

The committee wanted to know why Captain McVay was singled out for court-martial. The representative of the survivors' group pointed out that seven hundred other ships went down in World War II, and their captains were not court-martialed. Senator Smith asked:

> Did we look at every single one of those sinkings and look at the judgment of those captains prior to that? Did we analyze each one of those? Did we say, "Well, he did not zigzag; he did zigzag; he did know this; he did not know that?" I do not think we did. So, looking at the weight of the evidence, the weight of what was going on at the time, [McVay was] the only captain to be court-martialed out of hundreds of ships. The two superior officers, immediate superiors, recommend[ed] no court-martial because of the zigzag issue, yet it was still done at a higher-up level at the SECNAV. . . . It is, to me, bizarre that one individual would be court-martialed on a judgment. Would any of you gentleman wearing the uniform like to be court-martialed on an error in judgment that had no direct impact on the loss of lives? How would you feel if that were your son or you?

These comments were followed by an exchange between Vice Chief of Naval Operations Adm. Donald L. Pilling and Senator Smith.

ADMIRAL PILLING: If I could just respond, Senator. In the first place, as the Judge Advocate General pointed out, the role of a court-martial before 1950 was very different.

SENATOR SMITH: I understand that.

ADMIRAL PILLING: It is very difficult for us, 54 years later . . . to do the contact. . . . The second thing I would point out is that Fleet Admiral King, I mean, Nimitz, said he should not go to court-martial, but he should receive a letter of reprimand for a judgment error.

SENATOR SMITH: Well, that is a big difference. Let us face it. A big difference between a letter of reprimand and a court-martial. But you said that the Navy had a number of weaknesses, that is the term you used in your statement.

ADMIRAL PILLING: Right.

SENATOR SMITH: The way they noted and tracked ships, and weaknesses in survival equipment onboard. But it is interesting that when the Navy talks about their mistakes, they are not mistakes, they are weaknesses. When we talk about a possible mistake in judgment by Captain McVay, it is a court-martial offense. I would ask the JAG this: Were the individuals who allegedly received the SOS message court-martialed?

ADMIRAL HUTSON: No, sir. There were no other court-martials relating to the tragic loss. There were a number of letters of reprimand that were issued and were subsequently withdrawn by Secretary Forrestal. I would point out, too, that although you are absolutely correct about the judgment of Fleet Admiral Nimitz and Admiral Spruance, there were a number of other people, . . . including the Court of Inquiry with three flags, the Inspector General, Admiral Snyder, the JAG at the time, the CNO at the time, and then, ultimately and very importantly, the top civilian. We cherish civilian control of the military. It was ultimately Secretary Forrestal who decided that the appropriate thing to do was to refer this case to a general court-martial. So, there was, obviously, disagreement amongst some very senior people. But ultimately, the decision was made by the individual whose desk the buck stops on, and that was Secretary Forrestal.

CHAIRMAN WARNER [presiding]: That is a subject that intrigues me most, as having been the humble Secretary of the Navy, and Undersecretary for five and one half years. Is there anything in Forrestal's official records that reflects on his deliberations or process of thought, or is it just James V. Forrestal signed on some order?

ADMIRAL HUTSON: . . . So far as I am aware, there is not documentary evidence of his thought process at the time. In the end, his judgment was supported by the fact that a court, after hearing all of the testimony, listening to all of the evidence, a court made up of seven senior officers with combat experience, ultimately convicted Admiral McVay.

CHAIRMAN WARNER: Was it a unanimous verdict, or was it a recorded verdict? RADM Hutson's office (JAG) has read the record of the court-martial, and informs us that the recommendation for clemency was unanimous, but that the vote for the verdict was not recorded.

ADMIRAL HUTSON: We do not know. You know that at least, now, and I guess in 1945, two-thirds of the members have to agree. Whether it was unanimous or by something other than unanimity, it was lost to the . . . jury room.

CHAIRMAN WARNER: There is no official record of that.

ADMIRAL HUTSON: No, sir.

CHAIRMAN WARNER: I wonder if you would check it, to see whether or not . . . there was.

ADMIRAL HUTSON: Yes, sir.

Senator Warner then offered what might be considered an inference that influence and intimidation had been factors in the decision to court-martial Captain McVay: "I have to tell you, in those days, command influence, particularly from a Chief of Naval Operations, was felt down through all levels of the ranks."

Senator Smith continued with his tough and perceptive questioning of Admiral Pilling:

There were numerous examples of errors in judgment by the Navy here; numerous, not just Captain McVay. You singled out Captain McVay. All I am trying to point out, is in the context of the whole thing, hundreds of ships sunk. Admiral Nimitz, Admiral Spruance, both saying, "No court-martial"; [the matter] bumps all the way to the SECNAV, he does it. Nobody else court-martialed, with tremendous numbers [of] errors in judgment. Why? I mean, it makes no sense. . . . I [do not] think it is wrong to look back and say the Navy made an error in judgment here with this. We are not asking you to overturn the court-martial. That is not what our resolution says. You have admitted to half of it. . . . The other part of it is . . . that we should recognize McVay's lack of culpability for the loss of the *Indianapolis*. You also have said that. At least the court-martial said it.

So, what we have left is two other points. Number one, was McVay's conviction a miscarriage of justice that led to his unjust humiliation and damage to his Naval career? Apparently, you disagree with that. Well, it certainly damaged his Naval career. We know that. Was it a miscarriage of justice? I think you disagree with us on that. The second point is the court-martial charges against . . . McVay arising from the USS *Indianapolis* sinking while under his command were not morally sustainable. So how can you say that he did not cause the sinking of the ship and then claim that it is morally sustainable to court-martial him? How can you say that it was not unjust humiliation and damage to his Naval career if he did not cause the sinking of the ship?

Again, not trying to be a revisionist, in my view, you go back to the contemporary times, and you say, "Captain McVay, whether you make it across there or not"—let us assume he made it—"you need to be reprimanded, because you should have zigzagged. You risked the possibility of having your ship sunk. You got lucky." We did not do that. So we singled [him] out and you know full well he would not have been court-martialed had that ship not been sunk. . . . I have looked at cases like this before. I have come down on the side of the Navy many times, as the Navy people here know. But . . . this is just simply not right. It is not right.

ADMIRAL PILLING: Senator, if I could respond. I think my fellow panelists might have responses as well. On the issue of damage to his Naval career, he did not lose any seniority. He was not demoted. He, in fact, retired as a rear admiral. . . .

SENATOR SMITH: That was the law. The tombstone law. Every officer had the same thing.

ADMIRAL PILLING: No, sir.

Senator Smith made a cogent point when he noted that Captain McVay would not have been court-martialed for failing to zigzag had the ship arrived safely. He continued:

> The court-martial also indicates that the captain was not responsible for the sinking of the ship and the ultimate deaths of many of his men. So, what we now have to look at, with the perspective of historical hindsight, is the issue: On the night that Captain McVay gave the order to cease zigzagging, if that happened, the *Indianapolis* sailed safely into the port of Leyte. All 1,196 men came into port alive. The ship is good

shape. No 4 days of shark attacks. No exposure to the weather and the water. No fires. No botched search. No botched recovery effort. No botched withholding of evidence. No ignoring of enemy message traffic. Upon arrival of the crew and the ship, [if] one of these men or one of their colleagues [had said] . . . "Captain McVay did not zigzag," you are telling me that he would have been court-martialed. There is no way. You know it.

If he was not going to be court-martialed, then you made a mistake. If you tell me that he caused the death of those men, then OK, I might disagree with you. But at least the court-martial was justified. *But you cannot court-martial somebody for an error in judgment, and then not court-martial everybody else who made errors in judgment that cost the lives of more men. You did not do it.* That is why there is an injustice here. We should change injustices; not rewrite history, but change injustices.

That man wore the uniform just like you wore it. He wore it proudly. He was one hell of an officer. He would not have been given that bomb to take to the *Enola Gay* if he was not . . . and he endured the punishment that none of us could ever understand, probably, and paid the ultimate price for it. We have a chance, that he will never know about, to make it right. Not to overturn the court-martial; just simply to say that a mistake was made; that we did not apply the justice to the other members of the Navy who were involved here, that we did to Captain McVay. It was wrong. Therefore, that is all we are asking to do in this resolution. Not to overturn a court-martial. Not to demean the reputations of any of the other officers who may have made errors in judgment. . . . It was an injustice to a good man. We have a chance to do that. I cannot believe the Navy would view this as a precedent. I do not view it as a precedent. . . .

If you are going to speak to the principles of accountability, which you have done, and I cannot disagree with the principles of accountability, then you have to apply those principles to all officers who are involved in some way or another with the incident. You did not do that. The officer who received the distress signal, the SOS signal, was not held accountable. The officer who failed to report the arrival failure was not held accountable. The intelligence officer who withheld intelligence was not held accountable.

Let us go to command accountability. Where was the command accountability for those commanders whose leadership intelligence reports of any submarine activity was withheld from McVay? These are all judgments. I am not going to get into why. There may have been reasons that were valid at the time. It is easy to look back. But what I am saying to you is, if you are going to do this to one man who was involved in this incident, you have got to do it to everybody. You did not do that, which is what makes the court-martial, in my view, morally wrong.[23]

Again, Senator Warner raised the point of whether there had been pressure from the top.

CHAIRMAN WARNER: That is a key question, and the one that I was going to . . . probe, because we can only reflect here, these many years afterwards, on the element of fairness, and I will come back at some point, in the absence of what I call military politics. . . . Accountability at sea is just absolutely infallible. That is important, Admiral Pilling. You have stressed that. But it could have been an element of politics. That is where my research is going to continue in this case. I must say that I have watched, with some concern, as my dear colleague has pushed this issue. But this morning, my ship is righted a little bit, back on a very objective even keel as I look at this case. I intend to do, myself, some further inquiry.

Senator Warner was quite upset over Admiral Pilling's comment that Captain McVay's sentence was trivial:

CHAIRMAN WARNER: It resonates in my mind that Admiral Pilling used the word "this thing is trivial." What was the sentence that you were—used the word "trivially" in your testimony? You read it.

ADMIRAL PILLING: I do not remember saying it.

CHAIRMAN WARNER: Well, it certainly caught me. I looked over at the faces of these magnificent men—

ADMIRAL PILLING: Oh, in referring to the sentence . . . from the court-martial of losing 100 numbers. . . . For a court-martial, it is like a trivial sentence.

CHAIRMAN WARNER: This thing has, through the years, generated enormous interest throughout the United States. . . . There is more than triviality involved here.

ADMIRAL HUTSON: I think, sir, that the point is that one of the roles of courts in 1945 was to assess accountability. The court-martial in that case, not in a punishment or a criminal sense, assessed accountability, and then awarded—having done that, awarded trivial sentence, which was then ultimately remitted by Secretary Forrestal, indicating that the issue was not punishing, in any way Admiral McVay for his exercise of discretion, but simply assessing the accountability for his failure to zigzag.

CHAIRMAN WARNER: Well, I recognize that accountability at sea goes back to the times of the Phoenicians, the earliest of the sailors, and records of their trials at sea. But I will return to that in subsequent questions, but I was struck by your saying that all of the letters of reprimand had been rescinded. That is interesting. What was the predicate on which someone made that decision?

ADMIRAL HUTSON: The decision was made by Secretary Forrestal. Similarly, we do not know what his thoughts were in doing that. We can only conjecture.

CHAIRMAN WARNER: That is the trouble, we are leaving an awful lot to conjecture in this case. That act, alone, could indicate to me by way of hypothesis, that he felt he made a mistake in ordering that court-martial. So the most that he could do would be to alleviate the letters of reprimand.[24]

Senator Smith hammered home his point about the unfairness of the court-martial, introducing the term "scapegoat" in a backhanded way, then turned to the failure of Navy intelligence to warn Captain McVay of the submarine threat.

SENATOR SMITH: I think you can pretty well conclude that it would be pretty ridiculous to single out a captain with a record that he had and court-martial him if that ship went on safely. . . . I am not going to use the term "scapegoat," because I do not know that that is appropriate here. But I do not think we look at the big picture. Now, in Dr. Dudley's testimony, . . . Captain Naquin, the Surface Operations Officer at Guam, had personal knowledge that intercepted Japanese messages had revealed a group of four Japanese subs operating in the Philippine Sea. He did not inform the intelligence office at Guam. So, McVay never received the information. Now, that is clearly a judgment in error. . . . It is not only an error in judgment, I think it is negligence, if, in fact, that is the case. Is that not the case, Dr. Dudley?

DR. DUDLEY: May I respond to that . . . and a couple of other points? Captain Naquin is an interesting type to me. To me, he is the type of person who hoards information that he has; knowing it is incredibly valuable; knowing that the sources of that information must be protected; and is very reluctant to release that information to people whom he . . . thinks may not need it or . . . might use it . . . the wrong way. This reminds me of librarians who hoard books and archivists who do not want you to see the documents they are in charge of. That is the kind of thing. My feeling is that he was overzealous in his duties as an operations officer protecting intelligence. We can all agree or disagree on what is, exactly, his obligation here. My feeling, myself, was his obligation would have been to share the information and to protect the sources. . . an excessive kind of protection.

SENATOR SMITH: . . . Clearly, he had not only the authority, but . . . the capability to share that information with the captain and not share it with anybody else. That would have been very, very helpful. Whether or not it would have avoided the incident, we will never know, but it certainly would have been helpful. But my point is, he made a judgment.

DR. DUDLEY: That is correct.

SENATOR SMITH: For whatever reason. . . . Maybe he thought it was bogus. Maybe he did not, and was worried that it would get out. I do not know. But he did not share it with Captain McVay. He made a judgment. He was not court-martialed. He was not court-martialed. Yet, McVay made a judgment that did not lead to—well, you can say maybe it did, maybe it did not, but the point is, according to the Japanese commander, it did not. So, two judgments were made here. The one officer was court-martialed, and the other was not.[25]

The Navy's best response to that argument was that naval intelligence could not inform Captain McVay of the Japanese subs along the route of the *Indianapolis* lest the Japanese learn that their secret code had been cracked. Richard Von Doenhoff told the senators:

> The bottom line is that Charles McVay exercised his professional judgment based on information available to him, and ordered his duty officer to cease zigzagging and return to the base course late in the evening of 29 July 1945. The CINCPAC intelligence officers on Guam had predetermined that the security of Ultra dictated flag eyes only, and no deviation or exception was considered. These same intelligence officers also determined that national security considerations outweighed the interests of due process of law and Navy Regulations and consciously withheld relevant documentation from the *Indianapolis* Court of Inquiry and McVay's court-martial. The principal participants in these proceedings, the Judge Advocate and the defense, had no opportunity for appeal of these decisions to higher authority, simply because *the very existence of the documents and the decisions were unknown to them.*

Two thoughts come to mind. First, there appear to be inconsistencies in the Navy's security policy during World War II. The most fundamental principle in military security is the axiom, "Need to know." In that regard, it was determined that Captain McVay had a legitimate need to be aware of the nature of the nuclear cargo he transported from San Francisco to Tinian. Security surrounding the development of the atomic bomb was certainly no less stringent than the security of Ultra; nevertheless, *his lack of flag rank was no bar to his learning about the bombs.* If ever a commanding officer had a need to know that identified enemy submarines were operating in the area he was assigned to transit, this was one of those cases if only because *Indianapolis* was the first heavy warship to make this transit unescorted.

This brings us to the second point. Navy Regulations stipulate that a commanding officer is ultimately responsible for the safe operation of his ship and his crew. This most cardinal principle of Navy command was forcefully reiterated during the Court of Inquiry and the court-martial. In this instance, security procedures prevented Captain McVay from receiving full and complete intelligence regarding the area he was to transit. It stands to reason that the Navy Department should have taken this into consideration in its judgment of his conduct.

It is problematic to speculate on the impact of these cryptologic documents on McVay's original decision to cease zigzagging. Under the circumstances, and with the full benefits of 20/20 hindsight, we know that wiser heads should have looked more carefully at the circumstances of *Indianapolis's* transit and the available information, and allowed McVay the opportunity to make a complete and informed decision.[26]

It also came out at the hearing that the *Indianapolis* had sent an SOS, but nothing was done about it. The give-and-take at the hearing was an eye-opener. A witness stated, "I do not think the SOS problem came up at the court-martial. I think it was quashed."

SENATOR SMITH: I just want to make a final point, Mr. Chairman. At least, for my information, *Mr. Miner, you brought up something that I had not heard; that a statement on the record that a transmission of an S.O.S. had been sent.* Now, Mr. Scott, you have testified already, in questions that I asked you regarding those documents, but I just want to make sure everyone understands . . . I mean, this brings more credibility to the documents, in the sense that we now have testimony that somebody sent an SOS. . . . Would you just . . . simply say what [the] evidence of receipt of transmission was, because . . . it goes directly to what . . . the doctor just said here; that no action was taken on the judgment of these individuals who . . . we know [were aware that] a message was sent? Whether or not it was received was questionable, but *now we have three people who said they received it or heard it,* or whatever. So, just recap, quickly.

MR. SCOTT: The first one, Mr. Hetz, received the SOS, and it was regarded as a prank call by the Japanese to lure rescue ships into the area.

CHAIRMAN WARNER: Now, who was he and where?

MR. SCOTT: Russell Hetz. I believe he was in Tacloban, I think. . . . No. He was aboard the LCI-1004 harbor examination vessel in Leyte Gulf.

CHAIRMAN WARNER: He heard the SOS.

MR. SCOTT: He received the SOS. Then he received another one eight and one half minutes later. It was regarded as a prank by the Japanese to lure rescue vessels in the area.

CHAIRMAN WARNER: Did he or did he not pass that to his superiors? Did he make the decision it was prank?

MR. SCOTT: He did not make the decision. His superior officers or superior officer did.

CHAIRMAN WARNER: None of whom were court-martialed.

MR. SCOTT: No, sir. The second one was received by Mr. Clair B. Young. Mr. Young says he received the SOS and reported it to his boss, who was drunk at the time. His boss said, "No reply at this time. If any further messages come, notify me at once."[27]

Dan Kurzman, the author of an exhaustively researched book on the *Indianapolis* sinking, was asked to testify at the hearing:

MR. KURZMAN: You asked why was McVay convicted of a lack of judgment . . . or a lack of good judgment, when others were not. The fact is, I think, in doing my research, I did get some insight into that, because Mr. Hildago, . . . who was the Special Assistant to Secretary Forrestal, wrote in a memorandum to the Secretary, on February 16, 1945, . . . "We must squarely face a seeming inevitable question as to whether the Navy is to conduct additional investigations. If not, what disciplinary actions [have] been taken in addition to the McVay trial? My present understanding is that our investigations are at an end." Forrestal agreed. Now, the thing is, I think it is important—

CHAIRMAN WARNER: Can you check the date of that? You said February 16. . . .

MR. KURZMAN: Pardon me; 1946. . . . Now, the thing is, I think it is important . . . that there were other people who had done things which perhaps you could call bad judgment. *I think that there was a definite error to try to cover up the bad judgments, if you want to put it that way, of high people; highly placed people. There were a couple of lower placed people, so to speak, who were given some kind of punishment, minor punishment. But the higher ones were not. There was a deliberate effort to keep them from doing so.* I might just mention just a few examples.

Commodore Carter failed to warn McVay of the submarine danger, and issued the faulty order regarding the arrival of combatant ships.

Commander Layton, the combat intelligence officer in Guam, and his counterpart in Washington, Captain Smedberg, neglected to investigate the intercepted report from submarine I-58 that it had sunk an enemy warship.

Admiral McCormick . . . did not try to find out why the *Indianapolis* was overdue in Leyte.

Admiral Olendorf, who knew the ship was coming, but not when, made no inquiries after a reasonable time had passed.

Admiral Murray did not keep tabs on his subordinate, Naquin, to ensure that the man informed him of any submarine menace; especially one that, according to the Inspector General's report, would have appeared to have been sufficient reason for Murray's command to have diverted the *Indianapolis* from her routing.

Finally, Admirals King and Nimitz, and their Chiefs of Staff, had approved the ambiguous ship arrival order and had not required the combatant ships be escorted.

All of these, you can say, "Well, it was just a matter of judgment." That is the point. If it was a matter of judgment, why were not any of these officers, not one of them, brought up for questioning, at least, and were certainly not court-martialed? Yet, they go down to Captain McVay, and they get him for a judgment.[28]

One of the most difficult-to-accept comments, made by Admiral Pilling, was that the court-martial did not damage Captain McVay's future in the Navy.

ADMIRAL PILLING: He did not go home immediately after the court-martial. He served on Active Duty until 1949. He served 30 years in the Navy. So, I would disagree that it was damage to his Naval career. On the issue of zigzagging, there is a lot of speculation of what he knew and what he did not know, but we have not asked the question, why was he zigzagging during the day, and then made the judgment to stop zigzagging at night?[29]

Senator Smith considered the admiral had left something out and quickly responded by offering three reasons why Captain McVay had stopped: "Because (a) visibility was bad; (b) it was dark; (c) he had lights out."

The hearing also addressed an allegation that at the court-martial of Captain McVay in 1946, an attempt had been made to instruct witnesses on what their testimony would be. Survivor Dr. Giles G. McCoy, a Marine Corps PFC at the time of the sinking and the director of naval history in the Department of the Navy when he testified before the committee, told the members of the Senate hearing:

DR. MCCOY: The thing that I would like to bring up to show that they were really struggling, the prosecution was really struggling to try to find something to blame Captain McVay for and take the blame from themselves. That was because they tried to get him on a charge of failure to announce abandon ship properly.

Now, whenever I was waiting to be a witness and I was sitting back in the room, the prosecution came to me.

CHAIRMAN WARNER: This was at the court-martial, now.

DR. MCCOY: That is right, I was a witness at the court-martial. The prosecution came to me and presented me a paper. I cannot remember all the exact words, but he said, "Now, this is what you are going to testify to when you go before the hearing."

I looked at it. I said, "I cannot say that." What it said, it said that "I want you to announce that Captain McVay was negligent in not announcing an abandon ship." I said, "I will not say that, because that is not true. I could not have heard 'abandon ship,'" I told him then, "if the bugle was in my ear, because of all the noise and the screaming and the explosions and all." But I said, "No. I am not going to say that." But it was Captain Ryan. Captain Ryan says, "Now you are still in the service. I am a captain, and you are a PFC in the Marine Corps."

I said, "Well, I am not going to answer that, because that is not true."
The Marine major in charge of me, I asked him. I said, "Well, Major,
it looks like you have got another court-martial coming on, because I
am not going to say that."

He says, "You do not have to say that. You say the truth."

I know they were trying to find something in there to hit him for
abandon ship, as well as for failure to zigzag. So, somebody was really
trying to work this thing out, where they could go on and stick it to
someone besides taking the blame themselves.[30]

The court-martial prosecutor also had called as a witness Comdr.
Mochitsura Hashimoto, the captain of the Japanese submarine that sank
the *Indianapolis*. This move elicited severe criticism from throughout the
country, and was particularly upsetting to the survivors. Dr. McCoy commented at the Senate hearing:

> Well, the other thing, I was so embarrassed when I got on the stand and I looked
> over, . . . and there was the Japanese commander. I did not even know he was
> there. Here he was, testifying in the same courtroom that I was testifying. I could
> not believe that this man was called, and came over from his country. They took
> him out of uniform, put him in a civilian uniform, a civilian suit, and had him
> testify against our commanding officer. That was highly embarrassing to me. To
> this day, it just makes me raw to think that. Then to do the other thing and have
> this Captain Ryan trying to get me to say something against my commanding offi-
> cer, who was not guilty of anything.[31]

To the surprise of the prosecution, however, Hashimoto stated that it
would not have made any difference if McVay had zigzagged.

What was learned from the *Indianapolis* tragedy, and what corrective
action did CinCPac take immediately afterward? Several days after the court-
martial hearing, orders were issued that Navy ships traveling alone would be
considered overdue eight hours after their expected time of arrival, mer-
chant vessels twenty-four hours after ETA, and smaller craft and tows seventy-
two hours after ETA. Port directors were ordered to notify their area commander of overdue ships. The area commander would try to determine the
location of the missing ship and arrange for rescue measures if these proved

necessary. That directive established responsibility and provided instructions to prevent such a calamity from ever happening again.

Following the 1999 hearings, the Senate passed a resolution calling on the president to award a presidential citation to the crew of the USS *Indianapolis*. The resolution also expressed "the sense of Congress that Captain McVay's court-martial and conviction were not legally sustainable and were an unfair humiliation to an honorable officer." The resolution emphasized that "the survivors of the *Indianapolis* still living have remained steadfast in the support of the exoneration of Captain McVay." The survivors of the crew never placed any blame on Captain McVay and never gave up their efforts to clear his name. During the hearing, Admiral Pilling's remarks apparently raised a question about the survivors' support for Captain McVay.

CHAIRMAN WARNER: Before you step down, gentlemen, I would like to ask some questions here. You used the phrase, Admiral Pilling, "some of the survivors." Is there any evidence that other survivors took a position different than the one being advocated by this group today? Is there any evidence in the record that there is another—

ADMIRAL PILLING: No, sir. That was just because I did not know. The record stated: "The Navy knows of no contemporary testimony that indicated any of the survivors blamed McVay for the sinking." The only anti-McVay sentiment I'm aware of in 1945 came from families of the dead. A former commanding officer of the USS *Indianapolis* (SSN 697) personally met 80 of the survivors in May 1999, and none spoke of disagreeing with the effort to clear Capt. McVay's record.

Mr. Scott informed the committee that he had contacted every one of the 154 survivors still living. "Over 80 responded to my request for information," he said, "and filled out a questionnaire I sent to them. One of the questions was whether or not they felt Captain McVay's court-martial was justified and his conviction fair. All of the responses I got back were unanimous, and most were strongly worded in outrage and anger over the court-martial and conviction of their captain."

The survivors who spoke at the Senate hearing were emotional and ardent in expressing their respect and love for Captain McVay and their resentment over the Navy's treatment of him, as the following extracts from the record indicate. Lyle M. Pasket said he supported Joint Resolution 26, "which will help at last to restore the good name of our skipper Captain Charles Butler McVay, III." Buck W. Gibson stated, "Our skipper, Captain Charles B. McVay, III, was court-martialed on trivial and senseless charges. . . . Now is the time to right this wrong and give the aging survivors some peace in our twilight years." John A. Spinelli said, "There wasn't a man in his crew that wouldn't have sailed with him again. . . . His court-martial was a terrible thing, but may his soul rest in peace when you pass the Joint Resolution clearing his name." David F. Nelson said that the survivors' organization was "experiencing a ground swell of public support at the grass roots level for the effort to clear the name of Captain McVay." Woodie E. James said, "Captain McVay was the best commanding officer I ever served under. He was demanding, but fair. He cared for his crew. . . . None of us ever believed that he was to blame for what happened and we all would have gladly sailed with him again. He ran a good, efficient, and happy ship. It was the pride of the fleet." Edward J. Brown said: "For over 50 years my shipmates and I have been trying to get Captain McVay's good name restored after the U.S. Navy made him a scapegoat for the sinking of our very proud and glorious fighting ship, the USS *Indianapolis*. We have pleaded and begged Congress over and over through the years to correct this wrong. . . . We waited 5 days in shark-infested waters of the South Pacific to be rescued. We have waited over 50 years to get our Captain McVay's good name cleared by Congress. *Please pass this resolution in the Senate.* Do not make us wait any longer." Loel Dene Cox said: "We were proud to serve under Captain McVay. We knew that he had to be a top-notch captain to be chosen to command a flagship, and he proved to be just that. It was an honor to have served under him, and I don't know of a survivor that wouldn't be proud to serve under his command again if it were possible. . . . We survivors feel his court-martial was unjust and has left a stigma on our ship and the crew." Herbert J. Miner II summed it up beautifully when he said: "I can state without a moment's hesitation that, if Captain McVay had been given a new command after the *Indianapolis* was sunk, I would have been at the head of the line to request a berth on his ship. . . . We do not have the power to restore the lives of 880 men, but we do have the power to restore the good name of Charles Butler McVay, III and simultaneously repair some of the damage done by the court-martial to the reputation of the United States Navy."[32]

The Senate resolution passed in 2000 came far too late to help Captain McVay. The captain of the *Indianapolis* received hate mail from the families of some of those lost in the tragedy for twenty-three years, and finally could stand it no longer. On November 6, 1968, he took his own life with his service revolver.

Much can be said for Captain McVay's love for and loyalty to the Navy in spite of what it did to him. Kurzman made the point in *Abandon Ship*:

> McVay did not have to take the stand. A fairly good case had been presented on his behalf, and he could have stood on that. But right from the start he had wanted to tell his version of the events. Tension ran high as he began his story, because it was always the chance that he would make, or attempt to make, statements outside the narrow scope of the charges against him. But those who expected anything of this nature simply didn't know their man. McVay was prepared to defend his competence and his honor, insofar as the charges against him reflected on them, but he was far too Navy to go beyond that. He could have blown the thing wide open, and many fellow officers hoped he would, but his testimony was a model of correctness.[33]

He did not blow things wide open, as he could have, but fortunately he and the crew of the *Indianapolis* have now been exonerated.

Accountability and High-Level Errors in Judgment

In April 1961 the Kennedy administration attempted to overthrow the Cuban dictator, Fidel Castro, by sponsoring an invasion force composed of Cuban dissidents and CIA contract workers. The small army landed in Las Villas Province at the Bahía de Cochinos—the Bay of Pigs—planning to fan out over Cuba and generate a general uprising that would depose Castro. The invasion was a dismal failure. The Cuban army captured and imprisoned most of the men, and the repercussions of the incident swept through Washington, D.C., and around the world.

Adm. Thomas Moorer (CNO 1967–70, chairman of the Joint Chiefs

1970–74), who was present in Washington at the time, commented: "Kennedy was pretty well shaken by the Bay of Pigs, which McNamara and others tried by implication to suggest was the fault of the Joint Chiefs of Staff. He made the famous statement that it was the chiefs' fault but since they worked for him he would take the blame."[34]

President Kennedy deserves credit, however, for ordering an investigation of the events surrounding the invasion, and for bringing in Adm. Arleigh Burke as part of the investigating team. The fact that he wanted Burke is a clear indication that the president wanted answers, not a cover-up, and further acknowledges the administration's high regard for Burke.

In his oral history Admiral Burke discussed the failure of the Bay of Pigs invasion along with other aspects of the Kennedy administration's relations with senior U.S. military advisers:

> When Mr. Kennedy took office, he not only took office, but he brought a great big team in, not just his Cabinet officers, but also second-, third-, and fourth-echelon people, and placed them in various positions of government. Most of these people, nearly all of these people were ardent, enthusiastic people without any experience whatsoever in administering anything, including the president. He'd always been in Congress. He'd never had any sort of a job that required any administration. None of the rest of them had either. So they didn't understand ordinary administrative procedures, the necessity for having lines of communication and channels of command. The president himself would pick up the telephone and call people who were not connected with an operation, and give them orders or instructions or ask advice. He did this with me lots of times, and at first I thought it was just a question of information, but later I found out that he never paralleled that by going down the chain of command, for example. So I got in the habit, and so did the other chiefs, when we got a telephone call from the president, we informed all the other people as soon as we could of what it was, so that they would be informed of it.
>
> Well, there was a breakdown, a complete breakdown of channels, not only in the Bay of Pigs, but every other way. There was a change of plans at the last minute. There were conflicting orders given to different people. There was an unreasonable amount of secrecy involved so that people who should have known about the operation didn't know it. There was not enough checking by anybody, including the chiefs. The chiefs themselves did not realize how little the admin-

istration knew or how small their capability was for that kind of thing. And we didn't insist upon knowing. They would have told us probably, but we were not tough enough. Our big fault was standing in awe of the presidency instead of pounding the table and demanding and being real rough. We were not. We set down our case and then we shut up. That was a mistake.

Their big mistake was that they [the administration] didn't realize the tremendous importance of the operation or the effect it would have on the world. They didn't realize the power of the United States or how to use the power of the United States. It was a game to them. It was another election. They were inexperienced people.

Now, the trouble is that there were a lot of orders given that I don't know anything about. That operation was not under the military. We were told that every time we got anywhere near it—we had no responsibility for it, we were not supposed to comment on things, unless we were asked to. It was not our show, it was a CIA operation and you stay the hell out of it, we will not permit any regular force of the United States to become involved in this, and so you chiefs cannot become involved.

This was the president himself. Every time. And it was repeated over and over again. It was a military operation which was conducted by amateurs, all from top to bottom. And it was a horrible fiasco.[35]

There will probably never be an end to the discussions on why the administrations of President John F. Kennedy and Lyndon B. Johnson did not permit the U.S. military to conduct the Vietnam War in a fashion that might have brought us victory. Admiral Burke suggested that the reason for their reluctance to escalate was concern that Communist China might enter the war.

Well, many people were convinced of that. And the reason again is because Americans who haven't been in Oriental or foreign countries a lot have an idea that everybody thinks alike, that we're all equal in the way we think, but it's not true. Communists are realistic people. They're a bunch of bastards, but they're realistic. And they aren't going to go to war because you come close, or they aren't going to war because you're operating in a third country's territory, unless they have good reason to go to war anyway. Not for that reason. They wouldn't have gone to war just because we'd operated in North Vietnam. They would have gone to war if they'd thought they could have kicked the hell out of us in a hurry and have us capitulate. They would have gone to war then. But they would not have gone to war just because we entered. . . . They didn't have the military power to be successful. Now, before that time, Mao Tse-tung had laid down his principle "war is protracted conflict" in his *Little Red Book*. He had measured us pretty well in that book. I don't think there really was any danger. War is not something that most nations play with. We do. But most nations don't.[36]

Burke also addressed other mistakes made in the conduct of the Vietnam War:

When [we had] committed ourselves to military action, in South Vietnam, we should have committed ourselves to destroying North Vietnam—which we could have done. We could have fought in the enemy's territory instead of landing at Danang as a main landing. We should have put a small detachment, a battalion, or maybe a division, a striking force landed south of Hanoi and raised hell for a couple of months, destroying the military installations around there and destroying their ability to conduct war. We should have made them react to our surprise moves, and then we should have pulled out, quickly, and said to the South Vietnamese, you handle it now; and if they couldn't, if Communists came in again, we go back in again. This may happen two or three times, and then we should have trained the South Vietnamese to fight right away. The Vietnamization started much too late, as it did in Korea. But basically, we wanted to play at war, and war is nothing to play with. . . . Too bad because Mr. Kennedy, who I think was a bad president, was misled by a great many people, but he himself was not a bad man. I liked Jack Kennedy. But he permitted himself to jeopardize the nation, without being willing to carry through on an operation, and he did this over and over. He did it at the Bay of Pigs. He did not do it on the missile crisis.[37]

There is perhaps no greater challenge to a military officer's character (and equanimity) than his dealings with the media, which have a tendency to ferret out the truth and ensure military accountability. In spring 1987 the United States was having difficulty with Iran. The Iranians threatened to—and did—place mines in the Persian Gulf. We met this threat in part by changing the flags on foreign ships to the U.S. flag, making any damage to the ships an attack against the United States.

Adm. William J. Crowe Jr. (chairman of the Joint Chiefs of Staff 1985–89), commented:

The Kuwait tanker *Al Rekkab* was rechristened the *Bridgeton*. Unfortunately it struck a moored mine. It meant that Teheran had made the decision to risk the wrath of the United States. Fortunately, no one was injured in the explosion and the tanker was able to proceed. However, had it been one of our destroyer escorts, there might have been the loss of the ship and many casualties. The media were raking us over the coals about the *Bridgeton*. Why? The fact we did not leave minesweepers in place before escorting the tankers. . . . Our patrolling in advance of the convoy hadn't been all it should have been. . . . I was not in a position to complain. . . . The media attention to this matter didn't seem to go away. . . . One day I told Weinberger, the secretary of defense, that if he would let me, I would get hold of the press and kill the story. Weinberger's response was, "How are you going to do that?" My response was, "I plan to tell them we made a mistake when the *Bridgeton* got mined and that I was the one who made it. We should have had more minesweeping capacity out there and we should have looked at our intelligence data more critically." Weinberger's face flushed. "Do not do that," he said. "Never, never, never, never admit that you made a mistake. They will never let you forget it!" "Okay," I said. And I didn't do it.

But three weeks later, after Crowe made a speech in San Diego, an aggressive reporter from the *San Diego Tribune* got up and asked a long question about the *Bridgeton* mining, clearly intending to embarrass him. On this occasion Crowe failed to follow the secretary's advice and took the blame, stating, "Look, let me put this thing to rest right now. We were brand new and we had a lot to learn. I personally made a mistake on the *Bridgeton* mining." Crowe told me:

> The reporter gave me a strange look. He may never have heard such a response before. Then he sat down. Afterward he published a story reporting what I had said, and I never heard another word about the *Bridgeton* mining. Honesty often actually is the best policy. I always remembered Joseph Stilwell's comment after his defeat in Burma. When he finally hiked out of the jungle and got to India, a truly remarkable achievement, there was a press conference. The correspondent asked, "What happened?" And Stilwell said, "We got the hell beat out of us." The press loved Stilwell. There is a lot to be said for simply saying, "I was wrong."

There is an important caveat here. When admitting a mistake, *you* take the blame; you do not blame someone else. Crowe continued: "Of course, whoever does that must take the responsibility on his own shoulders. He cannot say, 'The president made a mistake.' He cannot go around including others in the blame. He cannot even use the word 'we.' He has to say, 'I did it and nobody else.' That is the beginning and the end of the mistake routine, but it has to be used sparingly. Otherwise, before too long, people will begin asking themselves, what is he doing there, if all he can do is make mistakes?"[38]

A good leader accepts responsibility for his or her mistakes and never blames superiors, even though orders or policies may originate with them. The same is true when orders come down from above that are likely to have an adverse impact on morale. Adm. James L. Holloway III (CNO 1974–78) related just such an incident that occurred when he was captain of the *Enterprise*.

In 1966, *Enterprise* was on the line at Yankee Station in the Gulf of Tonkin at Christmas time. Commander, Seventh Fleet, had scheduled a stand-down from offensive strike operations on Christmas Day to enable ships to serve a turkey dinner and for the crews to relax, attend church call, write letters home, and generally take a day off from war. The troops were really looking forward to a day without flight operations, replenishment, or field day. It wasn't a big deal, but it was Christmas Day off, and most Americans are very sentimental about Christmas.

On December 23, CTF-77 scheduled a major strike into the Hanoi area by the *Enterprise* air wing. It was a full-deck-load launch. Unfortunately, the results were not good. First, the weather in the target area was not favorable, but not so bad as to cancel the mission. There were heavy broken clouds in several overcast levels. Some sections of Hanoi were visible and other target areas were fully socked in. Second, the North Vietnamese defenses went all out. MiGs were airborne from Kep Airfield, and a barrage of SAMs filled the air as the strike group approached Hanoi. The weather conditions minimized the fighter threat because of the poor visibility. But the broken clouds in layers made defense against the surface-to-air missiles almost impossible. Countering a SAM requires the pilot to observe the missile tracking on his aircraft and then break [off] at the last moment in a sharp turn, too tight for the missile to follow. When the SAMs were obscured by the clouds, there is little a plane [could] do except depend on the passive electronic countermeasures, which were only effective when combined with maneuvering.

As the formation of strike aircraft encountered salvos of SAMs, individual planes took evasive action, became separated from their wingmen, and the cohesion of the group began to disintegrate. The desired effect of mutually supporting attacks was largely lost. The flight leader essentially lost control of the strike group before it got to the objective area. Individual planes did attack their assigned targets, but it was not a coordinated effort and the results were largely unobserved.

Our own losses in the strike were particularly painful. The executive officer of one of the two F-4 Phantom fighter squadrons, an experienced commander, along with his radar intercept officer, were lost to a SAM hit. The operations officer of the A-6 Intruder squadron, another experienced lieutenant commander, was shot down but managed to eject and was captured—and survived six long years as a POW. His bombardier-navigator was fatally injured when he ejected. . . . When the strike group returned to their ready rooms after the mission, the morale was rock bottom. They were hurting from the lack of mission success and from the loss of their shipmates. What a way to start a Christmas celebration. The one solace was Christmas Day off.

On the bridge of the *Enterprise* I was getting debriefed by the Hanoi strike leader even as the carrier was again launching aircraft against targets at Vinh and Thanh Hoa. As the dejected flight leader shuffled off in his sweat-soaked G-suit, the phone from the flag bridge rang. It was CTF-77 himself, who with his staff were embarked in *Enterprise* as his flagship. "Jim," he said matter-of-factly, "we have just reviewed the preliminary BDA [bomb damage assessment] photos for your Hanoi strike, and the principal targets have not been destroyed." I began to interject that the strike should have been canceled due to the adverse weather, but the admiral continued, "I know weather was a problem, but everyone up the line—Seventh Fleet, CinCPac, and Washington—wants those targets hit hard to show Hanoi we mean business, and that Hanoi is vulnerable to carriers. You are going to have send in another strike tomorrow." I simply answered, "I understand," and hung up. I called the CAG [air group commander] in his ready room and said I wanted to see him and his five squadron commanders in my sea cabin in ten minutes.

The sea cabin is a small room off the bridge with a bureau, bunk, and head—and lots of communications—where the carrier skipper lives when his ship is at sea. As the squadron commanders crowded in one by one—some were in khakis, some in flight gear getting ready to go on the next event, and two still in the grungy flight suits from the last hop—I knew what was on their minds. They expected me to console them for their losses and join them in blaming the weather for the strike's failure. There were six long faces in the crowd. What I was going to do was very tough, one of the hardest things I've ever had to do, but it had to be done. I said, "Today's strike was an out-and-out failure. The full weight of this ship's capabilities were assigned to these targets and not a single primary objective was destroyed. Two experienced air crews were lost in the process. I know the weather was not favorable, but this is a combat-experienced air wing, and it looks to me like there was a progressive loss of control when you ran into SAMs. Air discipline went to hell. This mission is going again tomorrow against the same target complex."

They had come in with their heads bowed, perhaps expecting sympathy or at least a kind word. Now they were facing me directly, looking me in the eye. I knew what they were thinking. "My God, Skipper, don't you know that is Christmas Eve?" After a pause I added, "I don't want to have to go through this again tomorrow afternoon and send you out on Christmas Day. Put your most experienced people on this flight, and I certainly consider that every squadron commander needs to be in on the strike planning and in the air leading his own people. I know tomorrow is Christmas Eve, but I want you to get that out of your minds. You are career naval officers and combat-experienced pilots. This is not mission impossible. Any questions?"

Not a word was spoken. The six pilots filed out of the sea cabin—but their heads were up. One of the squadron commanders tugged at my sleeve as he walked by and said, "I know how bad you feel, Skipper, but don't worry, we'll get it tomorrow." And they did; they got Christmas Day off.

Holloway did not place the blame on his superiors. He never even mentioned who gave the orders. Holloway added: "One of the cardinal sins of leaders is if a commander has an order he doesn't like and he says, 'Hey, I don't like this either. It's not my fault, it's what's coming down from upstairs.'"[39]

A good leader likewise never blames subordinates when something goes wrong. When I asked Adm. Carlisle A. H. Trost (CNO 1986–90) to describe his experiences as a senior leader with fixing the problem, not the blame, he said:

When a captain has a ship incident, some sort of disaster, sometimes you get excuses. I can recall one particular instance where a man, who had command of a destroyer, a very nice one, . . . ran it aground on the Roosevelt Roads channel down in Puerto Rico. He ran it aground proceeding at fifteen knots in a channel where that was just too fast for the area. He had disregarded the advice of his navigator, had turned when he saw a buoy, but it was not the buoy he thought it was. He simply ran aground and tore the sonar dome off. . . . In addition, there was other ancillary damage to the bottom of the ship. I relieved him for cause after the investigation. As a matter of fact, there were four investigations.

I saw him back in Washington when he requested to call on me. He had worked for me previously. I said: "What was on your mind?" He said, "It was getting dark and we had to get in." I said, "Did something dictate a time of getting in?" He said, "No." I asked, "Did somebody tell you that you had to travel at that speed?" "No, but," again he said, "I had to go that fast to get in before dark."

Then I said, "Did your navigation party screw up?" He said, "Yeah, they really let me down." By this time, the investigations had shown [that] . . . the navigator had previously asked him to slow down because they were having difficulty accurately fixing the ship's position. It is not an easy place, but it is not that hard a challenge. At high speed and with poor visibility, you clearly cannot set your positions accurately as you would like. So he told me the navigation party let him down and not that he ignored the navigation party's advice.

He told me, "I would like very much to get another command," and I said, "Not in the U.S. Navy. I told you, you are out, especially when you are at fault." Again he tried to put the blame on the navigator. His placing the blame on others when it was not so ended his naval career. He retired about a year later as commander, but the incident clearly ended his naval career. He would not have been promoted further. He would not have gotten a real trusted position thereafter, because he made excuses.[40]

When I discussed "Fix the problem, not the blame" with Adm. Jay Johnson (CNO 1996–2000), he told me:

Most leaders have had to deal with that, I recall the time I . . . was an air-wing commander, and as a senior commander . . . had to relieve one of my squadron commanding officers. It was very distasteful to me because he was a wonderful guy, and up to that event had been a pretty good leader. I won't retell the story here, but it centered on the CO's judgment wherein he blamed a younger pilot for something that happened while he was flying in the back seat of the younger pilot's aircraft. In my judgment, he offered up the pilot instead of taking responsibility himself. I didn't like that and therefore relieved him. He was an up-and-comer, and some couldn't understand why I did that, but it was the right thing to do. It's not easy, and I still feel badly about it in one way because it effectively ended that officer's naval career. But the entire air wing learned about accountability and responsibility.[41]

I discussed the aspect of blame with Adm. Charles R. Larson, twice the superintendent of the Naval Academy, as well, and he commented: "It was once said, there's no limit to what you accomplish as long as you don't worry about who gets the credit. I said this many times, and I truly believe it. You give credit to your troops for the things that they've accomplished, but you take the blame if it tends to go wrong." That is not an original statement. I heard it from several of the Army and Air Force generals I interviewed, but Larson added something meaningful: "Then quietly fix it, but you don't fix it by firing."[42]

The *Pueblo* Incident, January 23, 1968

On January 23, 1968, the USS *Pueblo,* a frigate on an intelligence-gathering mission, was attacked and seized by North Korean troops in international waters. While that action was outrageous, perhaps the most controversial and most discussed aspect of the incident was the American commander's surrender without a fight, breaking a proud U.S. Navy tradition that had stood since 1807.

Numerous books develop the incident in detail, among them *Bucher: My Story. The Ship That Never Returned* written by Comdr. Lloyd M. Bucher, USN, the *Pueblo*'s captain, with Eleanor Van Buskirk Harris; *My Anchor Held* by Stephen R. Harris, the officer in charge of naval security on the ship; *Mobility, Support, Endurance* by Edwin B. Hooper; *Second in Command* by Edward R. Murphy Jr.; *Bridge of No Return: The Ordeal of the USS* Pueblo by F. Carl Schumacher and George C. Wilson; *A Matter of Accountability: A True Story of the* Pueblo *Affair* by James Bamford; *The Last Voyage of the USS* Pueblo by Ed Brandt; and *The* Pueblo *Incident* by Rear Adm. Daniel V. Gallery, USN (Ret.). It is not my intent to rehash the content of these books; each speaks for itself. The issue here is, once again, accountability.

Rear Adm. Daniel V. Gallery called the *Pueblo* incident "a disgraceful humiliation unequaled in our history or in the history of any other great nation. It is much too big a blot on the national honor to call for scapegoats. There is shame enough in it for all, and the only shoulders broad enough to take the blame are those of Uncle Sam himself. . . . *But we can't just sweep the whole thing under the rug and forget it.* The blunders cry to heaven for exposure in the hope that perhaps they will not be repeated again too soon."[43]

Events unfolded as follows. The USS *Pueblo*, a Navy–National Security Agency intelligence ship, sailed from Sasebo, Japan, on January 11, 1968. Its mission was to patrol along the North Korean coast for sixteen days, collecting electronic information on North Korean naval activities and ports; then to move on to the Tsushima Straits to observe the activities of Russian *Riga*-class destroyers there until February 4, 1968; and then to return to Sasebo. None of these activities violated any national or international law, as long as the ship remained in international waters. The *Pueblo* was instructed to obtain oceanographic data on seawater temperature, salinity, depths, and currents in its assigned area, and, as part of its intelligence collecting, was to eavesdrop on Soviet ships and coastal defenses. The intelligence gathered would be analyzed by experts in Washington. Comdr. Lloyd M. Bucher was the commander of the ship, which had been refitted with electronic equipment relevant to its mission. While the *Pueblo* was being commissioned, he was present to oversee its refitting. As the work progressed, he requested the addition of a destruct system for the intelligence equipment. His request was denied.

The *Pueblo* was not the first of its type. The first ship refitted for this sort of intelligence mission was the USS *Banner*, which completed sixteen intelligence missions in the western Pacific between October 1965 and December 1967. During this period the *Banner* was harassed by North Korean boats on ten occasions; twice it had had to call for assistance. The *Banner* had numerous encounters with small craft that hung around, circled the ship, closed in and sniffed around the stern, and zigzagged across the bow. In spite of that evidence of past harassment, the Navy evaluated the *Pueblo*'s mission as low risk because its two earlier intelligence-gathering missions in the Sea of Japan had elicited no reaction from North Korea.

In the event of serious interference, assistance was theoretically available to the *Pueblo* from the Fifth Air Force, headquartered in Japan, and aircraft from the USS *Enterprise,* which was patrolling five hundred miles southwest of Wonsan. Since the *Pueblo*'s mission was classified as low risk, however, no contingency plan was devised to deal with aggressive activity by the North Koreans. The *Banner,* after all, had been harassed but never attacked. The *Pueblo*'s crew was completely unprepared to deal with an enemy boarding. They had not been drilled in emergency destruction of classified materials, and no gun drills had been held. Nor had they practiced possible reactions to boarding such as damaging the engines so the ship could not move, or disabling the anchor engine so the anchors could not be raised.

The Navy's false sense of security was shattered when a North Korean SO-1 gunboat with its crew at full battle stations approached the *Pueblo* at a rapid speed. Three torpedo boats soon joined the gunboats, and two MiG fighters flew over the *Pueblo* and fired rockets over its bow.

Several of the books cited above include minute-by-minute accounts of the seizure. Specifically, at noon on January 23, 1968, the *Pueblo*'s radio operator made a routine transmission. That message was followed by: "Company outside" at 1230; then, "Don't want to go down yet. We still got company outside. Will advise ASAP." At 1244: "Got company outside and more coming so will have to keep this up for a while. Will advise ASAP." Between 1326 and 1327, the *Pueblo* transmitted: "And they plan to open fire on us now, they plan to open fire on us now, they plan to open fire on us now." At 1330 the ship transmitted, "We are being boarded." Thirteen SOSs were sent, followed by eighteen more. The *Pueblo*'s crew then attempted to destroy the classified material onboard. At 1345 the *Pueblo* advised several times: "We are being escorted into probably Wonsan, repeat Wonsan," and four times asked, "Are you sending assistance?" At 1405, in Bucher's presence, the radio operator wired, "Have been requested to follow into Wonsan, have three wounded and one man with leg blown off, have not used any weapon nor uncovered 50-caliber machine guns. Destroying all key lists and as much electronic equipment as possible. How about some help? This group means business. Have sustained small wound in rectum, so not intend to offer any resistance." At 1432 the *Pueblo* wired, "Have been directed to come to all stop and being boarded at this time. Being boarded at this time" and "... four men injured and one critically and going off the air, now, and destroying this gear."

The North Koreans came onboard without meeting any resistance; not a shot was fired by anyone on the *Pueblo*. The North Korean boarding party was composed of two officers and ten men; the crew of the *Pueblo* comprised eighty-three officers and enlisted men. On paper, at least, the *Pueblo* had the North Koreans outnumbered and outgunned. After the USS *Liberty* was attacked by the Israeli Air Force in June 1967, the CNO had directed all U.S. Navy ships to carry defensive weapons. The *Pueblo* mounted two .50-caliber machine guns, one forward on the forecastle and one aft. They were old and unreliable, however, and jammed on every practice firing. One of the few gunnery practices held on the ship had as the target a five-gallon oil drum. When the gunners missed the target on both occasions, one of the sailors commented that he "hoped they were not attacked by a five-gallon barrel."

At the time of the attack, both deck guns were covered with canvas. In Commander Bucher's defense, Rear Adm. Frank L. Johnson stated at an investigative hearing that "the Commanding Officer of USS *Pueblo* was directed to keep the installed defensive armament covered or stowed so as not to elicit unusual interest, to employ weapons only when threat to survival was obvious and was advised that the application of force through the use of arms was authorized only as a last resort in self defense."[44] In all fairness, however, it should be added that Bucher had asked Admiral Johnson if he could use the guns against a boarding party and had been told yes. One of the criticisms of Bucher's action—or rather, inaction—was that he should have ignored the admiral's directive and immediately used the guns.

The small-arms locker onboard the ship contained ten Thompson submachine guns, one .30-caliber carbine, seven .45-caliber pistols, and fifty anti-swimmer grenades. No officer instructed Gunner's Mate, 2nd class, Kenneth R. Wadley to break out the small arms when it became apparent that the

Pueblo was under attack. No small arms practice had ever been conducted, and the men had never been instructed how to repel boarders.

As matters progressed, the situation appeared hopeless to Bucher. "Suddenly the complete uselessness of further resistance flooded my brain," he would later note. "It would only result in our being shot to pieces and a lot of good men killed to no avail, because the North Koreans would in the end get most of our secret documents. Instead of lunging for the annunciator and racking it back to ALL AHEAD FULL, I turned my back on it and walked out on the starboard wing of the bridge."[45]

Bucher's decision to surrender without a fight was severely criticized at the time, and many have never forgiven him for it. Article 1 of the "Code of Conduct for Members of the Armed Forces of the United States," established during the presidency of Dwight D. Eisenhower, states specifically: "I am an American fighting man. I serve in the forces which guard my country and our way of life. I am prepared to give my life in their defense." Article 2 states: "I will never surrender of my own free will. If in command I will never surrender my men while they still have the means to resist."

In addition, there is a two-hundred-year-old tradition in the U.S. Navy that a captain does not surrender his ship without a fight. No U.S. Navy ship had been boarded without a fight since 1807, when the USS *Chesapeake* was boarded and searched by HMS *Leopard* off the U.S. Atlantic coast. The British ship shanghaied four American sailors. Actions of this type by the British were, of course, one of the major causes of the War of 1812. The captain who surrendered the *Chesapeake* was James Barron. He later challenged Stephen Decatur of naval fame to a duel because Decatur openly criticized his decision to allow the boarding.

Later, during the War of 1812, the *Chesapeake* was lying off Boston Harbor and was once again boarded, captured by HMS *Shannon,* and sailed to a British port—but not without a fight. The *Chesapeake*'s captain, David Lawrence, was killed during the fight, along with a number of the crew. As he lay dying on the quarterdeck, Captain Lawrence uttered the immortal words, "Don't give up the ship!" Those words have been the watchword for the U.S. Navy ever since.

When he was commissioned as an ensign, Commander Bucher swore "to support and defend the Constitution of the United States . . . and to do so without any mental reservation or purpose of evasion." He failed this pledge when he did not lead the crew under his command to prevent the boarding. The intelligence information seized by the North Koreans seriously damaged the national security of the United States. What could Bucher have done to minimize the damage to the U.S. intelligence operation other than fighting the North Koreans? He could have scuttled the ship. Or the engines could have been disabled, requiring the *Pueblo* to be towed rather than going to Wonsan under its own power. Perhaps help might have arrived in the meantime.

Who, ultimately, bears responsibility for the *Pueblo*'s capture and the damage to U.S. security? Where did they fail? Bucher can be condemned for surrendering without a fight and for not scuttling the ship, but what were the responsibilities of the naval high command during the incident? Some critics have said that the high command should have sent help from the *Enterprise,* that fighter assistance should have been provided from the Fifth Air Force, that help from South Korea could have been requested, and that the United States could have gone into Wonsan Harbor the next day to retrieve the ship. None of these actions was ordered.

The Navy, as usual, convened a court of inquiry to find out what had occurred. A special subcommittee was established by the U.S. House of Representatives for the same purpose. Among the witnesses were Richard Helms, then director of the Central Intelligence Agency; six admirals; six generals; and a captain. In addition, the incident was reviewed by the Department of Defense. The bottom line in all of these investigations was that the senior Navy brass could not condone the *Pueblo*'s surrender without a fight. To do so would establish a precedent that would cause irreparable harm to the readiness of the U.S. Navy to defend the nation and any other areas it was called on to protect.

The naval court of inquiry recommended:

> that Commander Lloyd M. Bucher, U.S. Navy, the commanding officer of USS *Pueblo,* be brought to trial by general court-martial for the following five alleged offenses: permitting his ship to be searched while he had the power to resist; failing to take immediate and aggressive protective measures when his ship was

attacked by North Korean forces; complying with the orders of the North Korean forces to follow them into port; negligently failing to complete destruction of classified material aboard USS *Pueblo* and permitting such material to fall into the hands of the North Koreans; and negligently failing to ensure, before departure for sea, that his officers and crew were properly organized, stationed, and trained in preparation for emergency destruction of classified material.

The court of inquiry also recommended that Lt. Stephen R. Harris, USNR, the officer in charge of the research detachment aboard the *Pueblo,* be brought to trial by general court-martial for three alleged offenses of dereliction in the performances of his duties, in that he failed to inform his commanding officer of a deficiency in emergency destruction procedures and failed to take effective action to complete emergency destruction after having been ordered by the commanding officer to dispose of all remaining classified materials.

The court recommended that Lt. Edward R. Murphy Jr., USN, the executive officer of the *Pueblo,* be given nonjudicial punishment in the form of a letter of admonition for alleged dereliction in the performance of his duties as executive officer, in that he negligently failed to organize and lead the crew on the day of seizure, especially in the ship's major internal task of emergency destruction of classified material.

Rear Adm. Frank L. Johnson and Capt. Everett B. Gladding were likewise recommended for nonjudicial punishment in the form of letters of reprimand. The court alleged that Rear Admiral Johnson, then commander U.S. Naval Forces, Japan, was derelict in the performance of his duty in failing to plan properly for effective emergency support forces for contingencies such as occurred during the execution of the *Pueblo*'s mission and in failing to verify the feasibility of rapid emergency destruction of classified equipment and documents carried by the *Pueblo*'s research detachment. In the case of Captain Gladding, then director, Naval Security Group, Pacific, it was alleged that he was derelict in the performance of duty in failing to develop procedures to ensure the readiness of *Pueblo*'s research detachment for the mission assigned and to coordinate other services and agencies to provide intelligence support to *Pueblo* during the mission.

The secretary of the navy during the *Pueblo* seizure was John H. Chafee. On May 6, 1969, after the naval court of inquiry had handed down its recommendation, he handed down his verdict:

> I have reviewed the record of the court of inquiry and the recommendations of the Convening Authority and the Chief of Naval Operations. I make no judgment regarding the guilt or innocence of any of the officers of the offenses alleged against them. Such judgment could legitimately be reached by duly constituted authority only after further legal proceedings, such as trial by court-martial or the hearing required prior to issuance of letters of reprimand or admonition.
>
> I am convinced, however, that neither individual discipline, nor the state of discipline or morale in the Navy, nor any other interest requires further legal proceedings with respect to any personnel involved in the *Pueblo* incident.
>
> In reviewing the court's recommendations with respect to Commander Bucher, Lieutenant Murphy, and Lieutenant Harris, it is my opinion that—even assuming that further proceedings were had, and even going so far as to assume that a judgment of guilt were to be reached—they have suffered enough, and further punishment would not be justified. These officers were illegally imprisoned by the North Koreans for eleven months. During that time, their food and living conditions were marginal. They suffered extensively from physical abuse and torturous treatment. Their captors refused to accord them even the minimal humane treatment required under international law. When they were released from their captive status, each showed great loss of weight and other marks of cruel treatment.
>
> The court was of the opinion that, during his internment, Commander Bucher upheld morale in a superior manner; that he provided leadership by insisting that command structure be maintained and providing guidance for conduct; and that he contributed to the ability of the crew to hold together and withstand the trials of detention until repatriation could be effected.
>
> The charges against Rear Admiral Johnson and Captain Gladding relate to the failure to anticipate the emergency that subsequently developed. This basic, general accusation, however, could be leveled in various degrees at responsible superior authorities in the chain of command and control and in the collateral support structure.
>
> In light of the considerations set out above, I have determined that the charges against all of the officers concerned will be dismissed, and I have directed the Chief of Naval Operations to take appropriate action to that end.
>
> Every feasible effort is being made to correct any Navy deficiencies which may have contributed to *Pueblo*'s seizure. The Navy's leaders are deter-

mined that the lessons learned from this tragedy shall be translated into effective action.

The *Pueblo*'s officers had indeed "suffered enough." Commander Bucher's book describes his suffering in gruesome detail. On one occasion, for example, he was sitting in his cell when a guard came in with a drawn pistol, shouting, "Get up! Out now! Move quick!" He was taken to a interrogation room and told:

> "Now we must show you how we treat spies in our country!" He then stepped aside to let me be dragged out of the building through a side entrance. I felt a searing blast of freezing night air that turned my cold sweat to ice before being hustled into the protection of an automobile . . . whose plastic windows had been covered and its rear seat curtained off from the front one by an opaque screen. I was compressed between the hard quilted bodies of my guards in the back seat without any way of knowing where we were going after the driver started the engine and racked the gearshift to get us moving ahead. There were lots of bumps and wrenching turns during the next ten minutes, like we were traveling over a rough, winding country road. But as far as I could tell, we could also have been just driving around the barracks' compound to confuse me. At any rate, when we finally stopped and I was taken out, it was to be led inside a cement building very similar to our prison. But we did not go upstairs in this one. I was conducted down into one of those sinister cellar areas that have earned Communist police headquarters their gruesome reputation.
>
> We entered a barren room with a small casement window located close to the ceiling and a pair of strong spotlights focused on one gray wall where a human being was hanging . . . some six feet above the cement floor. The man was barely alive, stripped to the waist so that all the black bruises covering his torso were exposed, as was the compound fracture of one limp arm with a jagged piece of bone protruding through the torn flesh. His face was a pulp in which one eyeball dangled out of its socket in a dark ooze of fluid coagulating on his cheek. He had completely chewed through his lower lip that hung in shreds from between clenched teeth. With the first shock of seeing this horribly mangled wretch, I was stunned by the thought that he might be one of my own men, but then one of the interpreters announced: "This is a South Korean spy we have caught! Look at his just punishment." I could not take my eyes off that tortured pulp of humanity and saw through the torn and battered features that he was indeed a Korean, yet the shock remained and even intensified as I took in the details, completely overwhelming me with revul-

sion. It threw me into a sort of mental blackout that was like finding one's self in a horrible nightmare in which one consciously fights against a totally unbelievable experience and struggles to awaken to normalcy—but cannot! The dying South Korean hung there before my eyes from his strap, bleeding, twitching, frothing. . . . I tried to yell, but my vocal cords as well as the rest of my body, seemed to have been severed dreamlike from any controlling impulses of my brain.

I have no memory of being returned to our cellblock and suspect that I had to be bodily carried out of that torture chamber, dumped back in the command car and delivered into the custody of Super-C. When my blackout eventually dissipated in a gray daze, it was his face that dissolved into focus through the haunting specter of the South Korean's eviscerated eyeball, his eyes staring at me through tinted spectacles with a hooded smoldering intensity. "So now you have seen for yourself how we treat spies," he had his interpreter remind me. "Perhaps you will reconsider your refusal to confess?" It was pure stubborn reflex that made me shake my head.

"You must realize we are not playing games and may lose patience with you," the colonel continued in measured words. "You must surely remember you are responsible for the lives of your crew."

That struck a sensitive chord which jolted my mind back to full awareness. "Yes, I know I am," I blurted out. "But you are responsible for what is happening here. You are responsible for the atrocity of not caring for my wounded. You are responsible for the murder of one of my men."

I don't know if the interpreter was able to fully translate my faltering, slurred accusations, but the colonel got the gist of them and reacted with a gesture that turned his subordinates loose. . . . But he was more bent on talking than beating and quickly ordered the guards to drag me back into the chair and prop me up in it.

"You must be sincere. You must sign this confession as proof that you wish your crew to be treated leniently and humanely. The evidence is complete. Why do you not sign?"

"Because of all the lies it contains about my country," I gasped. "The world must know about the United States' imperialistic warmongering," he answered with a genuine note of agitation in his voice which warned me that he was really getting desperate for a confession to justify the North Korean's act of piracy.

"No, I won't sign it."

"We will see," he angrily shot back with an absolute conviction that made it quite different from any previous outbursts. "We will now begin to shoot your crew.

We will shoot them one at a time, right here in front of your eyes so that you can see them die. We will shoot them all, starting with the youngest one first and so on, . . . until you sign confession. And if you have not signed when they are all dead, then we still have ways of making you do it, and all your crew will be dead for nothing. So that's what we mean about you being responsible for their lives. You are not sincere. We now bring in the crew member Bland to be shot."

The name was read from a list of names he held. One of the guards left the room, presumably to fetch Fireman Howard Bland who I . . . knew as a boy of not much over twenty years. Would these animals dare kill him before my eyes? The vision of that tortured South Korean hanging from a strap with his compound fracture, blinded eye and multiple contusions reappeared on the wall of the room in full, horribly vivid reality. Yes, this breed of politics did not give a damn about the life or death of their own kinsmen—let alone any round-eyed Americans! They were well-molded beasts with the bare trappings of civilization. I could not even contemplate leaving Bland's life at their mercy for the blatantly obvious lies and propaganda. This dilemma was beyond my training as a naval officer, as captain of a ship, as a human being with deeply ingrained sensitivity for his fellow men. I had resisted as long as I could, but now I could do none other than finally give in to a totally foreign brutality. I made up my mind: "All right . . . I will sign."

Super-C gave a start and let out a snakelike hiss and thrust a pen into my hand, eagerly directly his minions to support me while I leaned over his desk and scrawled a trembling signature across the bottom of the paper. I could feel the triumphant relief of my tormentors who suddenly became very concerned with my state of health, and after helping me back to my cell, offered me a tray loaded with their warm milk, cookies, an apple and boiled eggs. I sat and stared at the tray, wanting to eat, but unable to.

I was too emotionally wrung out, too physically battered, to stay on my bunk and try to escape into sleep. No matter in what position I lay on the hard, musty mattress, one bruise would jab me into tossing against another. No matter how much I wanted to surrender to a numbing weariness, the torments in my mind kept fighting on.[46]

USS *Cole*, October 12, 2000

The national military strategy of the United States engages U.S. forces throughout the world to protect the freedom of Americans and citizens of many other countries. As a result, U.S. forces are constantly in harm's way.

On Thursday, October 12, 2000, the USS *Cole,* an *Arleigh Burke*–class destroyer, was damaged by terrorists while refueling in the port of Aden, Yemen. The ship patrolled the Mediterranean and made port calls at Barcelona, Spain; Villefranche, France; Malta; and Koper, Slovenia, before entering the Red Sea on October 9 en route to Aden, where the attack occurred. At 1120 on October 12, two men maneuvered a boat alongside the ship and detonated a bomb. The explosion ripped a thirty-two-by-thirty-six-foot hole in the *Cole*'s port side, killing seventeen of the crew, injuring another forty-two, and causing an estimated $240 million in damage. It was a carefully and cleverly planned and executed act. The blast occurred some forty-five minutes into the four-hour fueling procedure, just as the crew was starting lunch. No one had gone ashore, as refueling was the sole purpose of the stop.

Secretary of the Navy Richard Danzig reacted to news of the bombing at once, saying: "We feel very strongly that this situation demands accountability. In the process we cannot avoid our own responsibility for what the terrorist achieved. We owe it to those who suffer to provide the comfort of explanation, to the best of our ability." His statement set the stage for the investigations that followed the attack to determine, in the words of some, whether anyone was "to blame." I believe that it is preferable to determine accountability rather than to place blame, to focus on means of deterring, disrupting, and mitigating future attacks rather than vilify those responsible.

The attack on the *Cole* took place in an area of the world very dangerous for Americans. In January 1999 the threat possibility for U.S. ships calling in Yemen was changed from a medium to a high alert status that called for greater caution. Initially, the Yemen government provided harbor security for U.S. ships, even to the extent of patrolling around the ships as they refueled. As time progressed and there appeared to be no danger, these security measures were canceled, even though an attempt had been made to destroy the USS *The Sullivans* while it was refueling. The attempt failed because the attack ship was too heavy and sank before reaching its target. In the two years prior to October 12, twenty-five U.S. Navy ships had refueled at Aden. After the first two refuelings had been carried out without incident, requirements for harbor security were canceled. Predictably, the *Cole* followed a routine pattern of operations.

The Yemen government required twelve days' notice in advance of a refueling. Government officials and the U.S. embassy gave details of the refueling procedure to the refinery that did the refueling, the port authorities, and the ship chandler who provided supplies. There were thus many opportunities for leaks and ample time to plan the attack. There have been allegations that the harbor pilot was an accomplice in the attack and that armed forces hostile to the U.S. were positioned to assist the terrorists; some have even alleged that the Yemen government cooperated with the terrorists.

A review of the captain's responsibilities in the circumstances surrounding the attack is necessary to put the incident in perspective. No naval officer questions the ship captain's responsibility for the well-being and safety of his ship and crew. The standard instructions for commanders' rules of engagement at that time were, in effect, "Don't shoot until shot at." Such rules give a decided initial advantage to the attacker. The men who approached the *Cole* on October 12 showed no signs of hostile intent. While they were maneuvering alongside, the attackers were smiling and waving to the crew; some sailors even returned the greeting.

An important element of the investigation to determine accountability for the attack was the nature of any warnings given to Comdr. Kare Lippold, the captain of the *Cole*. Was he sufficiently alerted? Some naval officials take the hard line that the captain of a U.S. Navy ship is responsible for the well-being of his ship and crew regardless of such warnings and is responsible, moreover, for conducting his own risk assessment. This view is supported by Article 110 of the Uniform Code of Military Justice (UCMJ), which states: "Improper Hazarding of a Vessel: Any person subject to this chapter who negligently hazards or suffers to be hazarded any vessel of the armed forces shall be punished as a court-martial may direct." Negligence is defined as "the failure to exercise the care, prudence, or attention to duties which the interests of the government require to be exercised by a prudent and responsible person under the circumstances." Was there negligence? To determine accountability, two questions must be answered: First, were the decisions made and actions taken by the captain prudent and reasonable, given the expectations of his position? Second, were there measures not taken by the captain of the *Cole* that, if taken, might have prevented the attack or led to its defeat?

The Navy's study, termed the Judge Advocate General Manual (JAGMan) report, found serious faults in Commander Lippold's preparation of his ship. The report concluded that there was some negligence on the part of the captain and crew, but stopped short of recommending judicial punishment for either. It did note that the crew did not execute all of the provisions of their own force protection plan. In fact, the USS *Cole* had executed only thirty-one of the sixty-two force protection measures. The ship waived nineteen measures and failed to accomplish twelve others. Of the thirty-one measures not performed, it was reported that twelve might have prevented the suicide attack or mitigated its effects had they been implemented.

Vice Adm. C. W. Moore Jr., commander of the naval forces in the Middle East, was one of the three senior officers who reviewed the investigation. He concluded that the *Cole* had general information about the terrorist threat in Aden and that Lippold failed to "deliberately plan [or] deliberately implement and actively supervise a force protection plan . . . the watch was not briefed on the plan or their responsibilities, the bridge was not manned, service boats were not closely controlled, and there was little thought as how to respond to unauthorized craft being alongside."

It should be emphasized, however, that in going over the report with the other reviewing officers, Moore concluded that the attackers would not have been thwarted even if Lippold had followed all of the force protection requirements under the "ThreatCon Bravo" level designated for Aden, which did not require keeping small boats away from the destroyer. In addition, the investigators concluded that nothing in the intelligence information then available to Lippold pointed to an attack from the water. Accordingly, he focused his precautions on the possibility that any attack would come from the shore.

The *Cole*'s crew did not require identification from visitors; nor did they inspect the small boat that came alongside. Some of the investigators thought that more aggressive tactics could have prevented or mitigated the attack. Adm. Robert Natter, who was commander of the Atlantic Fleet when the attack occurred, forcefully rebutted those who took that position, stating that even a higher alert status would not have prevented the attack on the *Cole*. He emphasized that the bombers were waving as they puttered up; they showed no "hostile intent" that would have justified firing on persons who might have been harmless local citizens.

In addition to the JAGMan investigation, Secretary Cohen set up a second inquiry with Gen. William W. Crouch, USA (Ret.), and Adm. Harold W. Gehman, USN (Ret.), as co-commissioners. The commission was to examine the circumstances but not to assign culpability for the attack. The Crouch-Gehman report offered thirty findings and recommendations, many of which were not made public to avoid alerting "potential challengers and terrorists." Secretary Cohen asked the chairman of the Joint Chiefs of Staff, Gen. Henry H. Shelton, to review the recommendations and offer advice for follow-up, and to notify him if the report raised "any accountability issue that should be pursued further."[47]

It is often alleged that investigations by the military seek to protect their own. At a January 10, 2001, press conference, a reporter asked Secretary Cohen, in effect, whether the DoD investigation was "just looking for someone to blame." The secretary responded:

> Not at all. As a matter of fact, in . . . the Crouch-Gehman report, you'll find an expression to the effect that there should be no zealous search for a scapegoat, but for *accountability*. . . . There is a delicate balance that has to be maintained, . . . you want commanders to have the flexibility necessary on the front lines, but also be held accountable in the event that they fail out of what would be reasonably expected given the threat, given their equipment, given the training, and given their own command position. So it's not to try and pin the tail on anyone as such culpability, but simply to say to the families of those who have been lost, to all the men and women who are serving today, that we will insist upon standards, we expect that our commanders and those in charge of the lives of our men and women in uniform to measure up to those standards. But this is not a fault-finding investigation to try to find someone to pin the blame on and look for culpability, but rather to look to see whether or not certain actions could have been taken, should have been taken which may have either reduced the risk or mitigated the effect in this particular case. . . . I rather think we owe it to the fam-

ilies of those who are wounded and those who are lost, that accountability should be looked at.

Cohen added: "All of the recommendations are designed to make a good force protection system better so that our enemies will find it more difficult and more costly to interfere with our efforts to maintain peace and stability around the world."[48]

In sum, the Crouch-Gehman report concluded that the Navy needed to improve the training and equipping of its ships to carry out its missions in today's high-risk environment. The USS *Cole* bombing illustrated that there was insufficient intelligence, that training was not properly focused, and that there was not "appropriate equipment or on-scene security support to effectively prevent or deter such a determined, pre-planned assault on the ship."

The report strongly recommended that the Department of Defense develop an organization that more cohesively aligns policy and resources to combat terrorism, assigning a specific assistant secretary of defense to oversee efforts to combat terrorism and to ensure that DoD counterintelligence organizations are adequately staffed and funded to meet terrorism. In addition, the report emphasized the need for more coordination between the Navy and the State Department and other government agencies.

One extremely important recommendation was the need for greater human intelligence, a problem that has been known for years. It is hard to gather intelligence in countries where the United States does not have the cooperation of the local government or people. Lacking funds, it is difficult to train U.S. intelligence agents to speak the languages of foreign countries, or to obtain the services of other nations to assist in intelligence gathering. Developing such assets takes five to ten years, sometimes longer. The report emphasized that human intelligence must be given a higher priority by the U.S. government.

Stewart W. Bently in the January 14, 2001, *Washington Post* observed: "It is not surprising that certain basic force-protection measures were not in place before the bombing of USS *Cole*. At the heart of any force-protection plan is the presumption that individual servicemen and women, properly armed and equipped, have the authority to engage any threat using the force continuum." The article continued: "While the military's basic train-ing includes rifle marksmanship, military commanders are extremely hes-itant to allow troops to carry live ammunition in the weapons for fear of accidental discharges or improper use of deadly force." Bently also sug-gested that local commanders were concerned that young enlisted per-sonnel with loaded guns might make a mistake and the commander might have to answer for it. This suggests an atmosphere that could make Americans even more vulnerable to terrorism.

At the January 19, 2001, press conference Secretary Cohen announced his decision on the USS *Cole* attack: Commander Lippold would not be pun-ished; the guilt for the USS *Cole*'s vulnerability would be shared collectively, right up to the top of the chain of command; and many failures had led up to the bombing. Cohen specifically stated: "Given the nature of this partic-ular situation it would have been very difficult, if not impossible to protect against this type of incident." He concluded that Lippold had committed no acts of negligence that caused the bombing, but that "every level of the chain of command could have been better. . . . Navy leaders have concluded that the overall performance of the captain and his crew does not warrant puni-tive action, and I agree with that conclusion."[49]

Secretary Cohen demonstrated his character when he said at a second press conference on January 19, 2001: "It would have been easy for me to walk out of this office today and say it's 'somebody's else's responsibility,' but it happened on my watch, and I wanted to make that clear before I left."[50]

The official report on the *Cole* attack refers to the June 1996 terrorist attack on the Khobar Towers, a military housing complex in Saudi Arabia. Nineteen Air Force servicemen were killed when a car bomb demolished much of the barracks. The secretary of defense at that time was William J. Perry. An inves-tigation of the incident concluded that the Air Force commander, Brig. Gen. Terry J. Schwailer, had taken "reasonable and prudent" action to protect the servicemen living in Khobar Towers, and a second investigation found no grounds for action against him. General Schwailer had completed thirty-six of the thirty-nine recommended actions spelled out by the Air Force. Of the three not completed, he sought the funding needed for one, and the other two would not have prevented the Khobar bombing in any case.

Perry was replaced as secretary of defense by Cohen, who disregarded the findings of the two investigations and held Brigadier General Schwailer accountable for the disaster. There is an interesting contrast between Cohen's response to the *Cole* and Khobar Towers incidents. At a press conference on January 10, 2001, Secretary Cohen was asked to explain the difference. Neither Schwailer nor Lippold had fulfilled all the force protection measures called for, but only Schwailer had been punished. The secretary's response did not hit the issue head-on. He cited a number of differences in the two situations and refused to comment further until he had had a chance to review the JAGMan report.

Air Force Chief of Staff Ronald Fogelman objected to Secretary Cohen's decision and retired rather than have any part of making Schwailer a scapegoat. Richard J. Newman wrote in *U.S. News and World Report* that "Fogelman's departure expresses a principle that is broader and in a way more patriotic than standing up for what one believes in: the importance of the military's deference to its civilian masters. He has reinforced that idea at a time when growing military influence in matters of state has caused concern that it is acting beyond the limits of its authority. Military officers have recently become 'more willing to play the political game,' stated historian Richard Kohn, to get their way on budgets, security strategies, and other important issues." In resigning, General Fogelman maintained both principles: he followed his beliefs and he recognized the authority of the civilian secretary.

Adm. Vern Clark, the CNO, announced his position on the *Cole* attack in a statement released on January 1, 2001 (before Secretary Cohen's press conference of January 19, 2001). The CNO's decision regarding accountability offers a superb analysis of the issue. He dispatched it to all hands.

> There are some who are interested first and foremost in placing blame for the *Cole* explosion. There is no question that the primary blame for this event falls squarely on the shoulders of the terrorists who supported and perpetrated the 12 October action. Following the attack, however, it was incumbent on us to investigate the facts about what happened, determine lessons learned, and assess the accountability of those involved. The full report of the JAGMAN investigation provides a very complete picture of the events that transpired on Oct. 12, 2000. . . . Ultimately, both Secretary Danzig and I agreed with the second endorser's

determination that the commanding officer acted reasonably in adjusting his force protection posture based on his assessment of the situation as he knew it. I found the conclusion of the first endorser to also be compelling: specifically, that the perfect execution of ThreatCon Bravo measures would not have averted or mitigated this attack. I therefore concluded the facts do not warrant punitive action against the commanding officer or other members of the crew. We further concluded that the system—all the chain of command—bear[s] collective responsibility for this incident because we did not equip the skipper for success in the environment he encountered in Aden harbor that fateful day.

I want you to know why I came to the conclusion. And I want you to know what I mean by "collective responsibility." In my judgment the CO of *Cole*, and those in his wardroom and crew who were working the force protection challenge, developed a certain mindset about the Port of Aden, Yemen. That mindset was the summation of a million pieces of information and directives. I have read every piece of intelligence that I know was available to the *Cole*. I focused on the messages they received, and the impressions I believe they must have had as a result of what our military structure provided them. Then I looked at the requirements we placed on the ship via the ThreatCon posture which was specified on 12 October. I thought about what I expect of our commanding officers who are on the point: to evaluate their environment; to weigh alternative solutions; to assess risk; to protect their ship; and to be decisive. In, my view, CO *Cole* did what we expect commanding officers on the point to do. In 20-20 hindsight he didn't get everything right, but as I said in my endorsement to the investigation, I know of no intelligence he could have or should have considered which would have led him to change the posture which was specified for him by higher authority.

I have also come to believe that the tactics which any ship would utilize to implement the ThreatCon measures are as important as the measures themselves. One key ThreatCon Bravo measure has to do with placing boats in a fifteen-minute standby status rather than actually putting them in the water. Having boats deployed or not having boats deployed significantly impacted the methods to be used in executing the rest of the measures. It is very clear to me that the tactics employed, without boats deployed, were vital to the outcome for *Cole*. These tactics significantly weaken the effect of the ThreatCon Bravo FP measures. In my mind, the entire chain of command must bear responsibility for specifying these measures. I will not hold the commanding officer singularly responsible for this outcome. In the situation in Aden, *Cole*'s CO did not deem it appropriate to implement all ThreatCon Bravo FP measures. This action was correct because many of the measures were not applicable that day. But one caution: When we say we are going to do something, I expect us to do it. If we can't, then we need to communicate that with the chain of command and reset the expectation. . . .

There are some who believe my judgment is the result of my appreciation of the incredible job the leadership did in saving the ship. If you talk to anyone who holds this belief, dissuade them of it. Let me tell you, this had nothing to do with my judgment. To the contrary, if I had found even one action which directives had specified and was not accomplished that would have prevented the attack on *Cole,* rest assured, I would have judged differently regarding the correctness of punitive measures. Others might conclude I have judged this way because the ship was attacked. I assure you that is not the case. The ship was attacked, but all leaders are responsible for the way their subordinates execute, and I am satisfied that *Cole's* crew was well led and well trained.

The CNO also expressed his position on the lessons learned from this terrorist attack:

Some have asked me whether this changes the way we will judge other commanding officers in the future and whether this lack of punishment is fair when compared, for example, with a CO who is relieved for cause when his or her ship runs aground. My test goes like this: (1) Was the CO's action in accordance with the standards of performance we expect of our commanders? Did he exercise due care? and, (2) Did he fail to take a directed or expected action which would have changed the outcome and eliminated the hazard to the ship? In this case, *Cole* was attacked. In my mind, the commanding officer took due care; he acted decisively in putting together his FP response; his actions were reasonable given the intelligence available to him and the information he possessed, and the information he did not possess; he executed the applicable ThreatCon Bravo measures prescribed with tactics which were reasonable. I believe he did what we expect good commanding officers to do.

The strongest take away from this tragedy is the fundamental fact that we must improve the security of our transiting forces—ships in and around the world's littorals and overseas ports. Respecting the sovereignty of our host nations will be a challenge—but it is a challenge we must rise to, not shrink from. This was the first successful terrorist attack against a Navy vessel in modern times. It will not be the last attempt. This attack has been a sudden and deadly reminder that the world is full of risk and there are those who are determined to bring harm to America and America's Navy.

We are in the midst of a sea change. Since the end of the cold war, the threat of asymmetric warfare and terrorism has increased greatly. Just as we embrace the life-saving value of damage control procedures, force protection must also be an integral part of everything we do. While we have also increased our understanding and tracking of this type of warfare, we must now make a monumental leap in the attention we pay to this life-or-death issue. To that end, you will also be seeing results of the Navy's force protections task force convened to take a fresh look at every aspect of what we have done and what more we can do. The fleet commanders are also working on real change as we write this message. Take care not to make these changes obvious to our potential enemies; our task is to make his efforts incredibly difficult, and that's what we're going to do.

We cannot forget that, above all, we are leaders, we must lead our sailors. We must step forward and make the hard decisions. There are instructions and regulations that guide and direct nearly everything we do. But we all know that there is no set of rules that governs every scenario, every time. That is where leadership and judgment come in. We must be taking a hard look at all that we do and be ready, if we do not think we have been given the complete picture, to ask hard questions to ensure the safety of our people. The fact that we can make mistakes and learn from them is one of our greatest strengths as a nation and a navy. We have learned many lessons and we will be better because of this experience.

The actions of the *Cole*'s crew immediately following the blast are highly commendable. Undoubtedly through their discipline, training, and courage they saved their ship and many of their shipmates; without the efforts of every member of USS *Cole*, this tragedy could have been much worse. Under the harshest of conditions, they persevered through devastation and horror that many of us have never seen. They saved their ship and the lives of many of their shipmates. Their service is a wonderful example to us all.

Remember the message I sent each of you forty-eight hours after this attack; these words still apply: ours is a demanding profession, sometimes it is a dangerous profession. Stay sharp. Be proud. Be safe. Be ready!"[51]

Commander Lippold was not relieved of command of the USS *Cole*, but he retained his command for only a brief time because the ship was taken off active duty and sent to Pascagoula, Mississippi, to be repaired.

CHAPTER 9

Rickover and Zumwalt

Contrast and Contradiction

You must not confuse leadership with popularity. In its purest sense, military leadership is the art of inspiring people to do what they intrinsically do not want to do, . . . to the ultimate extent of putting their very lives at risk in battle—and to carry out these orders with enthusiasm and élan. Nor is military leadership synonymous with management. Good managers may be good leaders, but the two skills are not necessarily interchangeable. Leadership deals with people, and military leadership is unique.

Adm. James L. Holloway III, USN (Ret.)
Cheif of Naval Operations, 1974–78

Two men—Adm. Hyman G. Rickover and Adm. Elmo R. Zumwalt Jr.—are responsible for many of the fundamental changes made in the U.S. Navy during the post–World War II era. Both were highly controversial officers. Many of their innovations were not welcomed by a significant portion of the naval establishment, and not all of what they did was retained as policy or practice after they retired from active duty. The broad and radical changes they effected within the most hallowed precincts of the service made both officers reviled by a significant part of the uniformed ranks of the Navy; and yet they were revered by many others. Their leadership styles as well as the substance of the programs they initiated were the subject of criticism from detractors in the Navy, Congress, and the administrations under which they served.

Because of the many anomalies in the careers of these two four-star admirals, I believe a thorough examination of the leadership techniques each employed will be instructive. They were virtually opposites in their respective approaches to achieving their professional goals. Moreover, each was so critical of the other that their interpersonal relations actually reached the point of overt hostility.

While the foregoing chapters have largely focused on discrete components of an officer's character and personality that in the aggregate produce good leaders, this chapter reverses the process, exploring the philosophies and actions of two naval leaders and defining measurable and quantitative components of their leadership styles. In approaching this assessment, I have elicited the views of other senior officers who served with both men in positions of close association—their contemporaries and peers—who could objectively reveal a broad spectrum of the two admirals' official actions and personal attributes.

Admiral Hyman G. Rickover: Father of the Nuclear Navy

I interviewed a number of nuclear submariners, including some very senior admirals, in assessing the career of Admiral Rickover. Adm. Kinnaird R. McKee succeeded Admiral Rickover as director, Navy Nuclear Propulsion, in 1982, and served in that position for seven years. Adm. Bruce DeMars followed McKee with an eight-year tour. Admirals James D. Watkins, Carlisle A. H. Trost, and Frank B. Kelso II (all nuclear submariners and former CNOs) had personal knowledge of Admiral Rickover, as did Adm. Robert L. J. Long, former CinCPac, and Adm. Henry G. Chiles, who because of his exceptional character and leadership became the first four-star Navy flag officer to serve as commander, U.S. Strategic Command, and currently occupies a recently established chair of naval leadership at the U.S. Naval Academy. I also interviewed Adm.

Steven Angelo White, who served as a lieutenant in USS *Nautilus* during its first submerged polar crossing and later retired with four stars. None of these officers could share with me the classified aspects of nuclear submarine missions, although several suggested that I read *Blind Man's Bluff: The Untold Story of American Submarine Espionage* by Sherry Sontag and Christopher Drew, a thorough study of the role of nuclear submarines in the cold war. One of the book's reviewers wrote: "Espionage missions described in this book are among the most sensitive secret intelligence operations of the cold war."[1]

Submarines were an integral part of U.S. intelligence gathering in the cold war years—the period between the end of World War II and the collapse of the Soviet Union. Early on, diesel submarines were involved in the mission, but they did not have the espionage capabilities of the atomic-powered subs—they lacked the range of the later subs and could not stay submerged nearly as long. The sub had to come close to the surface daily to snorkel, ventilate, and recharge its batteries, potentially putting the ship and crew in grave danger. The air onboard diesel subs was heavy, had a foul smell, and even tasted bad. The sailors' bodies and clothes smelled of diesel oil for days after returning from a deployment. It was not easy duty, but it attracted a special breed of dedicated and courageous men who could tolerate the foul smells, long separation from their families, cramped quarters, risks, and dangers. There were a few amenities to make up for the discomforts. The men got to watch first-run movies (on 16-mm projectors), and submariners always ate well. Good food was consistently given the highest priority; it was a significant factor in the high morale. When the Soviet Union launched Sputnik in 1957, President Dwight D. Eisenhower ordered accelerated construction of nuclear-powered subs capable of firing cruise and Polaris ballistic missiles while underwater.

Nuclear propulsion enables modern submarines to remain submerged almost indefinitely and to operate at very high speeds. They can make oxygen and fresh water from seawater, discharging noxious respiratory by-products overboard. Compared with the throbbing of diesel engines they operate very quietly, becoming essentially invisible when they choose to do so. These and other factors give them virtually unlimited submerged endurance.

U.S. nuclear submarine forces in both oceans were a primary element of U.S. national defense during the cold war. They became our best defense against nuclear attack from the sea. Conducting difficult and often dangerous independent operations in both the Atlantic and Pacific (and several contiguous seas), they collected and brought home strategic as well as tactical intelligence. Submarine commanders conducted these operations with a clear awareness of the need for a proper balance between skillful aggressiveness and appropriate caution. Each fully understood the potential consequences of a mishap. There were several underwater encounters between Soviet and American subs during the cold war, but no submarines were lost on either side because of these operations.

After World War II, the Soviets were also quick to recognize the tactical and strategic utility of submarine nuclear propulsion. They had already begun work on their own program when the *Nautilus* went to sea in 1955. Their first *November*-class nuclear attack submarine went to sea in 1958, and they subsequently fielded a succession of new attack submarine designs, most of which were improved versions of their predecessors. About ten years later they deployed an SSBN similar in capability to our first Polaris boats. Not long after that, the American SSNs found that they could "trail" the Soviet boats undetected, sometimes over the course of an entire patrol.

Over time, U.S. SSNs developed a wide range of intelligence-collection capabilities against Soviet targets. Carrying special electronic intercept and communications-monitoring equipment manned by specialists in those fields (irreverently referred to by the submarine crews as "spooks"), they conducted a variety of sophisticated missions in many different areas, in shallow as well as deep water. These and other operations conducted by antisubmarine warfare (ASW) forces were supported by an undersea surveillance network laid in strategic parts of the world's oceans. This technology enabled the United States to maintain extensive coverage of submarine operations in those areas.

U.S. ballistic missile submarines patrolled both oceans within range of virtually all important strategic targets. Our attack submarines conducted critical intelligence-collection missions targeted against all classes of Soviet nuclear-powered subs; they also monitored the threat posed by sea-based strategic missiles by sitting off the coast of Soviet territory and observing the comings and goings of Soviet ships and subs. They were able to observe a variety of missile firings. In some cases specially equipped boats were even able to salvage pieces from the ocean floor after a missile was fired. We learned that Soviet submarines were carrying as many as twenty ballistic missiles, each of which could carry ten to twenty nuclear warheads.

Adm. Hyman G. Rickover did more to promote these submarine operations—and the U.S. nuclear navy in general—than any other single individual. Numerous biographies describe Admiral Rickover's career, including *Rickover* by Norman Polmar and Thomas B. Allen; *The Rickover Effect: How One Man Made a Difference* by Theodore Rickwell; and *Running Critical: The Silent War, Rickover and General Dynamics* by Patrick Tyler. The most recent (and probably the most accurate) is an authorized biography by Frank Duncan published in 2001. These biographies study Rickover's career in detail. In this chapter I will offer only a brief synopsis of the admiral's career before turning to an examination of his leadership developed through the insights of a number of the senior leaders of the Navy.

Rickover graduated from the Naval Academy in 1922 and went on to serve sixty years in the Navy. Before qualifying for submarines in 1930 he served in various surface ships. He pursued graduate training in 1928 in electrical engineering at Annapolis and then studied at Columbia University, receiving a master of science degree in electrical engineering in 1929. Because of his expertise in electrical engineering he was assigned to the Bureau of Ships, where he became chief of the electrical section. At the end of World War II he served as head of the Navy group working with the Manhattan Engineering District at Oak Ridge, Tennessee, his first exposure to the potential of nuclear power. He gradually assumed the authority he would require to develop an atomic-powered submarine. It was an idea to which he dedicated his life tirelessly.

The first post–World War II chief of naval operations, Adm. Chester W. Nimitz, spent the early part of his career in submarines. Rickover convinced him that nuclear propulsion was important—and feasible—for submarines, and Nimitz told him to go ahead with plans to develop it. Rickover subsequently became the chief of the Nuclear Propulsion branch in the Bureau of Ships and also served in a dual position as head of the Naval Reactors division of the Atomic Energy Commission. The latter association was to become increasingly important in achieving success in developing nuclear reactors and nuclear submarines.

Rickover was in charge of the Navy's nuclear power program from 1947 through 1982, holding this position under eight presidents. During that time he developed political power and influence that affected both naval policy and the personnel who served in the nuclear ships. He also developed enemies within the Navy. Some competitors for the naval budget argued that his accomplishments came at the expense of other, more important national defense programs.

The *Nautilus* Prototype Reactor (known as the Submarine Thermal Reactor) was successfully land-tested in March 1953. The *Nautilus,* the world's first nuclear-powered submarine, was launched in January 1954 and put to sea in 1955. No knowledgeable person would disagree that the individual most responsible for the design and development of the propulsion plant and the submarine it served was Rickover, whose efforts earned him the nickname "Father of the Nuclear Navy."

Rickover received promotion to commander on January 1, 1942. In late June of that year he was promoted to captain. In July 1951 he was passed over the first time he became eligible for promotion to rear admiral, then was passed over a second time in July 1952. This slight created a furor among the Rickover's many admirers in Congress. Indeed, it was announced on February 26, 1953, that because Rickover had not been selected for promotion, the Senate Armed Forces Committee was going to hold up the promotions of thirty-nine Navy captains, and was then going to proceed with an investigation of the Navy promotion system. The threat got results. On July 1, 1953, Rickover was selected for the rank of rear admiral. Adm. James L. Holloway Jr. (father of Adm. James L. Holloway

III), who was chief of naval personnel under Adm. Arleigh Burke for an unprecedented six years, worked behind the scenes to resolve the problem. In his unpublished reminiscences the elder Admiral Holloway wrote of Rickover:

> He's got plenty of G-U-T-S. . . . I think his compatriots in the EDO [Engineering Duty Officer] group were probably jealous as hell of him. So he was passed over. [He] got the *Nautilus* built five years ahead of what it would have been without him, just by being a little ornery pusher and fighting and giving them hell. . . .
>
> Well, they passed him over, and there was a hell of a roar on the Hill. I talked to Senator Henry Jackson, whom I know very well, and he said, "Admiral, I know he's probably obnoxious to a lot of people, but that fellow's got a following." And I said, "I . . . agree with you." So I went to Bob Anderson, the secretary of the navy, and I said, "There is machinery in the law which is very strict about the promotion and the Secretary can't dictate, but there is a way that you can write in a . . . certain qualification that you want, and we can write it so strongly that they can't accept anybody but Rickover." So I wrote a precept for a board of six line [officers] and three EDOs and . . . tied it up so that . . . only Rickover could qualify.[2]

Senior Navy admirals were worried that Congress was going to end the promotion system as it had been traditionally handled throughout this century. Under this system civilian secretaries could establish selection criteria, but the promotion board received no interference from the secretary other than establishing the criteria. The secretary could not tell the selection board the names of officers he wanted promoted. Admiral Holloway's response to those concerned about the Navy's traditional promotion system was, "No, it isn't. It isn't the end . . . because we've used a law to promote him . . . to make the will of the secretary felt. When we're too hidebound and reactionary, there's room in the law in Congress which would *really* be the end of the selection system."[3]

There are a number of theories on why the selection board initially passed over Rickover for promotion to rear admiral. He could be very abrasive, brash, outspoken, and openly critical. He was never intimidated by those senior to him in rank. He would not be ignored. He fought hard when anyone placed obstacles that would slow down or interfere with the development of nuclear ships. He would badger, write memos, and negotiate tirelessly for his projects. He got results through sheer force of will, often by methods that were unorthodox by traditional Navy procedures. There were those within the Navy who did not agree on the need for nuclear submarines or a nuclear surface navy and thought the Navy budget could be better spent on other ships and other technology, and they fought hard to stop Rickover. His stature grew with his success. He became a legend. He had the power to crush an officer's career but rarely exercised it.

The next crisis in Rickover's career arose when the time came for his selection for vice admiral; those not selected are retired from active duty. In October 1958 the Navy announced that Rickover would "fill a newly-created three-star rank authorized by President Eisenhower: Chief, Naval Reactors Branch, Atomic Energy Commission."[4]

In December 1963 President Lyndon B. Johnson nominated Rickover for the permanent rank of vice admiral and announced that Rickover would remain on active duty after the mandatory retirement age of sixty-two. When Rickover reached normal retirement at age sixty-two, he was immediately recalled to active duty, and his service was regularly extended for two-year periods until his retirement in 1982 at the age of eighty-two. He thus served an unprecedented—in this century—sixty years on active duty. Rickover was for many years the Navy's most senior admiral, and this longevity put him in a position to provide continuity in pursuing the development, operation, and maintenance of nuclear-powered ships. In 1973—without a recommendation by President Richard M. Nixon or comment from the Navy—the House and Senate passed resolutions promoting Rickover to four stars. Apparently it made no difference to the powers in Congress what the Navy had to say about Rickover's promotion to full admiral.

Rickover's refusal to follow many of the normally accepted rules was upsetting to much of the senior naval leadership, but he got things done: he reduced the lead-time in the development of the nuclear subs by an estimated five years while still demanding technical excellence in every aspect of development and operations. He did not do it alone, of course; he developed an intensely loyal staff driven by a contagious desire to be a part of the excitement of his vision. This tight-knit clique and political influence—in particular his rapport with Congress—were hallmarks of Rickover's leadership.

Rickover developed a remarkable ability to secure funding from Congress at a time when the military in general was being downsized. It did not hurt his cause that he named four attack submarines after important members of Congress, but his legendary efficiency helped as well. His projects were normally completed on time, often ahead of schedule, and often under budget. He held industry accountable for cost overruns in its shipbuilding like no other government agency ever had. Congress appreciated this and rewarded him for it. He was practical and more knowledgeable than perhaps anyone in the world in his discipline. He gave far more of himself than he asked of anyone else.

Rickover's shabby, austere office, with cinder-block walls, a paint-chipped rocker with frazzled green cushions, and Navy-issue metal desk, added to his legend. But Rickover did not spend much time there. He was constantly visiting job sites, meeting with his people, inspecting ships, asking probing questions to find, meet, and solve problems. His personal inspections gave him the ability to search out problems and potential problems.

His accessibility allowed his staff to present ideas to him directly. He did not hold back on his reactions. If he did not think much of what they had to offer, they were told right away. But someone who really believed in an idea could go back to him again. If he could be convinced, he had no hesitation in reversing himself, saying, "Only a fool never changes his mind."

Admiral Rickover did not surround himself with "yes men." I asked Adm. Henry G. Chiles, once one of Rickover's group, if Admiral Rickover tolerated people who stood up to him. "I think he did," he replied.

> I mean, there were times when you had to raise your voice to be heard. He was a man who showed his emotions. When he was angry, he showed it, but he got over it fairly quickly; in fifteen minutes he'd get over it. I never felt any hesitation about telling him what I thought. There was no intimidation or fear on my part. I believe very strongly that he appreciated it when you challenged him. He appreciated the fact that you would stand up for what you believed to be right and not only say, "I believe this is right," but follow that up with crisp arguments—concrete, well-reasoned scenarios and situations that would help him to understand where you were

coming from. So you needed to be able to not only tell him what you thought, you needed to be able to reason it through in crisp terms. . . .

There were several times when he . . . [turned down] people being interviewed for the nuclear program. I was one of the preliminary interviewers, and if I thought that a particular person should be accepted into the program, I said so. If he said no, I went back personally to ask for reconsideration. . . . We didn't win them all, but some of them. If he did agree he would just initial it and say, "Okay, you're responsible," and accept that person.[5]

With the help of his loyal staff Rickover managed a massive construction program that built a nuclear fleet. While his supporters called him the father of the nuclear navy, his critics believed that others would have been equally capable of developing the nuclear navy, but without the abrasiveness and high-handed methods Rickover used to get things done. Whether a less abrasive officer might have eased some of the growing pains of the nuclear navy seems less important than the fact that Rickover was the nuclear fleet's midwife.

An important factor in Rickover's success was his control over personnel selection. His philosophy was "Why not the best?" He wanted to be sure that Naval Reactors had the best people, drawing those with a technical aptitude from the Naval Academy and from civilian colleges and universities. His interviews were legendary; some called them cruel, weird, and insane. The interviews were intended to challenge the prospective candidates because he wanted officers able to stand up under stress. He demanded the best and wanted only those who would give their best, although he believed that people never lived up to their potential. He would always ask interviewees why they did not stand higher in their class. He wanted to determine a candidate's motivation, weaknesses, and strengths, how he or she handled stress. During his career he interviewed more than five thousand candidates, most drawn from the top 5 percent of the officer corps.

Adm. Thomas H. Moorer (CNO 1967–70, chairman of the Joint Chiefs 1970–74) said of his relations with Admiral Rickover:

I think when you get someone like Rickover who is dedicated to one program, in this case to nuclear submarines, and manages to build up the kind of reputation he has, you're faced with the political overtones of [the] image . . . he created for himself by dealing with the Congress, by his outspokenness in his testimony at congressional hearings, and so on. For instance, I agreed with Rickover on the high-speed submarine that we had such difficulty getting approved. . . . Rickover and I worked well together on that and we actually, in fact, got the submarine.

You have to deal with people like Rickover in such a way as to accent the positive. I mean Rickover has the capacity to make people furious with him, because sometimes he's abrasive and, of course, he is so intent on certain objectives that he just brushes off any objections. I made up my mind when I became CNO that I wasn't going to get into a big hassle with Rickover. During that time, we were trying to convince McNamara of the need for nuclear-powered destroyers, the DLGNs, as well as the high-speed submarine, both of which we did finally get. So, I think, on balance, I got along very well with Rickover. I don't recall any confrontation over a major issue. . . .

As I say, when you have an individual who has a great capability in a certain field, what you must try to do is make complete and total use of those capabilities without letting them stray off the reservation. Rickover is the kind of a fellow who must be handled differently than you do others. You don't give Rickover a direct order to stop doing what he's doing or to do something he's not doing, as you would in many cases. I've found that you have to handle each individual entirely differently. You can't just have a set of rules as to the way you're going to do it. You've got to deal with their personalities, their objectives, character, et cetera. What will work with Rickover won't work with somebody else and vice versa.

I think that bearing in mind, for instance, that Rickover has a tremendous following in the Congress and he was quite helpful to me in matters other than the nuclear program, because he had this entrée, and he could start talking about a nuclear submarine, then change the subject to something else. For instance, he was always a strong supporter of the aircraft carrier. So here was a man who had this image that he has: the father of the nuclear submarine and a great program manager. On the other hand, I know damned well if there had never been a Rickover, there would have certainly been a nuclear submarine. One must try, as I said before, to use the good points and strengths of people and follow them in that direction. If you know what their characteristics are, you don't intentionally just, you know, bring them to a boil. I think that's the job of the CNO. If you can set it up so that the people under you will be used to the best of their capacities, once you get that going, you really don't have to do very much yourself.[6]

Adm. William J. Crowe Jr. (chairman of the Joint Chiefs 1985–89) reflected on his experiences with Admiral Rickover—in particular his interview:

> There is a lot of mythology about that interview that is not always reported correctly. Actually, just before I went to graduate school in 1960, I had been trying to get in the nuclear submarine program for several years, indeed since about 1950. I don't know why Admiral Rickover never called me. I went to graduate school in 1960. I had been accepted for Princeton, and I was getting ready to go in a couple of months to Princeton. I got a call from Washington saying that Rickover wanted to interview me. I spent the whole weekend thinking this over. I told my wife that I didn't think I should go up there unless I was prepared to accept it, if he accepted me.
>
> I got advice from everybody, all of it contradictory. I talked to my wife, and my father, and everybody else. I finally called the detailer back and said, "I can't come. I'm going to graduate school. I've already been admitted, and I don't feel comfortable going up there." They said, "You are missing a great opportunity of your life," which to me was sheer nonsense, telling me, "You sure are making a big mistake."
>
> I went ahead and went to graduate school. I finished my first year at Princeton, I got another call telling me, "You are going to go see Rickover this week." I said, "I don't want to go." Well, this time they told me, "It is not as a volunteer, you have to go. He says he is insisting that he is not going to see anybody unless you come down there." So I went down and saw Rickover and initially he threw me out of the office once. I came back in, but I was very uncomfortable. I don't think I did very well interviewing.
>
> He was the kind of man that would irritate the hell out of me. He knew that, and he was intentionally irritating and abusive. Finally, he said, "If I accept you in this program are you ready to go?"
>
> I said, "Admiral, nothing would please me more than to be on this program, just as soon as I finish graduate school I will be ready to go." Then he really got mad, and he threw my ass right out of the office. . . . I never got back in the nuclear program. I had no idea then whether he would have accepted me or not, but I heard later that he was willing to accept me, but he couldn't afford to have junior officers go to a graduate school before he went into the nuclear program. He didn't like graduate school. A contemporary of mine, Harry Train, lieutenant commander on a boat, was turned down. He turned us both down, but we both made four stars.[7]

Adm. James L. Holloway III (CNO 1974–78) was the third captain of the first nuclear carrier, the USS *Enterprise*. An incident he related to me illustrated both how single-minded Rickover was about his nuclear reactors program and how human he could be as a private person. The *Enterprise* had returned to San Francisco in 1966 after a highly successful combat deployment to Vietnam, where the carrier set several records in daily totals of combat sorties that have never been surpassed. *Enterprise* at that time had an impressive cachet. It was the largest warship in the world, the first and only nuclear carrier, and its eight nuclear reactors gave it a speed of more than forty knots.

"It was a hero's welcome," Admiral Holloway recalled.

At that time the American people felt we were winning the war in Vietnam. The city had declared . . . "*Enterprise* Day," and any *Enterprise* crew member could get a free drink in most of the bars in San Francisco on that day. All three of the Bay Area's main newspapers devoted their full front pages on June 21, 1966, to the *Enterprise*'s return from Vietnam to its new homeport of NAS Alameda. One-inch headlines in the *Oakland Tribune* proclaimed "*Enterprise* Home": "This nation's most powerful lady returned from war today, her nuclear power churning her through the Golden Gate as thousands of welcomers cheered her on." The *San Francisco Examiner*'s front-page headlines stated "Wild Greeting for Carrier": "*Enterprise* steamed through the Golden Gate with a fleet of more than 40 small craft-sailboats, yachts and fireboats spouting spray . . . on hand . . . with Mayor John F. Shelley leading them." The *San Francisco Chronicle* had a full-front-page picture of *Enterprise* with one-inch headlines: . . . "*Enterprise* Homecoming Snarls Marin County Traffic: Two thousand persons lined the sidewalks of the Golden Gate Bridge to watch the homecoming of the *Enterprise*; . . . traffic on Highway 101 was backed up from the bridge to San Rafael. . . . Crowds gathered wherever they could to get a view of the Bay . . . all of the Bridge's parking lots were jammed and the overflow spilled into the Presidio and they too were quickly filled. . . . Despite the traffic there were amazingly enough no reports of accidents. They were moving too slow for anything to happen."

The *Oakland Tribune* summed it up: "The *Enterprise*, the largest warship in the world, has done her job. It is only fitting that her welcome should be the biggest in the Bay Area since that accorded the battered cruiser *San Francisco* during World War II." The homecoming was later written up in *Life* magazine, which had a picture of the *Enterprise* on the cover. The article also described the attitude of the crowds as reminiscent of World War II, welcoming a heroic ship of the U.S. Navy home from the wars. It was all very exciting.

When *Enterprise* came alongside the pier at Alameda, I could see my wife, Dabney, waiting for me with our two daughters, with Admiral Rickover next to her. As soon as the first gangway was over, Admiral Rickover took off at a fast pace to be the first aboard. A chief petty [officer] stepped in to block his way and sent Dabney aboard ahead of him. The chiefs knew their priorities—or at least they knew mine. I thought Admiral Rickover would be upset, but he wasn't at all. Admiral Rickover was so thrilled because of *Enterprise*'s successful cruise that he was in an unshakable good humor.

The combat experience of the *Enterprise* as the only nuclear-powered carrier had resulted in a great deal of ongoing press interest, and the coverage had been universally favorable. Rickover felt that his proposed program for a nuclear-powered fleet of aircraft carriers had been given a powerful boost and that the tactical advantages of nuclear propulsion had been vindicated—and he was probably right.

Dabney was brought up to the bridge, but I was still involved in getting the ship tied up. I hugged and kissed her. She said, "You're busy. I better get out of your hair." I said, "Why don't you go down to my cabin and I'll meet you down there when the lines are doubled up." Admiral Rickover had arrived with Dabney. He was bubbling over with the excitement of the homecoming. He congratulated me and then immediately launched into a discussion of how well the reactors had performed. He said his Naval Reactors staff had saved the day by directing the ship's Reactor Department in making repairs to number 7 reactor by satellite telephone. He said no other organization could have accomplished that feat. I agreed with him and then added, "Admiral, I'm trying to get this ship tied up and really I can't talk to you about those details now."

He said, "That's okay. I'll tell you what we'll do. . . . You pick a nice restaurant and we'll go out tonight and got a steak. You and I can sit there, enjoy your steak, and go over the whole cruise." My face must have fallen because Dave Leighton, who was Rickover's number-one assistant and always with him, spoke up and said, "Admiral Rickover, are you out of your goddamn mind? . . . Holloway has been at sea away from his wife and family for eight months. He doesn't want to talk to you. He wants to see his family." Rickover said, "I'm sure Holloway would like to talk to me about nuclear reactors!" Dave Leighton said to the Admiral, "Come with me," and he and Rickover departed without any fuss.

I invited Rickover to join me at breakfast in my cabin the next morning. He had to catch a plane back to Washington at 9:30 A.M. That breakfast was an enjoyable session. Rickover was still caught up in the excitement of the activity of homecoming and the national publicity that *Enterprise* was attracting.

Later, when I was CNO, Rickover became disappointed with me because I would not agree to make every new major warship nuclear powered. I was absolutely convinced we simply could not afford it in dollars or in skilled manpower. I did commit the Navy to a policy that would require every carrier and every submarine to be nuclear powered. That policy has remained in effect without exception to this day.

Leighton was very smart, a brilliant engineer, and impeccably loyal to Rickover. I have seen Rickover get furious with him. Rickover would have a tantrum and say to Leighton, "That's the dumbest thing I've ever heard. I don't know why I put up with your stupidity. You're not doing what I told you to do." Leighton would stand there, listen to Rickover, and then continue his conversation as if Rickover hadn't even spoken. Rickover would always simmer down and eventually agree with Leighton, once Dave had explained his position. He was just enormously patient and considerate of Admiral Rickover. I believe he always felt that these outbursts were Rickover's way of testing him, making sure Leighton was willing to stand behind his words without backing down. . . .

My two-year tour as commanding officer of *Enterprise* was ended in July 1967, and I . . . returned to the Pentagon, where . . . I became OP-34, director of strike warfare, which I considered to be the best job in the Pentagon. In that position I was responsible for all tactical aircraft and major combatant programs in the Navy except submarines and amphibious ships. Paramount among these programs were the plans for the construction of carriers. The Navy wanted all new aircraft carriers to be nuclear powered, but Secretary of Defense McNamara had disapproved a four-reactor follow-on to the *Enterprise*, stating that the Navy had not analytically proved the cost effectiveness of a nuclear-powered carrier over its conventional counterpart. So two conventional carriers, *America* and *Kennedy*, had been constructed after *Enterprise*, while the Navy struggled to convince McNamara's Whiz Kids of the advantage of nuclear power.

Although OpNav [the CNO's staff in the Pentagon] had the statutory responsibility of stating military requirements for the capabilities of weapon systems [i.e., ships and planes], Admiral Rickover, as director of Naval Reactors in the Ship Systems Command in the Naval Material Command, became an alternative spokesman for Navy carrier construction. He was not invited to do this officially;

it was simply his nature to become publicly involved in matters he cared about strongly. In so doing, he gave the Navy another voice, reaching another audience in support of nuclear power in carriers.

In the early days of *Enterprise* some aviation admirals with brilliant war records in World War II—and with a considerable constituency in the aviation community—were rejecting nuclear power for carriers as unnecessarily complicating a proven design, the *Forrestal*-class ships. One rear admiral stated, "I could care less about what kind of power drives the ship, it can be rubber bands, as long as I can ring up full power on the bridge and have the engine room respond." Other aviation captains when interviewed by Admiral Rickover for the nuclear program—and command of a nuclear carrier—told Rickover they didn't care about anything below the flight deck, they would simply depend upon a good engineering officer. These captains made it a matter of pride to be members of the "I Was Turned Down by Rickover Club."

So Rickover not only had to win over the Department of Defense and the Congress, but the support of the acknowledged naval professionals as well. During Admiral Arleigh Burke's tenure as CNO, Rickover found the support he needed at the top to get his Naval Reactors program off the ground. He had an organization of dedicated people of remarkable ability and a professional staff that was the best in the field when it came to the practical application of nuclear power. My first impression when I joined Rickover's staff in 1964 as a prospective commanding officer of *Enterprise* was that it was a bizarre collection of individual geniuses, which it was—not like any disciplined group I had ever served with before in the Navy. Working with them six days a week, twelve hours a day, three months at a stretch in the old World War I temp buildings in Washington and at the reactor site in Arco, Idaho, I quickly learned that theirs was a dedication I had never seen before in the Navy's shore establishment, and an ironclad but tacit discipline in their work and purpose that I had never seen before among civilians, and not often in a military organization. Their total motivation was a respect and admiration (bordering on adulation) of Rickover. This was a superlative collection of scientific engineers who recognized Rickover's genius, and who were willing to work their tails off for him. And he took full advantage of their devotion.

Under CNO Burke, Rickover's proposals for a nuclear-powered submarine (*Nautilus*), cruiser (*Long Beach*), and carrier (*Enterprise*) were approved and came to fruition. The support from a CNO of such wisdom and perspective as Admiral Burke became instrumental in the success of those initial projects. They were still not easy to pull off, but Rickover was able to do it without a hitch.

When George Anderson succeeded Burke, there were strong and deliberate efforts from the top to reduce Rickover's control and the influence that he was exercising through his various positions in the government, such as head of the Naval Reactors division in the Atomic Energy Commission, which was outside the authority of the Department of Defense. Rickover outlasted Anderson, whose normal four-year stint as CNO was aborted after two years because of his run-in with Secretary of Defense McNamara during the Cuban missile crisis. The term of Admiral McDonald as CNO was somewhat better for Naval Reactors, but there was no clear leadership at the head of the uniformed Navy for—or against—nuclear propulsion. Most of the vocal advocates for nuclear warships were in the Congress, where Rickover had gained the backing of a powerful group of legislators who were impressed by his accomplishments, his frankness, and his apparent humility.

Rickover was able to persuade the leadership of the House of Representatives to create the Sea Power Subcommittee of the House Armed Services Committee. This subcommittee was then filled with senior ranking representatives, all of whom were friendly with Rickover if not his out-and-out admirers. This committee was supposed to address all issues relating to naval affairs, but in fact seldom considered anything but matters of nuclear power. It is interesting that neither the Army nor the Air Force had similar advocacy committees in the Congress. It was Rickover who was able to charm the Congress into providing the Navy (or really Rickover) with his own sounding board.

When Admiral Tom Moorer became CNO, he recognized Rickover's contributions to the Navy, his continuing potential, and his impressive influence with the Congress. The new CNO wisely listened to Rickover and consulted with him on nuclear matters. He knew Rickover was too valuable to needlessly antagonize.

In 1966, *Enterprise* had completed her first cruise to the Seventh Fleet during the Vietnam War. It was the first time a nuclear-powered ship had engaged in combat operations. The cruise had been a monumental success. *Enterprise* set a record in daily totals of combat sorties, tons of bombs dropped, and the speed of replenishments of stores and ammunition. The eight-reactor propulsion plant had operated without a hitch. When number 7 reactor had developed a problem, it was repaired . . . from spare parts onboard and with no outside assistance except detailed directions from the engineers in Rickover's office by radio telephone. Rickover made sure that all of the details of the *Enterprise* cruise received wide public notice. The Sea Power Subcommittee met frequently to hold hearings at which Rickover testified on the advantages of a nuclear-powered carrier, based upon weekly unclassified operational summaries which I dispatched directly to him.

By the spring of 1966, the reports of the Sea Power Subcommittee, the interest of the Armed Services Committee, and the vocal support of such independent powers as Senator Scoop Jackson had resulted in a reversal of the attitudes in the Office of the Secretary of Defense with respect to nuclear-powered carriers. The contributions of the carriers in Vietnam . . . had given carriers in general and nuclear power in particular a new life. Rickover continued his efforts to win McNamara's support . . . taking him on visits to the Westinghouse and GE laboratories to see the latest developments in reactor technology. But McNamara . . . was not the person who would admit that he had been wrong by changing his mind. Dr. Harold Brown, who was director of defense research and engineering under McNamara, is quoted as saying, "Bob [McNamara] is in a box. He now supports a nuclear carrier but can't find a way to give in."

At the Bettis Atomic Laboratory, Rickover showed McNamara a 60,000 shaft horsepower [SHP] design (the DIW) intended for a single reactor cruiser power plant. McNamara asked Rickover if two of these could power an aircraft carrier. Rickover immediately answered "yes," and this was the breakthrough that led to McNamara's approval of a two-reactor carrier design that became the *Nimitz* class.

But that was merely the beginning of a new set of challenges. . . . Rickover had another hurdle, this time a technical problem. He had immediately agreed to a two-reactor carrier. He knew at the time that meant he was going to have to develop a single reactor of 120,000 SHP. An *Enterprise* reactor produced only 35,000 SHP. The experimental design at Bettis, which had not been fully constructed, was only 60,000 SHP. Rickover would have to double the output of the theoretical Bettis design. Leighton later confided in me that the 120,000 SHP reactor could not have been designed without the advances in computer technology that were occurring at the same time.

Nimitz was authorized in 1967, as CVAN 68, and commissioned in 1975 with President Ford doing the honors. Ten more *Nimitz*-class ships have been built; the CVAN 77 is currently under construction. These ships, built at an average cost of several billion dollars each, are tangible evidence of Admiral Rickover's contribution to the U.S. Navy. These carriers have gone where the action is. Every nuclear carrier in the fleet has launched its aircraft in combat operations in Vietnam, Kuwait, Serbia, Kosovo, Bosnia, Iraq, or Afghanistan.

Yet the nuclear-powered aircraft carrier program was only part of Hyman G. Rickover's legacy to the U.S. Navy. The Office of Naval Reactors under his personal direction was also responsible for the fleet of nuclear-powered submarines, both tactical attack boats and the Trident strategic ballistic missile submarines of the *Ohio* class—and the nuclear cruisers, frigates, and destroyers, which were fully successful as nuclear ships but not practical for the escort mission.

Admiral Holloway added, "The genius of Rickover is apparent."[8]

In his memoir, *On Watch,* Adm. Elmo R. Zumwalt Jr. described butting heads with Rickover.

> The fact that from the start of my watch to the end of it Vice Admiral, and then Admiral, Hyman G. Rickover was a persistent and formidable obstacle to my plans for modernizing the Navy did not at all surprise me. I had expected him to be. Over the course of my service I had encountered Admiral Rickover a number of times. I knew that he would stop at nothing, bureaucratically speaking, to ensure that nuclear-powered ships received priority over vessels of any other kind. I knew that he had enormous influence on Capitol Hill, far greater than that of any other military man, so great that one student of the scene remarked to me, "Congress doesn't really think of Rick as an admiral at all, but as a kind of Senator." I knew that his Division of Nuclear Propulsion was a totalitarian ministate whose citizens—and that included not just his headquarters staff but anybody engaged in building, maintaining, or manning nuclear vessels—did what the leader told them to, Navy regulations notwithstanding, or suffered condign punishment. In sum, I knew as soon as I was designated CNO that developing a productive working relationship with Rickover was among the toughest nuts I had been called upon to crack. In my exuberance over being chosen to head the Navy, I believed I could do it. I was wrong.

On Admiral Rickover's standing with Congress Admiral Zumwalt commented: "He headed an innovative and glamorous program of a kind that Congressmen like to have their names associated with, and because he is a master of public relations who, by providing certain influential Congressmen with publicity that delighted them, developed an image as one military man with the courage to speak plainly enough to make headlines and candidly enough to be worth inviting to testify at all sorts of hearings, in his field of expertise and out of it."

Their disputes were constant throughout Zumwalt's tenure as CNO. "Just one time," Zumwalt wrote:

was there a serious attempt to dematerialize Rick, and it failed ignominiously. That was in 1967. Paul Nitze, still secretary of the navy and increasingly disenchanted with Rickover's behavior, and the secretary of defense, Robert McNamara, an early "High-Low" man and therefore an opponent of Rickover's "All High" programs, had President Johnson convinced that if the concept of civilian control meant anything, Rickover must go. Lyndon Johnson was no Rickover fan himself. But the rumor that Rick's extension was in doubt came to the attention of Rickover stalwarts like Senators Everett Dirksen and Richard Russell. LBJ met such a storm of protest that he hastily changed his mind. Since then no one has made more than a token effort to question Rick's reappointment. I didn't the two times it came before me, much as I would have liked to. I was fighting too many hard battles I had a chance of winning to waste my time on one that was an almost sure loser.[9]

Anyone familiar with LBJ's understanding of how and when to use power—gained as Senate majority leader, vice president, and president—will recognize his retreat as a significant indication of Rickover's clout.

One of the major differences of opinion between Zumwalt and Rickover had to do with the balance between nuclear and conventional ships, referred to as the "high-low" mix. Zumwalt believed that the Navy simply could not afford the nuclear-powered escorts Rickover wanted to build. The two men developed a healthy dislike for one another as they competed for the Navy's budget. "The hair on the backs of our necks seemed to bristle when we encountered each other," Zumwalt said,

> especially when Congress was working on the budget. I suppose that was inevitable, given Rickover's status as an independent baron within the Navy. The budget is a presidential document that presumably arbitrates among the competing claims for money. It never gave Rickover everything he considered necessary [and] . . . consequently Rickover always was nudging Congress to give him a piece of my balanced program, and I was constantly fighting to maintain the balance within inadequate budget allocations. Henry Kissinger, no lover of independent baronies, asked me at least twice about the possibility of retiring Rickover for keeps. Both times I reminded him of what Congress had done to LBJ, and Henry dropped the subject.[10]

Kissinger, like LBJ, knew when and how to use power, and his backing away from the issue was another indication of Rickover's power.

Admiral Zumwalt summed up their relationship by saying: "There is almost no way for a CNO not to find himself in an adversary position to Rickover, because Rickover brazenly—though seldom openly—challenges the duly constituted authority of every CNO and indeed every secretary of the navy, every secretary of defense, and every president. After my summit with Rick I had a small hope for the best and a large expectation of the worst."[11]

In June 1976 the fight over how large a role nuclear-powered ships were to play in the U.S. fleet erupted in the media and into public discussion, throwing "two strong-willed men [Rickover and Holloway] into public confrontation, with Congress joining the debate, where the final decision will be made." An article in the June 7, 1976, issue of *U.S. News and World Report* focused on the dispute:

A fierce debate that will determine the shape of the future U.S. Navy has burst into the open. The White House, the Pentagon and Congress are all in the thick of it. The feuding started when the admirals now in charge of the Navy decided on a showdown with Hyman G. Rickover—the 76-year-old admiral who for a quarter of century has been a virtual one-man policy board on shipbuilding. Known as the father of the atomic submarine—which he is credited with developing almost single-handedly in the 1950s—Admiral Rickover now has won strong support in Congress for making all of the Navy's major surface warships nuclear-powered as well.

The Pentagon admirals, led by James L. Holloway III, Chief of Naval Operations, . . . viewed Admiral Rickover's goals as a challenge to their shipbuilding plans, which involve a mix of nuclear and conventional power. They have decided the time has come to break the stranglehold that Admiral Rickover has held on warship policy.

Their goal is to expand the present force of 478 ships to a 600-ship fleet that combines a few high-performance, nuclear-powered ships with a large number of conventional, oil-powered vessels. The dispute is not over whether a nuclear-powered ship is better, but rather how the nation can best spend its defense dollars. . . . Both sides are marshaling support in Congress, where the issue will be decided.

The Rickover plan, as his critics see it, would result in a gold-plated Navy too small to cover the worldwide U.S. responsibilities. The admirals' plan, as

Admiral Rickover sees it, might provide a larger fleet but one highly vulnerable because of its dependence on a network of oil tankers and fuel supply that could be cut off by an oil embargo or some other uncontrollable factor.

Ultimately Admiral Holloway prevailed, not an insignificant achievement in light of Rickover's power and standing with Congress. "As I recall, it was a crisis for everyone but me," Admiral Holloway told me.

I considered it all in a day's work. Bob Long, then a four-star and my VCNO, . . . came into my office after this article appeared and suggested I send a written apology to Rickover, and consider sending copies to members of Congress. My reply was, "Apologize for what? Doing my job as CNO?" Congressman Sam Stratton called me personally on the phone (he was the Republican ranking member on House Armed Services) to scold me severely. I scolded him right back.

The upshot was I made it Navy policy to discontinue nuclear power on all ships but carriers and submarines, and reaffirmed that they *must* be nuclear-powered. Within six years there were no more nuclear frigates, destroyers, or cruisers left in the fleet. Most had been decommissioned before their nominal service life. They were too expensive to operate for the benefit nuclear power provided. . . .

This dispute, which was reported widely in the press, was never alluded to by Rickover or myself in any of the many discussions we had when I was CNO. I never felt threatened by Rickover. In fact I was enormously grateful to him for the way he was running the technical side of the nuclear navy. What a tremendous commitment of time and energy it would have taken a CNO who did not have a person of Rickover's mind, dedication, and guts running this nuclear component of our Navy. I like to point out that the U.S. Navy has never had a nuclear incident [involving] . . . the release of fission products into [the] atmosphere. No other service in this country or any other can make such a statement. And of course the disasters in civil applications are well known and appalling—Three Mile Island and Chernobyl are grim examples.

I believed at the time that Rickover had a right to lobby for an expansion of nuclear power in the fleet. He was a public figure, and in his AEC hat he did not have to go through the CNO. By never failing to demonstrate his advocacy for naval reactors at every opportunity, I believe he strengthened rather than threatened the CNO's nuclear propulsion programs. I also believed at the time that Rickover understood my reasons for limiting the application of nuclear power. We each understood the other's need to take the position that we publicly espoused.

During my four years as CNO, Rickover was a frequent visitor to my office. He usually was accompanied by Dave Leighton, but often came alone. He always made an appointment and arrived at least fifteen minutes early. He would spend his time while waiting by engaging the CNO office staff in pleasant banter. They all thought Admiral Rickover was wonderful. He was always pleasant and they enjoyed his good humor. With me, in the office, he was businesslike and to the point in the presentation of his case. If I turned him down he simply left when his time was up without any remonstrations. I can only describe our relations as proper and cordial. I made every attempt to explain clearly the rationale of my position to Rickover, and that helped. If he really had a hot issue to pursue that he considered critical, he let Leighton do the arguing, I will admit that I sometimes shouted at Dave when he belabored a point or began repeating himself. Yet we too remain friends today. We knew what we each had to do.

Admiral Holloway added one final Rickover vignette.

I retired from the Navy as CNO on 1 July 1978, and moved out of Navy quarters to our home in Arlington directly after the change of command, which was held in Annapolis. Admiral and Mrs. Rickover had Dabney and me to supper in their apartment in Crystal City that evening. Admiral Rickover said he felt sorry for us having to leave the CNO quarters with all the staff and they wanted to help ease the transition. That was a little tongue in cheek, but I think it shows a human side of Hyman G. Rickover that not many people give him credit for. It was in fact a delightful evening, full of good conversation, with not a mention of the Navy or nuclear reactors.[12]

I asked Adm. Thomas B. Hayward (CNO 1978–82), a former carrier pilot, to describe his relationship with Admiral Rickover. He responded: "Until I was CNO, it wasn't very much. Earlier in my career I was not acceptable to him as a candidate on a nuclear carrier."

I asked: "Had you ever applied for it?"

"You're not allowed to apply for it," he answered.

You're chosen for it, so obviously I let him know I wanted it, but there was only one nuclear carrier, the *Enterprise*. I knew Rickover wasn't interested in me, but I would have gone that route if they had allowed me to do that. I was the fleet commander, and he came on and inspected the yard there. So we had an hour or so together talking, but basically we didn't know each other to speak of until I was CNO. Then we spent quite a bit of time together.

I've always believed that you respect rank, you respect age, you respect experience. He was the most senior officer in the Navy by a long shot, and I gave him the respect he was due, but I believed strongly that he should have retired way before he did, and I retired him. Jim Watkins and Bob Long were both quite helpful in building a strategy where we would be in a position to keep the nuclear program going if we lost Rickover and to get him retired at an appropriate time and an appropriate way without making a crisis out of it. Both were very close to Rickover and knew the system well.[13]

Adm. James D. Watkins (CNO 1982–86) experienced one of the legendary Rickover interviews just after completing his graduate degree.

I went for an interview with him after leaving Oak Ridge where I was completing my master's degree program. He chastised me roundly, telling me how stupid I was to write my thesis on mechanical engineering on an analog computer analysis of reactor responses under certain conditions, start-up conditions and so forth. He told me how dumb I was. He read my thesis. He did not like simulators in those days. Later on, he recognized the beauty of the simulator. In the old days of training, we were doing things before we had digitalized examinations of a core response. . . . We did not know what we were doing to the core when conducting certain emergency drills. We were probably overstressing some core elements, and not . . . aware of it. We knew it later on when we had better computer analysis of what went on. We could not conduct the kinds of training evolutions in the same manner done in the early days where you drop rods down, then immediately haul 'em out and start up the reactor again. That was a big dynamic, and you need to know exactly what's going on in the core. If you don't . . . you could burn out a fuel element. So simulators properly programmed could serve as training under these . . . reactor conditions without imposing any actual stresses on the operational training reactor. The concept was ultimately accepted by Rickover. But in the interview he threw me out, told me how dumb I was, but then I was accepted.

I mentioned that I heard bizarre stories about the interviews— something about a three-legged chair and being locked in a closet. He said, "That's nonsense, but it's not all nonsense. The candidate's initial interview was really run by three to five other top people that [Rickover] trusted. These interviews were lengthy, maybe forty-five minutes each. The candidate would spend most of the day there. Next, you were interviewed by Rickover. He had read everything about you from his trusted interviewers and would then lay right into you on the material before him."

I asked Watkins about Rickover's confrontational leadership style. Why did he conduct himself that way? "When Rickover jumped all over you, called you 'the dumbest Naval officer I have ever seen,' . . . and all that kind of stuff," Watkins answered, "he did that to people he still trusted and thought were potentially future leaders in the Navy. If he ever said to you, 'Dr. Puryear, you're doing a wonderful job here today, thank you very much,' that meant that you were finished, . . . whether you recognized it or not. So you had to know his technique, one backward to most people. I finally decoded his technique after working three years for him."

Admiral Watkins commented further on his tenure with Admiral Rickover:

> It was eighteen months after I reported to NR [Naval Reactors] in spring 1962 that I first began to understand the admiral's long-range goals and objectives related to enhancement of naval officer professionalism. Prior to that time, I experienced a degree of humbling not unlike that during plebe year at the Naval Academy seventeen years earlier. But, then, one morning, Mark Forsell and I arrived at the old N Building on Constitution Avenue about 7:15 A.M. . . . Promptly at 7:30, the call came down from the admiral, "Get Watkins up here." "What now, God?" I thought. But having been somewhat numbed by frequent trips down the hall over the prior one and a half years, I took the current impending trauma in reasonable stride. Clearly, I believed that this was just one more case of poor thinking and writing on my part, you know "like all those other dumb naval officers." But on this occasion, a miracle was about to take place. Apprehensively, I entered the admiral's office and he began yelling at me . . . but this time with a different ring to the voice. He said, "Watkins, go down the hall and tell Jack Grigg how to write a letter." He then dismissed me abruptly. Poor Jack obviously had his turn in the barrel that morning, as had we all at one time or another. On my way out, I said to the admiral's secretary, Jean Scroggins, "Jean, did you hear that?" Jean said to me rather matter-of-factly, "Mr. Watkins, today you have arrived." Well I walked down the hall toward Jack's office with a skip

and a smile, my first at NR. Admiral Rickover had "spooned" me in his own way. In fact, I can look back on his words that day as being the nicest compliment Admiral Rickover ever paid me in the more than two decades I worked for him. . . . At any rate, the light had just come on for me. I now understood his tactical plan to attempt to train all with whom he came in contact and through them, spread the good news throughout the Navy of the right way to do business. But I also realized that he would expend his energy only on verbally chastising those whom he still believed had the right stuff to help him achieve his goal of instilling a new sense of professionalism in future naval leaders, civilian and military. Woe to the person who was treated with kind words by the admiral—clearly someone he assessed as not having the right stuff and hence totally unworthy of his time, attention, and energy.

I asked Admiral Watkins if Rickover developed close personal relationships with any of those who worked with him. "No. Not that close," he answered. "He respected certain individuals and I was one of those." Why did Rickover respect him?

I guess because I learned from him. I wrote a better letter than I did when I got there. Gave a better speech; gave a better presentation; understood how training, education, and selection of Navy officers is important; how quality in individuals was important to readiness, to safety; how engineering was important to winning battles at sea at wartime, that is, to keep the weapon systems going; how much of engineering expertise . . . in the officer corps of the Navy had been lost since World War II. We changed that. I was part of the change. So was Holloway. For example, we started a mandatory formal training school for commanding officers going into non-nuclear-powered ships. This drove some of these officers crazy until after they went through it and realized how valuable it was to them when they took over as a skipper of an aircraft carrier, or a skipper of a destroyer. I don't want to say that Rickover was the end-all. Certainly, I would say that I would never emulate his leadership practices—but his approach was eminently successful. . . .

He read all the time and on almost any subject. They loved him on Capitol Hill because he was lucid. He was open with them; he was honest as the day is long. He despised industry that tried to take advantage of the federal government. He worked them over very hard. He was tough, but his goal was very clear, and that was to build a professional corps in the Navy, which he thought needed a major course change from the lessons learned—or what should have been learned—out of World War II and had been lost in the interim. He saw engineering going down the tubes in the conventionally powered fleet. So he decided to set an example with nuclear power practices which was picked up by Zumwalt, put into effect by his successors, carried on by me when I became CNO, and helped return engineering to the front of war-fighting readiness. . . . Eventually, nuclear-trained officers came up through the system to become CNO: Jim Holloway was the first; Tom Hayward was not; then I was, as were my immediate successors, Trost and Kelso; Boorda was not; Johnson was, and Vern Clark was not. Three in a row were nuclear submariners followed by a nuclear-trained naval aviator. Those in recent years who have not been nuclear trained have uniformly been very supportive of nuclear submarines and carriers. Admiral Rickover's long-term goal had been achieved and sustained since 1982.[14]

I asked Adm. Henry G. Chiles Jr. to tell me about his interview with Rickover and his subsequent relationship with the admiral.

The only interview I had with Rickover was in 1961 or 1962 to come into the program. It was a very short interview. We were in New London at submarine school. I trained down to Washington, and we had preliminary interviews, then I went in to see him. He asked me where I stood in the submarine class. I told him I was about number 5 out of 100, maybe out of 110. There was no leadership associated with that. It was strictly book learning and what we did when we rode the submarine at sea, learning. There was really no depth to that degree of training at that point in my life, so it was a very short interview. He told me to stand higher. Ultimately, I didn't. I stayed the same as I was when I went down there. He never made an issue out of it, never asked me to report back to him or do anything out of the ordinary.

I then went from the submarine school to nuclear power training, which was in New London, for six months, then six months in a prototype. I went from there to the *Trident* and directly to Hawaii for this department head tour on *Tecumseh.* . . . From that job in command I was early selected. When I came back here to Washington as a captain, I checked into Rickover's shop to run the prospective commanding officers' course in the propulsion plant. I was the senior naval officer on his staff for the last two years of his tour of duty at Naval Reactors. I stayed on a third year when Admiral Kin McKee relieved Admiral Rickover. I worked for Admiral McKee, doing the same job that I did in fleet liaison, working on the difficulties that came up, trying to help find solutions to the problems we were having.

Asked if the nuclear program would have been as successful under anybody else's leadership, Chiles said:

How many people are indispensable in this world? You might say General of the Army George C. Marshall was indispensable to President Roosevelt. But who is to say that someone else could not have done the job other than Rickover? I think Admiral Rickover moved that program faster in its early years than anyone available to the Navy could have done at that time . . . because he knew what he wanted, he understood the technology, and he brought together absolutely superb people to work the technical problems who were expert in their area. In the early days of his tenure, he got whoever he wanted. In my judgment most of the senior people in the submarine and nuclear surface program let Admiral Rickover get the best that he could get. . . . Admiral Rickover would bring the people in for interviews both to go out and to serve aboard nuclear ships, and to serve in Naval Reactors. He interviewed specifically for people for the jobs. He got some very good people to come into Naval Reactors from the naval ROTC, and other engineering graduates coming directly out of college. That was his principal recruiting source. Now, when he formed the program early in the late 1940s, he picked known quantities, but thereafter, he home-grew his engineers inside of Naval Reactors. . . .

Admiral Rickover's clout with Congress was relatively unprecedented because of his reliability. He did what he said he was going to do and had a magnificent track record . . . of not overloading his tail, and when he said he was going to do something, he did it. He knew that his people would be able to deliver it. I felt like he had a very strong background, not that he was the technical expert on every facet of that program, but he really built a wonderful team because he was good at picking the right people who would deliver for him.

The hierarchy of the Navy wasn't too crazy about him, and [he] never would have made admiral had it been up to the Navy hierarchy. . . . He was abrasive and he didn't suffer fools very kindly. He saw as his vision that nuclear power was the right future for the United States Navy and its capital ships, that you didn't need to be tied to a tanker or a logistics tether that was inordinately long, that you could put double the ammunition and one and a half times as much aviation fuel on your carriers by virtue of going with nuclear energy. The efficiency and operating capability before nuclear power was terrible on those ships.

There were other people that saw it as a real drain on physical resources and did not see eye to eye with him. There was only so many dollars in the budget within the Navy. It was a competitive environment. I don't think there's a significant hue and cry against the nuclear carrier today. I believe people realize the value of these ships. It certainly became the future, and it deserves careful attention to make sure we're buying the right ships for the future.

Should Admiral Rickover have stayed on active duty until he was eighty-two years old? Now that's a question I can't answer for you. His faculties were still good for his age, and you could have a good serious conversation with him. I don't think he wanted to retire. I think that his turnover with Admiral McKee was not the most pleasant in the world, but I'll let Admiral McKee talk to that.[15]

Admiral Watkins was present in Washington, D.C., when Admiral Rickover was finally retired. "A few of us worked hard to help ensure that a smooth transition to new leadership would take place," he told me.

In the fall of 1981 I was called back to Washington, D.C., at the behest of Admiral Hayward, then the CNO, and tasked to prepare everything necessary to assist in effecting a good transition from Admiral Rickover to his successor. I was CinCPacFlt at the time. I asked Bill Wegner to help me prepare the executive branch directives which would be required to accomplish this. Our first move was to discuss our planned approach with key supportive House and Senate leaders such as Scoop Jackson, Mel Price, and a number of other Armed Services Committee members, many of whom had served on the former Joint Committee on Atomic Energy during the early days when the Atomic Energy Commission was still in being. Our common objective, with their strong backing, was to put into place all the "best of Rickover," if you will, to insure against any raid on his well-proven standards or practices. Since time was then very short to effect legislative protection, Wegner and I set our sights on executive orders and related DoD directives, knowing that legislation would eventually be required to help guard against any future political mischief with the nuclear power program. We prepared all needed documentation, sent it forward from Navy to the secretary of defense, and to the White House. All this was done with congressional knowledge. Documents were then signed by the president, the secretaries of defense and navy, and were ready for implementation by the admiral's birthday, a date set by the administration for his retirement. Wegner and I were amazed at how easily we marched our documentation through the normally hazardous route for such matters. But the "old man" himself helped us. How? Well, he felt he had been rather shabbily treated by the administration in what he viewed as a stealthy forced retirement move. As a result, he let them have some of his well-known broadsides and the administration was then ready to sign almost anything at that point to move the process along . . . a classic Rickover maneuver. . . . The most important transition document was a presidential executive order which set the stage for everything else. This executive order was turned into statute in 1983 during Admiral McKee's tour. Admiral Rickover's visionary dream was now protected by law. By the way, it was another NR graduate, Mel Greer, who was a key member of the House appropriations staff at that time who helped shepherd this legislation through Congress. Those trained by Rickover were fast moving into other influential decision-making bodies in the government.[16]

Former secretary of the navy John Lehman took considerable credit for retiring Rickover, I noted to Admiral Hayward. "It was my impression, however, that you had the real responsibility for Rickover retiring," I said. "Am I correct?"

That is accurate. Without any details, because I don't think they need to be talked about, . . . as I recollect Admiral Rickover was eighty-one, and he had two or three minor heart attacks. So, one of the very first things I asked him to do was tell me what his plan was for his retirement. The plan to retire him started within a month of the time I was made CNO with Rickover's cooperation, but John Lehman, and unfortunately Cap Weinberger, disliked Rickover so badly, they wanted to drum him out. We went to significant effort to let the guy go out with some pride. He did an incredible job for this country. He just didn't recognize when it was time to go. We, on the uniform side, wanted in his retirement to treat him with the dignity he deserved.

I asked Admiral Hayward how he gained Admiral Rickover's support for the retirement.

Basically it was with recognition by me that right off the bat that I had the job of doing that. At some point I was going to do it, one way or the other, within the first month of the tour. I invited him over for lunch, which we had very frequently, and basically I said, "Admiral, you're eighty-one years old. No telling what can happen to you. You've already had a couple of heart attacks." Admiral Rickover wanted to know what my succession plan was for him. "Well, I don't have one," I told him. "Don't you worry about this . . . it's all taken care of." . . . I had to take it from there, build a succession plan, and execute it, but I didn't educate him. He would not cooperate to that extent, but he just knew it was going to happen. We were lucky in the sense that [some of] his very strong supporters in the Congress . . . had died. Senator Scoop Jackson and Senator Stennis were getting pretty old, but they recognized themselves that Rickover at eighty was old, and that helped us a lot. From captain on, every future promotion he got was through the Congress. Every two years he had to be reappointed, I would give him a lot of credit. He did one whale of a job when you figure we've got the best nuclear capability in the world.[17]

Adm. Kinnaird R. McKee was selected to succeed Admiral Rickover in 1982. The description of him in *Blind Man's Bluff,* quoted below, provides insight into his personality, character, leadership, and exceptional operational experience:

Kinnaird R. McKee, a lithe southern gentleman with bushy eyebrows and a showman's flair. He had set the standard for surveillance operations when he was on the USS *Dace* (SSN-607), and even [though] McKee's stellar command was nearly over . . . in 1969, he stood as an icon in the sub force. In 1967, McKee had not only photographed a Soviet nuclear-powered icebreaker as it was being towed, but he grabbed radioactive air samples that proved the ship had suffered a reactor accident. The next year, in one breathtaking mission, McKee collected the first close-up photographs and sound signatures of not one but two of the second generation of Soviet nuclear-powered subs: an attack sub and a cruise missile sub that NATO had named the "Victor" and the "Charlie." He had found one of the new subs in the waters off Novaya Zemlya, a large island between the Barents and Kara Seas that was one of the Soviets' main nuclear test areas.

. . . McKee had been detected. Indeed . . . he had snapped a photograph of a Soviet crew member standing on the deck of one of the subs and pointing right at the *Dace*'s periscope just before the Soviets began to chase. McKee had to outrace a group of Soviet surface patrols pinging wildly with active sonar. He finally managed his escape by driving *Dace* straight under the hazardous reaches of the Arctic ice. When it was safe to emerge, he continued his mission, locating the second new Soviet sub within a week.

"Gentlemen, the price of poker has just gone up in the Barents Sea," McKee announced on his return at a session with the Joint Chiefs of Staff and members of the Defense Department. With typical flair, he captured his audience with a briefing no less dramatic for his exclusion of the detection and his omission of the shot of the Soviet crewman pointing at *Dace*.

McKee's presentation and his slide show of other photographs shot through his scope went over so well that his immediate superiors never thought to criticize him for allowing his sub to be detected. Instead, for McKee, the mission was marred only by the fact that the Navy had refused to let him name the Soviet submarines he had found.[18]

I asked Admiral McKee if it was true that he had initially been turned down for the submarine service. He answered:

I was turned down two times for submarine school; twice for diesel boats. From the destroyer that was my first duty station, I applied for submarine training and didn't make the cut. I had to wait another year to apply. So I waited another year and applied again, but I didn't make the cut then either. I don't know why. They don't ever tell you that.

I thought, "Well, I've had my tail chewed a couple of times on this ship; maybe that's showing up in my fitness reports!" (It never did, as a matter of fact.) I thought, "I'm a pretty good destroyer officer, so I'm going to be all right," but at the next opportunity I put in for submarines again. I didn't make the cut that time either. At that point I was a little upset about the whole thing. So, I decided, "Well, I'm going to do something different." I applied for graduate education at MIT and was accepted. Then, at the last minute, the detailer called and said, "We've got a seat in this submarine school class; do you want it?" I thought about that for a long time, but finally said, yeah, I do.

After I'd qualified in submarines, my first skipper recommended me for nuclear power training in the first officer class of nuclear power trainees. I was not even selected for an interview, much less for the program. Then I went on to other things. I served on two other diesel submarines, then became officer in charge of the X-1, a five-man submarine. It was a midget submarine, similar to the X-craft that the British used to sink a German battleship during World War II. In that job, I was effectively in command. My title was "officer in charge" because it was in-service rather than a commissioned ship.

At the end of that tour I was called down for an interview. I said to myself, at least I'm going to get in this time. . . . The interview sort of followed the conventional process at the time. There was one difference. One of Admiral Rickover's very senior people interviewed me. I didn't spend a lot of time with the customary questions. My interviewer's principal questions were, "What is the

X-1? How does it work? What kind of problems do you have?" It was not a short interview. I went to the blackboard, drew engineering diagrams, and explained. . . . That was my interview. They must have decided that I was a reasonably good prospect if I could figure out how to make that little boat work.

My interview with Admiral Rickover was very short. He asked me why [I] had not done better at the Naval Academy and in submarine school. I told him I had stood fifty-one in the class and USNA. "That's not what it says here," he replied. I said, "Sir, you must have been misinformed." Then he said, "And you didn't do well at submarine diesel school." I said, "Well, I stood number two in the class." And he said, "It says right here—" And I said, "I don't care what it says right there; I stood number two." Then he said, "Get out!" I thought, well, that's the end of that. I wasn't feeling too bad because everything was working for me with X-1 at that time.

McKee subsequently served in four nuclear submarines, the first of which was *Skipjack* (SSN 585), commanded by Bill Behrens. From 1964 to 1966 Admiral McKee was on Rickover's Naval Reactors staff. Rickover was a demanding boss, but it was a reasonably structured schedule.

The good news was that you got to spend time with your family. Admiral Rickover's shop opened at eight and closed at six, unless there was something very important or unexpected going on. Most jobs in the Pentagon went into the late evening hours almost every day. On the other hand, we always worked Saturdays, and we usually worked holidays. There was no such thing as a holiday in NR. But it was worth it. I thoroughly enjoyed my association with the people in that organization. They were very professional, very tough, and very competent.

Some of Admiral McKee's comments offer insight into Admiral Rickover's success in developing an efficient and safe nuclear submarine.

One of my other responsibilities at NR was to present to Admiral Rickover the slate for CO, XO, and engineer assignments in each of the nuclear ships. The BuPers detailer made the slates, but Admiral Rickover approved the assignment of each CO, XO, and engineer. In the case of the carriers, he also approved the assignment of the reactor officer as well. I was the staff guy who had to take those recommendations to him for approval.

The submarine detailers would send over their recommendations. We would evaluate the officers concerned, based on what we knew about them in the areas where Naval Reactors had a direct interest. We did not comment on whether they might or might not be good tactical operators. That was the detailer's responsibility. On the other hand, we knew most of the eligible people in the submarine community. In addition, the PCOs [prospective commanding officers] all came to NR for three months' training. I ran that program at that time. Each PCO had already proved himself competent in his engineer and exec tours as far as the nuclear propulsion aspects of those roles were concerned, and was also depicted as "qualified for command."

Some people, usually those who were not fond of Admiral Rickover, tried to make the case that we just chose officers who would be good engineers with no regard for whether or not they were skilled tacticians. The idea was clearly wrong, and recently disclosed information makes that apparent. Everybody kept very quiet about SSN operations until *Blind Man's Bluff* was published last year.

From 1962 to 1964 I had served as executive officer of USS *Sam Houston,* a Polaris missile submarine. I had been told I would make three patrols. I was getting ready to go on the third one when the officer who had been Bill Behrens's relief on *Skipjack* became the officer detailer. He called me down to Washington and said, "You're going to command after this patrol." I asked for a ship that had recently completed a refueling overhaul and got my orders to command of *Seadragon* before we sailed on the third patrol in *Sam Houston.* I left feeling pretty good about everything.

However, about ten days from port on the way home from that patrol I received a familygram from my wife. It said, "Your orders [to command] are canceled. You will relieve Dan Summitt in Naval Reactors." It was almost a guarantee of being the last guy in my class to go to command. I didn't mind going to the job, but the timing was unfortunate. Jim Watkins, later the chief of naval operations, had something to do with those orders. He was just leaving the senior line officer slot in the NR staff. I would be number two of three line officers in NR. I asked the detailer who I would have to see to get the orders changed. He suggested that I talk to Admiral Rickover. Bill Behrens told me to "shut up and carry out my orders." I did that.

It was rarely fun to do anything with Admiral Rickover. He was very abrupt. He always managed to ask the question to which you didn't quite know the answer. He rarely agreed with anything the first time. He would really grill you about the subject at hand. "How do you know about this guy? What do you know?" And so forth. But that was the way he did business. I really couldn't fault him; I just didn't enjoy it much.

But an interesting thing happened in connection with my departure [from NR]. I was in position to exercise some influence over what ship I might get, had I chosen to exercise it. Of course, to some folks on the outside it might have appeared to be more than that, so I was reticent about being ordered to a new boat (something new and dashing). Therefore, I asked the detailer to send me to *Nautilus*. (I had been exec of that ship.) *Nautilus* was going through major overhaul. She would be a substantially better warship after that overhaul. . . . The detailer sent his recommendation over to that effect. Admiral Rickover disapproved it.

I was very surprised. Years later, I learned that he thought I should have a newer ship than that. At the time I was upset, but in the end, it turned out that he had done me a great favor. I went to *Dace*, an almost-new 594-class submarine, and had a successful command tour in that boat.[19]

I asked Admiral McKee to tell me about his selection to succeed Admiral Rickover after the latter's retirement in 1982.

I was not the only officer to be considered for the job. One other four-star submarine admiral was also considered. I believe that Rickover had initially agreed for me to take the job, but as soon as it was decided that I would be the one, he apparently had concluded that I had become part of a "cabal" that was trying to send him into retirement.

There was a lot of discussion about how to effect the relief. The administration's eagerness to have the relief go off smoothly put me in a good position to manage the process (and the job) to best advantage (I also had a lot of help from others). For example, John Lehman initially suggested that I go to NR as Admiral Rickover's deputy for six months to learn the job. I told him: "Absolutely not. The landscape is littered with heirs apparent to senior jobs—in industry, in the Navy, anywhere you want to go. I know Admiral Rickover well enough to know that that idea just won't work. The thing for me to do is just go over there and relieve him as quickly as possible." John agreed.

Admiral McKee spoke at length on the challenges he faced in relieving Admiral Rickover.

I have often been asked what it was like to relieve Admiral Rickover in an organization that had no other leader since its inception. The simple answer is that it was not an easy thing to do. In . . . an earlier and completely unrehearsed reply to the question I said: "It was sort of like trying to step in behind Bear Bryant as the Alabama football coach."

The relieving process began in late November 1981 when I was told that Admiral Rickover was to be retired and that I had been selected to replace him. He had run a great program, but would be 82 years old at the expiration of his latest two-year extension on active duty. It was through two-year extensions beyond the mandatory retirement age of 65 that Admiral Rickover remained in charge of the program. These extensions were sometimes approved with little opposition. At other times, they were bitterly contested at the highest levels of the administration in office at the time. In such instances, the issue had usually been resolved through congressional intervention.

This time, there would be no congressional intervention. The decision not to reappoint the admiral did not indicate a lack of respect for his past accomplishments, for his program, or for the people therein. It simply reflected the fact that the statistical chances of incapacity were increasing each year. It was time for a successor, but it was highly unlikely that Admiral Rickover would step down of his own accord. There was no heir apparent waiting in the wings to replace him. For years he managed the program without a formally designated deputy. He had acceded to Navy pressure to appoint one only following a heart attack some years before.

The CNO [Admiral Hayward] decided that Admiral Rickover's successor should be a naval officer with sound Naval Nuclear Propulsion Program credentials as well as experience in other parts of the Navy. I was selected for that assignment. . . .

Upon my arrival, it soon became apparent that Admiral Rickover had no intention of becoming directly involved in a traditional turnover; however, he would not allow anything to interfere with the relieving process. With his full knowledge and acquiescence, his staff and other key program personnel, including contractors, invested substantial effort in bringing me up to date and in educating me in areas which I knew very little.

I met individually with some twenty-two Naval Reactors section heads who reported directly to the admiral and with key prime contractor personnel on-site throughout the program. Without saying so, Admiral Rickover knew that this was exactly what I needed; not handholding from him. He also maintained a hands-off attitude toward our efforts to develop a presidential executive order that would codify the responsibilities and authority of the Director, Naval Nuclear Propulsion. He was also quite aware of extensive efforts by his staff who, working with former Naval Reactors officials and others, were quietly developing the language of that document.

President Reagan signed an executive order coincident with Admiral Rickover's retirement and Congress incorporated it into law the following year. That document would prove crucial to any success I might achieve as the director, insulating me and the program against those who might try to take advantage of his retirement to restructure the program and reduce its influence.

My first and final meeting with Admiral Rickover followed all of this. Not unexpectedly, it was very much to the point. I called on him for the first time on the last Saturday morning before he retired. I will never forget his sensitivity to my potentially difficult situation, or his appreciation of what would most set my mind at ease. In essence, he told me this: "When we are through talking today, I will go home. I will not return. When you arrive on Monday, this program will be your responsibility. I expect I will be asked from time to time what you are doing and how well you are doing it. I will tell them I do not know. That will be the truth. I will not attempt to get into your business unless you ask for my help." He kept his word, as I knew he would. That commitment was a very generous and critically important act on his part.

With my "training program" completed, I started my first day on the job knowing much more than I had ever known about the Naval Reactors program, but still well aware of how much there was to learn. The staff was ready and so was I. No significant loss of key personnel was expected unless I somehow evidenced less than their commitment to the high standards of the Program. There were no departures other than in due course. I also had a clear commitment of presidential and congressional support for the program as it was structured. . . . I would not make fundamental changes in the program or attempt to emulate Admiral Rickover's longevity on the job, but would plan to serve the prescribed eight years and would have one or more qualified successors in a position to relieve me. I would not try to emulate Admiral Rickover in his role as gadfly on public policy issues.[20]

How did he get along with Rickover's civilian staff?

One of my greatest fears about undertaking to relieve Admiral Rickover was that a number of his key staff might leave because of what they perceived as the high-handed way in which his departure was handled. Conventional wisdom had predicted that if he were forced out of office, a number of his senior people would walk away. He had extraordinarily talented and experienced people on his staff who continued to serve him well beyond the minimum times (either on active duty or in civil service), primarily out of loyalty to him and commitment to the job. None were adequately compensated for what they did, and they didn't have to stay. One of my senior section heads was solicited by a British industrial firm while I was there. They offered him over $300,000 per year to come to the U.K. and work in their nuclear propulsion program. He elected to stay at NR for his sixty or seventy thousand dollars a year, whatever it was at the time. That could have been a fragile situation. The key factor was that our principal players had come to believe that fundamental NR principles would not change when I relieved the admiral. They recognized that some details would have to change, because I'm a different guy—but the fundamentals upon which the program was established would remain in place.[21]

While he was careful in dealing with the brilliant civilians in NR, one of the most important things McKee did right after assuming the directorship of the program was to establish that *he* was in charge. "One other event that occurred right after I relieved was interesting," he related.

An old Rickover hand (who had been retired for some time) approached the secretary of energy with a proposal. (That secretary had no technical background at all.) His proposal was to establish a group of advisers (to whom I would report) with himself as chairman. They would oversee my work. The secretary of energy told me of the proposal and asked for my opinion. I told him it was unacceptable. He acknowledged his lack of technical background and said, "Well I just need a way to have confidence in what you are doing." I told him that if he did not have confidence in me he should find another officer to do the job. It was that simple. I didn't really care. This was not a job to become involved in without the independence and authority to do it the way it had to be done. NR was unlike any other job in the Navy. Relieving as any other four-star billet is a pretty straightforward process. This was unique. It was then and it still is.

I mentioned the presidential directive earlier. I had [the secretary of the navy's] agreement that it would be in law before I relieved (rather than a presidential directive). But the clock was running; we were at the end of the authorization and appropriation cycle, so it went forward as a presidential directive. It did so quietly, because there appeared to be some serious industrial opposition to a formal definition of NR's authority and responsibilities. Both of the submarine shipbuilders, as well as other industrial players, did not want to see these rules codified in law. They had seen Rickover's departure as an opportunity for the organization to be made more like the rest of the Navy.[22]

The presidential directive became law the following year.

Admiral McKee's successor as director of the Navy's nuclear program was Adm. Bruce DeMars. Like the others involved in the early years of the program, DeMars was personally interviewed by Admiral Rickover—in DeMars's case, twice. The first interview, he told me,

> didn't last very long. He asked me why I hadn't stood as well academically at submarine school as I had at the Naval Academy. They had told us to be honest, so I said, "Well, we lived in back in married officers' quarters essentially right next to the golf course. I played too much golf." He threw me out. They gave me some books to go off and study. I went off and studied for three months. He gave me a math book and physics books, and I had to come back and take an exam, which I did.
>
> I went back in for the second interview, and he asked me if I smoked cigars. I said, "Occasionally, sir." He was first admiral I ever talked to in the Navy. He pulled out a box and opened it up. It was a cruddy old dry cigar. He flipped it across and he said, "Go ahead and smoke that and write me a report on it." So I did that. I wasn't really sure what this was all about. Was he really serious? I had kind of a feeling that he was. I didn't want to appear too flip, so I wrote a very standard Navy form letter from Lieutenant Bruce DeMars to . . . Admiral Rickover, subject: cigar. And I said that it probably was a pretty good cigar at one time, but I recommended that he upgrade the storage facilities, Very Respectfully. . . . That went in. I sat around for three or four hours. Finally somebody came in and said okay, you've been accepted.

In discussing the obstacles Rickover had to overcome in his promotion to rear admiral, DeMars commented: "The system maybe didn't recognize him as it should have, and Congress had to rescue him, make him an admiral. But after that I think there was a recognition, grudging in some cases, that this man really was a genius, and they just overlooked his faults."[23]

During extensive interviews with Adm. Frank B. Kelso II (CNO 1990–94), I asked, "Would the nuclear program have gone as rapidly, as efficiently, and as safely without Admiral Rickover?" He responded:

Of course, that's a speculative question. From my observation of quite a few years in the Navy and this town [i.e., Washington, D.C.], I've never seen anybody else who could pull off a program that he pulled off. Have you ever seen a naval officer who had as much clout as he did with Congress? I haven't. He could not have accomplished what he did without the support of Congress. There's no question he would not have made admiral without the support of Congress. . . .

No one ever dreamed you could put a nuclear reactor in a submarine. . . . It was the genius of Rickover to have those kinds of ideas. I think he was a unique individual. A lot of people don't think Rickover was a leader. I don't agree with that. He was a different kind of leader—he was not the conventional kind of leader we think about. For instance, command—he never really had a command, but he was very prominent in the Navy long before nuclear power. He was chief of the Electrical Bureau of Ships in World War II. Many of the safety procedures developed during World War II were Rickover's ideas. A lot of people forgot that. For the people who worked with the old man every day, it wasn't a pleasant day, but they loved the fact he let them do their job. He might chew them out if he didn't like what they did, but he would talk to them. They could argue with him. He didn't care if you argued with him. A lot of people misunderstood Rickover, thought that if he called you and yelled at you, you were in bad shape. Instead, if he stopped calling you and yelling at you, you were in trouble. That meant he didn't have any confidence to talk to you anymore. Now that's not easy to live with. It's not a leadership style I would espouse, nor could I possibly ever do because that's not my personality.

He was the most impersonal man I have ever seen . . . but being impersonal allowed him to make very good decisions, because he did not let personal relationship get in the way of his decisions. Again, I wouldn't want to live that way, but that's the way I saw him. I worked for him for three years at Nuclear Power School in Bainbridge, Maryland, in command of the school, 1969 to 1971.

He was my direct boss. I remember when I went by to see him to go up there to work, I thought, "Well, this is going to be a hell of a job. I'm going to get yelled at every day." I walked into his office and he gave me about two minutes and he said to me: "You go up there and run that place like you own it and it will all go all right." That's all he said. So I went up there and started working. . . . I . . . worked for him for three years. I was a lieutenant commander. The school was over 2,500 kids. I had the largest Navy school in Bainbridge . . . at the time, as a lieutenant commander. You see, that was Rickover. He didn't care much about rank, he cared about competence. I don't mean he didn't want to get promoted, it's just that that was not his issue. I could have been a first-class boatswain's mate, and with his backing have been all right. He backed you to hell freezes over if he thought you were right. He would also be on your fanny if he thought you were wrong.

I remember I made a change once and it didn't work very well. I had not talked with him about the change before I made it. After that I made sure I talked with him—he told me about the change: "You dummy. We tried that ten years ago and it didn't work—when you're going to make any changes, let me know so I can tell you what's right and what's wrong." But he didn't tell me not to do it. He just told me after it was over with that it was a dumb idea. On two occasions he called me and told me I was doing a good job up there—keep at it—so he wasn't all bad. I enjoyed working for him, but there was very little discourse. He sent his people up to see what we were doing.

That was the first job I ever had where as an officer I could hold mast. This was a time . . . when . . . people were running off to Canada, so it was not an easy time to be taking care of 2,500 kids. Many chose the Navy because they were smart and didn't want to be drafted into the Army and go to Vietnam, so they were not all that excited when they got there to my school. A lot of those kinds of things were taking place, and I wouldn't say everything was sweet every day. Rickover accepted all that. He understood what was going on. His organization was, technically, very competent. . . .

He let [his staff] do their work. He listened to them—he yelled at them— but they could yell back at him. Lot of people say, "Rickover may be awful, but he was almost always right, when you look at it, he made the right decisions." You look back at the technical decisions he made, it was amazing the decisions he made, and how right he was. . . .

I willingly volunteered for the program because it was pretty clear . . . that . . . the way of the future was in nuclear submarines. . . . There wasn't going to be a future in submarines if you were not in nuclear submarines. In fact, most of my classmates that were in diesel submarines and remained in diesel submarines were limited in their career. There wasn't any chance for them for command because the diesel subs were all going away.[24]

My interview with Adm. Steven Angelo White produced an excellent illustration of Rickover's judgment in picking the best people. White confirmed a story I had heard about the chair used in Rickover interviews. One of the front legs had been made shorter than the other, he said, "so you felt uncomfortable." He was with a group of other young men being interviewed, and noted that the sessions with Rickover seemed to be going very quickly:

> They called the first guy out and he went to see Rickover. And about three minutes later, they called another guy out to see Rickover. About every three minutes, guys were going. They were short interviews. Very short. It was interesting because . . . I was in there for about twenty-five minutes. . . . It went on and on, and he asked me where did I stand in my high school class? I stood number two. "Why didn't you stand number one?" "Well, there was a girl that was smarter than I was." He said, "You let a girl be smarter than you?"
>
> "When did you mature?" he asked me. "You're twenty-six now [or whatever my age was]. When did you mature?" I said maturing was a lifelong thing, you mature constantly throughout life. He said, "You are twenty-six and you're not yet matured. Do you realize that Jesus Christ was twelve when he chased the money changers out of the temple?" I lost my temper. I said something sarcastic. At this point I figured I'm through. I said to myself, I've been here long enough that obviously he's toying with me and I've failed. I raised my voice and I said, "Don't compare me to Jesus Christ because I'm not Jesus Christ."
>
> Then he asked one more question and that was it. They had told us in this briefing beforehand that you'll know when it's over and when it's over get up, turn around, and leave the room. Don't say anything. Just get up and leave. . . . So I stood up and I turned around and walked toward the door, and he said, "White." I turned around and said, "Yes, sir." He held out his hand across the desk. I want to tell you that years later I reflected on all of this. Why did he do that? I came back and shook his hand and then left. And I thought why did he do that? What was it?[25]

The commanding officer of the nuclear school when Lt. Steven White attended was Comdr. Bill Behrens (later CO on *Skipjack*), who was horrified to learn that White had not taken mathematics in college. Behrens, White later discovered, "called Rickover and said, 'There's been a mistake.' Rickover said, 'What do you mean a mistake? What's the mistake?' 'We've got this guy here, Lt. (jg) White, and he's checked into the school. He's not had any college mathematics.' Rickover said, 'God damn it, Behrens, I pick them, you teach them.'"

White was a good choice for the school, as it turned out. He achieved the rank of admiral and was one of the candidates considered to replace

Rickover upon his retirement. "It was hard, hard work for me to succeed," he continued. "I would study until 2:00 A.M., up at 6:00 A.M., often getting up during that four-hour period to work a problem and go back to bed. I didn't own a slide rule or know how to use it. A classmate loaned me an extra one he had, and I proceeded to take a self-study crash program to learn to use it. I would never have succeeded without it."

I asked Admiral White if he thought the nuclear program would have developed as rapidly without Rickover. "No," he said, citing Rickover's vision, personality, toughness, and support in Congress. "He was a . . . unique individual. . . . The way he set it up was to set himself up with two hats—one Navy and one Atomic Energy Commission." When Rickover wanted to do something, White explained, he would write a letter from his Navy self to his AEC self, and the latter would give the former permission to proceed.

Rickover's rapport with Congress developed because he was so good at what he did. "For example," White said, "he'd go to a committee and he'd testify and they'd give him so much money. They'd give him this many millions of dollars and he'd come back the next year and say you know, I didn't use all that money and we were able to do some things, so I want to return some. What military guy ever returned money? So he got whatever he asked for because they said this guy is obviously doing everything he can. Would anyone else have been so successful? If you looked in those days at what he did, I'm not sure, you might find somebody else who could have done it, but I don't know who the hell it would have been.

Admiral White offered an excellent example of the lengths to which Rickover was willing to go to retain the people who made his program work. As a commander, White decided he was going to leave the Navy. "People were surprised to hear I was getting out," he told me. "I had been selected early for lieutenant commander, several years early, and then for commander, it was kind of fast. So Rickover looked at me and said, "It's money, then?" I said yes. He said: "All right, if it's money, I'll loan you what you need. I'll loan what you need and I won't even charge you interest." . . . So what could I say? I [had] just told him it was money, and he had really called my bluff. I stayed."[26]

Admiral Rickover died on July 8, 1986, at the age of eighty-six. The many obituaries and acknowledgments that commemorated his passing confirmed his contributions to the U.S. Navy. The *Washington Post*'s obituary, for example, called Rickover "one of the most influential military figures of the post–World War II era not only because he conceived and engineered the submarine nuclear technology that revolutionized the Navy, but because of a seemingly inexhaustible energy and flamboyance that mobilized broad public and congressional support for his programs. Both his technological vision, and the way he often bulldozed his way through bureaucratic roadblocks to pursue it, were recalled by his colleagues and admirers yesterday." The *Post* went on to quote President Ronald Reagan, who stated: "Admiral Rickover's commitment to excellence and uncompromising devotion to duty were an integral part of American life for a generation. . . . He was also a revered teacher who instilled in his pupils a desire to strive for the highest achievements. Countless thousands of sailors benefited from the skill and expertise of this talented public servant. Though he worked on tools of defense, he was a man of peace." Former president Jimmy Carter, who after his graduation from the Naval Academy entered Rickover's nuclear program, took Rickover's motto "Why not the best?" for his political slogan. "As president," he said, "I realized anew his great contributions to our nation's preparedness and to world peace."[27]

Admiral Rickover was not a patient man in his drive to serve and protect the United States. His abrasiveness extended beyond the Navy and civilian contractors he worked with on a daily basis. In a nationally televised 1958 interview with the revered reporter Edward R. Murrow on CBS, Rickover castigated Murrow for asking "stupid questions" about education in America. "The trouble with you is that you want easy answers, but you don't know the proper questions."

His *Washington Post* obituary commented: "Despite the fact that he trained thousands of officers for service aboard nuclear-powered ships, Admiral Rickover never made peace with the Navy establishment. He thought its rules were silly and its traditions a waste of time. 'We never had a book of Navy regulations in my office,' he said on *60 Minutes* in

December of 1984. 'One time some guy brought it in and I told him to get the hell out and burn it.'"

It takes time to evaluate a person's contribution to history and to his country—some historians believe fifty years must pass before an accurate evaluation can be made. At the ceremony celebrating the fiftieth anniversary of the Naval Reactors organization on August 30, 1998, Adm. James D. Watkins offered such an evaluation of Admiral Rickover:

> Shortly after his death, I was requested by Eleanore [Rickover's wife] to give Admiral Rickover's eulogy at the memorial ceremony which was held here at the National Cathedral in 1986. I opened my remarks by employing a simple quotation from Voltaire in which he tried to capture the essence of a purpose of life as follows: "Not to be occupied, and not to exist, are one and the same thing." And I can think of no man who better epitomized that tough standard. For Admiral Rickover *was* occupied. He was a unique individual who accomplished great deeds through hard work and struggle, and thereby gained the respect of a nation and the world. He was an original thinker who dared to peer beyond boundaries set by others, and therefore accomplished that about which others only dreamed. This was a special American: naval professional, visionary, intellectual, engineer, iconoclast, and most importantly, teacher.[28]

Admiral Elmo R. Zumwalt Jr., CNO 1970–1974

On July 1, 1970, Adm. Elmo Russell Zumwalt Jr. succeeded Adm. Thomas H. Moorer as chief of naval operations, jumping over thirty-three more senior admirals. The appointment capped a meteoric rise through the ranks. At forty-nine years of age, Zumwalt was the youngest four-star admiral in U.S. Navy history and the youngest ever to serve as CNO. The active strength of the Navy at that time was 696,000 men. Ten years before he became CNO he had been a relatively low-ranking commander. Five years earlier he had been the youngest naval officer ever promoted to the rank of rear admiral. Not since President Dwight D. Eisenhower selected Adm. Arleigh Burke as CNO, jumping ninety-two senior admirals, had a commander in chief reached so deeply into the ranks to select a new chief of naval operations.

Zumwalt was a 1943 graduate of the Naval Academy, graduating one year early because of World War II. His sea duty took place in surface ships.

The three previous CNOs—Adm. George W. Anderson Jr. (1961–63), Adm. David L. McDonald (1963–67), and Adm. Thomas H. Moorer (1967–70)—were former naval aviators. While he brought youth and image to the office, he did not have as much experience as his predecessors and had never held a major fleet command.

Admiral Moorer was openly opposed to his selection. Moorer commented on the appointment:

> I did not approve of Admiral Zumwalt. As a matter of fact, I wrote a letter to that effect to the secretary of the navy and secretary of defense. When Admiral Zumwalt was called to Washington for an interview, he stayed first with the undersecretary of the navy, John Warner. Then I invited him up to my quarters, the admiral's house. I told him, "Before you come into my house, I want to tell you that I did not recommend you for this assignment. I feel that you have had limited experience in major command. I feel that you are a man of great talents, but that being the case, I think it's unfair to the Navy to put you in a position where you will be retired at an early age and the Navy will not have an opportunity to take advantage of what you can do."

Admiral Moorer believed that his own somewhat adversarial relationship with Secretary of the Navy John Chafee was a factor in Zumwalt's selection. He reflected: "I really didn't get along well with Chafee, because we were so different in our thinking. He also thought that anyone who was older than he was an idiot. He set out to try to make certain that the admirals who were brought up were younger than he was. I think that was one of the reasons he was red-hot for Zumwalt to be my successor, a matter with which I disagreed in writing."[29]

Admiral Zumwalt assumed the responsibility of CNO at a challenging time for the Navy—indeed for all the military services. The Vietnam War was increasingly unpopular, and the administration's will to win, never very strong, was deteriorating. The cold war with the Soviet Union was escalating, and the USSR had a rapidly growing navy. The number of active U.S. fleet ships had declined from 769 to 512 between 1970 and 1974, and many of those still in service had been built during World War II and were obsolete or becoming so. The older ships required more and more maintenance, and once-routine repairs became harder and harder to accomplish. The constant struggle to keep the old ships operational put a severe strain on the Navy's resources. Morale was very, very low.

Zumwalt faced an uphill battle. The Navy's budget continued to decline, and he was required to make tough decisions on how to spend the scarce resources allocated in the defense budget. The CNOs who preceded him, aviators all, had made a strong effort to maintain the carrier force; and Adm. Hyman Rickover's popularity with Congress had ensured the allocation of funds to maintain the nuclear submarine fleet. But the surface navy needed immediate attention. Money had to be found to replace the aging ships.

Even with the seemingly boundless energy he brought to the job, Zumwalt could do very little to reverse the constant decrease in the budget, which was affecting the Navy's ability to carry out its mission of national defense. He spent some money on ship repairs and the balance on the production of new ships, following a "high-low" strategy. The concept is too complicated to be discussed in depth here, but the strategy's goal was to determine and give priority to the mix of ships best able to cope with the Soviet threat.

The Navy had serious personnel problems as well. Americans were increasingly opposed to the war in Vietnam, and young men resented the draft and the requirement to serve in harm's way in Southeast Asia. Many of the best sailors and officers were leaving the Navy when their obligated service was over. As a consequence, the retention rate in 1970 was only 9 percent, and recruiting was at a very low level. When the draft ended and the U.S. military became all-volunteer, personnel levels fell even lower. Young men and women were not enlisting. Something needed to be done to make service in the Navy more attractive to them.

Naval historian Norman Friedman maintained that Secretary of Defense Melvin R. Laird and Secretary of the Navy John H. Chafee picked Zumwalt because they believed he "would bring ideas to the billet and a different perspective given his background in the surface line."[30] The CNO selected in 1970 would have to be tough—someone who could determine priorities in allocating the increasingly scarce resources and fight the complacency that followed World War II.

Zumwalt was pessimistic about the Navy's readiness to take on the Soviet Union if the need should arise. In his estimation, the odds were in favor of the Soviet Union. As of July 1970 he projected that the United States had only a 55 percent chance of winning a conventional sea battle against the Soviets. If the budget continued as it was going, within the next year the chance would be only 45 percent, and in fiscal year 1973 only 35 percent. Nevertheless, in the increasingly antimilitary atmosphere, Zumwalt was considered an "alarmist" as he went about trying to improve U.S. readiness.[31]

Zumwalt began his tenure as CNO with vigor and determination. His memoir, On Watch, devotes one-fourth of its content to the personnel problems he was presented with and the steps he took to resolve them. He decided to do everything possible to improve motivation, incentive, and esprit de corps in the Navy. In particular, he wanted "to eliminate many of the most abrasive naval regulations and practices, standardize others which are inconsistently enforced throughout the fleet, and provide some general guidance reflecting my conviction that declining Navy retention rates will not be reversed until the worth and personal dignity of the individual are forcefully reaffirmed." He considered that he had been given a mandate by Secretary of Defense Melvin Laird and Secretary of the Navy John Chafee to "bring the Navy into the modern age."[32]

Taking an unorthodox approach, Admiral Zumwalt launched into solving the personnel problems at a furious pace. "While the retention study group program was getting underway," he recalled, "my staff was working on various personnel problems that sailors in Vietnam and the fleet told me about. By the end of July the staff had prepared or was preparing a score more of NAVOPS [naval operations messages] initiating new personnel policies or altering old ones to provide policy or guidance emanating personally from the CNO."[33] The fleet called the CNO's NavOps messages Z-grams. Zumwalt sent 120 such messages during his tenure as CNO, 69 of them during the first six months. He called it a shock approach:

> We were in a catastrophic situation, with the antiwar mood and the antimilitary bias in the country and with the tremendous sacrifices our people were having to make with very long deployments. Our reenlistment rate was at an historic low—9 percent. This meant that over 90,000 of every 100,000 sailors coming in

were leaving at the end of their four years. We had to turn that around. From the standpoint of management alone, [we had to shock the system.] Those were moves we would never make in today's [healthy] Navy.[34]

The Z-grams concentrated on liberalizing regulations currently in existence and establishing new regulations to address personnel problems, aiming toward improving retention and increasing recruitment. Among other things, the Z-grams

- authorized thirty days' leave for officers receiving a permanent change of station;
- started a program to have civilian classes onboard ships;
- started a program to implement a dependent air charter program whereby wives and dependent children could travel to liberty ports frequented by deployed ships, including assistance in obtaining hotel accommodations;
- authorized a sponsorship program for incoming Navy men and their families to assist in adjusting to new assignments;
- extended the hours during which officers could meet with detailers to discuss assignments and career goals;
- evaluated the advancement of certain deserving first-class and chief petty officers;
- permitted enlisted men to wear civilian clothes on all shore activities;
- eliminated many of the collateral duties of junior officers;
- allowed enlisted men to swap assignments with other personnel;
- liberalized check-cashing privileges;
- extended hours for offices processing urgent inquiries concerning pay and other financial matters;
- provided compensatory time off;
- improved basic living facilities;
- established procedures to give Navy wives an opportunity to present their complaints, views, and suggestions to COs;
- authorized and encouraged commanding officers to allow as much as 5 percent of their crews to be on leave when their ships were deployed overseas;

- initiated a pilot program to establish "hard rock" clubs to see if such activities would improve morale among junior officers;
- started a competition among junior officers in ship handling, with winners allowed to pick their next duty station;
- improved inputs of Navy personnel on the way exchanges and commissaries were run;
- allowed alcoholic beverages in room-type barracks and authorized the installation of beer-vending machines in senior bachelor enlisted quarters;
- made it possible for lieutenant commanders to have command of aviation squadrons where previously only commanders could do so;
- reduced where possible work on Sundays and holidays;
- established a policy under which ensigns and lieutenants (jg) could request sea duty as their first choice on their initial obligated service;
- encouraged the assignment of senior petty officers to officer-of-the-deck watches;
- implemented a program whereby flag officers and commanding officers of shore activities could offer increased help to the families of prisoners of war;
- opened a new office in the Bureau of Naval Personnel called PERS-P to ensure the fullest possible communications with individuals throughout the Navy;
- limited to sixty days the time for recommendation and final approval of awards and medals;
- encouraged the liberalizing of leave and liberty policies;
- authorized the annual publication of a list of available billets to permit junior officers to better plan their careers;
- asked for suggestions from the fleet and shore facilities to improve the Navy;
- ordered ships' stores to accept checks in payment for purchases;
- provided the opportunity whereby selected officers could pursue independent research and professional study;
- encouraged free exchange of ideas and recommendations between personnel and the command by asking all major naval installations to install an answering recording device on at least one telephone;

- set up a forum at the Naval War College to include discussions on means to improve the Navy, particularly those aspects relating to personnel policy, with the opportunity to present views directly to the secretary of the navy and the chief naval operations;
- directed each base to have the aircraft squadron commander appoint a minority officer or senior petty officer as an assistant for minority affairs, and ordered Navy exchanges and commissaries to stock food and grooming items designed for African Americans and to hire qualified barbers and beauticians to provide hair care for black personnel;
- offered preferential housing consideration for volunteers for naval advisory duty in Vietnam;
- improved sea/shore rotation provisions;
- offered awards for outstanding recruiters;
- provided copies of personnel fitness reports;
- offered pay advances when needed;
- initiated a drug rehabilitation program;
- established a sailor-of-the-year award; and
- instituted equal rights and opportunities for women.

Admiral Zumwalt issued 10 Z-grams in August 1972, 23 that September, 14 in October, 11 in November, and 6 in December. The Z-grams had enormous impacts on the Navy—some good, some bad, and some very controversial. Z-gram 57, which was issued November 10, 1970, was perhaps the most controversial of them all. Zumwalt planned initially to entitle it "Mickey Mouse, Elimination of," but was persuaded to call it "Demeaning and Abrasive Regulations, Elimination of." It was designed to eliminate a number of regulations that surveys of junior officers and enlisted personnel had indicated were abrasive and demeaning, and it liberalized Navy regulations or practices in a number of areas. The commotion it caused in the middle and upper levels of command surprised Admiral Zumwalt, who commented in his memoir:

> What did surprise me somewhat was how much confusion my way of doing things created among some of the members of the Navy's "middle management."

Looking back now, I can see why some of those captains and commanders and lieutenant commanders out in the field were confused. They had no experience of receiving directives about matters like beards and motorcycles directly from the Chief of Naval Operations, directives moreover that were couched in language as plain and simple as my staff and I could make it and took a tone as urgent as was consistent with common politeness. These individuals evidently took the Z-grams personally, as reproaches directed against them for past misdeeds and warnings to sin no more, rather than as the announcements of changes in policy that they were intended to be. Some concluded that since higher authority was taking such an unprecedented interest in details of personnel administration, the best thing for them to do was wash their own hands of further responsibility of such matters. Others really did feel that their rightful authority was being diluted and diminished, that I was going straight to the men without regard for the chain of command. My one regret about the way I handled my personnel program was that I did not consult sufficiently at the beginning with middle management, and did not bring its members up to speed on my ideas and plans at the outset. The great majority of them supported the program from the outset; most of the others did too, once they understood it, and no permanent harm was done, but for the first year or two their confusion was painful to them and it did slow things down somewhat.

My first attempt to deal with this confusion, which I became aware of within days of the dispatch of the first Z-grams, was to send, on 26 September, a six-page letter on the subject of "Command" to all flag officers, commanders, commanding officers, and officers-in-charge. Its fundamental message . . . was, "To accomplish what I have in mind, I think you need to achieve the very finest balance between the following: . . . a relaxed attitude and a responsible attitude, challenging your officers and crew and being considerate of them, adequate rewards but with proper restraint, polish and performance. . . ." A month later, on 23 October, I felt compelled to send to the same addresses Z-52, from which I quote the relevant passage.

During my four years as CNO, there must have appeared over my signature thousands of documents: letters, memoranda, orders, studies and analyses, posture statements, speeches, and what not. Of them all, none created more of a stir, inside the Navy and outside, than Z-57, issued on 10 November 1970. Its original title—my title—was "Mickey Mouse, Elimination of," but three days before it appeared, my superlative new Vice Chief, Admiral Ralph Cousins (who had just relieved Chick Clarey in that job), fearing that this would be considered flippant, changed it to "Demeaning and Abrasive Regulations, Elimination of."

Z-57 was an order specifically liberalizing Navy regulations or practices in twelve areas: (1) styles of hair, beards, sideburns, and civilian clothing; (2) uniforms for trips between living quarters and work sites ashore; (3) uniforms for visiting service facilities like snack bars, commissaries and disbursing offices; (4) requirements for officers and enlisted men to shift into uniform of the day for evening meals; (5) attire for enlisted and officers' clubs; (6) the meaning of the traditional phrase "optional uniform"; (7) preparing ships or stations for visits by senior officers; (8) conditions of leave; (9) the operation of motorcycles; (10) conditions for overnight liberty; (11) uniforms for certain kinds of conspicuous sea duty; (12) procedures for processing requests from individuals to higher authorities. It amuses me a little that I am known mostly as the CNO who allowed sailors to grow beards, wear mod clothes, and drive motorcycles. In truth, I spent almost all of my time pondering upon and seeking to make a contribution to American policy with respect to the U.S.-Soviet maritime balance, strategic arms limitation, naval modernization, and a number of other matters that most people would agree have more bearing on the fate of the nation than what a sailor wears to supper. There even were some Z-grams that ordered changes more profound than any in Z-57. Nevertheless, Z-57, because its subject matter was easy for servicemen and civilians alike to understand and because it dealt with practices that for years had unnecessarily irritated thousands of men and women every day, came to symbolize the Navy's effort to attune itself to the time. It caused great joy and great controversy and so it is worth discussing.

"Mickey Mouse"—or "chicken regs," as they are called just as often—is a term that covers, for one thing, those self-serving regulations and practices by which some commanders attempt to give an appearance of efficiency or smartness but which in fact make no contribution to either of those desirable conditions. Hastily painting over rust spots the day before inspection is that kind of Mickey Mouse, and so is making a sailor change out of dungarees into liberty uniform before going to the commissary for a candy bar. . . . The term . . . seem[s] to derive from an institutional notion that everyone below the rank of commander, say, is immature. Requiring a person going home on leave to prove he or she had the money for a round-trip ticket is that kind of Mickey Mouse, and so is refusing to provide parking spaces on naval stations for motorcycles on the ground that motorcycles (unlike nuclear submarines or guided missile frigates or helicopters) are too dangerous for sailors to ride.

Zumwalt was very sensitive to commanders' fears that the Z-grams were undermining their authority.

> I felt it necessary to include in one form or another in every Z-gram of even a faintly controversial nature a statement that I had no intention of undercutting or bypassing the authority of commanding officers, but rather relied on those officers to implement, in their own style, the new policies. I usually added to this that the relaxation in specific existing regulations or practices I was ordering did not imply that I favored relaxing traditional military discipline and obedience to orders. The reason for this last stricture, of course, was that just as there was a small minority of martinets who were reluctant to treat people like people, so there was a small minority of loafers who could be counted upon to abuse whatever added latitude they were given. I did not intend to have personnel reform in the Navy stultified by such people.[35]

One of Zumwalt's key decisions in initiating his personnel policies was that they should be public knowledge, which added to the program's controversy. He polled his senior admirals, the commanders in chief of the fleets, for their input. "Never has there been as much four-star input into an NAVOP," he said of their responses. "Many of the admirals' specific comments were well taken and incorporated into the final product. But one general recommendation they all agreed upon, that eliminating Mickey Mouse should be done quietly and privately, was one I had already considered and rejected. It was clear to me that the recruitment and retention situation called for a public and authoritative signal from the man in charge."[36]

He further elaborated on his open approach in his memoirs:

> Some who favored my personnel reforms as reasonable and long overdue were troubled by the public, not to say theatrical, manner in which I proclaimed them. They maintained that those reforms could and should have been initiated without creating a showy apparatus of retention study groups and Z-grams, without inspiring public jokes about "the Mod Navy" and getting the CNO on the cover of *Time*. I think they missed the point. "Going public" was a deliberate tactic based on my conviction that the Navy had to do more than to treat its people better in many big and little ways. It had to change, and change fast, the opinion, widespread among both sailors and civilians and having some basis in fact, that it was a humorless, tradition-bound, starchy institution owned by and operated for the

benefit of white males. This change could cause controversy. It seemed to me to be both right and necessary that I set up a system which made me personally the lightning rod for such controversy.

I do not think that my program would have had much of a chance if I had not made that first, all-out effort to tell the world about it. For basically it was not I, but the sailors in the fleet, and their families, and the media, and even certain members of Congress who overcame the inertia, or in some cases the opposition, of the system and forced the reforms through. What I did, in a sense, was to unleash those forces by seeing to it that the commitment to reform by the Navy's top leadership was posted on every ship's bulletin board, was featured on the evening news, and in the pages of *Time*. Once Z-68 got on the bulletin boards, I did not have to send emissaries around to make sure that petty officers were being permitted to keep civilian clothes in their lockers. The petty officers made sure of that. Once the media had reported that the Navy had committed itself to equal opportunity, they felt obliged to keep track of whether or not that commitment was being carried through, and thus helped keep up the pressure for it to be carried through.

I made the decision to go public knowing that it entailed risks and could arouse opposition among that perhaps 10 or 15 percent of officers and senior petty officers who felt that undisputed control of every aspect of a subordinate's life was a prerogative of military seniority. And indeed there was a considerable outcry about "going over the heads of commanders" and "washing dirty linen in public" from this small group of petty tyrants or, more commonly, sincere paternalists, though more often than not they spoke not with their own voices but through the retired community. All that did not surprise me. One could not spend a quarter of a century in the Navy without having numerous encounters with such folk; one of the first captains I served under as a young destroyer officer treated his entire crew, commissioned and enlisted, like backward and unreliable children, which once and for all set my mind against that style of leadership. My own philosophy about reform in the Navy was best stated by the first chief petty officer I worked with on board USS *Phelps* in 1942. He said, "Ensign Zumwalt, the Navy ain't what she used to be, and never was."[37]

According to Norman Friedman's profile of Admiral Zumwalt in *The Chiefs of Naval Operations,* "One of the reasons Secretary Laird chose Zumwalt to be chief of naval operations was because his views on the roles of blacks and women in the Navy were more liberal than those of other senior admirals. He did not think that the Navy had ever really tried to integrate blacks into the service and saw the general policy towards both blacks and women as tokenism. Not only did the Navy lag behind national standards, it was far behind the other services in accommodating liberal reforms."[38] Zumwalt himself reflected:

> There was no one of my duties as Chief of Naval Operations that I had had less practical experience with than race relations; in fact, when I took office I had no inkling that dealing with race relations should or would be among my most important duties. The most I can say for my appreciation of the problem was that my heart was in the right place. . . . However, . . . I had not yet done much . . . by October 1970 when my young assistant in charge of the retention study groups, Lieutenant Dave Halperin, who had a knack for discovering people of unusual ability, suggested that I see a certain Lieutenant Commander William Norman with a view toward making him a special assistant for minority affairs.
>
> Bill Norman was about to leave the Navy. After seven years of distinguished service as a Navy flight officer aboard carriers, an instructor at the Naval Academy, a White House aide, and a member of just about every committee or council or commission on race relations or minority affairs the Navy had set up in the previous half dozen years, he had decided that the unceasing strain of the conflict between being black and being Navy was greater than he was willing to bear any longer, and he had resigned his commission. He was in California when he received my invitation to come to see me and, he has since told me, he responded to the invitation with reluctance, having heard by then more than enough high-ranking pledges to implement the racial policies that, after all, Harry Truman had ordered the military to put into effect in 1947. And so what happened at our first conversation, whose ostensible purpose was for me to check him out, was that he checked me out. Evidently I passed his inspection, for he agreed to join my personal staff. I am not being facetious. Knowing what I know now, but did not know then, about the experience of minority people in the Navy, I think Bill Norman had every reason to look hard and skeptically at my motives and my intentions. I will add that I can't think of anyone who did more during my watch to make the Navy a better place to live in than Bill did in the two and a half years he was a member of my staff, first as "OOM," my special assistant for minority problems, then as "OOG," my special assistant for all personnel matters. . . .
>
> It was only months later, as our friendship became close, that I learned of Bill's own experiences as a black officer in a white Navy: the fact that as a young

officer he had rarely received a voluntary salute; of the time in Meridian, Mississippi, when the commander of the naval air station asked him not to come to the officers' club that night because his presence there would embarrass some local dignitaries who had been invited as guests; of the time he was returning to his ship from an evening in town in civilian clothes and the officer of the deck told him sharply that the enlisted men's gangplank was at the other end; of the time ashore in Japan when he intervened between a Japanese and a white chief petty officer who was abusing him and the chief had called Bill a "goddamn nigger" and punched him, and when Bill had put the petty officer on report, the captain of the ship had declined to punish him because the man had a "perfect record"; of the time he was assigned to the faculty of the Naval Academy and could not find anyone in Annapolis who would rent a black man decent living quarters and an Academy official had told him that was Bill's problem, not the Academy's; of the eternal temptation when he was with his own people to apologize for the uniform he wore. But if it was not until later that I learned those personal things about Bill, I learned right away that things like that were a matter of daily occurrence for the black men and women of the Navy. By the time Bill and I had our first business meeting on 5 November there was already in session a retention study group of black officers and their wives, which Bill and Dave Halperin had convened at only a few days' notice and which delivered its report on 6 November to as big a roomful as I could assemble of high-ranking officers and civilians, including Secretary of the Navy John Chafee.[39]

After presenting the results of the report and proposing solutions for the racial inequities his staff had so far uncovered, Zumwalt concluded:

This is the first of my reports to you on minority affairs. Secretary Chafee and I will be looking into all areas of minority affairs and will be issuing further reports as our problems become more clear and their solutions become more apparent. It is evident that we need to maximize our efforts to improve the lot of our minority Navymen. I am convinced that there is no place in our Navy for insensitivity. We are determined that we shall do better. Meanwhile, we are counting on your support to help seek out and eliminate those demeaning areas of discrimination that plague our minority shipmates. Ours must be a Navy family that recognizes no artificial barriers of race, color or religion. There is no black Navy, no white Navy—just one Navy—the United States Navy.[40]

The personnel policies brought about through the Z-grams were popular among the junior officers and younger enlisted personnel, but much less so among senior personnel, many of whom, as noted above, were disturbed by Zumwalt's unconventional methods and feared that their authority was being undermined. They were particularly concerned over the loss of discipline throughout the fleet. This concern went beyond the Navy.

The erosion of military discipline within the U.S. Navy was brought into national focus when sailors aboard two under-way carriers, the USS *Kitty Hawk* and USS *Constellation,* rioted. Both were warships, players in the Vietnam War, providing the vital tactical air component for Operation Linebacker, the U.S. campaign to end the war in Southeast Asia on terms favorable to the United States. The two incidents received wide media attention across the country. President Nixon was especially furious with the Navy when extensive TV footage was aired of the "mutineers" from the USS *Constellation* being off-loaded on the pier at San Diego before the carrier returned to the South China Sea.

Congressman F. Edward Hébert, the powerful chairman of the House Armed Services Committee, ordered a congressional investigation to look into "alleged racial and disciplinary problems" on Navy ships. Congressman Hébert appointed Congressman Floyd V. Hicks, a Democrat from Washington State, to chair a subcommittee to handle the investigation. The "Report of the Special Subcommittee on Disciplinary Problems in the U.S. Navy," which became known as the Hicks report, is a record of the investigation of the incidents aboard the *Kitty Hawk* and *Constellation,* but it also includes a number of thoughtful and pertinent observations concerning the broadest aspects of naval leadership from CNO to seaman apprentice. The very serious nature of the discipline situation in the Navy in 1972 and the broader context of the report relating to the command and discipline responsibilities of naval leaders make it worthwhile to reproduce parts of the Hicks report here.

"During the course of the 92nd Congress," the report noted,

> . . . there has been increasing concern in the House Armed Services Committee over the developing of more relaxed discipline in the military services. Substantial evidence of this practice reached us directly through subcommittee

investigative reports and messages from concerned service members, as well as indirectly through events reported in the news media.

While generally our men have performed in an outstanding fashion during battle and other in extremis circumstances, on occasion there has been an erosion of good order and discipline under more normal operations. More disturbing have been the reports of sabotage of naval property, assaults, and other serious lapses in discipline afloat. Further, lawful orders have been subject to "committee" or "town meeting" proceedings prior to compliance by subordinates.

Capping the various reports were the recent serious incidents aboard USS *Kitty Hawk* and USS *Constellation*—aircraft carriers of vital importance to the naval mission in Southeast Asia. . . . Immediately following air operations aboard the *Kitty Hawk* on the evening of October 12, 1972, a series of incidents broke out wherein groups of blacks, armed with chains, wrenches, bars, broomsticks and other dangerous weapons, went marauding through sections of the ship disobeying orders to cease, terrorizing the crew, and seeking out white personnel for senseless beating with fists and with weapons which resulted in extremely serious injury to three men and the medical treatment of many more, including some blacks. While engaged in this conduct, some were heard to shout, "Kill the son-of-a-bitch; kill the white trash; wipe him out!" Others shouted, "They are killing our brothers."

Aboard the USS *Constellation,* during the period of November 3–4, 1972, what has been charitably described as "unrest" and as a "sit-in" took place while the ship was underway for training exercises. The vast majority of the dissident sailors were black and were allegedly protesting several grievances they claimed were in need of correction. These sailors were off-loaded as a part of a "beach detachment," given liberty, refused to return to the ship, and were later processed only for this minor disciplinary infraction (6 hours of unauthorized absence) at Naval Air Station, North Island, near San Diego.

Because of the inherent seriousness of these incidents, the Honorable F. Edward Hébert, chairman, House Armed Services Committee, considered it necessary to appoint this special subcommittee on November 13, 1972, to inquire at once into disciplinary problems in the US Navy with particular reference to "alleged racial and disciplinary problems which occurred recently on the aircraft carriers USS *Kitty Hawk* and USS *Constellation.* "

During the course of its inquiry and hearing which commenced November 20, 1972, the subcommittee completed some 2,565 pages of . . . testimony, and assembled a large volume of reports, directives, military investigations and other papers which have been the basis for this report.

Many of the subcommittee's findings seemed to indicate that Admiral Zumwalt's "improvements" had had the opposite effect. Among the findings of the report were the following:

The subcommittee finds that permissiveness . . . exists in the Navy today. Although we have been able to investigate only certain specific incidents in depth, the total information made available to us indicates the condition could be service-wide.

The subcommittee has been unable to determine any precipitous cause for the rampage aboard USS *Kitty Hawk*. Not only was there not one case wherein racial discrimination could be pinpointed, but there was no evidence which indicated that the blacks who participated in that incident perceived racial discrimination, either in general or in any specific, of such a nature as to justify belief that violent reaction was required.

The subcommittee finds that the incident aboard USS *Constellation* was the result of a carefully orchestrated demonstration of passive resistance wherein a small number of blacks, certainly no more than 20–25, in a well-organized campaign, willfully created among other blacks the belief that white racism existed in the Navy and aboard that ship. The subcommittee, again in this instance as with the incident aboard *Kitty Hawk,* found no specific example of racial discrimination. In this case, however, it is obvious that the participants perceived that racial discrimination when, in fact, such was not the case.

The subcommittee was informed that a review, conducted by Naval Personnel Research Activity, San Diego, had found no racial discrimination in the punishments awarded by the Commanding Officer, USS *Constellation*. The subcommittee found no evidence that that conclusion was in error.

Discipline, requiring immediate response to command, is absolutely essential to any military force. Particularly in the forces afloat there is no room for the "town meeting" concept or the employment of negotiation or appeasement to obtain obedience to orders. The Navy must be controlled by command, not demand.

The generally smart appearance of naval personnel, both afloat and ashore, has deteriorated markedly. While the subcommittee appreciates efforts to allow maximum reasonableness in daily routines, there is absolutely no excuse for slovenly appearance of officers and men in the Navy uniform and such appearance should not be tolerated.

The members of the subcommittee did not find and are unaware of any instances of institutional discrimination on the part of Navy toward any group of persons, majority or minority.

After the incidents on *Kitty Hawk* and *Constellation,* a meeting was called by the Secretary of the Navy of all of the admirals in the Washington, D.C., area in which the CNO spoke to the failure of the Navy to meet its human relations goals. Immediately thereafter, his remarks were made available to the press and sent as a message to all hands. Because of the wording of the text, it was perceived by many to be a public admonishment by the CNO of his staff for their failure to solve racial problems within the Navy. Even though this was followed within 96 hours by Z-gram 117, which stressed the need for discipline, the speech itself, the issuance of it to the public press, and timing of its delivery, all served to emphasize the CNO's perception of the Navy's problems. Again, concern over racial problems seemed paramount to the question of good order and discipline even though there had been incidents on two ships which might be characterized as "mutinies." The subcommittee regrets that the condition of not criticizing seniors in front of their subordinates was ignored in this case.

The Navy's recruitment program for most of 1972, which resulted in the lowering of standards for enlistment, accepting a greater percentage of mental category IV and those in the lower half of category III, not requiring recruits in these categories to have completed their high school education, and accepting these people without sufficient analysis of their previous offense records, has created many of the problems the Navy is experiencing today.

The investigation disclosed an alarming frequency of successful acts of sabotage and apparent sabotage on a wide variety of ships and stations within the Navy.

The subcommittee is of the opinion that the riot on *Kitty Hawk* consisted of unprovoked assaults by a very few men, most of whom were of below-average mental capacity, most of whom had been aboard for less than one year, and all of whom were black. This group, as a whole, acted as "thugs" which raises doubt as to why they should ever have been accepted into military service in the first place.

The subcommittee expresses its strong objection to the procedures utilized by higher authority to negotiate with *Constellation* dissidents and, eventually, to appease them by acquiescing to their demands and by meting out minor nonjudicial punishment for what was a major affront to good order and discipline. Moreover the committee stresses that the actions committed aboard that ship had the potential for crippling a combatant vessel in a war zone.

The subcommittee believes that advice concerning decisions which had to be made with regard to *Constellation,* offered by personnel in human relations billets to line officers, was uniformly poor. The decisions made on the basis of that advice, proved unsuccessful in bringing the incident to a conclusion. Later decisions, reflecting a reversal of the policy of negotiations with the dissident sailors, resulted in the transfer of the men off the ship in a disciplinary status.

The statement that riots, mutinies and acts of sabotage in Navy are a product of "the time" is not valid. If those in positions of authority who profess such arguments really believe them, they have been negligent in not taking proper precautionary action to prevent their occurrence or to deal with such actions once they did occur. It is incredible that the Navy was totally unprepared to cope with such incidents as occurred aboard *Kitty Hawk* and *Constellation.* In view of the disturbances in recent years in the other military services, the Navy appears to have indulged in wishful thinking, apparently believing that similar incidents would not happen aboard ship.

Where human relations councils and minority affairs offices were manned solely by minority personnel, they became conduits for minority personnel to bypass the normal chain of command. Used properly, as another set of eyes and ears to keep the commander informed as to personnel problems, they can be worthwhile; but used as a vehicle for the settlement of individual minority grievances which should be resolved within the command structure, they are divisive and disruptive of good order and discipline and encourage further polarization. The equal opportunity and human relations programs of the Navy must not, in any way, dilute the authority of the chain of command.

The subcommittee detects a failure in the middle management area in that there has been a reluctance to utilize the command authority inherent in those positions.

The Navy's recruiting advertising appears to promise more than the Navy is able to deliver, especially to personnel who are unable to qualify for "A" school training. This can create frustration and discontent. The hopes held out by this advertising, plus statements made by some Navy recruiters, present an unrealistic picture of the Navy. Any such distortions should be corrected.

The subcommittee commends the Chief of Naval Operations for those of his programs which are designed to improve Navy life and yet maintain good order and discipline through the traditional channels of authority.

The subcommittee members were clearly disturbed by the declining standards of excellence and lack of discipline they discovered throughout the Navy during the course of their investigation.

The subcommittee found confusion as to what is "excellence" and what standards of excellence naval personnel are expected to meet. Clearly, in the area of good order and discipline, there has been confusion as to expected standards. That confusion reaches to the top levels of the service. If this had not been so, why, then, while denying that permissiveness does exist and claiming that firm discipline is the order of the day, was there a need on November 14, 1972, to issue Z-117 exhorting the Navy to strengthen and maintain its control over good order?

Instances of confusion and . . . misplaced perception of performance standards destroy the "conviction" so essential to good morale and esprit de corps.

The position that high morale is indicated by rising reenlistment rates is not entirely accepted by the subcommittee. The Congress has in the past two years, provided far more pay, allowances, and other related benefits than even the services themselves have requested. This was done to relieve the historically adverse effect of lower pay in the military than was available in comparable civilian employment. Higher enlistment and reenlistment rates were clearly influenced by these actions.

It may well be that, given the unfortunate state of the Nation's economy, with the lack of sufficient employment opportunities in the civil sector, military life now has a certain appeal based upon financial rewards. Certainly this aspect cannot be overlooked when considering the meaning of rising reenlistment rates.

The subcommittee was disturbed by the effect the CNO's relaxed standards of appearance was having on morale and discipline.

Traditionally indicative of high morale has been pride in the uniform. . . . The current relaxation of the standards of appearance for Navy men has caused a lessening in the pride that some sailors take in their appearance, and thus in their service. Admittedly, Z-57 and subsequent clarifying messages concerning the standards of appearance were not designed to permit Navy personnel to become sloppy and slovenly in their appearance and grooming. Nonetheless, such has been the effect.

Considerable testimony to the effect that the uniform seems to mean less today than it did several years ago was received by the subcommittee. Through its personal observation as well as the opinions given it by active duty personnel from all grades and ranks, including retired Navy personnel, and from private citizens, the subcommittee received clear and irrefutable evidence that the men of the naval service do not present the smart appearance that once was their unique trademark.

While this has undoubtedly been as a result of individual abuse of relaxed regulations, it has, in fact, caused a service-wide problem for all Navy personnel. Until such time as there is insistence on clear-cut standards for a smart appearance while in the uniform of the United States Navy, the general morale and discipline will be adversely affected.

The lack of discipline was showing up in the way orders were given and received as well.

"Aye, aye, sir," traditionally means, "I understand your orders and will comply with them, sir." It may well be that a general abandonment of this phrase has lessened the sense of immediacy that it implies. The subcommittee found a reluctance on the part of some petty officers, junior officers and seniors alike, to demand strict and immediate response to orders. Instead, there seems to be an attitude on the part of certain supervisory personnel that if they fail to explain in detail every order or command, the junior may not comply. Indeed, there is also the feeling that such failure to comply will be supported by various senior personnel and/or representatives of the juniors, be they council, committees, or representatives.

Young men and women, especially in an all-volunteer force such as the Navy, must know from the beginning of their service that immediate and unquestioning response is expected of them at all times and that failure to meet that expectation will result in disciplinary action.

This is not to say . . . that the reasons for a particular order should never be given. The subcommittee believes, however, that the option to explain an order must remain with the person issuing that order and that the response by junior will be immediate regardless of his senior's decision as to whether or not the directive is to be explained.

The subcommittee was particularly concerned to find that some petty officers and commissioned officers were willing to accept non-compliance until such time as they had fully explained the reasons for their orders. This attitude is not an acceptable.

The subcommittee commented on the decline in courts-martial in recent years.

The Navy has suggested that this decrease indicates that sailors are more respon-
sive to commands and, therefore, that discipline is being maintained at a greater
level than previously experienced. The subcommittee is concerned that the figures may indicate a tendency on the part of authority to ignore or appease rather
than to prosecute offenders.

The preponderance of testimony indicates that those in authority turn too
frequently to negotiation and then to appeasement rather than immediately to fair
and firm enforcement of existing regulations. As an illustration, we cite the efforts
on the part of senior officers to *deal with* the members of the so-called "beach
detachment" from USS *Constellation* rather than to invoke basic disciplinary procedures for offenses committed aboard ship. That the decision in this matter was
made far above the commanding officer of *Constellation* is clear. The result has been
the creation of an environment of leniency, appeasement, and permissiveness.

The maintenance of good order and discipline *relies* on certain knowledge
that offenses will not be tolerated and will be subject to swift and equitable action.
There is nothing wrong with punishment when it is deserved. A system which hes-
itates to punish when it is deserved is very wrong.

The subcommittee's investigation uncovered "literally hundreds of
instances of damage to naval property wherein sabotage is suspected. . . .
The magnitude of the problem both in the frequency of 'suspicious' incidents and in the total damage to Government property is alarming."

Also alarming to the subcommittee members was the extent of the
drug use they discovered.

During the course of this inquiry, it became abundantly clear that there continues to be illicit use of a variety of drugs aboard ship and that the drug abuse problem afloat has not abated to any significant degree, especially where there is a
supply of drugs available ashore. . . . There is, however, no evidence linking drug
abuse with the incidents aboard the *Kitty Hawk* and *Constellation*. . . . Apparently
there has been an abundant supply of illicit drugs available to our ships in the
Philippine Islands area. Further, during the recent declaration of martial law, that
source dried up almost completely. So, too, did the supply of illegal drugs aboard
naval vessels.

The subcommittee investigated charges that black sailors were dis-
criminated against in work assignments and advancement opportunities,
but concluded:

That this is racial discrimination is a false perception of the situation. But the perception problem is not limited to black seamen alone. The Chief of Naval Operations does not admit to any severe breakdown of discipline in today's Navy. He asserts that the Navy is operating under the most arduous conditions in its history and has proved itself to be combat effective. In his view, combat effectiveness is the proof of the Navy's maintenance of good order and discipline.

He feels, however, that there has been less than a full measure of success in assuring equal opportunity in the Navy and in fostering a successful program of race relations. Therefore, he has placed primary emphasis on a program to resolve racial problems. Because of this emphasis on racial problems, his subordinates may have perceived his attitude and his directives in a manner that has caused a lessening of discipline, creating a situation wherein racial problems have been overemphasized. . . . The record is replete with testimony that middle management, the junior officers and senior petty officers, perceived their authority to have been diluted by the Chief of Naval Operations when he addressed all naval personnel in a series of Z-grams which being general in nature, permitted individual interpretation of his directions.

It should be clearly understood that many of these perceptions are clearly contrary to the facts and do not necessarily represent the thinking of the major portion of the Navy. Nevertheless, as long as individuals perceive these to be the facts, the Navy will continue to have problems maintaining good order and discipline.

Among the most serious of the subcommittee's discoveries was

lack of leadership by middle management in the Navy . . . in dealing with the seaman. Examples of this lack of leadership are numerous: the poor personal grooming of the crew, the poor standards of cleanliness on at least one of the ships, the failure to counsel with subordinates concerning their "quarterly marks" or personal problems, the failure to take corrective action when corrective action was warranted, and the failure to demand an immediate response to lawful orders.

Undoubtedly, . . . as the Navy becomes more technical, grade or rank is obtained on the basis of technical skills rather than on leadership ability. There are insufficient on-going internal programs within the Navy to provide adequate training for petty officers, chief petty officers, and junior officers with respect to the basic elements of leadership.

One black chief petty officer described the change in discipline and attitude toward discipline, as "just one gigantic cop-out by people like us. When the CNO sends a direct message to everybody in the world, the senior petty officer community and the middle management officer community have thrown up their hands and said, 'He has taken all our power away and we can't do anything.'"

Obviously, there has not been any removal of the tools to maintain discipline aboard a ship or anywhere else in the Navy, but the attitude toward the use of such tools has changed. The change, in part, has been occasioned by the use of minority affairs representatives, human relations councils and human resources staffs which too frequently bypass the chain of command. When a seaman can go to some "special interest group" outside the chain of command to discuss his specific grievance without first attempting to resolve his problem through his immediate superior, and, in turn, when someone on that council or committee attempts to mediate that problem with the seaman's supervisor, then the authority of that supervisor is inevitably diluted. The result is that, too often, the supervisor later gives in to an unwarranted request or fails to take corrective action rather than fighting the auxiliary chain of command.

Also, because of a general feeling of permissiveness that we found prevailed among many personnel in the Navy, there is a tendency on the part of many junior officers, chief petty officers, and senior petty officers to take the attitude of "don't make waves." A good example of this was given the members of the subcommittee wherein a chief was preventing some men from going on liberty because of dirty shoes and unkempt appearance. A lieutenant told the chief to let them go on liberty and not rock the boat. This attitude breeds contempt by the seamen for their superiors and sows seeds for the destruction of the system.

We cannot and must not permit the middle management team to adopt a passive attitude which lets the men do anything they want to do. Superiors in the Navy are supposed to command, not give in to demands. Otherwise, there is no authority.

The subcommittee ended its report with a grave warning.

Discipline is the keystone of the armed services of any nation. If discipline collapses, a military force becomes a leaderless, uniformed mob capable only of accomplishing its own destruction. The United States Navy is now confronted with pressures, both from within and without, which if not controlled, will surely destroy its enviable tradition of discipline. Recent instances of sabotage, riot, willful disobedience of orders, and contempt for authority, instances which have occurred with increased frequency, are clear-cut symptoms of a dangerous deterioration of discipline.

The leaders of our Nation must make a critical decision—shall we tolerate a continued decline in naval discipline, or shall we adhere to traditional concepts of military discipline tempered with humanitarianism? That is the question. The subcommittee believes that the latter option is the only response which will provide an effective fighting force.[41]

"The Hicks report," reflected Admiral Holloway, "was probably kinder to Zumwalt than a lot of senior Navy people thought it should have been." He continued,

A group of former Navy CNOs headed by Admiral George Anderson . . . personally called on President Nixon in the White House, requesting that he relieve Admiral Zumwalt as CNO immediately. They, like much of the senior naval leadership who followed him as CNO, thought that changes were coming too fast, enlisting young people who were not properly educated or motivated, building up their expectations that the Navy was going to be fun, with rapid promotions, there would be no menial work, and that many regulations governing military conduct would be eliminated. Zumwalt felt that the report was unbalanced in that it did not show what he was trying to accomplish with his minority programs. He essentially suppressed distribution of the report within the Navy.[42]

Admiral Zumwalt offered his own reaction to the Hicks report in *On Watch*. "Perhaps it is hard for the reader to understand why this action of Eddie's [Hébert] so appalled and affronted me," he wrote. "Well, 'breakdown of discipline' is about as damning a charge as can be made against an entire military service, and to escalate incidents on three ships out of 596 in the fleet into 'breakdown of discipline,' incidents moreover that did not prevent any of the three from performing all her assigned missions, was to my mind neither more or less than a hatchet job against heroic, overcommitted, underfunded, undersupported sailors."

"Gratuitous, insulting and potentially damaging to the Navy though [the Hicks report] was," he continued, "it also was the kind of opportunity that no one in the executive branch ever could have given me to put my case for enlightened personnel policies in the armed services before the country." When his staff informed Zumwalt that "the Z-grams would be identified as the root of the permissiveness that was poisoning the Navy, because they had made it impossible for commanders to discipline their men," he had to respond directly. "That, of course, was a direct, personal challenge to the Navy from which I could not, and certainly would not if I could, back down."

He insisted on appearing personally before the subcommittee and was pleased with the result. He commented: "In sum, my going public appeared to be accomplishing what I hoped it would, which was to create so much overt support for twentieth-century racial policies in the Navy that the covert machinations of George Anderson and his coterie were frustrated."[43]

In the end, the Hicks report did not stop Zumwalt's efforts to update naval personnel policies. "The Hicks report received little attention," he noted.

> Within the Navy the report had next to no impact for a variety of reasons. . . .There no longer was an inordinate number of nonschool eligibles entering the Navy, and the hard cases that had come in the year before either had become accustomed to their new circumstances or were on their way out. . . . Most of the press had been with me from the beginning and, in the absence of further disturbances in the fleet, was not much titillated by the report. . . . I had had a nasty month or two, but the great torpedo that I feared would blow my policies clear out of the water turned out to be a damp little squib.[44]

Did Admiral Zumwalt's changes meant to make the Navy more attractive to recruits also cause a deterioration in discipline? The question should not be dismissed out of hand. The oral history of Vice Adm. Kent Lee, captain of the nuclear carrier *Enterprise* from July 1967 through August 1969, offers excellent insights on the subject. Admiral Lee, who enlisted in the Navy in 1939, was knowledgeable about the outlook of the enlisted man, having started his rise to three-star rank from enlisted status. He also had an excellent understanding of the nuances of shipboard discipline. He commented on his own experience commanding sailors:

> There were a certain number of men who were . . . amoral. They don't recognize right from wrong, and you see them back at mast, time after time after time. You begin to recognize them. You also recognize a youngster who's never been at mast before and who did something that he knows is wrong, whatever it might be, and who wants to take his punishment like a man and not do it again.

I think captains holding mast by and by get a pretty good grasp of when they have one of these amoral types and when they have a good sailor who made a mistake. I think captains should be given great leeway in this, because there are some youngsters that are absolutely first-rate sailors, but they have too many beers. Something happens, they get into trouble. If you get them back aboard ship and then take them to mast, and really hit them a hard lick, you can ruin them. They can become very discouraged.

So I think a captain has to be very perceptive in how he handles this. Men who had a good record, who were good performers, usually got a warning. It was always good to have the chief petty officer come to mast and describe the man. If the chief petty officer gives the man a good recommendation and it's a first offense, I would be very reluctant to do much, unless it's something really gross, borderline felony. But these amoral types, we showed no mercy on them. We tried to make a record, so to speak, and get them out of the Navy and off *Enterprise* as quickly as possible. . . . They take so much of the division officer's time and chief petty officer's time, so that as soon as we could pretty well recognize one of these characters, we tried to move them off the ship. I thought that was very good for the *Enterprise,* good for the Navy, and good for discipline. Their presence is really counterproductive. In the two years I was aboard, we probably transferred 50 or 100 of these types.

But other than that, with the bad apples, discipline was never a problem. It was less of a problem on *Enterprise* than I ever would have guessed, whether we were in port or otherwise. . . . There's absolutely nothing wrong with the American youngster of that generation, and I'm sure they haven't changed much to this generation. If they know they're getting a fair shake, they're willing to work hard. . . . Discipline certainly wasn't a problem in those years. I still am amazed at how many disciplinary problems the Navy apparently had during the Zumwalt era. Because we had no problems with blacks or anyone else before the Zumwalt era. No problems.

I think [Secretary of the Navy] Chafee got more than he bargained for with Zumwalt. I think Chafee's ideas for the Navy were rather modest. He's interested in people, and his ideas were good. He didn't want a revolution; my idea of Chafee was that he just wanted the process of evolution to be speeded up a little bit. But Zumwalt came in, and he wanted revolution. And Chafee didn't really know how to turn him off. He's damn hard to turn off. Not only that, I thought Zumwalt sort of turned on Chafee, and I was very sorry that Chafee caved in to him.

Let me tell you what I mean. Chafee was secretary of the navy; he hoped to run for Senate from Rhode Island. After Zumwalt had been there about a year, he announced that he was going to close the Naval Air Station [at] Quonset Point . . . and phase out basing destroyers in Narragansett Bay. I thought Zumwalt had a lot of chutzpah to do that to Chafee when Chafee wanted to go up there and run for the Senate. Zumwalt put it in such a fashion that Chafee had a very difficult time saying no. So he acquiesced. That may have been the reason he didn't make it to the Senate the first time around. So I thought Zumwalt treated Chafee very unfairly, and I thought Chafee early on had a chance to let Zumwalt know who was boss. But he didn't. He gave Zumwalt his head. I think it cost Chafee dearly in the end. This is my assessment. I really never discussed Zumwalt with Chafee. . . . I had two tours of duty in the secretariat. I learned that you only discuss the things with the secretaries that they bring up. . . . I would have liked to discuss Zumwalt with Chafee, but . . . he never brought it up with me. He muttered a little bit from time to time about closing out naval operations in Rhode Island and a few other things. . . . But I never, . . . I never brought up items or had my own agenda with those civilian secretaries because the aides that do are not very successful.

Lee's interviewer asked: "Is it possible that he didn't turn off on the personnel things because he was comfortable with what Zumwalt was doing?" Lee responded: "I don't think he was uncomfortable. But I had the feeling that he thought Zumwalt was going a little far in many areas." Asked for his own view of Zumwalt's changes, Lee replied:

I thought Zumwalt went overboard in many ways. The one thing that I liked about Zumwalt was his changing of the uniform, which Holloway changed back. [Prior to Admiral Zumwalt's tenure as CNO, enlisted men below the grade of chief petty officer wore traditional jumpers, "sailor" hats, and bellbottom trousers. Zumwalt instituted a uniform essentially similar to that of a chief petty officer for all Navy enlisted men. Admiral Holloway, who followed Zumwalt as CNO, restored the traditional uniform.] As you know, most of the personnel changes that Zumwalt put into effect disappeared without a trace under the two succeeding CNOs. I felt that those Z-grams took away the authority of the commanding officers. I thought that Zumwalt almost caused a revolution in the Navy. He caused a lot of discontent among the blacks. He raised expectations which couldn't be fulfilled, because we had to follow our standard promotion system for officers and enlisted men. It had stood the test of time. He alienated an awful lot of senior officers. He booted four-stars out and three-stars out right and left. Good people. . . . The absolute worst thing he did was erode the authority of the commanding officer. And he did that. We had riots on some of our carriers, which had never happened before. I think Zumwalt deserves full credit for those. So I think Zumwalt went much too far in many ways.

Some of the things he did or started I think were good. Changing the uniform I liked, because I had been a sailor myself. How can a first-class petty officer with a family of three be dignified wearing that little white hat? So I liked that. I think Army uniforms and Air Force uniforms for first-class petty officer pay grades are much better. But I think Zumwalt got carried away, went much too far.[45]

In his book *Naval Renaissance: The U.S. Navy in the 1980s,* Frederick H. Hartman addressed the aftermath of Zumwalt's tenure as CNO: "By June 1974, when Zumwalt turned over the watch as CNO to Admiral Holloway, the Navy was faced with problems everywhere it looked. In interviews in 1986 two senior four-star admirals used the same word to sum up the Holloway program: stability. Whether previous policies had saved the Navy or ruined it (both views were strongly held in the officer corps), Zumwalt had certainly made many changes quickly, and a steady hand was required. Holloway provided it."[46]

Admiral Holloway, who had been Zumwalt's vice CNO and then followed him as CNO, summed up his own views on Admiral Zumwalt's stewardship of the Navy as follows:

I am sure I will be censured by some of my colleagues in the Navy, both active and retired, for criticizing a fellow officer. Especially since Zumwalt and I had been good friends. From a name recognition aspect he was clearly the Navy's most famous CNO. But Admiral Zumwalt is too important a figure in modern naval history to be given a superficial assessment. George Santayana's well-worn but still-cogent axiom, "Those who cannot remember the past are condemned to repeat it," has a powerful relevance in this case. Zumwalt was our most controversial naval leader. Some say he was a great leader and others maintain he came close to wrecking the Navy. What is the truth? It really doesn't matter. What is important in a treatise on leadership is to understand that he had some successes and some failures. The intent of *American Admiralship* is to help future generations of naval officers become effective leaders by illuminating the bad as well as the good in the administrations of prior senior officers.

My thumbnail definition of military leadership is "the art of influencing those under your command to do what they would otherwise not want to do, and do it willingly and with spirit and élan." By this definition, Admiral Zumwalt does not qualify as a great leader because his command philosophy was not to lead but to accede to the wishes of the subordinate levels of the Navy. Unfortunately, he often did this without consideration of whether this permissiveness would be helpful to the overall mission of the Navy or hurt it. Admiral Zumwalt was a dashing figure, articulate and immensely popular with the junior officers and younger sailors who constitute the majority of the Navy. *But we must not confuse popularity with leadership, and a military organization is not a democracy.*

At the time of his retirement, Admiral Zumwalt was being openly criticized by the senior uniformed officers of the U.S. Navy, and [was] not highly regarded by the leadership of our allied navies and the generals of the other military services of the U.S. But the passage of time had altered his reputation so that at the time of his death, twenty-five years later, he had regained a folklore popularity. President Clinton attended his funeral and gave a moving eulogy. The *Washington Post* and the *New York Times* published extensive coverage of the funeral service, and the obituaries and op-ed pieces called him the Navy's greatest CNO.

There is a reason for this enlargement of Zumwalt's reputation over the past quarter century. Those contemporaries and senior officers who were so actively critical of Zumwalt's iconoclasm during his term as CNO had been largely dissipated by age and death when Zumwalt himself died. However, the leadership of the Navy in 1999 from the CNO on down was made up entirely of men who had been junior officers during the Zumwalt regime, and had known Admiral Zumwalt only as their champion and benefactor. They were not in positions to be aware of the collateral damage that was occurring to readiness and discipline. By the time they reached assignments at the level of command responsibility, the U.S. Navy had healed itself through the more professional approach of subsequent CNOs.

It is because of this controversy surrounding the Zumwalt era in naval history that some thoughtful and documented effort must be made to ensure that future generations of naval leaders are not misled by Zumwalt's fame and popularity into attempts to emulate his philosophy and style. On balance, Zumwalt's legacy was not helpful to the naval service except in his focus on race relations. And even here, although his objectives were magnificent, his techniques in their implementation were not well conceived. The Navy does not need another Zumwalt in its foreseeable future.

In a larger sense, the experience of the Zumwalt era must be driven home as a lesson to those in civilian control of the armed forces. Zumwalt's failure to live up to his promise of a great CNO was not his fault. He was thrust into the job by a secretary of the navy who totally disregarded the considered advice of every senior naval officer on active duty and the retired CNOs. He was too immature and professionally unprepared to be an effective CNO. Had Bud Zumwalt been permitted to wait four years and gain the experience of a numbered fleet command, a fleet CinC, and a joint theater command, I am convinced he would have not only been a great CNO, but could have gone on to be chairman of the JCS, and a superlative one at that. The nation would have had the benefit of six more years of that active and brilliant mind.

Admiral Holloway and I discussed his role as Zumwalt's vice CNO and the leadership qualities required to succeed him in that post and heal the deeply divided Navy.

I had gotten to know Bud Zumwalt long before I went to work for him as vice chief. First, we were classmates at the Naval Academy, although I did not know him well at that time. We were both picked for the National War College (NWC), now the National Defense University (NDU), for the class of 1962. Bud and I had both been selected a year early for captain in 1961, so were the first in our Academy class to attend the NWC.

Bud Zumwalt and I did not share the same professional interests. I was focused on fleet organization and operations. Bud was consumed with politico-military affairs. His thesis at the NWC was on the succession of the chief of state in the Soviet Union. Bud's oral presentation of his thesis was so good, among a host of outstanding briefings, that Zumwalt was selected by the faculty to give his presentation as part of the program for the Board of Visitors. Paul Nitze, then assistant secretary of defense for international security affairs, was in the audience and on the spot decided to have Bud ordered to be his executive assistant for his first duty assignment after graduation from the NWC.

After War College, Bud and I went our separate paths until 1967, when I returned to Washington after my two years in command of *Enterprise* to become the director of strike warfare on the OpNav staff. Admiral Moorer was CNO. Bud Zumwalt, now a rear admiral selectee just as I, had become executive assistant to Paul Nitze, the secretary of the navy. I found it universally perceived throughout the halls of the Pentagon that Bud had tremendous influence with the secretary, and that Nitze sought his advice in virtually every matter dealing with the secretariat. Their relationship had become a personal one, and the Zumwalt family was living in the guest house, the former gatekeeper's residence, on the Nitze estate. Bud spent many evenings after a full day in the office with Nitze in private intellectual discussions. Bud and I renewed our friendship upon my return to the Pentagon. He took the time to brief me and get me caught up on the palace politics. Ours was a pleasant relationship.

Bud left Nitze's office in 1968 when the secretary sent him to Vietnam with a promotion to three stars, an open job description, and a blank check. Bud's job was to bring the U.S. Navy into the war in-country, developing a combined capability with the South Vietnam Naval Forces to fight the Viet Cong in the extensive littoral areas of South Vietnam.

In the fall of 1969, when it was first rumored that Zumwalt would relieve Admiral Tom Moorer as CNO, I could not believe it was true. Since the creation of the position, the CNOs had been an orderly progression of senior admirals, experienced in a wide spectrum of assignments, usually including the command of one or two fleets—or three in the case of Tom Moorer. The only exception had been Arleigh Burke, where his age and experience exceeded his rank. His promotions had been slowed down by civilian politics for his role in the revolt of the admirals.

The reason for my surprise at Bud Zumwalt's selection was that I was a contemporary of his, and I could not conceive of myself serving competently as CNO at this point in my career or at my age. I could not see myself relieving Tom Moorer, who was ten years older than me, at the peak of his professional career, and the epitome of experience, wisdom, and dignity. Moorer had commanded the Seventh Fleet, been commander in chief, Pacific Fleet, commander in chief, Atlantic, and supreme allied commander, Atlantic, before becoming CNO. Bud had never commanded a force of major combatants at sea. . . .

I was director of strike warfare in OpNav when Bud took over as CNO, and he made a point of renewing our friendship. He wanted to send me to command of a carrier division immediately "to jump start" my future career in the youth movement he intended to initiate in the officer corps of the Navy. I could not but appreciate Bud's interest, but I had to ask him to leave me in the Pentagon for another few months. Admiral Moorer, before he had left the CNO job, had directed me to set up the office of the program coordinator for the nuclear-powered carrier program and to serve as its first incumbent, in addition to my strike warfare duties. I . . . wanted to see it well established and solidly on track before I left OpNav. Bud agreed, and I think he appreciated my willingness to extend my commitment in the bureaucracy. He promised his full and active support as CNO to the *Nimitz* program.

I was ordered to command Carrier Division 6 in the Mediterranean, which also carried the operational responsibility of commander, Striking Force, Sixth Fleet. The day after I took over, a Syrian armored column invaded Jordan and the Striking Force was activated and moved to the eastern Mediterranean. . . . Within a month the situation in Jordan was resolved by the presence of the Sixth Fleet Striking Force carriers off the Levantine littoral. The U.S. Navy was riding high, as neither the Army nor the Air Force had been able to respond to the crisis because of the nonavailability of the NATO bases. Zumwalt called me, as the operational commander, back to Washington to brief Secretary Chafee. . . .

Then in 1971, I was ordered to command the Seventh Fleet after less than a year as Deputy CinCLant. When Zumwalt called to tell me of these orders, he intimated that he had to work pretty hard to persuade Chafee, who wanted to send his senior aide to the job.

I asked Admiral Holloway what he thought had influenced Admiral Zumwalt to order him back as vice CNO.

I think there were several reasons. First, in 1971 the Seventh Fleet suddenly became the most important three-star assignment in the Navy. The U.S. was once again at war, and the Seventh Fleet was in the headlines, back in action. On 20 August 1971, as commander, Seventh Fleet, I embarked in the heavy cruiser *Newport News,* which led a four-ship bombardment group into Haiphong Harbor to attack targets in the airfield complex and the harbor facilities with naval gunfire. The foray made page 2 of the *New York Times,* complete with photographs and maps. Bud Zumwalt was delighted with the press coverage.

Later in 1972, the CNO made an official visit to the Pacific and spent two days with the Seventh Fleet, and I think he was favorably impressed. The Seventh Fleet had been built up to 153 ships, including seven carriers. It is hard not to be impressed with a fleet fighting a war with high morale and tremendous professional competence. There were no dress parades or personnel inspections as CNO Zumwalt visited the ships. That's the way the CNO wanted it. I spent the two days accompanying Zumwalt as he visited carriers, cruisers, destroyers, ammunition ships, and oilers at sea. He got an enthusiastic welcome from the sailors everywhere he landed.

I did not discuss Z-grams with Bud in our conversations. Our discussions were concerned with war-fighting matters, the availability of spare parts, the replacement of trained people, the adequacy of ammunition stocks, and the performance of the ship's commanders and flag officers. We spent a lot of time on this last topic. Bud pressed me hard for my views on the operational performance of a number of individuals. We pretty much saw eye to eye in our evaluations of the upcoming generation of COs and admirals. I didn't hold back either praise or criticism. In most cases Zumwalt agreed with my observations. We apparently had the same standards in judging flag officers.

So my selection as VCNO was probably based upon three things: first, my command of the Seventh Fleet. Second, as longtime friends, he knew me personally and professionally. There would be no surprises. Third, it is an unwritten policy that when the CNO is a surface officer or submariner, his VCNO is an aviator, and vice versa. So his VCNO field of candidates was limited to aviators, and he had to pick an aviator who was regarded as ready for promotion to four stars. Apparently I was on Bud's four-star list, he felt he would be comfortable working with me on a day-to-day basis, and he knew I was more a moderate than a conservative, and he liked that for the balance.

But when he called to tell me that he wanted me to be his VCNO, he said it was because of Dabney! . . . I was overwhelmed with the warmth of the welcome that we received. Bud had asked that we fly directly in from Japan and then I could take some leave after initially settling into the job. We flew from Japan in an Air Force VIP plane and arrived at Andrews Air Force Base about two o'clock in the afternoon. Both Bud and his wife, Mouza, were there to meet us. Mouza took Dabney in the official car and they drove into the CNO's quarters—which were then located on the Observatory grounds in the house now occupied by the vice president. Bud had a helicopter waiting for the two of us, and we flew into the helicopter pad at the Observatory grounds. Bud gave me a chance to wash up, and then we settled down in his study in the quarters with a cup of coffee and he gave me a comprehensive situation report on what was going on at the Pentagon. Bud was an extraordinarily articulate person, and he was certainly familiar with his subject. First he covered some of the very secret programs ongoing in the Navy and the Pentagon, so secret that even as commander, Seventh Fleet, I had not been cleared [to see]. Then he ran down the cast of characters in the Office of the Secretary of Defense, the Joint Chiefs of Staff, and his OpNav staff. Bud was utterly frank. He did not hold back on anyone. Bud wanted to share everything with his VCNO, and disloyalty and stupidity were two attributes that were at the head of his hit list. After a couple of hours of this very frank discussion, we joined Mouza and Dabney for a more social conversation, and at about five and Bud put us in the helicopter and sent us down to the Washington Navy Yard where we would be staying in the Visiting Flag Officer's Quarters until we could move into the permanent VCNO's residence.

I dwell on these events . . . because it was so unusual and in a way extraordinary. The Zumwalts could not have been nicer or more thoughtful and considerate to us. I look back on this with some guilty feelings. The Zumwalts were so anxious to get us well started on this tour and reestablish our close friendship of younger years as we worked together in my new job. My guilt stems from the fact that over the years I subsequently had become one of Bud's severest critics. But that negativism began later, starting about a year after I relieved him as CNO. The fallout from many of his policies began to emerge and reveal the damage that had been done to the military cohesion and character of our Navy by forcing people in the Navy to take sides: were you for human rights or for discipline? This is, of course, a very foolish characterization of our two philosophies, but unfortunately [it] came to be a perspective in which our two tours of duty as CNO were being compared.

Assuming the position of Zumwalt's VCNO was not difficult. I had relieved an especially fine four-star admiral in the job, Mickey Weisner, universally admired for his competence and integrity. He had been totally frank with Zumwalt but totally loyal as well. Bud admired Mickey and appreciated his support. I tried to fall into the same pattern as Weisner, and it worked well for me, and it made a smooth transition for Bud. Bud did not like surprises.

Bud continued to personally push those programs and projects in which he had an all-abiding interest, and pretty much left the business of fleet operations and military requirements up to me. He considered me his alter ego, as it should be in the CNO-VCNO relationship. I represented him as the Navy member of the Joint Chiefs of Staff when he was unable to attend a JCS meeting, and on one occasion took his place at the head of the dining room table in his quarters . . . at a formal dinner when he and Mouza had been called away for a family emergency. Bud was meticulous in rewarding his subordinates with a sincere pat on the back and a friendly well done, and I was a frequent recipient of these niceties, usually after I had stood in for him at a JCS meeting or some session in dealing with the Office of the Secretary of Defense.

My first surprise was how much Bud relied on his chief of information, second only to the VCNO. His public affairs officer, a dedicated Navy rear admiral, Bill Thompson, was in effect an image maker. Bud's approach to dealing with his people in the Navy was through the media of Z-grams, rap sessions, focus groups, all-hands sessions in the base auditorium, and videos. Quarterly, the chief of information would produce a very high-class and sophisticated half-hour movie entitled *The CNO Report.* This would consist mainly of clips of Admiral Zumwalt visiting the fleet, awarding medals, meeting with Navy families, digging the first spade of dirt in a new housing project, and more intimate scenes of his daily routine, including his exercise workout in gym clothes, jogging, or doing pushups. These films were professionally and skillfully done, and Bud suggested that some of his other senior commanders make periodic movies to reach out to their commands. One or two commanders actually tried, but the films got terrible reviews and were so embarrassing that no one else tried to get into this business of video reports to the troops. Bud could do it because he was photogenic, bright, articulate, and above all, passionate about his role as the personal head of the U.S. Navy. These CNO reports were distributed throughout the Navy to be shown to all hands.

The Z-grams are probably the best known of Zumwalt's communications. But it's important to understand that the Z-grams were an innovation only in their title. Ever since the Navy has had a signaling system, messages and dispatches have been going out from headquarters to the people in the fleet instructing them not only on fleet operations, but in matters of naval administration—uniforms, discipline, and leadership and housekeeping matters. In the past, all of these messages went out from the headquarters . . . as AlNavs, communications to all of the Navy. They came not from an individual by name such as Moorer, McDonald, Anderson, or Burke, but from the authority of the *office* of the chief of naval operations. Furthermore, although these OpNavs may have been posted on the bulletin boards of U.S. naval ships and stations around the world, their real implementation came through the commanding officer of each commissioned unit, who took the instructions in the AlNav and, as necessary, rephrased them in such a way . . . that they would apply directly to his command. . . . So the Z-gram was an AlNav which was personalized by the incumbent individual serving as CNO.

It is my recollection that, had I been asked who was the CNO when I was a young officer, it probably wasn't until I was a lieutenant commander I could have given the correct answer. In those days we knew our ship's skipper, our division officer, and sometimes the task force commander's name. But mainly we were working for our commanding officer, not some vague presence back in Washington. This is how the Navy was changed under Zumwalt, and it caused, in my mind, substantial problems until it all sort of went away on its own when Zumwalt departed.

The Z-grams had pretty much run their course by the time I arrived in OpNav. It was Bud's last year as CNO. By then he had launched most of his dramatic initiatives and he was fully engaged in making every effort to ensure that they were permanently institutionalized as a part of the Navy. To this end, a special office on his staff maintained a listing of all of the Zumwalt initiatives beginning with his first Z-gram. Each initiative remained in the uncompleted status of the list until the responsible officer in OpNav could convince Admiral Zumwalt that the actions prescribed by the initiative had been completed and were firmly integrated into official Navy doctrine or policy. This process in itself is not a bad management device, but it led to one of Admiral Zumwalt's greatest difficulties. That was an intense desire to get things done in a hurry, usually so fast that adequate time . . . was not taken to consider the side affects of these actions and the fallout that they generated downstream.

Asked to describe some of these hasty decisions and their ramifications, Admiral Holloway answered:

> Yes, nothing serves better than a palpable example. But first let me describe how most of these initiatives came about. Bud was appointed CNO with the forceful support of Secretary of Navy John Chafee, who reportedly had made a statement to the effect that, "Why shouldn't the Navy emulate industry, picking bright young people at the peak of their energy and productivity, without waiting for them to go through all of the mandatory hoops and check-off jobs?" Admiral Moorer had made it clear . . . that he did not support the appointment of Zumwalt because he did not have the necessary experience. Admiral Moorer wisely observed that Zumwalt probably should be CNO, and he would certainly support a man of Zumwalt's abilities in four years, after he had had an opportunity to serve at sea in command of major naval forces and in a theater command involving both Air Force and Army units. As Moorer said, "Think of how much better a CNO he would be." Zumwalt knew that the senior officers in the Navy, and his contemporaries as well, objected to this appointment.
>
> Bud in turn felt that the Navy was desperately in need of a major overhaul in every aspect, from its personnel policies to its war-fighting doctrines and its weapons. He recognized that he had been appointed to be the CNO in spite of a lack of support by the uniformed Navy. Therefore he considered it his mandate to drastically reform the Navy in all of its aspects. Bud was also smart enough to realize that to reform a traditional institution that has a two-hundred-year legacy could not happen under an administration doing business as usual. He knew that

he was going to have to get the attention of everyone in the uniformed Navy, in the Navy Secretariat, in the Office of the Secretary of the Defense, the Congress, and the White House to gain their support for these changes. He considered the best way, in fact the only way, to gain this attention was through shock tactics.

Bud Zumwalt had become convinced that the Navy had to change. But what and where? To determine this, Bud arranged for a succession of what might be called focus groups today, but which were referred to at the time as "rap sessions." He arranged to have representatives of identifiably discrete groups within the Navy meet with him in "shirt-sleeve" sessions and "let it all hang out." The first among these groups were the minorities, mainly the African Americans and Filipinos. From what I knew of Bud before he became CNO, he was not a crusader in the area of race relations or minority affairs. He first became a passionate advocate of reform as the result of his focus groups. Bud Zumwalt was so overwhelmed by the reports of discrimination, harassment, and downright brutality coming out of these sessions that as he told me later, it left an indelible scar on his conscience. Bud Zumwalt was horrified by some of the stories that he heard at sessions in which he said tears were liberally shed. Bud was a good man, a compassionate human being, and I understood how disturbed he must have been. So the initiative which gained the priority of time and resources in his program to transform the Navy was in the area of race relations. As we could expect, in the great haste and pressure to get things moving, mistakes were made. There were not enough professionally qualified minorities available to effectively fill the leadership positions proposed in some areas. Bud knew this and reluctantly accepted some failures, but only on the premise that the Navy not diminish its efforts to address those failures.

There were some—I'm not sure how many—officers in the Navy back in Zumwalt's CNO days who objected to the minority awareness projects and the equal opportunity programs. This situation alone was enough to add further justification in retrospect to Admiral Zumwalt's emphasis for corrective action in the area of the Navy's race relations. Today I don't know of anyone who went through that period with Bud who is not now convinced that he did the right thing in the way he had to do it, to make these changes . . . which if left uncorrected could bring nothing but shame and cause embarrassment to the Navy.

Zumwalt's approach to developing constructive solutions to the problems the focus groups identified, Holloway said, also followed the "rap session concept."

The minority participants were encouraged to make suggestions, with the assurance from the CNO that every idea would be carefully examined, no proposal would be rejected as being too extreme. So there were an awful lot of suggestions and a good many of them were not very sensible. But they had a desirable effect in letting the focus groups know that they were being listened to. The real problem, in my carefully considered opinion, was that the focus groups were not limited to minorities or even to groups that were subject to discrimination. It was very important to have the African Americans, the Filipinos, and the women in the service be given an opportunity to express complaints that they had never been able to surface before. But in addition to those groups, certain factions identified themselves as victims of discrimination who in my view did not qualify in the same sense as racial or gender denominations. These groups were young sailors and junior officers who complained that they did not get the same privileges as the "others" in the Navy. These "others" were the petty officers and field grade (commanders and above) commissioned officers—who had earned their perks through years of service in the lower grades. Another group that caught the CNO's sympathetic ear were the unsuccessful officers who had not gotten the assignments they wanted because they felt that they had been unfairly evaluated due to a "personality conflict" with their CO. Others considered assigning command of major ships such as aircraft carriers to the most outstanding officers as not "fair," [and thought] that everyone, including the lower-percentile performers, should have a chance to command the best.

Bud Zumwalt listened to all of these groups and directed his staff to come up with policies that would correct what were considered to be inequities. Then, unfortunately, because of the pressure placed by the CNO on quick action, decisions were made to implement policies that had not been adequately staffed or researched by experienced officers. The downstream problems were . . . horrendous.

Asked what he considered to be the main flaw in Zumwalt's philosophy, Admiral Holloway answered:

From our first days together in the front office I realized that there was a basic philosophical difference between Bud and myself on what life in the Navy should be like. Bud's premise was that Navy life should be fun, and his policies were to restore this element to the Navy. He often talked about the good old days on his destroyer when the crew would shift to whites in the afternoon and go ashore in an attractive liberty port in the Mediterranean or Caribbean. But times had changed. We were living through the cold war and Vietnam. The Navy's purpose was to fight and win wars. Fighting wars, people die. Dying and the prospect of dying are not fun. Even in peacetime, the separations for the deploying ships were becoming such hardships that it was impossible to make them "fun" in the old sense of the word.

My basic philosophy differed from Bud's in that I believed that the military career is a demanding profession and a tough life. It requires strong people with a determined dedication to serve in spite of hardship and sacrifice. I had seen this in my years in the Navy through World War II, Korea, Vietnam, and the cold war deployments. There was no way we could keep everyone in the Navy happy all of the time. I expressed these views to Bud on more than one occasion, early on. But he was adamant that changes were needed in pursuing his basic philosophies, and that shock tactics to the point of overkill were required. Although my own views were more conventional and conservative, when Bud made a decision, I took the lead in seeing they were properly carried out. Bud appreciated this and frequently commented on how important it was for his programs to be implemented by a VCNO who was an acknowledged traditionalist.

Subsequently, . . . I have concluded that the permissiveness and desire for personal recognition of the CNO as the proponent of "the good life" in the Navy drove most of those decisions which tended to erode the traditional command structure of the Navy, and in some cases threatened good order and discipline.

Zumwalt's directives also interfered with the chain of command, Holloway noted, and hampered the Navy's operations.

The chain of command was generally being bypassed throughout the Navy, although more prevalent in the rear echelons, where the sailors had more time to think about their perks than did their counterparts serving in combat in the western Pacific. By 1971 failure to follow the chain of command had become a pernicious malady that was beginning to affect the usefulness of our chief petty officers and division officers in the day-to-day running of the Navy. In several incidents a collapse of the chain of command had the potential for very serious consequences. In particular, I think of the decision of the CNO's staff in the Pentagon to countermand the orders of the commanding officer of the *Kitty Hawk* when he called out the marine detachment in battle gear to stop the rioters who were running wild through the ship's mess decks. The marines were immediately effective, and order was restored. But the rioters complained to the Pentagon that they were "being hassled" by the marines, and the commanding officer was directed to return the marine detachment to its compartment and . . . to negotiate directly with the ringleaders of the dissidents. I believe the commanding officer was able to avoid such a confrontation by remaining on the bridge and sending down a representative. Otherwise, I believe that an impossible precedent would have been set for the United States Navy.

[The general failure of the chain of command] was a natural progression from the philosophy that the Navy should be more fun, a kinder and gentler organization. The CNO, after his initial discussions with the African American minorities and his realization of the racial inequities . . . in the fleet, made a point of bringing in representatives from other constituencies and in the so-called rap sessions solicit[ed] their complaints and how they could be corrected.

For the younger officers and the nonrated sailors, whom I did not think deserved minority status or consideration, the major complaint was hairstyles and beards. At this time, the fashion for men in the civilian world was long hair . . . [and] the young men in the Navy wanted to wear their hair in the current fashion. Admiral Zumwalt decided that both officers and men could wear their hair just about any way they wanted as long as it was neat. If a man wanted to grow a beard, that was okay too. The CNO said publicly that extreme hairstyles did not affect the way a sailor or officer did his job. So the Z-grams allowed a wide range of head and facial hair arrangements. I personally had no problem with beards. When I had command of the *Enterprise* on its two deployments to the Tonkin Gulf, the sailors were allowed to grow beards . . . as long as the appearance was that of the traditional full beard sported by the salts in the old Navy. Bizarre styles such as Fu Manchu arrangements were not permitted, and it was the sailor's division officer and chief petty officer who decided whether a hairstyle or a beard was bizarre. What the chief said was the law.

When Admiral Zumwalt personally signed his name to the Z-gram concerning hairstyles, the sailor in the fleet felt that it was only the CNO himself who could stand in judgment of what was allowable, and that was the real problem. When a chief petty officer or a division officer attempted to regulate a hairstyle or beard, the sailor could cite the Z-gram, and extensive, time-wasting negotiations would become rancorous arguments, which led to dissension on the part of the sailors and exasperation on the part of the chiefs. It was a terrible waste of time, and bad feeling was developing between many sailors and their immediate supervisors. When the sailors became aware of the Z-gram that said they could appeal to the CNO, their commanding officers were obliged to hold the decision on that man's hair or beard until a new Z-gram was issued to further define the regulations. All of this back-and-forth resulted in petty quarrels which should have been quickly settled with a local command decision. But instead, something as ridiculous as the length of sideburns was being debated by the Navy staffs up to the office of the CNO. The petty officers, CPOs, division officers, and even the commanding officers had been divested of their authority of military command. The chief petty officers, who were primarily responsible for the sailors' good military discipline and appearance, were losing control. The crews' appearance was becoming unmilitary, but the chiefs couldn't do anything about it. It had to be referred to the Pentagon. It wasn't the appearance that was the problem. It was the disenfranchisement of the Navy's troop NCOs.

Then the shipboard sailors remonstrated to the CNO that they shouldn't have to chip paint because it was demeaning. Further, they said, it was for cosmetic reasons only, and did not contribute to the ship's fighting ability. This resulted in a Z-gram that essentially said sailors won't have to chip paint. Commanding officers will wait until the ship gets into port, and then civilian workers will be contracted to come aboard and chip paint. By the end of a six-month cruise, a U.S. Navy cruiser now looked like a rust-bucket, and Americans overseas, both military and civilian, wrote to the Navy Department complaining that the U.S. Navy ships in foreign ports were an embarrassment. This was a sad situation for a Navy that had always prided itself by its smartness.

At the same time, the mechanical condition of the ships began to suffer. This was due in part to a decline in the fleet maintenance account, which funded spare parts, but was exacerbated by a perceived lack of authority to require the sailors to do the dirty work of maintaining the ship's equipment in the corrosive environment of open-sea operations. If the sailors felt they were being asked to do demeaning tasks such as chip and repaint, remove rust and grime, and clean greasy engineering spaces, they could appeal to the CNO directly by telephone hotline, and thus avoid going through their chiefs, division officers, or commanding officers. So sailors and junior officers learned that if they were faced with unpleasant tasks—work, not fun—the CNO's policy was to be sympathetic with their complaints.

Most of the Z-grams were based upon good intentions and were an effort to make the Navy "fun" again. Yet many of these "harassments" and "chicken regulations" were part of the job of being in the Navy. The young authors of the Z-grams did not have the experience to foresee the side effects and the ramifications of the new policies, which so often were negatively reflected in the readiness and discipline of the fleet. In some segments of the Navy it was approaching a worrisome breakdown in discipline. The CPOs would continue to try to get the ship's work done in their traditional manner. The sailors would complain to the Pentagon that they were being hassled. The chiefs would be told to ease off. So in frustration the chiefs could do little but stick their hands down deep in their pockets and stare at the horizon.

Although Admiral Zumwalt's system was set up to respond to the inequities experienced by minorities, Admiral Zumwalt, because of his intense desire to please everybody in the Navy, was ready to listen to almost every tale of woe. Several aviation captains who were assigned to the CNO's immediate staff complained to him that they had not been selected for command of an aircraft carrier. Carrier commanders in the Navy, as a matter of established policy, were selected on the basis of their performance as naval officers and their . . . qualifications as an aviator by a selection board similar to that convened for . . . promotion[s]. The system was firmly established in naval aviation and was put in place after World War II to eliminate any taint of personal favoritism. Carrier command was a prerequisite to flag selection for an aviator. The procedure was for the selection board to arrange the eligible captains in relative order of merit, and the top twenty naval aviation captains in the Navy got command of the twenty carriers. Those captains who screened below the carrier cutoff point were ordered to command of naval air stations, as many as were available, in priority order. The rest did not get a major command. Admiral Zumwalt, after hearing the complaints of the aviation captains who were disappointed because they did not rank high enough to get a carrier, changed the policy. The new procedure was that the aviator captains would still be ranked on the major command list by merit, but would be alternatively assigned carriers and air stations. So the second, fourth, sixth, and so on best aviation captains in the Navy were arbitrarily excluded from carrier command in order to provide carriers for those captains ranked below the top twenty, "to be fair." In addition to depriving some truly fine and deserving officers of carrier command, the high point of their career, the carriers, which were the Navy's most complex and demanding weapons system, did not get the best-qualified officers as their commanders. As we well know in the Navy, command is everything. The sailors and the Navy suffered from this. An air station command was looked upon by the aviation community as a definite second best . . . like being the justice of the peace of a small town. So we had some very fine naval aviators go to naval air stations instead of a carrier command. Their talents were largely wasted this year during their most productive potential. And the carrier force, the main line of the battle fleet, did not get the best officers available in the Navy as operational and combat leaders.

The cause of this decision was a breakdown in the chain of command. The CNO did not consult with or take the advice of his number two in the chain of command, the VCNO—an aviator. Instead, the CNO made a decision to keep a small group "happy," seemingly regardless of whether they deserved it or of the impact upon the operational capabilities of the fleet.

It was also the direct result of Admiral Zumwalt's inexperience in aviation matters. He had never served as a task force or fleet commander, and therefore had never been aboard an operating carrier in the status of a responsible senior. Being a surface warfare officer, he never had carrier duty as an assignment, because it was the policy that up-and-coming surface warfare officers were not assigned duties aboard the carriers. Admiral Burke was also a surface warfare officer, but as a captain was recognized as a naval officer of outstanding future potential, and was therefore ordered as Marc Mitscher's chief of staff in Task Force 38 during World War II. When Admiral Burke became CNO, there were few officers on active duty who had seen more air combat operations from the bridge of a carrier and in its war room . . . and that experience was invaluable during his six-year tenure as CNO.

The problem of the lack of carrier experience by submariners and surface warfare officers has been corrected since Admiral Zumwalt's time. In 1975 the Bureau of Personnel initiated a policy that the top percentile of surface and submarine nuclear-trained officers would serve on carriers as engineering officers. This move not only broadened the future career opportunities of those officers, it caused the material condition of the carrier force to improve dramatically. Then in 1976, the Navy's operational organization underwent a major change when the CNO redesignated the attack carrier striking groups as battle groups, and battle group commanders were selected from submarine and surface warfare officers as well as aviators. They flew their flags aboard the aircraft carrier, which was the centerpiece of the battle group's striking power. These flag officers could then go on to fleet and theater commands with a full and practical understanding and appreciation of the employment of carrier aviation in the overall naval strategy and in its tactical dispositions.[47]

In his book *The Twenty-five Year War*, Gen. Bruce Palmer Jr., one of the Army's most respected and articulate general officers, offered his opinion of Zumwalt.

Admiral Elmo R. Zumwalt, Jr., succeeded Admiral Moorer as Chief of Naval Operations on 1 July 1970 and served until 19 June 1974. He was neither his predecessor's nor the Navy's sentimental choice for the job, as he was relatively junior and lacked major command experience. But he was bright and energetic and his systems analysis background was a big plus in dealing with the civilian bureaucracy in Defense. At JCS sessions he was sometimes naïve (particularly with respect to the conduct of the war) and often an irritant, but I admired his courage in tackling deep-seeded internal problems of the Navy.[48]

Bruce Palmer had been director of the Joint Staff and later was the Army's vice chief of staff, a regular attender of JCS meetings. His statement implies that Admiral Zumwalt's relations with the other chiefs were less than amicable. I asked Admiral Holloway to comment on this observation.

Remember, as VCNO, I never accompanied Admiral Zumwalt to the tank, I only met with the chiefs as his representative when he could not attend. But he rigorously debriefed me after each of his JCS meetings. Also he dictated an aide-mémoire of every session for his own personal use. Normally his OpDep, a three-star admiral who attended the meetings with him, also prepared a memo for the record.

From Bud's debriefs, reports from his OpDep, and my own presence in the tank as the CNO's representative, I early on came to the conclusion that Bud considered the tank not to be a collegial group to arrive at joint discussions, but an arena in which the Navy fought it out with the other services. His first priority was to establish the Navy position on a JCS staff paper as the joint position, [or,] this failing, to express a minority position in such strength that it became a persuasive document in its own right. When a JCS position paper was not at issue, Bud worked hard to have his views in any discussion dominate the JCS deliberations, and Bud was smart enough and could think on his feet so well that the Navy philosophy—as articulated by Admiral Zumwalt—was always a factor influencing the secretary of defense, who was present at every Friday meeting.

Much of the discussion in the tank in those days was associated with nuclear weapons policy, and Bud was particularly articulate in this area. This was not a popular subject with most members of the JCS, who believed nuclear weapons would never be released except for a strategic attack which would escalate—or degenerate—in minutes to an all-out maximum exchange that would obliterate both the U.S. and the USSR, their conventional forces, their economy, and their industrial bases. Consequently, the arcane strategies for limited nuclear war, nuclear war at sea, tactical nukes, were largely considered abstract exercises that had no real impact because they would never be employed or even considered because of the danger of escalation to mutual assured destruction. However, debate was Zumwalt's . . . forte, and being a nuclear strategist did not involve much—if any—prior military combat experience. So the nuclear issue attracted Bud. And he was quick to become involved in "what if" discussions which could become abstract and unreal in a short time.

Bud Zumwalt had a particular disdain for the Russians, and that attitude was reflected in his approach to the Strategic Arms Limitation Talks (SALT). He was a real hard-liner. I personally thought that the alternatives he espoused for the Navy position were so one-sided in our favor that the Soviets, first, would never take them seriously or, second, be so provoked with the transparent attempt to gain nuclear superiority that they would push us to the brink, where a nuclear crisis became more probable. Zumwalt always wanted to provoke, taunt, or if possible embarrass the Russians. It was an interesting predilection of his, but it was not useful in the JCS. It was not realistic as far as the SALT objectives were concerned, and that is what the JCS were being asked to comment on. Further, it was a problem for the Joint Staff people, who did not know how to address the Navy position because it defied a rational analysis—theories such as "nuclear war at sea" (but not on land). It simply wasn't realistic and as such, wasted a lot of time and created some doubt in the minds of the other chiefs. Was Zumwalt playing games with them? The CNO's evaluation of the Soviet Navy's number one-status also fell into this limbo when the Joint Staff was formulating joint plans. Was this interservice gamesmanship in pursuit of a larger share of the defense dollar? I believe the other services probably thought so.

There is an interesting example of Admiral Zumwalt's frame of reference for jointness and interservice rivalry. In Norman Polmar's monumental book *Rickover,* he reports asking Admiral Zumwalt, as CNO, what did he consider the greatest threat to the U.S. Navy. Admiral Zumwalt replied, "The Soviet Navy, Admiral Rickover, and the U.S. Air Force, in that order." Just before he retired, Zumwalt was asked this same question again by Polmar. "The threats are the same but I have changed their order of importance: the U.S. Air Force, Admiral Rickover, and the Soviet Navy." I personally cannot explain Bud's hang-up on the U.S. Air Force as a threat to the U.S. Navy. So I think I probably have to agree with General Bruce Palmer, that the other chiefs felt Zumwalt tended to stir things up in the tank without making much progress toward the creation of joint policies or the furthering of joint operations.

Zumwalt's insistence that the Soviet Navy was superior to the U.S. Navy was a sore point with Admiral Holloway.

There was one preoccupation of Bud's that really concerned me at the time, and it still bothers me when I think of it. He took the position that the Soviet Navy was superior to the U.S. Navy, and he testified to this before the Congress. He made a statement that he wished he were in Gorbachev's shoes, because the Soviet Navy had the support of the Soviet government. He said on many occasions that "if war started tomorrow, the Soviet Navy would whup our ass." Bud consistently reiterated this theme with his staff and also when he addressed groups of sailors. I personally felt that this was very wrong. We had only to look at current history and the scope and capability of the U.S. fleet, which was fighting a war in Vietnam with as many as seven carriers operating in the Seventh Fleet and at the same time keeping two to three carriers in the Atlantic and Mediterranean in a posture to deter a general war with the Soviet Union through both their conventional and nuclear capabilities. Furthermore, the Soviets had no real amphibious capability. It is doubtful that they could have put a thousand troops ashore in an opposed amphibious assault. Yet the United States was able to keep an amphibious ready group in the Mediterranean and a division of marines in the western Pacific, utilizing amphibious forces continually to land both U.S. marines and often [South Vietnamese] Army troops in amphibious operations during Vietnam.

I remonstrated with Bud on several occasions shortly after I arrived as his VCNO, pointing out that we were superior to the Russians in every category. He replied that the Russians had more ships than we did, almost fifteen hundred compared to our five hundred. I stated that we had sixteen aircraft carriers and the Soviets had none—their two carriers were both helicopter platforms. We had six or seven of these that were part of the Marine Amphibious Force. So numbers alone did not count, particularly since a very numerically large part of the Soviet Navy's fifteen hundred ships were patrol craft only slightly larger than PT boats that could not operate on the high seas.

I never really was able to determine in my own mind whether Bud really believed that we were number two or whether he was just saying this for political reasons in an effort to persuade the White House, the DoD, and the Congress to provide greater support for his shipbuilding programs. I never did hear him ever say anything to imply that the U.S. Navy was superior to the Soviet Navy, even in our most private conversations. Both of us agreed that in an all-out nuclear war, the surface ships on both sides would be destroyed. But then so would be Moscow, Washington, and all of the military bases and missile fields of the U.S., USSR, and their allies.

One undesirable aspect of this "the Russians are coming" preoccupation was the effect on our sailors. In my first week as CNO, I visited [the] Jacksonville, Florida, area, the site of a number of naval and air bases. I met with sailors from all of the local area commands in the very large base theater at the naval air station. This was my first public meeting as CNO. After my remarks I said I would answer questions. The first question was immediate: "Sir, are the Russians really number one and are we number two as the world's navies?" I didn't pause before replying: "The answer is no. The United States Navy is the finest in the world and is number one in comparison with any other navy. I do believe that the Soviets . . . are competitors with us, but they are just as clearly number two in the ranking of capability." With that, the entire theater spontaneously broke into applause. The sailors did not stand up. They didn't shout. They didn't wave their hands. They simply sat in their seats and applauded until I had to interrupt them. . . I was impressed with the dignity and maturity with which they received my answer.

I asked Admiral Holloway if their differences in philosophy caused difficulties in his relationship as VCNO with Admiral Zumwalt.

The answer is absolutely not. These may have been differences in philosophy, but they were not disagreements. I felt that I should speak up in those cases where I thought that his statements or policies or actions could go awry, or have side effects that he did not anticipate. But if after my inputs he persisted in his position, then that became CNO policy and I was a protagonist of that policy as long as I was VCNO.

At this point I must make an important and positive observation about Admiral Zumwalt. His most strongly expounded philosophy relating to major weapon system procurement was his "high-low mix" approach. This concept would limit acquisition of large, expensive ships [i.e., nuclear-powered vessels] in order to provide funds for simpler, less expensive units which could be procured in larger numbers in order to arrest the decline in the size of the fleet. The two major ship classes authorized by the Congress during Zumwalt's tenure were the *Oliver Hazard Perry*–class frigate in fiscal year 1973 and the *Ohio*-class SSNB in 1974. The *Perry* [exemplified] the low side of the mix and received Admiral Zumwalt's special attention during its development. The *Ohio* ballistic missile submarine was clearly high mix, the largest submersible ever constructed by the U.S. Navy and, of course, nuclear powered. But Zumwalt recognized its unique capabilities and the need for it in the national strategic arsenal, and he buried his animosity toward Rickover in this case and became a remarkably strong and effective advocate with the DoD and the Congress for its authorization and programming.

Zumwalt also inherited a number of other high-mix procurement programs from previous administrations, notably the *Nimitz*-class CVN, *Los Angeles*–class submarine, the *Spruance*-class destroyer, the S-3 Viking ASW aircraft, and the F-14 Tomcat. Zumwalt recognized the superior war-fighting capabilities in each of these systems and the essentiality of their place in the inventory of the future fleet. Again, he was unequivocal and determined in his support as CNO for these ongoing procurement programs. As his VCNO at the time, I can personally attest to his vigorous and powerful personal advocacy of the nuclear-powered carrier and the Tomcat. I was deeply impressed by his commitment to these programs he had inherited. It is also of interest to note that all of the classes of ships and aircraft referred to above as principal procurement programs during Admiral Zumwalt's four-year tour as CNO are still active as first-line fleet units, and were engaged in combat in the "Iraqi Freedom" war in 2003.

Asked if Admiral Zumwalt had discussed his possible successors as CNO, Holloway replied:

Yes, Bud was open about his plans for the next CNO. He told me when I arrived from the Seventh Fleet that I was one of his candidates. At the same time, Admiral Worth Bagley was in London as CinCUSNavEur with four stars, and was involving his command in some personnel welfare programs that were attracting a lot of the CNO's attention. During the early days of Zumwalt's tour as CNO, Vice Admiral Worth Bagley was an enthusiastic supporter of Bud's philosophy and a tireless worker in seeing its quick and effective implementation. Bud and Worth were not only simpatico, they worked well together. By putting Worth in CinCUSNavEur with four stars, just as he had brought me into VCNO with four stars, Admiral Zumwalt had positioned the two of us as contenders for the CNO job when he retired. There were other four-star admirals who considered themselves in contention as well, and one of them was Admiral Ike Kidd. However Admiral Zumwalt . . . could not support Kidd because . . . he was conservative to the point that he would move quickly to undo all of the changes that Zumwalt had made in the Navy. So in actuality, the competition for the CNO's job, with nine months to go, was pretty well confined to Admiral Worth Bagley and myself.

In the end, Worth had the support of Zumwalt; Holloway had the backing of the JCS chairman, Adm. Tom Moorer. Secretary of Defense James

Schlesinger selected Admiral Holloway. The ritual of notification was interesting. As Holloway described it:

> I was working at my desk in the VCNO's office on 12 May 1974 when I had a call from the secretary of the navy, John Warner. Warner said, "Get your cap, we are going to make a trip to the other side of the river. Stop by my office on the way to the River Entrance [of the Pentagon]." Secretary Warner was waiting when I got to the car, and we drove to the White House. We were met by the naval aide, who immediately led us to the Oval Office, where we were ushered in without waiting. President Nixon was there alone, obviously waiting for us. We sat down, and Nixon asked me a few innocuous questions about my Naval Academy class, my aviation experience, and then almost suddenly said as he stood up, "I know you'll make a good CNO, you have everybody's confidence." We shook hands, had our pictures taken, and holding me by the arm, he led me out. When we got to the door, he stopped and, confronting me, he said, "Admiral Holloway, get some discipline and pride back in the Navy. I'm an old Navy man and I'm not very pleased with what's going on in the Navy today."
>
> During my first interview with the press after becoming CNO, the obvious question was asked, "What changes are you going to make? Which direction is the Navy going?" I replied, 'There is a traditional expression that comes from the sailing Navy that says that the oncoming officer of the watch should not change the set of the sail in the first fifteen minutes of his watch. I'm going to wait a while before I consider changing the set of the sails." This was more than just an adage. I considered it the only wise course. There was turmoil in the Navy at that time. A lot of people didn't like Zumwalt because of his liberal policies. There were also a lot of people who didn't like me because they thought I would change things back to the way they were. We had to get our differences under control, heal, and unify the Navy again. The Navy didn't need more changes at that time.
>
> The Navy was in deplorable shape as far as discipline and morale were concerned. In Norfolk in the fall of 1974, a group of sailors armed with pistols and wearing ski masks rampaged through the enlisted barracks robbing their fellow sailors at gun point. This sounds almost unbelievable. My immediate and overwhelming reaction was, we've got to change things, and quickly. I was convinced that the Norfolk incident was just one manifestation of . . . discipline problems . . . throughout the Navy. We had to have positive actions by the leadership at the top and then assure our commanding officers they had the full support of the Department of the Navy to do whatever was necessary to fix this frightening breakdown in discipline.

It had to be our number-one priority. We couldn't accomplish any improvement in fleet readiness without discipline.

At first there seemed to be no real feeling of urgency on the part of some people in the Navy to get discipline back in the fleet. Their excuse seemed to be, "That's the way it is on the outside. Our sailors are just reflecting the post-Vietnam counterculture." As vice chief I had realized that we had discipline problems, but I didn't have a real appreciation of the extent. . . . I stayed in the Pentagon while Bud visited the fleet and the field activities. In my first week as CNO I was asked if I would go to Norfolk to inspect the new alcohol rehabilitation center that had recently been opened on the base. I had not realized that alcohol and drug rehab was a big issue in the fleet, so I was quite interested. I flew to Norfolk, transferred to a car, and drove around the naval base for a general overview. It was around 11:30 A.M. and the car literally had to crawl . . . because of the hundreds of sailors on the streets coming up from the waterfront. They were in dungarees. I asked the captain of the base, who was escorting me, where the sailors were going. He replied, "They're going to the Enlisted Club. We've got a great deal. Our E Club is really making money. During the week, from 11:30 to 12:30 we offer a martini happy hour, two drinks for the price of one, and we have topless go-go dancers, too. It has really put this E Club back in the black." I asked, "Are you in favor of this?" He said, "It has made the Enlisted Club solvent. We hardly need the slot machines anymore. It was proposed from our all-hands session at the base theater last year." This was a forum that had been established by an earlier Z-gram.

So I inspected the alcohol rehab center, which seemed underutilized, and then went to the waterfront, where all the fleet units—carriers, cruisers, destroyers, supply ships, and amphibious vessels—were tied up at the piers. On the waterfront, you expect to hear paint chipping and gear banging, but it was dead quiet. I went aboard a couple of ships and there was no work being done. I asked where the sailors were. I was informed, "Well, a lot of them have gone to the PX or are down in their berthing compartments."

I suggested to the captain, "If these sailors have been drinking at noon, you're not going to get any work out of them this afternoon." He said, "Well, even though they have a couple of beers at lunch, they still ought to be able to do a day's work." I said, "Let me be realistic. I'm a normal human being. If I had two double martinis in the middle of the day, I know I'd be through [with] any productive work. Physiologically, they're no different than I am. I can't believe they can be productive in the afternoon. I sure wouldn't want them working on my airplane." I got a couple of the ship skippers together and they told me, "It's terrible, Admiral. These young teenage sailors go up to the club almost every day in their dungarees. They come back to the ship, but they don't work. They just sort of drift around going through the motions of doing their job, but nothing really gets done after the middle of the day." Here was an example of permissiveness that was really hurting the Navy. It was supposed to be good for the young seamen's morale, subsidized booze and topless dancers in the middle of the working day. And it wasn't really legal; most of the young sailors weren't twenty-one. ID cards were never checked. The attitude seemed to be, "If a kid is old enough to fight, he's old enough to drink."

I decided this middle-of-the-day bingeing had to be stopped. But it just couldn't be limited to the enlisted clubs. When I got back to the Pentagon I personally drafted an order that said in effect, "There will be no alcohol served at any of the clubs on a naval base or station during working hours. The bars will not open until 5:00 P.M. and will close at midnight." The reaction was immediate. A fleet CinC called me and said I couldn't do this. "The retired officers and their wives in the local community use the officers' club, and they like to have a cocktail or beer or wine with lunch." My reply was, "I'm sorry that the retireds got caught up in this thing, but base clubs are primarily for active-duty people so they can dine without going off the base. If the retireds want to drink before 5:00 P.M., they can have it at home or at a local bar or restaurant. Norfolk and Virginia Beach are full of them. We have to run these base facilities primarily for active fleet people." The Navy needed to be operating at maximum efficiency to recover from the aftermath of Vietnam, and any policy concerning alcohol had to be consistent with everybody. We had to be tough on this issue.

A week later a related problem surfaced. The chief petty officers' clubs asserted that it had been a long-term traditional privilege for them to remain open and serve liquor twenty-four hours per day. Their reasoning was that chiefs sometimes work unusual hours. And if a chief has the graveyard shift, and he gets off at eight in the morning, he ought to be able to go to his club and get a drink. My first reaction was that the Navy should not sponsor drinking at eight in the morning. There is no counterpart to this in civilian life. If they have to, the chiefs can get their drink at home or in a local bar. I held fast to my dictum of bar hours from five to midnight. So all of the base clubs had the same bar hours. There were sporadic complaints for a couple of weeks, and then it was accepted. After that, the issue of drinking during the working day went away.

Another misfortune occurred during my first month as CNO. An amphibious group of five ships left Norfolk to cross the Atlantic to join the Sixth Fleet in the Mediterranean. Only one of them made it as far as Gibraltar under its own power. One never left the pier in Norfolk, and the other three broke down en route and had to be towed into port. Shortly thereafter, I appeared before the House Armed Services Committee to testify on fleet readiness. The poor material condition of our naval vessels was a principal concern of the congressmen. I took a lot of heat, and it was well deserved. The committee's allegation was that the ships were in terrible condition. I agreed but added, "Yes, but Congress has to bear some of the responsibility. You haven't appropriated the necessary funds for overhauls, repairs, or spare parts. The Navy's budget is at the lowest point since 1948 after World War II." The committee responded that their staff were reporting that the crews are not doing the maintenance they should. I replied, "There is some truth to that report, and there are two reasons. First, the work ethic in the fleet has eroded. We are working hard to correct that. But a more serious concern and a related cause is that we have a shortage of experienced petty officers, who are our real maintenance and repair technicians. The young sailors lack the training and experience to maintain much less repair this complex equipment. Our best sailors are not reenlisting," I continued. "They are frustrated in their jobs because they don't have the parts and equipment to maintain the ships and aircraft and they work long hours scavenging for temporary makeshift solutions. It is demoralizing for a responsible, conscientious sailor. We are working on that problem, too, training our new people. But you've got to give us some time."

The committee chairman said, "We'll help you. We could legislate a policy that for any ship that fails a readiness inspection, the captain will be relieved of his command." I said, "Please don't do that. The Navy is just as hard up for competent captains as experienced petty officers. And it's not necessarily the captain's fault. We've hit the point now where the more we push the crews, take their liberty away from them, and work them around the clock, the worse their morale becomes. Any more squeezing and they may give up altogether. It's a very delicate balance. We are routinely working them ten to twelve hours a day. But if it were to become sixteen hours a day, I'm afraid the men would become physically and psychologically exhausted." The committee's response was: "We don't think you're being tough enough." So, I had the Congress on my back as well.

So we moved slowly, restored discipline, and gave authority back to the petty officers. At the suggestion of Admiral Rickover and with the personal support of Vice Adm. Jim Watkins, the chief of naval personnel, we established a four-week school for prospective ship-commanding officers to learn machinery maintenance and repair at the trade-school level. It was something the nuclear program had done for years with great success. Then I held the commanding officers accountable for the good material condition of their ships, and the fleet commanders responsible for providing the number of people and the proper equipment allowed by the tables of organization and supply. Everyone in the chain of command at all echelons had to become productively involved.

I was working on the other disciplinary issues at the same time. I ordered there will be no bizarre facial hair. All sailors will be required to present a military appearance, defined by the commanding officers and regulated by the petty officers. However, the sailors still looked awful in their new uniforms, which was a single-breasted blue suit with a white shirt and black necktie. Unfortunately, a white shirt looks like hell if you don't put on a clean one every day. That meant these kids had to have six or seven shirts, which they could not afford nor stow or wash aboard ship. This was one of the initiatives that would require specific action to rescind the changes. It is interesting that the restoration of the bellbottoms was driven by the sailors themselves. Practically from the day that I moved behind the CNO's desk, my mail included letters pleading to bring back the traditional bellbottoms. A lot of these were from retired people and girlfriends, and they carried little weight. It was the mail from the active-duty sailors in the fleet that got my attention. Even more persuasive were my contacts with the bluejackets when I embarked in Navy ships. As I visited the working spaces— shops, berthing compartments, working areas, and engine rooms—small groups of sailors would congregate, and after the ice was broken, they brought up what was foremost in their minds. Invariably it was their uniforms. They really wanted to look like sailors. They were sailors, and very proud of it. It was when President Jimmy Carter visited the USS *Eisenhower* at sea that the issue really surfaced. Groups of sailors cornered both the president and the secretary of the navy and brought up the subject of returning the bellbottoms and jumper. President Carter thought it was a great idea, and Secretary Claytor said he would look into it. The crew also approached me on changing back the uniform, but I had already gotten BuPers looking into the details of cost, time to effect, and the other hard parts of the transition process.

When I returned to the Pentagon, I called a special meeting of the CNO Advisory Board—the CAB—which was made up of all of the flag officers in OpNav, the CNO's staff. There were about fifteen of them. I told them I was thinking about going back to the old uniform; bellbottoms, blouse, and round hat, and I wanted to get their views. After considerable discussion only one admiral had reservations; the rest of the CAB was all for it. With all this enthusiasm bubbling around the table I felt safe in saying, "Let's take a vote." That was a mistake. They all hesitated. They didn't think the Office of the Secretary of Defense would approve because of the expense. Comptrollers have a reputation of not being able to relate dollars to abstract values such as morale. Some of the officers felt to change back would indicate that the original decision was wrong. They were correct. I said to them, "Now that I have heard your concerns, which seem to be different from your desires, I will make a command decision. We will go back to the old uniform. Meeting dismissed." The CAB was delighted and asked for another vote to show their support. It was unanimous.

That got it started, but first I had to get it through Navy Secretary Graham Claytor. So after our meeting, I briefed the secretary of the navy that we were going back to the old uniforms. His reaction was, "I am all for it, but I am not sure you have the authority to do that, even though I agree." So he consulted his lawyers, and they informed him that the CNO is responsible for uniforms in the naval service, not the SecNav or SecDef. So Graham Claytor came onboard, and later when he became deputy secretary of defense under Harold Brown, he was very helpful in getting the decision through the bureaucracy of the SecDef staff.

Several months later, Admiral Holloway received a message that confirmed his judgment. It was a clipping from the *Washington Post* with a photograph of a sailor in bellbottoms and an article. On the clipping was handwritten: "Admiral Holloway, I am an old Navy man. I like your decision on the bellbottom trousers. Jimmy Carter, White House."[49]

What kind of marks does Admiral Zumwalt receive today, some thirty years after his stint as CNO, for his revolutionary personnel policies to improve retention? The figures indicate that the policies had at least that desired effect. Admiral Zumwalt himself stated that "first-term reenlistments had risen from a low of 10 percent during FY '70, just before I assumed office, to 32.9 percent during FY '74." Retention continued to improve throughout his tenure.

Several books written about Admiral Zumwalt evaluate his four years as CNO. Frederick Hartman, the author of *Naval Renaissance,* summed up Admiral Zumwalt and his policies as follows:

> Even today, senior naval officers disagree about the changes introduced by Admiral Zumwalt. Some feel that changes were overdue, given the changing temperament and outlook of American youth; others believe that he produced an

intolerable mess for his successor; all agree that he bypassed the traditional chain-of-command with his Z-grams and special advisory groups for racial problems and the like. In an interview in April 1986, Admiral James Watkins expressed his opinion succinctly: "We lost it in the chiefs' quarters."

Zumwalt supporters say his approach was necessary because otherwise bureaucratic stonewalling would have nullified his policies. His detractors point especially to the pernicious effects of undermining petty officer (and junior officer) authority in bypassing of the chain of command. Some straddle the fence: it was necessary to proceed as Zumwalt did, and it created a mess. Vice Admiral William H. Rowden recalled holding mast in those years and being told by the accused sailor that the CNO's Z-grams said he could not be tried! Vice Admiral Staser Holcomb, a definite supporter of Zumwalt, thought the Navy came into the Twentieth Century under Zumwalt, and would not have otherwise. The way he did it left a lot to be desired. "You came to work in the morning not knowing what new right had been granted overnight."[50]

Norman Friedman, in his article on Zumwalt in *The Chiefs of Naval Operations*, concluded:

When Elmo R. Zumwalt became chief of naval operations on 1 July 1970, he was the youngest man to hold the office. He will probably be remembered as the naval chieftain who tried to rock the boat, who sought to make fundamental changes in naval policy during an era dominated by generally conservative flag officers. As chief of naval operations, he appeared to offer the Navy revolutionary solutions to its gravest problems, rather than the evolutionary changes with which most of the naval community felt comfortable. And, in contrast to his predecessors and contemporaries, Zumwalt was flamboyant: his style resembled the charismatic, vigorous military leader of the past, rather than the colorless, bureaucratic manager of modern armed forces. Whereas another admiral might have stressed continuity, Zumwalt preferred to sharpen the differences between his innovations and previous practices in an attempt to change underlying trends in naval policy and thought.[51]

Thomas J. Cutler, in the profile on Admiral Zumwalt in his book *Quarterdeck and Bridge*, noted the difficulty inherent in trying to classify Zumwalt's accomplishments:

Many important figures in history are easily classified as either heroes or villains. Few but the iconoclastic historian would have difficulty categorizing the likes of

George Washington or Adolph Hitler. Some historical entities, however, fall into a different category altogether. The names of these individuals are guaranteed to provoke a reaction, if rarely a predictable one. The mere mention of the name Douglas MacArthur, for example, will almost always bring forth hymns of praise or venomous fulminations but rarely anything in between.

Whether permanently condemned to this purgatorial characterization or merely waiting for the mellowing effects of time, Admiral Elmo R. Zumwalt Jr. at the time of this writing, is one of these individuals. A history-making admiral merely by being the youngest U.S. Chief of Naval Operations (CNO), Zumwalt was not content to steer the familiar courses taken by his predecessors. From the very beginning of his tenure as CNO, he was a champion of change who dared to sail into the political mine fields sown by traditionalists and special interest groups and was ever willing to "rock the boat" in an attempt to correct what he perceived as the serious ills of the U.S. Navy during the early 1970s.

Because he was appointed to the Navy's highest military office over the heads of many more senior admirals, opposition to his policies might have been inevitable, but a more conservative approach on his part would surely have minimized it. By overturning strategic thinking, liberalizing the Navy's personnel policies and practices, daring to challenge the omnipotence of the Navy's long-standing nuclear czar, and using unconventional means to attempt many of these changes, Zumwalt was bound to earn either the profound respect or the fervid execration of those bearing witness to all of this revolutionary turmoil. Like MacArthur and other controversial figures before him, "Bud" Zumwalt is rarely the object of indifference, and he is frequently referred to as either the savior or the ruination of the Navy of the 1970s.[52]

CHAPTER 10

Selflessness

We are honored to have had the opportunity to serve our country under difficult circumstances. We are profoundly grateful to our commander in chief and to our nation for this day. God bless America.

Rear Adm. Jeremiah A. Denton, USN (Ret.)
Prisoner of War—Vietnam
July 18, 1966–March 28, 1973

Three Navy Heroes

During the Vietnam War, 771 American military pilots were captured and interned by the North Vietnamese. Several extensive studies of the experiences of American military prisoners of war during the Vietnam War have been published. They include *P.O.W.: A Definitive History of the American Prisoner-of-War Experience in Vietnam, 1964–1973* by John G. Hubbell; *Honor Bound: The History of American Prisoners of War in Southeast Asia, 1961–1973* by Stuart I. Rochester and Frederick Kiley; and *Voices of the Vietnam POWs* by Craig Howes. Because this book is a study of naval leadership, I will focus on the POW experiences of three Navy pilots: Jeremiah A. Denton, James B. Stockdale, and Everett Alvarez Jr. Their courage and dedication to duty reflect inspirational, selfless leadership and set an example for others of all services to emulate.

I have had many opportunities to interview Adm. Jeremiah Denton, who was a commander at the time of his capture. The following story describes his experiences in detail and puts into perspective the leadership qualities of senior American naval commanders under the harshest conditions.

Commander Jeremiah A. Denton

Commander Denton was the first POW to step off the Air Force plane that flew him, along with thirty-nine other POWs, from Hanoi to the Philippines on March 28, 1973.[1] Exiting the door, he threw back his shoulders and at the bottom of the ramp saluted the senior officers and spoke with them briefly. He then addressed the assembled group, offering the inspiring message quoted above. There could be no better testimonial of a warrior's selfless service.

On July 18, 1965, Commander Denton was the flight leader of a group of twenty-eight aircraft from the USS *Independence*. It was his twelfth combat flight over Vietnam, and he had been the flight leader on each mission. During his bombing run, his aircraft was hit at bomb release; within seconds he lost all internal and external communications equipment and the controls failed. He slammed his left foot so hard on the rudder pedal trying to keep his aircraft level that the left tendon in his thigh snapped and recoiled into his abdomen, making his leg useless.

After a harrowing ejection from his aircraft, his thoughts as he floated down were on escaping. A strong swimmer, his plan was to swim underwater to a marshy area of the river where he would hide, breathing through a hollow reed, until dark, when he might be picked up by a rescue helicopter. Things did not work out as he planned. His injuries were so serious that he could not use his left leg. Two civilians hoping for a reward pursued him in a canoe and, when they caught up to him, hit him on the back and neck with the flat side of a machete, cutting him deeply. Having lost his pistol during the ejection, he was defenseless. North Vietnamese soldiers standing along both sides of the embankments of the river fired at the civilians to stop them from harming him further. In the canoe his arms were tied behind him and he was taken to the bank of the river and dragged ashore, dazed and bleeding.

Reflecting later on his seven years and eight months of imprisonment he said, "My heritage, training, and background made me the very antithesis of everything my communist captors stood for. . . . My heart and soul belonged to God, country, and family long before the Navy got hold of me. My religious upbringing and my mother's strong influence shaped my character. . . . My mother, a Roman Catholic, brought her children up in an atmosphere that would have a profound effect on my life." This foundation would be his rock in the years he spent as a POW.

His injuries prevented him from walking, so he was put on a wooden plank. As he was being carried on the plank, an American A-4 flew over to assess the possibility of a rescue. Afraid for their lives, the North Vietnamese soldiers dropped Denton and the plank and ran for cover. The pain of the impact caused him to pass out. When the soldiers returned, he then was placed in a jeep, tied hand and foot, and blindfolded for the trip to Hanoi and a POW camp. The first picture taken of him as a captive shows a swollen face, evidence that he had been beaten.

His prison covered a full block in the middle of Hanoi. While being led to his cell he was heartened by sounds in the distance of a fellow POW whistling "Yankee Doodle." "My heart skipped a beat," Denton recalled, "and a joyful feeling flowed through my body. I was not alone." The prison was called Hoa Loa Prison by the North Vietnamese; Americans came to know it as the "Hanoi Hilton." It was given the nickname by Bob Schumaker, an inmate with whom Denton would form a close friendship.

His nine-by-eight-foot cell had two solid concrete beds that were three and a half feet high. Metal and wood stocks sat at the foot of the bed. A small pail served as a toilet. The window was barred. Two days after his internment, he was awakened and told he was to be questioned. The snapped tendon had broken through the skin and he could not walk, so his captors forced him, at the point of a bayonet, to crawl to the interrogation room. For the first time, he remembered, "I became acutely concerned with my welfare."

All captured American military personnel are required to live by the Military Code of Conduct, which allows a prisoner to give to captors only his or her name, grade, serial number, and date of birth. In Denton's initial interrogation, the North Vietnamese sought statements of propaganda value. The value of any military intelligence he might carry would decrease rapidly, so they were eager to find out immediately what he knew. After this session the guards took him to a latrine with toilets and washing facilities. It was small, filthy, and smelly. Finding a piece of broken glass, he hid it in his clothes, fearing that "prolonged torture would have broken me to the point that I would reveal enough about the airplane to dishonor myself." It was six days before they let him bathe, and then only with a bucket of water; it was nevertheless a moment of "rare luxury."

"The guards urinated in a gutter that ran along the outside door of the cell," Denton remembered,

> so the place stank. Roaches and flies covered the walls and floor, and sometimes my body. The food, by American standards, was wretched. We frequently saw the guards picking out the few tiny bits of meat and pig fat before the meals got to us. This was a steady source of irritation. By the time breakfast was shoved under the door about ten-thirty I was literally drooling. The food was meager, soup with some greens and occasionally a piece of pork fat, and rice, and I would leap at it and gulp it straight from the pewter plates. I was hungry again as soon as I finished eating, and it wasn't until about four-thirty that the next meal was shoved under the door. In more than two years there were few times when I wasn't desperate for food.
>
> My stomach hurt constantly from the snapped tendon, and there was the festering wound on the inside of my thigh where the other end of the tendon had broken through the skin. I sweltered on the bare concrete bunk, clad only in my underwear. I had no shoes or sandals, and I wasn't allowed to bathe. Worst of all, I was alone. I longed for the comfort, security, and companionship of the *Independence*.

On July 21, 1965, he experienced his first voice contact with another POW—Maj. Larry Guarino, USAF, whom the Vietnamese had put in irons. Guarino's words presaged Denton's own future: "Jerry, I'm in bad shape. They are giving me almost nothing to eat. I'm down to a hundred pounds and I haven't crapped in twenty-six days. I don't remember how long I've been in irons, but it's been weeks. I don't know whether I can make it."

In accordance with the Code of Conduct, the senior POW officer in the chain of command was determined by date of rank at that grade, regardless of service branch. It fell off and on to Commanders Stockdale and Denton. When one senior leader was completely isolated from the other POWs, the officer next in seniority took over the leadership.

On July 28, 1965, after interrogation, the North Vietnamese placed him in leg stocks for the first time. "The stock consisted of a lower wooden frame attached to the concrete bed, with a heavy metal piece hinged to it at one end," he recalled. "There were two spaces for the ankles, and the metal part could be swung down and locked in place, effectively pinning the prisoner. It was humiliating and terribly uncomfortable" because the wounds from the irons became infected. While he was confined in the leg stocks, the infections became worse. There were dark red streaks in his swollen thigh, and he had a severe fever. He became constipated. He was kept in the stocks almost twenty-four hours a day, and he had periods of delirium. And it got worse. "There would come a day," he reflected, "when the stock and that sweat-soaked, smelly bamboo mat would seem like my four-poster bed at home." As the days progressed in his initial confinement in the stocks, his foot became infected for the third time. "I had no bed. I was sleeping on a wooden pallet on the bare floor, and the roaches and spiders were playing tag across my body every night. Also, it was getting colder at sundown, and my thin pajamas afforded practically no protection."

His infection ultimately cleared up and he got a "bed"—a wooden pallet placed on top of two wooden sawhorses. Things got worse again. On November 1, 1965, the North Vietnamese began to starve the POWs, cutting their food back to almost nothing. Denton weighed 167 pounds when he was shot down; by the second month he was down to 140 pounds, and by the third month had shrunk to 120 pounds. Earlier, the rations had included cabbage, greens, pumpkin, and eight to twelve ounces of bread or a bowl of rice twice a day. Each starvation meal consisted of a bowl of water containing two shriveled pieces of cabbage with human waste on them. One of his interrogators came into his cell and in English asked, "Well, Denton, do you know that you are eating shit?" When Denton did not answer, the guard continued, "So you want to continue eating shit?"

Somehow Denton found the strength to pull himself to his feet. "Well, I hope there is some protein in it," he said. Finally, his captors started to wash the feces off the cabbage and served hot soup, a rare treat. "My mother frequently told me that the simple pleasures were best, but I had to go ten thousand miles to discover its truth," Denton noted.

As the prison population grew, a new camp, the "Zoo" (the name given to it by the POWs), was added to house the POWs after their initial indoctrination at the Hanoi Hilton. When Denton got out of isolation, he became the senior officer at the Zoo. He filled that role for most of 1966 and until he was moved back to the Hanoi Hilton in late January 1967. As time progressed, the severity of the treatment accorded the prisoners was determined by the course of the war and their captors' need for propaganda. His first exposure to real brutality came when his feet were placed in iron ankle cuffs at opposite ends of a five-foot cement-filled bar that hardly permitted walking. He was struck in the face and knocked down by a guard. Denton was stunned and angered. His face swelled and his nose bled, but he refused to write anything that they demanded. He was dragged by the cuffs to his cell, thrown to the ground, and left alone in complete darkness. Several hours later he was interrogated by the guard they had named "Smiley." He pulled Denton to his feet and hit him again, causing blood to stream down his face, then hit him in the stomach. Denton reacted by refusing to eat, showing determination to resist. He reflected:

> After what I judged to be four days and four nights of fasting and total darkness, I believed that I was beginning to lose my grip. I couldn't keep my mind occupied, and the deep, insidious cold had stiffened my body and penetrated my consciousness so thoroughly that on the few occasions when I could focus my mind, all I could do was mourn my condition. My wrists had become swollen, and in lucid moments I worried that I would lose my hands, which had been without feeling for days. There was plenty of pain in the rest of my body, however, especially in my shoulders and back.

Denton's captors apparently became concerned about his condition and decided to remove the cuffs, but his wrists were so swollen that the guards had difficulty removing them. They finally got one cuff off by squeezing Denton's hand, which was very painful, but the other cuff was buried in pus-filled flesh. It took four guards three hours to get his hand out of the restraint. His fingers were black and swollen to twice their normal size. "In lucid moments," he remembered, "I sought a reservoir of strength. To justify the sacrifice, I built an image of my country and knew that even with its imperfections, that it was the best in the world. Then I could truly say to myself: 'My country is worth any sacrifice.'"

A human being can take only so much torment. Denton did finally "break" and write the biography that the North Vietnamese demanded, but he made it fictitious. And each time they wanted more from him, they had to torture him again. Throughout the incarceration the POWs continued a policy of making torture necessary before supplying any information that might be used for propaganda. Denton never provided any classified information and instructed the other POWs, "We will die before we give them classified military information."

During one particular propaganda attempt by the North Vietnamese Denton showed his true mettle. In early May 1966 he was told by his captors that he was "going to meet with some members of the press. . . . In preparation for my performance, Mickey Mouse kept me up three nights in a row telling me the truth about the war." Denton was then taken on a ten-minute jeep ride and brought into a room that looked like a "gentlemen's club" with rugs, inlaid stone floors, and expensive-looking furniture. Denton was put in a side room and handed a bottle of beer, which he poured out when no one was looking. "I needed all the presence of mind I could muster," he said. Finally, he was shoved

. . . through some French doors into a large room. I blinked against the glare of a battery of floodlights and looked into the heavy face of a Japanese reporter, who grinned at me from behind a huge pair of horn-rimmed glasses and then motioned me to a chair in front of a table with sweets. . . . The reporter gestured at the table and asked me to smile, but I just stared at him. I also was going to answer his questions in a manner opposite to what the North Vietnamese wanted, but I had a feeling it would fail. They would dub the words or find some way to fake the whole thing. And I was terribly afraid of the torture certain to follow. I decided to be polite and wait for an opening.

The reporter asked some routine questions about my background and then launched into a diatribe about the bombing. I didn't listen to what he was saying. I gazed dully around the room, as though in a daze. The blinding floodlights made me blink, and I suddenly realized that they were playing right into my hands. I felt my heart pounding; sweat popped out on my forehead; the palms of my hands became slippery. I looked directly into the camera and blinked my eyes once, slowly, then three more times, slowly. A dash, and three more dashes. A quick blink, slow blink, quick blink. T . . . O . . . R . . . a slow blink . . . pause, two quick ones and a slow one, quick, slow, quick, quick. T . . . O . . . R . . . T . . . U . . . R . . . E. While the Japanese droned on in a high-pitched voice, I blinked out the desperate message over and over: TORTURE . . . TORTURE . . .

I . . . wondered why the roof hadn't fallen in on me. I concluded that my captors hadn't caught on yet. Perhaps they were taken off guard; under the circumstances, they could not have expected me to do what I had done. I assumed that the North Vietnamese would refuse to let the film leave the country. Astoundingly, as I learned years later, the tape got to Japan with only a few minor cuts. The only explanation I can offer is that the North Vietnamese would have lost too much face if they had refused to give the material to the reporter—especially as it was given in such a thoroughly controlled atmosphere. The reporter made out pretty well. His videotape was bought by a U.S. network and received wide circulation. Eventually, this information would get back to the Vietnamese and I would pay in blood for it. But it was worth it. I learned years later that naval intelligence had picked up my torture signals. It was the first clear message U.S. intelligence had received that we were being tortured.

Once the North Vietnamese realized what Denton had done, he was severely beaten and shackled to the concrete bar. "There is no way," he reflected, "to describe the excruciating pain in the ankle area without experiencing the rig."

In August, the beginning of his second year of captivity, the North Vietnamese demanded that he rewrite his confession into a special form they had created. He refused, so they placed him in a cell with no ventilation. The summer sun turned the cell into an oven. The heavy pajamas he was given to wear made him sweat, and his body became covered with boils. His hands were cuffed behind him, and ropes were placed around his ankles. At intervals the guards tightened the ropes to maintain the constant pain. When he continued to refuse, they raised him off the ground with his arms still tied behind him. "They kept this up for what seemed like hours, and I don't know how my arms didn't pop from their sockets. The pain was so intense that finally I could take it no longer. I gave in and copied my confession onto their standard form."

His captors began a new approach. "They were now spreading the harassment and torture over a longer period of time, trying to wear us down. I didn't like the method. If I was going to be tortured, I wanted it over very quickly." But throughout the torment, Denton followed the Code of Conduct, keeping faith with his fellow prisoners and his country. After the first two years of imprisonment he told his guards: "You'll never break us. There is no way to break our organization because the senior man will always take charge." "Late in September, I was called to a quiz with Flea. He ordered me to kneel, lectured me for about fifteen minutes, then asked me questions which I refused to answer. 'Denton,' Flea said, 'I think that no matter what we do, you will not tell us about Stockdale [the other senior POW] and the organization. Is that right?' 'That's right,' I replied. 'If you get rid of him, I will take over, if you get rid of me, the next man will take over.'"

His valiant resistance landed Denton and ten other hard-core resisters in the prison the POWs had named "Alcatraz." When his blindfold was removed, Denton recalled, "I blinked. My mouth fell open in disbelief. I was looking into the dark shadows of the tiniest, most barren cell I had ever seen. I heard a voice behind me. 'How do you like your new home?'"

"Alcatraz," Denton said,

> meant solitude, filth, hunger, and despair—and many other things that even now the ten survivors are sometimes reluctant to talk about. It was also a badge of honor. Each man had earned his way in. There were, of course, men elsewhere who possessed equal credentials but had been so clever or lucky that they had escaped this final horror.
>
> And horror it was. The cells were tiny; a standing area forty-seven inches square, plus a raised pallet area the length of a man's body. The pallet was nothing more than bamboo strips laid side by side. Mine had a nail that protruded near my right shoulder blade. There was no window, and the only ven-

tilation was from a few small holes drilled in a steel plate above the door and a six-inch space under the door, which was recessed. A dim bulb, ten watts or less, provided the only light. Most of the time there was only darkness and silence.

My possessions consisted of a toothbrush, a water jug, a cup, soap, a washrag, two blankets, a bucket, two sets of underwear and two shirts, a turtleneck sweatshirt, a torn mosquito net, and a pair of sandals which were only pieces of rubber with a strap. I didn't get socks until much later. When the heavy wooden door closed behind me on that first night and the bolt slid into place with a thump, a choking feeling welled up in my throat. The cell was so tiny, so dark. I could hear little crawling sounds as the roaches and spiders reacted to their new roommate.

Among the POWs sharing Alcatraz with Denton was Comdr. James Stockdale, Denton's Naval Academy classmate. Commander Stockdale was the senior officer for much of his incarceration, although he sometimes temporarily handed the role to the officer next in seniority when he needed time to recover from torture. His story is told later in this chapter, but Denton's description of him is a good introduction:

Jim Stockdale, who had been the air wing commander aboard the *Oriskany*, was considered a "high-grade criminal" by the North Vietnamese, and his BACK US program [see below] had frightened them. To add insult, he had once shown the BS signal [i.e., extended his middle finger] during a filmed confession and the signal got through. He had limitless courage. I remember watching him back in our Naval Academy days serving as cannon fodder against the huge Navy football team while he was a junior varsity player. Despite his relatively small size, Stockdale was always on the attack against the biggest players he could find.

His leg had been dislocated at the knee during shoot-down, and the North Vietnamese, citing a slogan, "Politics before medicine," had refused him treatment. He was in intense pain for many months, and his leg eventually froze at a right angle. From his central location at the Thunderbird, in the Little Vegas area of the Hilton, he had run a vigorous, successful resistance operation until the BACK US program had been traced to him during a torture purge. Because he had led the prisoners at Vegas so well, he had become the number-one target. He was the senior American officer at Alcatraz.

Denton invented a new form of POW communication at Alcatraz—the vocal tap code. "Communications remained the heart of our existence," he told me. "Without that slender and infrequent link with the others, I think I would have lost my mind. I came to truly love them." The taps informed the prisoners that something was going on one hot July day when the North Vietnamese tried to generate a propaganda coup.

"I had been in solitary for nearly a year," Denton recalled.

In that time, I had got fleeting glimpses of maybe a half-dozen Americans: Bob Shumaker, Bob Peel, Larry Guarino, Ed Davis, Phil Butler, and one or two others. Now I would see more than I wanted, under the circumstances. July 6 was hot from the beginning. Humid air lay like a wet blanket over Hanoi, heavy, depressing, deadening. I flopped listlessly in cell 1 of the Pool Hall [one of the POW camps] until about four o'clock, when I heard sounds of increased activity. Instinctively, I disliked it. Any change in routine usually meant trouble. There was some nervous tapping between cells as the prisoners began to sense the different atmosphere. Even guards making their rounds were more tense and curt than usual.

As darkness fell, Smiley came to my cell, flung open the door, blindfolded me, and took me to a quiz room filled with other prisoners. I was handcuffed to another American, and suddenly I was wild with joy. Gently, I pressed my knee against his, tapping out my name. Back came an answer: "Peel." Air Force Lieutenant Bob Peel had lived in a cell next to mine briefly in the Pool Hall and now lived in the Pigsty [another POW camp].

The prisoners, handcuffed together two by two, were put in the back of trucks, where we communicated by tapping on the knee of the man next to us. There were sixteen men in my truck, and as we moved ponderously through the streets of Hanoi, I got all their names.

After about a half hour, the convoy stopped in an alley off a main square, where we were unloaded and our blindfolds removed. As I blinked against the glare of headlights in the growing darkness, guards with pistols crowded around while JC and Mickey Mouse told us that the people of North Vietnam wanted to demonstrate their anger toward us. They warned that if we communicated or otherwise misbehaved, we would be killed. As other trucks were unloaded, I counted about forty Americans lined up in handcuffed pairs. In front of me was one of several trucks loaded with news correspondents, still cameras, and movie cameras. As we moved off, I gave the victory sign in front of one of the movie cameras.

The heat swept off the black asphalt in waves as our ragged group started down the street between two columns of people. At first, the crowd was sparse, well-dressed, and relatively quiet, obviously high-ranking party officials. As the crowd got thicker and louder, a guard shouted: "Bow your heads!" The words shot through me like a streak of lightning. I shouted: "You are Americans! Keep your heads up!" As my command rippled through the ranks, the guards prodded us with bayonets to get us to bow. Then they used their rifle butts, without success. As we trudged down a broad avenue, the crowd became nasty and threatening, and the guards, now troubled, became too preoccupied with crowd control to bother with our lack of bowing.

A middle-aged woman stood with a basket of rocks, and as I passed, she fell in behind and made me her special target. Four or five egg-sized rocks whizzed past before one struck me squarely in the back of the head. I fell flat on the ground, dragging Bob Peel down with me. I shook my head, and with Peel's help got to my feet in time for a Vietnamese man, perhaps eight inches shorter than I, to dart out of the crowd and deliver a sharp left hook to my groin. I was engulfed by nausea as the man ran back into the crowd, my curses for his cowardly act following him.

People now filled the broad sidewalks and spilled into the street, striking at us with their fists. We began to stagger and fall from the immense strain and the blows as the protective cordon of guards broke down. Out of the corner of my eye, I could see the man who had attacked me running through the crowd. He found an opening and came at me, his face twisted with rage, his fists clenched. I tried to dodge, but he got me again in the groin and knocked me down. When I got up, I looked into Peel's bloody face and said: "He's not going to get me again!" And right there, in the middle of that frenzied, murderous crowd, Peel and I practiced coordinating his left arm with my right, which were handcuffed together. At the count of "one" we took a stance. At "two" I threw a left jab. At "three" we swung an uppercut together with our manacled hands. Spot [one of the guards], our officer-escort, saw us swing and understood what we were up to. I shouted to him, "If that son of a bitch comes out again, I'm going to kill him."

He hesitated for a moment, and I could see the look of indecision in his eyes. It could have been the difference between life and death for us. But Spot saw the danger, and as the man came toward me again, he grabbed him by the shirt, shook him hard, pistol-whipped him across the face, and threw him back into the crowd. That was the end of my personal assailant, but the danger had not passed.

The crowd was now flailing us from both sides, and the guards were fighting a losing battle. The prisoners, some crawling on their hands and knees, were kicking and punching their way through the mob. We turned left at some point, and above a solid wall of howling people, the lights of a soccer stadium shone eerily through the muggy air.

The only thing that saved us was the stadium gates. We fought our way through the final thirty yards, using elbows, knees, and cuffs as weapons, until the guards pushed us through and closed the gates against the mob, now wild with rage because its prey had escaped. This was not the way the North Vietnamese had planned it. The Hanoi March had got out of hand.

While the bloody prisoners flopped exhausted on the cinder track bordering the field, the guards smiled and jabbered among themselves, relieved that it was over. For a while they didn't even try to stop us from talking. That respite soon ended, however, and on the return trip in the truck we were blindfolded and guarded closely again.

Back at the "Zoo," JC, upset and excited by my behavior during

the march, slugged me while I was still blindfolded and cuffed to
Peel. Then I was returned to my cell. But in a few minutes an officer
came to my cell, told me to drink some water, and turned me over to
a guard who took me outside to the office end of the compound. He
blindfolded and gagged me with two filthy rags which had been used
to bind my sandals during the march. He then pulled my arms
behind me around a tree and handcuffed them.

From various sounds, I guessed that I was one of several men
bound to trees. The guards began drifting away, and I tried to take
my mind off my predicament. My wrists and back ached, my groin
was sore, and blood continued to run from various cuts on my body.
Grit from the rag filled my mouth. I thought: Well, here I am, a sin-
ful man tied to a tree by savage enemies, like the thieves tied to the
crosses next to Jesus. "Lord," I prayed, "forgive me." I found that
despite the gag, I could make a muffled coughing sound. I coughed
twice, five times, paused, then once, then four times—my initials, JD.
I was a little shaken when the coughs coming back identified the
man on my left as "JC," but before I got carried away I realized with a
smile it wasn't Jesus Christ but Jerry Coffee.

After several hours, I heard the sounds of men being removed
from the trees and taken away. Now, at last, this horrible affair would
be over. I had to lean against the tree for support as a guard removed
the cuffs, gag, and blindfold. But instead of being returned to my cell,
I was taken at bayonet point directly to a quiz room, where Fox and JC
were sitting behind a long desk. I was prepared for the worst, but to
my surprise JC summoned a guard to wipe my face, which was covered
with blood, grime, and sweat. The guard blinked, as though he couldn't
believe what he had heard, and gave my face a cursory swipe.

JC told him to do a better job, and this time the guard wiped
my face carefully. Then JC told him to leave the room. The guard
went and stood outside by the door. Fox leaned over and whispered to JC, who went to the door and told the guard to go across
the road. This byplay was unprecedented, and my hopes picked
up sharply. JC sat down and acted as an interpreter for Fox, who

knew little English. Fox wanted to know what I thought of the march.

My eyes widened, and I felt the adrenaline begin to flow. Suddenly all the emotion pent up by a year's imprisonment and brutal treatment erupted. "You fools!" I half-shouted. "It's the biggest mistake you've made. Parading prisoners in the streets is a return to barbaric times. I have nothing but contempt for your utter cowardice. The spectacle of helpless prisoners being paraded through the streets will bring a wave of criticism from the world." The words came tumbling out. I paused from time to time to give JC the chance to translate. Ordinarily, such talk would bring a punch and a "shut mouth," but not this time. Finally I stopped, and JC asked respectfully if I was finished. I said I was.

Then Fox said through JC: "I have something to say to you and I request that you remember it for a long time. These words are important. Do you understand?" I said I did. "The march was not the idea of the Army of Vietnam. The march was the idea of the people," Fox continued. Again he asked me if I understood, and repeated the whole thing twice.

I understood perfectly. He was trying to tell me that the Communist party had ordered the march and that the army didn't agree with it.

It was, I later deduced, a manifestation of a deep split between the army and the party. The army was concerned that the United States would send paratroopers into North Vietnam and was trying to protect itself against being tried for war crimes should the country be conquered. Such was the North Vietnamese state of mind in 1966 as U.S. troops and equipment began to pour into the South. I believe it would have taken only an extra push by the U.S. to have ended the war right then.

Essentially, two enemy officers conceded to me that the Hanoi March was an illegal, barbaric act, and they wanted to assure me it was not the idea of the Vietnamese Army, but the idea of the party. The significance of this interview lies in the remarkable effort of two officers, one of them, Fox, being camp commander of the Zoo with the probable rank of lieutenant colonel, to step out of character from routine captor-captive relationship, to tell a captive, me, of information which they hoped I would believe and report after the war to U.S. authorities. This was the first of several more examples of this kind of effort with me, and the combined stories that I have related should contribute significantly to understanding the true attitude of the enemy toward the war and to refute the historical context in which the war now rests in U.S. history.

The purpose of their message was to remove themselves and their army from possible prosecution and punishment for involvement in the brutal Hanoi March in the event of postwar war crimes trials conducted by the United States, which they assumed would be ultimately victorious. The haughty, arrogant confidence that characterized what the officers normally expressed to us about the war was thus mimicking the Communist party line. Even at this early stage (mid-1966) the army, and I believe also the party, had doubts about the outcome of the war. By late 1969 and 1970 their doubts had become near certainty. It was a forgone conclusion in their minds that they were going to lose the war. And at this time, they were compelled to take extraordinary steps—the party joining the army in a clever effort to escape punishment at the hands of a U.S. war crimes trial, going so far as to afford scapegoats for punishment administered by the Vietnamese themselves, in order to get most of the army and party clear of prosecution.

In September 1969 something happened that would change our lives immensely. We had heard on the camp radio that Ho Chi Minh was ill, and on September 3 he died. Mickey Mouse came to me immediately to warn me about the guards, who he said would be very irritable and unpredictable. "You should tell everyone to be careful and not offend them at this time," he said, and I passed the order to cool it. The effect of Ho's death on the guards was disastrous. They broke into the storage cell next to mine and took drugs and wine, and while messages of condolence from other countries were being read endlessly on the camp radio they wept and got drunk. The officers were also badly shaken, and wandered through their duties in a daze. Ho's funeral took place about five blocks from Alcatraz, and as I listened under the door I could hear the sound of guns booming and the roar of many jet aircraft zooming in the traditional flyover. And there was the high-pitched wailing of thousands of voices as the founder and president of the People's Republic of Vietnam was carried to his grave.

We speculated on Ho's successor and hoped for a revolt. I suspected that his death would mean a change in our treatment, but I didn't know which way it would go. Almost immediately, subtle changes began to take place which I interpreted as a good sign. The camp administration was less harsh, and the purge petered out. In October, I was caught communicating and got my first real clue on the new treatment. I was taken to quiz with Softsoap [one of the guards], who said, "Denton, you have been caught communicating. You know what has happen before."

"Yes, sir," I said.

"I am going to surprise!" Softsoap said. "This time you will not be punish. We still have regulation and you have broken it, and I will criticize you for it. But as long as I am in authority, there will be no more punishment for communicating."

Night had turned to day! As I stood there, a chill ran through my body and the flesh on the back of my neck prickled with a sense of joy. I tried to appear unperturbed, but I had to exert great will to keep the tears from flowing. A guard took me back to the cell, and as soon as the door closed I got on the wall to tell the others what had happened. I said I thought the North Vietnamese might be coming off their torture line, and that our treatment would improve. The others were somewhat skeptical. Torture had become a way of life.

The next day I was again caught communicating, and off I went to another quiz with Softsoap. "Ah, Denton," he said, "you did it again. The guard is doing his duty, but you will not be punish." While we were talking, a guard came stomping into the room and threw his arm across his chest in salute to Softsoap. It was raining, and as water dripped from his slicker, the guard rather theatrically reported that he had just caught Sam Johnson communicating. Softsoap translated the report to me and repeated his pledge that no one would be punished for communicating. When I reported this scene to the others, they began to lose their skepticism. Johnson had indeed been caught but hadn't been punished.

This incident at Alcatraz indicated to me that the torture would be ended and the formerly harsh treatment would radically improve. . . . Softsoap told me I would be given the whole story of the new policy and improved treatment when I was moved to the next camp. . . . The move came about a week later. One night those of us left at Alcatraz, except Storz, who was dying, were moved via truck, blindfolded, back to Las Vegas. . . . I was taken to cell 6 in Stardust, the section where I had lived before. After Alcatraz, this new cell was like the presidential suite: large and airy with a big window opening toward the outside wall, and two sets of double bunks making me think I would soon get a cellmate.

My spirits were lifted as the move and the big cell seemed to be consistent with the promise made about improving our treatment. The other Alcatraz guys were also moved into Stardust except for Sam Johnson. Within a short time Mulligan was moved into the cell with me, and the other Alcatraz people were given cellmates in surrounding cells, except for Johnson and Stockdale, both of whose whereabouts were as yet unknown to me. . . . At about eleven P.M., the Alcatraz arrivees . . . got on the wall and started booming messages to each other to find their locations. Everyone in the camp within shouting distance soon knew the Alcatraz Gang was back. The din was so loud the guards were in a frenzy, and Bug, the sinister little torturer who had been terrorizing the camp, came to my cell, saying, "Denton, have your men be reasonable and quieter. Things are going to get better." Somewhat reluctantly I asked the guys to keep it down to a gentle roar.

But our communications effort went on as we urgently tried to learn what was going on at the camp. We learned that Bill Lawrence had been doing his best to act as SRO, but he reported to me that discipline among the POWs was terrible: some had become turncoats and were actively cooperating with the enemy in the antiwar propaganda efforts; many were meeting peace delegations on their visits to Hanoi; and many were writing papers on demand. About a half dozen POWs senior to me were present, but none had offered to take over as SRO, and Bill had assumed command. I assumed there were understandable reasons for this. I told Bill I would take over. And I issued orders, with the usual excellent assistance of my Alcatraz buddies, in an effort to get things squared away. The effort was generally successful, but the men who were still beyond the pale were unresponsive, less than a dozen.

I also told the camp about their promises to me about better treatment, especially no more torture. At that point, I have no idea how many POWs put much stock in those promises. The day after I arrived, Cat, the senior North Vietnamese officer running the POW program, confronted me after I came out of the shower (the shower building was located in the center of the compound, surrounded by bare earth). Cat was accompanied by a retinue of officers and guards. He was wearing a crisp uniform with highly shined shoes, and gave a big, false smile as he strode toward me with his right hand extended for me to shake. Somehow he looked unsure of himself, unlike the past. "Ah, Denton, I believe," he said, blinking in the bright sunlight. He knew damned well who I was. I ignored his hand and went to attention.

"Yes, Denton," I replied looking straight ahead.

"Long time since I see you, Denton," he said, slowly dropping his hand.

"Yes, not since the banana and the torture."

He ignored this. "Denton, you and I will be having many discussions soon," he said, and allowed me to pass by him and return to my cell. The next morning I was taken to quiz with him. . . . The setting . . . was a large room with an elevated portion at one end where Cat reposed on a thronelike chair. The beginning of it struck the tone for the entire . . . two weeks of meetings. He addressed me with courtly courtesy, inviting me to sit down in a comfortable chair in front of his huge desk. He offered me a cigarette, a cigar, and tea, all of which I declined. He began by saying he was going to give me a long list of important information [and] that to ensure we understood the meaning of every word he had on both sides of him respectively a Vietnamese-French dictionary and an English-French dictionary. The arrogance and sparkle were definitely gone. He appeared tired and distraught, and a nervous tic had developed over one eye. He settled into an overstuffed chair under a picture of Ho Chi Minh, with the two huge dictionaries beside him. It was obvious that this was to be a serious discussion, without the usual harangue. "I have some very important announcements, Denton," he said. . . . "I, other officers, and many of the guards had in our rage allowed ourselves to vent our anger on the prisoners and were responsible for deviations from our Vietnamese tradition of humane treatment."

I sat there silently, bemused and surprised at this unprecedented admission.

"I have been required to make public self-criticism for my mistakes," he went on, "and from now on you will be allowed to follow the Code of Conduct. I will prove by my deeds that my words are true, and I want ideas from you on how we can apply humane treatment, including games and movies. We shall have many discussions in the future. Maybe you would like to explain to girls in kitchen about menus," Cat said, emphasizing the word "girls."

I said, "No, we can't accept that."

Cat, the mastermind behind the torture campaign, was now almost conciliatory. "Just follow reasonable orders and don't insult guards," he said. I accepted a cup of tea and said I wanted to talk to the other prisoners about this new era. Noting the blood that was running from around a large callus on my knuckle, Cat smiled and said, "Ah, Denton, you have ways to talk to them." He meant he would look the other way while I tapped out the conversation on the wall, but he didn't want anyone communicating outside of the Stardust. I couldn't make any promises.

The quizzes with Cat went on almost daily for two weeks. He was continually trying to impress me with the new image. I figured the

North Vietnamese believed that President Nixon was going to try to carry the war to a successful conclusion, and that they might be held accountable for their crimes. They wanted us to go home in good condition. Although Cat didn't keep all his promises, from then on no one I know of was tortured for propaganda or military information. At the time, of course, I had no certain faith that he was telling the truth, but I passed the information on to the others for what it was worth. I was overwhelmed by Cat's new attitude, but I had to be careful about what to recommend. There should be no special favors for anyone, I told Cat, and everyone must get a roommate. And we must all be allowed to follow the Code of Conduct. We would accept games if everyone were allowed to play. I also asked the whereabouts of Jim Stockdale, and when he replied, "Stockdale is tranquil," I was frightened. He wouldn't explain further. I asked about Johnson, saying I knew he was still in solo, and I demanded that he be given a cellmate in accordance with the new treatment policy. He replied that Johnson needed a bit more attention, that he was like a misbehaving nephew. After further fruitless conversations about Johnson, I told Cat that if he kept him solo, I would do something very unpleasant for Cat. Later I called a voluntary hunger strike, and shortly Sam was brought to my cell, and I was assured he was getting cellmates, which turned out to be true. They did this to avert a resumption of the hunger strike. (I was aware they had to fatten us up for our return.)

The interviews [were] mostly about what treatment I wanted and what I would accept. We got ample time outside, a French version of pool, basketball, Ping Pong, etc. As things turned out later, Cat was true to his words except that I learned after the fact that some B-52 pilots had been tortured for info during Linebacker operations. We learned from some of the informant guards we developed that indeed some guards who had been brutal were returned to the front and some had been killed. I think it may have been true.

Denton was certain that the improved treatment of the POWs was a ruse intended to ensure that most of the guards would be found innocent if the United States held war crimes after the settlement and return of the POWs. Admiral Denton also described another incident that took place during his captivity, one that was portrayed incorrectly in the book he wrote about his experiences.

It was February 1973. The three-phase release of POWs was about to begin. The first group of three planeloads to be released had been segregated from the rest of the prisoners. Our moods were complicated and various. We had already absorbed that we were supposed to be released in accordance with the settlement, and were still finding it hard to believe, and entertained fears that something would still happen to delay it or cancel it. Some of the men were chattering incessantly in groups, some seemed to want to be alone and contemplate; some were doing both.

A few days before my release, I was unexpectedly and frighteningly called to a quiz, the purpose of which I had no idea. I was taken to a building I had never been in, and when I entered the large room a feeling of cold dread overcame me. What I saw as I entered was a rather ornate room, rectangular, perhaps forty by twenty-five feet, with twenty-five to thirty men seated against the far wall and the adjacent walls. Seated in the middle of them, and maybe slightly in front of them, was the senior man at a small desk. The thing that most impressed me about the men was their marked difference in appearance and bearing from any I had seen in Vietnam. They reminded me of a board of directors of a large company or the men who sat at meetings of the Joint Chiefs of Staff in the Pentagon. The other senior men I had met in Vietnam, compared to them, had the appearance of middle-level executives or middle-ranking officers. Also striking about them was the obvious tension in their expressions, postures, and body language. I thought, Oh, God, what is this—it seems important and signals some event that might result in my not going home.

The spokesman, who looked to be totally their leader and was throughout their sole spokesman, looked at me and spoke to me as if I was an important visitor with whom they had a most important matter to discuss. He greeted me with the words, "Commander Denton, Good afternoon. Would you sit down?" gesturing at a chair about ten feet in front of his desk. As I sat down, my senses were in an elevated state of alertness, and a constant anxiety pervaded my mind. I glanced around at the other attentive faces whose eyes remained fixed on me for the entire interview. The spokesman, after I had sat down, let a few seconds go by, and then said, with an almost friendly tone and with a faint smile, "Denton, we acknowledge that we have had little success here getting you to answer our questions, but we are going to ask you one now, and hope that you will consent to answer it."

I tried to look composed, but I was becoming increasingly convinced that this interview had the tone of one likely to result in my being pressed to say or do something impermissible and that they would not let me go home with the others. I said, "What is the question?"

Without hesitating, he said, "We are asking you what you will say in detail when you return home about the treatment you and your comrades received here."

Immediately I felt less anxiety, because I did not believe they were on a mission to try to torture me to say something untrue, but were, for reasons I was beginning to have an inkling of, intensely interested in my honest answer to their question. I answered, partly to buy time, "It seems unusual that you would place such importance on asking me that question. The subject is important, and I feel I have to ask my seniors whether they object if I give an answer."

He asked, "Which seniors?"

I said, "The two available to me are Risner and Stockdale. If they say yes, I will answer if you will answer two questions from me first."

There was a little murmur from the others, but without taking his eyes off of mine, he said, "Very well. You go back and ask your seniors, and we will see you here tomorrow."

I was dismissed. Quickly I found Risner and Stockdale together talking animatedly about something. They turned to me as I walked up, and I said I just had an interesting experience. I told them the V just asked me what I would say about the treatment when I got home. "I have told them I would ask my seniors if I could answer. If you tell me I can, I will tell them the truth." They said words to the effect, "Hell, why are you asking us, we know you will do right, and sure you have our permission." . . .

As the second interview approached, I felt that . . . their question to me now was closely connected to the context of Cat's long message, Ho Chi Minh's implied role in the ruse, and so on. When they came to get me the next day and brought me in, I felt a lot less tense but they looked even more tense than the day before. After I was greeted and seated, the spokesman cleared his throat and asked, "Well, did your seniors give you permission?" I said they had. "Then what are your two questions of me?"

I said, "First I want to know why you are placing so much emphasis on what I will say, when you know there are a number of American officers here who are senior to me."

He answered rather slowly but with emphasis, "Because we think you have credibility, Denton." He emphasized the word "credibility."

After a pause I said, "Okay. My second question is why are you so intensely interested in what we, including me, are going to say? It will all be pretty much the same obvious stuff which you know about."

He said, "No. By now, we know you all pretty well, and we suspect many of the prisoners will exaggerate about the treatment, resulting in a public opinion that will make it impossible for President Nixon to follow through with the promised concessions of the settlement, such as redevelopment of the Mekong Valley. Now, will you answer our question?"

I said I would. And I tried to hide my sense of satisfaction at the answer, which indicated that all the V cared about now was getting the promised postwar concessions, which while not unexpected to me, was still quite gratifying to hear, and almost humorous. . . . I cleared my throat and saw the tension and suspense in their faces as I began. "You will not hear anything surprising in what I am going to say. I will simply report the facts. I will tell that shortly after I was shot down you began torturing us to obtain confessions, biographies, and statements condemning our government's policies and praising your side in the war. You starved us, you gave us inadequate clothing, you isolated us from one another in many cases, and generally treated us worse than U.S. law allows animals to be treated." I went on for about five minutes describing the cruelty and illegality of the treatment, included the Hanoi March and many individual instances of brutality and some of death. Their faces showed no reaction to any of this. They seemed to be waiting for something vital. Then I said the few words they were waiting for.

"But then in October 1969, the treatment changed. It was like going from night to day. Although it never approached Geneva standards, you stopped torturing us (at this time I did not know of the torture of the B-52 guys), gave us the best food I think you had, let us exercise outside, play games, etc." As soon as the words "October 1969" came out of my mouth they knew that the foundation of their ruse was intact and assumed that along with the rest of the truth, I would also report Cat's explanation and apology. Their show of relief was superobvious, a huge exhale, big smiles replacing frowns, and the exchange of murmurs of relief. Of course, as things turned out they never had to employ this ruse. And now they would never admit they had ever planned to.

Then Admiral Denton pulled together the significance of the stories related above.

Let me try to add some information and observations shared by all the POWs which place the episodes described above in more precise context. Although the incidents indicate enemy doubt early on and especially near the end about their likelihood of success in the war, none of the episodes except the last, in the sense of having presented evidence of the enemy's sense of defeat, compare to the evidence presented by facts surrounding the Linebacker II operations (the bombing of Hanoi) of December 1972. All the POWs saw the following overwhelming facts:

The critical and decisive change beginning 18 December 1972 from a U.S. strategy involving ineffective and too gradually escalating attacks with overly limiting rules of engagement to a strategy of applying massive destructive power in large-scale attacks essentially devastating the enemy's capacity to wage further war and eliminating their will to do so. The effect on the enemy capabilities and will was never revealed to the American public. The enemy's infrastructure of logistics, air defense, electric power, communications, and transportation were rendered incapable of any kind of effective military operations.

The POWs witnessed or learned about nightly attacks by three waves of eighty B-52s, at crucial military targets never before hit in and around Hanoi and Haiphong.

All the POWs witnessed the breaking of the wills of every enemy officer and man they saw during and after these attacks. And I personally witnessed convincing evidence that the political and military leadership was deprived of any further war ambitions except for hoping that the peace agreement struck would hold. President Nixon would come through with promised aid to them and they would not suffer greatly from war crimes trials.

Almost every POW of my acquaintance shares my opinion from his own observations that Linebacker II broke the enemy's will and won the military war. The victory was insanely handed back to the enemy by the congressional actions, motivated by political catering to the media, academic, and public antiwar activities, which tragically compromised a loud, violent, ignorant minority of our people who were swept along in the days of national dissolution.

The North Vietnamese themselves in the episodes related by me showed that in spite of the early and prolonged flawed strategy of the U.S. that they were confident all along that the U.S. would finally adjust to reality, use our available overwhelming power, and defeat them. The true historic context of the Vietnam War becomes obvious when facts comprise its basis. As a result of the false impressions in the United States imparted by the media and book publishers, the following disastrous events took place:

1. The South Vietnamese people whom we had committed to save from communism were betrayed and abandoned.
2. Thousands of senior military officers, intelligence officials, Pentagon civilian officials, along with all other informed people who knew the truth, had suffered and are still suffering from the knowledge that the country was misinformed into the betrayal and abandonment.
3. Hundreds of thousands of veterans dead and alive were betrayed and demoralized about the commitment they so valorously made which was appallingly unappreciated and apparently wasted. Many of these veterans are psychopathic wrecks because of this (in spite of there having been some recent public appreciation belatedly given). They deserve the truth about the war in which they fought.
4. Posterity and the soundness and integrity of future military planning deserve and need the truth.

These false impressions and the false historical context in which the war has been placed cannot be allowed to go unchallenged and unrefuted. I have hope that this book . . . will contain a sufficient number of authoritative testimonies on this subject. I have further hope that in the better journalistic climate of today there are enough objective media commentators and publishers to recognize the truth in this book and follow up with writings which prove the case that the U.S. won the military war with North Vietnam, and that before and during the time of the settlement of the war the North Vietnamese will was utterly broken and the U.S. had won the war in the sense of Sun Tzu's classic definition of victory: the object of war is to break the will of the enemy.

My own perspective is not solely based on the POW experience. For fifteen consecutive years followed by six more years later in the U.S. Senate I was exposed to and involved with learning the events and context of the war in Vietnam. My involvement began with formal scholastic study including a year of study and close examination of the prospects for the war at the Naval War College (1963–64), an advanced degree in international affairs from George Washington University, followed by some non-POW combat participation in the war earning the Distinguished Flying Cross, then the POW experience, followed by over four years following the war in consultation with people who had been intimately aware of the conduct of the Vietnam War: admirals generals, and civilian officials including President Nixon, many members of his and President Johnson's, Carter's, and Reagan's administrations—many of whom were speakers at the Armed Forces Staff College during my three and a half years tenure there as commandant 1974–77. These speakers were routine guests at luncheons at the college and dinners in my home where they laid out to me their thoughts on Vietnam.

These speakers included a chairman of the Joint Chiefs of Staff (General George Brown) two NATO supreme allied commanders (Generals Andrew Goodpaster and Alexander Haig), a supreme allied commander, Atlantic (Admiral Ralph Cousins), to name a select few. I had the honor to co-host a major NATO symposium with General Brown and Admiral Cousins. Another man with whom I had many relevant discussions with was Admiral Tom Hayward, CNO while I was senator, and close friend.

Another example of hearing seniors discuss the issue occurred when I was summoned along with Risner and Stockdale to the White House by President Nixon. This was shortly after we had returned. On my way to the White House the helo dropped me off to pay my respects at the Pentagon to the secretary of defense and the chairman of the Joint Chiefs Admiral Thomas Moorer. As soon as Admiral Moorer greeted me he said, "Jerry, I want you to know I did everything I could starting at the beginning of the war to escalate it properly. In the month you were shot down I as CinCPac strongly recommended the mining of Haiphong Harbor and other strong measures. It was extremely exasperating for me to see the way the war was conducted."

I informed him that I knew about the mining because I was the officer who was diagramming the minefield in the harbor which my squadron was planning to hit and I was dumbfounded when the mining was called off.

He and I had other discussions later on the subject and the four-star admiral (like so many other relevant senior officers) had views with which I totally agreed and I had realized from the beginning that the civilian leadership beginning with McNamara was not sufficiently following the advice of our military.

It was President Nixon in December 1972 under whose leadership the corrective strategy was finally applied. We POWs feel a great debt to him. It was basically the same kind of strategy used in Desert Storm and planned for Iraq. I believe that that strategy had it been applied at the outset could have decided the Vietnam War in a couple of weeks as it did in Desert Storm.

In conclusion, with all the mistakes made in Vietnam, the war had one good result. The expenditures made by the Soviet Union during that conflict were an important factor in finally allowing the U.S. to win the cold war. The Soviet final failure came in the form of an economic failure in their inability to continue to pursue a policy of world domination against the Free World led by the United States. Vietnam veterans can take full credit, and realize that their sacrifices were not wasted. As President George W. Bush said in his first State of the Union Address, the U.S. realizes that God is the author of all human rights including Liberty, and the United States of America proves its belief in that concept by sometimes fighting for the freedom of strangers. Vietnam veterans have exemplified that proof.

John T. Mason Jr. interviewed then–Rear Adm. Jeremiah Denton when he was president of the Armed Forces Staff College in Norfolk, Virginia. Extracts from that interview provide further insight into the character and leadership Denton showed as a POW.

MASON: Tell me about the whole process of coming home.
DENTON: Well, even at the time it was almost like a dream. The announcement that we would come home was made in accordance with the cease-fire agreement. It was scrupulously observed, but it was an anticlimax to us, especially to me. . . . We knew they were finished. The guards were obviously jelly. The officers were jelly. They started acceding to our demands. They started catering to our goodwill, and sort of "you remember me, I wasn't bad," and that type attitude. And as the release sequence came along, they asked us how many feet from us would we tolerate photographers? Could photographers come with us on the bus? And we would tell them yes, no, maybe, and this sort of thing. For the first time, . . . the senior officers were actually telling the North Vietnamese what to do, and they did it.

So going through with it was, in a way, an anticlimax and, in another way, a test of restraint because you didn't want to go mad with joy. You just didn't want to go insane with joy. You had to try to keep telling yourself, "Now, come on, twenty years from now this won't be a real big deal!"

MASON: Or maybe something will happen to prevent it?

DENTON: True, I was hanging on that. You didn't want to doubt that either. But there was a time in the first release sequence in which I was involved, we were on our way to the airport and they told us when the plane was supposed to land and we were supposed to leave, and it didn't happen that way. They were delayed. I've forgotten now the actual cause of the delay, but we began to worry. . . . I was the senior officer in the first release group. I tried not to show them how worried I was, but, boy, my stomach. I just about lost it when I saw that it was getting late and I didn't know what the hell had happened. But finally the plane did land and when I saw that C-141 out there, it was the most beautiful sight I've ever seen in my life. It was so clean and all new and the Air Force guys with all these fancy flight suits and the nurses all crisp and clean. It was the first time we'd seen any physical evidence of American power recognized by the North Vietnamese. They were awed. The crowd out there was awed by that airplane, awed by the military smartness of the people that came out of there. . . . And getting in the plane, I was just trying to suppress my own excitement. I was also very painfully aware that on that first plane we had [Comdr. Walter] Wilbur [USN] and [Lt. Col. Edison] Miller [USMC], who were traitors, and I didn't know how they would spoil the arrival, if they chose to. Stockdale initiated legal proceedings against them, filing a formal indictment, but the Navy and Marine Corps officials elected to drop the charges, and decided not to prosecute. Letters of censure were filed on Wilbur and Miller and they were retired.

MASON: How did the other boys treat them on the plane?

DENTON: Just ignored them. They were too much caught up in the elation of getting there. It was my sack to worry about it. I was the senior guy. They let me worry about that, and I did. I worried about it quite a bit. I went up to either Seiverts [of the State Department] or [Roger] Shields [of the DoD] and told them that we had those two creeps aboard and I wanted to know what the hell they were doing there because we were supposed to come out in order of shoot-down, and the sick and wounded first. That was our insisted policy, which the North Vietnamese agreed to honor.

MASON: And these two men were later shoot-downs?

DENTON: Yes, but I was later told by the prisoners who were on the airplane who knew who was where over in the New Guy Village sector—that's where Wilbur and Miller were (it was a sort of sick bay part)—that they had apparently been ill and that they were coming out as sick. I didn't know whether that was true or not and I didn't trust the two gentlemen enough to ask them, but at least I didn't have to stand on ceremony. They were coming out as sick men and they had been in the sick bay, and the guys who had been with them said they did believe they had been ill, and these were loyal men who said that. So I didn't have to say, okay, the plane can't take off, and cause an international incident there, but I did have to cope with what the hell am I going to do with them.

So I told Shields and Seiverts about it, and Shields said, "Well, what do you want to do?" First, Shields came to me and said: "Jerry, there's probably going to be some kind of an opportunity to say something when we get off the airplane and there will probably be a good many people watching." That just went right over my head. All I knew was he said, "CinCPac will be there," and I thought that's a big deal, but we already had for years, probably the first year, developed the policy that the senior officer on the returning airplane, ship, or bus would be the spokesman for the group, and he was responsible for getting the men further transportation. We had all that already laid out, so that was expected of me, and I'd been thinking about what I was going to say for five or six years if I happened to be senior, so that was no problem for the general sentiments.

I thought the main threat was whether Wilbur and Miller were going to get off the plane and make an antiwar statement of some kind and kind of mess the thing up. That was his concern, too, and he asked me what I thought we ought to do, so I said, "Let me go have a chat with them." . . . Wilbur and Miller looked at me with what I would consider controlled expressions, and as I recall, the general tenor of what

I said to them went like this: "I know who you are. . . . This is a matter for your conscience and for the government to handle. I'm not interested in that right at the moment. What I am interested in is what you're doing on the plane and what your intentions are when you land at the field. I don't feel empowered on my authority to prevent you from saying whatever it is you choose to say." . . . So I made it clear that I didn't want to bully them around and I respected their right to their points of view, and it was going to be, as I say, the government's and their consciences that rule when they got home. But I was interested, since we, the main body of prisoners, had planned for the senior officer to be the spokesman, and I wanted to know was that all right with them. I told them generally what I was going to say. I told them I was going to generally say that we were honored to serve there and give the impression that we were conscious that we had been continually members of the U.S. Armed Forces, and that we were grateful for what the country and the president had done to get us out of there. And I wanted to know if they objected to that or felt that they had to say something at that time.

They said no, they didn't. They preferred to remain completely low profile and they didn't want to make any kind of public demonstration . . . at that time. Then I had to check with them on the way they wanted to depart the aircraft. There were two ways to leave, one out the regular ramp and one out the rear ramp, which was for the sick and wounded. I didn't want it to appear that those creeps had been allowed to come out of there out of turn as well men, since they were aboard as sick and wounded. So I gave my opinion that since they were listed as sick and wounded on the flight, I thought they might choose to go out with the rest of the sick and wounded. They immediately acceded to that, so that was the end of that problem. They weren't visible, they just went out with the other guys, the other sick and wounded, some of whom were quite recently shot down, B-52 crewmen and so forth.

That was a crisis that I got over and then I made up my little thing. I asked the guys to give me a thumbs-up if they liked what I had said . . . and to give me a thumbs-down if they didn't like it, and give me a hand up if they wanted to ask questions, or add or subtract. I wanted them all to have input because it was something that represented them all and, since I had time, I wanted to make sure that I tapped all their opinions. . . . They all gave me a thumbs-up and were pretty cheerful, so that's the way it went.

    . . . I kind of stumbled going down the ramp, and I saw Admiral Gallery. I reported back to him: "Admiral Gayler, Commander Jeremiah A. Denton Jr.," and I gave him my old file number, 485087 USN, "reporting back for duty in the Navy," or some words that allowed for the fact that I had been on duty, but now I was coming back for regular assignment. I believe he mumbled something about—he didn't know what I was going to say either—"would you like to," and he pointed at the mike. I said, "Yes, sir," and I walked over there and said my little saying.[2]

Commander James B. Stockdale

On August 5, 1965, Comdr. James Stockdale was shot down over North Vietnam while on a bombing mission. He ejected from his aircraft, floated down in his parachute, and became caught in a tree. His memoir tells the story of his capture:

> Snagged, I bob down onto main street like a puppet on a string. No time to think. With my right hand I pop the two quick-release latches on either side of my chest and the parachute straps snap up and away into the tree as I become conscious of a thundering herd bearing down on me from my right.
>
>   They are right on top on me, the town roughnecks, running pell-mell from the south, carrying clubs and screaming. I am off-balance and it is the quarterback sack to end them all; every kid has to show off to the crowd, get his licks in, as I am pummeled, bashed, rolled up in a ball. They grab my arms and legs and twist and kick, and then somebody zonks me over the head and I start to get woozy. Through my dim consciousness, I hear a police whistle blowing. The action is fast— they are down to those red polka-dot shorts. Dear Syb [his wife], help me! Now even the shorts we bought are cut away, lying in shreds in this muddy street.
>
>   There go some men with my parachute, wadding it up to hide it; white parachutes draw trouble from the air. What's the man in the pith helmet trying to

say? Pointing down—boots? I take 'em off? My God! Look at it! My left leg shattered at the knee, angling out to the side where it isn't supposed to be; no skin broken, but it is bent at least 60 degrees from straight up and down. That changes the whole picture. That is *real* trouble! I am crippled. I will never run again. And just when I need all my strength! I was going to give myself the shot of morphine and run up over the hill. After all those hurdle races I'd run. And I haven't even felt the pain of it yet.

There is the morphine, there is the miniature radio [part of his survival gear]—there it is all out in the street; the kids are rifling my strewn-about gear and cut-up clothes. Another kid rushes up; he has *three* American wristwatches on his arm. He motions for mine. Another shock: My left wrist is clean; my left arm won't raise; arm flail during that high-speed ejection; I forgot to grab my right wrist with my left hand when I used the emergency handle. Now a broken back or shoulder or both. And the old Abercrombie & Fitch, whipped off and out in the weeds somewhere, "JBS, 1942, Love Dad," lost forever.

I am conscious of aircraft-engine noises overhead as I am lugged naked down the street and laid in a clear area. My guys are up there, in and out of the low clouds, trying to figure out where I am. It's not worth the risk, guys; I've had it. I'll be here quite a while—in this land of night-soil smell. . . . My leg and shoulder were quite painful now, but like the civilians before, none of the soldiers was the least bit interested in my gestured requests for help in getting them back into their sockets. Cold muscles and swelling were locking them into their misshapen places.[3]

As he was being taken to POW camp, the guards placed him temporarily in a house.

There was tension in the room among the two or three men who remained with me. A crazed man suddenly burst in with a little milking-type stool and brought it down in the middle of my stomach with two blows before being grabbed and ejected. (I had a vague recollection of some disturbed man being repulsed in a charge against me back in the village about the time I passed out, and now I had the feeling he was still trailing me.) But the real shocker came about twenty minutes later. Again he rushed the door and lunged at me as he came through it. Although the men acting as my guards knocked him off-balance, he managed to fire a big pistol toward me, point-blank, twice. The flashes blinded us and acrid smoke filled the little room as he was thrown out for good. His aim had been deflected; the shots hit below my torso, one creasing my foreleg but not hitting bone, and both rounds splintering the bed slabs, showering wood splinters all over me and that corner of the room. . . .

The leg was terribly swollen and distorted. The skin was stretched tight over some pretty jumbled-up bones near the surface; but even at the inside of what had been the knee joint, the skin was not quite broken. The doctor also examined my shoulder and back, and moved the arm enough to determine the degree of restriction and sensitivity. Then he took what looked like a big veterinary needle and filled it full of clear fluid. I had to lie back down and expose the inside of my right elbow. Then he shoved the big needle in. I started to count, but before I could get to "three" I was out like a light. . . .

I, being immobile in my crippledness and what was left of my leg cast, both man and woman left me alone in the truck and walked forward to the prison gate. Little did I know on that morning in 1965, as I looked lazily at the old French Ministry of Justice on one side and the wall of seventy-year old Hoa Lo Prison on the other, that I would never again be without blindfold or handcuffs on a Hanoi street until I walked out that gate in 1973. . . .

After I had eaten what I could, Dipshit [the name given to one of the guards] rolled me out of the stretcher, took out his knife, and cut the rest of my leg cast off. I was shocked at the appearance of my leg; there was no knee anymore, just a wide strip of irregularly swollen meat that connected my calf to my thigh. The lower leg seemed to flop to an unnatural position just about as it had when I saw it in the street of that little town—swung outboard about 45 to 60 degrees, its axis of bending 90 degrees from the natural one. Eagle came in and helped Dipshit put me up on a high table, and I watched my lower leg sway back and forth like a pendulum as I was moved. It was very painful by then, and I was in and out of consciousness. . . .

I lay awake that night of October 25, 1965, for a couple of hours, heart pounding in excitement. I had not received one word of advice about when I could put weight on this leg. There was a big scar down the center of the knee where they had just taken the stitches out. The leg was toed-in, ugly, and crooked, but under me; there was no joint action at all. The tendons behind what had been the knee were all changing shape. I was amused to discover that if I lay back and extended the stiff leg directly over my head, I could count my own heartbeats by watching a misplaced pulsating vein on the top of my left foot.[4]

With all of this suffering it is no wonder that he told himself, "An ominous depressed feeling overcame me inside these walls." Stockdale's book *In Love and War: The Story of a Family's Ordeal and Sacrifice during the Vietnam*

Years, from which these quotations are taken, provides insight into the tortures he and others went through. Perhaps the cruelest torture of all was the isolation, and the POWs were willing to suffer whatever was necessary to communicate among themselves. Communication was vital to the POW's ability to resist and was a significant factor in maintaining sanity over years of essentially solitary confinement interrupted by unspeakable torture.

One of Stockdale's most courageous and selfless acts was—to every extent possible—to prevent the Vietnamese from using him for propaganda purposes. For example, sensing the start of another effort by the guards to extract propaganda, and aware that his earlier efforts at self-disfiguration had successfully dissuaded his captors from photographing him for propaganda purposes, he deliberately inflicted a near-mortal wound to himself in order to convince his captors of his willingness to give up his life rather than capitulate. He described this event in his book:

> I had lived enough years close to Cat's horns to realize that the stage was set for my imminent personal exploitation in public. I had to use my initiative to do something to derail it. My only hope was to disfigure myself.
>
> Already I had the plan. To hell with washing—work fast! Pigeye will be back in a minute! To look authentic, I stripped. Faucet on, wet the soap and get it sudsing, blade into the razor, now stoop forward over the faucet, direct your bare ass to the peephole. Head under the faucet for a splash, now lather your hair and cut a swath right down the middle of your head, from way back right down to your forehead. Make it a "reverse Cherokee," cut it right down to the skin. *Pop!* goes the peephole. "Queek!" yells Pigeye, then it pops closed. I'm up to the count of two and the bolt has not been thrown. Good! Pigeye is going about more chores. Cut, cut, cut. God, my old hair is matted and tough from a week of sweat and tears. What's this? Blood! I must be tearing up my scalp trying to rip this hair out! Cut, cut, cut. *Pop!* goes the peephole. "Don!" screams Pigeye. *Clunk* goes the bolt, and he swings the door open. By this time, there is blood all over my hands and the floor, and in my soapy hair. Pigeye grabs me by the arm, screaming, "Eeoow!" Out we rush into the central court, I totally naked, blood running down my shoulders now, civilians all over the courtyard, men and women, standing aghast.

"Rabbit," the guard assigned to prepare Stockdale for this attempt at propaganda exploitation, saw him:

Rabbit looked at me, wheeled, and nearly expired of shock. I was slow to realize that, seeing all the blood, he thought I had tried to kill myself. I felt good, felt that I was on the track. I figured I had the ropes coming, so I sat down in position for Pigeye to put on the straps and get it over with. Rabbit and Chihuahua [another guard] both started yelling, "No! No! Get on your feet!" Typical Vietnamese face-savers, I thought. It was my idea to take the ropes, so they say, "No! You are not entitled to the ropes!"

I stood up as Chihuahua was shouting, "Why are you taking your own life? I know you want to kill yourself, but you must not do it. You have things to do. You have an appointment to keep tonight. The general staff officer wants to see you downtown tonight. . . ." I was to have been secretly recorded at that rehearsal in case I clammed up tonight before the movie camera. . . . "You will make the movie tonight! We will get a hat!" All three of them—Pigeye and the two officers—strode out of room 18 into that late-afternoon sun, locking the door behind them. . . . I had stumbled into winning . . . I was well into a hunger strike, I was unpresentable in public and would take pains to reblacken my cheeks every day. . . . I had learned how to make these sons of bitches work every step of the way.[5]

To further prevent the Vietnamese from using him, he frequently made himself sick with "puke balls," pieces of soap that he hid in his pajama pocket. "When alone in the daylight, I was seldom away from the peephole, and the approach of a guard or interrogator with a key meant a quick gulp of soap and a brisk walk to the slop bucket in the corner. By the time the door was open, I was retching. When asked what was wrong with me, I said I had a disease known as a "nervous stomach." They took this information to the old doc several times, and apparently he was puzzled, but he was not permitted to call on me because a Camp Authority rule denied his access to those in punishment.[6]

Stockdale's success at beating himself up and making himself sick derailed his captors' plan to make a film using the American POWs, which was to be entitled *The Secret Plan to End the War*. One of the most important aspects of Stockdale's leadership in the POW camp was what he called the spirit of "unity over self." This required remarkable and courageous leadership, particularly when the two senior POWs, whom Stockdale in his book called "Bob" and "Ed," gave in to the Vietnamese to avoid discomfort and torture. While Stockdale and Jeremiah Denton were in Alcatraz, separated from the other POWs to eliminate their leadership, these two men

> talked freely, and obviously without prior torture, about the illegality of the war. I shuddered as I thought how that self-serving tape by that pair of misfits was guaranteed to destroy the morale of any young aviator who heard it. Hearing things like that, which *nobody* in Alcatraz would have tolerated for a minute, was dismaying. I spoke aloud to myself: "What the hell has happened to American spirit in this place? What American is running this camp?" It seems like we are going backward; our hard-won gains, our unity, our sense of responsibility for each other, are slipping away in a vacuum of zero leadership."[7]

He and other senior POW leaders

> kept the prisoner communications lines full of BACK US—we all go home together—no repent, no repay and general "hang together" philosophy. We were capitalizing on the chance of a lifetime to unify all American prisoners in North Vietnam. . . . My whole concept of proper prisoner-of-war behavior was based on sticking together. We were in a situation in which loners could make out. If, after the initial shakedown, you refused to communicate with Americans, there was tacit agreement that the Vietnamese would leave you alone; there would likely be no more torture, no confessions, no radio broadcasts, maybe not even another tough military-information interrogation. One interested only in keeping his own nose clean could score lots of points by remaining a loner. I asked everybody to give up this edge of individual flexibility and get in the swim, communicate, level with your American neighbors on just what-all you compromised, what information you had to give up in the torture room, to freely enter into collusions with Americans, to take your lumps together and, if necessary, all go down the tubes together. In this circumstance our highest value had to be placed on the support of the man next door. To ignore him was to betray him. The bottom line was placing prisoner unity over selfish interests. It was "Unity over Self."
>
> This first set of Hanoi-wide laws was put out in easy-to-remember acronym form—Bow, Air, Crime, Kiss, Unity over Self, BACK US. These orders were absolutely prohibitory—that is, you were required to take torture, forcing the Vietnamese to impose significant pain in you before acceding to these specific demands. In the spring of 1967 the orders were carried to every camp in the Hanoi prison system under my name as the senior American communicating in that system.

The North Vietnamese released some POWs early if they agreed to return to the United States and assist in their propaganda campaign against the people of the United States, hoping to destroy America's will to continue the war. Stockdale related: "I gave their new release program a name: FRP—the 'Fink Release Program,'—and that was the way it was to be known. I also issued an order that started on its way to the other cell-blocks of Las Vegas and with subsequent movers to the camps elsewhere in the city and outside it: "No early release; we all go home together."[8]

On March 4, 1976, Captain Stockdale was awarded the Congressional Medal of Honor by President General Ford.

Lieutenant Junior Grade Everett Alvarez Jr.

Lt. (jg) Everett Alvarez Jr. was shot down and captured on August 5, 1964, during the first sortie of the Vietnam War. His captivity lasted "103 months, or 446 weeks, or 3135 days," the longest of any prisoner of war in North Vietnam.[9] Alvarez's vivid memories of his imprisonment are recorded in his book, *Code of Conduct* (1991), which is the source of the information that follows.

Although he was moved from one place to another, Alvarez usually found himself in a cell that was

> seven feet by seven feet, blank concrete walls and concrete floor, small ventilation ducts near the fifteen-foot ceiling, two concrete slabs as beds, heavy steel reinforced door that might have a pinhole bored through by a termite. Belongings for each inmate consisted of a straw mat, a mosquito net, a washer jug, a metal cup, one blanket, a set of prison pajamas, two pairs of shorts and a "Bo," a small bucket that served as a commode, sink, stool. Nothing whatever was provided for a prisoner to occupy his time. Some of us lived alone in such cells for up to two or three years.
>
> For almost all of our waking moments, there was nothing to see. One could just as well have closed his eyes and kept them closed. There was very little to touch or feel. And most of us who spent a very long period of time in solitary confinement may just as well have lost the ability to talk. We had no one to talk to. . . . The only time we saw human beings other than fellow prisoners or jailers was when we were put on display, as in the infamous march through Hanoi.

The loneliness and isolation presented an almost indescribable hardship for the POWs. The tapping and other means of communication they developed over the years assisted greatly in their ability to endure. "There were brutal individuals among the guards," Alvarez said, "men who reveled in their work of torture, and I would admit to hating them. For the most part our guards were misfits in their society, men who for one reason or another couldn't qualify for service at the front or in higher posts of the government."[10]

Most of the POWs did not immediately discuss their experiences after release, but as time went by, Alvarez and other POWs began to talk more about their confinement. One day, as Alvarez was talking to a group of students, "I found myself telling them about the worms—how the first time I saw a worm in my stool I screamed for the guard. He told me that everyone in North Vietnam had worms. 'It's good,' he said. 'If you don't have worms, your stomach bloats.'" The POWs, with prison humor, made a game of the intestinal parasites. "Eventually," he said, "we POWs had contests to see who could pass the longest worm, and I scored with a twelve-incher."[11]

On their return to the United States, a group of the POWs were at Bethesda Naval Hospital recovering. Alvarez reflected: "For the first time we talked about the torture. Risner said that he had been tied into a ball so tight that his toes pushed against his mouth and his shoulders popped out of their sockets, and yet he said truly that a stretch of six months of solitary was harder to take. I remembered what it felt like being forced to sit for days on a stool without sleep or food, lousy food, the loneliness in solitary, the beatings."

But there was more hardship for him than physical torture. The Vietnamese made a point of telling him that his sister Delia had become an antiwar activist and was publicly saying: "The war is wrong and is hurting America more than anything else." Her statements were announced over the radio and broadcast throughout the entire POW camp. His wife suing him for divorce hurt him terribly, he said, but "dealing with my sister Delia's defection from the cause I'd nearly died for and suffered a long time for was more difficult." The Vietnamese also made sure Alvarez learned that his wife, Tangie, had decided to divorce him. "Unquestionably, the news of her desertion . . . brought a long down period in prison."[12]

The North Vietnamese made extensive efforts to splinter the POWs' unity, particularly trying to use race and nationality as fracture points. Alvarez, a Mexican American, commented: "believe me they tried, especially working on me and Fred Cherry, a black Air Force pilot. They wanted us to feed their propaganda machine with material about mistreatment as members of oppressed minorities. For me the concept of being a minority person had never entered my head. Both Fred and I maintained that we were Americans and proud of our country, under all pressure and against all temptation, and our fellow captives accepted us as such."[13]

The conduct of Alvarez, the longest-held prisoner of war in Vietnam, was a source of pride for the other POWs as well as for himself: "One of my very few sources of satisfaction in captivity had been the recognition I was given by my fellow POWs. When new prisoners were marched through the compound, my cellmates would boost me on their shoulders so that I could be seen over the dividing wall. The message was: look at Alvarez; if he could take it this long, so can you. Well, I would do my best as required by the code of conduct that had sustained me so far." Alvarez showed enormous self-discipline during his captivity. He told his father, "I could have come home earlier if I had given the North Vietnamese propaganda material, except that I couldn't have lived with myself, couldn't have considered myself a man if I'd done that." His father responded, "You've made me proud." During all the years of suffering, the torture, and the loneliness, Alvarez never lost faith in America's leaders. And when he was finally freed and en route to Travis Air Force Base in San Francisco, he was selected to be the spokesman for the group of POWs when they landed. His brief statement was: "For years and years we dreamed of this day and we kept the faith. Faith in God, in our president and in our country. It was this faith that maintained our hope that some day our dreams would come true and today they have. We have come home. God bless the president and God bless you, Mr. and Mrs. America. You did not forget us."[14]

Alvarez described the source of his inner strength and discipline: "I know that it was my . . . belief in the United States and in the code of conduct to which I subscribed that enabled me to survive with a sense of honor throughout the isolation and torture of long imprisonment." When he met President

Richard M. Nixon at a reception for the returning POWs in May 1973, Alvarez told him: "It is my belief in all the intrinsic values which are inherent in just being an American, faith in my God, my fellow Americans, and you, Mr. President, that carried me through these long years of imprisonment."[15]

Sources of Selfless Leadership
The Role of the U.S. Naval Academy

In one of my many discussions with Adm. James L. Holloway III (CNO 1974–78), I asked if the Naval Academy had a motto similar to West Point's "Duty, Honor, Country," because West Point graduates, it seemed to me, emphasized its importance as a guideline in their military careers. Admiral Holloway's answer did much to explain why America was so fortunate to have naval officers with the character of Denton, Stockdale, and Alvarez.

> The motto of the Naval Academy is *Ex Scientia Tridens*. The literal translation would be, "Out of knowledge comes sea power." That's not exactly the sort of battle cry we rallied around over the years. During my years at the Academy, world events increasingly cast their long shadow over our lives as Europe became engulfed in . . . World War II. As soon-to-be officers in the fleet, our curriculum and routines were adapted to better prepare us for wartime service. My class, originally scheduled to graduate in 1943, was moved up to a June 1942 date. This acceleration was accomplished by eliminating nonessential courses, lengthening the work week, and canceling the Christmas and summer leave periods. The hardships of this strenuous regimen were partly compensated for by a strengthened sense of purpose and the anticipation of an early commissioning. The grinding schedule served mainly to remind us that being in the military at this time was serious business. Then Pearl Harbor occurred just six months before our scheduled graduation. The class ahead was off to the fleet a month after the war began, and for a precious but impatient five months, we were the seniors on the campus. But the anticipated joys of first classman privileges were limited. We were full-fledged members of a Navy that was now at war.
>
> We graduated and were commissioned on June 19, 1943, and America was not winning the war. The Navy was fighting the Germans in the Atlantic and the Japanese in the Pacific, and we were losing in both theaters. The disaster at Pearl Harbor had been followed by successive losses of the Philippines, Guam, and

Wake Island; defeats in the Java Sea and the Solomons; and the seizure by the Japanese of the Aleutian Islands in Alaska. The United States was yet to claim a single victorious battle or campaign. The Battle of Midway had occurred in early June, but at the time, the significance of the outcome was not clear.

Many of our former upperclassmen we had served with in Bancroft Hall from the years of 1940, 1941, and 1942 had been killed in action. As all our class had received orders to sea duty our own immediate prospects upon commissioning clearly involved wide and lengthy separations from friends and families aboard the combatant ships of the fleet engaged in all-out conflict with determined enemies who seemed to be unstoppable.

Yet our morale was high. We were confident that the Naval Academy had fully prepared us for the demands and trials that lay ahead. We considered ourselves better trained technically than our counterparts graduating from reserve programs. We felt ready to join the fleet as competent professional officers, trained in the art of naval warfare and inspired by the traditions of the service and the heritage of the United States Naval Academy. We were motivated to give all we had, to ensure the success of our ship in its wartime mission. We were very serious about our métier, an attitude that often caused some amusement on the part of our non-Academy shipmates. This attitude of pride in our service had been ingrained in our character as midshipmen, largely without our conscious awareness. As officers in the fleet, we were absolutely determined not to let down our country, our Navy, our Academy, or our classmates. Many of us had suffered through a sophomoric cynicism of those concepts as midshipmen. But under the realities of war, with others' lives depending on our performance of duties, those special responsibilities of our profession became inherent.

It was this subtle inculcation of a dedication to "duty, honor, country"—as the Military Academy puts it—that is the true raison d'être of the service academies. For my thirty-nine years in the Navy—which included combat in three major wars, long periods of family separations, and the frustrations of bureaucracy—this powerful sense of dedication had sustained me. Stripped to its leanest fundamentals, the gift of the Naval Academy to its graduates is this mindset of a dedication to an extraordinary set of moral values that go beyond our own selfish concerns and are committed to serving the common good.

Given the opportunity to impress these deep moral values upon the formative and receptive minds of the young men and women who seek the service as a career and the Naval Academy as their college, the Academy has done well. A simple "Who's Who" list of Naval Academy graduates successful in all career fields is a convincing testimonial to its institutional competence in producing leaders of national caliber. Yet, it is important that these famous names do not obscure those legions of other alumni who have served with equal honor but with perhaps less visible success in creating a Navy and a nation that can both be characterized as the best in all of history.

The character of the leadership offered by the graduates of the Naval Academy is well illustrated by a story related by Admiral Holloway during one of our interviews:

A young officer came by to see me when I was CNO. He had just been repatriated after six years as a POW. He had served with me some years ago. Subsequently, he had been a carrier pilot flying in Vietnam, was shot down, taken prisoner of war, and spent six years in captivity. When he got out of prison camp and came home, BuPers had offered him any duty station he wanted, within reason. This was the Navy's policy with the returning Vietnam POWs. I asked him where he wanted to go now that he had his choice of any duty station. Some were going to Jacksonville to improve their golf, others going to an NROTC assignment near their home. But he said, "I'm going to the Naval Academy." I said, "That surprises me. You're not a Naval Academy graduate, are you?" "No, I'm not," he replied. "That's why I'm going." I asked, "What do you mean?"

He answered, "Well, I have a story to tell you. When I went to my first squadron, about half the pilots were Naval Academy graduates. I had been an aviation cadet and we referred to the Academy officers as the 'ring knockers.' We reserves thought they were too serious, always consumed with business, no acey-deucey in the squadron ready room. I guess we were more happy-go-lucky. To be honest with you, we sneered a little bit at the ring knockers. Then I was shot down, and I went to prison camp. It was a terrible shock. The other POWs were unshaven, they were unwashed, and their morale was awful. They weren't taking care of each other. Each one was concerned only about his own lot. Then one day everything changed. Jim Stockdale, the air wing commander on the *Oriskany*, had been shot down, and he came into our camp. He was the senior officer in rank and therefore nominally in charge. He announced, 'Okay, things are going to be different. I'm in charge now. I want you guys clean-shaven and shaped up. And I want you to start resisting our jailers. Do only what the Geneva Convention requires of a POW. Give only your name, rank, and serial number. Don't cooperate!' It just absolutely turned our lives around. But as you know, because of this, Stockdale was badly beaten. . . . He continued to resist, so he was put into solitary confinement.

Jeremiah Denton took over as senior officer while Stockdale was put away in solitary. Jerry did the same thing as Jim and so too was tortured and put in solitary. Then came Bill Lawrence, he was an inspirational leader and also badly tortured for leading the POW resistance. In every case, these guys were Naval Academy graduates. I said to myself, 'If the Naval Academy can get these guys so pumped up with that attitude, I want to find out how.' So I want to go to the Naval Academy and serve as a company officer and find out what there is at the Naval Academy that is so inspiring."

. . . After I had retired, I ran into him again and asked: "How did your tour at the Naval Academy go?" He said, "It was something. I liked it so much I requested an extension. However, they couldn't do it. A nice thing happened, though. I was made an honorary member of the Class of 1984."

I think it's a great story because you will hear many people smirk about the ring knockers and the "professionals." We are sometimes even referred to as "lifers." So there was something very special about his experience that I deeply understood and appreciated.

Let me get back to your question. How is this dedication instilled in people? I don't believe it can be just by a motto. I'm not a believer in mottoes as an excuse for action. One thing that bothered me during the Korean War was the army trucks with big bumper stickers saying, "Kill Commies." I thought that was phony. The Marines didn't advertise, they just did it! Military people react to unit pride. The smaller the unit, the more intense the pride. [I] was [in] the second flight division in VF-52. The four of us were a band of brothers who flew together in all kinds of weather and got shot at together. Then our loyalty was successive to our squadron, our carrier, carrier aviation, naval aviation, the Navy, and the nation, with some diminution of enthusiasm at each level. Loyalty and unit pride stem from sharing the same experiences, vicissitudes, and dangers. At the Naval Academy it was sharing the discipline, the intense conformance to duties and regulations, and the tough mental strain of the curriculum. We considered ourselves to be a special breed of young men to put up with these pressures, and we shared that commitment with our fellow midshipmen and with the naval heroes of the past. Unit pride is "I can't let my buddies down." At the Naval Academy, it was pride in the 12th Company, loyalty to Fourth Battalion, and a pure satisfaction of being a Naval Academy midshipman. It was pride in the Naval Academy because we had made a great effort to get there and substantial sacrifices to remain. While my contemporaries from high school were at Princeton having fun, I was in the Navy, and they kidded me for wearing a "sailor suit."

During the Korean War we shared a common source of pride in being in Fighter Squadron 52. We had a rough time, but morale remained high. I was the squadron exec, and eventually I took command of the squadron after the commanding officer had been shot down. I also lost my wingman to Chinese AA fire early on the deployment. Eight of our aircraft were destroyed by enemy ground fire, but only two pilots were lost. We felt no one was doing more for our country than we were, and we were proud of it. I am sure that Jim Stockdale, Jerry Denton, and Bill Lawrence felt the same way. We had signed up for naval aviation and we are not going to let our institution or our comrades down.[16]

In talking about the role of the Naval Academy in the development of his character and leadership, Admiral Holloway referred to the "commitment with other midshipmen and with naval heroes of the past." Admiral Denton reflected on the importance of history in his own Naval Academy experience:

Force of arms is one way to protect [our country]. Another and most vital way is through a spiritual awakening within each of us and a return to the basic values which made this country the greatest in history. In my Naval Academy years, where my sense of duty and honor were developed and refined, I copied some quotations onto the flyleaf of a schoolbook. Among them was a strangely prophetic one by David Glasgow Farragut, the Civil War hero of Mobile Bay: "There are comparatively few men from whom one cannot learn something, and a Naval officer should always be adding to his knowledge. . . . It is hard to say what a naval officer might not have to do."[17]

Prophetic indeed. Admirals Denton and Stockdale were asked to do more—to suffer more and lead more—than most Americans will ever have to do. They earned the title "hero." Their leadership and character traits are worthy of emulation.

I asked Adm. Thomas Hayward (CNO 1978–82) to describe the role of the Naval Academy in the development of his character and leadership ability.

I have a couple of comments on that. First, I was raised in a very straightforward and squared-away environment. As a result of that, I adjusted very easily to the discipline; the whole idea of West Point and Annapolis I approached with sparkling eyes. Basically, I loved the Academy and all of the routine we had to adjust to. I thought it was terrific, and I had very little trouble in adjusting. So it was very easy for me to fit into that milieu.

From the standpoint of education, I never thought I would last a year. I didn't see my first "A" on a high school report card until my senior year. I . . . honestly had a lot of doubt about how well I would do. With the Naval Academy experience, I walked out of there at graduation with what came across clear to me then and has always been a guiding post that I helped others with—other officers and enlisted—that you can accomplish anything. The Academy teaches you how to accept responsibility and that if you work hard enough at it, you can do anything. I really feel very strongly about that. I'm very convinced of that; it was certainly very much so in my case. I graduated in the top 10 percent of my class, I wasn't the top 1 percent, but hard work, determination, and self-discipline, all . . . things [that] are fundamental in character building, played an enormous role with me. From that experience I have persuaded and mentored a lot of people that there is nothing you can't do.

"As you practice, so you play!" is more than a platitude. It is a predominant characteristic of most leaders. I asked Admiral Hayward about the character training he received at the Naval Academy, the caliber of the faculty, and what he learned about naval history while he was there. "Remember, first, we had a war going on," he said, "and consequently the general motivation that you start with was pretty high. The people are serving their country while going to school. The war ended before I graduated, so in World War II I never shot at anybody. But it certainly worked in respect to understanding the character of our prior leaders, the big leaders, like John Paul Jones; that he had a lot to do with it. You take from the study of naval history . . . at the Academy the elements of greatness and try to use them as your guidepost."[18]

In my interview with Adm. Carlisle A. H. Trost (CNO 1986–90) I asked a similar question. He told me:

> I guess all of us who were there at the time certainly had a desire to serve our country. It was almost bred into us, having been teenagers in World War II, and I had graduated from high school just shortly after the end of that war. We were led by some very fine people at various levels. We were also given examples of leadership that we would not emulate in future years, examples of how not to lead. There were a few of those, but there are some in every organization. I can recall being extremely impressed by some of the people who were in leadership positions at the Academy. We had excellent instructors, both military and civil-

ian, who impressed upon us the history of the Navy, the traditions, which I think meant more than anything else to us.

We were raised in an environment that was steeped in tradition. Also, having the opportunity not just to learn about the Navy, but to make these summer cruises, having those training experiences where we were interfacing with the real fleet and learning what it was like to work as an enlisted sailor in our initial cruise, then fleeting up and having an opportunity to do the kinds of things that we would do as junior officers. It was extremely important in our professional development.

Also at the Naval Academy, there was this constant stepping up to greater responsibility . . . each year after you left your plebe year, when you were the trainee. You had a little more responsibility for yourself, and . . . that was probably a new thing to many young people because there is no longer mom to take care of your clothes, to tell you what to do, and when to do it. You are on your own all the way, and the decisions that you make are your decisions. You are guided by people with experience in your profession. You learn self-sufficiency to a degree that you have not had to up to that point in your life.

I think what impressed me as much as anything was the caliber of some of the officers, and some of those who had served in World War II, and in various capacities, including some of the younger officers. One of those who probably had the greatest influence on me was a fellow named Lando Zech. Lando retired as a three-star nuclear submariner. . . . In addition to commanding two diesel-powered submarines, [Lando] was commander of the *Nautilus*. He was a lieutenant when I knew him first. . . . He was my company officer for my last year and a half at the Naval Academy. He was simply a very impressive man and a *man of character*. He clearly was a leader, and of *absolute integrity*. He impressed upon us a great sense of responsibility that we had to have, especially in our last year at the Naval Academy as people in a leadership position with other midshipmen. He was so successful, I suppose, that it influenced people. Of the thirty-nine new officers from my company who were commissioned, which included several who went into the Air Force, sixteen of them became submarine officers. So, I would say that his influence was very considerable.[19]

"I really believe that the Naval Academy had a significant role in my character and leadership development," reflected Adm. Jay Johnson.

When I was CNO, I spent a lot of time at the Naval Academy. I would often talk to the classes, meet with them in various venues. There's not a day that goes by that I'm not thankful that I went to the United States Naval Academy. . . . It put me on the pathway to where I am today and really made me what I consider to be a responsible adult, who is proud of having given a whole career of service to his country. Now, that gets imbued at the Naval Academy. . . . The focus at that time, I think, on Vietnam had something to do with it. The fact that, hey, this isn't like going to other schools. It's different here; there's a mission here, you know. It really helped me grow up. The leadership I saw there. The leaders I saw, albeit it was from the perspective of a midshipman.[20]

I asked Adm. Frank B. Kelso II (CNO 1990–94) if he had ever been tempted to leave the Navy. His answer addressed the role of the Naval Academy in his decision to make the Navy his career and in his development.

Yes, on many occasions. I think when you reach your obligated service time in your career, most officers look around. The grass often looks greener somewhere else, and one has to make a decision as to whether to stay or leave. In my case, the decision to leave was never too serious. My wife accepted Navy life, I liked the people with whom I worked, I enjoyed the work, and every time I thought about the issue, two questions came to mind: Is the job important, and if it is who will do the job when I leave? It always came down to a conclusion that the job was important and I had been trained to do it. I did think about leaving when my first obligated service was up and again at twenty years when I was eligible to retire. Then I was a commander completing submarine command when I was selected a year early for captain and that ended the idea of leaving the Navy.

I pointed out to him that graduates of West Point put stock in their motto, "Duty, Honor, Country," to guide their careers and asked if the Naval Academy had a similar motto or inherent quality that affected his character development and commitment to service.

There's no question in my mind [that] the commitment to service was reinforced at the Naval Academy. . . . Most of the people I met and saw there I could look at as role models. A lot of them were veterans of the Second World War. All of the superintendents, in fact, that I had when I was there were veterans of the Second World War. One of them was Admiral Turner Joy, whom I remember in particular. He came back to be a superintendent after he had been a U.S. nego-tiator for the Korean War. He had cancer, but we didn't know that at the time, and he passed on shortly after that. He was a very impressive gentleman.

There were no leadership courses anything like there are today, no formal courses of leadership. As I remember it, there was one course maybe one semester, but nothing similar to what they have today. Leadership was taught more by example in my time than it was by you going to get it out of a book.[21]

I asked a similar question of Adm. James D. Watkins (CNO 1982–86). "In the beginning," he responded,

I did not give much thought to a naval career. The education was my great motivator, and the people in the small town in which I lived looked upon an appointment to the military academies with great favor. I was not opposed to a career, but in truth I did not know much about a Navy career. At seventeen there are a lot of steps for most young people before they lock into any career. There is no question, the time in the Academy had great influence on my subsequent decision to choose a career in the Navy. It reinforced my love for this great country and offered me the opportunity to serve.[22]

Adm. Charles R. Larson served two tours as superintendent of the Naval Academy. What role, I asked, did his experience at the Naval Academy have in the development of his character and leadership? He replied: "Well, we had leadership classes when I was at the Naval Academy, but quite frankly, I can't remember much about them. We used to call them 'leader-sleep.' I think some of them were probably more practical things. We talked about some of the practical things you had to know to be ready to go to fleet. I'm sure there were some basic precepts or concepts of leadership in those classes, but there's nothing that really jumped out at me and said that really motivated me to stay."

I asked him whether there were officers at the Academy he tried to emulate because of their character and leadership. "Certainly," he said, "they had large impact on me, their example: officers that walked the walk and talked the talk; people who lived what they preached and really gave you the sense that they believed in what they were doing and they cared about people. They were people of integrity that really cared about our development."[23]

The Selflessness of Admiral Arleigh Burke

Several chiefs of naval operations have demonstrated the importance of selflessness as a vital part of character and leadership. One of the most able naval leaders ever to serve the United States was Adm. Arleigh Burke (CNO 1955–61). In 1959 Admiral Burke was asked by President Eisenhower to serve an unprecedented third two-year term as CNO. "I was quite reluctant to accept the reappointment," reflected Admiral Burke.

> I had been asked by the president and the SecDef and the secretary of the navy. I didn't want to accept very much. You're caught on something like that. It's a great honor and anybody would want that sort of an honor. It's a great privilege. . . . There were a lot of nice things about being reappointed, but there [are] a lot of things that can go very wrong, too. In the first place, it can be bad for a man to stay too long in a top spot. It stifles some promotion. You get stagnant in the job. You get a feeling that you've studied that problem before and you already know the answer, when the answer might be different. You're stereotyped in Congress, your relationship to Congress. And besides that you get very tired. It takes a lot of stamina for that job. You work seven days a week, and you're lucky if you can get seven hours' sleep a night, and you have a lot of social work in addition to other work. Your personal life is nil. So all and all, I thought for the good of the Navy, I ought to retire.
>
> Nobody can judge himself, whether he's any good or not. Because you've seen an awful lot of people who stay on a job, both in civilian life and military, stay on too long, and then nobody wants to tell them frankly, "You're overstaying your usefulness." I'm having a little difficulty persuading a man in civilian life now, who's a very important man—he believes that because he's reached seventy, he should retire. Actually he's very important to the company, but he doesn't want to stay on too long. Well, I can't persuade him that he's not going to. He knows he's not staying on too long now, but he doesn't know when that time will come. Well, the only thing that will make him stay on, I'm sure, is for me to arrange for a committee to be appointed that will tell him frankly when he ought to get out.
>
> Now, I had these same thoughts, too, that I ought to get out. My personal desire was to get out—I wanted to be home a little bit, I've got a nice wife, I want to keep her, and I was tired. But the big thing that I was fearful of was, people were just being kind to me and generous and saying polite things and they didn't really mean it. I don't know how you can evaluate things like that. Actually what convinced me finally was when I went over to see President Eisenhower, and he didn't try to argue at all, he just said, "It's your duty to stay," and that ended it. I accepted the third two-year term without any further discussion. . . . But I don't

think six years is advisable normally. Surely, there are a lot of good people in the Navy, an awful lot of them, and a lot of them can take over that job and do an adequate job. . . .

When I finally did retire—I had trouble the next time, too, as I knew I was going to, so I submitted my request for retirement before the election, before Mr. Kennedy, so that there wouldn't be any political connotations about it. And then after Mr. Connally was SecNav, and Mr. McNamara SecDef, President Kennedy wanted me to stay on. But that I knew would be wrong. I had no doubt then that I ought to get off.[24]

Admiral Burke's selflessness even led him to turn down a promotion. As was discussed in chapter 6, Adm. Marc A. Mitscher, who commanded one of the aircraft carrier task forces in World War II, initially resented the assignment of Burke, a surface ship commander, as his chief of staff, but Burke ultimately won Mitscher's respect and trust. Burke became extremely valuable to Mitscher because of his sound judgment and ability to develop and carry out plans. Indeed, Mitscher put Captain Burke in for promotion to rear admiral. Burke commented:

[Mitscher] wrote a personal letter to Admiral Nimitz and suggested that I be made rear admiral on his staff, and gave the reasons why it would facilitate my doing my job, and then after he sent the letter he showed it to me. I told him I didn't think I should be, and being a rear admiral wouldn't make a bit of difference in the way I was running that job, and I don't think it would have. And I told him why and asked him if he had any objections if I were to go see Admiral Nimitz and explain to him next time I went back to Pearl, why I shouldn't be [promoted]. He said no. So next time I went back I did see Admiral Nimitz and told him why, and he never put it in, and I think rightly so because . . . it's all right to go a bit farther, but if you get too far out of step, you're overcoming too many obstacles, there's too much experience you do not have, so much you don't understand. But worse than that is if you get people in high places too soon, they've got to get out of high places too soon, so it's very costly and expensive to the service to have too young people in it, because of retirement pay.

For example, even though I served six years as CNO, I still got out, there was no place for me to go—I retired when I was fifty-nine, and at that time I was a better officer than I'd ever been before. It would have been gold if the Navy would have used that, used me for a couple of more years. It would have saved that much retirement pay, saved that many officers; and as it was, why, I went out, and the Navy lost that service. Now, of course, that's a question of opinion as to whether or not I was worth it . . . but still that's generally true.

Admiral Burke was on several occasions tempted to leave his naval career. He related an experience during his active-duty years when he had to decide whether or not to take a very lucrative opportunity in the civilian sector:

> I note in my files several letters from Randy Lewisohn. They reminded me of a question I am sometimes asked by some of the young officers, i.e., did I ever think about getting out of the Navy during my career. Well, I did, and Randy nearly persuaded me once that the opportunities outside the Navy were more rosy than inside. Randy was a member of the Lewisohn family who built the Lewisohn stadium and other important edifices around New York. I was in the inspection division of the Naval Gun Factory just before the war and during the early days of the war. Young Lewisohn, in his thirties I would guess, reported to my antiaircraft gun mount section as an assistant, either just before the war or shortly after it started. We were looking frantically for manufacturing facilities that could possibly make gun mounts. After several months' training, Randy made a pretty good inspector. We had found that manufacturers of printing presses were accustomed to fine workmanship and were used to holding to the very small tolerances required in the manufacturer of accurate gun mounts. So we got all the printing press plants under contract as soon as we could. . . .
>
> One big trouble with those plants was that they had been manufacturing one type of apparatus for so long that . . . they were not used to flow sheets, fast work, large outputs, etc. The workmen were all very experienced in machining on the work they were used to, but were not very susceptible to the needs of getting accurate mounts out in a hurry. They were willing enough, but it was just like teaching old dogs new tricks. Many of the plants were family owned, too, and the leading men and supervisors had built up little systems they thought were pretty good, but we knew wouldn't get the job done either soon enough or good enough. Family-owned businesses meant that there was more than a little nepotism around, too.
>
> We had to have new machines put in, arrange flow of material, make machinery layouts, adapt their old machines, arrange for workloads, possible bottlenecks, and all the other things necessary to start up a plant and get it operat-

ing at full speed in a hurry. The technical and mechanical things were bad enough, but the worst difficulty was in getting new systems introduced and having supervisors who could get the people to continuously turn out good work and not resent the supervisor . . . when he rejected a piece of work. We worked out, because we had to, a good system of supervision and inspection and ways of handling these good men. . . . Although I spent most of my time in the gun factory, I was usually at a new plant when they first started to roll mounts or when something happened and the local inspector sent for me. For some reason or other I took Randy along on many of these troubleshooting trips, and since he learned fast and was good, eventually, I sent him out by himself. He became very good and could usually get a plant rolling without help from me.

Well, after the war Randy recognized that there were hundreds of plants that had to convert from manufacturers of war material to peacetime things, and they would have as much trouble doing that as they did to convert to wartime manufacturing. He got an idea that we would make them profitable, buy a share of the plant, and in addition have a fee based on the degree of profitability. Good idea, especially when he would put up most of the money. I had no money, but he said I could arrange to borrow it. He was certain we would be millionaires within three or four years. I was pretty sure it would work, too, and I was tempted to get out of the Navy and give it a whirl. But I still thought Navy life was better. Randy urged me quite a bit, but I finally convinced him that was not for me. He went into that business by himself and sure enough, within three years he had made his million and it came in faster thereafter. Only he died from overwork and a heart attack within ten years.[25]

Adm. James L. Holloway III did his job as CNO in spite of the many frustrations it entailed, serving his country with the selflessness that high leadership demands.

Dealing with the bureaucracy could be so frustrating. I served through a change of administration as CNO from the Republicans to the Democrats. From President Ford, who had been on the House Appropriations Committee, Armed Services Subcommittee, who understood the military and who had in Jim Schlesinger a very good secretary of defense, to President Jimmy Carter, who was dedicated to disarmament. The transition was a turbulent time.

Whenever there is a change in administration, there is a complete turnover at the top when the new senior people are brought in. But at the lower levels of the Pentagon many of the civilians are civil service and go from one administration to the next. As a result, there are in the Office of the Secretary of Defense the hobby shops, a little office with one GS-10 who has a pet project. One such project was the flying battleship! Every time there was a change of administration, into that vacuum came his proposals. The flying battleship was a large, heavily armored airplane that allegedly could defend itself against ground fire and fighter aircraft because of its many guns and missiles. Its proponent compared it to a battleship because of its survivability. Then, there was the hobby shopper who proposed a PT boat that launched intercontinental missiles. These proposals were ridiculous and impractical, but they each had to be formally considered and rejected, which took our time and effort.

General Bernie Rogers succeeded to chief of staff of the Army after his predecessor, General Abrams, died in office. After Bernie Rogers had served for three years, he had an opportunity to take over CinCEur, and he said, "That's where I'm going." When I asked him why, he said, "I can't take this Pentagon crap anymore." . . . One fellow who was put in the job found it over his head, and he committed suicide—that Mike Boorda. The CNO before Mike Boorda was Frank Kelso. Frank had to retire early because of an illness that was brought on by the stress of the job. The chief of naval operations is a tough position. Just recently the chief of staff of the Air Force, General Ron Fogleman, retired early because he said he couldn't take the crap. He refused to have any part in finding a scapegoat to blame for the bombing of the barracks in Saudi Arabia [Khobar Towers] that killed a number of airmen.

When I retired, I found that during the final weeks of my tour, I could hardly wait to retire. I was absolutely exhausted. The frustrations were so great. At an Armed Forces Policy Council meeting chaired by Secretary of Defense Harold Brown, I was explaining the reasons our carriers had to be so large. This was because our planes have become bigger in order to develop the power to have the range and altitude to intercept Soviet-designed aircraft representing the latest in aerospace technology. Before I could conclude he said to me, "The trouble with the Navy is that you have no imagination. If you had smaller planes and smaller carriers, you could buy more of them. But you don't even try; you just stick with the big nuclear carriers. You Navy people just don't have any imagination." I replied, "Mr. Secretary, do you call it not having imagination when we have fourteen submarines under the water at all times, nuclear submarines capable of launching while deeply submerged, enough nuclear-tipped missiles to obliterate all of Russia? Does that show a lack of imagination, in terms of a weapons system? Do you think it is a lack of imagination that we can move an entire tactical air wing at six hundred miles per day to any place around the seven-tenths of the world made up of international waters, and supply all their fuel, ammo, and maintenance support?" . . .

There were times during my tour as CNO I wanted to quit, either because I was fed up with the frustration or to demonstrate my opposition to a policy or program. And there were times when it was suggested that I quit in protest.

Life in the armed forces is a life of sacrifice. I asked Admiral Holloway, who was born into a Navy family, to comment on the selflessness that Navy life required—not just of him, but of his family as well.

I believe that one of the reasons that I was able to endure it was that my family was in the Navy so I knew what I was getting into. My parents had no outside income, and yet they sent both me and my sister to boarding schools. It was the only way we could get a decent high school education. My father moved three times during my four years in high school. Without a good high school record, getting into a good college was impossible. My parents made the sacrifices necessary to send us to private schools.

My wife, Dabney, knew what she was getting into by marrying into the Navy. Her father was an active-duty Navy captain when we were engaged. Dabney and I also realized the importance of a stable high school education for our own children. I was deployed during much of the time our children were at the age that they needed stability and family support. I was deployed to Korea in a carrier squadron for twenty months during 1951–53. Our youngest daughter was born when I was in the Sea of Japan on the USS *Valley Forge*. I didn't see her until she was six months old. I was deployed in command of an A-4 squadron on USS *Essex* for eleven months from January to December of 1958. We went to the Sixth Fleet in the Mediterranean, covered the Lebanon landings in September, went through the Suez to augment the Seventh Fleet in the Formosa Straits during the Quemoy-Matsu crisis. We came home via Cape Town and Rio de Janeiro. Eleven months is a long time in "peacetime." In 1962, my son's senior year in high school, I was again deployed, to command the USS *Salisbury Sound,* a seaplane tender operating out of Okinawa. Families were not permitted to join their husbands in the ship's company. Then, as commanding officer of *Enterprise* during Vietnam, I was deployed for two seven-month cruises in the Gulf of Tonkin from 1965 through 1967.[26]

Adm. Robert J. L. Long served as vice CNO under Admiral Holloway from 1977 to 1979, during the Carter administration. "This was a time when we lost money for personnel," reflected Admiral Long in one of my personal interviews with him.

> We lost money for maintenance during this period, so the readiness of the Navy and all of the armed forces went downhill. As a matter of fact, when I went to the job of CinCPac in 1979, 25 percent of the Pacific Fleet ships were in readiness category C-4. That means that they were not capable of carrying out their missions, a low point. We really struggled at that time.
>
> Harold Brown was the secretary of defense, a very bright guy. I'd say he probably was more interested in technical and programmatic aspects than in operational matters. The secretary of the navy was a wonderful guy, Graham Claytor, and Jim Woolsey was the undersecretary. I had a good rapport with them, but we had lousy budgets, and lousy readiness people were leaving, and our retention rate was poor.
>
> There was also another experience . . . that shaped my thinking for the future. I was the acting chief of naval operations, and in that capacity attended Joint Chiefs of Staff meetings. When the chairman discussed issues going to the president and the secretary of defense, I never will forget that someone would say, "Let's give the president only our military advice. Let's not give him the political stuff. Let's just keep it pure military advice." Of course, on reflection, that advice wasn't worth the paper it was written on, because you cannot separate out . . . military factors from political factors or economic factors when you're dealing with national security.

Selflessness is a factor taken into consideration by the selection board for rear admiral. Admiral Long continued:

> I remember [serving] on one plucking board [which decided when two-star admirals were to retire]. I think you probably get even more pressure when you're dealing with flag officers. We had this one senior flag officer who really was putting pressure on the board. So finally we said, "Okay. How about this guy? Do you want to keep him or not?" One guy, whom I greatly respect, spoke up and said, "Look. I've been told that this guy won't come to Washington unless we make him three stars. If the son of a bitch doesn't want to come back here and count altimeters along with the rest of us, to hell with him." So we didn't continue him. When you're dealing with a continuation board, most of these people are personally known to the members of the board. That makes it even harder, but as I say, I don't know of a better way to do it.

Part of selflessness is willingness to serve in a staff assignment, particularly in Washington. Admiral Long continued:

> There has been a bias in the Navy against people that, unless they're actually in operating units, have not served in Washington. Washington is perceived in peacetime as where the future of the Navy is decided. So for a guy to be an attaché someplace is not considered to be as demanding as a guy who is on duty in OpNav in the Pentagon. That sometimes is not in the best interest of the Navy. As an example, . . . instructor billets of the Naval Academy require good people, but sometimes it's difficult to get the Navy to provide good officers there because they want to have the most outstanding in operations or serving at the Pentagon.

Naval officers have always been underpaid compared with the civilian sector. To make matters worse, they lose money every time they move to a new posting. Each move normally costs the family money beyond what might be reimbursed. Long said of his first Pentagon tour:

> It was a fascinating tour for me. We moved the family up and we didn't have a lot of money. We did sell that house in Norfolk for $18,000. So we made a lot of money—$1,000. But we couldn't find anything in Washington that we could afford, so we decided to rent. We rented a house for which we paid something like $150 a month. I guess at that time I was a lieutenant commander, so we lost money. We could not save any money living in Washington at that time. That was before they increased pay, and I didn't draw submarine pay while ashore.

After a lifetime of service to his Navy and country, did Admiral Long feel any regret when he took off the uniform for the last time?

> I think it was not so much regret as complete bewilderment as to what this new life consisted of. I should tell you that I was privileged to remain four years as CinCPac, and at that time the tour length was two years with one-year extensions. The normal retirement age was sixty-two, and I was kept on by the president until I was sixty-three. One of the things that was interesting was that in 1982, Mr. Weinberger queried me as to whether I would be willing to be the chief of naval operations. I said no, and I still think that was a good decision. I don't think you need a CNO who is sixty-two to sixty-six.

It was certainly selfless of Long to turn down the opportunity to be CNO so that the post could go to a younger man.

Adm. Stansfield Turner likewise showed selflessness when he gave up what he most wanted to do in order to head the CIA.

> President Carter told me he would like to know my reaction to the possibility of my becoming director of central intelligence. He didn't really offer me the job. He said, "What would you think about this?" I told him, "Mr. President, I would prefer to continue to serve you in the military." I said, "If I have the characteristics you've been so kind as to attribute to me, I think you need those qualities in the military that badly today and I'd like to serve you there. I'd like to be the vice chief of naval operations." I was audacious enough to pick my job. I wouldn't pick chief of naval operations because that would have meant firing the incumbent. I said I'd like to be the vice chief because he could go on to something else. My point was, and I said then, "Mr. President, in a year and a half when Admiral Holloway's term is up, you could decide whether I was qualified to move up to take the job. You could have a year and a half to evaluate me as the vice chief."

I asked if it would be fair to say that by accepting the appointment to head the CIA he sacrificed his career ambitions—that is, continuing in the Navy and perhaps becoming chief of naval operations.

> You have to understand that the law specifies that the chief of intelligence may be an active-duty officer, a retired officer, or a nonmilitary person. [The president] didn't say it at the time, but the law also provides that if it's an active-duty military officer, he or she will not participate in any decision making about military affairs. I would have to keep my hands out of the military if I were head of the CIA. I should not be up on the Hill lobbying for aircraft carriers. He encouraged me to stay on active duty. At the end of two years, neither the president nor I raised the issue of whether I'd be considered for the next chief of the Navy.
>
> I had become enmeshed in the CIA, and I had started many programs, I was so controversial, busy reforming the place. To pull out would have been difficult and looked bad. I never appreciated how much more important on the national scene the director of central intelligence was than the chief of the Navy. That's not to say I shouldn't have kept my ambition to be the chief of the Navy, because maybe I could have done more over the long run because I would have had a bigger impact on the Navy perhaps than I would have had on this new strange organization.[27]

Selflessness became a part of the Naval Academy midshipmen's experience under the tenure of Admiral Larson when midshipmen began contributing significant time to public service projects. In Larson's last year as superintendent, the midshipmen performed 150,000 hours of voluntary community service. Although the service program started before his first tour as superintendent, it gathered momentum in his second tour because of his interest and emphasis. I asked him what the midshipmen did.

> They were cleaning up beaches, cleaning up parks, building houses for Habitat for Humanity. During one of the rainstorms where [road conditions were] hazardous . . . all the midshipmen with four-wheel-drive vehicles went out and transported patients to and from the hospitals. They performed this service on weekends on their own time, and it was coordinated to a midshipmen action group. To show that we supported them, my wife and I went down with the midshipmen action group one weekend and cleaned up a whole tenement area in Washington, D.C. We wore civilian clothes, Levis, port shoes, sweatshirts, and golf hats. It was an interesting reaction by the tenants who lived with this horrible trash across the street from them that used to be a park. We'd made arrangements with the city to bring trucks to pick up the trash that we collected. Because we started making real progress, you could start seeing the light of day. Pretty soon, their children started coming out and helping. Then, toward the end, the tenement people started coming out to help. Then they started lighting charcoal grills, breaking out the hot dogs, and the midshipmen were included in a cookout. We had two buses and about one hundred midshipmen who cleaned up.
>
> There were a lot of ways we tried to do things to work with the community. One of the other things that I did was to take all of the department heads of the city—fire, police, security, financial, . . . and invite them in to spend a day with our counterparts at the Naval Academy so they could understand what we do here. Then we had a big luncheon for them at the superintendent's house and we all got to know each other. We asked the mayor to come and review the parade.[28]

Gen. George S. Brown, USAF, was chairman of the Joint Chiefs of Staff from 1974 to 1978, and in that capacity served the Army, Navy, Air Force, and Marine Corps. He summed up the role of selflessness as it applies to military service. Selflessness, he said, is "a steadfast dedication and total commitment to the nation and all that it stands for. That dedication must be deep-felt and unwavering." He went on to say that selfless service requires "a willingness to sacrifice, . . . the setting aside of personal desires, comfort, and security when the safety of the country is at stake." One who enters military service "gives up some personal freedoms of choice that civilians enjoy; they acknowledge that they can be called upon for long hours of work, additional duties, and significant hazards; that you put yourself and your family in an environment that may necessitate frequent uprooting; that you can be asked to give up your life, if necessary, for your country. All this is part of the sacrifice of military service." Young people who enter military service, he said, "must find fulfillment in hard work, in giving and sacrifice—and be willing to serve in the absence of expressed appreciation. In America's goal of maintaining peace and preserving freedom lies our inspiration to serve. . . . As men of action we are inclined to show our appreciation more by deeds—by serving you to the best of our professional capacity—than by words."[29]

CHAPTER 11

Elements of Command

Self and Family

Their eyes were always on the thing that would lead to command, . . .
they were born to command and this was the objective,
and anything else was a diversion.

Rear Adm. Chester W. Nimitz Jr.

Why Command?

Rear Adm. Chester W. Nimitz Jr., son of Fleet Adm. Chester W. Nimitz, grew up knowing the senior naval leaders of World War II—Fleet Admirals William D. Leahy, Ernest J. King, and William F. Halsey, and Adm. Raymond A. Spruance, among others—and served with many in a junior capacity. The epigraph that begins this chapter reflects his observations of those men.[1] Is it true, as he said, that some people are born to command? Adm. William J. Crowe Jr. (chairman of the Joint Chiefs of Staff 1986–90), on leaving his assignment in the Pentagon, reflected on his service as aide to Adm. Bernard Austen three decades earlier:

> When I left Austin's office [in 1957], it was to take command of the USS *Trout*, the Navy's newest diesel submarine. . . . Nuclear submarines were beginning to

come along, but since I was not in the nuclear program this was a first-rate assignment. I was exhilarated about receiving command of the *Trout*. The meaning of life for most Navy men is to go to sea, and the goal of 98 percent of young officers is command. That is what they aspire to, and despite my growing interest in the political-military world, that was my aspiration as well.

I couldn't help conveying my feelings to Austen. He himself had held many commands: a submarine, two destroyers during World War II, a destroyer division in Arleigh Burke's famous "Little Beaver" squadron. "That's just wonderful," he said after listening to me go on a bit. "But you'll discover that after you've had one command they're generally all alike and there isn't much more to learn. If you have seven commands it's like having one command seven times." God, I thought, what a statement! Heresy. How could a man of his talent and background say such a thing?

Whatever the truth of Austen's comment, an officer's first command is a high point. A young man receiving his orders to command can taste the excitement. Life seems free and intense and charged with purpose. There was a time in the Navy when a captain was truly an autonomous ruler, a king in his realm. Once he lost sight of land, he was literally on his own; nobody heard from him for months at a time. Space-age communications have relegated that era to history, but a ship commander . . . still enjoys a sense of authority that few other people ever experience.[2]

Perhaps no words describe the essence of a sea command better than Joseph Conrad's in "The Prestige, Privilege and the Burden of Command":

In each ship there is one man who, in the hour of emergency or peril at sea, can turn to no other man. He is the one who alone is ultimately responsible for the safe navigation, engineering performance, accurate gunfire, and morale of his ship. He is the commanding officer. *He is the ship.*

This is the most difficult and demanding assignment in the Navy. There is not an instant during the tour of duty as commanding officer that he can escape the grasp of command responsibility. His privileges in view of his obligations are ludicrously small; nevertheless, command is the spur which has given the Navy its great leaders. I think most people have some appreciation of the responsibility, but few understand the unique accountability that must accompany that responsibility in the context of command at sea.

In one of my interviews with Adm. James L. Holloway III (CNO 1974–78) I asked what made him want to command. He told me:

I think it all begins back [in] the United States Naval Academy when you become a naval officer. You graduate and you go to a destroyer and you are on the bottom rung. You look at the lieutenants and you say I can run a department better than that guy could. He's kind of a dumbbell. Well, he isn't really. You are only looking at his mistakes. You don't realize how may good things a fellow is doing.

I think that's it. We are professionals. We want our opportunity to make use of what we have learned as subordinate officers. We are self-centered enough to think that we can do a better job. I think ambition is an inherent factor in the character of all mankind. Everybody wants things a little better. You might say why is my house today larger than the one I lived in as a lieutenant? Why have I collected this library? We are constantly expanding our interests and as we grow older and wiser we want the satisfaction of accomplishment. In the end, it is the commander who, rightfully so, gets credit for the accomplishments of the command.

The important thing is that you must not, as a young officer, start on how you will run your first command. Don't even look forward to becoming a division officer. Concentrate on tomorrow. Determine that you are going to be the best ensign on the ship. Take it one day at a time. The people who lose their way are usually those who as young officers start thinking about how they are going to run their squadron command. You can't command a squadron until you have been a good wingman, then a good section leader, a good division leader, and a good exec. You will not succeed in any of those jobs unless you've determined at each of those stages that you were going to do the very best you could as you served in each successive job. I never thought about commanding an aircraft carrier before I got my orders.

Up to then, I was too busy doing my current job. The way it works is that by doing well in an assignment you get selected for promotion and another assignment; and so the capable officer progresses. I found that all of the cumulative jobs that I had over the years had equipped me to command the *Enterprise*. I understood nuclear power. I had flown airplanes. I knew ship handling from my days on a destroyer.

I was qualified for command of the *Enterprise*. How? By qualifying as officer of the deck on destroyers in World War II, flying as a wingman in a dive bomber squadron, serving as an exec and then CO of a squadron in combat, and going through the nuclear power program. Those things qualified me for the job. Then there was the satisfaction of being selected for command of the first and only nuclear carrier in the Navy, and the thrill of standing on the bridge and conning her out of the channel to the open sea. All those hours in seemingly routine duties, the days away from home, the months of learning, and the years of waiting had earned me my big command. The apprenticeship had paid off.[3]

I asked Adm. Thomas Hayward (CNO 1978–82) for his thoughts on command.

The Navy gives our junior officers enormous amounts of responsibility and authority, and holds them accountable. This is a strong part in the development of the young officers that causes them to stand out, or not stand out. They learn during that time where they want to go and they also learn very quickly that if you really want to go very high up, you have to take on more and more responsibility. You have to be ready for it and you have to be willing to do that; you have to aspire to that. The environment you are working in, a squadron or ship, you are looking up to the commanding officer. You're not looking to Washington, you don't even know who the CNO is. You don't know who the CinCLant leader is, but you sure need to know who your commanding officer is. That's where you're getting your inspiration—saying to yourself, "I want that job. I can do it as well or better than that guy." It drives you on, and that's what you aspire to. In my case, an aviator's case, the command of a squadron, then an air wing, and then a carrier.[4]

Adm. Carlisle A. H. Trost (CNO 1986–90) told me: "I wanted command first of all because I thought I could do it. It was a challenge. I thought the Navy had trained me for a command. I thought I could lead people. I felt I could successfully run a ship or any other command; that I could meet whatever mission goals that came along. I found that command is the most satisfying thing I've ever done." I asked him why. "Because you could see the direct results of your own activity," he said. "You could see it not only in your people, but also in the results, and that to me is very important. What kept me in the Navy very frankly was the fact that the challenge never stopped and satisfaction never ceased. It was a very gratifying experience."[5]

Adm. Frank B. Kelso II (CNO 1990–94) told me:

When I was a midshipman at the Naval Academy I didn't know anything about the Navy. When I left the Naval Academy the only thing I cared about, ambition-wise, was to get command of a ship. I never thought about anything else. I think it came from the history of the Navy, the tradition, about our great naval leaders that you don't get anywhere important—never get anywhere in the end—without command. How you do in command fundamentally affects what your future potential is. I don't think I understood that part of it in the beginning. Most young officers don't understand until they get much older what the importance of command is. But I knew that I wanted to have command of a ship. I didn't have any ambition beyond it. I think most of every step in leadership is to get you to command. That's how I saw command. I didn't know what command was when I left the Naval Academy. Some people knew they wanted to fly; some people wanted to go into submarines. I was pretty sure I didn't want to fly because I didn't feel I had the aptitude for it. . . . But if you are an aviator, it is a squadron for your early command. . . . I don't think command is any different from what an Army officer experiences. They don't go anywhere if they don't have command experience either. Essentially, very few ever go beyond 0-6 [Navy captain or Army colonel] if they don't. Why command? I don't think you can express military leadership except in getting to command. My command tour was wonderful.

I asked him why he was a successful commander. "Because under my command," he said, "we were capable of doing what we were asked to do and produced good results. We got away on time and did our job when we got there. People who observed us were complimentary of how well we worked together and what we did. There isn't any other measure. We passed our inspections, we did well on them, our people got promoted, and our reenlistment rate was high. Those are the measures that are visible."[6]

I asked Adm. Jay L. Johnson (CNO 1996–2000) why he wanted command. He responded:

Well, I think, in many respects, it was considered the pinnacle of the naval career. . . . I think a lot of it may have to do with just the nature of the Navy. When you're in command of an organization in the Navy, like a ship or a squadron, you really are in command. You're out all over the world. There's nobody else around to take charge and carry it out. I mean, you've got the responsibility. It's a tremendous responsibility, but it's also a tremendous opportunity. I think just the nature of deployed operations and what command means may be subtle in the junior days, but I think the closer you get to it, the more you say, wow, it's quite remarkable, that opportunity. My first command was in 1983, . . . Fighter Squadron 84, F-14 Tomcats, aboard USS *Nimitz*. We had about a dozen airplanes, about eighteen pilots, and about fifty air crew. . . .

One of the Navy's smartest leadership moves was the establishment of a course in Newport, Rhode Island, for prospective commanding officers. Parts of the Navy had been doing that for years, but naval aviation hadn't been a part of that. So, one of the things that happened in the last few years, and I got to implement it, was this leadership training continuum. It really started with Frank Kelso and Mike Boorda. I matured it a little bit as I got to execute it. . . .

Looking back, I now realize how much I didn't know when I was a commanding officer, the first time, about being a commander. I just picked it up as best I could. We had no structure to pass along the good things from one commanding officer to the next, other than just the normal turnover you'd have. We needed to institutionally pass along the good things, and also to pass along the speed bumps and the bad things that you had to deal with that you learned from. So, we tried to create an environment where we could share these kinds of things with the prospective commanding officers and, frankly, that they could hear from the people who'd gone just before them about what it's really like. It started back with Frank Kelso. It was shaped with Admirals Kelso and Boorda. I felt like I knew how to be a commanding officer, but as I looked back years later, I realized I could have been much better prepared for that. That was one of the reasons I felt good about us formalizing a bit more than we had before, the training for aviation in particular, but all command officers.

When I was a one-star battle group commander, it was one of the highlights of my career. Yesterday or the day before [2001], they were showing the *Theodore Roosevelt* battle group on television as it left Norfolk. That was my battle group. I did that. This brought a wonderful rush of memories.

When I was a battle group commander, the four-star CinC over in Norfolk was a wonderful mentor, Admiral Paul David Miller. He told me one day when he came to visit the ship and we were in my cabin, "You know, Jay, enjoy this tour. There's never going to be another one like it." I said, "What do you mean?" He told me, "This is the last time in your naval career that you'll really feel like you've got your arms around your command, and that you really can control what's going on." Only later did I realize that he was absolutely right. The more senior you get, you do, in a sense, lose that direct connection, that direct feedback, that direct personal bond that you've got, just because it gets too big after that.[7]

As CNO, Admiral Johnson talked about command with newly selected flag officers.

I used to talk to the flag officers a lot about examples and about . . . grooming. . . . I used an analogy that's a little simplistic, maybe, but I didn't know another way to describe it. I used to tell them, "The truth of it is that you've just moved into a glass house. Everything you say, everything you do, every move you make, somebody's watching, twenty-four/seven, anywhere in the world. Think about that a minute. You may not like that; in fact, you may not even believe it. But, I'm here to tell you it's real. Having said that, don't take that as some kind of a bad thing. This is your time. This is your opportunity to make your imprint on the next generation. There are very few people in the grand scheme of things that get to do that. You won't live in that glass house for long. It's measured in years . . . maybe a handful, at most two handfuls; meaning you only have so many years as rear admiral, vice, or full admiral. Your time will go by very quickly. . . . So, don't miss the opportunity while you live in that glass house to show how it's supposed to be done. Everything that you do will be observed. . . . Pick the most remote place from where you normally live, someone will know you. I'll be out there pumping gas in my car, and somebody'll say, 'Hey, Admiral, how you doing?' It's a sailor who's on leave just like I am. You're making an impression on somebody wherever you are. So, set the example. Revel in that."[8]

Sometimes command requires patience. Adm. Kinnaird R. McKee, who succeeded Adm. Hyman Rickover, needed that quality while he waited for his first sea command:

I was only in *Nautilus* for a little over a year. At the time, the submarine shipyards were turning out new Polaris submarines in great numbers. I expected to do two years as exec in *Nautilus,* then go on to command. That's what I hoped to do, but when we got back from a special operation I had orders to go as the gold commissioning crew exec of *Henry Clay* (SSBN 624). That was one of the few times in my career that I became upset with my detailer. I wanted command. I said, "Look, I've already had two exec tours—*Marlin* and *Nautilus.* I qualified for command in *Marlin*." At the time I was about two-thirds of the way through the tour. There's nothing like the arrogance of youth. . . . I thought nothing would come of that, but why not try? Well, I got orders to the X-1 by return mail; that was great. It was the most exciting set of orders I ever received, including my orders to command of *Dace.*

While a naval officer seeks command for the exhilaration and the challenge it entails, command always poses a risk. A ship command offers authority, but also accountability. The accountability, as any commander knows, has no parallel in military service. The commanding officer of a ship at sea has more independent authority than any officer of the same rank in a land assignment; it is absolute. But with authority is an equally absolute accountability. A ship's commander is responsible for his own actions, or inactions, and for those of every crew member under his command. This has been so for centuries and is a cornerstone of the U.S. Navy tradition. When there is a problem, the commander can expect that his actions will be scrutinized.

I asked Admiral McKee why he sought command. "One of the best things about my job," he answered, "is the opportunity it gives me to work with the young officers and enlisted men who take nuclear warships to sea. They are a handful, less than a tenth of the Navy's strength, but without them over 40 percent of our first-line combatant ships could not get under way. I see them in every facet of our business—in interviews; in training, qualifying, and serving at sea; and finally as prospective commanding officers en route to their new commands."[9]

Adm. Thomas H. Moorer (CNO 1967–70, chairman of the Joint Chiefs of Staff 1970–74) also emphasized his love of working with young people: "I loved responsibility. I loved working with young people. I looked forward to every day. The commander in the Navy is in a position to observe the execution of his command. You can see the results of your leadership right away."[10]

In a similar discussion of command with Adm. Paul David Miller, he told me:

> I love responsibility. I think it is unique and that is one of the challenges of leadership. At sea you're . . . responsible for the after-steering room, . . . the front of the ship, and everything in between, in weather fair and foul, and in all kinds of sea conditions, calm and rough. There are so many dimensions to it that you can't step away from it. It's yours twenty-four hours a day. I just loved it. . . . I sought command because it was that assignment that you were totally responsible for all the activities within that unit. That's what I wanted to do, I wanted responsibility. There is an intrinsic reward; it is satisfying a need to be able to project a certain amount of order and discipline to yield results. That's your reward, that you did it. I always hoped to be able to get bigger and bigger responsibilities. I sought it, but it was not ambition, because I could walk away from it without feeling sad.[11]

Prior to his incarceration in North Vietnam, discussed in chapter 10, Comdr. James B. Stockdale was sent by the Navy to Stanford University for two years of graduate study. The master's degree he received presented both opportunity and a dilemma:

> I was told that I could go up the operational aviation command chain or go for a PhD and become a specialist, but not both. I wrestled with that decision, but Syb [his wife] read through me. I loved to fly and had a feel for the sea, and Syb knew that and loved me and made my decision easy. "Do what you do best: take the command route and go to sea."
>
> So I took the master's degree in June 1962 and accepted the old admiral's "oversight" of not ordering me back to a squadron until after I had finished a special philosophy program he knew I particularly wanted to continue in summer school. In September our family headed for Coronado, near San Diego, where my fighter squadron was waiting.
>
> Syb had been right. Now that the war was starting, I could never have lived with myself knowing that I had dodged the ultimate challenges of what I had spent my life preparing for: I had to take command of that air group.[12]

Sybil Stockdale understood her husband's need to return to operations and supported him wholeheartedly:

> The most memorable day for me had been Jim's change of command when he took over as carrier air-group commander 16. On that February day, he became the "CAG" of the air group aboard the aircraft carrier *Oriskany*. That made him the senior aviator aboard ship who still flew from the carrier. He was in charge of six squadrons flying five different kinds of airplanes. He flew all of them himself as he felt required to do in his leadership position.
>
> We were thrilled when he got his orders for this job. CAG was the apex of every naval aviator's flying career, and only a few ever attained the position. We accepted the loneliness of another nine-month separation without complaint; we knew a hundred others would jump at the chance. Anyway, this would be the last cruise before shore duty; then we'd probably go to Washington, where Jim would do a payback tour at the Pentagon, applying his Stanford University education.[13]

Early in the Vietnam War, Commander Stockdale really began to understand the thrill and challenge of command. On August 4, 1964, he recalled, there was a sense of urgency, a change of emphasis, about the ship during the hours and days immediately following the PT-boat incident. Now it was all "ship defense." On Monday, August 3, I had flown two "combat air patrol" hops up into the Gulf, on guard against a Communist answer to our PT-boat sinking of Sunday. On Tuesday I was scheduled to lead two more such flights.

I lay in bed awhile that morning, relishing my life of change and flexibility, thanking Providence for the totally unexpected joy of having command during a period of such instability that I could do damned near anything I wanted to—provided the squadron delivered under pressure. I hated the "by-the-numbers" rules of the Navy. On this cruise we were anything but "by-the-numbers": we were completely off the page. It seemed to me imperative that we have the independence to act on our feet, by instinct, when defending our ships from the North Vietnamese or Red Chinese forces.

Captain Bart Connolly, skipper of the *Oriskany* and a living jewel in the combat environment, was very tolerant of my ever-more-flagrant rule-bending in my attempt to maintain tactical autonomy for the sake of effectiveness and safety. Bart watched me like a hawk, and as long as I met his standards, all the pilots aboard—those regularly assigned to my air group and the many that were being sent out from shore bases to temporarily reinforce us—were mine to work with as I saw fit.[14]

After his ordeal as a POW, Stockdale still sought command. His wife wrote:

One Friday evening at about 6:30, some six weeks after Jim's return, while he and yet another naval officer continued their conferences in the den I sat in the kitchen crying and blubbering to Jimmy that this was not the way I'd thought it would be at all. We hadn't had any time to ourselves since his return. . . .

This wasn't my first cry since his return. That had come about two weeks after he came home. While I was soaking in the bathtub, Jim had said that most of all he wanted command of an aircraft carrier as soon as possible. That would take him to sea for many more months, I reminded him, and was dismayed and dissolved into tears at his calm acceptance of this possibility. In April I was saved from this prospect when Admiral Zumwalt, who had been CNO since 1971, telephoned early one morning to tell Jim he had been selected for the rank of rear admiral. As I held my breath in the next room, I heard Jim say, "I believe this is one of the greatest moments of my life." Later that month we went to Washington, where Jim wore his admiral's uniform for the first time while visiting with President Nixon alone in the Oval Office.[15]

But more than command is required for a successful naval career. Staff duty, particularly in Washington, D.C., is also important—perhaps more than it should be. Admiral Moorer reflected in his oral history:

> I'm afraid that there's a tendency today to reward officers and recognize officers based on their performance in Washington. While that's important to a certain degree certainly, when you get right down to it the only reason we have a Defense Department is to be able to fight. I am very concerned about this tendency to give maximum recognition to those here in the sight of the mighty, so to speak, *vice* those guys that are standing watches out there in the driving rains and wind.
>
> . . . I did a fair job of shunning staff duty myself until I was a captain. . . . But even so, I think that in order to round out your outlook and understanding of the whole complexity of the Defense Department one must, of course, come to Washington. But generally speaking you simply cannot . . . do anything . . . that would decrease the desire on the part of the uniformed Navy to go to sea. The worst thing that can happen is to get into the minds of the young officers that the way to get promoted is to come to Washington. The Navy budget is not to support activity in Washington; it supports activity on the ocean. And you should have your best people on the ocean. Bearing in mind that in order to get their support for them, you've got to have people who know what their problems are and come to Washington to do their share toward formulating the budgets, accepting and developing equipment, etc.—all the things you have to do, talking to the Congress and the White House, etc.
>
> But I've told many a young officer who has come in to see me and said, "Admiral, please let me stay in my ship—or let me stay in my squadron, or let me stay in my submarine—I don't want to come to Washington. I'm an operator and I want to stay out there." But I always say, "Now, young man, I understand your feelings because I had the same feeling myself, and that's fine and don't you ever lose it. But I'll tell you so far as I'm concerned I have to order some of you young men to Washington because I'm in the same position as the farmer who hitched his prize bull to the plow to teach him there is more to this than just romance."[16]

The Role of the Navy Spouse

I had the good fortune in doing the research for this book to visit many times in the homes of numerous admirals. I had the same opportunity to visit the homes of the Army and Air Force generals I had interviewed for my book *American Generalship: Character Is Everything*. To my surprise, I observed a contrast between families of the respective services: there was a very special relationship in the marriages of the Navy families I visited. I learned that the challenges of family life were greater in the Navy than in the Army or Air Force. One of the major differences was that a naval career involved constant separations because of sea duty. While members of today's Army and Air Force now experience similar separations because of America's worldwide commitments as a superpower, members of the Navy have always faced this challenge.

In a personal interview that took place in April 2002, I asked Adm. Thomas H. Moorer to describe the role his wife had played in his naval career. He replied:

> A few months ago I received the Naval Academy's Distinguished Graduate Award. I reviewed a full dress parade by the Brigade of Midshipmen. I made a speech. They kept telling me I always talk too long. It was Parents' Day, so the mothers and fathers were there. I talked to them about how important it was to bring to the Academy [young people] with the [right] mental, moral, and physical qualities. . . .
>
> Then I turned to the midshipmen and told them I had stood where they were standing and I thought I knew what they were thinking. "You are wondering why the admiral doesn't shut up and sit down." I said to them, "I just have one more thing to say, so hold onto your rifles a little longer. What I want to talk about is marriage in the service. My wife and I moved twenty-five times during our career. We have four children, ten grandchildren. I just want to talk about my wife. She has always supported me. She has never complained. I want everyone in this audience to realize if it wasn't for my wife, Carrie, I wouldn't be standing here today." What a special tribute to a great lady.[17]

Admiral Moorer reminisced about his marriage: "We had this prohibition on getting married prior to the end of two years. So shortly after I commenced flight training, I did get married on Thanksgiving Day of 1935. It was a long-standing romance that had been going on for years. I think I had my first date with . . . Carrie when she was about thirteen years old."

Asked if his wife supported his decision to go into aviation, he said: "She had been very wonderful about that. I know that many, many wives discouraged their husbands from going into aviation at that time. It was far more dangerous than it is today, primarily because of material failures. I mean the equipment was not nearly as reliable because, of course, at that point it was under development in many areas. So many wives discouraged their husbands, but mine had never discouraged me at anything that I set out to do. She never even commented on it.[18]

Adm. Arleigh Burke's (CNO 1955–61) marriage may or may not be typical for naval leaders. I discuss it in detail here because it was a partnership worth emulating—one that provided support for both partners throughout their Navy life together. Burke was introduced to his wife, Roberta "Bobbie" Gorsuch, by his Academy roommate. Burke was a big, blond Swede; Bobbie was only five feet tall and weighed less than one hundred pounds. They courted throughout his four years as a midshipman and were married on June 7, 1923—Graduation Day.

Burke was stationed in Long Beach right after their marriage, and the only quarters they could afford was a furnished apartment in San Pedro, not at that time a particularly nice neighborhood. But they wanted to be together. His initial assignment was on the battleship *Arizona*. Shortly thereafter he was assigned to Torpedo Training School in San Diego, and although it was only a four-month course, Bobbie went with him. They always tried to stay together in spite of their limited funds and the difficulty of finding a place they could afford.

Once, out of loyalty to the *Arizona*, Burke bet on his ship's crew in a rowing contest with the crew of the *Concord*. The *Arizona*'s crew lost, and Burke lost the funds he had set aside for Bobbie's living expenses. He owned up to what he had done in a letter, and she wrote back to say that he had done exactly what he should have done and that she had taken a job to tide her over until payday.[19]

After they had been married four years, Burke was assigned to a school in New York. Between the two of them they had only $120 to last until payday at the end of the month. All they could get in the way of quarters was a rented room so small there was not even space for a chair. Often, all they could afford to eat was doughnuts. At the end of the month they had only $2 left. In spite of the financial challenge, both described this time "as among the happiest of their lives."[20]

Separations were frequent during Burke's early career. On his first assignment in World War II he wrote to Bobbie every day, mailing his letters whenever the ship was in port. They were separated for two years during the war, but still they both corresponded almost daily. He always provided as full a description of the battles he was involved in as the censors would allow.

When Burke was assigned to Norfolk after World War II, Bobbie rented a small apartment, hoping to see more of him. She didn't. He was given a demanding job that required him to go to work early and stay late. Bobbie met him at the dock at the end of each day. One of his colleagues, Don Griffin, recalled, "Arleigh Burke's wife would come down to the dock to pick up Arleigh and take him home. She would drive up, park her car on the dock. Sometimes she would sit there until eight or nine o'clock waiting for him to come down."[21]

Chapter 5 described how Capt. William R. Smedley warned Burke to get out of town quickly because Secretary of the Navy Forrestal wanted Burke's help in writing his memoirs, a job that would take him away from sea duty. As soon as he received the warning, he called Bobbie and asked her to pack. He left the building he was working in and met Bobbie, who was waiting for him in their Dodge with all his gear. At Westover Airfield he managed to find an outgoing cargo flight and went out to the car where she was waiting. "I think I've got a way out," he told her. "I'll get my baggage and you shove off for Washington." So off she went on a five-hundred-mile trip in the middle of the night, alone except for their Great Dane and with no place to stay along the way.[22]

Burke's next assignment was as commanding officer of the *Huntington*. His ship was suddenly detailed from the Sixth Fleet to make goodwill calls on the east coast of Africa and in South American ports. He was gone for a considerable period. When the ship returned to the Philadelphia Navy Yard, Bobbie was there to meet him, having rented a furnished apartment even though they would have only a month before he returned to sea. They did not have even that long. He received a telephone call on his arrival ordering him to the Pentagon "without delay," so they left before dawn, driving straight to Washington.

When they arrived at the Pentagon, he jumped out of the car and dashed inside. E. B. Potter's biography of Burke describes what happened next: "Bobbie waited. And waited. This sort of thing had happened many times before. No telling when Arleigh would be out. It was up to her to find a motel where they could spend what was left of the night. . . . And to serve notice of eviction on the tenants to whom they had rented their home. Bobbie had dedicated her life to looking after Arleigh, and willingly so, but there were moments like this when she felt her allegiance to the Navy slipping."[23]

The separations and long workdays occurred throughout their career. Potter noted that Adm. Thomas H. Moorer was among those who recognized her contributions to Burke's career.

> Bobbie was so gentle and unassertive that few people discerned the vital role she played in her husband's career. Moorer, however, through his long association with the Burkes, recognized that Arleigh, in any circumstances a great man, was a greater one thanks to Bobbie's advice and support. She was his steadying influence, cheering him out of his glooms and restraining his impulsiveness. He consulted her on all matters, social, professional, and administrative. She lacked his technical training and his broad, hard-earned knowledge, but she was unusually gifted with patience, common sense, and inner strength, and she devoted herself unstintingly to her husband's needs.[24]

On August 1, 1967, Admiral Burke retired after six years as CNO. The secretary of the navy at the time was John B. Connally. While the secretary sent Burke the normal congratulations and praises for his contribution and achievements, he sent him a special note as well:

Dear Admiral Burke:

When a man achieves greatness, he is almost always backed and aided every foot of the way by a wonderful and devoted wife. It is beyond my official powers to award Mrs. Burke the decoration she so richly deserves, however, I want to say that you have been most fortunate in your wife's choice of a husband.

To Mrs. Burke and to you, may the best of everything be yours for many years to come.[25]

A Navy wife can have an enormous effect on her husband's career. A wise commander, as Arleigh Burke was, realizes that and takes it into account. When Admiral Burke was selecting his staff as CNO, he looked beyond the job candidates:

> I didn't choose the staff. I'd tell the Marine Corps that I would like to have a Marine aviator, a lieutenant colonel with these qualifications. Send me one. . . . I finally learned to talk to the wives before I made a final decision. The wife's attitude toward the service—what she believes her husband's duty to the country is—that's a very important factor. If she believes her husband has a tremendous duty, he does, too. Never, though, when the selection process got down to where I was talking to a wife, never once did she fail. I had six years there and a staff of maybe fifty people and they were a high-performance staff.[26]

I asked Admiral Holloway to describe the role his wife played in his success. He told me:

> I think I had the talent to have made captain on my own, maybe rear admiral. But . . . I would never have gotten beyond that stage without her. One of the things she did is she kept me from getting into trouble. I might suggest I was going to do something and she would say: "That's the dumbest thing I ever heard. If you do that, you will just look stupid." She was very tough-minded, especially about not letting me get a swelled head. She brought me down to earth repeatedly.
>
> Also she was so solid at home during the long deployments. The other wives tended to congregate at our house, not for bridge parties, but for reassurance, support, and just companionship. If they had a problem, they came to her. "Dabney, what should we do?" It just seemed natural for them to do it because they had such respect for her judgment. They would go to her for advice.

Regarding his flying, he said:

> She knew it was dangerous. She knew because the two of us had to so often call on a pilot's wife to break the news that her husband had been killed in a crash. When I was CO of VA-83 on the USS *Essex* cruise of WestPac with the Seventh Fleet, two of the four squadron commanders were killed in landing accidents coming aboard the carrier. When I was XO of VF-52 during the Korean War, both my skipper and my wingman were shot down. I know Dabney was concerned, but she did her best not to show it. Dabney has always been very good at being able to handle things like that.

She knew it would just be another worry for me to worry about her. I'm only finding out now how she felt about the long deployments. At the time, she never let me know it. I only found out two or three years ago how much it bothered her, how tough it was for her, particularly during the Vietnam War, when I had two successive Christmases away from home.

My aircraft went down twice in Korea. She knew about it. Her response was, "You promised you'd be careful." She accepted the fact that as a career naval officer I was flying F9Fs [a jet fighter] in combat in Korea. She could not help but know that the casualty rate was between 20 to 25 percent for the pilots, but this never came up.

Our second daughter was born when Dabney was by herself out on the West Coast. I was in Korea. My mother came out from Washington, D.C., by train to be with her when the baby was born. She got another Navy wife to take her to the hospital. I didn't see my daughter Jane until she was five months old.

On *Enterprise,* I was gone both Christmases to the Tonkin Gulf for the war in Vietnam. Those things were pretty tough, but never a whimper from her. . . . It was so important for me to get encouraging, positive letters from Dabney. There was never any hand wringing. If the allotment check was late she didn't tell me about it. If the children were sick she didn't tell me about it. She did indicate she wished I was home and that she missed me and that the children missed me. She accepted my being gone as part of my American duty and not just as a career naval officer.

When Holloway had the opportunity to enter Admiral Rickover's nuclear program, he asked for Dabney's input. She knew how demanding it would be, but her answer was, "That's your decision." And when Admiral Holloway became CNO, his wife was expected to shoulder a huge burden too.

There was something that was very bothersome to me. Mrs. Zumwalt and . . . Dabney knew each other long before I became CNO. Mrs. Zumwalt told her, "Now, you, of course, are going to be responsible for all of the wives in the Navy. We've already organized the naval officers' wives clubs, to organize and give guidance to the enlisted wives' clubs." Dabney said, "I don't think Jim would be in favor of that."

When she told me about the conversation I agreed, "You're absolutely right. We're going to stay completely out of what the wives do. That's not our business. We're not going to organize the wives. If they want to do it themselves, that's one thing. We will do all we can to keep them informed and to help them find housing and take care of their families. But we will do that officially through individual commanding officers, base housing officers, and the Navy and Marine Corps Relief Organization. Navy wives' clubs should not have an official role but help as needed in referring . . . spouses in need to the proper officers' organization designated to take care of their needs and then provide any help that a support group can in terms of morale and understanding."[27]

Adm. Stansfield Turner, who headed the CIA during the Carter administration, pointed out some of the difficulties for a Navy spouse:

> My first wife, Patricia, . . . was with me through the CIA and a couple of years after. She did an excellent job. . . . In the Navy, you have a greater sense of family, because the wife is the commanding officer of the wives when the ship is overseas. The wives who have problems tend to go to the commanding officer's wife. That puts a great strain on the wife because for six months she's mother and father. It's difficult for a group of women to be stranded when their husbands are three thousand miles away. It makes for a family environment in the Navy more than it does in the other services.[28]

Admiral Trost spoke of his wife's role in his career:

> I would say [it was] considerable. She would say none, but I would say very considerable. First of all, when you are deployed, the wife becomes dad, mom, and everything else. When I left Charleston, South Carolina, as commander of the nuclear sub *Sam Rayburn* to go on patrol [in] December 1968, I sailed down the river and waved to my wife on the bank over at the officers' club with my little kids standing there. It wasn't easy. It was just before Christmas, and I would not be home for Christmas. Our ship would be on patrol for seventy days.
>
> I particularly think of her and the hardships when I was the executive officer of the *Scorpion,* a submarine that was lost five years later. At the time we had deployed quite a bit. I was on the ship for nineteen months, and we were deployed for more than half the time. We were in and out all the time. So my wife was suddenly also faced with being the mother confessor for wives whose husbands were on the ship as well as for everybody else. It is a tough responsibility. She tells the story about the time when one of the young enlisted wives called and said, "Mrs. Trost, I am sorry to bother you, but I have a washer problem." Pauline told me, "I said to myself, have I run into a blood bath?" She asked, "What

is wrong with it?" And she said, "It doesn't run." Pauline asked, "Well, what kind is it?" It was a Sears brand, and my wife said to herself, "Thank God," with a flash of inspiration. And she said, "Call Sears. That's what I would do." She had a lot of responsibility, and . . . she had confidence in her ability to handle the challenges, and although she didn't seek it, she was superb. We are not social butterflies by any means, but she is one of the better diplomats that this country has ever had.

. . . I think we had twenty-eight or twenty-nine moves in a total of thirty-six years, some of them just six-month tours of schooling, like going to New London for a . . . six-month submarine school. Then I went back to New London for six months for nuclear power training. My family went with me. Then, I went to Idaho for six months of nuclear prototype training, and we had other six-month moves, and relocations of that nature. The wife is critical through all of this. I would say I was especially fortunate with my wife because she did a wonderful job. The nice thing about it is that I am going back this afternoon because I would rather be with her than not be with her.[29]

I discussed the role of the wife with Admiral Hayward, who agreed that a supportive spouse is an important element of a successful naval career.

Certainly I would endorse those statements of Admiral Moorer and Holloway on the role of the wife. We lived in a generation in which marriage as an institution was founded on an admiration from both sides, male and female. Not that many of our age group are still with wives and . . . married for years and years—I'm coming up on my fifty-fifth. Loyalty and shared commitment are a built-in part of our character to begin with, a calling for a strong team effort, and you know it's going to be for the rest of your life. That is so very important and helpful to the durability of a partnership.

There are two ways to look at the wife's role, first when the officer is a junior officer, the other is when he is a senior officer. The roles for the wife are quite different in each circumstance. When I was a jg to lieutenant . . . I went on two cruises to Korea, eleven months each time [1950–51]. Long cruises, with two young children left behind. Think of it. You have this young wife with two very young daughters, . . . providing basically the whole family support since her family was on the East Coast. Alone, Peggy managed to deal with all the sickness, car trouble, the plumbing, and the rest of that, at the same time worrying about whether she was going to get her husband back; and we lost a lot of guys. Because of our relationship and my confidence in her strength, I was able to do my job without having the burden of worrying about what is going on back home. Same thing occurred in Vietnam. I had a different level of responsibility at that time. I was a commander and then captain. I went to Vietnam first as an air wing commander, [then] commanding a deep-draft ship. Then I returned soon after that as the commanding officer of the USS *America* [a conventional carrier]. If you consider the overall time spread of those three commands, I was gone a lot of the time when my children were in junior high and high school. Vietnam attitudes were developing rapidly, the early drug scenes were upon the country, civil rights were active. It was a very tough time. In looking back on that time, I am in awe of how incredibly the wives held their family together and did a great job. They deserve a medal that none of the men would have deserved. They provided tremendous support.

. . . When I was Seventh Fleet commander, CinCPac, and CNO, Peggy's role became much more diverse and enjoyable at a time when our children were on their own. We shared a lot of interesting travel, meeting important people, with Peggy's role much more directly support. . . . Additionally, by meeting with other wives [and] helping to find [out] things not self-evident to me she played a crucial role, . . . keeping [me] . . . advised as to what is really happening. . . . Wives are truly important to helping you do your best. I can't imagine doing an acceptable job with no wife, or enduring trouble at home. There was never a time when Peggy ever tried to influence me to leave the Navy.[30]

Admiral Kelso pointed out:

You've got to remember, when we deploy, the wife's at home. She carries all the load. When I go off to sea, she's got four kids to take care of, and most of the time she couldn't even reach me because we didn't send the kinds of communications that we have today. We are much more lenient with communications today than we were then. So the wife plays an absolutely necessary role in your career. I would never have been able to do the things I did without her being willing to make my life a happy one at the same time she was taking on both roles when she was home. That was not easy, particularly with teenage boys.[31]

I asked Admiral Kelso how he met his wife.

That's a long story, but it's a good story. Once a year her family visited my hometown, sometimes more often than that. My dad would say, "You ought to go see that pretty little girl." I never had anything to do with her. . . . I was home for Christmas my freshman year at Annapolis, and my dad made me get out of the car and go see Landis. So I did. That started a long romance. We dated from about the second year on. She came to Washington when I was a junior and senior working for a congressman, and she supported me in a style that I've never forgotten.

They were married a week after graduation. "We've been very close since then," he said,

. . . but in my early career, we were away as much as we were home, so when your children are young, it is very difficult. I don't think you can find very many successful naval officers who do not have a wife [who supports] their career. There may be one or two. The wife provides so much support to you, particularly if you have a family. You can hardly survive without her. A young mother always wants to take care of her children, but a Navy wife must become father as well, and often how children feel about the father depends on what the mother/wife tells them when he is gone. She provides enormous support to the wives of the personnel on the ship when their husbands are deployed. In many cases she is the one who is called for support by the other wives. Normally she spends an enormous amount of time doing that. Without her blessing . . . it is pretty hard to have a career in the Navy. In other words, if it is unacceptable to her, then the officer, or sailor, is not going to be very happy. Because under the circumstances you are consistently being pulled in two different directions. Many wonderful officers have to leave the Navy because the wife cannot accept his career. They don't want to separate and lose their wife. The role of a wife is so important in a Navy career. . . . By the time an officer is selected to be a three- or four-star admiral, the function of the wife is very visible. I don't mean she makes him an admiral; he earns the stars, but he is unlikely to get there without the strong support of her and the Navy.

You sort of put a lot of things together in an officer's career—is he healthy? Is he competent? Does he have a stable family situation? All those things play into the total equation. I can't emphasize enough how important it is to have a wife who accepts his career and supports him. In my case, Landis always knows how to keep my hat size the same. The stars with my children are always on her shoulders.[32]

Admiral Johnson spoke of the many moves his family made as his career progressed and how they affected his family.

I think Garland, my wife, would say the same thing. It got harder with every deployment, not the other way around. People say, hey, you know, you get used to it, it gets easier as you go. I don't think so. Garland's got this written down at home because she used to—in her *Joy of Cooking* cookbook, in the back cover—write down every address we ever had. It was either twenty-six or twenty-seven in thirty-two years. We had one child, our daughter. I think she handled it very well. But it was tough. We spent a lot of time apart. There's a part of me that regrets that, but we also understood that it was the business we were in. A lot of what I was able to do in the United States Navy was enabled by my wife. She focused me. She had the great ability to put my head in the right place, center my thinking, and keep me focused. She also kept my ego in check. Reminds the emperor when he has no clothes, those kinds of things. That sounds trite when I say them, but she had a huge impact. . . . I really don't think I'd be where I am today if I hadn't married her. That's how strongly I feel. There's no question about that in my mind. It could be a tough life. We don't need to be apologetic about that, but we also have to be fairly pragmatic. It's tough. We ask a lot of our families, absolutely.[33]

Adm. Robert L. J. Long remembered one of his less pleasant assignments:

I'd have to say my next assignment was somewhat unnerving. I had orders to go as the executive officer of a brand-new antisubmarine submarine, the *K-1*, which, incidentally, President James E. Carter was also assigned to. But then my orders were changed to go to be the exec of *Cutlass*. That boat had gone through two or three skippers in one year and two or three execs in one year. It was a real problem. And it was at Key West, Florida, where there was no real housing to speak of. So we were less than enthusiastic about, one, going to a place where housing was difficult and, two, going to a submarine that was screwed up.

So, anyway, we went and arrived down there, with two babies and no place to live, mosquitoes that almost could carry the children away. We moved into a motel. It was Sunday, so I went down and walked aboard *Cutlass*. All the officers were there, including the skipper, Lieutenant Commander Charles Styer Jr. The officers were all sitting in the wardroom while the exec was reading the deck logs aloud to make sure that they were properly worded. I said to myself, "Well, that doesn't look very good to me." Then I went in to see the captain, who was a very close friend of mine.

He said, "Bob, we're going to sea tomorrow for two weeks, and I'd like to have you go with us." I said, "Captain, I just arrived here. I don't have a place for my family. They're sitting in a crummy motel out here. I'd prefer not to." He says, "Well, I really want you to go. We'll make some time available to you when we get back."

I was so mad, I went back to the motel, sat down, and wrote out my resignation from the Navy. I said, "If this is the way the Navy treats its people, I don't want any part of it." Fortunately for me—or maybe unfortunately—my wife, Sara, got on the telephone to her father and told him, "I don't think Bob should do this." Her father was a guy I really respected, a great guy, and he talked me out of it. He said, "Hey, this is a temporary thing. My observation is that you are ideally suited for the Navy. You have a lot to offer. Don't let this one incident destroy that." So, anyway, I went aboard.[34]

Adm. Kinnaird R. McKee, who succeeded Adm. Hyman Rickover in 1982 as head of the Naval Reactors program, said of his wife:

She was part and parcel to everything I did. It was she who encouraged me—I'll tell you a story about that. I met my first wife and we became engaged very soon after that. When we told her mother that we were engaged, she said, "That's fine," or words to that effect. Didn't register a lot of emotion. But the next morning at breakfast, she sat down with her daughter—my fiancée—and said, "You've got to be sure you really know what you really want to do, because that young man knows what he wants to do, and he knows where he's going to go."[35]

Admiral McKee pointed out a historical precedent for the Navy wife's role:

Daniel Boone's wife, Rebecca, shared his life for fifty-six years. She gave him ten children, and grieved with him when two were killed during his campaigns. She could mold bullets, shoot a flintlock, and skin a deer. She spent much of her life alone for long periods of time, not knowing if her husband was alive or dead. Submarine wives would fit an updated version of that description. They don't mold bullets or shoot a flintlock, but they still have to carry the load alone, for long periods of time—and still they do not know. They have to be just as talented and independent as their men. And they are—I know that better than most. They share the same commitment and accountability, and nobody has a bigger stake in the outcome.[36]

Admiral McKee's wife was the sponsor of the USS *Louisville* (SSN 724) in 1985. He made the principal address, then turned to her and said, "I can't find the words to say more, Sweetheart, except that none of what has been credited to my account would have been possible, or would have had any meaning, if I had not been able to share it with you and with our children."[37]

The wife of a successful career officer must be just as selfless as he is. Adm. Charles R. Larson said that his wife "had to give up her own career and her own life, really, to totally support me. I guess one of the problems with making admiral as early as I did, that was just about the same time the kids were getting ready to go off to college, where she could then go and do her own thing. She really ended up pretty much doing the things that she needed to do to support me, particularly when you consider seven years at the Naval Academy, where we've got social events at least five nights a week, and then eight years as a four-star."[38]

I noted to Admiral Larson that traditionally, Navy spouses have endured longer separations—and the added responsibilities these entail— than other service spouses. He agreed: "I think the Army and the Air Force started learning this lesson during Desert Storm, what it's like to have people gone for six months, because they really were not used to it; even when they went to Europe, the families went with them. So they never experienced this. My wife spent a tremendous amount of time as kind of a representative of the wives when we were gone on deployments. The wives of the senior officers had a more important leadership role."[39]

Among the most interesting experiences I had in writing this book were my several interviews with Adm. Paul David Miller. He had a remarkable career and retired as a full admiral after twenty-eight years of service. I asked him what role his wife had played in his success. He responded:

> Ah, bless her heart. Lots. She still does it today. I do very little at home. She takes care of all the finances at home. She raised the boys more than I did because I was gone so much. She comes from a small town in Illinois. She didn't know what she was getting into, but if you asked her, she wouldn't change a thing. She handled the deployments, the long and frequent separations brilliantly. She's a beautiful lady, and she was an outstanding representative of this nation. The NATO people loved her. She was able, particularly while the boys were growing up, to never permit them during the long absences to lose touch. We were still a family even though we were apart. She had them write little notes on her letters to me. I responded to everybody. I have stored away some of the things they said.
>
> The Navy today is so much different. We stayed in touch with Colby [his son on active duty in the Navy] in the Persian Gulf with e-mail almost daily. We would

get pictures of him every couple weeks about what was going on on the ship. It made the deployment go a lot faster.[40]

Admiral Miller commented that he loved what he was doing in his naval career so much that he rarely took leave. I asked him if his wife ever complained about that. "Complain is probably too strong a word," he answered. "She handled it and moved forward. I was unable even when I was in command to ever leave it. She would tell me that every time I was at home that my mind was worried about something aboard ship, every time."[41]

Leadership and command can be very lonely, particularly in wartime, when tough, agonizing decisions must be made. Admiral Burke's daily correspondence with his wife, mentioned above, filled much of the vacuum and loneliness and helped give him the strength he needed for command. In his biography on Nimitz, E. B. Potter made the point that when Nimitz assumed command in the Pacific, "he felt the loneliness of high command, for nobody in the Pacific theater could share his appalling responsibility." Actually, that is not quite true; he could and did share it with his wife. He received a great deal of support from her in their correspondence during those lonely times. As the war developed, he shared many of his thoughts with Mrs. Nimitz in his correspondence, particularly personal and personnel matters. His letters to her were as important as hers to him because he could tell her things he could tell no other person.

In October 1942, a time of crisis as U.S. forces were involved with the recapture of Guadalcanal, he took the time to tell her about a dinner he had on October 16 with the governor of Hawaii; and on October 21 he wrote about a popular speech he had given at the University of Hawaii, sharing with her: "At least a number of people came to compliment me." One letter written in September 1942 referred to a personnel change involving Vice Admiral Towers. Mrs. Nimitz knew that her husband did not approve of Towers's methods, so he "hastened to assure her by letter" that "I am to have a new air advisor. Never mind. We will get along fine."[42]

While, as I noted in chapter 6, Admiral Nimitz initially retained Adm. Husband Kimmel's staff when he assumed the post of CinCPac in December 1941, he gradually rotated them out. But he did that only after sufficient time had elapsed to expunge the stigma of the surprise attack on Pearl Harbor. In addition, he believed in regularly reinvigorating his staff with officers fresh from combat and wanted to give his own staff a variety of experiences, particularly sea duty and combat. He shared another reason with his wife: "My staff will gradually change from those I found to those I choose." When Nimitz had to relieve Vice Adm. Robert L. Ghormley, a friend of many years, as commander, South Pacific, he shared his doubts with his wife: "Today I have replaced Ghormley with Halsey. It was a sore mental struggle and the decision was not reached until after hours of anguished consideration. I hope I have not made a life enemy. I believe not. The interests of the nation transcend private interests." Nimitz also enjoyed passing on good news. He had received a letter from Secretary of the Navy Frank Knox telling him, "all of us here are very proud of the way you are handling your job." Nimitz wrote to Mrs. Nimitz: "Good news. Perhaps I can last out the year."[43]

Adm. Raymond A. Spruance also knew the loneliness of command and leaned on his wife, Margaret, for support. His correspondence with Margaret throughout their long separation in World War II was vital to his well-being. In February 1942 he wrote to her, "I need my wife to keep me cheered up. . . . Life has certainly lost its interest for me since you left, and the worst of it is that I have no definite date to look forward to when I shall see you again." Always careful not to violate censorship, he had a clever way of keeping her informed. For example, when Halsey's activities were written up in *Life* magazine, he suggested she read it, knowing, of course, that it covered his activities too.

Spruance's thirteen months as Nimitz's chief of staff were, he wrote to his wife, "an inspiration . . . and I hope watching him has taught me more patience and tolerance. He is one of the finest and human characters I have ever met, yet has all the energy, courage, determination, and optimism that is needed in a great military leader." Another letter told her: "My staff has been working up to midnight every night and I have been working during the day, but I refuse to go on the night shift."[44] Admiral Spruance kept Margaret informed of his daily activities; with the planned invasion of the Gilbert Islands looming, he told her she would not hear from him for several weeks because "I shall be too occupied with the other matters to do any writing." He unloaded to her his contempt for the press: "Everyone in the country seems at liberty to express his opinions on the strategy of the war and to publish his ideas to the largest audience that will listen to him." Social events were a necessary part of his activities as a commander. "At times like this and at social events when names fail me I need you very badly," he wrote.[45]

As the war intensified, he told his wife how much her letters meant to him. "My letters will be irregular from now on, but keep writing regularly yourself. Mail will reach me at intervals and it means a great deal to me to hear from you." When he received notice on February 10, 1942, that he had been promoted to full admiral—at age fifty-seven the youngest man to reach that pinnacle—he wrote: "Getting this rank was something that was beyond my utmost expectations." As the war drew to an end and assignments of flag officers were being determined, he told Margaret that he would be happy to replace Nimitz as CinCPac. "Don't ask me where I would have my headquarters, or what I would be able to do about you, for I don't know yet. I am in favor of our high command getting back on board ship during peace, so as not to lose touch with the fleet. You know well enough that wherever I may be, I want to have my family near me. I know you must be disappointed over this, but you know my feeling that a line officer must be willing and anxious to go to sea and to remain at sea. So just be patient for a while longer and wait and see what happens."[46]

Children are, of course, an integral part of Navy families. Children and parents have mutual responsibilities toward one another, and the relationship often involves selflessness and sacrifices on both sides. Among the memories of Rear Adm. Chester W. Nimitz Jr., son of the great naval leader, are some that provide insight into the family life of naval officers.

> Dad had probably the most highly developed sense of duty, as a public servant, and devoted himself first, foremost and always to that aspect of his life, and perhaps secondly to his wife. I believe the children were a natural outgrowth of marriage, and . . . my guess is that his basic belief . . . was, the children were expected to perform and conform and enhance the stature of the family, and so long as they did and were not delinquents, really, that was pretty much the responsibility of the father. . . . Dad was . . . away a tremendous amount of time, so that when

he did come home, all of us children understood absolutely and instinctively from our mother that by golly, we made the time he was at home relatively [quiet]—he'd contest this, I'm sure, but by our lights it was relatively serene. It was far more serene than when we were with Mother alone.[47]

Asked about his father's role in the home, Chester Jr. responded:

> Let me say in the first place, Father was a completely dedicated naval officer. I think such leadership and influence as he did exert in the home, and mind you, in the days we were brought up it was certainly largely an upbringing by the mother because the father was away a good deal of the time—his method was simply the same method he used everywhere else, to express sublime confidence in the dedication and right thinking point of view on the part of his children and of their understanding of the almost necessity of doing well at what they undertake. It certainly was not a close personal kind of a—this is the way you do things because in the long run that's the way you succeed. It was a considerably more formal sort of standard setting. I really think that the Navy consumed an extraordinary percentage of his thoughts and energies.[48]

Admiral Nimitz's daughter-in-law, Joan, provided further insight into the driving force in his life. It was not money, she said, but service to his country and his beloved Navy. She commented: "I remember that when he retired, I'm sure that Chester's mother hoped that he would do something to occupy himself. Here he was, just full of energy and ability and good mind and everything else. He wouldn't take a business job of any sort. He was totally disinterested in finances or money. He never handled any of the money in the family, you know. Mother did all of that. And he didn't care about money at all, so he didn't want a job for money, and he didn't feel that he could take a sort of a commercial type of job."[49]

Flag wives fill an important leadership role in their relations with other Navy wives, but they can also play a role in the development of the junior officers. Adm. James F. Fife was a junior officer under Admiral Nimitz before World War II. During that time Admiral Nimitz's wife offered genuine family hospitality to him and to other junior officers. "For many years Mrs. Nimitz used to say that she brought me up," he recalled. "This was later on, after [Nimitz] was chief of naval operations in Washington, and I've always had very proud feelings that she would feel that way and would say so . . . she had a great influence on my whole career."[50] She did an excellent job. Fife retired as a full admiral.

The following remarks from Admiral Holloway reiterate the importance of the spouse's role in a naval officer's career, particularly as the officer moves up the command hierarchy.

> The influence of a wife on the career of a naval officer can be enormous. I have never known an officer to be promoted to a position of responsibility on the basis of his wife. Yet I am aware of many situations when a naval officer—particularly in the grades of captain and above—was not given a favorable assignment or even failed for selection because of his wife. This unfortunately has occurred because the wife has had a drinking problem or even a personality conflict that has made her an embarrassment when appearing publicly with her spouse. I don't say that these cases of a woman ruining her husband's career are common, but they are not infrequent, based upon my experience as a senior officer sitting on selection boards and as the chief of naval operations responsible for the appointment of all flag officers in the Navy.
>
> That's the negative side of the picture. What about the positive? A Navy wife can be an asset to her husband, and this influence is exerted almost entirely through her relationship with her spouse, not in lobbying other senior officers in his behalf. That latter activity is an absolute taboo, and almost inevitably results in almost fatal problems to the person she is trying to help. I can say from experience that senior officers do not like to hear about . . . [a] subordinate's professional competencies from that subordinate's wife. It is obviously totally subjective and generally does nothing but plant the seeds of suspicion in the mind of the senior that the couple is attempting to hide something.
>
> The good Navy wife endures separations and accepts the additional burdens of doing her job as homemaker and the husband's job as "paterfamilias" without a complaint, at least to her husband. She has the children always seeming in good spirits and well mannered whenever the husband returns from one of his long sea duty jaunts. There is much more to being a good Navy wife than simply accepting with stoicism the vicissitudes of the service. It takes leadership on their part as well.[51]

After reporting what senior naval officers have had to say about Navy wives, it seems only fair to approach the subject from the wife's point of view. The wife of a senior admiral talked about what she considered to be the most difficult part of being a naval officer's wife. Let her remain anonymous, because she spoke for many wives.

My husband was a naval aviator, a carrier pilot, and during his flying days there were special concerns. First was the constant threat of a fatal accident. Had we not lost so many close friends and classmates in crashes, I might have been able to put it out of my mind. But then when I had almost forgotten that ever-present danger, we would get the news of the loss of another friend. It didn't help when the men brought home the aviation safety magazine. It had all of the brutal statistics. Flying off a carrier was listed as the most dangerous profession going. But our guys loved the flying, so I just had to be fatalistic and not think about an accident happening to my husband.

The long deployments were also a problem, especially when the children were still at home. They missed their father and never quite understood why he had to be gone so long. Actually it wasn't the separation that bothered me the most; it was the fact that the more days he was gone on a carrier, the more chances he had to get killed. That's where so many losses seemed to occur. On almost every cruise a squadron would expect to lose one or two pilots in crashes. . . . When my husband stopped flying, the deployments weren't so bad. I missed not having him around those months, but I was sure he would be coming home, an assurance I did not have when he deployed in a squadron.

There was one other aspect of being a naval aviator's wife that was difficult, and for me, unanticipated. We had to share our men with the squadron. I hadn't realized the intense camaraderie that exists in a squadron where everyone from the skipper on down is risking his life every day together in this very dangerous profession. As the squadron gels during the re-forming phases after each cruise, with a new commanding officer and replacement pilots, the spirit becomes intense. The pilots are competing in air-to-air combat with other Navy squadrons, and winning an intersquadron competition means everything.

Happy hour was the biggest headache for the wives. After a full day of flying, the pilots from each squadron would gather at the bar of the air station "O" club and get pumped up, singing squadron songs and holding arm-wrestling contests with the other squadrons. I guess in current jargon that is known as male bonding, but I wanted my husband to come home and help me with the kids. Of course, about half the squadron were young, unmarried, and pretty happy-go-lucky. They had no families to go home to. So all too often, the whole bunch would transfer the party to the home of one of the senior officers when happy hour broke up. So as a skipper or exec's wife, I did get my husband home, but with a half a dozen starry-eyed but hungry young ensigns and jaygees who had to be fed and nurtured. So it was scrambled eggs or carryout pizza and Chinese for dinner after feeding the kids and putting them to bed.

The admiral's wife added,

Don't underestimate the pull of the squadron camaraderie. The night before deploying to the Korean War, the squadron held a "beer muster" at the . . . local watering hole, and even the married pilots showed up—with their wives. I know the same thing happened during the Vietnam War. It was virtually a ritual for the pilots who were deploying to combat to bid the noncombatants goodbye in a raucous farewell party. I didn't understand it at the time, and it was sort of hard to take. I understand now that it is part of the role of being the Navy wife.

CHAPTER 12

The Pattern

There is a pattern in the fundamental traits of character that can
be identified with the successful military leader.

Edgar F. Puryear Jr.

This book has examined important aspects of naval leadership using the
wisdom and knowledge of some of America's greatest military leaders. My
primary sources were the top World War II naval leaders: Fleet Admirals
William D. Leahy, Ernest J. King, Chester W. Nimitz, and William F. Halsey,
and Adm. Raymond A. Spruance; and nine postwar admirals, including
three who were selected to be chairman of the Joint Chiefs of Staff: Arthur
Radford, Thomas A. Moorer, and William J. Crowe Jr.; and CNOs James L.
Holloway III, Thomas Hayward, James D. Watkins, Carlisle A. H. Trost,
Frank Kelso II, and Jay L. Johnson.

The leadership profiles of the admirals examined in this study reveal a
pattern in the qualities necessary for successful leadership. All of these
great men exhibited a selfless desire to serve; the ability to accept the
responsibility for decision making, the essence of leadership; and a "feel"
or "sixth sense" for decision making. They were not "yes men" in serving

their seniors and did not tolerate yes men among their subordinates. They read widely and accepted opportunities to serve under senior officers who selected and mentored them, their reward being longer hours, greater challenges, and greater sacrifices for themselves and for their families. They were concerned for and considerate of their people, and they realized that the ability to delegate determined how far they would go and how successful they would be. When problems surfaced, they tried to fix the problem, not the blame.

All showed early in their careers that they were self-driven leaders. They shared the desire to command and the willingness to work selflessly toward that goal. There are many officers who think they want command but are not willing, either consciously or subconsciously, to expend the effort required. There are some who get command and lose it, either because they are incompetent and fail or because they are unwilling to serve after learning what the responsibilities of command entail. Let us summarize, one by one, the characters great leaders have in common.

Decision

Senior admirals could not be successful military leaders without the ability to make decisions quickly and well. To again quote General of the Army Dwight D. Eisenhower:

> Making decisions is the essence of leadership—handling large problems whether or not you are at war or peace. When you make these decisions it is not done with any reaching for the dramatic. It is almost everyday and commonplace. You reach a conclusion based upon the facts as you see them, the evaluations of the several factors as you see them, the relationship of one fact to another, and, above all, your convictions as to the capacity of different individuals to fit into these different places. You come to a decision after you've taken all these things into consideration. Then you decide and say, "That's what we'll do."[1]

Command involves loneliness—the higher the command position, the lonelier the commander. At no time does a leader feel loneliness more deeply than when having to make a critical, high-level decision dealing with life and death, success or failure, victory or defeat. But making decisions is part of leadership; the wartime leader who does not have the strength to make decisions and the judgment to be right a large percentage of the time does not remain long in a position of high command.

During his time as president, Harry Truman was presented with numerous critical decisions that required immediate attention, among them: Should the United States use the atomic bomb on Japan? How was the occupation of a defeated Germany to be handled? Should the United States continue to encourage the Soviet Union to declare war against Japan? What should be done about the puppet communist regimes the Soviet Union was establishing in Eastern Europe? Others involved the Truman doctrine to save Greece and Turkey from communism, the Marshall Plan, the occupation of Japan, the Berlin blockade, and the Korean War. It is no wonder that Truman entitled the first volume of his memoirs *Year of Decisions*. In the preface to his book, he wrote:

> The presidency of the United States carries with it a responsibility so personal as to be without parallel. Very few are ever authorized to speak for the President. No one can make decisions for him. No one can know all the processes and stages of his thinking in making important decisions. Even those closest to him, even members of his immediate family, never know all the reasons why he does certain things and why he comes to certain conclusions. To be President of the United States is to be lonely, very lonely at times of great decisions.[2]

Perhaps the most difficult of many difficult decisions General Eisenhower had to make in World War II was when and where to launch the Allied invasion of France. The invasion had been scheduled for June 5, 1944, and the invasion troops were massed and ready on the coast of England. The worst storm of the season was blowing in the English Channel, but further delay was risky as well. The meteorologists were promising a brief window of good weather on the sixth. Eisenhower's advisers, meeting on the fourth, were evenly divided over whether to launch on the fifth. Eisenhower alone was empowered to decide. Wait one day, was his decision; launch on the sixth. History proved him correct.[3]

What goes on in a commander's mind after making such a monumental decision? Ike later said of this occasion: "Again I had to endure the interminable wait that always intervenes between the final decision of the high command and the earliest possible determination of success or failure in such ventures." He occupied himself with visiting his troops and sending them on their way with his best wishes. Although he was surrounded by people before, during, and after decisions, Ike nevertheless wrote to a friend during the war: "The worst part of high military command is the loneliness."[4]

Adm. Chester Nimitz felt the loneliness, too. His daughter, Catherine Nimitz Lay, remembered an occasion when her father spoke with some schoolchildren: "One of the questions was: 'How did you feel when you found that you were the commander-in-chief?' And he said, 'Lonely,' and then went on to say, . . . 'a person in that position is bound to be lonely even though you have wonderful people to help you.'"[5]

Gen. Colin Powell, as chairman of the Joint Chiefs of Staff, commented on the U.S. military intervention in Panama to remove Gen. Manuel Noriega from power: "Command is lonely. . . . The last night before the invasion, sitting alone in the dark in the back seat of my car . . . I felt full of foreboding. . . . Had I been right? Had my advice been sound? . . . Was it all worth it? I went to bed gnawed by self-doubt."[6]

Gen. Norman Schwarzkopf was the commander of the forces that pushed Iraq out of Kuwait in Operations Desert Shield and Desert Storm. "I didn't sleep very well in the Gulf," he recalled. "Even after the plan was locked in concrete, every night I would be in bed and say, 'What have I forgotten? What have we missed? Is there something more we can do . . . ?' I think it takes that kind of driving of yourself as a commander if you care about soldiers."[7]

Wartime admirals are faced with innumerable difficult and grave decisions. And, unlike historians, who have the benefit of hindsight, they must base their decisions *on the facts available at the time*. Admiral Halsey made a tough decision when he opted to launch Doolittle's B-25 flight to bomb Tokyo earlier than planned, lengthening the trip and thus making it even more hazardous. Admiral Nimitz had to relieve a vice admiral who had been a friend since their Naval Academy days because he was indecisive. Admiral Burke, too, understood that the human factor—toughness in particular—

is a vital part of decision making: "You have to make tough, hard decisions and make them after you've analyzed as much as you can within the time that you've got, make them as right as you can, but then you have to stand by them, and sometimes force the decisions on people that hurt people. You can't do anything productive without adversely affecting some people." He continued: "President Eisenhower did not want problems coming up to him, he wanted them settled down below, and it was one of the things that he had difficulty with me the whole time, and with the other chiefs. Eisenhower tried to have unity of the services, but I believe now that it's not so important to have unity; what is important is to make sure that all the facts and all the factors pertaining to the problem are each brought out clearly and then if there are differences of opinion, the president has to make a decision."[8]

One of the toughest decisions Admiral Hayward made as CNO was to fight the Navy-wide drug problem by instituting a policy of no tolerance. He faced strong criticism, but his decision ultimately benefited all the services.[9] Admiral Trost told me the toughest decision he had to make as CNO was to challenge the secretary of the navy when he interfered with the decisions of a captains' promotion board. Trost took the matter over the head of the secretary to Secretary of Defense Casper Weinberger, who supported Trost.

Sixth Sense

Critical to good decision making is a "feel" or "sixth sense" for the right thing to do. It is a quality that all top military leaders have. Study, experience, and preparation help leaders develop a feel for the situation that is a kind of intuition. This combined with sound judgment allows a successful leader to make decisions quickly and well. General Eisenhower, for example, commented: "One must never lose touch with the *feel* of his troops. He can delegate tactical responsibility and avoid interference in the authority of his selected subordinates, but he must maintain the closest kind of factual and spiritual contact with them or . . . he will fail. This contact required frequent visits to the troop themselves."[10] He believed that a properly led unit should function well in the commander's absence.

He believed that if he could get soldiers to talk with the brass, they would not be afraid to talk with their sergeants, lieutenants, and captains. This openness would in turn produce meaningful ideas, ingenuity, and initiative, which would increase readiness and performance and the quality of the decisions made. Ike believed that the army's business was success in war and that "attention to the individual was the key to success."

On May 2, 1942, Admiral Nimitz had a "hunch" that the Japanese would attempt to invade Midway, so he flew out there—1,135 miles from his headquarters—to inspect the defenses and get a personal feel for the situation. His visit both alerted the defenders and instilled confidence in them, and they successfully defended the island. Nimitz maintained a feel for his command through a policy that required each ship commander report to him. If a commander impressed him, he would comment, "There's an officer we must watch. He's going to be one of the good ones." Another staff officer added, "He wanted a chance to size them up and for them to know they had an identity with the fleet commander." Of his visits with the officers and sailors, Nimitz said, "Some of the best help and advice I've had comes from junior officers and enlisted men."[11]

The battle for Guadalcanal was a difficult and bloody fight. During a lull in the action, Admiral Halsey decided to tour the island to get a firsthand impression of the situation. The Marine Corps commander, Maj. Gen. A. Archer Vandegrift, remembered that Halsey "flew in like a wonderful breath of fresh air." He talked with a number of marines, praising them, telling them as he left, "I wish to God that every man and woman in our great country could know and see what you are doing. God bless you." It was actions such as that that made him an effective leader and morale builder.[12]

While serving as Vice Adm. Marc Mitscher's chief of staff, Arleigh Burke decided that if he was going to serve with aviators, he should understand what they went through in combat. He decided to fly on a reconnaissance mission "to get the feel. I don't know anything about air combat," he told Admiral Mitscher, "but I want to get the feel of it and I can't do that sitting here in the ship or from listening to somebody else." He was almost shot down, but he went on to become one of the greatest CNOs ever to serve the Navy.[13]

Admiral Moorer told me that he talked to his troops when he wanted to maintain his feel for command. "I asked them to tell me what they were going to do this morning. . . . I never placed any restraints on them. I wanted them to say what they thought. I didn't want any rank-conscious intervention. . . . I always made a point to talk with chief petty officers."[14]

As captain of the *Enterprise* Admiral Holloway kept in touch with all aspects of his command by visiting the people who needed attention. "I went down into the gasoline pumping stations and asked 'Well, how are you guys doing?' They were filthy, overworked, and seldom saw much of the actual flight deck operation. Their work was dirty and smelly. Yet without their total effort, we could never have made a launch on schedule. I would tell them results of our missions . . . it was important to inform them the results of their efforts."[15]

Admiral Trost commanded the Seventh Fleet before becoming CNO in 1986. "I was tasked with visiting the countries in Asia, South Asia, and East Asia, on a cycle of no less frequently than six months," he told me. "I tried to get out to the ships . . . I generally talked to all the sailors . . . I usually got pretty well through the ships I visited." Earlier in his career he commanded a nuclear submarine. "My routine when I commanded *Sam Rayburn* was basically to make a point of seeing every sailor at least once a day. . . . I would stop and talk to them about their jobs, and talk to them about what was happening back home . . . it can get pretty lonely out there."[16]

"The higher you get, the harder it is to reach all the people you would like to see," Admiral Kelso told me. "There is no question of the importance of visiting with your subordinates. They need to see you and know that you respect them and the jobs they are doing. Their morale and yours is dependent on face-to-face contact. The troops want to know you will listen to them; . . . the American sailor is brutally frank and will tell you candidly how he or she feels."[17]

Admiral Johnson, as CNO, also recognized the importance of visiting to get that feel: "I always believe, and I told others, particularly admirals stationed in Washington—indeed, anybody, anywhere—you have got to get out. You have to go to the troops. You have to go to the deck plates to really find out what the heck is going on. Go to their spaces, where they work, where they live. You've got to go to them. . . . That's where you find out what's going on." When he spoke to a large number of troops he would tell them, "'I'm going to turn my transmitter off and my receiver on. I want to hear what's on your mind.' . . . I relied very heavily on input, fresh from the fleet . . . that's why I went out and talk to them . . . to create an atmosphere where they felt free to talk with their leaders."[18]

Admiral Stansfield Turner reflected, "You've got to stay in touch with your people." As Captain of the USS *Rowan,* for example, he made it a point to visit an area of the ship that some captains ignored, the boilers: "They're the undesirable places to work. It's hot, it's dirty and sweaty. Most captains go months without going into one; some never did. . . . I said to myself, I've got to make those sailors understand that they've got a dirty, gritty job down there, but they're important. I can't run the ship if the engines don't work."[19]

Admiral Long said, "Inspection is a major part of any command. . . . I'd go out for a few days and make my own observations, and those were useful to me . . . it made the crew feel good when [I came] visiting back in their spaces."[20]

All of the admirals I interviewed claimed to have that sixth sense. Admiral Holloway, for example, said, "Yes, absolutely . . . intellect alone is not enough to be effective leader."[21]

Admiral Watkins likewise responded: "Absolutely. I have never, as CNO or any other time, ever doubted (I mean as a senior officer . . .) my ability to address or solve problems no matter how thorny they were. I always felt comfortable with whatever challenge."[22]

Admiral McKee's comment about "feel" was: "If you understand the ship—if you 'know the boat,' as we say on submarines—and you demand the same of your crew, when the time comes, she'll talk to you. She'll truly become an extension of your fingertips." He described awakening suddenly with a "sense of something different" and contacting the bridge just in time to prevent a collision with a surface ship.[23]

Admiral Larson "had the kind of instinct that if I felt something just was right, I had that feeling in the pit of my stomach . . . if it wasn't just right, I didn't do it."[24]

Adm. Henry G. Chiles commented on Admiral Holloway's statement that "the ship talks to you, and . . . you'd better listen." He related an experience similar to Admiral McKee's as a sub captain. On a clear night, something about the operation of the ship was bothering him. "Something just didn't seem right. . . . My senses told me to check on things. . . . I just picked the right timing to go take a look. . . . It was just a hunch that something was not right." He also made it a point to visit his crew, stopping to talk with many individually. "What's going on that I need to know about?" he would ask. "What can I help you with? . . . I loved it."[25]

All the admirals I interviewed believed that a feel for command can be developed, although some added that certain qualities may be present from birth. General of the Army Omar Bradley developed a feel for situations through collecting information, "little bits of it," as if his brain were a computer. Then, he explained, "when you are suddenly faced in battle with a situation needing a decision, you can give it. When people would call me on the phone and give me a situation, I would push a button and have an answer right then."[26]

George S. Patton Jr., the outstanding World War II field commander, called this ability "military reaction." He explained: "What success I have had results from the fact that I have always been certain that my military reactions were correct. No one is born with them any more than anyone is born with measles. You can be born with a soul capable of correct military reactions or a body capable of having big muscles, but both qualities must be developed by hard work."[27]

Admiral Holloway told me: "I think it's like so many things, [command feel comes] only through experience . . . you can't learn these things in a textbook.[28]

Admiral Trost "always felt I had a gut feeling for things; what is right and what is wrong, and which way to go. . . . It is directly a matter of how you have been raised, and what you have experienced, and what you have read, and how you reacted to different situations."[29]

Admiral Kelso commented: "I don't think it's God-given. I think it's learned." Like a mother who wakes up the instant her child cries in the night, "a good commander of a ship has got that same sense. I could sleep through anything, but if one blower stopped running that ought to be running, I would wake up. . . . You don't get that by not paying attention. . . . It's an experience level. You learn from experience; but you can have experiences and learn nothing from them, or you can have experiences where you learn a lot from them . . . it's really a set of experiences you put together. It's what I call a memory bank."[30]

Admiral Larson thought the feel for command is probably part talent and part learned: "I think it's probably both, but I think a lot of us develop it and experience it." As CinCPac before becoming CNO, he said, he "visited virtually every naval base in the Pacific. I walked around and visited individual units, talked to the troops as I was doing it. . . . Their comments might not be correct," he said, ". . . but perceptions are important as well as reality."[31]

A leader can delegate authority and minimize interference in the authority of his or her subordinates, but a good leader always maintains the closest possible contact with them all the way down the line.

Yes Men

Fleet Adm. Ernest J. King's biographer wrote that the admiral "despised yes-men." Fleet Adm. Chester W. Nimitz exhibited that quality as well. Immediately after he was appointed to replace Adm. Husband Kimmel as CinCPac, but before leaving Washington to take command, he told Secretary of the Navy Frank Knox that he wanted a certain Captain Jacobs to replace him as chief of the Bureau of Navigation. When Secretary Knox objected because "FDR doesn't like him," Nimitz exploded, telling Knox, "God damn it, he's the only man who can do the job." Jacobs got the job.[32] Secretary of the Navy James Forrestal said that with the possible exception of Admiral King, Nimitz was the most stubborn officer he had to deal with.

Adm. Raymond Spruance, after achieving a brilliant victory against the Japanese in the Pacific, was instructed by Secretary Knox to make himself available to journalists so that the success could be publicized. Spruance said, "No. If they want somebody to come out here and fight a publicity war, then they can relieve me."[33]

As a destroyer commander in World War II, Capt. Arleigh Burke accepted then-Lt. Byron "Whizzer" White as his intelligence officer. He later reflected, "If I had time, and I always had time, to tell him what I was going to do, he'd criticize it. It got so that I dreaded listening to his criticism just before fighting the battle. I dreaded that more than I did fighting the battle." But Burke conceded, "Well, those things helped."[34]

In 1953 Burke served on the UN commission charged with negotiating an end to hostilities in Korea. Burke and some of the other commission members were so violently opposed to a direction from Washington that they told Army Gen. Matthew Ridgway, "we just weren't going to do it, and if they wanted someone to do that, they'd have to get someone else." Ridgway told Burke and the other objectors, "You are military people. I dislike these orders just as much as you, but we are military people . . . and you will carry out your orders." Burke responded: "We'll carry out these orders, but that's the last thing we do."[35]

On being selected to serve on the General Board after World War II Burke reflected, "There is no room for a yes man in any outfit like this." When he became CNO in 1954, he said, "I looked around to find a man who would disagree with me, but who was straightforward and had great integrity—and great experience, too. I didn't want just a stubborn man, but I wanted somebody who was very intelligent, from a different background, different personal characteristics, so that I could discuss matters with him."[36]

Perhaps the strongest evidence of Burke's refusal to be a yes man was his insistence as CNO on a draft for the Navy. The secretary of the navy and secretary of defense were opposed to the draft, but Burke insisted on taking the issue to President Eisenhower. Burke prevailed, but the president told him: "'Burke, you put me in a hell of a spot!'" But he eventually became a confidante of the president, who appointed Burke to an unprecedented third two-year term.[37]

The entire senior naval carrier force showed they were not yes men by standing up to Secretary of Defense Louis Johnson when he canceled construction of the carrier USS *United States*. The carrier constituency ultimately prevailed, but the rebellion cost Adm. Louis E. Denfeld his post as CNO.

On August 2, 1961, Adm. George W. Anderson succeeded Admiral Burke as CNO. Even as he was being selected for the post he was discussed as a possible choice for chairman of the Joint Chiefs when Gen. Lyman L. Lemnitzer's term ended. Anderson rose no higher in Washington, however; in fact, his tenure as CNO ended after his first two-year term. The reason? He refused to be a yes man. During the Cuban missile crisis of 1962, when Secretary of Defense Robert S. McNamara tried to interfere in the Navy's operations, Anderson told him to go back to his office and "let the Navy run the blockade."[38]

Admiral Holloway insisted on the importance of "no men": "Like-minded leaders will differ, and a CNO must be prepared to disagree." He certainly did when he tangled with Secretary of State Henry Kissinger over the SALT II Treaty. Kissinger wanted him to agree with the Soviet Union's proposal to eliminate America's arsenal of Tomahawk missiles. The presidential election was approaching, and the treaty was very important to President Gerald Ford, but Holloway prevailed. History has proven the value of this missile. "The president was obviously upset with me," Holloway recalled, "but he said: 'Admiral, I asked for your view and you gave it to me.'"

When President Jimmy Carter announced at a JCS meeting in 1978 that he wanted to cut the military budget by nine billion dollars, Admiral Holloway spoke up when all the other chiefs were silent, respectfully challenging the president's decision. Holloway reflected, "The president was clearly upset." But he could not agree with Carter's suggestion that the chiefs tell Congress that "a cut in defense of nine billion dollars could make the nation stronger." He challenged the attempts by Secretary of Defense Harold Brown to force a small-carrier concept on the Navy. In a congressional hearing on the matter, Holloway openly stated his objections to the smaller carrier, despite Brown's instructions not to speak openly on his views. Holloway pointed out it was his obligation to state his own personal views.[39]

Admiral Watkins, a Roman Catholic, as CNO took on his church when the bishops drafted a proposal stating that a practicing Roman Catholic could not be involved in a military that had nuclear weapons. Because of his intervention, the subsequent report was balanced and reflected the views of the military.[40]

Admiral Trost "brought people into my office who were known entities who knew my thought process, and who would disagree with me when appropriate. . . . I am not that hard to talk with, and I don't have an ego that needs stroking, and so they could talk with me if they disagree with something."[41]

Admiral Kelso summed up his position on yes men as follows: "I've always felt the most disloyal subordinates are the ones who won't tell you . . . the truth, but what they think you want to hear. . . . I tried to make it clear to people who worked for me I could take bad news." He added that if they did not give him the facts, they could not make use of his experience in solving their problems.[42]

But having strong personalities on your advisory team can be disconcerting. Admiral Crowe, for example, commented: "I'm human. Sometimes a 'no man' really upsets me. . . . But those are the kind of guys who really matter."[43]

I discussed yes men with Air Force Gen. Nathan F. Twining, who was chairman of the Joint Chiefs of Staff from 1953 to 1957. "In leadership," he told me, "you have got to have the ability to sit back and listen to your staff or an individual who briefs you—men who can speak with authority. You have got to have the courage to sit down and listen, have them say what they think is right, no matter how sore you might get at them. You also need a commander who will come in and tell you off when he thinks you are wrong. I have had that happen to me many times, and it has been helpful to me. It sure takes the ego out of you, too."[44]

Refusing to be a yes man involves risks. Admirals Denfeld and Anderson were fired; then–Captain Burke was removed from the promotion list by the secretary of the navy, but went on to serve six years as CNO; Admiral Radford, a carrier pilot, challenged the cancellation of the USS *United States* but went on to become chairman of the Joint Chiefs. Admiral Chiles fought with Adm. Hyman G. Rickover when the latter turned down applicants to the Navy's nuclear program that Chiles considered qualified, and often persuaded him to reverse his position.

I could cite many more examples, but these prove the point. Rank can give validity to decisions and can silence contrary opinions from subordinates. Successful leaders and decision makers need and value the inputs and thoughts of those who work for them and must create an atmosphere that supports the free exchange of ideas until such time as a decision is made. Very few leaders are successful when deprived of the opinions of their subordinates.

Books: The Importance of Reading

After interviewing more than one hundred four-star officers over the last thirty-five years, I have observed that those who were avid readers had a depth of knowledge and perception superior to those who were not readers. Their interest in reading biography and military history played a role in the development of their character and leadership, but so did their interest in the works of Socrates, Plato, Aristotle, and Shakespeare, for example. As youths they read adventure books by Sir Walter Scott, Rudyard Kipling, and James Fenimore Cooper, and these sparked their interest in the adventures of a military career. But they also read poetry, which developed their sensitivity and understanding, and enhanced their judgment.

Many of today's young officers say that their schedules are too demanding to allow time and energy for reading. I say this is a lame excuse for laziness. Gen. Charles E. "Shy" Meyer, who was jumped over fifty-seven generals to become chief of staff, told me: "While in the army, I got up early every morning at three-thirty or four-thirty and read for my own information. That was my own precious time to read. . . . I jealously guarded that time. . . . I found that if I didn't set aside time to read, it wouldn't get done. Today, to be a reader, you have to work at it."[45]

The wife of Gen. George C. Marshall thought that reading energized her husband. During World War II, the general would come home in the evening too tired to talk. She would send him to the library for a pile of books, and he would go through it like a "swarm of locusts devouring a green field."[46]

While the planning was going on for the defense of Guadalcanal during World War II, a young lieutenant asked Nimitz if it was true that he read a lot at night. "Yes, I do," replied the admiral. "I read from three until five every morning."

"Three until *five*! When do you sleep, sir?"

"Well, I turn in at ten and I sleep till three, and then I catch another wink from five till six-forty-five," the admiral replied.[47]

Adm. Raymond Spruance's wife, Margaret, said that "he was . . . curious about the world and loved to explore things and places while he walked or to pursue abstract ideas in men's minds and in books. He was an avid reader of . . . biographies and histories, which he preferred in [his] early years. . . . He owned two well-thumbed books . . . one was the Bible."[48] Spruance believed that those with a liberal education in art, literature, and music had an advantage over people with only a technical education, such as himself, commenting: "a knowledge and an appreciation of these subjects enriches their lives and makes them more interesting to their friends and acquaintances."[49] Spruance made it a point to be conversant with world affairs. He thought it was the duty of every well-educated American to be familiar with the broad field of government, extending into the field of international relations. He believed strongly that "*those with the mental equipment to do so had a special duty to inform themselves on world affairs and to help educate and guide the rest of the country in that respect*. During his first tour of duty in the Philippines he inquired into and took great interest in Filipino politics and legislative affairs, an interest which helped make him an understanding and informed ambassador to the Islands forty years later."[50]

Admiral Burke's interest in reading was sparked by his mother, Clara, who "devoted herself to nurturing his intellect," as his biographer, E. B. Potter, noted.

> Under her tutelage he had already in his preschool days begun identifying printed words. . . . Stimulated by the competition of his fellow students, he made rapid progress and early began reading in his free time, mostly adventure stories. Clara, ambitious to have him read more substantial fare, obtained a library card for him, and each Saturday when family members went to town for shopping, she had him draw books. She encouraged him to read at least two a week, and when

he had read three books of his own choosing, she insisted that he alternate with three she chose for him. . . . Thus she gradually raised his intellectual appetite so that his own selection of reading material steadily matured.[51]

When Burke was appointed chief of staff for then–Vice Adm. Marc Mitscher, he "devoted every spare moment to his first rapid reading course" to learn his job. But, as Potter noted, Burke came to recognize the need for broader knowledge as well.

During much of his career he had applied himself so vigorously to the problems at hand that he had little energy left for serious general reading. Within the field of his specialties he was without peer, but he had become somewhat of a narrow specialist. Gradually he came to realize that the world of informed citizens was leaving him behind. Too often he saw references in newspapers or heard references in conversations to things he didn't understand. To rectify this defect, Arleigh . . . devour[ed] books and articles that might fill in the blanks in his knowledge of history, economics, science, politics, and international relations.[52]

Admiral Moorer described what he saw as the value of studying history: "I'm a big believer in learning from other people's mistakes, even if they happened a century ago. I'm not anxious to go out there and experiment myself if I already know the answer. And it's very dangerous." Moorer said that an effective and successful military leader never stops studying. He believed strongly in understanding the technical side of the Navy profession as well as its history. He commented: "The Navy . . . is a highly technical thing. . . . Any successful operator or commander at sea must have a burning technical curiosity about how things work, including his bilge pump, his steering engine, right on up to his supersonic jet. No one is going to tell him those things. He's got to go out and find out for himself."[53]

Admiral Holloway reflected on the difference between training and education:

In 1946 as a lieutenant, I was very young for an executive officer of the squadron. Normally the XO was a lieutenant commander. Professionalism had been instilled in me in the fleet as a destroyer gunnery officer during in the war, and I was just beginning to grasp the distinction between training and education. Training covers the technical side of the specifics of your plane and your job in the squadron. Education is acquiring the ability to comprehend more obtuse subjects—leadership, engineering, principles, and the art of writing. This education was gained from reading books. Training was the first essential for the squadron pilot. It was a question of survival in the air. Learning was for when you left the squadron area. In the evening was the time to settle down with a good book, not hanging out at the bar. . . .

Reading in general, a wide exposure to fiction, drama, and art, gave me an opportunity to socialize with a wider group of people. When we went out to a party, I didn't have to go in the kitchen with the men and drink bourbon and talk about the Navy or flying. Dabney and I could make friends with people outside the Navy and talk about things other than flying and babies.

Few officers have affected more naval careers than Adm. Hyman Rickover, who was head of the Navy's nuclear research program. Admiral Holloway provided insights into Rickover's reading habits: "Admiral Rickover was an avid reader. . . . He and his wife preferred to remain at home and read rather than join his fellow officers and their wives at bridge or dinner parties. The Rickovers did not play bridge or enjoy cocktail parties. They preferred to read or visit historical or cultural sites. . . . Yet Rickover never regretted his introspective ways. . . . He told me several times that it enabled him to pick and choose his company, and talk on topics of his choice. He was interested in everything."[54]

Vice Adm. Kent Lee also understood the distinction between training and education. "The education to be a commanding officer of an aircraft carrier is a kind of do-it-yourself thing. I got all the literature available on the technical aspects of running the ship. . . . There are . . . instructions on how to handle storms, and you get all the books on ship handling. I think all ships' captains do a great deal of reading in this area, especially carrier captains. So yes, I had read and reread all the instructions on books in this area."[55]

Reading, in sum, is the foundation on which a true professional builds a successful career.

Mentorship

Reading and experience are two of the factors that help officers develop sound leadership and decision-making abilities. General Eisenhower offered another: "Be around people making decisions." Mentorship—both seeking guidance from a mentor and being a mentor to others—is an important part of successful leadership. Some officers seeking advancement become sycophants trying to ride on the coat-tails of a superior. True mentorship requires study, preparation, and hard work, on both sides. It reflects an awareness that when war occurs we must place our finest officers in the top command positions to protect and preserve our country and lead our fighters.

Admiral Nimitz was mentored early in his career by Capt. Samuel S. Robinson, who took him to Europe during World War I to study British submarine strategy. Rear Adm. William Moffett as chief of the Bureau of Aeronautics encouraged Ernest King and William Halsey to enter Navy carrier aviation. Admiral Moorer was mentored by the Naval Academy superintendent. Arleigh Burke was a mentor for many senior U.S. naval leaders. He had a terrific feel for people, understood all aspects of naval warfare, and was skilled in bureaucratic infighting in Washington.

All those who became CNO first gained meaningful experience as aides to civilian service secretaries. As a captain, Admiral Moorer served as an aide to the secretary of the navy. In that role he screened all papers that came into the office, attended top-level meetings with the secretary, traveled around the world with him, wrote his speeches, and prepared briefings for his congressional hearings. After that experience, he told me, "it wasn't strange to me when I had to go myself as CNO and chairman."[56]

Admiral Crowe was an aide to three flag officers. From one he learned what not to do as a leader. Vice Adm. George Clifford "Turkey Neck" Crawford "was hard to live with and hard to work with," Admiral Crowe recalled, and not a leader he would "want to emulate." Vice Adm. Stuart S. Murray, in contrast, was "so considerate and cheerful that he was known throughout the Navy as 'Sunshine.' He was one of the kindest, most gracious men I had ever met. In those days, kindness was not a trait that many admirals had."[57]

Admiral Watkins's first mentor, Admiral Clarey, was "a Navy Cross winner, a fabulous person, as was his wife," Watkins recalled. Clarey "was not only great professionally, but great personally and socially. He never forgot a name. He was someone whom you would want to emulate. He was inspirational to me and one of the reasons why I decided to make a career of it." Another mentor for him was Capt. Gene Fluckey, a Medal of Honor winner: "He was a terrific leader, natural, friendly; you could talk to him, he listened to you . . . he is the kind of person with whom I would want to go to war . . . he was going to win and come back." Admiral Rickover taught him that "a professional's number-one duty was to train men properly."[58]

Adm. Stansfield Turner had what he described as "a terrible skipper" in his first sea duty. A Rhodes scholar, Turner wanted to postpone going to Oxford until after he had completed his Navy duty and was "a free man. Then I could do what I wanted." He went to see his mentor, Ferd Eberstadt, to discuss the matter with him and was told: "'Turner, we've worked hard to get this Rhodes scholarship, you get your ass to Oxford.' . . . I went to Oxford. If it hadn't been for my mentor, I'd have been a civilian."[59]

Admiral Kelso commented, "My first job as an officer out of the submarine world was as an executive assistant to Admiral Isaac Kidd, when he was commander in chief, Atlantic. He openly said that his job was to teach me, and he spent a lot of time providing me with information that was of use to me in latter parts of my career." A true mentor, Kelso added, is someone who tries "to provide young people [with] information and knowledge about how to do the job better," not someone who tries to get his or her protégé promoted." Kelso told me, "I tried to use my senior leaders to assist in identifying those who would be most successful. You can't know everybody . . . so you need . . . other leaders to tell you what kind of leaders the subordinates are, what kind of leaders they think they will provide the greatest success in the next assignment. . . . I felt, to be fair to the officers, that I needed to hear what other senior Navy leaders thought of them."[60]

In Admiral Trost's view, "a mentor is, first of all, a leader who is responsible for developing those subordinate to him." Capt. Shannon Kramer was a diesel and nuclear submariner whom Trost considered a mentor because he had qualities Trost tried to emulate: "consideration for people. He was exceptionally competent and honest, and had the highest possible integrity. He had a great interest in the professional development of the people who worked for him."[61]

Admiral Johnson learned a great deal from Captain Barron, one of his COs. "The officers that set the best example for me," he said, "were those who looked after their people. He taught me lot about how to be a leader."[62]

Admiral Crowe emphasized the importance of chief petty officers as mentors when he was addressing young officers: "If I could for a moment, I would recommend that early in the game every ensign latch on to the leading petty officers in your unit and absorb their wisdom. You will benefit greatly from what experience has taught them and the depth of their knowledge. If you are genuinely willing to learn, they will be happy to share with you."[63]

Mentorship does not and should not mean favoritism. Admiral Moorer told me, "I never got involved in the flag officer promotion, and I wouldn't even talk to the president of the board about any individual; . . . some people don't believe that. They think that the CNO calls the president of the board in and says, 'Now you select Jack Jones and I'll give you another star.' They think that goes on all the time, but it doesn't in the Navy. I think our system is the fairest of all." All the CNOs I interviewed handled the flag promotion boards in that same "hands-off" way.[64]

Consideration

Of great importance to leadership success is a basic love and concern for people. An admiral can get his or her subordinates to carry out orders through fear, but never will they give their all to such a commander. The people under a leader's command—staff, commanders, officers, noncommissioned officers, all the way down to the lowest-ranking sailor—can sense whether he or she has a thoughtful and sympathetic regard for them. This quality was a hallmark of the admirals surveyed in this study.

Admiral Moorer summed up the importance of consideration in successful military leadership: "In every position; a commander's crew will want to know how much he cares for them far more than they will ever care how much you know."[65] Admiral Holloway explained:

> In general, "consideration" . . . means that the leader has a concern for the feelings or comfort of his subordinates that rise above his required responsibilities. The leader who is "tough but fair" seldom is considerate. He does what the regulations require, and the regulations are mute when it comes to a leader sacrificing his own time or his privileges to go beyond the official requirements of his duties toward his subordinates. For a commander to provide aid, comfort, and benefits to his subordinates simply to conform with regulations is not consideration. There must be some aspect of "giving" or self-sacrifice on his part."[66]

Consideration, discussed in chapter 6, was illustrated with numerous examples. Admiral Nimitz, for example, retained Adm. Husband Kimmel's staff when he took over command in Pearl Harbor; gave up Admiral Spruance as his chief of staff to allow him to return to a command; and had his photograph taken with the sailor who bet his buddies that he could get in to see CinCPac so that the man would have proof of his success. Admiral Halsey's demand that the surgeon ride in the ambulance with the sailor injured in a motorcycle accident is another example of consideration for subordinates.

The post–World War II period offers many examples of consideration as well: Admiral Burke's refusal to provide a list of successors because a leak might embarrass a fellow officer showed great consideration. The engineering training school Admiral Holloway established for officers endeared him to the chief petty officers. Admiral Watkins improved the pay and quality of life for sailors; and Admiral Larson improved officer and enlisted housing.

Delegation

How far a leader rises in responsibility and effectiveness depends in large part on his or her ability to delegate. Admiral Burke put this essential ability into perspective when he stated: "We believe in command, not staff. We believe we have 'real' things to do. The Navy believes in putting a man in a position with a job to do, and let him do it—give him hell if he does not perform—but be a man in his own name. We decentralize and capitalize on the capabilities of our individual people rather than centralize and make automatons of them. This builds that essential pride of service and sense of accomplishment. . . . This is the direction in which we should move."[67]

In the process of delegating authority, a successful leader must be able to distinguish the vital from the less consequential—must be able to grasp the essentials and refuse to let nonessentials take up his or her time. In order to delegate successfully, the leader has to have the ability to pick good people, to get the best out of everyone, more than they ever thought they could produce. Self-confidence and the willingness to delegate are measures of a commander's ability. As Admiral Holloway put it, "delegation is a tool of command."

What inspires a person to give that something extra? Sometimes it is enough simply to be given a job and then left alone to do it. The leader periodically checks to see how things are going, always available to help if help is needed. He places trust in his subordinates, and they respect this vote of confidence and respond accordingly, not bothering the commander with small decisions. Subordinates want to give their best—they do not want to disappoint their leader and violate the leader's trust. But the leader must keep aware of what his or her subordinates are doing, always monitoring what is going on, without getting bogged down in detail.

"Admiral Burke," commented Admiral Moorer,

> was a man that knew how to select people and then give them their lead and let them go. He didn't kibitz you move by move at all. So he was easy to work for. I thought it was a very stimulating experience because *he didn't try to tell you how to run your business.* He wanted certain results, and he would say, "I think we ought to go in this direction" in the broadest sense, but he permitted you to make the best use of the people you had. That was his real strong point. It's not totally true that he didn't want to do things himself; he just wanted other people to make him look good—he was a good manager.[68]

Fleet Adm. Ernest J. King, Fleet Adm. Chester W. Nimitz, and Adm. Raymond A. Spruance, among America's most important naval leaders in World War II, could not have accomplished their overwhelming responsibilities without delegating. Speaking of King, Nimitz, and Spruance, biographer Thomas B. Buell commented:

> Their philosophy was to tell the subordinate commander what you wanted done, give him the necessary resources, provide as much information as you could about the enemy, and then *let him alone so he could accomplish his mission.* King would upbraid any commander for the sin of oversupervising subordinates with complex, overly detailed directives. *The intent was to encourage the on-scene commander to use his initiative and not to inhibit his freedom of action.* Spruance's personal belief was that the commander responsible for accomplishing the mission should develop the necessary plans; the proper role of the next highest command echelon was to establish the objective and to *suggest* how the objective might be achieved.[69]

In his biography of Admiral Nimitz, E. B. Potter described the admiral's views on delegating as follows:

> A principle of Nimitz's training plan was to give every man as much responsibility as he could handle, which was often a great deal more than the man thought he was capable of handling. By increasing the competence of his junior officers, he could give them responsibilities their immediate seniors were exercising and thus push the latter into higher responsibilities until, at last, he himself could confine his activities to those broad areas of command, administration, and ceremony that only he, as captain, could carry out. *It was Nimitz's abiding rule that he should never do anything his juniors could do,* least of all mere ship handling. "Conning the ship," he said, "is ensigns' work."[70]

The most consistent opponent of interference in the chain of command I found in my examination of naval leadership was Admiral Nimitz. There were occasions when Spruance, his chief of staff, would recommend sending long-range advice to combat commanders. Nimitz always refused. "Leave them alone," he would say. "Looking over their shoulder only inhibits them. As long as the local commanders have the responsibility, they must retain the initiative to do what they think best."[71]

Admiral Spruance had two functions at Pearl Harbor—directing CinCPac and advising Admiral Nimitz. Biographer Potter wrote:

> In his first capacity he was not the bright, harassed, nail-biting chief of staff of the stereotype. Bright he was, *brilliant* is probably a better word, but he never let him-

self become harassed. He was, by his own admission, inclined to be lazy—the kind of smart, indolent character said to make the best commanding officer. *When Nimitz passed details down to Spruance, Spruance promptly passed them on down the chain of command.* Like Nimitz, he was a master organizer, who organized himself as much as possible out of the staff picture. Also like Nimitz, he was *adept at picking men, delegating authority to them, then leaving them alone to perform.*[72]

Admiral Halsey reflected on one of his experiences: "My message to Admiral Bayly, simply informing him that I was proceeding to assist, may sound presumptuous, but it would have been silly to request instructions. *The Admiral himself always pointed out that the man on the spot had so much better information than the man at headquarters, it was impossible for HQ to give proper instructions. This is a lesson that has stood by me all through my naval career.*"[73]

After World War II, as the Soviet threat to America loomed ever greater, Admiral Mitscher was assigned to organize and train the Eighth Fleet. Arleigh Burke was again his chief of staff. "He pushed the responsibility down to give his subordinates just as much responsibility as he could possibly do," Burke said. "He kept the responsibilities that were his, but he gave his subordinates authority and responsibility, and they loved it. This is how he would get so very much done."[74]

Fix the Problem, Not the Blame

General of the Army George C. Marshall, chief of staff in World War II, secretary of state, and secretary of defense, stood by his policy of "Fix the problem, not the blame." It was a significant factor in his leadership success and certainly played a role in the loyalty his subordinates gave to him. We can learn nothing from tragedies if the ensuing investigations attempt to cover up events or channel blame away from those accountable toward someone else or some other agency.

We examined the issue of blame by selectively analyzing events such as the relief of Adm. Husband Kimmel after the surprise attack on Pearl Harbor, the court-martial of Capt. Charles B. McVay III of the USS *Indianapolis,* the refreshing acceptance of the blame for the terrorist attack on the USS *Cole* all the way up the naval chain of command, the indecisiveness of Comdr. Lloyd M. Bucher in surrendering the USS *Pueblo* without a fight, and Adm. William J. Crowe Jr.'s insistence on accepting the responsibility for the mining of the *Bridgeton* and thus ending a media controversy.

Accountability is a must in naval leadership. In speaking about Adm. Hyman Rickover, the father of the nuclear navy, Admiral Watkins offered Rickover's definition of the concept:

> Responsibility is a unique concept. It can only reside and inhere in a single individual. You may share it with others, but your portion is not diminished. You may delegate it, but it is still with you. You can disclaim it, but you cannot divest yourself of it. Even if you do not recognize it or admit its presence, you cannot escape it. If responsibility is rightfully yours, no evasion or ignorance or passing the blame can shift the burden to someone else. Unless you can point your finger at the man who is responsible when something goes wrong, then you have never had anyone who is really responsible.[75]

General Eisenhower understood responsibility as well as any military leader ever has: "Leadership," he told me, "consists of nothing but taking responsibility for everything that goes wrong and giving your subordinates credit for everything that goes well." His best illustration of this was his plan to accept full responsibility for the failure of the June 6, 1941, D-day invasion, had that been necessary. On that day he had in his pocket a note that he planned to read to the press in the event of the invasion's failure. It stated: "Our landings have failed. . . . If any blame or fault attacks to the attempt it is mine alone."[76]

The Role of the Adviser to the Decision Maker

Wartime decision makers generally have strong and dedicated professionals as advisers. One cannot take the advice of such people lightly. When they are all opposed to a top admiral's conclusion, the decision-making process becomes far more difficult. Admiral Nimitz, for example, consulted his staff when making plans to capture Kwajalein, Wotje, and Maloelap. Nimitz wanted to take Kwajalein first, but his staff—Vice Adm. Raymond A. Spruance, Maj. Gen. Holland M. Smith (USMC), and Vice

Adm. Richard K. Turner—were strongly opposed. The earlier invasion of Tarawa had resulted in horrendous losses, and they feared that invading Kwajalein would have the same result. After much serious, even heated, discussion, Nimitz told them Kwajalein was to be it. "If you don't want to do it," he said, "the department will find someone else to do it." They decided they wanted it. Nimitz was right. The invasion was immensely successful with limited casualties.

Extensive interviewing of admirals with responsibility for making life-and-death decisions brought out the fact that these men invariably sought out the best people to do particularly tough jobs. A good leader is always training his or her successor, and these younger leaders train their successors, so leadership development snowballs. The responsibility of the person at the top is to create an environment in which subordinates can use their full horsepower. Part of that is understanding the problems the top person is dealing with, the factors that surround these problems, and the top leader's personal philosophy. A good leader does not surround himself or herself with yes men. One of the grave hazards of command is that too many people will tell a leader what they think he or she wants to hear. A good leader works hard at creating an atmosphere that supports discussion and disagreement. It is not easy. If a commander takes decisive action, subordinates are apt to think it will be held against them if they disagree. The successful commander understands that no one is smart enough to think of everything and values the views of the support staff. Somebody may have an idea or a thought that might change the course of action if the commander knew it. But once the decision is made, all hands are expected to carry out the decision. If an atmosphere of trust has been established, people are more likely to be happy and work well.

Adm. Charles R. Larson learned important lessons about decision making and yes men while serving as an aide to President Richard Nixon:

> The second thing I learned from him and a number of people under whom I served is to convey to my people at every new command that they shouldn't think that just because I'm the admiral that I'm perfect and I'll never make a mistake. I really needed to hear from them if they disagreed with me. I wanted people who have the courage to say, "Wait a minute. Does that really look like that's the right

thing to do? Let's think about this." I looked for two or three people who would challenge me. I found in going back to the rosters of my command that there were a number of people who worked for me in senior advisory positions more than once. Those were the people that felt quite free to come and argue with me. And particularly, when they felt strongly, I was able to close the door and listen to them.[77]

It takes courage to be a decision maker. Some decisions—both in peacetime and war—will cost lives. Many prefer staff positions simply because they want to be involved in decision making but are not willing or able to accept the responsibility for these decisions. It also is inevitable that, sometimes, wrong decisions will be made.

Selflessness

Although this is a study of *naval* leadership, some of the great military leaders of the other services can tell us much about leadership qualities. General of the Army Dwight D. Eisenhower, one of the greatest leaders ever to serve America, faced many challenges on his way to success. In my interview with him I asked about the most necessary quality for a commander. In response, he told me that on June 12, 1944, a week after the D-day invasion, he took Gen. George C. Marshall; Gen. H. H. Arnold, commander of the Army Air Forces; and Adm. Ernest King, the CNO, on an inspection trip. They toured the beachheads in jeeps, stopping at noon at a field mess. As they sat on ammunition boxes eating lunch, Marshall turned suddenly and said, "Eisenhower, you've chosen all these commanders or accepted the ones I suggested, and I have accepted all but one whom you recommended. What's the principal quality you look for?" General Eisenhower told me, "Without thinking, I said *selflessness*. This is what guided my life and my career."[78]

An avid student of history, Eisenhower clearly understood that selflessness is part of the makeup of every good leader; it is a quality dating back to America's first military commander, Gen. George Washington. Eisenhower he told me that the qualities of great leaders "excited" his admiration, but it was in particular "Washington's stamina and patience in adversity, first, and then his indomitable courage, daring, and capacity for self-sacrifice" that he most admired.[79]

The selflessness of America's great naval leaders is evident throughout this book in their own words and in the descriptions of others. Perhaps the most frequently quoted statement from a presidential inaugural address concerns that quality. In 1961, immediately after taking the oath of office, President John F. Kennedy addressed the nation with these inspiring words: "My fellow Americans: Ask not what your country can do for you—ask what you can do for your country." But America's military leaders understood the concept of selflessness long before that.

Henry L. Stimson was a remarkable public servant. He served as secretary of war in the administration of President William Howard Taft from 1909 to 1911, as secretary of state from 1928 to 1932 for President Herbert Hoover, and served again as secretary of war from 1939 to 1945 for President Franklin D. Roosevelt during World War II. After spending four decades in service to his country, he had distinguished two types of public servants: "I had been accustomed throughout my life to classify all public servants into one or the other of two general categories: one, the men who were thinking what they could do for their job; the other, the men who were thinking what the job could do for them." Lawrence Lowell, president of Harvard University, likewise understood selflessness. In 1911 he noted: "A man who desires to do his duty without making any sacrifices for it is like one who seeks to be a soldier without risking his life. He may parade in a uniform in time of peace, but he is not the real stuff that soldiers are made of."[80]

I have collected the thoughts and insights of several hundred key American military leaders, and many of them had insights to offer on selflessness. The chairman of the Joint Chiefs of Staff belongs to all the services. Highly decorated Air Force General George S. Brown was chairman from 1974 to 1978; his career was the epitome of selflessness and sacrifice. A 1941 graduate of West Point, he achieved the rank of full colonel in October 1944, only three years and four months after graduation. He retired in June 1978 after a brilliant career. In one of his final speeches he told a group of ROTC students that a career in the military would require "steadfast dedication and total commitment to the nation and all that it stands for. That dedication must be deep-felt and unwavering." They would also need, he said, a willingness to sacrifice, . . . [to set aside] personal desires, comfort, and security when the safety of the country is at stake. . . . You must find fulfillment in hard work, in giving and sacrifice—and be willing to serve in the absence of expressed appreciation. . . . In America's goals of maintaining peace and preserving freedom lies our inspiration to serve. . . . As men of action we are inclined to show our appreciation more by deeds—by serving to the best of our professional capacity—than by words. As I leave active service, I am moved by the same deep feelings that have sustained me over the years:

By love for this country, which continues to be the world's best hope for
　　freedom;
By gratitude for the opportunities of service and responsibility;
By pride in our people in uniform—those who have gone before and those
　　who remain—who make sacrifices willingly, and who do their arduous and
　　dangerous tasks so magnificently;
By faith in the American people, who when armed with the facts will make dif-
　　ficult choices and do what is right.

　　My life has been split between service to my country and to my family—perhaps at times to the detriment of the latter. However, both remain the objects of my devotion. I am especially grateful to my family, who have accepted the work, the inconveniences and demands of military life . . . ; to good and faithful friends, who have lightened the burdens and shared the joys; to courageous comrades who have shared the sacrifices. They deserve a full measure of the rewards and appreciation with which you have honored me today.[81]

In a speech on February 15, 1977, before the Los Angeles World Affairs Council, Brown observed that one who enters military service "gives up some personal freedoms of choice that civilians enjoy [and] acknowledge[s] that they can be called upon for long hours of work, additional duties, and significant hazards. . . . You put yourself and your family in an environment that may necessitate frequent uprooting; . . . you can be asked to give up your life, if necessary, for your country. All this," he said, "is part of the sacrifice of military service."[82]

Admiral Holloway told me:

The two most important personal attributes of moral character for a naval officer are *integrity* and *dedication*. There are, of course, . . . many other qualities important in life or useful in the pursuit of a chosen vocation, but for a naval officer, the guiding fundamentals that sum it all up are integrity—truthfulness, honor, and the adherence to high moral principle; and dedication—hard work, unselfishness, and courage.

Some years ago, intrigued with the question of what does it take to be a successful leader, I attempted to analyze the biographies of a number of naval heroes. I picked examples from various nationalities in different periods of history, such as Drake, DeTrompe, John Paul Jones, Horatio Nelson, Yamamoto, Nimitz, and Arleigh Burke. I found a wide variance both in their backgrounds and in the career paths that they followed to the top. Even more varied were their physical traits and personalities. However, a single thread was common throughout. In every case, these naval leaders were men of the most profound professional integrity and of absolute dedication to their naval careers. I concluded that these were the main attributes of the character essential to successful naval leadership.[83]

Admiral Burke put into perspective the importance of character, trustworthiness, reliability, and dependability:

When a man is in battle . . . he is absolutely dependent upon other people doing things properly; and it can be a seaman, it can be the captain, who can do things right or wrong, but you're absolutely dependent upon them all doing things right, and doing it right means they have to do it generally in the same way. You have to be able to depend on everybody down the line to do things in a certain way so that you know that . . . you can do your job in your certain way. You must all work together toward the common end. It's got to work this way in battle, people going down to sea in ships do get that way or they lose their ships in war. There are many different parts of the Navy, and sometimes in a destroyer billet, particularly, they don't work enough with one another often enough to know exactly what the other group is going to do. That causes consternation sometimes or just confusion. So there has to be a lot of cross-exchanging of information so that the submariners know what the aviators are doing, the aviators know what the surface people are doing, and they all know what each other can do for the common cause and to help each other. They are all mutually supporting. They have to get the maximum amount of mutual support and yet, at the same time, not depend on support any more than they have to. There's that fine distinction. You shouldn't build your organization so that mutual support is required unless it is absolutely necessary. Every unit should be able to do as much as it can for itself without depending upon anybody else. But you can never do that completely. You're always depended upon.[84]

Command

Adm. Chester W. Nimitz's son, Rear Adm. Chester W. Nimitz Jr., who grew up knowing the senior naval leaders of World War II, observed that all shared at least one character: "their eye was always on the thing that would lead to command; . . . anything else was a diversion they really didn't care too much for."[85]

What does command entail? The previous chapters have examined the qualities a successful commander must possess. A successful commander must be willing to devote twenty-four hours a day, seven days a week, to his or her responsibilities. Spouse and family will often have to take a secondary role to the mission. The commander and his family must be willing to live in a goldfish bowl because their actions will be closely observed by both subordinates and superiors. The commander must be willing to learn, teach, and live the fundamentals necessary to develop his unit and still believe his talents for "bigger things" are not being wasted. He must like to be with young people and able to live with their energy and the problems they create.

Commanders of large units must be able to delegate and must be willing to accept the responsibility for any failures of their subordinates. Command is complex, and the commander must be able to simultaneously handle training, maintenance, tests, administration, inspections, communications, messes, supply, athletics, discipline, job proficiency, awards, and public relations.

The commander must be able to take orders, for no leader is ever really autonomous. A good commander can compete with other military units without losing the spirit of cooperation and the knowledge that all the individual units together make up the whole team. Often he is expected to accomplish the impossible with inadequate means. If things go wrong, the successful commander accepts the blame, even though the failure might rest with his or her staff, subordinates, or superiors. He must be able to do the best he can with whatever he has, which on occasion might be very little. It is the commander's job to inspire subordinates of average abilities to put out to the maximum effort required to build a superior unit.

The responsibility for a unit's success or failure to perform a mission rests with the commander, and failure generally results in relief from command. Command requires a person who can cope, physically and emotionally, with responsibility and strain without losing effectiveness or patience. Often, the only compensation is personal satisfaction. There is generally little reward or glory, particularly in time of peace, and the reward may go to a superior rather than to the person most responsible for the performance of the unit or the accomplishment of the mission.

When the overwhelming tasks, the sacrifice, the pressure, the responsibility, the hard work, and the just and unjust criticism faced by the commander are taken into account, a second question arises: Why do men and women seek command? Although that question is discussed in detail in chapter 11, it is worth reconsidering here. All too often, command means taking the blame and watching the credit for success go to others. Nevertheless, natural leaders seek out command—as if, in Chester Nimitz Jr.'s words, they were born to it. Adm. Kinnaird McKee focused on this crushing responsibility in one of our discussions: "It is cruel, this accountability of good and well-intentioned men. But the choice is that or an end to responsibility, and finally, as the cruel sea has taught us, an end to the trust and confidence in men who lead. For other men will not trust leaders who feel themselves beyond accountability for what they do.[86]

Command at sea is particularly challenging. As Joseph Conrad's brilliant description makes clear, "the captain *is* the ship."

> Only a seaman realizes to what extent an entire ship reflects the personality and ability of one individual, her Commanding Officer. To a landsman this is not understandable, and sometimes it is even difficult for us to comprehend,—but it is so.
>
> A ship at sea is a distant world in herself and in consideration of the protracted and distant operations of the fleet units the Navy must place great power, responsibility and trust in the hands of those leaders chosen for command.

In each ship there is one man who, in the hour of emergency or peril at sea, can turn to no other man. There is one who alone is ultimately responsible for the safe navigation, engineering performance, accurate gunfiring and morale of his ship. He is the Commanding Officer. He is the ship.

This is the most difficult and demanding assignment in the Navy. There is not an instant during his tour of duty as Commanding Officer that he can escape the grasp of command responsibility. His privileges in view of his obligations are most ludicrously small; nevertheless command is the spur which has given the Navy its great leaders.

It is a duty which most richly deserves the highest, time-honored title of the seafaring world—"CAPTAIN."[87]

Why, then, do naval officers seek command? Admiral Crowe thought it the natural goal for a Navy man. "The meaning of life for most Navy men is to go to sea, and the goal of 98 percent of young officers is command. That is what they aspire to . . . a ship commander still takes his organization away from the rest of the world. He enjoys a sense of authority that few other people ever experience."[88]

Admiral Holloway told me: "We are professionals. We want our opportunity to apply what we have learned as subordinate officers. We are self-centered enough to think that we can do a better job. . . . I think ambition is an inherent factor in the events of mankind. Everybody wants to do things a little better."[89]

Admiral Trost's comment to me was, "The Navy gives our junior officers enormous amounts of responsibility and authority, and holds them accountable. . . . That's where you're getting your inspiration—saying to yourself, I want that job. I can do it as well or better than that guy." Trost also told me: "I wanted command first of all because I thought I could do it. It was a challenge. I thought the Navy had trained me for a command. I thought I could lead people. I felt I could successfully run a ship or any other command. . . . I found command is the most satisfying thing I've ever done . . . because you could see the direct results of your own ability."[90]

Admiral Kelso developed his desire for command at the Naval Academy. "When I was a midshipman at the Naval Academy, I didn't know anything about the Navy. When I left the Naval Academy the only thing I cared about, ambition-wise, was to get command. . . . I think most every step in leadership is to get command, then how you perform in command. . . . My command tour was a wonderful tour because under my command we were capable of doing what we were asked to do and produced good results."[91]

Admiral Johnson said, "When you're in command in the Navy, like a ship or a squadron, you really are in command. . . . It's a tremendous responsibility, but it's also a tremendous opportunity." Admiral McKee enjoyed "the opportunity it gives me to work with the young officers and enlisted men who take nuclear warships to sea." Adm. Vern Clark "wanted to prove I could do it." Admiral Moorer said, "I loved responsibility, I loved working with young people. I looked forward to every day. Every day to me was just like a day off."[92]

The lives and careers of the senior admirals examined in this volume reveal a pattern for success that is available to every officer—indeed to every person. Success, up to the limits of one's innate abilities, is available to all who dedicate themselves to their career, who are willing to work long and hard to prepare themselves, who recognize and develop the high character necessary to successful leadership, who love their fellow humans and show concern for their well-being, and who can communicate with other officers in a manner that inspires confidence and devotion to duty.

Notes

Chapter 1. Decision

1. Interview: Gen. Dwight D. Eisenhower with Edgar F. Puryear Jr., May 2, 1962.

2. William D. Leahy, *I Was There* (New York: Whittlesey House, 1995), pp. 2–3.

3. Ibid., pp. 96–97.

4. Ibid., pp. 98–99.

5. Ibid., pp. 101–3.

6. Ibid., p. 105.

7. Emmet P. Forrestal, *Admiral Raymond A. Spruance* (Washington, D.C.: U.S. Government Printing Office, 1966).

8. E. B. Potter, *Nimitz* (Annapolis: Naval Institute Press, 1976), p. 265.

9. Ibid., pp. 221–22.

10. James M. Merrill, *A Sailor's Admiral: A Biography of William F. Halsey* (New York: Thomas Y. Crowell, 1976), p. 32.

11. William F. Halsey and J. Bryan III, *Admiral Halsey's Story* (New York: Whittlesey House, 1947), p. 102.

12. James H. Doolittle, *Doolittle: An Autobiography* (New York: Bantam Books, 1991), p. 5.
13. Merrill, *A Sailor's Admiral*, p. 35.
14. Potter, *Nimitz*, p. 191.
15. Ibid., pp. 196–97.
16. Ibid., p. 197.
17. Ibid.
18. Ibid.
19. Ibid., p. 199.
20. Charles T. Jones and R. Manning Ancell, eds., *Four Star Leadership for Leaders* (Mechanicsburg, Pa.: Executive Books, 1997), p. 11.
21. Ibid., pp. 11–12.
22. Ibid., pp. 10–11.
23. Ibid.
24. Ibid., pp. 13–14.
25. Ibid., p. 10.
26. Oral history: Adm. Arleigh Burke, USN (Ret.), with John T. Mason Jr., November 14, 1972, vol. 5, pp. 21–22, U.S. Naval Institute, Annapolis, Md. [hereinafter USNI].
27. William J. Crowe Jr., *The Line of Fire* (New York: Simon and Schuster, 1993), pp. 265–70.
28. Interviews: Vice Adm. Kent L. Lee, USN (Ret.), with Edgar F. Puryear Jr., January 4, 2001, and several other interviews.
29. Ibid.
30. Oral history: Vice Adm. Kent L. Lee, USN (Ret.), with Paul Stillwell, November 18, 1987, p. 288, USNI.
31. Ibid., December 21, 1987, pp. 476, 477, 548, 549.
32. Ibid., pp. 617, 719.
33. Ibid., pp. 718–19.
34. Interviews: Adm. Thomas B. Hayward, USN (Ret.), with Edgar F. Puryear Jr., May 23, 2001, and January 5, 2003, and numerous other interviews.
35. Interview: Adm. Stansfield Turner, USN (Ret.), with Edgar F. Puryear Jr., April 3, 2001.
36. Interviews: Adm. Carlisle A. H. Trost, USN (Ret.), with Edgar F. Puryear Jr., July 18, 2001, and September 13, 2001.
37. Ibid.
38. Ibid.
39. Interview: Adm. Jay L. Johnson, USN (Ret.), with Edgar F. Puryear Jr., September 21, 2001.
40. Ibid.

41. Ibid.

42. Interview: Adm. Henry G. Chiles Jr., USN (Ret.), with Edgar Puryear Jr., February 21, 2001.

43. Interview: Adm. Charles R. Larson, USN (Ret.), with Edgar Puryear Jr., April 10, 2001.

44. Ibid.

45. Ibid.

46. Interviews: Adm. James L. Holloway III, with Edgar F. Puryear Jr., July 18, 2001, and numerous other interviews.

47. Harry S. Truman, *Year of Decision* (Garden City, N.Y.: Doubleday, 1955), p. ix.

48. Walter Isaacson and Evan Thomas, *The Wise Men* (New York: Simon and Schuster, 1986), p. 255.

49. Ibid., p. 256.

50. Walter B. Smith, *Eisenhower's Six Great Decisions: Europe, 1944–1945* (New York: Longmans, Green, 1956), p. 35.

51. Dwight D. Eisenhower, *Crusade in Europe* (New York: Doubleday, 1948), p. 251.

52. Interview: Catherine Nimitz Lay with U.S. Naval Institute, February 16, 1970, p. 94.

53. Burke oral history, October 9, 1980, pp. 302–4.

54. Edgar F. Puryear Jr., *Stars in Flight: A Study in Air Force Character and Leadership* (Novato, Calif.: Presidio Press, 1981), p. 276.

Chapter 2. Sixth Sense

1. Interview: Gen. Dwight D. Eisenhower with Edgar F. Puryear Jr., May 2, 1962, emphasis added.

2. E. B. Potter, *Nimitz* (Annapolis: Naval Institute Press, 1976), p. 78.

3. Ibid., pp. 78, 85, 104, 192–93.

4. Ibid., p. 223.

5. Ibid., p. 225.

6. Ibid., p. 373.

7. William F. Halsey and J. Bryan III, *Admiral Halsey's Story* (New York: Whittlesey House, 1947), p. 47.

8. James M. Merrill, *A Sailor's Admiral: A Biography of William F. Halsey* (New York: Thomas Y. Crowell, 1976), pp. 57–58, emphasis added.

9. Adm. Arleigh Burke, *Readers Digest*, September 1973, p. 120.

10. Oral history: Adm. Arleigh Burke, USN (Ret.), with John T. Mason Jr., November 21, 1978, pp. 268–69, USNI.

11. Ibid., January 12, 1973, pp. 211, 213.

12. Oral history: Adm. Thomas H. Moorer, USN (Ret.), with John T. Mason Jr., January 13, 1976, pp. 684–86, USNI.

13. Ibid., p. 686.
14. Ibid., pp. 963–64.
15. Ibid., August 17, 1976, pp. 909–10.
16. Ibid., April 17, 1975, p. 291.
17. Ibid., pp. 505–6.
18. Interviews: Adm. James L. Holloway III with Edgar F. Puryear Jr., July 18, 2001, and numerous other interviews.
19. Ibid.
20. Ibid.
21. Interview: Adm. Robert L. J. Long, USN (Ret.), with Paul Stillwell, February 26, 1993, pp. 286–87.
22. Ibid.
23. Interviews: Adm. James D. Watkins, USN (Ret.), with Edgar F. Puryear Jr., February 2, 2001, and January 7, 2003.
24. Interviews: Adm. Carlisle A. H. Trost, USN (Ret.), with Edgar F. Puryear Jr., July 18, 2001, and September 13, 2001.
25. Interview: Adm. Frank B. Kelso II, USN (Ret.), with Edgar F. Puryear Jr., March 28, 2001.
26. Interview: Adm. Jay L. Johnson, USN (Ret.), with Edgar F. Puryear Jr., September 21, 2001.
27. Interview: Adm. James A. Lyons, USN (Ret.), with Edgar F. Puryear Jr., April 27, 2001.
28. Interview: Adm. Stansfield Turner, USN (Ret.), with Edgar F. Puryear Jr., April 3, 2001.
29. Ibid.
30. Interview: Adm. Henry G. Chiles, USN (Ret.), with Edgar F. Puryear Jr., February 21, 2001.
31. Ibid.
32. Ibid.
33. Interview: Charles R. Larson, USN (Ret.), with Edgar F. Puryear Jr., April 10, 2001.
34. Ibid.
35. Interview: Adm. Kinnaird McKee, USN (Ret.), with Edgar F. Puryear Jr., September 26, 2001.
36. Eisenhower interview.
37. Interview: Gen. Omar N. Bradley with Edgar F. Puryear Jr., February 15, 1963.

Chapter 3. Yes Men

1. William D. Leahy, *I Was There* (New York: Whittlesey House, 1950), p. 95.
2. E. B. Potter, *Nimitz* (Annapolis: Naval Institute Press, 1976), p. 31.
3. Ibid., pp. 9–10.

4. Ibid., pp. 322–23.

5. Ibid., pp. 326–27.

6. Ibid., p. 292.

7. Ibid., p. 382.

8. Ibid., p. 216.

9. William F. Halsey and J. Bryan III, *Admiral Halsey's Story* (New York: Whittlesey House, 1947), pp. 188–89.

10. Oral history: Adm. Arleigh Burke, USN (Ret.), with John T. Mason Jr., November 24, 1972, pp. 66–69; June 21, 1979, pp. 110–18, USNI.

11. Ibid., June 21, 1979, 110–18.

12. Ibid., pp. 116–18.

13. Ibid., May 3, 1979, pp. 3–4.

14. Ibid., pp. 12–15.

15. Ibid., pp. 154–55.

16. Ibid., June 21, 1979, p. 155, emphasis added.

17. Ibid., p. 159.

18. Ibid., pp. 192–94, emphasis added.

19. Ibid., pp. 227–28.

20. Ibid., November 24, 1972, pp. 62–64, emphasis added.

21. Ibid., pp. 53–54.

22. Ibid., November 19, 1972, pp. 25–26.

23. Ibid., pp. 103–6, emphasis added.

24. Ibid., pp. 29–37.

25. Ibid., p. 22.

26. Ibid., June 21, 1979, pp. 125–27.

27. Omar N. Bradley and Clay Blair, *A General's Life: An Autobiography by General of the Army Omar Bradley* (New York: Simon and Schuster, 1983), p. 502.

28. Ibid.

29. Ibid., p. 714.

30. Jeffrey G. Barlow, *Revolt of the Admirals: The Fight for Naval Aviation (1945–1950)* (Washington, D.C.: Brassy, 1998), p. 254.

31. *Time*, October 24, 1949.

32. Arthur W. Radford, *From Pearl Harbor to Vietnam: The Memoirs of Admiral Arthur W. Radford* (Stanford, Calif.: Stanford University Press, 1980), pp. 205–6.

33. Ibid., pp. 205–7.

34. Ibid., pp. 209–10.

35. Ibid., p. 211, 214.

36. Bradley and Blair, *A General's Life*, p. 507.

37. Radford, *From Pearl Harbor to Vietnam*, pp. 208–10.

38. Ibid.
39. Bradley and Blair, *A General's Life,* p. 659.
40. Radford, *From Pearl Harbor to Vietnam,* p. 312.
41. Ibid., pp. 313–15, emphasis added.
42. Ibid., p. 323.
43. Oral history: Adm. Felix B. Stump, Columbia University, p. 245; and Barlow, *Revolt of the Admirals,* p. 279.
44. Barlow, *Revolt of the Admirals,* pp. 279–80.
45. Ibid.
46. David McCullough, *Truman* (New York: Simon and Schuster, 1992), p. 798; Barlow, *Revolt of the Admirals,* pp. 174–76.
47. Bradley and Blair, *A General's Life,* p. 503.
48. Ibid.
49. Ibid.
50. McCullough, *Truman,* pp. 792–93.
51. Ruby Abramson, *Spanning the Century: The Life of W. Averell Harriman, 1891–1986* (New York: William Morrow, 1992), pp. 457, 456.
52. McCullough, *Truman,* pp. 741–42.
53. Dean Acheson, *Present at the Creation* (New York: W. W. Norton, 1969), pp. 373–74.
54. McCullough, *Truman,* p. 798.
55. *New York Times,* August 2, 1961.
56. Ibid.
57. *Washington Post,* May 7 and 8, 1963.
58. Robert William Love Jr., ed., *The Chiefs of Naval Operations* (Annapolis: Naval Institute Press, 1980), p. 329.
59. Ibid., p. 326.
60. Ibid., p. 324.
61. *New York Times,* May 8, 1963.
62. *Washington Post,* May 8, 1963.
63. Ibid., emphasis added.
64. Ibid.
65. *Washington Post,* May 7, 1963.
66. *New York Times,* May 11, 1963.
67. Interviews: Adm. James L. Holloway III, USN (Ret.), with Edgar Puryear Jr., July 18, 2001, June 20, 2002, and numerous other interviews.
68. Ibid.
69. Ibid.
70. Interview: Adm. William J. Crowe Jr., USN (Ret.), with Edgar Puryear Jr., May 16, 1997.

71. Interviews: Adm. Robert L. J. Long, with Edgar F. Puryear Jr., February 23, 2001, and May 21, 2001.

72. Interview: Adm. Stansfield Turner, USN (Ret.), with Edgar F. Puryear Jr., April 3, 2001.

73. Ibid.

74. Interview: Adm. Frank B. Kelso II, USN (Ret.), with Edgar F. Puryear Jr., March 28, 2001.

75. Interviews: Adm. Carlisle A. H. Trost, USN (Ret.), with Edgar F. Puryear Jr., July 18, 2001, and September 13, 2001.

76. Interview: Adm. James. D. Watkins, USN (Ret.), with Edgar F. Puryear Jr., February 2, 2001.

77. Interview: Adm. Charles P. Larson, USN (Ret.), with Edgar F. Puryear Jr., April 10, 2001.

78. Interview: Adm. Jay L. Johnson, USN (Ret.), with Edgar F. Puryear Jr., September 21, 2001.

79. Interview: Adm. Henry G. Chiles, USN (Ret.), with Edgar F. Puryear Jr., February 21, 2001.

80. Interview: Adm. Kinnaird R. McKee, USN (Ret.), with David Winkler, March 21, 2001, pp. 30–32; and interviews with Edgar F. Puryear Jr. on February 23, 2001, and September 26, 2001.

81. Holloway interviews.

Chapter 4. Books: The Importance of Reading

1. Interview: Gen. Dwight D. Eisenhower with Edgar F. Puryear Jr., May 2, 1963.

2. Dwight D. Eisenhower, *At Ease* (Garden City, N.Y.: Doubleday, 1967), pp. 39–41.

3. Richard Brookheiser, *Founding Father: Rediscovering George Washington* (New York: Free Press, 1996), p. 139.

4. Ibid., p. 137.

5. Ibid., p. 140, emphasis added.

6. Catherine Drinker Bowen, *The Most Dangerous Man in America* (Boston: Little, Brown, 1974), p. ix.

7. Benjamin Franklin, *The Autobiography of Benjamin Franklin* (New York: Barnes and Noble, 1994), p. 13.

8. Ibid., p. 15.

9. Ibid., pp. 18, 89.

10. Ibid., pp. 113–14, 121–22.

11. Kenneth Ray Young, *The General's General: The Life and Times of Arthur MacArthur* (Boulder, Colo.: Westview Press, 1994), p. 302.

12. Ibid., p. 314.

13. Ibid., p. 323.

14. Douglas MacArthur, *Reminiscences* (New York: McGraw-Hill, 1964), p. 31.

15. William Manchester, *American Caesar* (Boston: Little, Brown, 1978), p. 23.

16. Ibid., p. 177.

17. Ibid., p. 324.

18. Ibid., p. 145.

19. Eisenhower interview.

20. Ibid.

21. Ibid.

22. David Eisenhower, *Eisenhower: At War 1943–1945* (London: Collins, 1986), p. 57.

23. George C. Marshall, *Interviews and Reminiscences*, with Forrest C. Pogue (Lexington, Va.: George C. Marshall Research Foundation, 1991), p. 67.

24. Ibid., pp. 54–55, 58.

25. Ibid., pp. 95–96.

26. Omar N. Bradley and Clay Blair, *A General's Life: An Autobiography by General of the Army Omar Bradley* (New York: Simon and Schuster, 1983), p. 17.

27. Ibid., pp. 17–19.

28. Ibid., p. 38.

29. Ibid., pp. 47, 53–54.

30. Interview: Gen. Omar N. Bradley, with Edgar F. Puryear Jr., February 15, 1963.

31. Interview: Gen. Matthew Ridgway with Lt. Col. John M. Belair, November 24, 1971.

32. Ibid.

33. E. B. Potter, *Nimitz* (Annapolis: Naval Institute Press, 1976), pp. 135, 134, 146.

34. Ibid., p. 175.

35. Ibid., p. 383.

36. Ibid., p. 455.

37. Emmet P. Forrestal, *Admiral Raymond Spruance* (Washington, D.C.: U.S. Government Printing Office, 1966), p. 7, emphasis added.

38. Thomas B. Buell, *The Quiet Warrior: A Biography of Admiral Raymond A. Spruance* (Boston: Little, Brown, 1974), pp. 37, 39, 123.

39. Ibid., p. 213.

40. Ibid., pp. 345–46.

41. Ibid., p. 348.

42. E. B. Potter, *Admiral Arleigh Burke* (New York: Random House, 1990), p. 4.

43. Ibid., p. 121, emphasis added.

44. Oral history: Adm. Arleigh Burke, USN (Ret.), with John T. Mason Jr., May 9, 1979, USNI.

45. Potter, *Admiral Arleigh Burke*, p. 298.

46. Burke oral history, January 11, 1979, pp. 340–42.

47. Ibid., December 12, 1972, pp. 189–90.

48. Oral history: Adm. Thomas H. Moorer, USN (Ret.), with John T. Mason Jr., September 15, 1975, vol. 1, pp. 506–7, USNI.

49. Ibid., p. 507.

50. Ibid., pp. 32–36, 62.

51. Interviews: Adm. James L. Holloway III, with Edgar F. Puryear Jr., July 18, 2001, and numerous other interviews.

52. Interview: Adm. Thomas B. Hayward, USN (Ret.), with Edgar F. Puryear Jr., May 23, 2001.

53. Interviews: Adm. Carlisle A. H. Trost, USN (Ret.), with Edgar F. Puryear Jr., July 18, 2001, and September 13, 2001.

54. Interview: Adm. Jay L. Johnson, USN (Ret.), with Edgar F. Puryear Jr., September 21, 2001.

55. Interview: Adm. Stansfield Turner, USN (Ret.), with Edgar F. Puryear Jr., April 3, 2001.

56. Oral history: Vice Adm. Kent L. Lee, USN (Ret.), with Paul Stillwell, December 14, 1987, vol. 2, p. 402, USNI.

57. Ibid., pp. 331, 335.

58. Ibid., pp. 334–35.

59. Interview: Vice Adm. Kent L. Lee, USN (Ret.), with Edgar F. Puryear Jr., January 4, 2001.

60. Lee oral history, November 16, 1987, vol. 1, pp. 304–5.

61. Krassimira J. Zourkova, *Princeton University Alumni Magazine,* spring 1997.

62. Edgar Puryear Jr., *American Generalship: Character Is Everything* (Novato, Calif.: Presidio Press, 2000), pp. 182–83.

Chapter 5. Mentorship

1. Interview: Gen. Edward C. Meyer, USA (Ret.), with Edgar F. Puryear Jr., July 14, 1997.

2. E. B. Potter, *Nimitz* (Annapolis: Naval Institute Press, 1976), pp. 129–30.

3. Ibid., pp. 130–31.

4. Ibid., p. 132.

5. Ibid., pp. 138–39, 141.

6. Ernest J. King, *Fleet Admiral King: A Naval Record* (New York: W. W. Norton, 1952), p. 193.

7. Oral history: Adm. Thomas H. Moorer, USN (Ret.), with John T. Mason Jr., February 10, 1975, vol. 1, pp. 19–20, USNI.

8. Ibid., p. 20.

9. Ibid., pp. 22–23.

10. Ibid., pp. 26–29.

11. Ibid., pp. 25–26.

12. Ibid., May 31, 1981, pp. 1581–82.

13. Ibid., March 3, 1981, pp. 1345, 1595–97.

14. Ibid., pp. 1600–1601.

15. Ibid., pp. 350–53.

16. Ibid., May 9, 1975, pp. 374–75; interviews: Adm. Thomas H. Moorer, USN (Ret.), with Edgar Puryear Jr., March 21, 2003, and numerous other personal interviews.

17. Moorer oral history, pp. 1567–72.

18. Oral history: Adm. Arleigh Burke, USN (Ret.), May 3, 1979, pp. 28–31, USNI.

19. Ibid., pp. 93–94.

20. Interviews: Adm. James L. Holloway III, with Edgar F. Puryear Jr., July 18, 2001, and numerous other interviews.

21. Ibid.

22. Ibid.

23. William J. Crowe Jr., *The Line of Fire* (New York: Simon and Schuster, 1993), p. 34; and interview with Edgar F. Puryear Jr., November 13, 2000.

24. Interview: Adm. Robert L. J. Long, USN (Ret.), with Paul Stillwell, February 26, 1993, p. 143.

25. Ibid., pp. 233–36, 305.

26. Ibid., pp. 212–13.

27. Interviews: Adm. James D. Watkins, USN (Ret.), with Edgar F. Puryear Jr., February 2, 2001, and January 7, 2003.

28. Ibid.

29. Interview: Adm. Stansfield Turner, USN (Ret.), with Edgar F. Puryear Jr., April 3, 2001.

30. Ibid.

31. Interview: Adm. Frank B. Kelso II, USN (Ret.), with Edgar F. Puryear Jr., March 28, 2001.

32. Ibid.

33. Ibid.

34. Interviews: Adm. Carlisle A. H. Trost, USN (Ret.), with Edgar F. Puryear Jr., July 18, 2001, and September 13, 2001.

35. Interview: Adm. Charles R. Larson, USN (Ret.), with Edgar F. Puryear Jr., April 10, 2001.

36. Interview: Adm. Jay L. Johnson, USN (Ret.), with Edgar F. Puryear Jr., September 21, 2001.

37. King, *Fleet Admiral King,* p. 20.

38. Trost interviews.

39. Long interview.

40. Holloway interviews.

41. Interviews: Adm. Thomas B. Hayward, USN (Ret.), with Edgar Puryear Jr., May 23, 2001, and January 5, 2003.

42. Interview: Adm. Kinnaird R. McKee, USN (Ret.), with Edgar Puryear Jr., February 23, 2001.

43. Oral history: Adm. Thomas H. Moorer, USN (Ret.), with John T. Mason Jr., February 10, 1975, pp. 38–39, USNI.

44. Burke oral history, June 21, 1979, pp. 187–89.

45. Interview: Adm. Jay L. Johnson, USN (Ret.), with Edgar Puryear Jr., September 21, 2001.

46. Ibid.; interview: Adm. Charles R. Larson, USN (Ret.), with Edgar Puryear Jr., April 10, 2001.

47. Ibid.

48. Interview: Adm. William N. Smith, USN (Ret.), with Edgar Puryear Jr., July 26, 2001.

49. Interview: Adm. Paul David Miller, USN (Ret.), with Edgar Puryear Jr., July 25, 2001.

50. Interviews: Adm. Kinnaird McKee with Edgar Puryear Jr., February 23, 2001, and September 26, 2001.

Chapter 6. Consideration

1. Interviews: Adm. James L. Holloway III, with Edgar Puryear Jr., July 18, 2001, and numerous other interviews.

2. E. B. Potter, *Nimitz* (Annapolis: Naval Institute Press, 1976), p. 21.

3. Interview: Rear Adm. William Waldo Drake, USN (Ret.), with Etta-Belle Kitcher, June 15, 1969, pp. 4–5.

4. Potter, *Nimitz,* p. 55.

5. Ibid., p. 17.

6. Ibid.

7. Ibid., p. 239; Thomas B. Buell, *The Quiet Warrior: A Biography of Admiral Raymond A. Spruance* (Boston: Little, Brown, 1974), p. 182.

8. Ibid.

9. Potter, *Nimitz,* p. 239.

10. Interview: H. Arthur Lamar with John T. Mason Jr., May 3, 1970, p. 29, USNI.

11. Potter, *Nimitz,* p. 167.

12. Drake interview, pp. 12–13.

13. Interview: Vice Adm. Lloyd M. Mustin, USN (Ret.), with John T. Mason Jr., March 10, 1970, p. 6, USNI.

14. Lamar interview, pp. 83–84.
15. Ibid.
16. Potter, *Nimitz,* p. 398.
17. Lamar interview, p. 78.
18. Potter, *Nimitz,* p. 354.
19. Ibid., p. 391.
20. Ibid., p. 224.
21. Ibid., p. 391.
22. Ibid., p. 400.
23. Ibid., p. 416.
24. Ibid., p. 429.
25. Ibid., p. 427.
26. Interview: Rear Adm. Chester W. Nimitz Jr. with John T. Mason Jr., April 14, 1969, pp. 1–2, USNI.
27. William F. Halsey and J. Bryan III, *Admiral Halsey's Story* (New York: Whittlesey House, 1947), p. xvi.
28. Ibid., p. 132.
29. Potter, *Nimitz,* p. 189.
30. Halsey and Bryan, *Admiral Halsey's Story,* pp. 165–66.
31. Buell, *The Quiet Warrior,* p. 169.
32. Ibid.
33. Oral history: Adm. Arleigh Burke, USN (Ret.), with John T. Mason Jr., November 14, 1972, vol. 5, pp. 19–20, USNI.
34. Ibid., March 1, 1979, pp. 545–46.
35. Ibid., May 3, 1979, p. 57.
36. Ibid., November 14, 1972, pp. 14–15.
37. Ibid., pp. 64–65.
38. Ibid., August 30, 1979, pp. 306–7.
39. Ibid., December 12, 1972, pp. 204–5.
40. Charles T. Jones and R. Manning Ancell, eds. *Four-Star Leadership for Leaders* (Mechanicsburg, Pa.: Executive Books, 1997), p. 15.
41. Interviews: Adm. Thomas H. Moorer, USN (Ret.), with Edgar Puryear Jr., March 21, 2003, and numerous other personal interviews.
42. Oral history: Adm. Thomas H. Moorer, USN (Ret.), with John T. Mason Jr., November 29, 1976, p. 1059, USNI.
43. Ibid., February 25, 1976, pp. 739–40.
44. Ibid., January 13, 1976, p. 686.
45. Ibid., February 21, 1975, p. 77.
46. Ibid., August 17, 1976, p. 892.
47. Moorer interviews.

48. Moorer oral history, January 13, 1976, p. 688.

49. Ibid., p. 694.

50. Ibid., April 11, 1975, pp. 226–27.

51. Holloway interviews.

52. Ibid., July 18, 2001.

53. Interview: Adm. Thomas B. Hayward, USN (Ret.), with Edgar F. Puryear Jr., January 5, 2003.

54. Interview: Adm. James D. Watkins, USN (Ret.), with Edgar F. Puryear Jr., January 7, 2003.

55. Interview: Adm. Frank B. Kelso II, USN (Ret.), with Edgar F. Puryear Jr., March 28, 2001.

56. Interviews: Adm. Carlisle A. H. Trost, USN (Ret.), with Edgar F. Puryear Jr., July 18, 2001, and September 13, 2001.

57. Interview: Adm. Robert L. J. Long, USN (Ret.), with Paul Stillwell, March 5, 1993, p. 376, USNI.

58. Ibid., pp. 361–62.

59. Interview: Adm. Charles R. Larson, USN (Ret.), with Edgar F. Puryear Jr., April 10, 2001.

60. Ibid.

61. Interview: Adm. Stanfield Turner, USN (Ret.), with Edgar F. Puryear Jr., April 3, 2001.

62. Interview: Vice Adm. Kent L. Lee, with Edgar F. Puryear Jr., January 4, 2001.

63. Interviews: Adm. James L. Holloway III, USN (Ret.), with Edgar F. Puryear Jr., September 18, 2001, and numerous other interviews.

64. Moorer interviews.

Chapter 7. Delegation

1. William D. Leahy, *I Was There* (New York: Whittlesey House, 1950), p. 97.

2. Ibid., pp. 103–4.

3. Ibid., p. 4.

4. Thomas B. Buell, *The Quiet Warrior: A Biography of Admiral Raymond A. Spruance* (Boston: Little, Brown, 1974), p. 136, emphasis added.

5. E. B. Potter, *Nimitz* (Annapolis: Naval Institute Press, 1976), pp. 47, 156.

6. Interview: Rear Adm. Odale D. Waters Jr., USN (Ret.), with John T. Mason Jr., July 14, 1969, pp. 4–5, USNI.

7. Interview: H. Arthur Lamar with John T. Mason Jr., May 3, 1970, pp. 59–60, USNI.

8. Interview: Capt. James T. Lay, USN (Ret.), with U.S. Naval Institute, February 16, 1970, pp. 3–6, USNI.

9. Potter, *Nimitz*, p. 10, emphasis added.

10. Ibid., p. 43.
11. Ibid.
12. Ibid., pp. 336, 337.
13. Buell, *The Quiet Warrior*, p. 87.
14. Ibid., p. 88.
15. Ibid., pp. 75–76.
16. Ibid., p. 89.
17. Ibid., p. 88.
18. Oral history: Adm. Thomas H. Moorer, USN (Ret.), with John T. Mason Jr., May 9, 1975, vol. 1, p. 402, USNI.
19. Potter, *Nimitz*, p. 373.
20. Ibid., p. 371.
21. Ibid., pp. 393–94.
22. Ibid., pp. 229, 253.
23. Buell, *The Quiet Warrior*, pp. 173, 219.
24. Ibid., p. 183.
25. Ibid.
26. Ibid., p. 338.
27. Ibid., p. 252.
28. Ibid., p. 245.
29. William F. Halsey and J. Bryan III, *Admiral Halsey's Story* (New York: Whittlesey House, 1947), pp. 33, 34.
30. Ibid., pp. 72–74.
31. Ibid., pp. 105–6.
32. Ibid., p. 136.
33. Potter, *Nimitz*, pp. 196–200.
34. Ibid., p. 197.
35. Oral history: Adm. Arleigh Burke, USN (Ret.), with John T. Mason Jr., pp. 261–66, USNI.
36. Ibid., March 1, 1979.
37. Ibid., pp. 480–90.
38. Moorer oral history, August 17, 1976, pp. 910–11; June 8, 1981, pp. 1638–39.
39. Interviews: Adm. James L. Holloway III, with Edgar F. Puryear Jr., July 18, 2001, and numerous other interviews.
40. Interviews: Adm. James D. Watkins, with Edgar F. Puryear Jr., February 2, 2001, and January 7, 2003.
41. Ibid.
42. Interview: Adm. Jay L. Johnson, USN (Ret.), with Edgar F. Puryear Jr., September 21, 2001.

43. Interview: Adm. Robert L. J. Long, USN (Ret.), with Paul Stillwell, February 26, 1993, p. 200.

44. Interview: James D. Holloway III, with Edgar F. Puryear Jr., July 18, 2001.

Chapter 8. Fix the Problem, Not the Blame

1. Finding XVII, Navy Court of Inquiry, July 24–October 19, 1944, quoted in Husband E. Kimmel, *Admiral Kimmel's Story* (Chicago: Henry Regnery, 1954), emphasis added.

2. Ibid.

3. Ibid., emphasis added.

4. Husband E. Kimmel, *Admiral Kimmel's Story* (Chicago: Henry Regnery, 1954), pp. 170, 171, 172, 184–85, emphasis added.

5. Ibid., p. 185, emphasis added.

6. Ibid.

7. James O. Richardson, *On the Treadmill to Pearl Harbor* (Washington, D.C.: Navy History Division, Department of the Navy, 1973), pp. 442, 449–50, 453–54, 455–56, emphasis added.

8. Kimmel, *Admiral Kimmel's Story*, pp. 147–50, 151–57.

9. Ibid., pp. 186–87.

10. Ibid., pp. 182–83.

11. Quoted in ibid.

12. Quoted in ibid.

13. Edwin P. Hoyt, *Yamamoto: The Man Who Planned Pearl Harbor* (New York: Time Warner Books, 1991), p. 179.

14. Memorandum for the Deputy Secretary of Defense from Edwin S. Dorn entitled "Advancement of Rear Admiral Kimmel and Major General Short," December 15, 1995.

15. William F. Halsey and J. Bryan III, *Admiral Halsey's Story* (New York: Whittlesey House, 1947), pp. 133–34.

16. Don Kurzman, *Left to Die: The Tragedy of the USS Juneau* (New York: Pocket Books, 1994), pp. 144, 147, 163, 169, 187.

17. Halsey and Bryan, *Admiral Halsey's Story*, p. 134.

18. Kurzman, *Left to Die*, p. 233.

19. Ibid., pp. 233, 234.

20. Richard F. Newcomb, *Abandon Ship! The Saga of the USS Indianapolis, the Navy's Greatest Sea Disaster* (New York: HarperCollins, 2000), pp. ix–x.

21. Hearing before the Committee on Armed Services, U.S. Senate, 106th Congress, 1st session, September 14, 1999 (Washington, D.C.: U.S. Government Printing Office, 2000), p. 36; paragraph integrity not maintained for quotations from this source.

22. Ibid., p. 93.

23. Ibid., pp. 6, 80–81, 83–84, 88, 89, 101–2, emphasis added.

24. Ibid., p. 88.

25. Ibid., pp. 87–88.

26. Ibid., p. 82.

27. Ibid., p. 124, emphasis added.

28. Ibid., p. 100, emphasis added.

29. Ibid., p. 99.

30. Ibid., p. 86.

31. Ibid., pp. 91, 95, 96.

32. Ibid., pp. 12–17.

33. Dan Kurzman, *Fatal Voyage: The Sinking of the USS* Indianapolis (New York: Atheneum, 1990), pp. 145, 279–80.

34. Oral history: Adm. Thomas H. Moorer, USN (Ret.), with John T. Mason Jr., September 30, 1975, p. 524, USNI.

35. Oral history: Adm. Arleigh Burke, USN (Ret.), with John T. Mason Jr., January 12, 1973, pp. 216–19, USNI.

36. Ibid., November 24, 1972, pp. 176–78.

37. Ibid., January 12, 1973, pp. 174–75.

38. Interviews: Adm. William J. Crowe Jr., with Edgar F. Puryear Jr., May 16, 1997, and November 13, 2000.

39. Interviews: Adm. James L. Holloway III, with Edgar F. Puryear Jr., July 18, 2001, and numerous other interviews.

40. Interviews: Adm. Carlisle A. H. Trost, USN (Ret.), with Edgar F. Puryear Jr., July 18, 2001, and September 13, 2001.

41. Interview: Adm. Jay L. Johnson., USN (Ret.), with Edgar F. Puryear Jr., September 21, 2001.

42. Interview: Adm. Charles R. Larson, USN (Ret.), with Edgar F. Puryear Jr., April 10, 2001.

43. Daniel V. Gallery, *The* Pueblo *Incident* (Garden City, N.Y.: Doubleday, 1970), p. 83, emphasis added.

44. Special Subcommittee on the USS *Pueblo, Inquiry into the USS* Pueblo *and EC-121 Plane Incidents,* 91st Congress, 1st session, July 28, 1969, lt. A.S.C. No. 91-10 (Washington, D.C.: Government Printing Office), p. 737.

45. Lloyd M. Bucher, *Bucher: My Story* (Garden City, N.Y.: Doubleday, 1970), p. 192.

46. Ibid., pp. 242–46.

47. U.S. Department of Defense, USS *Cole* Commission Report, Executive Summary, January 9, 2001.

48. Ibid.

49. Ibid.

50. Ibid.

51. Ibid.

Chapter 9. Rickover and Zumwalt: Contrast and Contradiction

1. Sherry Sontag and Christopher Drew, *Blind Man's Bluff: The Untold Story of American Submarine Espionage* (New York: Perseus Books, 1998), cover.

2. Quoted in Norman Polmar and Thomas B. Allen, *Rickover* (New York: Simon and Schuster, 1982), p. 203.

3. Ibid., p. 204.

4. Ibid., p. 214.

5. Interview: Adm. Henry G. Chiles, with Edgar F. Puryear Jr., February 21, 2001.

6. Interviews: Adm. Thomas H. Moorer, USN (Ret.), with Edgar F. Puryear Jr., April 23, 2002, March 21, 2003, and numerous other personal interviews.

7. Interviews: Adm. William J. Crowe Jr., with Edgar F. Puryear Jr., November 11–13, 2000.

8. Interviews: Adm. James L. Holloway III, USN (Ret.), with Edgar F. Puryear Jr., July 18, 2001, and numerous other interviews.

9. Elmo R. Zumwalt Jr., *On Watch* (New York: New York Times Book Company, 1976), pp. 85, 98, 100.

10. Ibid., p. 108.

11. Ibid., p. 107.

12. Holloway interviews.

13. Interviews: Adm. Thomas B. Hayward, USN (Ret.), with Edgar F. Puryear Jr., May 5, 2001, and January 5, 2003.

14. Interviews: Adm. James B. Watkins, USN (Ret.), with Edgar F. Puryear Jr., February 2, 2001, and January 7, 2003.

15. Interview: Adm. Henry G. Chiles, with Edgar Puryear Jr., February 21, 2001.

16. Watkins interviews.

17. Hayward interviews.

18. Sontag and Drew, *Blind Man's Bluff,* pp. 137–38.

19. Interviews: Adm. Kinnaird R. McKee, USN (Ret.), with Edgar F. Puryear Jr., February 23, 2001, and September 26, 2001.

20. Ibid.

21. Ibid.

22. Ibid.

23. Interview: Adm. Bruce DeMars, USN (Ret.), with Edgar F. Puryear Jr., January 4, 2001.

24. Interview: Adm. Frank B. Kelso II, USN (Ret.), with Edgar F. Puryear Jr., March 28, 2001.

25. Interview: Adm. Steven St. Angelo White, USN (Ret.), with Edgar Puryear Jr., May 19, 2000.

26. Ibid.

27. Burt Barnes, *Washington Post,* July 9, 1986.

28. Watkins interviews; Watkins speech at meeting celebrating 50th anniversary of the Naval Reactors organization, August 30, 1998.

29. Oral history: Adm. Thomas H. Moorer, USN (Ret.), with John T. Mason Jr., November 29, 1976, p. 1059; May 13, 1981, pp. 1603–4, USNI.

30. Norman Friedman, article on Elmo Zumwalt Jr. in *The Chiefs of Naval Operations,* ed. Robert W. Love Jr. (Annapolis: Naval Institute Press, 1980), p. 369.

31. Frederick H. Hartman, *Naval Renaissance: The U.S. Navy in the 1980s* (Annapolis: Naval Institute Press, 1990), p. 35.

32. Zumwalt, *On Watch,* p. 192.

33. Ibid., p. 172.

34. Hartman, *Naval Renaissance,* p. 18.

35. Zumwalt, *On Watch,* pp. 179–80, 182.

36. Ibid., p. 193.

37. Ibid., pp. 178–79.

38. Friedman, article on Elmo Zumwalt Jr., p. 376.

39. Zumwalt, *On Watch,* pp. 199, 200–201.

40. Ibid., pp. 203–4.

41. Report of the Special Subcommittee on Disciplinary Problems in the U.S. Navy of the Committee on Armed Services House of Representatives, 92nd Congress, January 2, 1973.

42. Holloway interviews.

43. Zumwalt, *On Watch,* pp. 245–47.

44. Ibid., p. 259.

45. Interview: Vice Adm. Kent L. Lee, USN (Ret.), with Paul Stillwell, November 30, 1987, pp. 435–37, 697–700, USNI.

46. Hartman, *Naval Renaissance,* p. 20.

47. Holloway interviews, emphasis added.

48. Bruce Palmer Jr., *The Twenty-five Year War: America's Military Role in Vietnam* (New York: Da Capo Press, 1984, 1990).

49. Holloway interviews.

50. Hartman, *Naval Renaissance.*

51. Friedman, article on Elmo Zumwalt Jr., p. 365.

52. James C. Bradford, ed., *Quarterdeck and Bridge: Two Centuries of American Naval Leaders* (Annapolis: U.S. Naval Institute Press, 1997), p. 416.

Chapter 10. Selflessness

1. Admiral Denton's story is taken from numerous interviews with Edgar Puryear Jr. and John Mason Jr., and from his book, Jeremiah A. Denton, *When Hell Was in Session,* with Ed. Brandt (New York: Readers Digest Press, 1976).

2. Ibid.

3. Jim Stockdale and Sybil Stockdale, *In Love and War: The Story of a Family's Ordeal and Sacrifice during the Vietnam Years* (New York: Harper and Row, 1984), pp. 102–3.

4. Ibid., pp. 106, 107, 113, 115, 153, 332.

5. Ibid., pp. 333, 336, 338.

6. Ibid., p. 339.

7. Ibid., p. 264.

8. Ibid., pp. 252, 254.

9. Everett J. Alvarez, *Code of Conduct* (New York: Donald I. Fine, 1991), p. 6.

10. Ibid., pp. 10, 91–92.

11. Ibid., p. 193.

12. Ibid., pp. 15, 13, 30, 37.

13. Ibid., p. 132.

14. Ibid., pp. 3, 8–9, 13.

15. Ibid., p. xvi.

16. Interviews: Adm. James L. Holloway III, USN (Ret.), with Edgar F. Puryear Jr., July 18, 2001, and numerous other interviews.

17. Interviews: Rear Adm. Jeremiah Denton, USN (Ret.), with Edgar F. Puryear Jr., April 7, 2001, and numerous other interviews.

18. Interviews: Adm. Thomas B. Hayward, USN (Ret.), with Edgar F. Puryear Jr., May 5, 2001, and January 5, 2003.

19. Interviews: Adm. Carlisle A. H. Trost, USN (Ret.), with Edgar F. Puryear Jr., July 18, 2001, and November 13, 2001; emphasis added.

20. Interview: Adm. Jay L. Johnson, USN (Ret.), with Edgar F. Puryear Jr., August 21, 2001.

21. Interview: Adm. Frank B. Kelso II, USN (Ret.), with Edgar F. Puryear Jr., March 28, 2001.

22. Interviews: Adm. James D. Watkins, USN (Ret.), with Edgar F. Puryear Jr., February 2, 2001, and January 7, 2003.

23. Interview: Adm. Charles R. Larson, USN (Ret.), with Edgar F. Puryear Jr., April 10, 2001.

24. Oral history: Adm. Arleigh Burke, USN (Ret.), with John T. Mason Jr., January 12, 1973, pp. 208–11, USNI.

25. Ibid., pp. 9–10.

26. Holloway interviews.

27. Interview: Adm. Stansfield Turner, USN (Ret.), with Edgar F. Puryear Jr., April 3, 2001.

28. Larson interview.

29. Edgar F. Puryear Jr., *George S. Brown, General, U.S. Air Force: Destined for Stars* (Novato, Calif: Presidio Press, 1983), pp. 296–97.

Chapter 11. Elements of Command: Self and Family

1. Interview: Rear Adm. Chester W. Nimitz Jr. with John T. Mason Jr., April 14, 1969, p. 55, USNI.

2. William J. Crowe Jr., *In the Line of Fire* (New York: Simon and Schuster, 1993), p. 45.

3. Interview: Adm. James L. Holloway III, USN (Ret.), with Edgar F. Puryear Jr., July 18, 2001.

4. Interviews: Adm. Thomas B. Hayward, USN (Ret.), with Edgar F. Puryear Jr., May 23, 2001, and January 5, 2003.

5. Interviews: Adm. Carlisle A. H. Trost, USN (Ret.), with Edgar F. Puryear Jr., April 22, 2002, July 18, 2001, and September 13, 2001.

6. Interview: Adm. Frank B. Kelso II, USN (Ret.), with Edgar F. Puryear Jr., March 28, 2001.

7. Interview: Adm. Jay L. Johnson, USN (Ret.), with Edgar F. Puryear Jr., September 21, 2002.

8. Ibid.

9. Interview: Adm. Kinnaird R. McKee, USN (Ret.), with Edgar F. Puryear Jr., February 23, 2001.

10. Interview: Adm. Thomas H. Moorer, USN (Ret.), with Edgar F. Puryear Jr., March 21, 2003.

11. Interview: Adm. Paul David Miller, USN (Ret.), with Edgar F. Puryear Jr., April 8, 2001.

12. Jim Stockdale and Sybil Stockdale, *In Love and War* (New York: Harper and Row, 1984), p. 60.

13. Ibid., p. 77.

14. Ibid., p. 89.

15. Ibid., p. 445.

16. Oral history: Adm. Thomas H. Moorer, USN (Ret.), with John T. Mason Jr., January 13, 1976, pp. 681–82, USNI.

17. Interview: Adm. Thomas H. Moorer, USN (Ret.), with Edgar F. Puryear Jr., April 23, 2002.

18. Interview: Adm. Thomas H. Moorer, USN (Ret.), with John T. Mason Jr., February 21, 1975, pp. 44–45, USNI.

19. E. B. Potter, *Admiral Arleigh Burke* (New York: Random House, 1990), p. 35.

20. Ibid., p. 38.

21. Ibid., p. 291.

22. Ibid., pp. 302, 304.

23. Ibid., pp. 306, 308, 311.

24. Ibid., p. 406.

25. Ibid., p. 439.

26. Interview: Adm. Arleigh Burke, USN (Ret.), with John T. Mason Jr., March 1, 1979, USNI.

27. Holloway interview.

28. Interview: Adm. Stansfield Turner, USN (Ret.), with Edgar F. Puryear Jr., April 3, 2001.

29. Trost interviews, July 18, 2001, and September 13, 2001.

30. Interviews: Adm. Thomas B. Hayward, USN (Ret.), with Edgar F. Puryear Jr., May 23, 2001, and January 5, 2003.

31. Kelso interview.

32. Ibid.

33. Johnson interview.

34. Interviews: Adm. Robert L. J. Long, USN (Ret.), with Edgar F. Puryear Jr., February 23, 2001, and May 21, 2001.

35. McKee interviews, February 23, 2001, and September 26, 2001.

36. Ibid.

37. Ibid.

38. Interview: Adm. Charles R. Larson, USN (Ret.), with Edgar F. Puryear Jr., April 10, 2001.

39. Ibid.

40. Miller interview, July 25, 2001.

41. Ibid.

42. E. B. Potter, *Nimitz* (Annapolis: Naval Institute Press, 1976), pp. 36, 189, 203.

43. Ibid., pp. 109, 197, 199.

44. Thomas B. Buell, *The Quiet Warrior: A Biography of Admiral Raymond A. Spruance* (Boston: Little, Brown, 1974), pp. 119–20, 129, 185, 200.

45. Ibid., pp. 211, 234.

46. Ibid., pp. 234, 241, 248, 409.

47. Nimitz interview, pp. 18–19.

48. Ibid., pp. 7–8.

49. Interview: Mrs. Joan Nimitz with John T. Mason Jr., April 14, 1969, p. 49, USNI.

50. Interview: Adm. James R. Fife, USN (Ret.), with John T. Mason Jr., May 31, 1969, USNI.

51. Holloway interview.

Chapter 12. The Pattern

1. Interview: Gen. Dwight D. Eisenhower, with Edgar F. Puryear Jr., May 2, 1963.
2. Harry S. Truman: *Year of Decisions* (Garden City, N.Y.: Doubleday, 1955), p. ix.
3. Walter B. Smith, *Eisenhower's Six Great Decisions: Europe, 1944–1945* (New York: Longmans, Green, 1956), pp. 53–55.
4. Edgar F. Puryear Jr., *American Generalship: Character Is Everything* (San Francisco: Presidio Press, 2000), p. 50.
5. Interview: Catherine Nimitz Lay with U.S. Naval Institute, February 16, 1970, p. 94, USNI.
6. Colin Powell, *My American Journey* (New York: Random House, 1995), p. 427; interview: Gen. Colin Powell, USA (Ret.), with Edgar F. Puryear Jr., October 16, 1997.
7. Interview: Gen. H. Norman Schwarzkopf, USA (Ret.), with Edgar F. Puryear Jr., October 12, 1995.
8. Oral history: Adm. Arleigh Burke, USN (Ret.), with John T. Mason Jr., October 9, 1980, USNI.
9. Interviews: Adm. Thomas Hayward, USN (Ret.), with Edgar F. Puryear Jr., May 23, 2001, and January 5, 2003.
10. Dwight D. Eisenhower, *Crusade in Europe* (New York: Doubleday, 1948), pp. 213–14.
11. E. B. Potter, *Nimitz* (Annapolis: Naval Institute Press, 1976), pp. 78, 223.
12. James M. Merrill, *A Sailor's Admiral: A Biography of William F. Halsey* (New York: Thomas Y. Crowell, 1976), pp. 57–58.
13. Burke oral history, January 12, 1973, pp. 208–11.
14. Oral history: Adm. Thomas H. Moorer, USN (Ret.), with John T. Mason Jr., January 13, 1976, pp. 684–86, USNI.
15. Interview: Adm. James L. Holloway III, USN (Ret.), with Edgar F. Puryear Jr., July 18, 2001.
16. Interview: Adm. Carlisle A. H. Trost, USN (Ret.), with Edgar F. Puryear Jr., April 22, 2002.
17. Interview: Adm. Frank B. Kelso II, USN (Ret.), with Edgar F. Puryear Jr., March 28, 2001.
18. Interview: Adm. Jay L. Johnson, USN (Ret.), with Edgar F. Puryear Jr., September 21, 2002.
19. Interview: Adm. Stansfield Turner, USN (Ret.), with Edgar F. Puryear Jr., April 3, 2001.
20. Interviews: Adm. Robert R. J. Long, USN (Ret.), with Edgar F. Puryear Jr., February 23, 2001, and May 21, 2001.
21. Holloway interview.

22. Interview: Adm. James D. Watkins, USN (Ret.), with Edgar F. Puryear Jr., January 17, 2003.

23. Interview: Adm. Kinnaird McKee, USN (Ret.), with Edgar F. Puryear Jr., February 23, 2001.

24. Interview: Adm. Charles R. Larson, USN (Ret.), with Edgar F. Puryear Jr., April 10, 2001.

25. Interview: Adm. Henry G. Chiles Jr., USN (Ret.), with Edgar F. Puryear Jr., February 21, 2001.

26. Interview: Gen. of the Army Omar N. Bradley with Edgar F. Puryear Jr., February 16, 1962.

27. Letter from Gen. George S. Patton Jr. to his son, Cadet George S. Patton II, dated June 6, 1944, quoted in Edgar F. Puryear Jr., *Nineteen Stars: A Study in Military Character and Leadership* (Novato, Calif.: Presidio Press, 1971, 1981), p. 362.

28. Holloway interview.

29. Trost interview.

30. Kelso interview.

31. Larson interview.

32. Potter, *Nimitz*, pp. 9–10.

33. Ibid., p. 292.

34. Burke oral history, November 24, 1972, pp. 66–69.

35. Ibid., pp. 116–18.

36. Ibid., June 21, 1979, p. 155; November 24, 1972, pp. 62–64.

37. Ibid., November 14, 1972, pp. 29–37.

38. Robert William Love Jr., ed., *The Chiefs of Naval Operations* (Annapolis: Naval Institute Press, 1980), p. 329.

39. Holloway interview.

40. Watkins interview.

41. Trost interview.

42. Kelso interview.

43. Interview: Adm. William J. Crowe Jr., with Edgar F. Puryear Jr., November 13, 2000.

44. Interview: General Nathan F. Twining, USAF (Ret.) with Edgar F. Puryear Jr., March 3, 1977.

45. Interview: General Charles E. Meyer, USA (Ret.), with Edgar F. Puryear Jr., July 17, 1997.

46. Katherine Tupper Marshall, *Together* (New York: Tupper and Love, 1946), p. 17.

47. Potter, *Nimitz*, p. 175.

48. Thomas B. Buell, *The Quiet Warrior: A Biography of Admiral Raymond A. Spruance* (Boston: Little, Brown, 1974), p. 37.

49. Ibid., p. 39.

50. Emmet P. Forrestal, *Admiral Raymond A. Spruance, USN* (Washington, D.C.: U.S. Government Printing Office, 1966), p. 7, emphasis added.

51. E. B. Potter, *Admiral Arleigh Burke* (New York: Random House, 1990), p. 4.

52. Ibid., p. 298.

53. Oral history: Adm. Thomas H. Moorer, USN (Ret.), with John T. Mason Jr., pp. 326, 662, USNI.

54. Holloway interview.

55. Oral history: Vice Adm. Kent L. Lee, USN (Ret.), with Paul Stillwell, December 14, 1987, vol. 2, p. 492, USNI.

56. Moorer oral history, pp. 350–53, 374–75.

57. William J. Crowe Jr., *The Line of Fire* (New York: Simon and Schuster, 1993), p. 34; interview with Edgar Puryear Jr., November 13, 2000.

58. Watkins interview.

59. Turner interview.

60. Kelso interview.

61. Trost interview.

62. Johnson interview.

63. Crowe interview.

64. Moorer oral history, pp. 1567–69.

65. Moorer interviews.

66. Holloway interview.

67. Burke oral history.

68. Moorer oral history, p. 402, emphasis added.

69. Buell, *The Quiet Warrior,* p. 136, emphasis added.

70. Potter, *Nimitz,* p. 156, emphasis added.

71. Buell, *The Quiet Warrior,* p. 173.

72. Potter, *Nimitz,* p. 229, emphasis added.

73. William F. Halsey and J. Bryan III, *Admiral Halsey's Story* (New York: Whitney House, 1942), p. 34, emphasis added.

74. Burke oral history, pp. 261–66.

75. Watkins interview.

76. Eisenhower interview.

77. Larson interview.

78. Eisenhower interview.

79. Ibid.

80. Puryear, *American Generalship,* p. 1.

81. Ibid.

82. Gen. George S. Brown, speech before the Los Angeles World Affairs Council, February 15, 1977.

83. Holloway interview.

84. Burke oral history, pp. 280–81.

85. Interview: Rear Adm. Chester W. Nimitz Jr., USN (Ret.), with John T. Mason Jr., April 14, 1969, p. 55, USNI.

86. McKee interview.

87. Joseph Conrad, "The Prestige, Privilege and the Burden of Command."

88. Crowe interview.

89. Holloway interview.

90. Trost interview.

91. Kelso interview.

92. Johnson interview; McKee interview; interview: Adm. Vern Clark, USN (Ret.), with Edgar F. Puryear Jr., July 18, 2002; interviews: Adm. Thomas H. Moorer, USN (Ret.), with Edgar F. Puryear Jr., April 23, 2002, December 4, 2002, March 21, 2003, and numerous other interviews.

Index

A1Navs, 459

A-5, 22

Abrams, Creighton W., 62

Acheson, Dean, 45, 128, 129

Adams, John, 156

Adelman, Ken, 19

Afghanistan, 138, 143

aircraft carriers, 113–14, 116–18,
    141–43, 253–54, 261–62, 395–98,
    466–67, 583. See also *Constellation,*
    USS; *Kitty Hawk,* USS

aircraft selection, 23–24

aircraft, tactical, 133

air defense, attempts to unify, 111–12

Air Force, 111–12, 117, 133, 469

Air Force Squadron Officer's School
    (SOS), 193

Air Warning Service, 315

Alamo, USS, 188–89

Alcatraz, 489–98, 517

alcohol, 474–75. *See also* drug use

Allen, Benny, 227

Allen, Thomas B., 385

Al Rekkab, 355

Alsop, Joseph, 134–35

Alvarez, Everett, Jr., 518–21

America, USS, 256, 395, 560

Anderson, Bob, 387

Anderson, George W., 130–35, 152,
    245, 397, 426, 448, 583, 584

Andrews, Adolphus, 317

Argonne, 168

Arizona, 553

Armstrong, Neil, 207

Army Pearl Harbor Board, 300

Arnold, Henry H., 3, 49–50, 598

At Ease: Stories I Tell My Friends
    (Eisenhower), 155

Atlanta, 321

Atlas Corporation, 112

Atomic Energy Commission, Naval
    Reactors Branch, 388, 397–99,
    405–6, 408–9, 413–21, 423

Augusta, 275–76

Austen, Bernard L., 208, 279, 541–42

Australia, 76

B-36, 112–13, 117, 118

BACK US program, 490, 517

Bagley, David, 209

Bagley, Worth, 472
Baird, Chuck, 210
Baldwin, Robert H. B., 203, 209–10
Bamford, James, 360
Bannerman, Jim, 210
Banner, USS, 361–62
Barb, 212
Barlow, Jeffrey G., 125
Barron, James, 364, 591
Barrow, Bob, 28
Barrow, John, 217–18
Baruch, Bernard, 126
Bayly, Sir Louis, 286, 287, 595
Bay of Pigs, 299, 351–53
Beale, USS, 286
Behrens, Bill, 223–24, 413, 414, 422
Benevolence, 239
Bently, Stewart W., 375–76
Bertolette, Levi Calvin, 234
Bettis Atomic Laboratory, 398
Biesemeier, Harold, 317
Bland, Howard, 370
Blind Man's Bluff (Sontag and Drew), 383, 411, 414
Blue Fish, 73
Boeing, 133
Boorda, Mike, 34, 534, 546
Bowen, Catherine Drinker, 157
Bowen, "Hal," 208–9
Bowsher, Chuck, 210
Bradley, John Smith, 165
Bradley, Omar N., 85, 97, 113–20, 127–28, 165–67, 580
Brandt, Ed, 360
Bridgeton, 355–56, 596
Brookheiser, Richard, 156
Brown, Edward J., 350
Brown, George, 38, 136–39, 507, 539–40, 599–600

Brown, Harold, 141–43, 153, 259, 398, 534, 536, 583
Browning, Miles, 287, 322, 325
Brown, Julian, 287
Bryan, J., III, 241–42
Brzezinski, Zbigniew, 139
Buchanan, Charlie, 204
Bucher, Lloyd M., 360–65, 367–70, 596
Buckner, Simon B., 90
Buell, Thomas B., 171–73, 243, 274–75, 594
Burke, Arleigh: air combat experience of, 467; and Bay of Pigs, 352; Omar Bradley on revolt of, 119; consideration of, 243–48, 262, 592; and decision making, 13–16, 47–49, 575–76; decline of fourth term as CNO, 131; and delegation, 282, 288–91, 592–93, 595; and Eisenhower's support of unification, 118; independent thinking of, 114; and leadership qualities, 58–60, 601–2; on marriage, 553–56, 565; and mentorship, 199–201, 225–27, 589; as Marc Mitscher's chief of staff, 285, 577; on nuclear powered submarines, 396; on personnel decisions, 204; promotion to rear admiral, 124–26; reading habits of, 173–76, 586–87; respected by James Holloway, 205; selflessness of, 529–33; on Vietnam War, 353–54; and "yes men," 94–111, 152, 582, 584
Burke, Clara, 173, 586–87
Burke, Roberta "Bobbie" (Gorsuch), 553–55
Burns, General, 129
Burr, Aaron, 156

Bush, George, 30, 40
Bush, George W., 508
Butler, Lee, 35
Butler, Phil, 491
Butterfield, C. Wyatt, 324

Calhoun, Bill, 326
Callaghan, William M., 242
Callaghan, David J., 321, 322
Carlucci, Frank, 20
Carney, Robert B., 13, 103–4, 107, 326
Carpenter, Charles L., 325
Carter, James B., 346
Carter, Jimmy: James Holloway on,
    533; on *K-1,* 562; military budget
    of, 138–43, 152–53, 583; on Hyman
    Rickover, 424; selection of
    Stansfield Turner as CIA head, 29,
    213, 538; on uniforms, 477, 478
Castro, Fidel, 351
Central Intelligence Agency (CIA),
    29–30, 76–77, 538
Chafee, John H., 61, 367–68, 426–28,
    437, 450–51, 456, 460
chain of command, 29, 77, 294,
    433–35, 463–67
Champayne, Joseph D., 58
Cherry, Fred, 520
Chesapeake, USS, 364
Chiang Kai-shek, 10
Chief of Naval Operations, responsi-
    bilities of, 103–5, 239–40
Chief of Staff to the Commander-in-
    Chief of the Army and Navy, 87
chief petty officers, 218–31, 463–66,
    475, 479, 578, 591. *See also* petty
    officers
Chiefs of Naval Operations, The (Korb), 132
Chiles, Henry G., Jr., 35–36, 77–80, 84,
    150, 382, 389–90, 407–9, 580, 584

Churchill, Winston, 86, 87, 179
Clarey, Chic, 211–12, 589–90
Clarke investigation, 300
Clark, Vernon, 210, 377–80, 605
Clausen investigation, 300
Claytor, Graham, 141–42, 477, 478,
    536
Cleland, Max, 333
Clements, William, 39–44, 136
Clinton, Bill, 34, 453
CNO Report, The, 459
Code of Conduct, 364, 483–85, 489,
    501
Coffee, Jerry, 494
Cohen, William S., 374–75, 377
Cole, USS, 299, 370–80, 595
Collins, J. Lawton, 97
completed staff work, 296–97
computer-assisted distribution mecha-
    nisms, 258
Congress, 318, 386–89, 391, 397–402,
    420, 423
Connally, John B., Jr., 531, 555
Conner, Fox, 162–63
Connolly, Bart, 550
Conrad, Joseph, 542, 603–4
Constellation, USS, 59, 438–49
courts-martial, 444–45
Cousins, Ralph, 432–33, 507
Covington, USS, 286
Cox, Loel Dene, 350
Cramer, Shannon, 216
Crawford, George Clifford, 208,
    589
Crommelin, John G., 119
Crouch, William W., 374–75
Crowe, William J., Jr.: and *Bridgeton*
    mining, 354–56, 596; on command,
    604; experiences with Hyman
    Rickover, 392; and mentorship,

Crowe, William J., Jr.: (*continued*)
207–8, 218, 541–42, 589, 591; and
"yes men," 143–44, 584; on zero bal-
listic missiles formula, 16–21
Crow, Tom, 29
Cunningham, Bill, 306
Cutlass, 562
Cutler, Thomas J., 479–80

Dace, USS, 82, 411–12, 415, 547
Dalton, John, 262–63
Danzig, Richard, 371, 377
Davis, Arthur C., 285
Davis, Ed, 491
Decatur, Stephen, 364
Deckers, George H., 134
Delaney, Captain, 316
DeMars, Bruce, 31–32, 382, 419
Demilitarized Zone (DMZ), 38–46
Denfeld, Louis E., 114–17, 119–20,
130, 152, 331, 582, 584
Dennison, Robert L., 97–98, 114, 125, 132
Denton, Jeremiah A., 481–512; cap-
ture of, 482–83; on conditions at
Hoa Loa Prison, 483–86; on Hanoi
March, 491–95; on improved treat-
ment, 497–501; leadership shown
by as POW, 524; on Naval
Academy, 525; on release of POWs,
508–12; on ruse of Vietnamese,
502–4; torture of, 486–89; on vic-
tory in Vietnam War, 505–8
deployments, length of, 256–57, 261–62
"dial a sailor," 76
Dirksen, Everett, 400
discipline, 441, 443–50, 465–66, 473–77
Doolittle, James H., 9–11, 575
Dorn, Edwin, 320
Dorn report, 320
Douglas, McDonnell, 24

Draemel, Milo F., 233
draft, 107–10, 152, 259, 582
Drake, William Waldo, 233–34, 236
Drew, Christopher, 383
drug use, 27–29, 445, 474. *See also*
alcohol
Dudley, William S., 342
Dulles, John Foster, 124
Duncan, Charles K., 60
Duncan, Frank, 385
Duncan, William, 104

Eberstadt, Ferd, 213, 590
Eisenhower, David, 163
Eisenhower, Dwight D.: on George
Anderson, 131; and Arleigh Burke,
13, 105, 108–10, 126, 530; code of
conduct established under, 364; creation of Chief, Naval Reactors
Branch, Atomic Energy
Commission, 388; and decision making, 46–47, 573–76, 588–89, 596; on
draft, 152, 582; on Joint Chiefs of
Staff, 16; on leadership, 1–2, 596;
reading habits of, 154–56, 162; relationship with soldiers, 51–53, 71;
selection of Arthur Radford as chair
of JCS, 121, 123–24, 152; on selflessness, 598; on sixth sense, 83, 576–77;
on submarine construction, 383; on
unification, 118
engineering, 252–54, 256
Enlisted Clubs, 474–75
Enola Gay, 339
Enterprise, USS: James Holloway on,
63–64, 84, 205, 266–71, 356–58,
393–96, 535, 543–44, 578; Kent Lee
on, 22–23, 266, 449–50; and *Pueblo,*
362; Hyman Rickover's attention
to, 397

Essex, USS, 535, 556

F-14 Tomcat, 472
F-16, 25–26
F-18, 21–27
family service center, 258–59
Farago, Ladislas, 87
Farragut, David Glasgow, 525
Fechteler, William Morrow, 97
Felt, Harry Donald, 104, 245–46
Fife, James F., 568–69
Finback, 70
Fitch, Jake, 326
Flatley, James A., Jr. (Jim), 71, 151–52
Flatley, James A., III (Jim), 210
Fluckey, Gene, 212, 590
Fogelman, Ronald, 377, 534
Ford, Gerald, 38, 39, 136–38, 398, 518, 533, 583
Formosa, 89–91, 152
Forrestal, E. P., 170–71
Forrestal, James V.: and Arleigh Burke, 204, 554; on construction of aircraft carriers, 117; on Carl Moore, 285; on Chester Nimitz, 581; on publicity of war, 91; on sinking of *Indianapolis*, 330–31, 336–37, 341, 345
Forsell, Mark, 405
Founding Father: Rediscovering George Washington (Brookheiser), 156
France, 46–47
Frankfurter, Justice, 307–8
Franklin, Benjamin, 157–59
Frederica, Queen of Greece, 246–47
Freeman, Douglas Southall, 170, 180
Friedman, Norman, 427, 435, 479
Frosch, Bob, 210

Gallery, Daniel V., 360–61, 512
Gates, Thomas H., 201–2, 245

Gehman, Harold W. (Hal), 34, 374–75
General Board, 98–100, 173–74
General Dynamics, 133
Ghormley, Robert L., 11–13, 287–88, 566
Gibson, Buck W., 350
Gilbert Islands, 283–84
Gilpatric, Roswell, 132
Gladding, Everett B., 366, 367
Glasgow, Chief, 219
Glass, Richard, 125
"Gonzo Beer," 257
Goodpaster, Andrew, 507
Gorbachev, Mikhail, 16–17
Gorsuch, Roberta "Bobbie." *See* Burke, Roberta "Bobbie" (Gorsuch)
Gray, Gordon, 127
Greer, Mel, 410
Griffin, Don, 554
Griffis, Chuck, 217
Grigg, Jack, 405
Grumman, 23–24, 133
Guadalcanal, 54, 57–58, 83, 320–22, 577
Guarino, Larry, 484, 491
Guzowski, George, 225–27

Habib, Philip, 40, 42
Haig, Alexander, 507
Halperin, Dave, 436
Halsey, Bill (son), 242–43
Halsey, William F.: on bombing of Tokyo, 9–11; consideration of, 241–43, 592; and decision making, 575; and delegation, 274, 278–79, 286–87, 595; and Guadalcanal, 321, 577; independent thinking of, 91–92; on Douglas MacArthur, 92–94; mentorship of, 589; on naval aviation, 115; and POWs, 239; relief of Robert Ghormley, 12, 566; on sinking of *Juneau*, 322,

Halsey, William F.: (*continued*)
325–27; sixth sense of, 57–58, 83,
577; on visiting troops, 83
Hamilton, Alexander, 156
Hanoi March, 491–96, 518
Harding, Edwin Forrest, 166
Harmon, Millard F., 90
Harriman, Averell, 45–46, 128
Harris, Stephen R., 360, 366, 367
Hart inquiry, 300
Hartman, Frederick H., 452, 478–79
Hart, Tommy, 197
Hasayampa, 254
Hashimoto, Mochitsura, 348
Hatcher, Andrew T., 135
Hayward, Peggy, 559–60
Hayward, Thomas B.: on command,
544; on consideration, 256–57; and
decision making, 576; on drug
problem, 27–29; and F-16, 25; on
mentorship, 222–23; on Naval
Academy, 525–26; on Navy spouses,
559–60; reading habits of, 185; and
Hyman Rickover, 403–4, 409–11,
416; on Vietnam War, 507
Hébert, F. Edward, 438, 439, 448
Helena, USS, 321, 322, 325–27
Helms, Richard, 365
Helm, Thomas, 332
Henry Clay, 547
Hetz, Russell, 344–45
Hewitt inquiry, 300
Hickman Air Force Base, 263
Hicks, Floyd V., 438–49
"high-low" mix, 400–401, 427, 471–72
Hilbert, William E., 331
Hildago, Edward, 345
Hill, Henry W., 125
Hoa Loa Prison, 483, 514
Ho Chi Minh, 496–97

Hodes, Henry, 96–97, 226
Holcomb, Staser, 479
Holdman, Rob, 227
Hollandia, 59
Holloway, Dabney, 178–79, 182–83,
394, 457, 535, 556–57
Holloway, James L., III: on accountability, 356–58; and chain of command, 29, 463–67; as CNO,
472–78; on command, 542–44, 604;
and consideration, 232, 253–56,
266–71, 592; on delegation, 292,
294–97, 593; on draft, 107; on Kent
Lee and F-18, 24–27; on mentorship, 205–7, 221–22; on murder of
Americans in DMZ, 38, 40–46; on
Navy spouses, 556–58, 569; and
nuclear powered ships, 406, 407;
reading habits of, 177–85, 587–88;
on Hyman Rickover, 63, 205,
393–99, 401–3; and selflessness,
521–25, 533–35, 600–601; on sixth
sense, 63–65, 77, 84, 578–80; on
Soviet Navy, 469–71; on uniforms,
451; as vice CNO, 454–60, 466, 468;
on visiting troops, 84, 578; and "yes
men," 135–43, 151–52, 583; on
Elmo Zumwalt, 452–54, 460–63,
471–72
Holloway, James L., Jr. (father), 178,
205–6, 386–87
Holloway Plan, 205–7
Hooper, Edwin B., 360
Hoover, Gilbert C., 322, 325–27
Hoover, Herbert, 599
Hornet, 10
housing, 61, 250, 260, 262–63
Howe (Judge Advocate), 314, 316–17
Howes, Craig, 481
Hubbell, John G., 481

Huntington, 554
Hutson, John D., 336–37, 341

Ikle, Fred, 138
Indianapolis, USS, 89, 299, 328–51, 595
INF Zero Option, 20–21
inspections, 63–64
Iowa, 206
Iran, 354–56
Iwo Jima, 89–91

Jackson, Henry, 387, 398, 409, 411
Jacobs, Randall, 88–89, 581
Jameson, Dirk, 35
James, Woodie E., 350
Jefferson, Thomas, 156
Johnson, Frank L., 363, 366, 367
Johnson, Garland, 561–62
Johnson, Jay L.: on accountability, 359–60; on command, 545–47, 605; and decision making, 33–35; on delegation, 293; on family life, 561–62; on mentorship, 217–18, 227–28, 591; on Naval Academy, 527–28; reading habits of, 186–87; relationships with people, 84, 149; on visiting troops, 74–75, 578–79
Johnson, Louis, 113–15, 118, 126–30, 582
Johnson, Lyndon B., 353, 388, 400
Johnson, Sam, 498, 501
Joint Chiefs of Staff: on arms limitation, 136–38; on Bay of Pigs, 352; Arleigh Burke on favoritism shown by, 105; on Jimmy Carter's military budget, 138–41; and decision making, 16–21; establishment of, 3; on flush deck carrier project, 116–18; on murder of Americans in DMZ, 40, 43–44; Arthur Radford as chair of, 120–24, 131; and Franklin Roosevelt, 273; on

SALT II Treaty, 110–11; and Strategic Planning Division, 101–2; Elmo Zumwalt on, 468–69
Jones, Dave C., 139
Jones, Don, 32
Joy, Turner, 96–97, 528
Juneau, USS, 299, 320–28

K-1, 562
Kalbfus, Edwards C., 317
Kelso, Frank B., II: on command, 544–45, 604–5; on consideration, 259–60; and leadership training, 546; on mentorship, 214–15, 590; on Naval Academy, 528–29; on Navy spouses, 560–61; and nuclear powered ships, 407; and Hyman Rickover, 382, 419–21; on sixth sense, 69–74, 85, 578, 580–81; stress of job on, 534; on visiting troops, 84, 578; on "yes men," 146–47, 584
Kelso, Landis, 560–61
Kennedy, John F.: and George Anderson, 130, 131, 134, 135; and Bay of Pigs, 351–53; and Arleigh Burke, 245, 531; on selflessness, 599; and Vietnam War, 353, 354
Kennedy, USS, 395
Kessing, Oliver Owen "Scrappy," 92
Kestral, HMS, 286
Key West Agreement, 117–18
Khobar Towers, 376–77
Kidd, Isaac, 214–15, 472, 590
Kiley, Frederick, 481
Kimmel, Husband: and Chester Nimitz, 235, 565–66, 592; and Pearl Harbor, 299–320, 595; replacement of, 53, 88, 233; resignation of, 302; on Roberts Commission, 309–12; on sending planes to Wake Island, 286–87

King, Ernest J.: appointment as CNO, 318; character and leadership of, 87–88; and delegation, 274, 593–94; inspection after D-day invasion, 598; and invasion of Formosa, 89–91; on invasion of Guadalcanal, 321; on Joint Chiefs of Staff, 3; and mentorship, 196–97, 218–19, 589; on naval aviation, 115; on personnel, 285, 288; and relief of Robert Ghormley, 12; and sinking of *Indianapolis,* 331, 334, 346; as special aide to secretary of navy, 240; on "yes men," 152, 581

Kinkaid, Tom, 93, 115

Kinnear, Gus, 207

Kissinger, Henry, 38, 39, 43, 136–38, 152, 400–401, 583

Kitty Hawk, USS, 438–49, 463–64

Knox, Frank, 88, 91, 299–301, 307, 566, 581

Kohn, Richard, 377

Korb, Lawrence, 132, 133

Korea, 39–44, 96–97

Kramer, Shannon, 590–91

Kurzman, Dan, 323–24, 327–28, 332, 345–46, 351

Kwajalein, 7, 596–97

Laird, Melvin R., 427, 428, 435

Lamar, H. Arthur, 55–56, 236–39, 276, 282–83

Larson, Charles R.: on accountability, 360; on consideration, 262–64, 592; and decision making, 36–38, 597–98; on mentorship, 217, 228–29; on Naval Academy, 529, 538–39; on Navy spouses, 564; on sixth sense, 80–81, 85, 579, 581; on

"yes men," 148–49, 597

Lawrence, Bill, 498–99, 524

Lawrence, David, 364

Lay, Catherine (Nimitz), 47, 168–69, 575

Lay, James T., 129–30, 276–77

Layton, Edwin T., 238, 346

Leahy, William D., 3–6, 86–87, 152, 273–74

Lech, Raymond B., 332

Lee, Kent L., 21–25, 188–90, 266, 449–52, 588

Lehman, John, 31–33, 138, 261, 410, 415

Leighton, Dave, 394, 395, 398, 403

LeMay, Curtis E., 134–35

Lemnitzer, Lyman L., 131, 134, 583

Leopard, HMS, 364

Lewisohn, Randy, 532–33

Liatis, Alexis S., 247

Liberty, USS, 363

lightweight fighters, 25–26

Linder, Sam, 268–70

Linebacker operations, 501, 505

Linhard, Robert, 17

Lippold, Kare, 372–73, 376–80

loneliness, 45–47, 565–66, 573, 575

Long Beach, USS, 396

Long, Robert L. J.: on delegation, 293–94; on family life, 562–63; on long deployments, 261–62; and mentorship, 208–11, 217, 220–21; on nuclear powered ships, 402; refusal to be "yes man," 144–45; and Hyman Rickover, 382, 404; selflessness of, 535–37; on sixth sense, 65–66, 84, 579; on visiting troops, 84, 579

Long, Sara, 563

Los Angeles-class, 472

Louisville, USS, 563
Lovell, Jim, 207
Lowell, Lawrence, 599
Lyons, James A. "Ace," 75–76

Maas, Peter, 328
MacArthur, Arthur, 159–61
MacArthur, Douglas, 90, 92–94, 154, 160–61, 239, 248, 283
Madison, James, 156
Maloelap, 7, 596
Manchester, William, 161
Marlin, 151, 547
Marshall, George C., 3, 130, 154, 163–65, 298, 311, 585, 595, 598
Marshall Islands, 7–8, 285, 596
Mason, John T., Jr., 47, 508
Matthews, Francis P., 114, 120, 125–26
Maumee, USS, 195
Maxwell Air Force Base, Alabama, 193
May, Andrew J., 304
McCormick, Lynde D., 346
McCoy, Frank R., 308
McCoy, Giles G., 347–48
McCullough, David, 126–28, 130
McDaniel, Red, 64
McDonald, David L., 61, 397, 426
McKee, Kinnaird: on accountability, 298–99; on chief petty officers, 223, 231; Henry Chiles under, 407–8; on command, 547–48, 603, 605; and hazing at Naval Academy, 255; on Navy spouses, 563; refusal to be "yes man," 150–51; and Hyman Rickover, 382, 411–19; on sixth sense, 77, 81–82, 84, 85, 579
McLucas, John, 25
McMorris, Charles H., 99, 173–74, 233, 282

McNamara, Robert S.: on Bay of Pigs, 352; and Arleigh Burke, 531; confrontation with George Anderson, 131–35, 152, 397, 583; and nuclear powered ships and carriers, 391, 395, 398; personnel selection of, 210; and Hyman Rickover, 400
McNarney, Joseph T., 308, 314–16
McVay, Charles B., III, 328–51, 595
Merrill, James A., 57, 59
Meyer, Charles C., 141
Meyer, Edward C. "Shy," 194, 215, 585
Michelsen, Twain, 304
Midway, 53–54, 321, 577
Midway, USS, 40, 43
Miller, Colby, 564–65
Miller, Edison, 509–11
Miller, Paul David, 210, 230–31, 546, 548, 564–65
Miner, Herbert J., II, 350–51
Mississippi, 279–81
Missouri, 282–83
Mitscher, Marc A.: and Arleigh Burke, 58, 99, 173, 175–76, 467, 531, 577, 587, 595; consideration of, 244–45; and delegation, 285, 288–91, 595; mentorship of Thomas Moorer, 199
Mitscher, Mrs. Marc, 244–45
Mix, George Edward, 304
Moellering, John, 17, 18
Moffett, William A., 196–97, 589
Montgomery of Alamein, Viscount, 46, 241
Moore, Charles J. (Carl), 172, 236, 284–85
Moore, C. W., Jr., 373
Moorer, Carrie, 552–53

Moorer, Thomas H.: on Bay of Pigs, 351–52; on Bobbie Burke, 555; on command, 548, 551, 578, 605; and consideration, 248–53, 260, 271, 591–92; and delegation, 282, 291–92, 593; on history in leadership, 176–77, 587; and James Holloway, 205, 472; on mentorship, 197–203, 224–25, 589, 591; on personnel assignments and promotions, 203–4; qualifications of, 455; refusal to be "yes man," 148; and Hyman Rickover, 390–91, 397; on sixth sense, 83–85; on Vietnam War, 507; visiting of troops, 60–63, 83–84; wife of, 552–53; and Elmo Zumwalt, 426, 460

Moreau, Arthur S., Jr., 211

Most Dangerous Man in America, The, (Bowen), 157

Munsan-ni, 225–26

Murfin, Orin G., 317

Murphy, Edward R., Jr., 360, 366, 367

Murphy, Paul J., 331

Murray, George D., 346

Murray, Stuart S., 207–8, 589

Murrow, Edward R., 424

Mustin, Lloyd M., 237

Myers, Chuck, 25, 26

Naquin, Oliver F., 342, 346

Nash, Frank, 121

National War College (NWC), 454

Natter, Robert, 373–74

Nautilus, USS, 383, 384, 386–87, 396, 415, 527, 547

Naval Academy, 36–38, 255, 521–29, 538–39

Naval Air Systems Command, 24

Naval Maritime Strategy (1986), 66–67

Naval Nuclear Power School, 69–70

negligence, 372–73, 376

Nelson, David F., 350

Newcomb, Richard F., 328, 332

Newman, Richard J., 377

Nimitz, 71

Nimitz, Catherine (daughter). *See* Lay, Catherine (Nimitz)

Nimitz, Catherine (wife), 240, 565–68

Nimitz, Chester W.: and consideration, 233–41, 243, 592; and decision making, 9, 575, 596; and delegation, 273–79, 282–84, 287–88, 593–95; and William Halsey, 58, 242; on Gilbert Hoover, 326; independent thinking of, 88–89, 91–92; and invasion of Formosa, 89–90; invasion of Guadalcanal, 320–21; on invasion of Marshall Islands, 7–8; leadership qualities of, 53–57; loneliness of, 47, 575; marriage and family life of, 565–68; mentorship of, 195–96, 589; on naval aviation, 115; and promotion of Arleigh Burke to rear admiral, 531; reading habits of, 168–70, 586; relief of Robert Ghormley, 11–13; and sinking of *Indianapolis,* 331, 334, 336, 337, 346; on sixth sense, 83, 577; Raymond Spruance on, 566; and submarines, 386; on visiting troops, 237–38, 577; and "yes men," 581

Nimitz, Chester W., Jr., 168, 240–41, 541, 567–68, 602

Nimitz-class aircraft carriers, 398, 472

Nimitz, Joan (daughter-in-law), 568

Nimitz, Nancy (daughter), 168, 170

Nitze, Paul, 129, 209, 210, 400, 454–55

Nixon, Richard: Everett Alvarez on, 521; and Charles Larson, 37, 217, 597; promotion of Hyman Rickover, 388; on riots on aircraft carriers, 438; and selection of James Holloway as CNO, 473; strategy for Vietnam War, 507–8; on treatment of POWs, 501, 504, 505; visit with James Stockdale, 550; on Elmo Zumwalt, 448

Norfolk, 473–74

Norfolk Navy Lodge, 250

Noriega, Manuel, 575

Norman, William, 436–37

Nouméa, 11, 13

NROTC program, 206

nuclear powered surface ships, 391, 395–98, 400–403, 406–9. *See also* submarines, nuclear

Nuclear Power School, 420–23

nuclear weapons policy, 468–69

O'Connor, Bishop, 148

Odlum, Floyd B., 112

Ofstie, Ralph A., 119

O'Hare, Butch, 151

Ohio-class, 399, 471

Okinawa, 56–57, 67, 89–91

Olendorf, Jesse B., 346

Oliver Hazard Perry-class, 471

Operation Torch, 11

Oriskany, USS, 218, 490, 549, 550

Osborne, 280

Overman, Eleanor, 304–5

Palmer, Bruce, Jr., 467–68

Pasket, Lyle M., 350

Patton, George S., Jr., 580

Pearl Harbor, 233–38, 299–320, 595

Peel, Bob, 491–93

Perle, Richard, 17, 18

Perry, William J., 376–77

Petersen, Forrest, 24

petty officers, 435, 476–77, 479, 591. *See also* chief petty officers

Phelps, William Lyon, 191–92

Philippines, 89

Pilling, Donald L., 34, 335–38, 340–41, 346–47, 349

Pirie, Bob, 205

Poindexter, John, 17

Polmar, Norman, 385, 469

Poor Richard's Almanac (Franklin), 157

Portland, 321

Potter, E. B.: on Arleigh Burke, 173, 174, 555, 586; on Ernest King, 87; on Chester Nimitz, 9, 53–54, 88–89, 168, 233–36, 238, 278, 565, 594–95; on Raymond Spruance, 89

Powell, Colin, 575

POW-MIAs, 37–38, 239, 498–99, 501–2. *See also* Alvarez, Everett, Jr.; Denton, Jeremiah A.; Stockdale, James B.

presidents, 45–47

Price, Mel, 409

promotions, 31–33, 203–4, 215, 386–88, 466–67, 591

Pueblo, USS, 299, 360–70, 596

Pye, William S., 234–35

Quonset Point Naval Air Station, 451

race relations, 435–42, 445–46, 449, 461–62, 464

Radford, Arthur W.: Omar Bradley on, 119, 120; Arleigh Burke on, 105; on cancellation of *United States*, 152, 584; as chair of Joint Chiefs of Staff, 120–24, 131; on Louis Denfeld's congressional hearing, 115, 117; and Dwight Eisenhower's support of unification, 118; independent thinking of, 114

Ramsay, Sir Bertram H., 46
"rap sessions," 461–62, 464
Rayburn, Sam, 118
Reagan, Ronald, 16–21, 136, 257, 417, 424
Reeves, Joseph W., 126, 198–99, 308, 314
Regan, Donald, 18
revolt of the admirals, 115, 118–19, 126, 128
Revolt of the Admirals (Barlow), 125
Reykjavik summit, 16–21
Richardson, James O., 306–9
Rickover, Eleanore (wife), 425
Rickover, Hyman G., 382–425, 584; on accountability, 596; on communication, 65; death of, 424; early career of, 385; and education and training for officers, 253–54, 476–77; on *Enterprise*'s return to California, 394–95; and James Holloway, 63, 205, 393–99, 401–3; influence in Congress, 386–89, 391, 397–402, 420, 423; longevity of, 388; mentorship of James Watkins, 212–13, 590; personality of, 387–89, 400–401, 403–7, 408, 414, 420–21, 424–25; personnel decisions of, 211, 390, 392, 408, 413–14, 421–22, 584; promotion to rear admiral, 419; reading habits of, 183–85, 189–90, 588; relationship with civilian staff, 417–18; retirement of, 409–11, 415–17; Carlisle Trost on, 260–61; and "yes men," 144–45, 148–50, 389–90; and Elmo Zumwalt, 381–82, 469
Rickwell, Theodore, 385
Ridgway, Matthew B., 96–98, 167–68, 582

Risner, Robinson, 503, 507, 519
Robert A. Owens, 219
Roberts Commission, 300–303, 305, 307–18
Roberts, Owen J., 301–3, 305, 307–18
Robison, Samuel S., 195–96, 589
Rochester, Stuart I., 481
Rogers, Bernie, 20, 534
Roosevelt, Franklin D.: creation of Joint Chiefs of Staff, 3; delegation by, 272–73; and James Doolittle, 11; on *Indianapolis*, 328; and William Leahy, 86–87; and Arthur MacArthur, 159–60; on Chester Nimitz as commander of Pacific Fleet, 88; nomination of William Halsey for four stars, 241; and Pearl Harbor, 299, 319, 320; James Richardson on, 309; and Henry Stimson, 599
Rowan, USS, 76, 265–66, 579
Rowden, William H., 479
Royall, Kenneth, 127
Rumsfeld, Donald, 38, 136–38
Russell, Jim, 246
Russell, Richard, 400
Ryan, Thomas J., Jr., 347–48

S-3 Viking ASW aircraft, 472
SALT II Treaty, 110–11, 136–38, 152, 469, 583
Sam Houston, USS, 414
Sam Rayburn, 67–68, 558, 578
San Francisco, 321
Schlesinger, James, 25–26, 472–73, 533
Schultz, Carl, 217
Schultz, George, 17
Schumacher, F. Carl, 360
Schumaker, Bob, 483, 491

Schwailer, Terry J., 376–77

Schwarzkopf, Norman, 575

Scorpion, 558

Scott, Hunter, 332–33, 344–45, 349

Scott, Norman, 242, 321–22

Scroggins, Jean, 405

Sea Cat, 150–51

Seadragon, 414

sea pay, 258, 259

Sea Power Subcommittee of the House Armed Services Committee, 397–98

Seiverts, Frank, 509–10

Seventh Fleet, 456, 556

Shannon, Harold, 54

Shannon, HMS, 364

Shelley, John F., 393

Shelton, Henry H., 374

Shepherd, Lemuel C., Jr., 97

Sherman, Forrest, 90

Shields, Roger, 509–10

Short, Dewey, 117

Short, Walter C., 300–312, 320

Simard, Cyril T., 54

Sirago, 216

Skipjack, 413

Skowcroft, Brent, 40–42

Smedberg, William R., 213–14, 346

Smedley, William R., 204–5, 554

Smith, Bob, 333, 335–44, 347

Smith, Holland M., 7–8, 236, 596

Smith, Jerry, 210

Smith, Levering, 209

Smith, Walter B., 46–47

Smith, William N., 229–30

Smith, William W., 233

Snyder, Charles P., 336

Sontag, Sherry, 383

Soviet Union, 426–28, 468–71, 508

Spinelli, John A., 350

Spruance-class, 472

Spruance, Margaret, 171, 566–67, 586

Spruance, Raymond A.: and consideration, 243, 592; and delegation, 274, 279–86, 593–95; independent thinking of, 89–91, 152; on invasion of Marshall Islands, 7–8, 596; marriage of, 566–67; on Charles McVay's court-martial, 331, 334, 336, 337; on naval aviation, 115; and Chester Nimitz, 235–36; reading habits of, 169–73, 586; refusal to publicize war, 581

Standley, William H., 308, 310, 314, 315

Stardust, 498–501

Stark, Harold R. ("Betty"), 300–301, 307, 311, 318

Stennis, John, 411

Stillwell, Joseph, 355

Stillwell, Richard G., 38–39, 41–44

Stimson, Henry L., 599

Stockdale, James B., 485, 489, 490, 501, 503, 507, 509, 512–18, 523–25, 549–51

Stockdale, Sybil, 549, 550

Stone, Harlan F., 308

strategic bombing, 112

Strategic Plans Division, Office of the Chief of Naval Operations, 100–103, 152, 174

Stratton, Sam, 402

Stump, Felix, 244

Styer, Charles, Jr., 562

submarines, nuclear, 383–86, 388–90, 394–96, 399, 411–15, 421. *See also* nuclear powered surface ships

Sullivan, John L., 114, 128

Sullivan, Leonard, 25, 26

Swenson, Lyman K., 322
Symington, Stuart, 112–13, 117, 123

Taft, Robert A., 128
Taft, William Howard, 159, 599
Tamura, Admiral, 252–53
Tedder, Sir Arthur, 46
Tenth Fleet, The (Farago), 87
terrorism. See *Cole,* USS
TFX (Tactical Fighter Experimental), 133–34
Thach, Jimmy, 151
Theobald, Robert A., 310, 312–14
Theodore Roosevelt, 143
The Sullivans, USS, 371
Thomas, Charles S., 108–10
Thompson, Bill, 458
ThreatCon Bravo, 373, 378–79
Thunder Below (Fluckey), 212
Thurber, H. Raymond, 242
Tokyo, 9–11
Tomahawk missiles, 136–38, 583
Towers, John H., 99–100, 173–74, 278, 565
Train, Harry, 392
Trost, Arlena, 186
Trost, Carlisle A. H.: on accountability, 358–59; on command, 544, 604; on consideration, 260–61; and decision making, 30–33, 576; and mentorship, 215–17, 219–20, 229, 590–91; on Naval Academy, 526–27; and nuclear powered ships, 407; reading habits of, 185–86; and Hyman Rickover, 382; on visiting troops, 67–69, 84, 578; and sixth sense, 69, 85, 580; on wife, 558–59; on "yes men," 147–48, 584
Trost, Mardelle L., 186

Trost, Pauline, 558–59
Truman, Harry S., 6, 45–46, 97–98, 125–30, 274, 305, 436, 574
Turner, Kelly, 235–36, 326
Turner, Patricia, 558
Turner, Richard K., 7–8, 597
Turner, Stansfield: on consideration, 264–66; on difficult decisions, 29–30; mentorship of, 213–14, 590; on Navy spouses, 558; reading habits of, 187–88; refusal to be "yes man," 145–46, 153; relationships with people, 84; selflessness of, 538; on sixth sense, 76, 579
Twining, Nathan F., 584
Tyler, Patrick, 385

Udall, Stuart, 264
Underhill, USS, 334
unification, 111–23
uniforms, 451–52, 477–78
United States, USS, 113–15, 117–19, 128, 152, 582, 584
urinalysis, for drug testing, 28
U.S. Navy court of inquiry, 300, 317–18

Van Buskirk Harris, Eleanor, 360
Vandegrift, A. Archer, 54, 56, 57, 83, 282, 321, 577
Vandenburg, Hoyt S., 97, 112, 113, 116–18
Van Zandt, James E., 112
Vietnam War, 62, 249, 251–52, 353–54, 397–98, 427, 481–82, 505–8
Vinson, Carl, 112, 117–20
Volador, 212
Von Doenhoff, Richard A., 334, 343–44

Wadley, Kenneth R., 363
Wake Island, 278, 286–87

Walker, Walter H., 167

Wang, Charles, 323–24

Warner, John, 250, 260, 333, 336–37, 340–41, 344–45, 347, 349, 473

Washington, George, 156–57, 180, 598

Washington Special Action Group (WSAG), 39–43

Waters, Odale D., Jr., 275–76

Watkins, James D.: on consideration, 257–59, 592; on delegation, 292–93; and education and training for officers, 253–54, 476–77; and John Lehman, 261; and Kinnaird McKee's relief of command, 414; and mentorship, 211–13, 217, 589–90; on Naval Academy, 529; refusal to be "yes man," 148, 583–84; and Hyman Rickover, 382, 404–7, 409, 425, 596; on sixth sense, 66–67, 84, 579; on visiting troops, 84; and Elmo Zumwalt, 479

Wegner, Bill, 409

Weinberger, Casper, 18, 32–33, 410, 537, 576

Weisner, Mickey, 458

White, Byron R. "Whizzer," 94–96, 582

White, Steven Angelo, 383, 421–23

Wiesner, Maurice F., 260

Wilbur, Walter, 509–11

Williams, Alfred, 197

Wilson, Charlie, 108, 109, 121, 124

Wilson, George C., 360

Wilson, Lou, 136, 139

women, 435, 462

Woodward, Bob, 30

Woolsey, Jim, 536

Worth, Cedric, 113, 118

Wotje, 7, 596

Wouk, Herman, 178–79

Wright, Jerauld, 198, 200

Yamamoto, Isoroku, 320

Years of Decisions (Truman), 45

Yorktown, 54

Young, Kenneth Ray, 160

Zech, Lando, 216, 527

Zephyr, HMS, 286

zero-ballistic-missiles-in-ten-years (ZBM) formula, 17–21

zero tolerance drug policy, 28–29

Z-grams, 428–34, 438; on discipline, 441, 443; and Enlisted Club in Norfolk, 474; Hicks investigation of, 446, 448–49; James Holloway on, 459–60, 464–66; Kent Lee on, 451; "Mickey Mouse, Elimination of," 431–34, 443–44, 464–65

"Zoo," the, 486, 493–94

Zourkova, Krassimira J., 190–91

Zumwalt, Elmo, Jr., 425–80; evaluations of, 452–54, 478–80; and Hicks report, 448–49; on Joint Chiefs of Staff, 468–69; Thomas Moorer on, 249–50; and nuclear powered ships, 407; overview of career, 425–26; passion for reform, 460–61; personnel problems of, 428–52; philosophy of, 462–63, 471–72; popularity of, 453; problems faced by, 426–27; on race relations, 435–42, 445–46, 449, 461–62, 464; and Hyman Rickover, 381–82, 399–401; selection of James Stockdale for rear admiral, 550; style of, 435; on successor, 472; Stansfield Turner on, 76

Zumwalt, Mouza, 457, 557

About the Author

Edgar F. Puryear Jr. earned a Bachelor of Science degree at the University of Maryland in 1952, and also holds Master and Doctorate degrees from Princeton University and a law degree from the University of Virginia. He is a professor emeritus at Georgetown University, where he taught from 1983 to 2000. Over the last forty years he has lectured on military character and leadership at numerous American military institutions and installations. He is the author of *American Generalship: Character Is Everything, Nineteen Stars: A Study in Military Character and Leadership, Stars in Flight: A Study in Air Force Character and Leadership,* and *General George S. Brown, USAF: Destined for Stars.* Dr. Puryear currently practices law in Madison, Virginia.